New National Framework
MATHEMATICS 9

M. J. Tipler   K. M. Vickers

Text © M J Tipler and K M Vickers 2004
Original illustrations © Nelson Thornes Ltd 2004

The right of M J Tipler and K M Vickers to be identified as authors of this work has been asserted by them in accordance with the Copyright, Designs and Patents Act 1988.

All rights reserved. No part of this publication may be reproduced or transmitted in any form or by any means, electronic or mechanical, including photocopy, recording or any information storage and retrieval system, without permission in writing from the publisher or under licence from the Copyright Licensing Agency Limited, of 90 Tottenham Court Road, London W1T 4LP.

Any person who commits any unauthorised act in relation to this publication may be liable to criminal prosecution and civil claims for damages.

Published in 2004 by:
Nelson Thornes Ltd
Delta Place
27 Bath Road
CHELTENHAM
GL53 7TH
United Kingdom

04 05 06 07 08 / 10 9 8 7 6 5 4 3 2 1

A catalogue record for this book is available from the British Library

ISBN 0 7487 6755 X

Illustrations by Harry Venning
Page make-up by Mathematical Composition Setters Ltd

Printed and bound in Great Britain by Scotprint

Acknowledgements
The authors and publishers would like to thank Jocelyn Douglas for her contribution to the development of this book.

The publishers thank the following for permission to reproduce copyright material.

Corel 1: 113; Corel 28 (NT): 199; Corel 62 (NT): 367; Corel 233: 386; Corel 248 (NT): 367; Corel 315 (NT): 35; Corel 381 (NT): 128; Corel 600: 119; Corel 737 (NT): 143; Corel 778: 103; Corel 783 (NT): 111, 249; Digital Stock 1: 397; Digital Stock 6 (NT): 255; Digital Vision 11: 140; Digital Vision 12 (NT): 106; M.C. Escher's "Belvedere" © 2004 The M.C. Escher Company – Baarn – Holland. All rights reserved: 285; Peter Adams/Digital Vision BP (NT): 18; Photodisc 22: 28, 80; Photodisc 40: 388; Photodisc 45 (NT): 161; Photodisc 66 (NT): 367; Jeff Lepore/Science Photo Library: 317

The publishers have made every effort to contact copyright holders but apologise if any have been overlooked.

INCLUDES QCA QUESTIONS

Contents

Introduction		**v**
Number Support		**1**

Place value and powers of ten; Multiplying and dividing by 10, 100, 1000; Rounding; Putting decimals in order; Integers; Divisibility; Prime numbers, prime factors; HCF; LCM; Powers; Mental calculation; Estimating; Written calculations; Checking answers to calculations; Order of operations; Fractions; Converting between fractions, decimals and percentages; Comparing and ordering fractions; Finding fraction of and percentage of; Ratio and proportion

1 Place Value, Ordering and Rounding — 20
- Powers of ten — 21
- Multiplying and dividing by powers of ten — 25
- Rounding to powers of ten — 28
- Rounding to decimal places — 31
- Summary of key points — 33
- Test yourself — 35

2 Integers, Powers and Roots — 37
- Adding, subtracting, multiplying and dividing integers — 38
- Prime factor decomposition — 42
- Common factors of algebraic expressions — 45
- Divisibility and algebra — 46
- Powers — 47
- Multiplying and dividing numbers with indices — 49
- Square roots and cube roots — 51
- Summary of key points — 55
- Test yourself — 56

3 Calculation — 59
- Multiplying and dividing by numbers between 0 and 1 — 60
- Order of operations — 61
- Mental calculations — 63
- Solving word problems mentally — 69
- Estimating — 72
- Written calculation — 76
- Choosing a strategy for calculation — 81
- Using a calculator — 85
- Summary of key points — 86
- Test yourself — 89

4 Fractions, Decimals and Percentages — 92
- Fractions, decimals and percentages — 93
- Comparing proportions — 97
- Adding and subtracting fractions — 102
- Fraction and percentage of — 107
- Multiplying fractions — 110
- Dividing fractions — 112
- Summary of key points — 114
- Test yourself — 116

5 Percentage and Proportional Changes — 119
- Percentage change — 120
- Proportionality — 130
- Ratio — 134
- Solving ratio and proportion problems — 137
- Summary of key points — 141
- Test yourself — 142

Algebra Support — 146
Equations; Expressions; Simplifying expressions; Substituting into expressions; Formulae; Sequences; Functions; Graphs

6 Algebra and Equations — 157
- Understanding algebra — 158
- Identities — 159
- Inequalities — 160
- Solving equations — 162
- Equations with unknowns on both sides — 166
- Solving non-linear equations — 168
- Algebra and proportion — 172
- Summary of key points — 176
- Test yourself — 178

7 Expressions and Formulae — 180
- Simplifying expressions — 181
- Writing expressions — 186
- Factorising — 191
- Adding and subtracting algebraic fractions — 193
- Substituting into expressions — 195
- Substituting into formulae — 197
- Changing the subject of a formula — 200
- Finding formulae — 202
- Summary of key points — 205
- Test yourself — 206

8 Sequences and Functions — 210
- Generating sequences — 211
- Describing and continuing sequences — 213
- Quadratic sequences — 214
- Sequences in practical situations — 216
- Finding the rule for the nth term — 221
- Functions — 222
- Inverse of a function — 225
- Summary of key points — 227
- Test yourself — 229

9 Graphs of Functions — 232
- Graphing functions — 233
- Gradient of a straight line — 239
- Distance–time graphs — 243
- Drawing, sketching and interpreting graphs — 247
- Summary of key points — 251
- Test yourself — 252

Contents

Shape, Space and Measures Support — 255
Lines and Angles; 2-D shapes; Constructions; Locus; 3-D shapes; Coordinates; Symmetry; Congruence; Transformations; Measures; Bearings; Perimeter, area and volume

10 Lines and Angles — 272
Conventions, definitions and derived properties — 273
Finding angles — 273
Interior and exterior angles of a polygon — 278
Summary of key points — 282
Test yourself — 283

11 Shape, Construction and Loci — 285
Triangles, quadrilaterals and polygons — 286
Tessellations — 290
Circles — 291
Constructions — 294
Locus — 297
3-D shapes — 302
Cross-sections — 305
Summary of key points — 306
Test yourself — 307

12 Transformations and Scale Drawings — 311
Congruence and transformations — 312
Combinations of transformations — 314
Symmetry — 317
Enlargement — 320
Scale drawing — 324
Summary of key points — 327
Test yourself — 329

13 Measures, Perimeter, Area and Volume — 331
Metric conversions, including area, volume and capacity — 332
Working with measures — 334
Perimeter and area — 338
Circumference and area of a circle — 341
Surface area and volume of a prism — 347
Summary of key points — 350
Test yourself — 352

Handling Data Support — 355
Planning and collecting data; Mode, median mean, range; Displaying and interpreting data; Comparing data; Probability

14 Planning a Survey and Collecting Data — 367
Planning a survey — 368
Two-way tables — 375
Summary of key points — 378
Test yourself — 378

15 Analysing and Displaying Data — 380
Mode, median, mean — 381
Displaying data — 384
Scatter graphs — 389
Interpreting graphs and diagrams — 396
Misleading graphs — 401
Comparing data — 402
Surveys — 405
Summary of key points — 406
Test yourself — 408

16 Probability — 413
Language of probability — 414
Mutually exclusive events — 417
Calculating probabilities of mutually exclusive events — 418
Calculating probability by listing all the mutually exclusive outcomes — 423
Estimating probabilities from relative frequency — 426
Comparing experimental and theoretical probability — 430
Summary of key points — 434
Test yourself — 435

Test Yourself Answers — 439

Index — 452

Introduction

We hope that you enjoy using this book. There are some characters you will see in the chapters that are designed to help you work through the materials.

These are

This is used when you are working with information.

This is used where there are hints and tips for particular exercises.

This is used where there are cross references.

This is used where it is useful for you to remember something.

These are blue in the section on number.

These are green in the section on algebra.

These are red in the section on shape, space and measures.

These are yellow in the section on handling data.

v

Number Support

Place value and powers of ten

The **place** of a digit tells you its **value**.

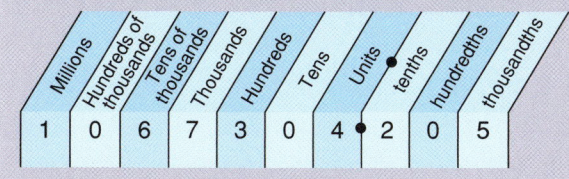

Millions	Hundreds of thousands	Tens of thousands	Thousands	Hundreds	Tens	Units	tenths	hundredths	thousandths
1	0	6	7	3	0	4 •	2	0	5

This is a *place value* chart.

To **add or subtract 0·001**, add or subtract 1 to or from the thousandths digit.

Examples 6·372 − 0·01 = 6·362
8·999 + 0·001 = 9·000

Practice Questions 1, 51

Multiplying and dividing by 10, 100, 1000

To **multiply by 10, 100, 1000** move each digit **left** one place for 10, two places for 100, three places for 1000.

To **divide by 10, 100, 1000** move each digit **right** one place for 10, two places for 100, three places for 1000.

Examples

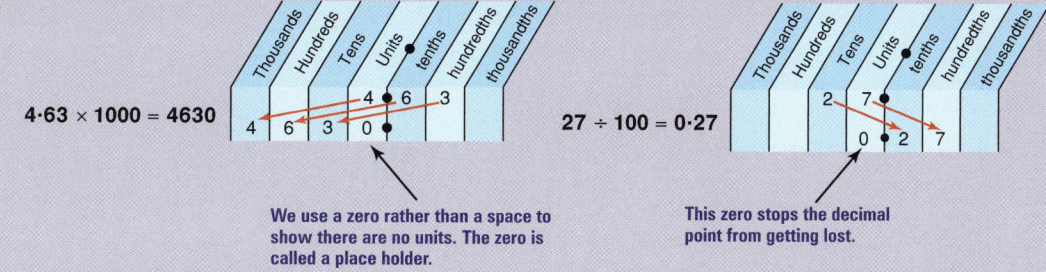

4·63 × 1000 = 4630

We use a zero rather than a space to show there are no units. The zero is called a place holder.

27 ÷ 100 = 0·27

This zero stops the decimal point from getting lost.

Practice Questions 2, 24, 53

Rounding

Rounding to 10, 100, 1000, 10 000, ...

367 498 to the nearest thousand is 367 000,
to the nearest ten thousand is 370 000,
to the nearest hundred thousand is 400 000.

When a number is halfway between two numbers we round up.

Example 8 500 000 to the nearest million is 9 000 000.

Rounding to the nearest whole number

To round to the nearest whole number we look at the digit in the first decimal place.
If this digit is 5 or more, we round the units up. Otherwise the units digit is left the same.

Examples 12·39 to the nearest whole number is 12.
49·505 to the nearest whole number is 50.

Practice Questions 40, 52, 54, 63

1

Number

Putting decimals in order

To put **decimals in order**, compare digits with the same place value. Work from left to right to find the first digits that are different.

Example   10·6537 > 10·6528   Starting at the left the digits are the same until we get to the digits 3 and 2.
3 > 2 so 10·6537 > 10·6528

Practice Questions 6, 25, 55, 62

Integers

We can **add and subtract integers** using a number line.

Adding

Examples

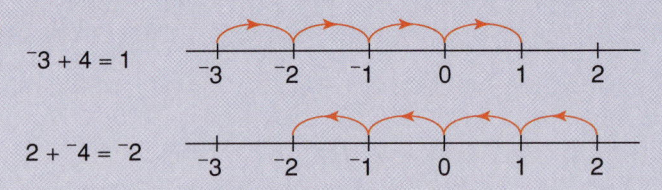

⁻3 + 4 = 1

2 + ⁻4 = ⁻2

To add a positive number move right.
To add a negative number move left.

Subtracting

Examples

⁻2 − 3 = ⁻5

⁻2 − ⁻3 = 1

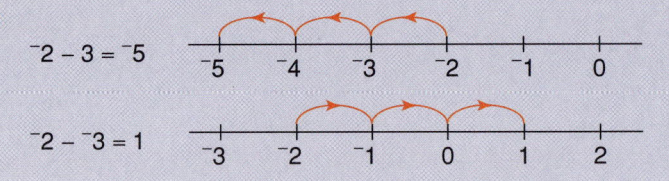

To subtract a positive number move left.
To subtract a negative number move right.

Multiplying

When we multiply a positive number and a negative number we get a negative answer.   ⊕ × ⊖ = ⊖
⊖ × ⊕ = ⊖

Examples   4 × ⁻3 = ⁻12   ⁻5 × 6 = ⁻30

When we multiply two negative numbers we get a positive answer.   ⊖ × ⊖ = ⊕

Examples   ⁻4 × ⁻5 = 20   ⁻6 × ⁻8 = 48

Dividing

When we divide with a positive and a negative number we get a negative answer.   ⊖ ÷ ⊕ = ⊖
⊕ ÷ ⊖ = ⊖

Examples   ⁻6 ÷ 2 = ⁻3 $\frac{-10}{5}$ = ⁻2

When we divide with two negative numbers we get a positive answer.   ⊖ ÷ ⊖ = ⊕

Examples   ⁻8 ÷ ⁻4 = 2 $\frac{-20}{-4}$ = 5

Practice Questions 7, 18, 30

2

Divisibility

A number is **divisible by 2** if it is an even number.
A number is **divisible by 3** if the sum of its digits is divisible by 3.
A number is **divisible by 4** if the last two digits are divisible by 4.
A number is **divisible by 5** if its last digit is 0 or 5.
A number is **divisible by 6** if it is divisible by both 2 and 3.
A number is **divisible by 8** if half of it is divisible by 4.
A number is **divisible by 9** if the sum of its digits is divisible by 9.
A number is **divisible by 10** if the last digit is 0.

For **divisibility by large numbers** we check for divisibility by factors.

Example   To check if a number is divisible by 18, check for divisibility by 2 and 9, not 3 and 6. We check by dividing by two numbers which multiply to 18 but which have no common factor other than 1.

Practice Questions 26, 27, 56

Prime numbers, prime factors, HCF, LCM

A **prime number** has exactly two factors, itself and 1.
1 is not a prime number.

A **prime factor** is a factor that is a prime number.

Example   The factors of 24 are 1, 2, 3, 4, 6, 8, 12 and 24.
The prime factors of 24 are 2 and 3.

To write 240 as a **product of prime factors** we can use a table or factor tree.

Divide by the smallest prime number.

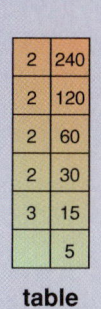

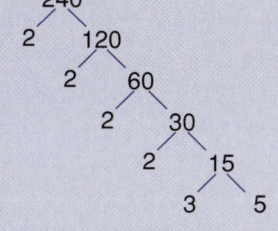

2	240
2	120
2	60
2	30
3	15
	5

table

factor tree

$240 = 2^4 \times 3 \times 5$

We can use a diagram to find the highest common factor, HCF, and lowest common multiple, LCM, of two numbers.

Example   To find the HCF and LCM of 240 and 168, write them as a product of prime factors.
$240 = 2^4 \times 3 \times 5$
$168 = 2^3 \times 3 \times 7$
Fill in the diagram as shown.
HCF = $2 \times 2 \times 2 \times 3 = 24$
   — multiply the common factors

LCM = $2 \times 5 \times 2 \times 2 \times 2 \times 3 \times 7 = 1680$
   — multiply all the numbers in the diagram

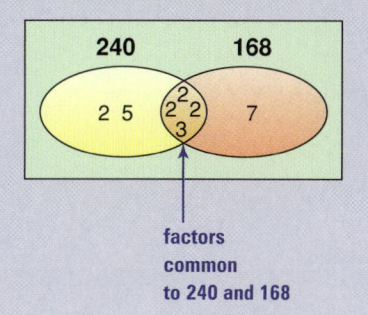

factors common to 240 and 168

Practice Questions 29, 41, 65a, 74

Number

Powers

2^5 is $2 \times 2 \times 2 \times 2 \times 2$.
2^5 is read as 'two to the power of 5'.

↑
index

> The plural of 'index' is 'indices'.

The first four **triangular numbers** are 1, 3, 6 and 10.

Squares and cubes

$3^2 = 3 \times 3 = 9$ 9 is called a **square number**.
$5^3 = 5 \times 5 \times 5 = 125$ 125 is called a **cube number**.

On a calculator, squares are keyed using $\boxed{x^2}$,
cubes are keyed using $\boxed{x^3}$.

Examples $2 \cdot 4^2$ is keyed as $\boxed{2 \cdot 4}$ $\boxed{x^2}$ $\boxed{=}$ to get 5·76.
$4 \cdot 5^3$ is keyed as $\boxed{4 \cdot 5}$ $\boxed{x^3}$ $\boxed{=}$ to get 91·125.

The first twelve **square numbers** are 1, 4, 9, 16, 25, 36, 49, 64, 81, 100, 121 and 144.

The first five **cube numbers** are 1, 8, 27, 64 and 125. The cube of 10 is 1000.

Square roots and cube roots

$\sqrt{64}$ is read as 'the square root of 64'.
8 is the square root because $8 \times 8 = 64$.

On a calculator, square roots are keyed using $\boxed{\sqrt{}}$.

Example $\sqrt{96}$ is keyed as $\boxed{\sqrt{}}$ $\boxed{96}$ $\boxed{=}$ to get 9·8 (1 d.p.).

$\sqrt[3]{125}$ is read as 'the cube root of 125'.
5 is the cube root of 125 because $5 \times 5 \times 5 = 125$.

Practice Questions 65b, 66, 67, 75

Mental calculation

These strategies can be used to **add and subtract** mentally.

1 Complements in 1, 10, 50, 100, 1000

Example $4 + 44 + 56 + 6 = 4 + 100 + 6$
$= 10 + 100$
$= \mathbf{110}$

> 44 and 56 are complements in 100.

2 Partitioning

Examples $6 \cdot 7 + 4 \cdot 2 = 6 + 0 \cdot 7 + 4 + 0 \cdot 2$ $8 \cdot 75 - 0 \cdot 67 = 8 \cdot 75 - 0 \cdot 6 - 0 \cdot 07$
$= 6 + 4 + 0 \cdot 7 + 0 \cdot 2$ $= 8 \cdot 15 - 0 \cdot 07$
$= 10 + 0 \cdot 9$ $= \mathbf{8 \cdot 08}$
$= \mathbf{10 \cdot 9}$

3 Counting up

Example $15 \cdot 7 + 3 \cdot 6$
$15 \cdot 7 + 3 \cdot 6 = 15 \cdot 7 + 0 \cdot 3 + 0 \cdot 3 + 3$
$= \mathbf{19 \cdot 3}$

+0·3   +0·3   +3
15·7   16   16·3   19·3

4

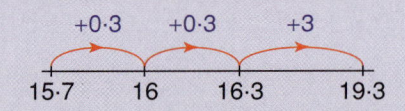

Number Support

4 Nearly numbers

Example
$12.8 + 7.9 = (13 - 0.2) + (8 - 0.1)$
$= 13 + 8 - 0.2 - 0.1$
$= 21 - 0.2 - 0.1$
$= 20.8 - 0.1$
$= \mathbf{20.7}$

5 Adding or subtracting too much then compensating

Examples
$8.76 + 3.8 = 8.76 + 4 - 0.2$
$= 12.76 - 0.2$
$= \mathbf{12.56}$

$11.47 - 3.91 = 11.47 - 4 + 0.09$
$= 7.47 + 0.09$
$= \mathbf{7.56}$

6 Using facts you already know

Example
$0.36 - 0.19$
We know that $36 - 19 = 17$
so $0.36 - 0.19 = \mathbf{0.17}$

Practice Questions 3a, 5, 8, 9, 10, 28, 34, 42, 45

These strategies can be used to **multiply and divide mentally**.

1 Place value

Example

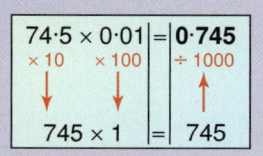

74.5×0.01	=	**0.745**
$\times 10 \quad \times 100$		$\div 1000$
745×1	=	745

> We multiplied by 1000 altogether so we must divide the answer by 1000.

2 Partitioning

Examples
$14 \times 2.4 = (10 \times 2.4) + (4 \times 2.4)$
$= 24 + 9.6$
$= \mathbf{33.6}$

$430 \div 5 = (400 \div 5) + (30 \div 5)$
$= 80 + 6$
$= \mathbf{86}$

3 Factors

Examples
$4.5 \times 20 = 4.5 \times 2 \times 10$
$= 9 \times 10$
$= \mathbf{90}$

$480 \div 16 = \mathbf{30}$ because $480 \div 4 = 120$
$120 \div 4 = 30$

4 Near tens

Examples
$34 \times 11 = 34 \times 10 + 34$
$= 340 + 34$
$= \mathbf{374}$

$25 \times 39 = 25 \times (40 - 1)$
$= 25 \times 40 - 25$
$= 1000 - 25$
$= \mathbf{975}$

$25 \times 40 = 25 \times 4 \times 10$
$= 100 \times 10$
$= 1000$

5 Known facts

We know that $5 = 10 \div 2$, $\quad 25 = 100 \div 4$, $\quad 50 = 100 \div 2 \quad$ and $\quad 25 = 5 \times 5$.

Examples
$324 \times 50 = 324 \times 100 \div 2$
$= 32\,400 \div 2$
$= \mathbf{16\,200}$

$625 \div 25 = 625 \div 5 \div 5$
$= 125 \div 5$
$= \mathbf{25}$

$625 \div 5 = 600 \div 5 + 25 \div 5$
$= 120 + 5$
$= 125$

Number

6 Doubling and halving

Examples

$$24 \times 16 = 24 \times 2 \times 2 \times 2 \times 2$$
$$= 48 \times 2 \times 2 \times 2$$
$$= 96 \times 2 \times 2$$
$$= 192 \times 2$$
$$= 384$$

halve double

$$2 \cdot 4 \times 3 \cdot 5 = 1 \cdot 2 \times 7$$
$$= 1 \times 7 + 0 \cdot 2 \times 7$$
$$= 7 + 1 \cdot 4$$
$$= 8 \cdot 4$$

Practice Questions 5, 10 c ii, 19, 28, 31, 32, 33, 38, 39, 42, 58, 64, 72

Estimating

To **estimate the answer to a calculation** we round the numbers so that we can do the calculation in our head.

Examples $492 \times 23 \approx 500 \times 20$ $318 \div 25 \approx 300 \div 20$
$ = 10\,000$ $ = 15$

We try to round to '**nice numbers**' when estimating.

Example $\frac{62}{7} \approx \frac{63}{7}$ We round to 63 rather than 60.
$\phantom{Example\ \frac{62}{7}\ } = 9$ 63 can be divided by 7.

Practice Question 68

Written calculations

When we **add and subtract decimals** using pencil and paper we line up the decimal points.

Example $64 \cdot 9 - 7 \cdot 14 + 16 \cdot 7 \approx 65 - 7 + 17 = 75$

```
  5 1 8 1
  64·90         and      57·76
 -  7·14                + 16·7
  ──────                ──────
  57·76                  74·46
                          1 1
```

Check the answer with the estimate.

This shows two different ways we can **multiply numbers**.

Example $58 \cdot 2 \times 6 \cdot 7$

$58 \cdot 2 \times 6 \cdot 7 \approx 60 \times 7 = 420$

×	50	8	0·2
6	300	48	1·2
0·7	35	5·6	0·14

check
↓
349·2
40·74

$335 + 53 \cdot 6 + 1 \cdot 34 = \mathbf{389 \cdot 94}$

or

$58 \cdot 2 \times 6 \cdot 7$ is equivalent to $58 \cdot 2 \times 10 \times 6 \cdot 7 \times 10 \div 100$
or $582 \times 67 \div 100$.

```
    582
  ×  67
  ─────
  34920    60 × 582
   4074     7 × 582
  ─────
  38994
```
Answer $38\,994 \div 100 = \mathbf{389 \cdot 94}$

We can **divide using written methods**.

Example 97·6 ÷ 27

27)97·6 97·6 ÷ 27 ≈ 100 ÷ 25 = 4
 81·0   27 × 3
 ────
 16·6
 16·2   27 × 0·6
 ────
 0·40
 0·27   27 × 0·01
 ────
 0·13

Answer 3·61 R 0·13
          3·6 (1 d.p.)

When we **divide by a decimal** we do an equivalent calculation.

Example 62·8 ÷ 3·6 is equivalent to 628 ÷ 36. $62·8 ÷ 3·6 = \frac{62·8 \times 10}{3·6 \times 10} = \frac{628}{36}$

Practice Questions 3b, 12, 43, 46, 59, 71

Checking answers to calculations

We can **check an answer to a calculation** in one of these ways.

1 Check that the answer is sensible.

2 Check that the answer is the right order of magnitude by estimating.

   Example Marnie worked out the answer to 96 × 2·8 as 268·8.
              Estimate 96 × 2·8 ≈ 100 × 3 = 300
              So 268·8 is the right order of magnitude.

3 Check using inverse operations.

   Example 76·8 ÷ 2·4 = 32
              Check 32 × 2·4 = 76·8   Multiplying by 2·4 is the inverse of dividing by 2.4.

4 Check using an equivalent calculation.

   Example 36 × 12 = 432   can be checked by calculating 72 × 6   or   72 × 3 × 2   or
                               36 × 4 × 3   or   12 × 3 × 12

5 Check the last digits.

   Example 46 × 2·3 = 105·6 is wrong because 6 × 3 = 18.
              The last digit should be 8.

Practice Questions 69, 70

Order of operations

We work out brackets first, then indices, then do × and ÷, then do + and −.

Example   ⁻6 − 3 × ⁻2 = ⁻6 − ⁻6   ⁻2(− 5 + 2) = ⁻2 × ⁻3
                       = 0   = 6

> Brackets
> Indices
> Division and Multiplication
> Addition and Subtraction
> BIDMAS

Practice Questions 4, 57, 68

Fractions

When writing one number as a fraction of another, the numerator and denominator must have the same units.

Example 35 minutes as a fraction of an hour is

$\frac{35^{\,7}}{60_{\,12}} = \frac{7}{12}$ We write 1 hour as 60 minutes.

> Always write the fraction in its simplest form.

Number

Equivalent fractions

$\frac{1}{3}, \frac{2}{6}, \frac{3}{9}, \frac{4}{12}, \frac{5}{15}, \ldots$ are equivalent fractions.

We find equivalent fractions by multiplying or dividing both the numerator and denominator by the same number.

Example

$\frac{3}{5} \xrightarrow{\times 2} \frac{6}{10}$ $\qquad$ $\frac{3}{5} \xrightarrow{\times 5} \frac{15}{25}$ $\qquad$ $\frac{3}{5} \xrightarrow{\times 6} \frac{18}{30}$

Cancelling fractions

We write a fraction in its **simplest form** by **cancelling**.

Example $\frac{18\;^3}{42\;_7} = \frac{3}{7}$ To cancel we divide the numerator and denominator by their HCF. The HCF of 18 and 42 is 6.

Improper fractions have a larger numerator than denominator.

Mixed numbers have a whole number part and a fraction part.

Example   To write $\frac{34}{8}$ as a mixed number we divide 34 by 8.

$34 \div 8 = 4$ with remainder 2.

$\frac{34}{8} = 4\frac{2}{8}$

$= 4\frac{1}{4}$

Example $3\frac{2}{5} = 3 + \frac{2}{5}$

$= \frac{15}{5} + \frac{2}{5}$

$= \frac{17}{5}$

Adding and subtracting fractions

We **add and subtract fractions** which have the same denominator like this.

$\frac{7}{12} + \frac{7}{12} - \frac{1}{12} = \frac{7 + 7 - 1}{12}$ ← keep the denominator

$= \frac{13}{12}$

$= 1\frac{1}{12}$

We can find a fraction of a quantity or multiply **integers and fractions**

Examples $\frac{2}{3}$ of 39 = 26 $5 \times \frac{1}{6} = \frac{5}{6}$ $5 \times \frac{3}{8} = 5 \times 3 \times \frac{1}{8}$

$\frac{1}{3}$ of 39 = 13 $= 15 \times \frac{1}{8}$

$\frac{2}{3}$ of 39 = 2 × 13 $= \frac{15}{8}$

$= 26$ $= 1\frac{7}{8}$

Practice Questions 11, 20, 21, 22, 36, 48

Converting between fractions, decimals and percentages

Percentages to decimals or fractions

'Percent' means number of parts per hundred.

$84\% = \frac{84}{100}$ $72\% = \frac{72}{100}$ $135\% = \frac{135}{100}$

$= \frac{21}{25}$ ← always put fractions in lowest terms $= 0\cdot72$ $= 1\cdot35$ or $1\frac{7}{20}$

8

Number Support

Fractions or decimals to percentages

Either **a Write with denominator of 100**

Examples $\frac{7}{50} = \frac{14}{100}$ $0.67 = \frac{67}{100}$
$= 14\%$ $= 67\%$

or **b multiply by 100%**

Examples $\frac{8}{15} = \frac{8}{15} \times 100\%$ key 8 ÷ 15 × 100
$= 53.3\%$ (1 d.p.)

$0.625 = 0.625 \times 100\%$
$= 62.5\%$

Fractions to decimals

Either **a use known facts**

Example $\frac{1}{8} = 0.125$ so $\frac{3}{8} = 3 \times 0.125$
$= 0.375$

b make the denominator 10, 100 or 1000

Examples

$\frac{7}{25} \xrightarrow{\times 4} \frac{28}{100} = 0.28$ $\frac{24}{40} \xrightarrow{\div 4} \frac{6}{10} = 0.6$

c divide

Example $\frac{5}{9} = 5 \div 9$

```
  9)5·0
    4·5       9 × 0·5
    0·50
    0·45      9 × 0·05
    0·050
    0·045     9 × 0·005
    0·005
Answer  0·555 R 0·005
        0·56 (2 d.p.)
```

or **d use a calculator**

$\frac{36}{43}$ key 36 ÷ 43 = to get 0·84 (2 d.p.)

Fractions always convert to either a
terminating (one that ends)
or a **recurring decimal** (has one or more digits that repeat).

Examples $\frac{1}{5} = 0.2$ terminating decimal $\frac{5}{11} = 0.454545...$ recurring decimal
$= 0.\dot{4}\dot{5}$

> The dots above the 4 and 5 show that these repeat.

Decimals to fractions

Write with denominator 10, 100, 1000, ... and cancel if possible.

Examples $0.65 = \frac{65}{100}$ $0.535 = \frac{535}{1000}$
$= \frac{13}{20}$ $= \frac{107}{200}$

9

Number

You should know these.

$\frac{1}{10} = 0.1 = 10\%$ $\frac{1}{100} = 0.01 = 1\%$

$\frac{2}{10} = 0.2 = 20\%$ and so on. $\frac{2}{100} = 0.02 = 2\%$

$\frac{1}{2} = 0.5 = 50\%$ $\frac{1}{4} = 0.25 = 25\%$ $\frac{3}{4} = 0.75 = 75\%$

$\frac{1}{5} = 0.2 = 20\%$ $\frac{1}{3} = 0.\dot{3} = 33\frac{1}{3}\%$ $\frac{2}{3} = 0.\dot{6} = 66\frac{2}{3}\%$

$\frac{1}{8} = 0.125 = 12\frac{1}{2}\%$

Practice Questions 13, 14, 15, 16, 42, 49, 73

Comparing and ordering fractions

We can **compare and order fractions** by

1 converting them to decimals
2 writing them with a common denominator.

Example $\frac{3}{4} > \frac{5}{8}$ because $0.75 > 0.625$

or $\frac{3}{4} > \frac{5}{8}$ because $\frac{6}{8} > \frac{5}{8}$ $\frac{3}{4} \xrightarrow{\times 2} = \xrightarrow{\times 2} \frac{6}{8}$

Practice Question 44

Finding fraction of and percentage of

In maths 'of' means multiply.

Examples $\frac{1}{5}$ of 120 $= \frac{1}{5} \times 120$ 5% of 80 = 36 because   10% of 80 = 8
                    $= 120 \div 5$ 40% of 80 = 4 × 8 = 32
                    $= 24$

$\frac{2}{5}$ of 120 = 24 × 2   5% of 80 = 4
            = 48   45% of 80 = 32 + 4
                                                                                              = 36

We can find '% of' using a calculator.

Example   Find 18% of 96.

Using fractions	**Using decimals**	**Finding 1% first**
18% of 96 = $\frac{18}{100} \times 96$	18% of 96 = 0.18 × 96	1% of 96 = 0.96
key 18 ÷ 100 × 96 =	key 0.18 × 96 =	18% of 96 = 18 × 0.96
to get **17·28**.	to get **17·28**.	key 18 × 0.96 =
		to get **17·28**

Practice Questions 35, 37, 47

Ratio and proportion

Ratio compares part to part.

Proportion compares part to whole.

Examples

The ratio of red to blue is 5 : 7.
The proportion of red squares is $\frac{5}{12}$.
The proportion of blue squares is $\frac{7}{12}$.

Number Support

We write ratios in their **simplest form by cancelling**.

Examples ÷5 (5 : 25 = 1 : 5) ÷5   ÷9 (45 : 54 = 5 : 6) ÷9

We can **solve problems using ratio and proportion**.

Example 6 packets of nuts cost £15.
So 12 packets cost twice as much, £30.

We sometimes **divide an amount in a given ratio**.

Example Susie and Rachel paid for a £20 raffle ticket in the ratio 2 : 3.
Altogether there are 5 shares (2 + 3).
One part = $\frac{20}{5}$ = £4
2 parts is £8 and 3 parts is £12.
Susie paid £8 and Rachel paid £12.

Practice Questions 17, 23, 50, 60, 61, 76, 77

Practice Questions

Except for questions 12, 43, 46, 49 and 66.

1 What is the value of the digit 6 in these? **a** 0·642 **b** 5·026 **c** 12·56

2 Find the answers to these.
 a 32 × 10 **b** 32 × 100 **c** 32 ÷ 10 **d** 32 ÷ 1000 **e** 0·3 × 100
 f 4·6 ÷ 10 **g** 4·65 × 1000 **h** 64·7 ÷ 100 **i** 0·7 ÷ 1000 **j** 0·008 × 100

T 3 Use a copy of these.
What numbers go in the top box?

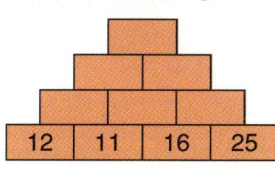

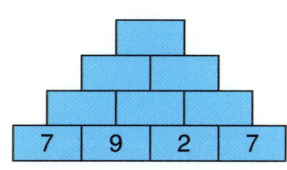

| 12 | 11 | 16 | 25 |

| 7 | 9 | 2 | 7 |

 a In the red boxes, two numbers are added to get the number above.
 b In the blue boxes, the number on the right is multiplied by the number on the left to get the number above.

4 Work these out.
 a 3 + 4 × 2 **b** 4 × 3 + 6 × 5 **c** 7 + 2 × ⁻2

T 5 Use a copy of this.
Look at these prices.
 a Use the prices to fill in the gaps below.
  The total cost of 2 muffins and 1 drink → ___
  The total cost of 3 apples → ___
  The total cost of 1 roll and ___ → £1·90
 b There are many different ways to make the total cost £1·70.
  Use the prices to fill in the gaps.
   £1·70 → the total cost of 1 pie and 1 crisps
      → the total cost of _____
      → the total cost of _____
      → the total cost of _____

rolls	£1·30
pies	£1·20
muffins	60p
yoghurt	55p
crisps	50p
apples	55p
drinks	£1·15

Number

6 Jude has four number cards and a decimal point card.

| 8 | 6 | 3 | 0 | . |

   a Put the four cards together in as many different ways as possible so that there is only one number card before the decimal point.
   b What is the biggest number you made?
      Write this number in words.
   c What is the smallest number you made?
      Write this number in words.
   d Use the four cards to make the number that is as close as possible to 7.

7 **a** $7 + 4 + {}^{-}2$ **b** $17 - 8 - {}^{-}4$ **c** $0.6 + 1.2 - 0.2$ **d** $9 - 8 - {}^{-}4 + 2$

8 Work these out mentally.
   a $60 + 50$ **b** $90 - 35$ **c** $64 + 27$ **d** $630 + 780$
   e $560 - 380$ **f** $367 + 309$ **g** $735 - 419$ **h** $2107 - 234$

T 9 Use a copy of this magic square.
Fill it in.

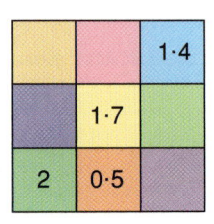

		1·4
	1·7	
2	0·5	

10 **a** What number should you add to 23 to make 100?
    b What number should you subtract from 100 to make 73?
    c Work these out.
       i $68 + 69$ **ii** $84 \div 7$ **iii** $2059 + 507$ **iv** $5637 - 590$

11 Write 3 fractions which are equivalent to each of these.
    a $\frac{1}{4}$ **b** $\frac{2}{5}$

12 Write down the answers.
    a Add 257 to 479, then subtract 263.
    b Multiply 278 by 16, then add 726.
    c Add 88 to half of 976.
    d How much less than 1000 is 49×17?

T 13 Use a copy of this.
Fill in the first gap in each with a decimal and the second gap with a percentage.
    a $\frac{1}{4} = \_\_ = \_\_\%$ **b** $\frac{6}{10} = \_\_ = \_\_\%$ **c** $\frac{2}{5} = \_\_ = \_\_\%$
    d $\frac{1}{3} = \_\_ = \_\_\%$ **e** $\frac{37}{100} = \_\_ = \_\_\%$ **f** $\frac{7}{25} = \_\_ = \_\_\%$

14 Fill in the first gap in each with a fraction and the second gap with a decimal.
    a $70\% = \_\_ = \_\_$ **b** $43\% = \_\_ = \_\_$ **c** $45\% = \_\_ = \_\_$
    d $8\% = \_\_ = \_\_$ **e** $120\% = \_\_ = \_\_$

> Give the fractions in their simplest form.

15 **a** Change these decimals to fractions.
       i 0.7 **ii** 0.27 **iii** 0.03 **iv** 0.36 **v** 0.65 **vi** 1.4
    b Write the decimals in **a** as percentages.

Number Support

16 a What fraction of this shape is purple?
  b Write your answer to **a** as a decimal.
  c What percentage is blue?
  d Write your answer to **c** as a decimal.

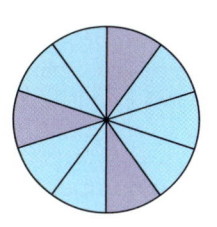

17 a Write these ratios in their simplest form.
  i 6 : 24   **ii** 5 : 45   **iii** 18 : 28   **iv** 42 : 63
  b Harley and Sarah shared a 48-hour gardening job in the ratio 5 : 3.
  How many hours did Sarah work?

T

18 Use a copy of this
The arrow by this thermometer shows a temperature of 20 °C

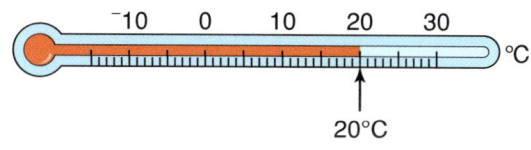

[SATS Paper 1 Level 4]

  a Draw an arrow by the thermometer to show 7 °C.
  Label your arrow 7 °C.
  b Draw an arrow by the thermometer to show ⁻5 °C.
  Label your arrow ⁻5 °C.
  c In New York the temperature was ⁻2 °C.
  In Atlanta the temperature was 7 °C warmer.
  What was the temperature in Atlanta?
  d In Amsterdam the temperature was 3 °C.
  In Helsinki the temperature was ⁻8 °C.
  How many degrees warmer was it in Amsterdam than in Helsinki?

19 How much does it cost to park for 60 minutes?
Show your working.

CAR PARK
25p for 12 minutes

20 Write these as mixed numbers.
  a $\frac{12}{11}$ **b** $\frac{17}{15}$ **c** $\frac{26}{8}$ **d** $\frac{44}{7}$

21 Write these as improper fractions.
  a $1\frac{3}{4}$ **b** $3\frac{2}{5}$ **c** $2\frac{3}{8}$ **d** $5\frac{6}{11}$

22 a $\frac{3}{8}+\frac{1}{8}$ **b** $\frac{5}{9}+\frac{2}{9}$ **c** $\frac{7}{10}-\frac{3}{10}$ **d** $\frac{1}{5}+\frac{2}{5}+\frac{1}{5}$
  e $\frac{5}{6}-\frac{1}{6}-\frac{1}{6}$ **f** $\frac{7}{12}+\frac{5}{12}$ **g** $\frac{5}{11}+\frac{4}{11}-\frac{3}{11}$ **h** $\frac{5}{8}+\frac{7}{8}-\frac{1}{8}$

23 The ratio of protein to carbohydrate in a breakfast cereal is 2 : 15.
How many grams of protein are there if there is this much carbohydrate?
  a 15 g   **b** 30 g   **c** 150 g   **d** 45 g

24 Heather is going to make some necklaces for presents.
She needs 72·5 cm of thread for each necklace.
How much thread does she need to make 10 necklaces?

25 Does < or > go in the box?
  a 23·45 ☐ 23·54   **b** 16·523 ☐ 16·52
  c 9·05 ☐ 9·025   **d** 0·024 ☐ 0·04

26 Which of these are divisible by both 2 and 6?
  84   326   432   573

13

Number

27 Which of these are divisible by both 5 and 8?
96   520   645   1040

28 Use +, −, ×, ÷ to make each calculation correct.
a 4 ☐ 5 = 12 ☐ 3
b 12 ☐ 4 = 4 ☐ 4
c 3 ☐ 1 = 12 ☐ 3
d 5 ☐ 5 = 10 ☐ 10

29 There are four different ways to put 15 people into equal size groups.

1 group of 15
15 groups of 1
3 groups of 5
5 groups of 3
(15 people)

a Show the six different ways to put 18 people into equal size groups.
b Which of these numbers are factors of 30?
1   2   3   4   5   6   7   8   9   10   11   12
13   14   15   16   17   18   19   20   21   22   23   24
25   26   27   28   29   30
c Which of the factors of 30 are prime factors?

T 30 When the wind blows it feels colder.   [SATS Paper 1 Level 4]
The stronger the wind, the colder it feels.
Use a copy of this table. Fill in the gaps.
The first row is done for you.

Wind strength	Temperature out of the wind (°C)	How much colder it feels in the wind (°C)	Temperature it feels in the wind (°C)
Moderate breeze	5	7 degrees colder	⁻2
Fresh breeze	⁻8	11 degrees colder	....
Strong breeze	⁻4	.... degrees colder	⁻20
Gale	....	23 degrees colder	⁻45

31 Work these out mentally.
a 30 × 80   b 16 000 ÷ 400   c 300 × 9   d 6000 ÷ 200   e 32·6 × 0·01

32 Work these out mentally.
a 45 × 2   b 580 × 2   c 32 × 30   d 84 ÷ 2   e 250 ÷ 5   f 24 × 11

33 Work these out mentally.
a 8 × 0·6   b 0·7 × 2·4   c 1·5 ÷ 5   d 740 ÷ 5
e 572 ÷ 4   f 96·6 ÷ 3   g 450 ÷ 15   h 32 × 8

34 Holly had these number cards.

0 1 2 3 4 5 6 7 8 9

She placed all the cards in the diagram so that each side added to the same total.
Fill in the missing numbers on the cards.

(diagram shows cards arranged with 2, 9, and 4 8 3 visible)

35 Find these.
a $\frac{1}{6}$ of 30 mℓ b $\frac{1}{8}$ of 48 g   c $\frac{2}{5}$ of 35 ℓ d $\frac{7}{10}$ of 700 ℓ
e $\frac{3}{5}$ of 85 mℓ f $\frac{5}{6}$ of £3·60   g $1\frac{1}{2}$ of 68 g   h $1\frac{1}{3}$ of £2·70

Number Support

36 Find these.
   a $3 \times \frac{1}{5}$ **b** $6 \times \frac{1}{11}$ **c** $4 \times \frac{3}{5}$ **d** $2 \times \frac{5}{8}$

37 Find these percentages.
   a 25% of 80   **b** 30% of 120   **c** 70% of 340   **d** 15% of 40
   e 35% of 120   **f** 8% of 60   **g** $66\frac{2}{3}$% of 300   **h** $12\frac{1}{2}$% of 160

38 Write down the next two lines of these patterns.
   a $4 \times 3 = 12$ **b** $0.2 \times 8 = 1.6$ **c** $5 \times 1.2 = 6$
        $4 \times 0.3 = 1.2$ $0.2 \times 0.8 = 0.16$ $0.5 \times 1.2 = 0.6$
        $4 \times 0.03 = 0.12$ $0.2 \times 0.08 = 0.016$ $0.05 \times 1.2 = 0.06$

39 In a science experiment, Rosalie had to put 0·6 g of sodium carbonate into each of four test tubes.
How much sodium carbonate does she need to weigh out altogether?

T 40 Use a copy of this table.
Fill it in.

	Round to nearest 10	Round to nearest 100	Round to nearest 1000	Round to nearest 10 000	Round to nearest 100 000
34 392					
848 312					
8 050 802					
775 500					

41 a Which column, A, B, C, D, E or F, has the most prime numbers?
How many are in this column?
   b If we continued this table, the only prime number in column B is 2.
How do we know this? Explain.

A	B	C	D	E	F
1	2	3	4	5	6
7	8	9	10	11	12
13	14	15	16	17	18
19	20	21	22	23	24
25	26	27	28	29	30

42 a What goes in the gaps?
   $31\frac{1}{4} + \_\_ = 35$ $120 - \_\_ = 35$
   25% of $\_\_ = 35$ $\frac{1}{3}$ of $\_\_ = 35$
   b What numbers go in the gaps to make these correct?
   $\_\_ \times \_\_ = 35$ $\_\_ \div \_\_ = 35$
   $\_\_ + \_\_ = 35$ $\_\_ \times \_\_ + \_\_ = 35$

43 The table shows how much it costs to go to a cinema. [SATS Paper 2 Level 4]
Mrs Jones (aged 35), her daughter (aged 12), her son (aged 10) and a friend (aged 65) want to go to the cinema.
They are not sure whether to go before 6 p.m. or after 6 p.m.
How much will they save if they go **before** 6 p.m.?
Show your working.

	Before 6p.m.	After 6p.m.
Adult	£3·20	£4·90
Child (14 or under)	£2·50	£3·50
Senior Citizen (60 or over)	£2·95	£4·90

44 Which of <, > or = make these correct?
   a $\frac{3}{5} \square \frac{2}{5}$ **b** $\frac{3}{8} \square \frac{1}{4}$ **c** $\frac{5}{6} \square \frac{10}{12}$ **d** $\frac{2}{3} \square \frac{3}{4}$

15

Number

45 Nick recorded the amount of rain that fell one week.
  a What goes in the gaps?
      The most rain fell on ___.
      The least rain fell on ___.
  b How much more rain fell on Saturday than Thursday?
  c How much rain fell altogether on Monday, Tuesday, Wednesday, Thursday and Friday?
  d Give your answer to **c** in millimetres.

Results	amount in cm
Monday	0·3
Tuesday	0·7
Wednesday	0·45
Thursday	0·25
Friday	0·6
Saturday	0·9
Sunday	0·05

T **46** Use a copy of this.
  a Fill in the missing numbers in the circles below.

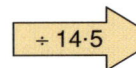

   15 → + 57 → ◯ → × 14·5 → ◯

   ◯ → ÷ 14·5 → 40

  b Fill in the missing numbers in the arrows below.

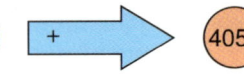

   270 → + → 4050

   270 → × → 4050

47 There are 20 classes in a school.
  a 35% of them went on a school trip to the beach. How many classes went?
  b In total 210 students went on the trip. $\frac{3}{5}$ of them had never been there before. How many had never been there before?

48 Use cancelling to write these fractions in their lowest terms.
  a $\frac{6}{18}$ b $\frac{7}{28}$ c $\frac{15}{25}$ d $3\frac{6}{10}$ e $\frac{56}{63}$

49 Beth got 42 questions out of 63 correct in a science test.
What percentage did she get correct?
Round to the nearest percent.

50 a What is the ratio of red : blue in this shape? Write it in its simplest form.
  b What is the proportion of blue in the shape? Write it as a fraction, decimal and percentage.

51 a 6·27 + 0·01   b 5·976 − 0·01
    c 12·149 + 0·001   d 21·490 − 0·001

52 Round each of these to the nearest whole number.
  a 45·67   b 5·403   c 5·025   d 7·99

Number Support

53 The number 9 is halfway between 7 and 11.
What number is halfway between these?
    a 4 and 10   **b** 7·5 and 12·5   **c** 2 and 6·8   **d** ⁻3 and 2

54 Matt had these number cards.

    [5] [0] [2] [3] [8] [5]

    a Make 2 numbers that round to 500 to the nearest 10.
    b Make 2 numbers that round to 4000 to the nearest 1000.

55 Which of > or < or = goes in the box?
    a 450 m ☐ 4 km   **b** 7350 g ☐ 7·3 kg   **c** 7·3 km ☐ 7300 m   **d** 702 mm ☐ 72 cm

56 Which of 216, 504, 732, 756 and 1722 are divisible by
    a 12   **b** 18   **c** 21?

57 a Write the answers.
        (6 + 3) × 4 = ___   6 + (3 × 4) = ___
    b Work out the answer to this.
        (3 + 5) × (4 + 5 + 1)
    c Put brackets in the calculation to make the answer 64.
        3 + 2 + 3 × 8
    d Now put brackets in the calculation to make the answer 43.
        3 + 2 + 3 × 8

58 Sara needed 6 m of fabric to make a costume.
    a How much did it cost to the nearest penny?
    b How much change did she get from £20?

    Fabric £2·20 per metre

59 Give the answers to these to 1 d.p. if you need to round.
    a 288 ÷ 16   **b** 567 ÷ 21   **c** 677 ÷ 18   **d** 419 ÷ 38

60 The ratio of milk to water in a chocolate drink is 4 : 3.
How much milk is in the drink if there is this amount of water?
    a 30 mℓ   **b** 120 mℓ   **c** 15 mℓ   **d** 60 mℓ

61 Amy poured 2 cartons of apple juice and 3 cartons of orange juice into a big jug.
    a What is the ratio of apple juice to orange juice in Amy's jug?
    b Tom pours 1 carton of apple juice and $2\frac{1}{2}$ cartons of orange juice into another big jug.
What is the ratio of apple juice to orange juice in Tom's jug?
    c Chandri pours 2 cartons of apple juice and 2 cartons of orange juice into another big jug.
But she wants only half as much apple juice as orange juice in her jug.
What should Chandri pour into her jug now?

62 a Sarah weighed some samples of chemical in her science laboratory. Write her results in order from largest to smallest mass.
        7·3871 g   7·8351 g   7·38 g   7·0835 g
    b These times were recorded in an athletics record book.
Write them in order from the fastest time to slowest time.
        0·4782 min   0·7482 min   0·0072 min   0·0728 min   0·7 min

Number

63 David rounded a whole number to the nearest 10 000 and got 80 000.
Alex rounded the same number to the nearest 1000 and got 78 000.
   a What is the smallest number it could have been?
   b What is the largest number it could have been?

64 a Georgie bought 5 bananas.
Their total mass was 727 g.
About what was the mass of each banana to the nearest gram?
   b In Design and Technology, 8·1 m of braid was shared equally by 6 students.
How much did each get, to the nearest metre?

65 a I am a prime number.
I am a factor of 35.
What number am I?
   b I am a square number.
I am a multiple of 4.
The sum of my digits is divisible by 3.
What number am I?

66 Use your calculator to find these.
   a $\sqrt{169}$ **b** $1\cdot3^2$ **c** 16^3 **d** $\sqrt[3]{2744}$ **e** $\sqrt{8\cdot7}$ **f** $15^3 - 11^2$

67 Which is bigger, the square of 22 or the cube of 12?

68 Estimate the answers to these. Show how you found your estimate.
   a 8×19 **b** $102 \div 9$ **c** 19×22 **d** $88 \div 31$ **e** $21\cdot9 \times 6\cdot2$
   f $492 \div 4\cdot8$ **g** $\frac{3\cdot1 \times 4\cdot8}{5\cdot2}$ **h** $\frac{2\cdot6 + 6\cdot1}{7\cdot2 - 3\cdot8}$ **i** $8\cdot5 \div (7\cdot7 - 4\cdot8)$

69 Check the answer to these using inverse operations. Which ones are wrong?
   a $35 \times 7 = 245$ **b** $595 \div 7 = 84$ **c** $156 + 397 = 653$ **d** $17\cdot2 \times 4\cdot8 = 82\cdot56$

70 How can you tell this answer is wrong without doing the calculation?
$3\cdot64 \times 1\cdot7 = 6\cdot186$

71 a A club wants to take 2000 people on a trip to London.
The club organiser says:
'We can go in coaches.
Each coach can carry 52 people.'
How many coaches do they need for the trip?
Show your working.
   b Each coach costs £390.
What is the total cost of the coaches?
   c How much is each person's share of the cost?

72 ☐☐
   × ☐
   ─────
   1 8 0

Write down all the different numbers that could go in the boxes.

73 In a maths test, Jake got 92%, Amy got 0·89 and Susie got 9 out of 10.
Who got the highest mark?

74 a Use a table or factor tree to write 264 as a product of prime factors.
   b Copy this diagram and complete it for the prime factors of 264 and 84.
   c Find the HCF of 264 and 84.
   d Find the LCM of 84 and 264.

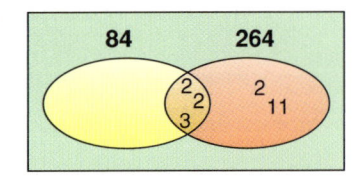

Number Support

75 a I am thinking of a two-digit square number with a units digit of 9.
   __ 9
   What is the square root?
b I am thinking of a three-digit square number between 100 and 200.
   It has units digit 1.
   1 __ 1
   Could its square root be a prime number?

76 Dressing is made by mixing oil and vinegar.
Recipe A says to mix 1 part oil with 2 parts vinegar.
Recipe B says to mix 1 part oil with 3 parts vinegar.
a In recipe A, how much oil should I mix with 250 ml of vinegar?
b In recipe B, how much oil should I mix with 450 ml of vinegar?
c How much oil and vinegar would I mix to make 600 ml of dressing in Recipe B?
d Is this correct?
   50% of recipe A is oil.
   Explain your answer.

77 These labels give the amount of fat in some muesli bars.

Energy Bar	Life Bar	Tandem Bar
mass 250 g	mass 300 g	mass 200 g
fat 8 g	fat 12 g	fat 7·5 g

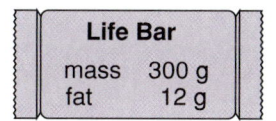

a What is the ratio   *fat : total mass*   in the 3 bars?
b Which bar has the highest percentage of fat?
c What percentage of fat does it contain?

1 Place Value, Ordering and Rounding

You need to know

✓ place value and powers of ten — page 1
✓ multiplying and dividing by 10, 100, 1000 — page 1
✓ rounding — page 1
✓ putting decimals in order — page 2

Key vocabulary
exponent, indices, index, power, round, standard form, to the power of n

▶▶ Staying alive with 5 on Planet X

The number system on Planet X has only these five number symbols.

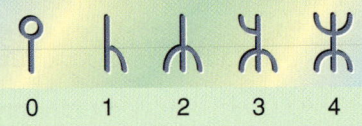

♀ Һ ⋏ ⋎ ⋇
0   1   2   3   4

On Planet X when they get to 5 they have no more symbols.

They have to write 5 as 1 lot of five and 0 ones.

Һ   1 lot of five
     and
♀   0 ones

These are how some numbers are written.

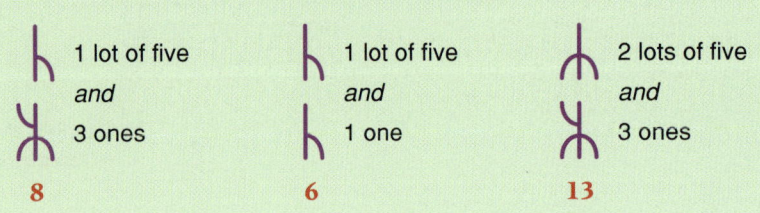

Һ 1 lot of five   Һ 1 lot of five   ⋏ 2 lots of five
    and   and   and
⋎ 3 ones   Һ 1 one   ⋎ 3 ones

8   **6**   **13**

Write these numbers in the Planet X number system.

    7   18   24

How do you think 38 might be written?

Place Value, Ordering and Rounding

Powers of ten

Remember
The **decimal number system** is based on **powers of ten**.

$10 = 10^1$
$100 = 10 \times 10 = 10^2$
$1000 = 10 \times 10 \times 10 = 10^3$
$10\,000 = 10 \times 10 \times 10 \times 10 = 10^4$

$10^1, 10^2, 10^3, 10^4, ...$ are called **powers of ten**.

The little $^1, ^2, ^3, ^4$ of $10^1, 10^2, 10^3, 10^4, ...$ are called **indices** or **exponents**.

Discussion

$10^2 = 10 \times 10$
so $\frac{1}{10^2} = \frac{1}{10 \times 10}$
$= \frac{1}{100}$
$= 0{\cdot}01$

To find 10^2 on the calculator we could key $\boxed{10}\;\boxed{x^y}\;\boxed{2}\;\boxed{=}$.
Try this.

To find 10^{-2} on the calculator we key $\boxed{10}\;\boxed{x^y}\;\boxed{(-)}\;\boxed{2}\;\boxed{=}$.
Compare your answer to 10^{-2} with $\frac{1}{10^2}$.

Compare $\frac{1}{10^3}$ with 10^{-3}.
Compare $\frac{1}{10^4}$ with 10^{-4}.

Make a general statement about $\frac{1}{10^n}$ and 10^{-n}. **Discuss**.

$10^2 = 100$ $\qquad 10^1 = 10$ $\qquad 10^0 = 1$

$10^{-1} = \frac{1}{10} = 0{\cdot}1$ $\qquad 10^{-2} = \frac{1}{10^2} = \frac{1}{100} = 0{\cdot}01$ $\qquad 10^{-3} = \frac{1}{10^3} = \frac{1}{1000} = 0{\cdot}001$

The number system we use is the **base 10 number system**.
This **place value chart** shows the base 10 number system.

Millions	Thousands			Hundreds					
Millions	Hundreds of thousands	Tens of thousands	Thousands	Hundreds	Tens	Units	tenths	hundredths	thousandths
10^6	10^5	10^4	10^3	10^2	10^1	10^0	10^{-1}	10^{-2}	10^{-3}

$\times 10$ between each place. Each place to the left is ten times larger.

We say $8{\cdot}6 \times 10^3$ as 'eight point six times ten to the power of 3'.

The thickness of a piece of thick paper is $0{\cdot}0089$ mm.
We can write this as $8{\cdot}9 \times 10^{-3}$ mm.
We say $8{\cdot}9 \times 10^{-3}$ as 'eight point nine times ten to the power of negative three'.

Number

Exercise 1

1. Write these without the index.
   Write **e**, **f** and **g** as decimals.
   a 10^3 **b** 10^6 **c** 10^0 **d** 10^1 **e** 10^{-2} **f** 10^{-1} ***g** 10^{-5}

2. Write these as powers of ten.
   a ten **b** ten thousand **c** a million **d** one **e** one tenth
   f one thousandth ***g** one hundred thousandth

3. Copy and complete these. The first one has been done for you.
   a $10^{-1} = \frac{1}{10^1} = \frac{1}{10} = $ **0·1**
   b $10^{-2} = \frac{1}{\_\_} = \frac{1}{100} = \_\_$
   ***c** $\_\_ = \frac{1}{10^4} = \_\_ = \_\_$
   ***d** $\_\_ = \_\_ = \frac{1}{1000} = \_\_$

   This is linked to science.

4. Write the numbers in red in words.
   a The world's highest observatory is $4 \cdot 3 \times 10^3$ m above sea level.
   b Jupiter's largest moon is $1 \cdot 07 \times 10^6$ km from Jupiter.
   c The thickness of a piece of paper is about 6×10^{-2} cm.
   d The thickness of a hair is about $1 \cdot 5 \times 10^{-5}$ m.

*5. Write the numbers in green as powers of 10.
   a The distance to the nearest star is about
      10 000 000 000 000 km.
   b The length of the Earth's orbit around the sun is about
      1 000 000 000 km.
   c In a hydrogen bomb explosion, about **0·001** kg of mass converts into energy.

Review 1 Write each of these without the index.
Write **b** and **c** as decimals.
a 10^4 **b** 10^{-3} ***c** 10^{-6}

Review 2 Write these as powers of ten.
a one thousand **b** ten million **c** one hundredth

Review 3 Copy and complete these.
a $10^{-3} = \frac{1}{10^3} = \frac{1}{\_\_} = \_\_$
b $\_\_ = \frac{1}{\_\_} = \frac{1}{100} = \_\_$

Review 4 Write the numbers in red in words.
a The shortest distance between Mars and Earth is $5 \cdot 58 \times 10^6$ km.
b A light year is $9 \cdot 4 \times 10^{12}$ km.
c The distance of the Sun from the Earth is $1 \cdot 6 \times 10^{-5}$ light years.
d The power output of a speaker is $2 \cdot 1 \times 10^{-3}$ watts.

***Review 5** Write these numbers as powers of ten.
a 1 000 000 **b** 10 000 **c** 0·01 **d** 0·0001

Place Value, Ordering and Rounding

Standard form

$1 \cdot 86 \times 10^{-2}$

one digit before the decimal point

times ten to a power

We say that a number written in this way is written in **standard form**.

$8 \cdot 735 \times 10^4$ and $7 \cdot 08 \times 10^{-3}$ are written in standard form.

$14 \cdot 73 \times 10^{-1}$ and $0 \cdot 0863 \times 10^4$ and $3 \cdot 86^4$ are *not* written in standard form.

Exercise 2

1 Are the numbers in purple written in standard form?
Write yes or no.
  a Neptune takes a bit more than $1 \cdot 6 \times 10^2$ Earth years to orbit the Sun.
  b Neptune's largest moon is $27 \cdot 1 \times 10^2$ km in diameter.
  c Neptune is $4 \cdot 497 \times 10^9$ km from the Sun.
  d The wavelength of light we can see is $5 \cdot 0 \times 10^{-5}$ cm.
  e The mass of a magnesium atom is 40×10^{-24} g.

2 Pick the one out of each of the following lists that is **not** written in standard form.
  a $5 \cdot 3 \times 10^2$, $8 \cdot 643 \times 10^{-3}$, $5 \cdot 3^7$, 4×10^{-1}
  b $3 \cdot 4 \times 10^{-7}$, $0 \cdot 842 \times 10^4$, $3 \cdot 68 \times 10^3$, $7 \cdot 28 \times 10^9$

*3 Copy these and fill in the gaps so that the final answer is in standard form.
  a $27\,300 = 2730 \times 10 = 273 \times 100 = 27 \cdot 3 \times 1000 = 2 \cdot 73 \times \underline{} = 2 \cdot 73 \times 10^{\underline{}}$
  b $8662 = 866 \cdot 2 \times 10 = 86 \cdot 62 \times \underline{} = 8 \cdot 662 \times \underline{} = 8 \cdot 662 \times 10^{\underline{}}$
  c $567 = 56 \cdot 7 \times \underline{} = \underline{} \times \underline{} = \underline{} \times 10^{\underline{}}$

Review   Which of these are written in standard form?
a $4 \cdot 7 \times 10^3$ **b** $86 \cdot 4 \times 10^5$ **c** 90×10^{-1} **d** 830×10^7
e $4 \cdot 36 \times 10^{-1}$ **f** $0 \cdot 84 \times 10^{-2}$ **g** $3 \cdot 6842 \times 10^7$ **h** 7×10^0

A **kilo**metre is 1000 metres.   **Kilo** is 10^3.
A **centi**litre is $\frac{1}{100}$ of a litre.   **Centi** is $\frac{1}{100}$ or 10^{-2}.

These **prefixes** are associated with the given powers of 10.

Power	Prefix	Power	Prefix
10^9	giga	10^{-2}	centi
10^6	mega	10^{-3}	milli
10^3	kilo	10^{-6}	micro
		10^{-9}	nano
		10^{-12}	pico

The prefixes are usually used with the following units.

   metre (m)   gram (g)   litre (ℓ)   second (s)

Number

Exercise 3

1 Mel measured her wrist as 15 centimetres.
She wanted to convert this to metres.
She wrote

$$\text{centi} = 10^{-2}$$
$$= \frac{1}{10^2}$$
$$= \frac{1}{100}$$

so 1 centimetre is $\frac{1}{100}$ of a metre.

$\frac{1}{100}$ of 15 = 15 ÷ 100
         = 0.15 m

Look at what Mel wrote to help you decide what to put in each gap.

Copy and fill in the gaps to work out these conversions.

a 8.4 kilograms to grams
kilo = 10^3
= ___
So 1 **kilo**gram is ___ grams.
8.4 kg = 8.4 × ___ grams = ___ grams

b 894 millimetres to metres
milli = 10^{-}
= $\frac{1}{10^{-}}$
= $\frac{1}{-}$
So 1 **milli**metre is ___ of a metre.
___ of 894 mm = (___ ÷ ___)m
= ___ m

* **c** 5 megabytes to bytes
mega = ___
= ___
So a **mega**byte is ___ bytes.
5 megabytes = 5 × ___ bytes

2 Copy and fill in the gaps. The first one is done.
a 3 kilograms = 3 × **10^3** grams
b 5 gigabytes = 5 × ___ bytes
c 8 centimetres = 8 × ___ metres
d 24 nanoseconds = 24 × ___ seconds

[T] *3 Five nanometres could be written as 5×10^{-9} m.
Use a copy of this.
Find an equivalent in the square for each of these measurements. Shade the box it is in.
The shading makes a letter. Which letter?
a 2 gigabytes
b 2 megabytes
c 2 kilobytes
d 8 centimetres
e 8 millimetres
f 8 micrometres
g 8 picometres
h 8 nanometres
i 20 gigabytes
j 200 kilobytes
k 800 nanometres
l 80 micrometres
m 2 bytes

8×10^{-3} metres	8×10^{-5} metres	2×10^6 bytes	8×10^{-9} metres
8×10^{-7} metres	2×10^{-6} bytes	2×10^{-10} bytes	20×10^7 bytes
2×10^{10} bytes	2×10^9 bytes	2×10^3 bytes	8×10^5 metres
8×10^{-12} metres	8×10^3 metres	8×10^6 metres	8×10^2 metres
2×10^5 bytes	2×10^0 bytes	8×10^{-6} metres	8×10^{-2} metres

Review 1 Copy and fill in the gaps to work out these conversions.
a 8.75 kilometres to metres
kilo = 10^{-}
So 1 kilometre is ___ metres.
8.75 km = ___ × 1000 metres = ___ metres

b 3.4 centilitres to litres
centi = $10^{-} = \frac{1}{-} = \frac{1}{-}$
So 1 centilitre = ___ litres.
3.4 cℓ = (3.4 ÷ ___) litres = ___ litres

24

Place Value, Ordering and Rounding

Review 2 Match each of these measurements with an equivalent one from the box.
a   9 nanoseconds
b   9 milliseconds
c   9 microseconds
d   9 picoseconds
e   900 nanoseconds

A	9×10^{-3} seconds
B	9×10^{-12} seconds
C	9×10^{-7} seconds
D	9×10^{-9} seconds
E	9×10^{-6} seconds

Multiplying and dividing by powers of ten

Remember
To **multiply by 10, 100, 1000, 10 000** ... we move the digits one place to the left for each zero in 10, 100, 1000, 10 000, ...

To **divide by 10, 100, 1000, 10 000** ... we move the digits one place to the right for each zero in 10, 100, 1000, 10 000, ...

Examples
$\quad\quad$ U·t h $\quad\quad\quad\quad$ HTU·th $\quad\quad\quad\quad$ ThHTU $\quad\quad\quad\quad$ T U·t h th tth
$\quad\quad$ 8·42 × 100 = 842· $\quad\quad\quad\quad\quad\quad$ 8642 ÷ 10 000 = 0·8642

Multiplying by 0·1 is the same as dividing by 10. $\quad$ because $5 \times 0.1 = 5 \times \frac{1}{10} = 5 \div 10$
Multiplying by 0·01 is the same as dividing by 100. $\quad$ because $8 \times 0.01 = 8 \times \frac{1}{100} = 8 \div 100$
Dividing by 0·1 is the same as multiplying by 10. $\quad\quad$ because $7 \div 0.1 = 7 \div \frac{1}{10} = 7 \times 10$
Dividing by 0·01 is the same as multiplying by 100. $\quad\;$ because $6 \div 0.01 = 6 \div \frac{1}{100} = 6 \times 100$

Examples $\quad 9 \cdot 8 \times 0 \cdot 1 = 9 \cdot 8 \div 10 \quad\quad\quad\quad 7 \cdot 93 \div 0 \cdot 01 = 7 \cdot 93 \times 100$
$\quad\quad\quad\quad\quad\quad\quad\quad\quad\;\; = 0 \cdot 98 \quad\quad\quad\quad\quad\quad\quad\quad\quad\quad\; = 793$

1 m² = 10 000 cm²

$\quad\quad$ 1 m $\quad\quad\quad$ 100 cm
1 m [1 m²] = 100 cm [10 000 cm²]

Worked Example
In design and technology, Fiona made a small table for her mother's birthday.
She worked out the area of the top surface as 2000 cm².
She needed to convert this to m² to work out how much varnish to buy.
What is the area of the table top in m²?

Answer
To convert m² to cm² we multiply by 10 000.
So to convert cm² to m² we divide by 10 000.
$\quad$ 2000 cm² = (2000 ÷ 10 000) m²
$\quad\quad\quad\quad\quad\;\; = 0 \cdot 2$ m²
The area of the table top is **0·2 m²**.

Link to metric conversions on page 000.

Discussion

Denny was asked to multiply 8·64 × 0·1. He got 0·864.

I must have done something wrong. The answer should be bigger than 8·64 because I multiplied.

Is Denny correct? **Discuss**.

When we divide, is the answer **always** smaller than the number being divided? **Discuss**.

Number

Exercise 4

1 Work out the answers to these.
Put the answers in order from smallest to largest.
What word do the letters make?

| D | 0·94 ÷ 100 | E | 6940 ÷ 10 000 | G | 7094 × 10 000 | I | 3·82 × 100 |
| N | 56 × 1000 | R | 8·6 ÷ 1000 | R | 86·4 ÷ 100 | O | 5·7 ÷ 1000 |

2 a Damian measured the height of a cupboard as 1250 cm.
How many 10 cm high boxes can be stacked, one on top of the other, in the cupboard?
b Justine bought 100 second-hand CDs for £2·25 each.
How much did this cost altogether?

T 3 Use a copy of this.
Match the equivalent calculations with a line.

| 5·6 ÷ 0·1 | 5600 × 0·1 | 5·6 × 0·1 | 0·056 ÷ 0·01 | 0·56 × 0·01 | 0·0056 ÷ 0·1 |

| 5·6 | 0·0056 | 56 | 560 | 0·056 | 0·56 |

4 a Rosie showed that 7·8 × 0·1 is the same as 7·8 ÷ 10.

$$7·8 \times 0·1 = 7·8 \times \frac{1}{10}$$
$$= 7·8 \div 10$$

Use Rosie's way to show that
8·3 × 0·01 is the same as 8·3 ÷ 100.

*__*b__ Madhu explained why 14 ÷ 0·1 is the same as 14 × 10.

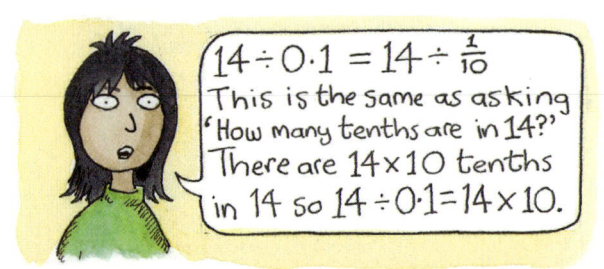

$14 \div 0·1 = 14 \div \frac{1}{10}$
This is the same as asking
'How many tenths are in 14?'
There are 14 × 10 tenths
in 14 so 14 ÷ 0·1 = 14 × 10.

Use Madhu's way to explain why 12 ÷ 0·01 is the same as 12 × 100.

5 a 5 × 0·1 **b** 6·4 × 0·1 **c** 0·37 ÷ 0·1 **d** 0·68 × 0·01
e 4·98 ÷ 0·01 **f** 8·47 × 0·01 **g** 32 ÷ 0·01 **h** 0·092 ÷ 0·1

See page 2 for multiplying positive and negative numbers.

6 a ⁻4·2 × 0·1 **b** ⁻0·64 ÷ 0·1 **c** ⁻0·24 ÷ 0·01 **d** ⁻48·2 × 0·01

7 Harry filled 8 test tubes with 0·02 litres of acid.
He worked out how much he had used like this.

$8 \times 0·01 = 8 \times 2 \times 0·01$ 0·02 = 2 × 0·01
$= 16 \times 0·01$
$= 16 \div 100$
$= 0·16$ litres

Work out how much he would use to fill
a 5 jugs with 0·5 litres **b** 6 beakers with 0·08 litres **c** 80 bell jars with 1·2 litres.

Place Value, Ordering and Rounding

8 What goes in the box?
  a 0·5 × ☐ = 50   **b** 0·8 ÷ ☐ = 80   **c** 12 × ☐ = 1·2   **d** 85·3 ÷ ☐ = 853   **e** 187 × ☐ = 1·87

9 The big square is 1 unit by 1 unit.
Each small square has sides of 0·1.
Explain how you could use the diagram to show these.
  a 0·4 × 0·7 = 0·28   **b** 0·12 ÷ 0·2 = 0·6

1 cm^2 = 100 mm^2
1 m^2 = 10 000 cm^2
1 cm^3 = 1000 mm^3
1 m^3 = 1 000 000 cm^3

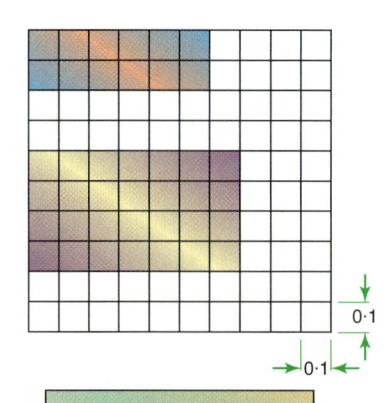

10 Use the facts in the box to help.
  a What goes in the gaps?
   7 cm^2 = ___ × ___ mm^2
        = ___ mm^2
  b i Faye worked out she needed 3 m^2 of carpet for a wardrobe.
   How many cm^2 is this?
   ii Janna worked out the volume of a cube of sugar was 8 cm^3.
   What is the volume in mm^3?
   iii A rubbish skip has a volume of 5 m^3.
   What is this in cm^3?

*__11__ Use the facts in the box in question **10** to help.
  a What goes in the gaps?
   50 000 cm^2 = (___ ÷ ___) m^2
           = ___ m^2
  b Convert these.
   i 80 000 mm^3 to cm^3 **ii** 5600 mm^2 to cm^2 **iii** 86 000 000 cm^3 to m^3

T

Review 1

0·073	24·5	7·3	52·1	8	24·5	52·1		29	56	521	521	81	81		2·41	8	7·3
B																	
2·45	81	81	24·5		8	2	56	5·3	24·5	5·6		7·3	0·073	24·5	29	81	
52·1	2·41	81		81	0·073	0·8	2·41	52·1	81	81	24·5	52·1	2·41				
29	81	24·5	52·1	5·3	2	0·2											

Use a copy of this box. Write the letter beside each calculation above its answer in the box.

B 24·5 ÷ 10 = **2·45**   **S** 0·073 × 100   **C** 0·029 × 1000   **U** 0·0053 × 1000
E 0·81 × 100   **Y** 200 ÷ 1000   **D** 0·056 ÷ 0·01   **I** 7·3 × 0·01
A 8000 × 0·001   **N** 245 × 0·1   **F** 0·521 ÷ 0·001   **O** 0·56 ÷ 0·01
G 80 × 0·01   **R** 0·002 ÷ 0·001   **H** 24·1 ÷ 10   **T** 52 100 × 0·001

Review 2
  a Show that 4·23 × 0·001 is the same as 4·23 ÷ 1000.
   You could use Rosie's way from question **4**.
*__b__ Show that 5·76 ÷ 0·01 is the same as 5·76 × 100.
   You could use Madhu's way from question **4**.

27

Number

Review 3 This square is 1 unit by 1 unit.

Each small square is 0·1 by 0·1.

Explain how you could use the diagram to show these.
a 0·4 × 0·8 = 0·32
b 0·27 ÷ 0·3 = 0·9

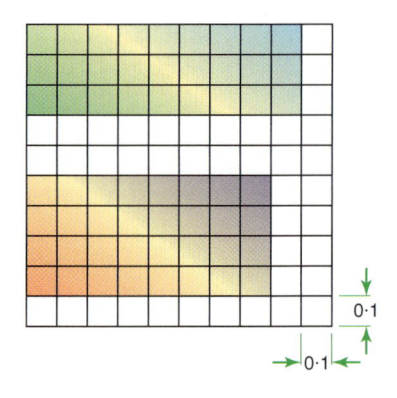

Rounding to powers of ten

We often **round** numbers when **estimating**.

Example A newspaper reporter might round 28 362, the number of people at a concert, to
28 000 (nearest thousand)

or 30 000 (nearest ten thousand).

Example 342 × 78 is about
300 × 80 = 24 000

rounded to nearest hundred   rounded to nearest ten

Worked Example
The population of England is about 60 million.
The populations, to the nearest hundred thousand, of the five largest cities are:

London	6·4 million
Birmingham	1·0 million
Liverpool	0·5 million
Sheffield	0·4 million
Leeds	0·4 million

Remember: when a number is exactly halfway between we round up.

a What is the greatest population London could have?
* **b** The tenth largest city is Coventry with a population of 0·3 million. Estimate the percentage of the population of England who live in the ten largest cities.

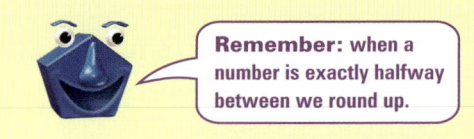

Answer
a 6·4 million is 6 400 000 and has been rounded to the nearest hundred thousand. The greatest number that would be rounded to 6 400 000 is **6 449 999**. If it was one more, 6 450 000, it would be rounded to 6·5 million.

* **b** The sixth to the ninth largest cities must have populations between 0·3 million and 0·4 million. We estimate that the mean population of these four cities is 0·35 million.
Total millions in ten largest cities = 6·4 + 1 + 0·5 + 0·4 + 0·4 + 4 × 0·35 + 0·3 = 10·4 million
Percentage in ten largest cities = $\frac{10 \cdot 4}{60} \times 100\%$
= **17%** to the nearest per cent

Place Value, Ordering and Rounding

Exercise 5

1 Round these population figures.
  a 864 to the nearest 10
  b 3864 to the nearest 100
  c 17 983 to the nearest 1000
  d 486 247 to the nearest 10 000
  e 79 500 to the nearest 1000
  f 78 402 to the nearest 100
  g 81 647 to the nearest 1000
  h 842 010 to the nearest 100 000
  i 7 082 400 to the nearest million.

2 Write down an estimate you could do to find an approximate answer for these.
  a 721 × 81   **b** 82 × 290   **c** 2912 × 127

There is more about finding an estimate on page 72.

3 Jack has these number cards. 8 3 5 7 2 0

  a Jack made the closest number he could to 570 000 using all of his cards. What number did he make?
  b Jack made this number. 2 7 5 3 0 8
    He rounded it to 275 000.
    Did he round to the nearest 1000 or nearest 10 000?
  c Jack was given another card, 5.
    He made the number 5 2 7 5 3 0 8
    He said 'I have made a number just bigger than five million.'
    His friend said 'It's nearer to five and a half million.'
    Who is more accurate, Jack or his friend? Explain.
  d Jack made a number that, when rounded to the nearest 10 000, was 580 000.
    What might his number have been?
    Is there more than one answer?

Find all the possible answers.

4 Make up a salesperson's speech for this vacuum cleaner using rounded numbers.
Consumers want the price, noise and weight to be low and the reach to be high.

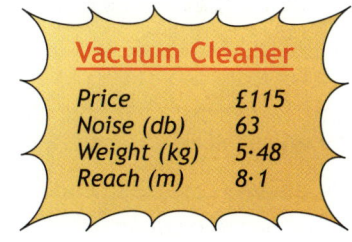

Vacuum Cleaner
Price   £115
Noise (db)   63
Weight (kg)   5·48
Reach (m)   8·1

5 Charlotte read in the newspaper that, to the nearest thousand, the local park upgrade cost £18 000.
  a What is the smallest amount of money this could have cost?
  b What is the largest amount?
  c Charlotte read in another newspaper that it had cost £18 400 to the nearest hundred. What are the smallest and largest amounts now?

6 Sam had some money saved in his bank account.
He estimated the amount as £3500 to the nearest hundred.
He told his mother the amount was £4000 to the nearest thousand.
Write down three amounts Sam might have saved.

29

Number

7 This table gives the population of the five largest countries in Europe.

Population	
Russian Federation	105 984 000
Germany	81 912 000
United Kingdom	58 144 000
France	58 375 000
Italy	57 193 000

  a Round each population to the nearest million then add these rounded figures.
  b Add the five populations, then round the answer to the nearest million.
  c Explain why the answers to **a** and **b** are different.
  d The estimated population of Europe is 688 million.
     Estimate the percentage of people in Europe who do **not** live in the five largest countries.
 *e The population of the tenth largest country, the Netherlands, is 15 517 000.
     Estimate the percentage of people in Europe who live in the ten largest countries.

*8 About 74·5 million barrels of oil were produced one year.
  a This figure has been rounded to the nearest hundred thousand.
     What is the greatest and smallest number of barrels that could have been produced?
  b One report said 'Nearly seventy-five million barrels were produced'.
     Another said 'Just over seventy million barrels were produced'.
     Which report is more accurate? Explain.
  c This table gives the amount of oil produced by the five top oil-producing countries.
     The eighth top producer is Venezuela and it produced 3·2 million barrels.
     Estimate the percentage of the world's oil produced by the top eight oil-producing countries.

Million barrels	
Saudi Arabia	9·1
USA	7·7
Russian Fed	6·5
Iran	3·8
Mexico	3·5

Review 1 Round
 a 7921 to the nearest 100
 b 45 682 to the nearest 1000
 c 63 845 to the nearest 10 000
 d 159 845 to the nearest 1000.

Review 2 Cindy, David, Helen and Stuart were each given five playing cards from a pack. Cindy was given clubs, David diamonds, Helen hearts and Stuart spades. They were each given the same numbers, 1, 3, 4, 6 and 9.

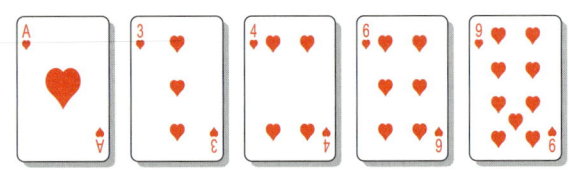

The Ace is 1

They were asked to make a number as close to 55 000 as possible.

Their answers were   Cindy   63 149,
                      David   61 439,
                      Helen   46 931,
                      Stuart   49 136.

 a Who was closest to 55 000?
 b Can you make a number closer to 55 000 using the same cards? If so what is it?
 c Stuart took another spade, the 7 of spades. He made the number 376 914 and asked David to round it to the nearest thousand. What should David's answer have been?

Review 3 Make up a salesperson's speech for this refrigerator by rounding the numbers.

Consumers want the price and energy usage to be low and the volume to be large.

Refrigerator
Price   £045
Capacity   373 litres
Energy usage   719
(KWh/year)

Place Value, Ordering and Rounding

* **Review 4** The land areas (in km^2) of some European countries are

British Isles	243 056
France	544 893
Germany	350 776
The Netherlands	33 272
Italy	297 677
Spain	492 588

a Put these numbers in order from largest to smallest.
b Add the land areas then round the answer to the nearest 1000 km^2.
c Round each land area to the nearest 1000 km^2 then add these rounded areas.
d Explain why the answers to **b** and **c** are different.

Rounding to decimal places

Remember
Follow these steps to **round to a given number of decimal places**, for example, to round 19·638421 to 2 decimal places.

1 Keep the number of digits you want.
2 Before 'throwing the rest away', look at the next decimal place.
3 If this digit is 5 or greater, increase the last digit you are keeping by 1. Otherwise leave it as it is. Throw the unwanted digits away.

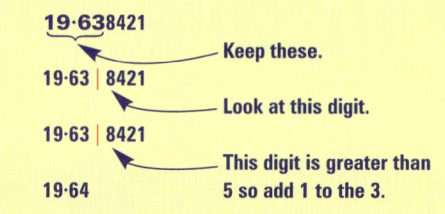

19·638421 — Keep these.
19·63 | 8421 — Look at this digit.
19·63 | 8421 — This digit is greater than 5 so add 1 to the 3.
19·64

Worked Example
Round 3·627253 to 2 d.p.

Answer
a We want 2 digits after the decimal point.

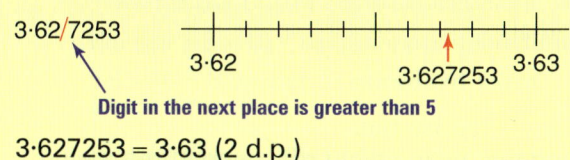

3·62|7253
Digit in the next place is greater than 5

3·627253 = 3·63 (2 d.p.)

Rounding to **the nearest whole number** is the same as rounding to **0 d.p.**

Example 3·8527 rounded to the nearest whole number is 4.

Sometimes the answer to a calculation has one or more repeating digits.

Example 17 ÷ 3 = 5·666666 ···
         = **5·6̇ or 5·67 (2 d.p.)**

5·6̇ is called a recurring decimal. The dot above the 6 shows that the digit repeats.

Note: We round 14·0342 to 1 d.p. as 14·0, not 14.
This shows that we have rounded to 1 d.p. and not to the nearest whole number.

Discussion

Never round until the final answer is found.

Suppose $A = \frac{0·34}{26·1}$ and $B = 5·9A$.
You are to find the answer to B to 2 decimal places.

What answer do you get for B if you round the answer to A?
What answer do you get for B if you do *not* round the answer for A? **Discuss**.

Number

C   **Multiplying and dividing by powers of ten**

To **multiply by 10, 100, 1000, 10 000**, ... we move the digits one place to the left for each zero in 10, 100, 1000, 10 000, ...

To **divide by 10, 100, 1000, 10 000**, ... we move the digits one place to the right for each zero in 10, 100, 1000, 10 000, ...

Multiplying by 0·1 is the same as dividing by 10.
Multiplying by 0·01 is the same as dividing by 100.
Dividing by 0·1 is the same as multiplying by 10.
Dividing by 0·01 is the same as multiplying by 100.

Examples   43·45 × 0·01 = 43·45 ÷ 100   6·4 ÷ 0·1 = 6·4 × 10
                      = 0·4345   = 64

Example   1 m^3 = 1 000 000 cm^3

Mr Todd worked out he needed 3 000 000 cm^3 of soil for a garden plot.
He had to convert this to m^3 to work out how much to order.
To convert cm^3 to m^3 we divide by 1 000 000.
3 000 000 cm^3 = (3 000 000 ÷ 1 000 000) m^3
                    = 3 m^3
He needs to order **3 m^3** of soil.

D   **Rounding to powers of ten**

We often **round** numbers when we **estimate**.

Example   The population of the world is about 5300 million.

The populations of the four largest cities are:
    Mexico City 21·5 million, Sao Paulo 19·9 million, Tokyo 19·5 million,
    New York 15·7 million.
The 10th largest city is Rio de Janeiro with a population of 11·9 million.
We can estimate the populations of the 5th, 6th, 7th, 8th and 9th largest cities as having an average population of $\frac{15·7 + 11·9}{2}$ = 13·8 million.
The total population of the ten largest cities is then
21·5 + 19·9 + 19·5 + 15·7 + 5 × 13·8 + 11·9 = 157·5 million.
The approximate percentage of people in the world who live in the ten largest cities is $\frac{157·5}{5300}$ × 100% = 3·0% (1 d.p.).

E   When **rounding to a given number of decimal places** we keep the digits we want. If the digit in the next decimal place is 5 or greater, we increase the last digit we are keeping by 1.

Examples   4·5362 to 1 d.p. = 4·5
                26·3774 to 2 d.p. = 26·38
                17·038 to 1 d.p. = 17·0
                25·5 to 0 d.p. or the nearest whole number = 26

Place Value, Ordering and Rounding

Test yourself — Except for questions 15, 16 and 17.

1. Write each of these without the index.
   Write **c** and **d** as decimals.
   a 10^4 **b** 10^0 **c** 10^{-3} **d** 10^{-4}

2. Write these as powers of ten.
   a one thousand   **b** ten   **c** one hundredth   **d** one ten thousandth

3. Write the numbers in red in words.
   a Mount Everest is $8 \cdot 848 \times 10^3$ metres high.
   b The mass of a magnesium atom is about 4×10^{-23} g.

4. Which of these are written in standard form?
   a $3 \cdot 4 \times 10^4$ **b** $5 \cdot 6^7$ **c** 80×10^{-1}
   d $5 \cdot 65 \times 10^6$ **e** $4 \cdot 27 \times 10^{-2}$

5. Copy and fill in the gaps.
   a 6 kilometres = 6 × ___ metres   **b** 14 megabytes = 14 × ___ bytes
   c 9 millilitres = 9 × ___ litres   **d** 32 nanoseconds = 32 × ___ seconds

6. Which measurements in the box are the same as these?
   a 7 centimetres   **b** 7 kilometres
   c 7 nanometres   *__d__ 70 micrometres
   *__e__ 700 picometres   *__f__ 0·7 kilometres

A	7×10^{-10} metres
B	7×10^{-9} metres
C	7×10^{-5} metres
D	7×10^{-2} metres
E	7×10^{2} metres
F	7×10^{3} metres

7. Find the answers to these.
   a $6 \cdot 02 \times 100$ **b** $6 \cdot 02 \div 10$ **c** $6 \cdot 02 \div 100$ **d** $6 \cdot 02 \times 1000$

8. Show that $9 \cdot 5 \times 0 \cdot 1$ is the same as $9 \cdot 5 \div 10$.

9. Find the answers to these.
   a $4 \cdot 35 \times 0 \cdot 01$ **b** $4 \cdot 35 \div 0 \cdot 1$ **c** $4 \cdot 35 \div 0 \cdot 01$
   *__d__ $^-4 \cdot 35 \times 0 \cdot 1$ *__e__ $^-4 \cdot 35 \div 0 \cdot 01$

10. Jody walked 0·8 times as far as Tim to school.
    If Tim walked 600 metres to school, how far did Jody walk?

11. $1 \text{ cm}^2 = 100 \text{ mm}^2$
    $1 \text{ m}^2 = 10\,000 \text{ cm}^2$
    Use the above information to fill in the gaps.
    a $6 \text{ cm}^2 = $ ___ mm^2 **b** $7 \text{ m}^2 = $ ___ cm^2
    c $10 \text{ cm}^2 = $ ___ mm^2 *__d__ $200 \text{ mm}^2 = $ ___ cm^2
    *__e__ $8000 \text{ mm}^2 = $ ___ cm^2 *__f__ $30\,000 \text{ cm}^2 = $ ___ m^2

12. Round
    a 326 to the nearest 10   **b** 4671 to the nearest 100
    c 21 500 to the nearest 1000   **d** 4 699 000 to the nearest 10 000.

35

Number

13 Jessie read that there were 15 000 people, to the nearest 1000, at a football match.
   a What is the smallest number of people that could have been there?
   b What is the largest number?
   c Jessie heard on the radio that there were 15 200 people, to the nearest 100, at the match.
   What are the smallest and largest number of people now?

14 Use a copy of this. Fill it in.

Number	Nearest whole number	to 1 d.p.	to 2 d.p.
46·075			
0·625			
16·995			

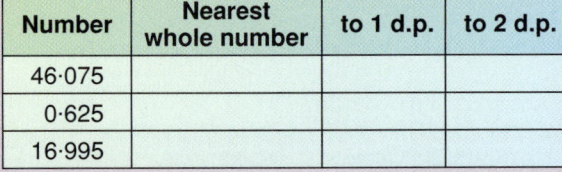

15 Write the answer to these as recurring decimals or round to 2 d.p.
   a $56·4 \div 11$ **b** $6·045 \div 7$ **c** $\frac{31·6}{9}$ **d** $\frac{0·0275}{4}$

16 Round the answers to these sensibly. Say what you have rounded them to and why you chose that.
   a A 6 kg bag of fruit and nuts was shared equally by 14 people.
   What mass did each person get?
   b The area of a rectangular mat is 36·5 m².
   One side of the mat is 7·5 m.
   What is the length of the other side?

*17 The population of the world is about 5300 million.
The approximate numbers of people who speak the three most widely spoken languages in the world are:
   Chinese 780 million   English 455 million   Hindi 320 million
About 260 million people speak Russian, the fifth most-widely spoken language.
Estimate the percentage of the world's population who speak one of the five most widely spoken languages in the world.

2 Integers, Powers and Roots

You need to know

✓ integers — page 2
✓ divisibility — page 3
✓ prime numbers, prime factors, HCM, LCM — page 3
✓ powers — page 4
  — squares and cubes
  — square roots and cube roots

Key vocabulary

cube, cubed, cube root, highest common factor (HCF), indices, index, index law, lowest common multiple (LCM), prime factor decomposition, square, squared, square root

Shaping up!

1

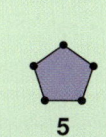

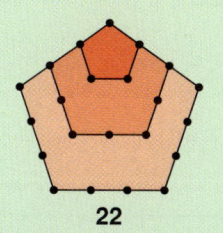

1, 5, 12, 22

These diagrams show the first four pentagonal numbers. Why are 1, 5, 12, 22 called pentagonal numbers?

Draw a diagram to find the fifth pentagonal number. What is it?

2

1, 6, 15

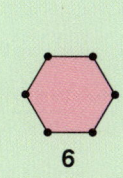

These diagrams show the first three hexagonal numbers. Why are 1, 6, 15 called hexagonal numbers?

Draw a diagram to show the fourth hexagonal number. Write down the first four hexagonal numbers.

Number

Adding, subtracting, multiplying and dividing integers

Remember

Adding and subtracting

Adding a positive number or **subtracting a negative** number is the same as **adding**.

Examples $^-8 + {}^+2 = {}^-8 + 2,$ $5 - {}^-2 = 5 + 2,$ $^-4 - {}^-3 = {}^-4 + 3$
  $= {}^-6$ $= 7$ $= {}^-1$

Adding a negative number or **subtracting a positive** number is the same as **subtracting**.

Examples $4 + {}^-2 = 4 - 2,$ $^-3 + {}^-2 = {}^-3 - 2,$ $^-5 - {}^+3 = {}^-5 - 3$
  $= 2$ $= {}^-5$ $= {}^-8$

Multiplying and dividing

When we **multiply a positive and a negative number** we get a negative answer.   ⊖ × ⊕ = ⊖
or
⊕ × ⊖ = ⊖

When we **multiply two negative numbers** we get a positive answer.   ⊖ × ⊖ = ⊕

When we **divide with a positive and a negative number** we get a negative answer.   ⊕ ÷ ⊖ = ⊖
or
⊖ ÷ ⊕ = ⊖

When we **divide with two negative numbers** we get a positive answer.   ⊖ ÷ ⊖ = ⊕

Worked Examples
a $^-7 \times 3$ **b** $^-5 \times {}^-7$ **c** $^-12 \div 3$ **d** $\frac{^-30}{^-5}$

Remember: multiplying and dividing are inverse operations.

Answers
a $^-7 \times 3 = {}^-21$ $7 \times 3 = 21$ and ⊖ × ⊕ = ⊖   **b** $^-5 \times {}^-7 = 35$ $5 \times 7 = 35$ and ⊖ × ⊖ = ⊕
c $^-12 \div 3 = {}^-4$ $12 \div 3 = 4$ and ⊖ ÷ ⊕ = ⊖   **d** $\frac{^-30}{^-5} = 6$ $30 \div 5 = 6$ and ⊖ ÷ ⊖ = ⊕

To key a negative number on a calculator use the (−) key.

Example To find $3 \cdot 82 - {}^-2 \cdot 16$
Key [3·82] [−] [(−)] [2·16] [=] to get 5·98.

Discussion

Discuss how to find the answers to these.

$\frac{5 + {}^-7}{2 \times {}^-1}$ $6({}^-5 + {}^-2) \times {}^-1$

Exercise 1

Except for question 6.

T **1** Use a copy of this. Shade the answers.
What does the shading make?
a $5 + {}^-4$ **b** $3 - 9$ **c** $^-2 + {}^-3$ **d** $^-3 + 14$
e $^-2 - {}^-2$ **f** $2 - {}^-2$ **g** $^-6 - 6$ **h** $^-1 + 10$
i $^-5 + {}^-3$ **j** $^-3 + 13$ **k** $^-4 - {}^-1$ **l** $^-12 + 5$
m $^-12 + 25$ **n** $^-12 + 6 + 4$ **o** $^-17 - {}^-19$ **p** $^-8 + {}^-4 + {}^-5$
q $^-39 + 58$ **r** $^-18 + 27 - 16 + 10$

0	6	3	⁻1	⁻6
⁻2	⁻10	1	8	⁻7
⁻5	5	2	⁻11	⁻3
13	12	⁻17	⁻9	11
⁻12	⁻13	4	7	19
⁻8	⁻14	10	14	9

38

Integers, Powers and Roots

T **2** Use a copy of this.
Fill in the circles and gaps.

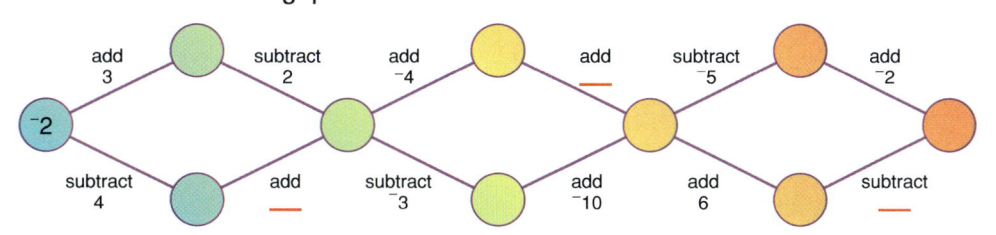

3 Calculate these using a mental or written method.
  a 6 + ⁻6   **b** ⁻36 + 36   **c** ⁻40 + 32   **d** 29 + ⁻32   **e** 41 − ⁻22
  f 24 − ⁻8   **g** ⁻240 + 180   **h** ⁻320 − ⁻170   **i** ⁻89 − ⁻73   **j** ⁻72 + ⁻39
  k ⁻4·2 + 1·8 **l** 42·1 − ⁻37·4 * **m** 18·07 − 6·3 − ⁻3·96 * **n** $\frac{-2}{3} - \frac{-3}{4}$

4 **a** 50 + ⁻30 + 20 + ⁻40   **b** ⁻20 + ⁻20 − 30 + 50   **c** 12 + ⁻8 − ⁻7 + ⁻9
    d 24 − ⁻13 − 29 + ⁻27   **e** ⁻18 + 37 + ⁻29 − ⁻16   **f** 53 − 29 + ⁻32 − ⁻48

5 Only negative numbers can go in the boxes.
  a What numbers might they be if they are both integers?
  b What numbers might they be if they are both decimals?
    i ☐ − ☐ = 4   **ii** ☐ − ☐ = ⁻4

6 Use a calculator to find the answers to these.
  a ⁻386 + ⁻857   **b** 52 × ⁻794   **c** ⁻847 + ⁻352 + 643   **d** ⁻936 ÷ ⁻36
  e 72 × ⁻8 ÷ ⁻2   **f** 12(⁻8 + ⁻4) ÷ ⁻2 **g** $\frac{-384 \times 4}{-8 \times 2}$

T **7** Use a copy of these multiplication squares. Fill them in.

  a
×	⁻5	⁻3	7
8			
12			
⁻20			

  b
×			⁻8
⁻6			
		63	⁻56
	12	⁻27	

8 Multiplying by ⁻4 is the inverse of dividing by ⁻4.
What is the inverse of dividing by ⁻5?

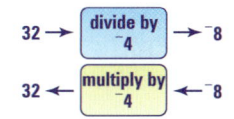

32 → [divide by ⁻4] → ⁻8
32 ← [multiply by ⁻4] ← ⁻8

9 **a** 24 ÷ ⁻6   **b** ⁻18 ÷ 3   **c** ⁻12 ÷ ⁻4   **d** 36 ÷ ⁻9   **e** 48 ÷ ⁻8
    f ⁻30 ÷ ⁻5   **g** ⁻100 ÷ ⁻20 **h** 72 ÷ ⁻9   **i** ⁻64 ÷ 4   **j** ⁻108 ÷ ⁻9

T **10** Use a copy of this.
  a Multiply each pair of numbers to get the number above.
  What number goes in the red rectangle?

	⁻2	6	
⁻1	2	3	⁻2

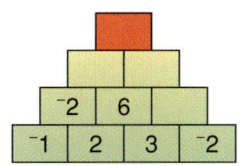

  b Divide the number on the left by the number on the right
  to get the number above.
  What number goes in the red rectangle?

  | ⁻144 | ⁻4 | 2 | ⁻1 |

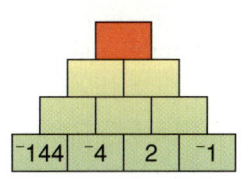

11 **a** How many ⁻3s are in ⁻12?   **b** How many ⁻8s are in ⁻48?

39

Number

12 What numbers might go in the boxes?
At least one must be a negative number.

  a ☐ × ☐ = ⁻24   **b** ☐ × ☐ = 24
  c ☐ ÷ ☐ = 6   **d** ☐ ÷ ☐ = ⁻6

13 Use the order of operations to find the answers.

  a $3 + 2 \times {}^-3$ **b** $\frac{{}^-8}{2} + 3$ **c** $5({}^-3 + {}^-4)$ **d** ${}^-5(7 + {}^-3) - 5$
  e $\frac{8 + {}^-5}{{}^-3}$ **f** $5 - {}^-6 \times {}^-3$

14 a Put one of these digits in each gap to make this true.   7, ⁻4, ⁻3

  ___(___ − ___) = ⁻7

  b Make up one addition, one subtraction, one multiplication and one division that has an answer of ⁻10.

I got an answer of −10.

15 Here are some number cards.

  2   ⁻4   ⁻6   6   10   ⁻10   ⁻14

  a Which two could make this true?   ☐ + ☐ = ⁻4
  b Choose another two cards that would also make it true.
  c Choose two cards to make this true.   ☐ × ☐ = ⁻24
  d Which three cards will make the biggest answer?   ☐ + ☐ − ☐ =

16 a Two numbers **multiply** together to make ⁻15.
They **add** together to make **2**.
What are the two numbers?   [SATs Paper 1 Level 6]

  b Two numbers **multiply** together to make ⁻15, but **add** together to make ⁻2.
What are the two numbers?

  c Two numbers **multiply** together to make 8, but **add** together to make ⁻6.
What are the two numbers?

T *****17** Use a copy of this.
Each pair of circles is multiplied to give the circle above.
Find two ways to fill it in using integers.

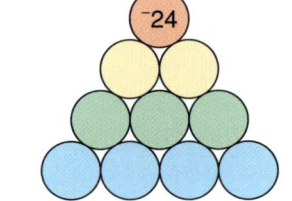

*****18** Here are six number cards.

  ⁻6   5   ⁻3·2   8·3   4·1   ⁻5·2

You can add, subtract, multiply or divide three of these numbers to make a target number.

Example $8·3 + {}^-3·2 - 4·1 = 1$ or ${}^-3·2 \times 4·1 - {}^-5·2 = {}^-7·92$

  a Find three numbers to make a target number of 30·1.
  b Add or subtract three numbers to make the largest target number possible.
  c Multiply three numbers to make the largest target number possible.

Integers, Powers and Roots

Review 1 Use a copy of this.
Shade the answer to each question.
The shading will tell you my lucky number.

a ⁻3 × ⁻7
b ⁻2 × ⁻6 × ⁻3
c ⁻15 − 11
d ⁻6 + ⁻4
e ⁻4 × ⁻4
f ⁻3 × 16
g ⁻24 ÷ ⁻3
h ⁻14 + 6 − 8
i 5 − 7
j ⁻2 − ⁻16
k ⁻37 + 32
l 48 ÷ ⁻4
m ⁻28 ÷ ⁻4
n ⁻6 + ⁻2
o 5 − 9 − ⁻3
p ⁻57 + 27
q ⁻5 × 11
r 4 − 11
s ⁻7 − ⁻3
t 15 − 18

⁻2	3	⁻36	14	⁻8	4	7
21	⁻11	0	5	⁻12	15	⁻10
⁻5	10	40	⁻7	⁻26	⁻15	⁻4
⁻1	9	11	32	⁻55	24	8
⁻3	⁻18	16	⁻30	⁻16	18	⁻48

Review 2

```
__  __  __  __  __  __  __  __    __  A   __  __    __  __  __  __
5   12  ⁻9  ⁻8  1   8   ⁻3  ⁻8    ⁻6  10  ⁻1  8     ⁻9  5   ⁻4  8

__  __  __  __  __
⁻9  5   12  12  25
```

Use a copy of the box. Write the letter beside each question above its answer in the box.

A 2 + 3 × ⁻4 = ⁻10
O ⁻2 × (3 + ⁻9)
B ⁻4 − (2 − ⁻3)
S ⁻56 ÷ (3 − ⁻4)
D 4 − 7 × ⁻3
T ⁻1 × ⁻1 × ⁻1 × ⁻1
E 5 − ⁻13 + ⁻10
U $\frac{⁻8 − 4}{3}$
H ⁻3 + 6 ÷ ⁻2
V ⁻1 × ⁻1 × ⁻1
L $\frac{⁻15 + ⁻5}{⁻4}$
R 17 + ⁻4 × 5

Review 3
a A person was born in 21 BC and died in AD 41.
   How old was he when he died?
b John had £127·50 in his bank account. He went shopping for new clothes and spent
   £203·69. How much would his account be overdrawn if he paid by cheque?

Review 4 Write down the numbers for L, M, N and P in the story.
On a cold day last winter the temperature in Llanberis was ⁻9 °C at 5 a.m. By 8 a.m. the temperature had risen 4° and was L °C. By 1 p.m. the temperature was 3 °C, so it had risen M °C since 8 a.m. By 5 p.m. the temperature had fallen 5° to N °C and by midnight the temperature was ⁻6 °C, a further drop of P °C.

Review 5
a Two numbers add together to give 3.
   They multiply together to give ⁻28.
   What are the two numbers?
b Two numbers add together to give ⁻3.
   They multiply together to give ⁻28.
   What are the two numbers?

*__Review 6__ Use three copies of the diagram.
Put the integers 7, 5, 3, 1, ⁻1, ⁻3, ⁻5, ⁻7, ⁻9 in the circles, so that the integers on each side of the triangle add to
a 2   b ⁻4.
Try to arrange the numbers to make a third total. Remember each set of 4 numbers must add to the same amount.

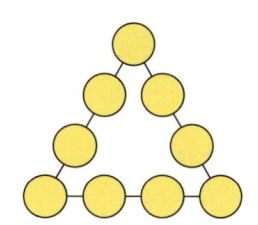

Number

? Puzzle

⁻4	⁻5	1	⁻4	⁻3	2	⁻2	⁻1	2	5	⁻5	0	⁻4	⁻4	2	⁻2
1	6	⁻2	⁻4	⁻5	⁻6	1	3	⁻2	⁻5	⁻6	1	0	1	4	1
⁻4	1	⁻1	1	4	⁻1	0	2	⁻4	⁻1	2	⁻1	5	⁻5	⁻2	⁻1
⁻1	⁻5	4	3	⁻1	4	⁻2	⁻5	1	⁻4	⁻5	1	⁻3	0	3	⁻6
⁻2	⁻3	⁻1	⁻6	0	3	⁻2	⁻1	4	⁻3	⁻2	⁻2	3	⁻2	⁻3	5
2	1	6	2	⁻4	⁻1	4	5	⁻2	⁻6	1	1	1	⁻4	⁻1	⁻4
0	⁻4	⁻2	⁻1	⁻2	1	⁻2	4	⁻6	⁻5	0	⁻1	4	⁻2	⁻2	1
3	1	4	1	⁻6	2	⁻8	⁻3	2	5	⁻1	⁻4	⁻7	⁻2	⁻5	0
3	⁻8	2	0	⁻3	⁻2	3	⁻3	⁻6	2	⁻1	⁻2	7	5	2	⁻7
⁻4	0	⁻3	⁻5	2	2	0	⁻1	⁻3	3	⁻9	2	⁻1	0	⁻3	0

Score: 100 or more Excellent
60–99 Very good
20–59 Good
fewer than 20 Keep trying

Find as many 'triple statements' as you can. A 'triple statement' is a true statement formed from 3 adjacent integers, either horizontally or vertically or diagonally.

For instance, the ringed numbers are a triple statement since ⁻1 − (⁻2) = 1. You may use the operations +, −, ×, ÷.

★ Practical

You will need a graphical calculator.

Use the list facility to practise adding and subtracting integers.

Use the random number generator to fill the first two lists.

The command for this is Int(21 Ran # − 10).

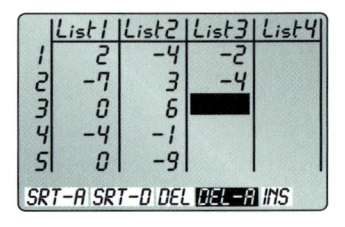

Prime factor decomposition

Remember
The **HCF (highest common factor)** of two numbers is the largest factor common to both.

Example   8 is the HCF of 24 and 32.

1, 2, 3, 4, 6, ⑧, 12, 24
1, 2, 4, ⑧, 16, 32

See page 3 for more on HCF and LCM.

The **LCM (lowest common multiple)** of two numbers is the smallest number that is a multiple of both.

Example   24 is the LCM of 6 and 8.

6, 12, 18, ㉔, 30, ...
8, 16, ㉔, 30, ...

42

Integers, Powers and Roots

We can use prime factors to find the HCF and LCM.

Example   72 and 60

We find the prime factors of 72 and 60 using a table or tree diagram.

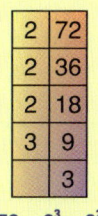

2	72
2	36
2	18
3	9
	3

$72 = 2^3 \times 3^2$
table

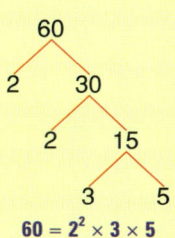

$60 = 2^2 \times 3 \times 5$
tree diagram

We can then find the HCF and LCM using a Venn diagram.
HCF = 2 × 2 × 3 = 12 (common factors)
LCM = 2 × 3 × 2 × 2 × 3 × 5 = $2^3 \times 3^2 \times 5$ = 360

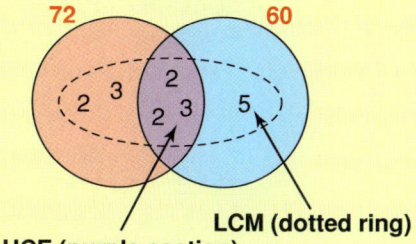

The LCM can be found by multiplying the highest power of each prime factor.

HCF (purple section)
LCM (dotted ring)

Discussion

A number is a multiple of 3 and 4. It has 3 digits.

What is the smallest number it could be? **Discuss**.

What if the numbers were 12 and 21?

Exercise 2

1 $144 = 2^4 \times 3^2$
This is 144 expressed as a product of prime factors in **index notation**.
Express these in the same way.
Use a factor tree or table to help.
   a 45   **b** 72   **c** 576   **d** 2160

2	144
2	72
2	36
2	18
3	9
	3

$144 = 2 \times 2 \times 2 \times 2 \times 3 \times 3$
$= 2^4 \times 3^2$

2   Find the HCF and LCM of these.
You could draw Venn diagrams to help.
   a 24 and 18   **b** 45 and 54   **c** 112 and 154   **d** 525 and 25

*3   The HCF of 20 and another number is 5.
What might the other number be? Write down more than one answer.

*4   A pair of numbers have an HCF of 8 and an LCM of 480.
What might they be?
Find all the answers.

*5   Use each of the digits in the box once to make two three-digit numbers with an HCF of 24.

| 1 | 5 | 0 |
| 8 | 6 | 4 |

43

Number

Review 1 Express these as products of prime factors.
a 96 **b** 945

Review 2 Find the HCF and LCM of each of these.
a 48, 80 **b** 105, 231

Puzzle

Tristram found this method of finding the HCF and LCM in his sister's maths book.

> To find the LCM and HCF of 30 and 48:
> Divide both by the same smallest prime possible   2 | 30 48 $30 \div 2 = 15, 48 \div 2 = 24$
> Divide both again by the smallest prime possible   3 | 15 24 $15 \div 3 = 5, 24 \div 3 = 8$
>   5   8
>
> It is not possible to divide both 5 and 8 by the same prime number so stop.
> HCF = 2 × 3 = 6
> LCM = 2 × 3 × 5 × 8 = 240

Use this method to find the HCF and LCM of these.
a 12 and 30 **b** 24 and 30 **c** 16 and 20 **d** 20 and 30
e 20 and 48 **f** 48 and 100 *__g__ 96 and 144

When cancelling fractions, the HCF of the numerator and denominator is the largest number that will divide into both.

Example To cancel $\frac{60}{72}$,   divide by the HCF, 12.

$\frac{^5 60}{^6 72} = \frac{5}{6}$ dividing both numerator and denominator by 12

When we add and subtract fractions, we find the LCM of the denominators.
This LCM is the **lowest common denominator**.

Example $\frac{3}{72} + \frac{9}{60} = \frac{15 + 54}{360}$ ⟵ $\frac{3}{72} = \frac{15}{360}$ and $\frac{9}{60} = \frac{54}{360}$

$= \frac{69}{360}$

$= \frac{23}{120}$

Exercise 3

1 Cancel these fractions by finding the HCF of the numerator and denominator.
a $\frac{12}{20}$ **b** $\frac{36}{80}$ **c** $\frac{18}{40}$ **d** $\frac{32}{56}$ **e** $\frac{42}{72}$ **f** $\frac{72}{120}$
g $\frac{144}{180}$ **h** $\frac{90}{144}$ **i** $\frac{105}{240}$ *__j__ $\frac{120}{288}$ *__k__ $\frac{164}{280}$

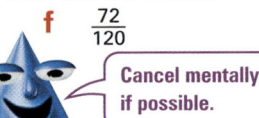

Cancel mentally if possible.

Link to adding and subtracting fractions.

2 Add these fractions by finding the LCM of the denominators.
a $\frac{1}{8} + \frac{3}{4}$ **b** $\frac{1}{5} + \frac{2}{3}$ **c** $\frac{7}{20} - \frac{3}{15}$ **d** $\frac{3}{15} + \frac{8}{35}$ **e** $\frac{7}{12} - \frac{9}{20}$
f $\frac{1}{24} + \frac{7}{36}$ **g** $\frac{7}{32} + \frac{11}{48}$ *__h__ $\frac{23}{56} + \frac{39}{70}$ *__i__ $\frac{19}{28} - \frac{7}{38}$ *__j__ $\frac{48}{72} - \frac{3}{20}$

44

Integers, Powers and Roots

*3 $\dfrac{5}{\boxed{B}} + \dfrac{\boxed{A}}{12} = \dfrac{9}{8}$

The HCF of A and B is 2.
The LCM of B and 12 is 24.
What numbers might A and B be if they are different?

Review 1 Cancel these fractions by finding the HCF of the numerator and denominator.
a $\dfrac{55}{88}$ b $\dfrac{30}{75}$ c $\dfrac{36}{90}$ d $\dfrac{52}{84}$ e $\dfrac{28}{120}$

Review 2 Add these fractions by finding the LCM of the denominators.
a $\dfrac{5}{18} + \dfrac{1}{12}$ b $\dfrac{13}{20} - \dfrac{7}{15}$ c $\dfrac{3}{14} + \dfrac{7}{21}$ d $\dfrac{5}{36} + \dfrac{9}{40}$ e $\dfrac{21}{28} - \dfrac{14}{38}$ f $\dfrac{83}{96} - \dfrac{17}{28}$

Investigation

Number of factors

1 $45 = 3^2 \times 5^1$
The indices are **2** and **1**.
Add one to each index to get 3 and 2.
Multiply these new numbers. $3 \times 2 = 6$

45 has **6** factors.   1, 3, 5, 9, 15, 45

$36 = 2^2 \times 3^2$
If we add one to each index and multiply the new numbers together, does this give us the number of factors of 36? **Investigate**.

Test to see if this method gives us the number of factors for these numbers.
     24   48   60   125

*2 Find the smallest number that has 18 factors.

*3 Find the smallest number greater than 50 that has the same number of factors as 50.

Common factors of algebraic expressions

Remember
A factor is a number that divides exactly into another number.
In algebra, letters stand for numbers.

We can find **common factors of algebraic expressions**.

Example $2n = 2 \times n$
$3n = 3 \times n$
Both $2n$ and $3n$ can be divided exactly by n.
n is a common factor of $2n$ and $3n$.

Example $2xy^2z$ and $3wxy$ can both be divided exactly by x and by y.
xy is a common factor of $2xy^2z$ and $3wxy$.

Number

Exercise 4

1 Write down the common factor of each of these.
  a $5n$ and $8n$
  b $3m$ and m
  c $5b$ and b^2
  d $2n$ and $2n^2$
  e $3p$ and p
  f n and $2n$
  g $8x$ and 2
  h $3a$ and $6a$
  i $5m$ and $10m$
  j $5xy$ and $3yz$
  k $4ab$ and $8bc$
  l $5a^2b$ and ab
  m $3x^2y$ and x^2y
  n $5pq^2$ and $4pq$
  *o $8a^2bc$ and b^2c
  *p $12xy^2z$ and $4xy$

Review Write down the common factor of each of these.
  a $5a$ and $7a$
  b $3x^2$ and x
  c $5n$ and 10
  d $8pq$ and $16q$
  e $4a^2b$ and $6ab^2$

Divisibility and algebra

We can use **algebra** to prove some **divisibility** rules.

See page 3 for more on divisibility.

Worked Example
The numbers 21, 42 and 63 are all divisible by 7.
In each, the tens digit is twice the units digit.

Prove that any two-digit number in which the tens digit is twice the units digit is always divisible by 7.

'Prove' means it must be true for every case. We usually use algebra to prove something.

Answer
If the number of units is t, then the number of tens must be $2t \times 10 = 20t$.
The number has the form $20t + t$
                             tens units

We must multiply by 10 to get the number of tens.

$20t + t = 21t$

$21t$ is always divisible by 7 because 21 is divisible by 7.

Exercise 5

1 Adele started with 59.
  She reversed the digits to get 95.
  She found the difference, $95 - 59 = 36$.
  She did this with some other two-digit numbers.
  Adele thinks the difference is always divisible by 9.
  a **Show**, using three examples that Adele could be correct.
  b Adele started to **prove** that the difference is always divisible by 9.
     Copy and finish Adele's proof.

     Call the number you chose $10t + u$.
     When you reverse the digits, the number is $10u + t$.
     The difference between these two expressions is $10t + u - (10u + t) = 10t + u - 10u - t$
     $=$

  *c Prove that this is also true for a four-digit number.

     Hint: Call the number you choose $1000s + 100h + 10t + u$.

Integers, Powers and Roots

2 583, 264, 781 and 374 are all divisible by 11.
Boris noticed that in all of these numbers, the sum of the hundreds digit and the units digit equals the tens digit.
He started to prove that all three-digit numbers of this type are divisible by 11.

Let the number be $100h + 10(h + u) + u$.
$100h + 10(h + u) + u = \ldots$

Copy and finish the proof.

Hint: Multiply out the brackets and then simplify.

*3 Prove this statement.
Any three-digit number is divisible by 9 if the sum of the digits is divisible by 9.

Review Carlota noticed that all of the two-digit numbers where the tens digit is equal to the units digit are divisible by 11.
11, 22, 33, 44, 55, 66, 77, 88 and 99 are all divisible by 11.
She wanted to prove this, using algebra.
Show how she could do this.

Powers

Remember
We write $3 \times 3 \times 3 \times 3$ as 3^4.
3^4 is read as 'three to the power of 4'.
The 4 in 3^4 is called an **index**.
The plural of index is **indices**.

On a calculator, squares are keyed using $\boxed{x^2}$
cubes are keyed using $\boxed{x^3}$.

Example $(^-8.1)^3$ is keyed as
$\boxed{(}\,\boxed{(-)}\,\boxed{8.1}\,\boxed{)}\,\boxed{x^3}\,\boxed{=}$ to get $^-531.441$.

We need the brackets around $^-8.1$ so that we find $^-8.1 \times\, ^-8.1 \times\, ^-8.1$.

On a calculator, indices are keyed using $\boxed{x^y}$.

Example 21^5 is keyed as $\boxed{21}\,\boxed{x^y}\,\boxed{5}\,\boxed{=}$ to get $4\ 084\ 101$.

Discussion

Use your calculator to find the value of these.

$10^0 \qquad 18^0 \qquad (\tfrac{1}{2})^0 \qquad 116^0 \qquad 256^0 \qquad (^-3)^0 \qquad 5.7^0$

What do you notice? **Discuss**.

Any number to the power of zero equals 1.
$x^0 = 1$

Number

Exercise 6 Except for questions 1, 8, 11, 12 and Reviews 1–4.

1 Use your calculator to find the value of these.
Give the answers to **e**, **g** and **h** to 2 d.p.
 a 14^3 **b** 1.4^2 **c** 6^6 **d** 23^4 **e** 5.6^4 **f** $(^-5)^4$
 g $(^-2.3)^5$ *__h__ $(\frac{1}{4})^3$ *__i__ $7^2 \times 6^3$ *__j__ $12^3 \times 3^2$

2 a What does 8.3^0 equal?
 b What does $(^-7.4)^0$ equal?
 c What does x^0 equal?

3 In an experiment it was found that the number of bacteria cells doubled each hour, as shown in this table.
How many cells will there be after
 a 6 hours   **b** 12 hours   **c** a day?

Hour	Number of cells
0	1 = 2^0
1	2 = 2^1
2	4 = 2^2
3	8 = 2^3
.	.
.	.
.	.

4 Show that 6.547^2 is about 43.

5 $9 \times x$ is a square number.
What is the smallest value of x?

6 We can write powers of ten using indices.

Examples $1000 = 10^3$ $0.1 = 10^{-1}$
Write these using indices.
 a 10   **b** 1   **c** 10 000   **d** 0.01   **e** $\frac{1}{100}$ **f** $\frac{1}{1000}$

There is more about powers of ten and indices on pages 21 and 49.

7 Give a number raised to a power that has a value of
 a 1   **b** 25   **c** 27   **d** 16?

8 a What power of 2 has a value of 64?
 b What power of 3 has a value of 243?
 c What power of 2 multiplied by a power of 3 gives 864?
  Hint: Use prime factors.

9 $28 = 1^3 + 3^3$
Write 35 as the sum of two cubes.

10 $10^2 - 8^2 = 36$
 a The difference of the squares of two other consecutive even numbers is 44.
   What are these even numbers?
 *__b__ The difference of the squares of two consecutive even numbers less than 30 is a square number. What are these even numbers?

*__11__ **a** Look at these numbers.   [Sats Paper 1 Level 7]

  1^6 2^5 3^4 4^3 5^2 6^1

  i Which is the **largest**?   **ii** Which is equal to 9^2?
 b Which **two** of the numbers below are **not** square numbers?

  2^4 2^5 2^6 2^7 2^8

Integers, Powers and Roots

*12 $8^3 = 512$
The units digit is 2.
Without using a calculator, work out the units digit of 8^{12}.
Explain how you did this.

*13 Find the smallest number that can be written as the sum of two cubes in two different ways.

*14 Use your calculator to find these.
Write the answer as a decimal and as a fraction.
a 3^{-1} **b** 2^{-3}

Review 1 Find the value of these. Give the answers to **c** and **e** to 1 d.p.
a 8^4 **b** 7^6 **c** 8.1^5 **d** $(^-3)^3$ **e** $(^-2.4)^4$ **f** $(\frac{1}{2})^2$ **g** 6.5^0 **h** 10^{-3}

Review 2 A liquid is cooling under special conditions. Its temperature halves every hour.
a If its temperature at the start was 360 °C, what was its temperature after
   i 1 hour   **ii** 2 hours   **iii** 5 hours?
*b After how many hours will its temperature be less than 2 °C?

Review 3
a When you raise the number 5 to any power, the answer always ends in 5. $5^2 = 25$
$5^3 = 125$
$5^8 = 390\,625$
...

Two other single-digit numbers also have this property.
One of them is 1. What is the other?

Investigation

Squares of sums
Safia thinks that adding two numbers and then squaring is the same as squaring each number and then adding.

Investigate whether this is never true, sometimes true or always true.

Multiplying and dividing numbers with indices

Discussion

• $2^5 = 2 \times 2 \times 2 \times 2 \times 2$ $2^3 = 2 \times 2 \times 2$ $2^8 = 2 \times 2 \times 2 \times 2 \times 2 \times 2 \times 2 \times 2$
   $= 32$ $= 8$ $= 256$

So $2^5 \times 2^3 = 32 \times 8$
$= 256$
$= 2^8$

So $2^5 \times 2^3 = 2^{(5+3)}$
$= 2^8$

Number

Would $2^4 \times 2^3 = 2^7$? **Discuss**.
What would $3^5 \times 3^4$ equal? **Discuss**.
What would $2^3 \times 3^5$ equal? **Discuss**.
* Can you make up a general rule for this?

• $2^6 = 2 \times 2 \times 2 \times 2 \times 2 \times 2$ $2^2 = 2 \times 2$ $2^4 = 2 \times 2 \times 2 \times 2$
    $= 64$ $= 4$ $= 16$

So $2^6 \div 2^2 = 64 \div 4$
           $= 16$
           $= 2^4$

So $2^6 \div 2^2 = 2^{(6-2)}$
           $= 2^4$

Would $2^8 \div 2^5 = 2^3$? **Discuss**.
What would $3^8 \div 3^6$ equal? **Discuss**.
What would $4^8 \div 3^5$ equal? **Discuss**.
* Can you make up a general rule for this?

The **index laws** are:
   Indices are **added** when **multiplying**.
   Indices are **subtracted** when **dividing**.

Worked Example
Write each of these as a number with a single index.
a $7^4 \times 7^9$ **b** $7^8 \div 7^2$
Answer
a $7^4 \times 7^9 = 7^{(4+9)}$ **b** $7^8 \div 7^2 = 7^{(8-2)}$
           $= 7^{13}$ $= 7^6$

> The base numbers you are multiplying must be the same.
> $3^4 \times 3^5 = 3^9$
> same

Exercise 7

1 Bella started to explain why $5^2 \times 5^3 = 5^5$.   Finish her explanation.
$5^2 = 5 \times 5$ $5^3 = 5 \times 5 \times 5$ $5^5 = 5 \times 5 \times 5 \times 5 \times 5$
   $=$ ___ $=$ ___ $=$ ___

$5^2 \times 5^3 = (5 \times 5) \times (5 \times 5 \times 5)$
         $=$ ___ $\times$ ___
         $=$ ___

$5^5 = 5 \times 5 \times 5 \times 5 \times 5$
    $=$ ___

2 Copy and fill in the gaps.
a $4^3 \times 4^2 = ($___$\times$___$\times$___$) \times ($___$\times$___$)$ **b** $7^5 \div 7^2 = \dfrac{\_\_\_ \times \_\_\_ \times \_\_\_ \times \_\_\_ \times \_\_\_}{\_\_\_ \times \_\_\_}$
                $= 4^{\_\_}$ $= 7^{\_\_}$

3 Write these as single powers of 5. The first one is done.
a $5^3 \times 5^6 = 5^{(3+6)}$ **b** $5^4 \times 5^3$ **c** $5^4 \times 5^4$ **d** $5^7 \times 5^{10}$ **e** $5^6 \div 5^4$ **f** $\dfrac{5^8}{5^4}$ **g** $5^7 \div 5^3$
         $= 5^9$

4 Simplify.
a $3^4 \times 3^6$ **b** $6^3 \times 6^2$ **c** $4^7 \div 4^3$ **d** $\dfrac{10^{11}}{10^9}$ **e** $\dfrac{8^6}{8^5}$ **f** $7^5 \times 7^5$
g $27^3 \times 27^4$ **h** $\dfrac{16^9}{16^7}$ **i** $11^8 \times 11^4$ **j** $24^{24} \div 24^{16}$

Integers, Powers and Roots

5 Use the index laws to simplify these. Then find the answers using a calculator.
  a $2^4 \times 2^3$ **b** $3^2 \times 3^3$ **c** $\frac{5^7}{5^5}$ **d** $\frac{3^9}{3^9}$ **e** $4^2 \times 4^3 \times 4^0$ **f** $2^2 \times 2^3 \times 2^2$
  g $\frac{4^3 \times 4^6}{4^7}$ *__h__ $\frac{2^{13}}{2^4 \times 2^5}$ *__i__ $\frac{7^{11} \times 7^4}{7^9 \times 7^6}$ *__j__ $\frac{5^7 \times 5^3}{5^2 \times 5^5}$

6 Which of these are true?
  a $4^3 \times 4^2 = 4^6$ **b** $4^3 + 4^2 = 4^5$ **c** $4^3 \times 2^2 = 8^5$ **d** $4^8 \div 2^3 = 2^5$ **e** $4^5 - 4^3 = 4^2$

7 Gemma thinks that $2^3 \times 3^2 = 6^5$. Is she correct? Explain why or why not.

8 Sarah thinks that the index laws are true for algebra as well as arithmetic.
  She wrote $a^4 \times a^2 = (a \times a \times a \times a) \times (a \times a)$
  $= a^6$
  So $a^4 \times a^2 = a^{(4+2)} = a^6$
  a How could she show that the index laws are true for $m^3 \div m^2$?
  b Show that the index laws are true for these.
   i $n^4 \times n^3 = n^7$ **ii** $p^8 \div p^3 = p^5$

*__9__ Use the index laws to simplify these.
  a $a^4 \times a^5$ **b** $n^7 \times n^5$ **c** $p^8 \div p^2$ **d** $m^6 \times m^4$ **e** $b^9 \div b^7$
  f $r^6 \times r^{11}$ **g** $d^{12} \div d^4$ **h** $x^7 \times x^{12}$ **i** $\frac{n^{10}}{n^4}$ **j** $a^0 \times a^4$
  k $\frac{y^6}{y^2}$ **l** $\frac{b^{20}}{b^5}$ **m** $\frac{a^{10}}{a^{10}}$ **n** $b^2 \times b^4 \times b^5$

Review 1 Copy and fill in the gaps.
a $2^5 \times 2^3 = (\_\_\_ \times \_\_\_ \times \_\_\_ \times \_\_\_ \times \_\_\_) \times (\_\_\_ \times \_\_\_ \times \_\_\_)$
$= 2^{\_\_}$
b $5^6 \div 5^3 = \frac{\_\_ \times \_\_ \times \_\_ \times \_\_ \times \_\_ \times \_\_}{\_\_ \times \_\_ \times \_\_}$
$= 5^{\_\_}$

Review 2 Simplify these, then find the answer using a calculator.
  a $4^3 \times 4^1$ **b** $3^2 \times 3^2$ **c** $\frac{4^6}{4^4}$ **d** $3^2 \times 3^1 \times 3^2$ **e** $\frac{5^2 \times 5^3}{5^5}$ **f** $\frac{2^{11}}{2^2 \times 2^4}$ **g** $\frac{8^5 \times 8^6}{8^3 \times 8^7}$

*__Review 3__ Use the index laws to simplify these.
  a $y^5 \times y^8$ **b** $m^{20} \div m^4$ **c** $a^3 \times a^0$ **d** $\frac{p^9}{p^3}$ *__e__ $b^3 \times b^4 \times b^5$

Square roots and cube roots

Remember
$\sqrt{81}$ is read as 'the square root of 81'.
We must find what number squared equals 81.

$9 \times 9 = 81$ **and** $^-9 \times\ ^-9 = 81$

9 is the positive square root and $^-9$ is the negative square root.

$\sqrt{81}$ means the positive square root, 9.

$\pm\sqrt{81}$ means the **positive** and **negative** square roots, 9 and $^-9$.

Squaring and finding the square root are inverse operations. So are cubing and finding the cube root.

51

Number

$\sqrt[3]{27}$ is read as 'the cube root of 27'.
We must find what number cubed equals 27.
$\sqrt[3]{27} = 3$ because $3 \times 3 \times 3 = 27$

On a calculator we use $\sqrt[3]{\ }$ to find cube roots.

Example $\sqrt[3]{91}$ is keyed as $\boxed{\sqrt[3]{\ }}$ $\boxed{91}$ $\boxed{=}$ to get 4·5 (1 d.p.).

Some calculators do not have a $\sqrt[3]{\ }$ key.

Discussion

- The cube root of a positive number is always positive.

  Discuss Chelsea's statement. Is she correct?

  Find these.
  $^-3 \times {}^-3 \times {}^-3 = ({}^-3)^3 = \square$
  $^-4 \times {}^-4 \times {}^-4 = ({}^-4)^3 = \square$
  $^-1\cdot 2 \times {}^-1\cdot 2 \times {}^-1\cdot 2 = ({}^-1\cdot 2)^3 = \square$

  What can you say about the cube root of a negative number? **Discuss**.

- Chelsea put the number 6·31 into her calculator and cubed it.
  What must she do to get back to the starting number?
  Why is it sometimes not possible to get back exactly to the starting number? **Discuss**.
  What if she had found the square root of 6·31 instead?

- Calculate $\sqrt{4} + \sqrt{1}$.
  Calculate $\sqrt{5}$.
  Does $\sqrt{4} + \sqrt{1} = \sqrt{5}$?
  Does $\sqrt{9} + \sqrt{16} = \sqrt{25}$?
  Does $\sqrt{25} + \sqrt{49} = \sqrt{74}$?
  Is $\sqrt{a} + \sqrt{b}$ equal to $\sqrt{a+b}$? **Discuss**.

Exercise 8

Except for question 4 and Review 4.

1 The square of 8 is 64.
   The square of another number is also 64.
   What is that other number?

2 Find these.
   a $\sqrt[3]{16}$ **b** $\sqrt[3]{49}$ **c** $\sqrt{36}$ **d** $\sqrt{144}$ **e** $\sqrt[3]{100}$

52

Integers, Powers and Roots

3   Joel found the square root of 324 by factorising.

$$\sqrt{324} = \sqrt{9 \times 36}$$
$$= \sqrt{9} \times \sqrt{36}$$
$$= 3 \times 6$$
$$= 18$$

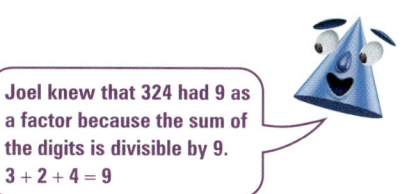

> Joel knew that 324 had 9 as a factor because the sum of the digits is divisible by 9.
> $3 + 2 + 4 = 9$

Find the square root of these by factorising.
   a $\sqrt{256}$ b $\sqrt{441}$

4   Use your calculator to find these.
    Give the answers to 2 d.p.
   a $\sqrt{304}$ b $\sqrt[3]{7}$ c $\sqrt{842}$ d $\sqrt[3]{367}$ e $\sqrt{187-46}$
   f $\sqrt{26^2 - 8^2}$ g $\sqrt[3]{32^2 - 17^2}$ h $\sqrt{27} + \sqrt{39}$ *i $\sqrt[3]{3} + \sqrt[3]{5}$

5   What goes in the gap, **positive** or **negative**?
   a There are two square roots of a _____ number. One is _____ and the other _____.
   b The cube root of a positive number is _____.
   c The cube root of a negative number is _____.

6   Which of these are true?
   a $\sqrt{25} + \sqrt{9} = \sqrt{25+9}$ b $\sqrt{25} - \sqrt{9} = \sqrt{25-9}$
   c $\sqrt{5} \times \sqrt{5} = \sqrt{25}$ d $\sqrt{4} \times \sqrt{9} = \sqrt{4 \times 9}$

7   $\sqrt[3]{-46\,656} = 36$.   Explain how you know this is wrong without doing the calculation.

8   a A three-digit square number has a units digit of 1.
      __ __ 1
      What could the units digit of the square root of this number be?
    b A six-digit square number has a units digit of 4.
      __ __ __ __ __ 4
      Could its square root be a prime number?
      Explain your answer.

*9 $\sqrt[3]{n} = {}^-m$
    m is a positive number.
    Is n positive or negative?

Review 1   Give the positive and negative square roots of these.   a 81   b 100

Review 2   Find these by factorising.   a $\sqrt{196}$ b $\sqrt{729}$

Review 3 $\sqrt{5}$ lies between 2 and 3. Explain how you know this without doing the calculation.

Review 4   Use your calculator to find these. Give the answers to 1 d.p.
   a $\sqrt[3]{86}$ b $\sqrt{16-3}$ c $\sqrt[3]{152-61}$ d $\sqrt{8^2+5^2}$ e $\sqrt[3]{5^3+3^3}$

Review 5
   a A four-digit square number has a units digit of 6.   __ __ __ 6.

   What could the units digit of the square root of this number be?
   Could the square root be an odd number?
   Explain your answer.
   b A five-digit square number has a units digit of 9.   __ __ __ __ 9.

   Will the square root of this number be even or odd?

53

Number

Discussion

- How could you estimate $\sqrt[3]{20}$? **Discuss**.

- Sharyn was using a calculator which didn't have a ☐√ or ☐∛ key.

  She decided to use trial and improvement to find $\sqrt{19}$ to 2 decimal places. She began as follows.

  19 lies between the two square numbers 16 and 25.
  $\sqrt{19}$ lies between $\sqrt{16}$ and $\sqrt{25}$.
  $\sqrt{19}$ lies between 4 and 5.

Try 4·5	4·5 × 4·5 = 20·25	too big
Try 4·3	4·3 × 4·3 = 18·49	too small
Try 4·4	4·4 × 4·4 = 19·36	too big

  I now know that $\sqrt{19}$ lies between 4·3 and 4·4

  | Try 4·32 | 4·32 × 4·32 = 18·6624 | too small |

  Discuss Sharyn's method. How could Sharyn continue?
  Find $\sqrt{19}$ to 2 decimal places. **Discuss**.

Exercise 9

1 Use trial and improvement to find these, to 2 d.p. Do not use the ☐√ or ☐∛ key.
   a $\sqrt{8}$ **b** $\sqrt{24}$ **c** $\sqrt[3]{50}$ **d** $\sqrt[3]{81}$

Review Use trial and improvement to find these, to 2 d.p. Do not use the ☐∛ or ☐√ key.
   a $\sqrt{35}$ **b** $\sqrt[3]{16}$

Practical

You will need a spreadsheet.

Ask your teacher for ICT worksheet **Estimating square roots and cube roots**.

Investigation

Painted Cubes

The outside of a cube made from 27 smaller cubes is painted pink.

How many small cubes have no faces painted pink?
What about 1 face? 2 faces? 3 faces? **Investigate**.

Integers, Powers and Roots

Summary of key points

A   **Adding a positive** number or **subtracting a negative** number is the same as **adding**.

Examples $^-6 + {^+4} = {^-6} + 4$ $^-7 - {^-4} = {^-7} + 4$
                   $= {^-2}$ $= {^-3}$

Adding a negative number or **subtracting a positive** number is the same as **subtracting**.

Examples $5 + {^-3} = 5 - 3$ $^-4 - {^+3} = {^-4} - 3$
                $= 2$ $= {^-7}$

When we **multiply or divide with a positive and a negative number** we get a negative answer.

Examples $^-6 \times 4 = {^-24}$ $15 \div {^-3} = {^-5}$

When we **multiply or divide with two positive or two negative numbers** we get a positive answer.

Examples $^-6 \times {^-3} = 18$ $^-24 \div {^-8} = 3$ $\dfrac{^-36}{^-4} = 9$

We use the (−) key on a calculator to key a negative number.

Example $4 \cdot 62 - {^-3} \cdot 43$ is keyed as

      4·62   −   (−)   3·43   =   to get 8·05.

B   When **cancelling fractions**, we divide the numerator and denominator by their **highest common factor** (HCF).

Example $\dfrac{^4 \cancel{24}}{_7 \cancel{42}} = \dfrac{4}{7}$ divide numerator and denominator by the HCF, 6

When **adding and subtracting fractions**, we first find the **lowest common multiple** (LCM) of the denominators.

Example $\dfrac{5}{6} + \dfrac{4}{9} = \dfrac{15 + 8}{18}$ The LCM of 6 and 9 is 18. $\dfrac{5}{6} = \dfrac{15}{18}$ and $\dfrac{4}{9} = \dfrac{8}{18}$
                $= \dfrac{23}{18}$
                $= 1\dfrac{5}{18}$

C   We can find **common factors of algebraic expressions**.

Example $3bc^2$ and b^2c have a common factor of bc

D   We can use algebra to prove some **divisibility rules**.

Example   Any two-digit number in which the tens and units digits are the same is divisible by 11.

If the number of units is d, then the number of tens is $10d$.

The number is then $10d + d = 11d$.

$11d$ is always divisible by 11.

55

Number

E On a calculator indices are keyed using x^y.

Example 32^5 is keyed as [32] [x^y] [5] [=] to get 33 554 432.

Any number to the power of zero equals 1. $x^0 = 1$

F On a calculator we use [$\sqrt[3]{\ }$] to find **cube roots**.
The cube root of a positive number is positive.
The cube root of a negative number is negative.
Examples $\sqrt[3]{216}$ is keyed as [$\sqrt[3]{\ }$] [216] [=] to get 6.
$\sqrt[3]{^-27}$ is keyed as [$\sqrt[3]{\ }$] [(−)] [27] to get $^-3$.

Note All positive numbers have a positive and negative square root.
Example $\sqrt{36} = +6$ or $^-6$ $6 \times 6 = 36$ and $^-6 \times {^-6} = 36$

G We can estimate the value of $\sqrt[3]{16}$ using **trial and improvement**.
See the Discussion on page 54 for an example.

H **The index laws**
When multiplying, add the indices.   *Example* $5^4 \times 5^7 = 5^{(4+7)} = 5^{11}$
When dividing, subtract the indices.   *Example* $\frac{9^{12}}{9^5} = 9^{(12-5)} = 9^7$

> The base numbers must be the same.

Test yourself
Except for questions 17, 18 and 22.

1 Use a copy of these.

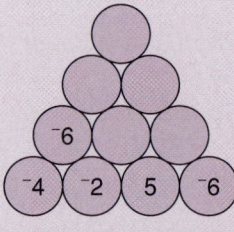

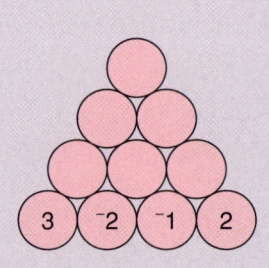

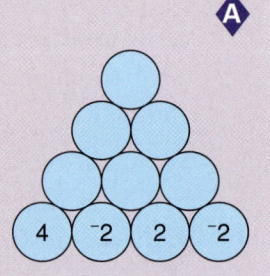

Purple pyramid bottom row: $^-4$, $^-2$, 5, $^-6$ (with $^-6$ shown in second row)
Green pyramid bottom row: 6, 8, $^-2$, 5
Pink pyramid bottom row: 3, $^-2$, $^-1$, 2
Blue pyramid bottom row: 4, $^-2$, 2, $^-2$

What number goes in the top circles?
a In the purple circles, two numbers are added to get the number above.
b In the green circles, the number on the right is subtracted from the number on the left to get the number above.
c In the pink circles, two numbers are multiplied to get the number above.
d In the blue circles, the number on the left is divided by the number on the right to get the number above.

Integers, Powers and Roots

2 Use a copy of these addition and multiplication squares.
Fill them in.

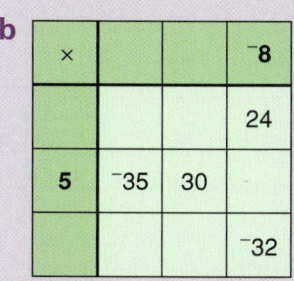

a
+	⁻3·2	1·6	⁻2·4
4·5			
⁻2·7			
⁻1·4			

b
×			⁻8
			24
5	⁻35	30	
			⁻32

3 a 28 ÷ ⁻7   b ⁻32 ÷ 4   c ⁻45 ÷ ⁻9   d 56 ÷ ⁻7

4 What numbers might go in the boxes?
At least one must be a negative number.
a ☐ + ☐ = ⁻17   b ☐ − ☐ = ⁻5
c ☐ × ☐ = ⁻36   d ☐ ÷ ☐ = 4

5 a Two numbers multiply to give ⁻18.
They add to give 3.
What are the two numbers?

b Two numbers multiply to give 12.
They add to give ⁻8.
What are the two numbers?

6 a 3(⁻3 + ⁻2)   b 4 × ⁻2 + 3 × ⁻6   c 6 − ⁻4 × ⁻5   d $\frac{7 + {}^-19}{{}^-4}$

7 Put one of these digits in each gap to make this true.   5, 3, ⁻2
___ (___ − ___) = 25

8 Here are some number cards.

⁻8 7 3 ⁻5 ⁻12 6 ⁻6 ⁻2 9

a Which two cards could make this true?

☐ + ☐ = ⁻5

b Choose another two cards that would also make it true.
c Choose two cards to make this true.

☐ × ☐ = ⁻30

d Which three cards will make the biggest answer for this?

☐ + ☐ − ☐ =

e Two number cards are added together to get the
number above.
Which of the number cards make this true?

⁻5

9 Find the HCF of these.
a 24 and 42   b 60 and 96   c 56 and 98   d 80 and 144

10 Use the HCFs found in question 9 to help you cancel these.
a $\frac{24}{42}$ b $\frac{60}{96}$ c $\frac{56}{98}$ d $\frac{80}{144}$

11 Find the LCM of these.
a 9 and 20   b 24 and 30   c 80 and 120

57

Number

12 Use the LCMs found in question **11** to help you to add and subtract these.
   a $\frac{2}{9} + \frac{7}{20}$ b $\frac{11}{24} + \frac{9}{30}$ c $\frac{9}{80} + \frac{53}{120}$

13 Two numbers have an HCF of 4 and an LCM of 24.
   What might they be?

14 Write down the common factor of these.
   a $6x$ and $7x$ b $5a$ and a^2 *c $3d^2$ and $3d$ *d $4x^2y$ and $8xy^2$

15 What digit will $8 \cdot 6^2$ end in?

16 A four-digit square number has a units digit of 6.
   __ __ __ 6
   a What could the units digit of the square root of this number be?
   b Can the square root of any number with last digit 6 be an odd number? Explain.

17 Find the value of these using your calculator.
   Give the answer to **c** to 2 d.p.
   a 6^7 b $1 \cdot 7^4$ c $0 \cdot 36^4$ d $(^-6)^4$ e 96^0

18 $8 \times y$ is a square number.
   What is the smallest possible value of y.

19 Find these. Give the answers to **c**, **d** and **e** to 2 d.p.
   a $\sqrt[4]{36}$ b $\sqrt{64}$ c $\sqrt[3]{48}$ d $\sqrt{22^2 - 7^2}$ e $\sqrt[3]{28^2 - 19^2}$

20 $\sqrt[3]{x}$ is a negative whole number.
   Which of these numbers could x be?
      8     $^-27$ $^-12 \cdot 167$ 125

21 Use trial and improvement to find these to 2 d.p.
   Do not use the √ or ∛ key. Show your working.
   a $\sqrt{11}$ b $\sqrt[3]{45}$

22 Write these as single powers.
   Then find the answers using a calculator.
   The first one is started.
   a $4^5 \times 4^6 = 4^{(5+6)} =$ b $8^3 \times 8^4$ c $7^{11} \div 7^6$ d $5^0 \times 5^4 \times 5^2$ e $\frac{5^3 \times 5^4}{5^2}$

23 Show that the index laws are true for these.
   a $x^3 \times x^4 = x^7$ b $x^9 \div x^4 = x^5$

   Start by writing $x^3 \times x^4 = (x \times x \times x) \times (x \times x \times x \times x)$.

*24 $2^2 \times 2^2 = 2^{2+2} = 2^4$
   $2^4 = 16$ and 16 is a square number.
   Is 4^4 a square number? Explain.

*25 a $26 = 3^3 - 1^3$
      Write 37 as the difference between 2 cubes.
   b The difference of the squares of two consecutive odd numbers less than 20 is 40.
      What are the numbers?

*26 Prove that any three-digit number, when repeated to give a six-digit number, is divisible by 7.

   Example If we start with 462 and repeat the digits to give 462 462, then 462 462 is divisible by 7.

3 Calculation

You need to know

- ✓ mental calculation — page 4
    - — add and subtract mentally
    - — multiply and divide mentally
- ✓ estimating — page 6
- ✓ written calculations — page 6
- ✓ checking answers to calculations — page 7
- ✓ order of operations — page 7

Key vocabulary

best estimate, complements, discount, order of operations, quotient

▶▶ A multiple of mysteries!

1. $$\begin{array}{r} **\\ \times\ **\\ \hline *2* \end{array}$$
    What digit does * stand for?

2. **a** A number when divided by 5 leaves no remainder.
    When divided by 6 there is a remainder of 5.
    It is between 20 and 50.
    What could it be?

    b A number is between 0 and 70.
    When divided by 3 or 7 there is no remainder.
    When divided by 4 there is remainder 2.
    What number is it?

    c A number is a multiple of 4.
    It leaves remainder 4 when divided by 5.
    What could the number be?
    Is there more than one answer?

    d A number has a digit sum of 9.
    It is divisible by 8.
    What number could it be?
    Is there more than one answer?

Number

Multiplying and dividing by numbers between 0 and 1

Discussion

- $40 \times 5 = 200$
  $40 \times 50 = 2000$
  $40 \times 500 = 20\,000$
  $40 \times 5000 = 200\,000$
  $40 \times 50\,000 = 2\,000\,000$

  You could use a spreadsheet to help.

  Discuss how to use the number pattern in the box to find the answer to the following multiplications.

  40×0.5 40×0.05 40×0.005

  When we multiply 40 by a number greater than 1 we get an answer greater than 40. What if we multiply 40 by a number between 0 and 1? **Discuss**.

- **Discuss** how to use the number pattern in the box to find the answers to these divisions.

  $\dfrac{8000}{0.4}$ $\dfrac{8000}{0.04}$ $\dfrac{8000}{0.004}$

  $\dfrac{8000}{4000} = 2$
  $\dfrac{8000}{400} = 20$
  $\dfrac{8000}{40} = 200$
  $\dfrac{8000}{4} = 2000$

  Is the answer greater or smaller than 8000 when we multiply 8000 by
  a number greater than 1?
  a number between 0 and 1? **Discuss**.

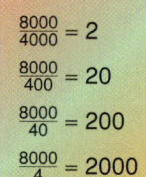

Worked Example

Which of these will have an answer greater than 0·72?
Which will have an answer less than 0·72? Explain.

a 0.72×1.8 **b** $0.72 \div 1.8$ **c** 0.72×0.27 **d** $0.72 \div \dfrac{3}{4}$

Answers
a The answer will be greater than 0·72 because we are multiplying by a number greater than 1.
b The answer will be less than 0·72 because we are dividing by a number greater than 1.
c The answer will be less than 0·72 because we are multiplying by a number between 0 and 1.
d The answer will be greater than 0·72 because we are dividing by a number between 0 and 1.

Exercise 1

1 Which of the following calculations will have an answer less than 200?
Do not calculate the answers.
a 200×0.4 **b** $200 \div 0.2$ **c** 200×0.5 **d** $200 \div 0.004$ **e** $200 \div \dfrac{1}{20}$
f 200×0.004 **g** 200×4.5 **h** $200 \div 1\dfrac{1}{2}$ **i** $200 \div 54$ **j** 200×54

2 Which of the following calculations will have an answer greater than 0·4?
Do not calculate the answers.
a $0.4 \div 0.1$ **b** $0.4 \times \dfrac{1}{10}$ **c** $0.4 \div 0.02$ **d** $0.4 \div \dfrac{1}{2}$ **e** 0.4×0.002
f 0.4×0.04 **g** 0.4×2.4 **h** $0.4 \div 24$ **i** $0.4 \div 2\dfrac{1}{2}$ **j** 0.4×24

Calculation

3 Choose the calculation which has an answer *less* than 1·04.
   a A 1·04 × 2·6   B 1·04 ÷ 2·6   C 1·04 ÷ 0·26
   b A 1·04 ÷ 0·58   B 1·04 × 5·8   C 1·04 × 0·58
   c A 1·04 ÷ 29   B 1·04 ÷ 0·29   C 1·04 × 29
   d A 1·04 × 1·04   B 1·04 ÷ 0·104 C 1·04 ÷ 1·04
   e A 1·04 ÷ 0·9   B 1·04 × 0·99   C 1·04 × 9·9

4 Kezia did this calculation.
Explain how you can tell, without doing it, that it is wrong.

    3·06 × 0·4 = 12·24

5 When we multiply a positive number, n, by 0·6 we get an answer less than n.
   a What is the inverse of multiplying by 0·6?
   b If we divide a positive number, p, by 0·6, is the answer more or less than p?

6 What goes in the gap, **greater** or **less**?
   a When we multiply a positive number, n, by a number between 0 and 1, the answer will be ___ than n.
   b When we divide a positive number m, by a number between 0 and 1, the answer will be ___ than m.

*****7** Which of these are true for *all* positive values of p and q?
   a $p > 1$ and $q > 1$ so $pq > 1$ **b** $p > 1$ and $q > 1$ so $\frac{p}{q} > 1$
   c $p > 1$ and $0 < q < 1$ so $pq < p$ **d** $p > 1$ and $0 < q < 1$ so $\frac{p}{q} > p$

Review 1 Which of these will have an answer greater than 1·83? Explain.
a 1·83 ÷ 2·7   **b** 1·83 × 0·27   **c** 1·83 × 2·7
d 1·83 ÷ 0·27   **e** 1·83 ÷ $\frac{27}{100}$ **f** 1·83 × $\frac{27}{100}$

Review 2 Decide which of these statements could be correct (✓) and which are definitely wrong (X). Justify your decision. Do not calculate the answers.
a 5·02 × 0·3 = 15·06   **b** 2·75 ÷ 0·02 = 1·375   **c** 6·24 × 1·2 = 7·488
d 8·127 ÷ 1·4 = 58·05 ***e** 2·75 × 1·1 < 2·75   ***f** 2·75 ÷ 0·8 > 2·75

Order of operations

Remember
We carry out operations in this order.
Work from left to right.

   Brackets
   Indices (powers)
   Division and **M**ultiplication
   Addition and **S**ubtraction

Use **BIDMAS** to help you remember.

Worked Example
Find $48 ÷ (7 + 5) - 6 + 4 × 3^3$ mentally.

Answer
$48 ÷ (7 + 5) - 6 + 4 × 3^3 = 48 ÷ 12 - 6 + 4 × 3^3$ calculating the brackets (7 + 5) = 12
$= 48 ÷ 12 - 6 + 4 × 27$ calculating 3^3 $3^3 = 27$
$= 4 - 6 + 4 × 27$ calculating 48 ÷ 12 = 4
$= 4 - 6 + 108$ calculating 4 × 27 = 108
$= \mathbf{106}$ calculating 4 − 6 + 108 = 106

Number

> **Discussion**
>
> **Discuss** the best way to do these.
> Find the answers.
>
> $\sqrt[3]{25 + 39}$ $\qquad$ $\left(\dfrac{5}{2}\right)^2$ $\qquad$ $\dfrac{18 + 72\cdot4 - 3 \times 4^2}{2(1\cdot9 + 0\cdot6)^2 - (3^2 + 3)}$

Exercise 2

1 Find the answer to these mentally. You may need jottings for some.
  a $15 \div (3 + 2)$
  b $3 + 4 \times 8$
  c $\dfrac{80}{4 \times 5}$
  d $\dfrac{35 + 14}{7}$
  e $6 \times 2 \div (5 - 3)$
  f $(2 + 1)^3 \div 3$
  g $(5 + 4)^2 - 11$
  h $(^-4)^2 - 3$
  i $(^-11)^2 - 3(5 + 2)$
  j $(25 - 17 + 2 + {}^-5)^3$
  k $4(5 - 3)^2 - 2$
  l $18 - 3 \times 2^2$
  ***m** $\left(\dfrac{5}{3}\right)^2$
  ***n** $24 \div (4 + 8) - 6 + 3 \times (10 \div 2)^2$

2 Find the answers to these mentally.
  a $\dfrac{25}{8 - 3}$
  b $\dfrac{16}{(3 - 1)^2}$
  c $\dfrac{5 \times 6^2}{10}$
  d $\dfrac{(5 \times 6)^2}{5 \times 4}$
  e $\dfrac{^-8^2 + 4}{7^2 + 1}$

3 Find the answers to these mentally.
  a $\sqrt{37 - 12}$
  b $\sqrt[3]{136 - 11}$
  c $\sqrt{4 + 5 \times 9}$
  d $\sqrt{5^2 + 24}$
  e $\sqrt[3]{2^2 - 3}$

4 Write down the letters that are beside the correct answers.
  The letters when unjumbled make the name of a famous Irish lead singer.
  N $3^2 \times 5^2 = 225$
  D $(12 + 8 - 17)^2 = 269$
  B $\sqrt{12 + 13} = 5$
  O $\sqrt[3]{57 + 68} = 5$
  A $(2 - 5)^2 = 25$
  O $(22 - 15 + 4 - 7)^3 = 64$

5 Explain the difference between $^-4^2$ and $(^-4)^2$.

***6** Put $+$, $-$, $\times$ or $\div$ into these calculations to make the answer correct.
  a $(3 \underline{\ \ } 8) \underline{\ \ } 9 \underline{\ \ } 3 = 30$
  b $\dfrac{5 \underline{\ \ } 7}{3^2 \underline{\ \ } 3} = 2$
  c $5(8 \underline{\ \ } 4) - (2 \underline{\ \ } 3)^2 = {}^-5$

***7** I am between 40 and 50.
  I am made from the numbers $^-4$, 7, $^-2$ and the operations $+$, $(\ )$, ^{2}.
  What number am I?

T ## Review 1

$\dfrac{1}{9}$	$\overline{16}$	$\overline{112}$	$\dfrac{1}{9}$	$\overline{10}$	$\overline{5}$	$\overline{6}$	$\overline{6}$		$\overline{9}$	$\dfrac{1}{9}$	**N** $\overline{1000}$
$\overline{7}$	$\overline{88}$	$2\dfrac{7}{9}$	**N** $\overline{1000}$	$\overline{100}$		$\overline{16}$	$\dfrac{1}{9}$	$\overline{6}$	$\overline{87}$	$\overline{125}$	$\dfrac{1}{9}$ $\overline{87}$ $\overline{112}$ $\overline{88}$

Use a copy of this box.
Write the letter beside each calculation above its answer in the box.

  N $(7 + 3)^3 = 1000$
  D $15 - 4 \times 2$
  C $(11 - 14)^2$
  T $9^2 + 6$
  R $(^-9)^2 + 7$
  W $(36 - 21 - 7 + 3 - 6)^3$
  K $(22 - 6 \times 2)^2$
  U $\dfrac{(3 + 2)^2}{3 \times 2 - 1}$
  A $\dfrac{5 - 2^2}{(2 + 1)^2}$
  I $\left(\dfrac{5}{3}\right)^2$
  E $\dfrac{(7 \times 8)^2}{7 \times 4}$
  S $\dfrac{7 \times 8^2}{7 \times 4}$
  G $\sqrt[3]{635 + 365}$
  L $\sqrt{10^2 - 8^2}$

62

Calculation

Review 2 Find the answer to these mentally.
- **a** $(^-3)^2 - 3^2$
- **b** $(^-3)^3 - 3^3$
- **c** $\frac{(3 \times 4)^2}{3 \times 4}$
- **d** $35 + 6(7 - 13) + 5$
- **e** $\frac{^-5 - ^-9}{2}$
- **f** $30 - 15 \div 5 - 4 \times 3$

*** Review 3** $\frac{(8+8)}{8} + 8 = 10$

Use seven 8s and any of +, −, ×, ÷ or brackets to make 1000.

Puzzle

Use the digits 3, 4, 5 and 6, the operations +, ×, −, ^{2} and two sets of brackets to get the answer 32.
Use each digit and operation just once.

Mental calculation

We can **add and subtract mentally** using
- complements
- partitioning
- counting up
- nearly numbers
- compensation
- facts you already know.

See pages 4 and 5 for examples of these.

We can **multiply and divide mentally** using
- place value knowledge
- partitioning
- factors
- near tens
- known facts
- doubling and halving.

See pages 5 and 6 for examples of these.

Exercise 3

This exercise is to be done mentally.

1 Answer these questions as quickly as possible.
- **a** Multiply eight by eight.
- **b** Add seven to the square of four.
- **c** What number should you add to negative three to get two?
- **d** What number is five cubed?
- **e** Multiply twenty-six by ten.
- **f** What is one quarter of thirty-six?
- **g** Subtract four from negative three.
- **h** Write down the factor pairs of 36.
- **i** Find the HCF of 24 and 36.
- **j** What is the value of x if $x + 28 = 104$?
- **k** $39 = 50 - x$
  What is the value of x?

63

Number

1
  l $x^2 = 25$
     What are the two possible values of x?
  m What is the next number in this sequence?
       8, 3, ⁻2, ⁻7, ...
  n What is one half of one hundred and fifty-six?
  o $p = 3q - 8$
     What is the value of p when $q = 2$?
  p How much must you add to 3087 to get 5000?
  q Find the LCM of 15 and 20.

T   **2**   Use a copy of this.
Shade the answers to these on your diagram.
  a 36 + 64   **b** 8 + ⁻2 + ⁻5
  c 18 + 39   **d** 0·6 + 0·8
  e 530 + 260   **f** 6·7 − 0·8
  g 4600 − 2800 **h** 5·6 + 1·7
  i 342 + 639   **j** 5·23 + 1·5
  k 5·07 − 3·8   **l** 8·64 + 5·36
  m 7·24 + 4·76 **n** 16 − 4·37
  o 5·63 + 3·37
What shape does the shading make?

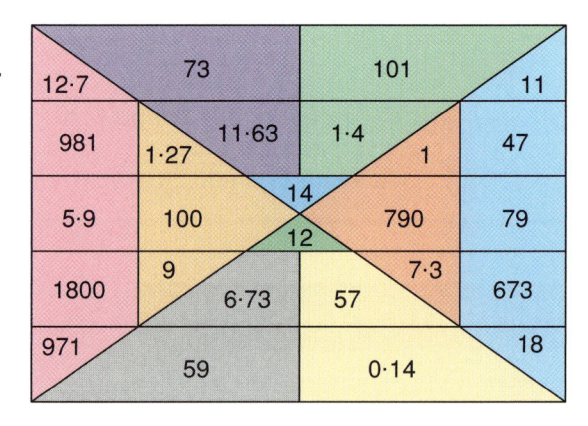

3 The number 4 is halfway between 2·5 and 5·5.
  a What goes in the gap?
      The number 4 is halfway between 1·8 and ___.
      The number 4 is halfway between ⁻10 and ___.
  b Work out the number that is halfway between 37×46 and 43×46.

4 Here are six number cards.

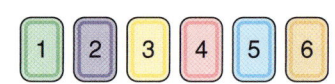

    | 1 | 2 | 3 | 4 | 5 | 6 |

Arrange the six cards to make these calculations.

  a 579 = ☐☐☐ + ☐☐☐   **b** 1146 = ☐☐☐ + ☐☐☐

  c 660 = ☐☐☐ + ☐☐☐   **d** 324 = ☐☐☐ − ☐☐☐

5 To fill in this puzzle you **add two numbers** to work out the number above them.
Find a way to fill in this puzzle.

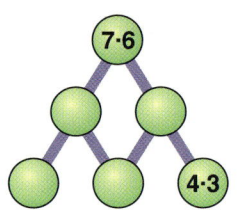

(Top: 7·6; bottom right: 4·3)

6 Find a and b in each part of this question.
  a The sum of a and b is 7.
     The product of a and b is 12.
  b The sum of a and b is ⁻10.
     The product of a and b is 24.
  c The difference between a and b is 3.
     The quotient of a and b is 2.
  d The difference between a and b is 4.
     The quotient of a and b is ⁻1.
  e The sum of a and b is 1·2.
     The product of a and b is 0·32.

Remember: The quotient is the answer to a division.

Calculation

7 a 20 × 30 b 300 × 50 c 500 × 8000 d 300 ÷ 600
   e 54 000 ÷ 900 f 2800 ÷ 70 g 180 × 4 h 324 × 4
   i 214 × 6 j 12 × 18 k 18 × 25 *l ⁻11 × 21
   *m ⁻19 × ⁻34

T 8 Use a copy of this.
     Find the answers on the dot grid.
     Join the dots in order. The first two are done.
   a 4·5 × 0·1 = **0·45** b 0·68 × 0·1 = **0·068**
   c 5·7 × 0·01 d 0·5 ÷ 0·1
   e 0·052 ÷ 0·1 f 0·3 × 0·02
   g 5·7 ÷ 0·01 h 5 × 0·6
   i 5 × 0·4 j 0·5 × 0·9
   k 0·04 × 0·6 l ⁻0·07 × 4
   m ⁻0·09 × ⁻8 n 0·2 ÷ 4
   o 0·04 ÷ ⁻5 p 0·6 ÷ 0·4
   q 0·07 ÷ 2 r ⁻0·09 ÷ ⁻2
   s 0·036 ÷ 6 t 0·26 × 0·4
   u 500 × 0·8 v 81 ÷ 0·9
   w 0·052 ÷ 0·1
   What shape have you made?

   Dot grid values:
   38   5·7   0·57   0·057   5   90   400
   104 40   0·068 50   9   0·52 0·104
   6   0·45 3·5   2   3   570 0·006
   24   0·024 57   35   20 15   0·045
   2·8 ⁻0·28 0·72   0·05   ⁻0·008 1·5 0·035

9 a 1·3 × 14 b 6·2 × 21 c 8·2 × 18 d 23 × 11 e 65 × 29

10 a 30 ÷ 0·5 b 16 ÷ 0·8 c 300 ÷ 0·6 d 180 ÷ 0·6 e 30 ÷ 0·06 f 45 ÷ 0·09

11 What goes in the box?
   a 0·01 × ☐ = 1·5 b ☐ ÷ 0·01 = 2·4

12 Look at these number cards.

   | 0·4 | 4 | 10 | 0·1 | 0·05 | 1 |

   a Which two cards multiplied together will give the
      smallest possible answer?
      What is this answer?   ☐ × ☐ =
   b Choose two of the cards to give the answer 100.   ☐ ÷ ☐ = 100

13 ☐ × ☐ × ☐ = 0·08
   What might go in the boxes?
   Find at least four different ways to fill them.

14 a 2·4 × 4·5 b 3·4 × 2·5 c 0·24 × 2·5 d 3·4 × 1·2

   Try doubling and halving.

15 a 270 ÷ 6 b 846 ÷ 4 c 2·68 ÷ 4 d 186 ÷ 12 e 13·8 ÷ 6
   f 112 ÷ 16 g 918 ÷ 18

*16 Given that 40 × 25 = 1000, find these.
    a 40 × 24 b 39 × 25 c 41 × 25 d 40 × 26

*17 Given that 36 × 35 = 1260, find these.
    a 36 × 34 b 35^2 c 72 × 35

65

Number

*18 The product of two numbers is four times their sum.
The sum of their squares is 180.
What are the two numbers?

*19 Put the digits 1, 2, 3, 4, 5 and 6 in place of boxes to make this true.
□□ × □ = □□□

Review 1 Answer these questions as quickly as possible.
a Multiply twenty-eight by one hundred.
b Find a fifth of forty-five.
c What is the square of the sum of seven and three?
d What is the difference between five and negative six?
e What are the next two numbers in the sequence 25, 18, 11, 4, ...?
f What is the value of ab^2 if $a = 2$ and $b = 3$?
g Find x if $48 = x + 75$.

Review 2 Using each of the numbers 1, 2, 3, 4, 5, 6, 7, 8 and 9 once, copy and fill in the blanks.

$$+\dfrac{\quad \_\_\ \_\_\ \_\_\ \_\_\ }{\quad \_\_\ \_\_\ \_\_\ \_\_\ }$$

This can be done in many different ways.
Find at least five.

Review 3
a What number is halfway between ⁻3·5 and 2·5?
b 6 is the number halfway between 8·3 and ___ .
*c 3 is the number halfway between 7·5 and ___ .

Review 4 Find a and b if
a sum of a and $b = 11$, product $= 24$
b sum of a and $b = 1$, product $= ⁻12$.

[T] **Review 5**

		A				A							
4·7	23	0·6	1·6	0·3	4·7	0·6	1·6	80	1·8	1000	1000	720	180	80

			A				
0·45	45	1·5	0·6	180	1·5	80	1·6

Use a copy of the box.
Put the letter beside each question above its answer in the box.

A $0.36 \div 0.6 = 0.6$ K 5×0.06 S $0.047 \div 0.01$ C $9 \div 6$ M 20×50
T $0.9 \div 2$ E $40 \div 0.5$ N 300×0.6 H $2.3 \div 0.1$ O $360 \div 8$
U 30×24 I 3.6×0.5 R 0.008×200

Remember
Fractions, decimals and percentages are all ways of expressing **proportions**.

$0.1 = \frac{1}{10} = 10\%$ $0.01 = \frac{1}{100} = 1\%$

$0.2 = \frac{1}{5} = 20\%$ $0.02 = \frac{1}{50} = 2\%$

$\frac{1}{8} = 0.125 = 12\frac{1}{2}\%$ $\frac{1}{3} = 0.\dot{3} = 33\frac{1}{3}\%$ $\frac{2}{3} = 0.\dot{6} = 66\frac{2}{3}\%$

66

Calculation

Discussion

Mira: *I know 50% = 0.5 so 5% = 0.05.*

Is Mira correct? **Discuss.**

How could you write these as decimals?

    0·5% $67\frac{1}{2}$% $17\frac{1}{2}$%

• Ruby found $1\frac{1}{2}$ of 18 mentally like this.

    $\frac{1}{2}$ of 18 = 9

    $1\frac{1}{2}$ of 18 = 18 + 9
              = 27

Discuss how Ruby could find these mentally.

    125% of 120 kg   35% of £60 $\frac{2}{5}$ of 16·5 m $1\frac{3}{8}$ of 3200 ℓ

Worked Example   Find $12\frac{1}{2}$% of 80.

Answer   10% of 80 = 8   **or** $12\frac{1}{2}$% = $\frac{1}{8}$
           1% of 80 = 0·8 $\frac{1}{8}$ of 80 = **10**
           2% of 80 = 1·6
           $\frac{1}{2}$% of 80 = 0·4
           so $12\frac{1}{2}$% of 80 = 8 + 1·6 + 0·4
                                      = **10**

Exercise 4

This exercise is to be done mentally.

1 Answer these questions as quickly as possible.
   a Express $\frac{1}{4}$ as a decimal.
   b Express $\frac{3}{5}$ as a percentage.
   c Convert $\frac{3}{4}$ to a decimal.
   d Convert 0·8 to a fraction.
   e $\frac{1}{8}$ = 0·125, what is $\frac{3}{8}$ as a decimal?
   f Convert $7\frac{2}{3}$ to an improper fraction.
   g Convert $\frac{38}{5}$ to a mixed number.
   h Express 0·625 as a percentage.
   i Express 10·5 as a percentage.

Remember to write fractions in their simplest form.

Number

j Simplify $\frac{85}{100}$.
k Simplify $\frac{450}{630}$.
l Convert 0·45 to a fraction.
m Convert $\frac{4}{25}$ to a decimal.
n Convert 1·2 to a percentage.
o Convert 165% to a decimal.
p Increase 200 by 10%.
q 25% of a number is 8. What is the number?
r 20% of a number is 12. What is the number?
s Increase 500 ℓ by 12%.
t Decrease 200 mm by 15%.
*__u__ Increase 360 m by 30%.
*__v__ Increase 7 by 150%.

T

2 Use a copy of this.
What goes in the gaps?

Fraction	Decimal	Percentage
$\frac{2}{5}$		
	0·$\dot{3}$	
		175%
		12$\frac{1}{2}$%
$\frac{3}{15}$		
	0·03	
		37·5%
	0·625	
12$\frac{1}{2}$		

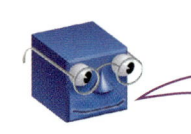

There is more practice at calculating fractions, decimals and percentages mentally in Chapters 4 and 5.

3 Find these answers mentally.
a $\frac{2}{5}$ of 40   **b** $\frac{7}{12}$ of 24   **c** $\frac{3}{8}$ of 64   **d** $\frac{2}{3}$ of 36
e $\frac{3}{5}$ of 150   **f** $1\frac{1}{3}$ of 18   **g** $1\frac{1}{4}$ of 1200   **h** $2\frac{3}{4}$ of 16
i 30% of 20   **j** 60% of 40   **k** 125% of 20   **l** 175% of 200
*__m__ $\frac{3}{5}$ of 10·5   *__n__ $\frac{3}{8}$ of 5600   *__o__ 20% of £2·50   *__p__ 35% of £5
*__q__ 85% of 15 mm   *__r__ $1\frac{3}{5}$ of £20·50   *__s__ $2\frac{5}{12}$ of 3600 kg   *__t__ 2% of 5% of 100 m

4 Robert bought a shirt, a pair of shoes and a coat.
How much did he save on each?
a   **b**   *__c__

25% OFF — £60
20% OFF — £85
30% OFF — £120·50

Calculation

*5 Find the sale price of a hat that was £45 and is reduced by 30% in a sale.

*6 There is a discount of 15% on a £65 fishing rod in a sale.
By how much is the rod's price reduced?

Review 1 Answer these questions as quickly as possible.
a Write these as decimals.   i $\frac{3}{4}$ ii $\frac{4}{5}$ iii $\frac{7}{50}$ iv 32%   v 4%
b Write these as percentages.   i $\frac{1}{5}$ ii $\frac{3}{12}$ iii $\frac{3}{20}$ iv $\frac{60}{50}$ *v 0·025
c Write each of these as a fraction in its simplest form.
  i 15%   ii 24%   iii 0·36   *iv 0·004
d Find   i $\frac{5}{8}$ of 72   ii 20% of £64   iii $2\frac{1}{3}$ of 150   *iv $12\frac{1}{2}$% of 240

Review 2
a Jane bought some books for £5 each. She wanted to make some money so she increased the price of each by 40% before she sold them. What did she make on each book?
b In a sale, a camera which cost £175 is reduced by 30%. How much would I save if I bought it in the sale?

ALL CAMERAS reduced by 30%

Solving word problems mentally

Example   Mel bought a new coat in this sale.
Its original price was £95.
The new price can be worked out mentally.

A 20% reduction is the same as 80% of the original price.
We need to find 80% of £95.
   10% of £95 = £9·50
so 80% of £95 = 8 × £9·50
             = 2 × 2 × 2 × £9·50
             = 2 × 2 × £19
             = 2 × £38
             = **£76**

SALE all coats reduced by 20%

Worked Example
What is the area of a rectangular tile of sides 5·5 cm and 8 cm?

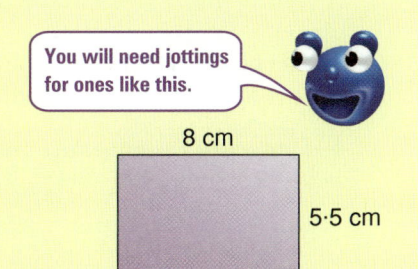

You will need jottings for ones like this.

8 cm
5·5 cm

Answer
Area = 5·5 × 8   or   5·5 × 8 = 5 × 8 + 0·5 × 8
     = $\frac{11}{\underset{1}{2}} \times 8^4$ = 40 + 4
     = **44 cm²**   = **44 cm²**

69

Number

Exercise 5 This exercise is to be done mentally.

1 Write the answers to these as quickly as possible.
  a How many faces has a cube?
  b A bird flies at an average speed of 30 kilometres per hour. How far will it fly in 1 minute at this speed?
  c How many seconds are there in two and a half minutes?
  d Last year Tim grew from 1·56 m to 1·8 m. How much did he grow in centimetres?
  e Two angles of a triangle are 37° and 95°. What is the other angle?
  f You get A$100 for £80. How much do you get for A$300?
  g What is the area of this triangle?
  h A fair spinner has eight equal sections. Five are red and three are blue. What is the probability I will spin red?
  i The scale on a map is 2 centimetres to 1 kilometre. On the map, the distance to the airport is 12 centimetres. How many kilometres is it to the airport?
  j What is the volume of a cuboid measuring 3 cm by 5 cm by 4 cm?
  k How many pairs of parallel sides does a parallelogram have?
  l In a test I got eighteen out of twenty questions correct. What percentage did I get correct?
  m a, b and c are equal angles. What is the size of angle a?
  n Multiply $2y$ by $4y$. Give your answer in its simplest form.
  o Find the area of a triangle with base 4·5 cm and height 12 cm.
  *__p__ 100 miles per hour is about 44 metres per second. About how many metres per second is 75 miles per hour?
  *__q__ Find the volume of a cuboid with dimensions 8 cm by 3·5 cm by 6 cm.
  *__r__ Find the area of a parallelogram of base 16 mm and height 2·1 cm.
  *__s__ Half the tickets for the school play were bought by parents, one-third by siblings and the rest by relatives. What fraction were bought by relatives?
  *__t__ The ratio of sugar to flour in a recipe is 5 : 8. There are 280 g of sugar. How many grams of flour are there?

2 a Eight people bought tickets for an animal park. Each paid £5·60. What was the total cost?
  b A group paid £61·60 for their tickets to the animal park. How many were in the group?

3 Use a copy of this table.
Show all the ways you could pay exactly 70p.

Number of 10p coins	Number of 20p coins	Number of 50p coins
7		

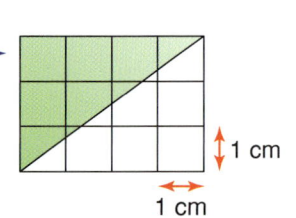

Drinks 70p
Use 10p, 20p or 50p coins

NO CHANGE GIVEN

Calculation

4 Phoebe measured the distance between two towns on a map as 4 cm.
The scale on the map is 1 : 150 000. What is the actual distance between the two towns?

Link to geography.

5 The probability that Emily will beat Tom at golf is 0·6. Out of 40 matches, how many would you expect her to win?

6 Some boys and girls have £30 between them. Each boy has £3 and each girl has £5. How many girls are there?

***7** Thirty years ago, Britain used pounds, shillings and pence.
There were 20 shillings in £1.
A gallon of petrol cost 7 shillings thirty years ago.
Today it costs about £3·90.
By how much has the cost of petrol risen in the last thirty years?

***8** Write **one** of the prime numbers 5, 7, 11, 13, 17, 19 and 23 in each circle so that the three primes in each line add to the same number. Use each number only once.

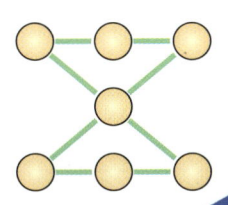

***9** **a** Use 3, 4, 5 and 6 once each with some of ×, ÷, +, − and brackets to make 30.
   b $4 \times 3 + 6 - 5 \times 3 + 1$
   Put brackets into this to make as many different answers as you can.

Remember BIDMAS, page 61.

   c Use any of +, −, ×, ÷, √ and brackets, and four 4s to make these.
   i 17   **ii** 9   **iii** 20

***10** Arnie wrote these jottings to help him work out the volume of this square-based cuboid.

$3 \cdot 5 \times 3 \cdot 5 \times 8 = \frac{7}{2} \times \frac{7}{2} \times 8$

3·5 cm
3·5 cm
8 cm

   a Copy and finish Arnie's jottings to find the answer.
   b Show another way you could work out the volume mentally.

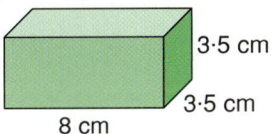

Review 1 Answer these mentally as quickly as possible.
a What is the name of a triangle with all its sides equal?
b What number is zero point one less than three?
c Write $\frac{4}{20}$ in its simplest form.
d I think of a number, call it n.
I square my number then add 3.
Write an expression to show the result.
e Subtract zero point six five from five.
f What is two point seven divided by 2?
***g** Two thirds of the class took part in 'Maths Week' and one quarter of the participants won prizes. What fraction of the class won prizes?
If 4 students won prizes, how many students were in the class?

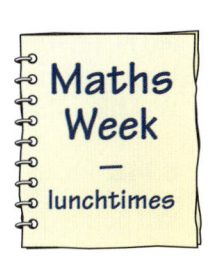

Maths Week — lunchtimes

Review 2 The cost of visiting an aquarium is given.

Adults £8·50 • Children £4
Family Pass (2 adults, 2 children) £22·50

How much would a family of 2 adults and 2 children save by buying a family pass?

71

Number

Review 3 On my map 2 cm represents 5000 metres. If the distance from Cambridge to Huntingdon is approximately 11 cm, how far are the towns apart, in kilometres?

Review 4 Jess was going to visit her Aunt in Australia. She was given £40 to spend. How many Australian dollars would she have if £100 is approximately equal to A$250?

Puzzle

Use a copy of the table.
Rewrite each number given in each row within the table using the numbers at the left of that row.
You may use +, −, ×, ÷ and brackets.
As an example, the first row has been completed.

Numbers	Use 2 of the numbers	Use 3 of the numbers	Use 4 of the numbers	Use all of the numbers
2, 3, 16, 8, 5	$4 = \frac{8}{2}$	$9 = 5^2 - 16$	$1 = \frac{16}{8} + 2 - 3$	$18 = 2(16 - 8) - 3 + 5$
1, 2, 7, 3, 4	$10 =$	$8 =$	$42 =$	$17 =$
4, 5, 12, 1, 9	$7 =$	$8 =$	$9 =$	$10 =$
6, 5, 13, 7, 4	$28 =$	$27 =$	$22 =$	$24 =$
3, 4, 15, 8, 2	$7 =$	$0 =$	$7 =$	$12 =$
3, 9, 18, 1, 4	$36 =$	$13 =$	$1 =$	$4 =$

Estimating

Discussion

- Robbie is painting his bedroom.

  He needs to calculate the area of the walls to work out how much paint to buy.
  He measures the lengths and heights to the nearest 10 cm, then calculates the area.
  Will his estimate for the area be accurate enough? **Discuss**.

- **8348**

  We could give a number of approximations to this.
  We could give 8000 or 8300 or 8350 or 8500 or 10 000.
  Think of situations where each of these approximations for 8348 might be used.
  Discuss.

- What does '**degree of accuracy**' mean? **Discuss**.

Calculation

Exercise 6

1 Decide the degree of accuracy needed for these.
   a A vet uses the mass of a cat to calculate how much medicine to inject.
   b A builder calculates the amount of wood he needs to buy to build a shed.
   c A chef calculates how much flour and sugar are needed for a cake.
   d A reporter calculates the number of people who have attended an art exhibition in the last week.

> **A.** As accurate as possible.
> **B.** A rough estimate will do.
> **C.** An estimate is fine but it must be reasonably accurate.

2 a Maria rounded the length and width of her bedroom to the nearest metre. She then calculated the area so that she could work out the cost of recarpeting. Would her estimate for the area be accurate enough? Explain.
   b Thomas bought the same book for all of his 10 cousins for Christmas. He worked out the length of paper, to the nearest cm, needed to wrap one book. He used this to estimate the total length of paper he would need. Will his estimate be accurate enough?

Review 1 Write down two calculations where the answer must be as accurate as possible and two where a rough estimate is good enough.

Review 2 Rose rounded the length of one curtain to the nearest 10 cm and then worked out how much material she would need for 24 curtains of this length.
Will her estimate be good enough?

Discussion

- Is $8 \div 2$ or $9 \div 2$ a better approximation for $8.59 \div 2.37$? **Discuss**.

- Is 5×4 or 5×5 a better approximation for 4.5×4.5? **Discuss**.

Remember
$\approx$ means '**is approximately equal to**'.

Guidelines for estimating

1 Look for '**nice**' **numbers** that enable you to do the calculation mentally.

   Example $200 \div 5.7 \approx 200 \div 5$ rather than $200 \div 6$.

   Example $\dfrac{72.6 \times 347.05}{0.89} \approx \dfrac{100 \times 350}{1}$

> $\approx$ means 'is approximately equal to'.

2 Look for **numbers that will cancel**.

   Example $\dfrac{12.48 \times 487.31}{3.69} \approx \dfrac{12^3 \times 500}{4^1} = 1500$

> There is often more than one possible estimate for an answer.

3 When **multiplying** two numbers, try to **round one up and one down**.

   Example   It is better to estimate 2.5×3.5 as 2×4 or 3×3 rather than 3×4.
   $2.5 \times 3.5 = 8.75$ so $2 \times 4 = 8$ or $3 \times 3 = 9$ both give a closer estimate than $3 \times 4 = 12$ or $2 \times 3 = 6$.

73

Number

4 When **dividing** two numbers, try to **round both numbers up** or **both numbers down**.

Example   It is better to estimate $\frac{83.2}{8.5}$ as $\frac{80}{8}$ rather than $\frac{83}{9}$.

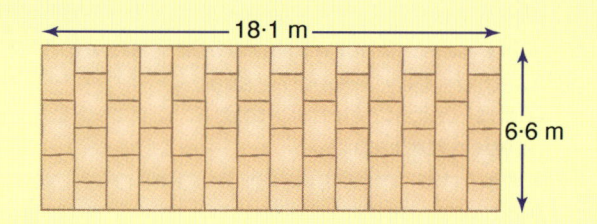

$\frac{83.2}{8.5} = 9.79$ **(2 d.p.) so** $\frac{80}{8} = 10$ **gives a closer estimate than** $\frac{81}{9} = 9$.

Worked Example
Find the approximate area of this patio.

Answer
Area = length × width
≈ 20 × 7
= **140 m²**

Worked Example
Estimate the answers to these.

a 8.98×24.6 b $\frac{198 \times 71.6}{11.3 \times 0.83}$ c 0.09×59.6.

Answer
a $8.98 \approx 10$, $24.6 \approx 25$
An estimate is $10 \times 25 = 250$.

b $198 \approx 200$, $71.6 \approx 70$, $11.3 \approx 10$, $0.83 \approx 1$
An estimate is $\frac{\overset{20}{200} \times \overset{7}{70}}{\underset{1}{10} \times 1} = 1400$.

c $0.09 \approx 0.1 = \frac{1}{10}$, $59.6 \approx 60$
An estimate is $\frac{1}{10} \times 60 = 6$.

Exercise 7

Except for questions 5, 10 and Reviews 2 and 3.

1 Choose the best estimate for these:
   a 4.5×5.5 **A** 5×6 **B** 5×5 **C** 4×5
   b $41.3 \div 6.6$ **A** $42 \div 7$ **B** $42 \div 6$ **C** $48 \div 6$
   c 8.4×7.8 **A** 7×7 **B** 8×8 **C** 8×7
   d $96.4 \div 12$ **A** $96 \div 15$ **B** $90 \div 10$ **C** $100 \div 10$

2 Estimate the answers to these.
   a 111×89 b 382×63 c $585 \div 27$ d $521 \div 23$ e 5627×839

3 Estimate the answers to these. Justify your estimates.
   a 7.6×4.123 b $67.34 \div 9.3$ c 7.24×18.07 d $(10.14)^2$
   e $\frac{19.6 \times 34.7}{4.35}$ f $\frac{7.62 + 2.21}{5.23}$ g 81.2×0.27 h $\frac{102 \times 0.46}{4.1}$
   i $\frac{28.6 \times 24.4}{5.67 \times 4.02}$ j $\frac{18.3 + 11.1}{57.03}$

   'Justify' means give reasons why you did it that way.

4 a Choose the **best** estimate for the answer to this.
       $72.36 \div 8.92$
       A 6   **B** 7   **C** 8   **D** 9   **E** 10   **F** 11

   b Choose the **best** estimate for the answer to this.
       32.6×0.47
       A 1.2   **B** 1.6   **C** 12   **D** 16   **E** 120   **F** 160

   c Estimate the answer to $\frac{9.31 + 22.4}{5.26}$.

   d Estimate the answer to $\frac{29.3 \times 24.6}{6.12 \times 4.08}$.

74

Calculation

5 Use a calculator to find the answers to these. Round the answers sensibly.
Check that the answer is reasonable by making an estimate.
  a 37.64×23.1 **b** $44.9 \div 8.76$ **c** 0.47×19.1 **d** $\frac{38.4 + 22.5}{18.4}$
  e $\frac{31.2}{0.24}$ **f** $(3.24)^2$ **g** $\frac{87.9}{1.3 + 5.01}$ **h** $\frac{4.7 \times 49.2}{0.18}$

6

Penn: I think $6 \div 2$ is the best approximation for $6.69 \div 2.46$.

Nadia: I think $7 \div 2$ is the best approximation for $6.69 \div 2.46$.

Decide who **you** think is right. Give a reason for your answer.
You could choose either as long as you give a reason for your choice.

7 A nautical mile is approximately 1·853 km.
Estimate how many km are in 214 nautical miles.

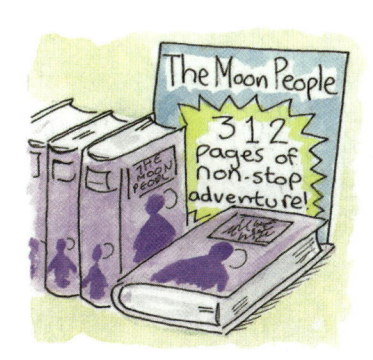

8 Kareema is reading this book.
She takes an average of 2 minutes 5 seconds to read a page.
Estimate how long it will take her to read the book.
Give your answer in hours and minutes.

The Moon People — 312 pages of non-stop adventure!

9 An ounce is about 28·35 grams.
Estimate the number of ounces in 600 grams.

10 Estimate, then use your calculator, to find the answers to the following. If rounding is needed, round your answers sensibly.
  a Find the cost of 9·7 m of material at £8·19 per metre.
  b Find the perimeter of this triangle.

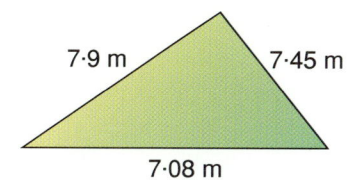

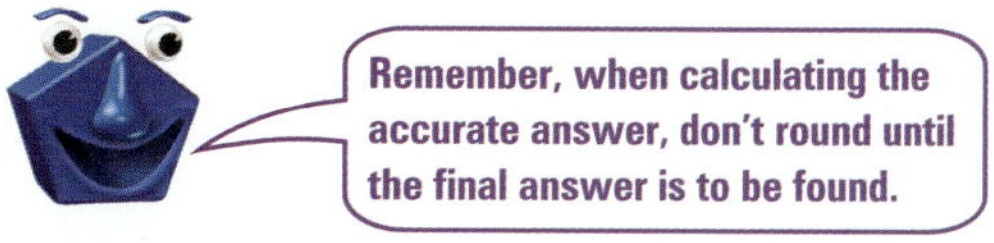

  Triangle sides: 7·9 m, 7·45 m, 7·08 m

  Remember, when calculating the accurate answer, don't round until the final answer is to be found.

  *****c** A formula for finding the area of a trapezium is
  $A = \frac{1}{2}(a + b) \times h$.
  a and b are the lengths of the parallel sides and h is the distance between these sides.
  Find the area of this trapezium.

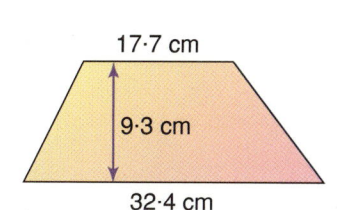

  Trapezium: 17·7 cm (top), 9·3 cm (height), 32·4 cm (bottom)

  *****d** A formula for finding the area of a circle is $A = \pi r^2$.
    i Using $\pi = 3.14$, find the area of a circle with radius 26·7 cm.
    ii Using $\pi = \frac{22}{7}$, find an estimate for the area of a circle with radius 26·7 cm.
    iii Did you get the same estimate for **i** and **ii**?
    Did you get the same answer, to the nearest cm², for the calculation?

  There is more about areas of circles on page 343.

Number

*11 Mason estimated the answer to $\frac{31.3}{5.27 - 3.14}$ as $\frac{30}{2} = 15$.
Write down four more calculations that could have an estimated answer of 15.
Use at least two of the operations +, −, ×, ÷ and squaring in each calculation.

Review 1 Estimate the answer to each of these. Show your working. The first question is done for you.
a $3.75 \times 4.26 \simeq 4 \times 4 = 16$
b $172 \div 46$
c $68.9 \div 6.83$
d 562×24
e $\frac{14.23 + 31.8}{7.86}$

Review 2 Estimate your answer to each of these questions then use your calculator to find the exact answer.
a $\frac{5.35 + 9.83}{0.66}$
b $8.7^2 - 5.2^2$
c $2.6^2 + \sqrt{84.64}$
d $7.82(8.56 - 20.04)$

Review 3 Estimate, then use your calculator, to find the answers to the following.
a On holiday Joe's family travelled 125·6 km the first day, and on the next four days they travelled 233·8 km, 64·3 km, 189·8 km and 291·4 km.
  i How far did they travel altogether?
  ii How much petrol did they need if the car went 28 km on 1 litre of petrol?
b A book is 3·8 cm thick. The front and back covers are 3 mm thick cardboard. Each leaf is 0·78 mm thick. How many leaves has the book?

Written calculation

Adding and subtracting

Remember
We **add and subtract decimals** by lining up the decimal points. Always estimate the answer first.

Example These are the areas of three small islands.

  1583 km²   890·006 km²   8·0035 km²

The total area of all three is
2481·01 km² (2 d.p.)

```
   1583
    890·006
+     8·0035
  2481·0095
    1 1 1
```

Exercise 8

1 a 84·72 + 1·39
   b 7·35 + 186·4
   c 0·057 + 32·8
   d 23·2 − 1·96
   e 560·3 − 7·82
   f 86·09 − 4·3
   g 19 − 4·97 − 4·6
   h 21 − 5·72 − 6·8
   i 4936·27 − 83·9 − 0·06
   j 96 + 4·38 − 24·7 + 3·72
   k 9683 + 294·308 + 0·0067
   l 79 632·4 + 83·096 + 5·007
   m 8326 + 4·094 + 38·62

2 Evelyn bought a stereo for £1086, a CD rack for £58·70 and a CD cleaning tissue for £0·85. How much did this cost altogether?

Calculation

3 What is the perimeter of this shape?

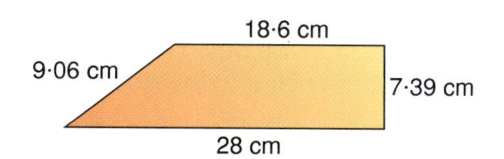

18·6 cm
9·06 cm
7·39 cm
28 cm

*4 The largest mammal ever measured was a blue whale, 31·996 m long.
The smallest mammal ever measured was a pygmy white-toothed shrew, 5·98 cm long.
What is the difference in length between these two mammals?

Review 1
a 186·4 + 7·982
b 83·4 − 9·79
c 83·72 − 68·4 − 0·89 − 5·72
d 8672 + 36·4 + 0·0073 − 5·802

Review 2
Marie weighs a container of igneous rock. It has a mass of 0·839 kg.
The container has a mass of 0·062 kg.
What is the mass of the rock in grams?

Multiplying and dividing

Example A vet needs to give a dog 4·3 mℓ of antibiotic per kilogram of mass.
The dog has a mass of 19·2 kg.
The vet must give the dog 19·2 × 4·3 mℓ.
   19·2 × 4·3 ≈ 20 × 4 = 80 mℓ
   19·2 × 4·3 is equivalent to 192 ÷ 10 × 43 ÷ 10 = 192 × 43 ÷ 100.
First multiply the integers.

```
    192
 ×   43
   7680    ← 192 × 40
    576    ← 192 × 3
   8256
    1 1
```

19·2 × 4·3 = 8256 ÷ 100
           = **82·56**

Example To find the current in an electrical circuit, Dylan had to divide
the voltage of 86·7 volts by 16.
He needed to know the answer to 1 decimal place.
   86·7 ÷ 16 is approximately 100 ÷ 20 = 5.

```
16)86·7
 − 80·0      16 × 5
    6·7
 −  6·4      16 × 0·4
    0·30
 −  0·16     16 × 0·01
    0·14
```

Answer   5·41 R 0·14
         5·4 to 1 d.p.

> Dylan wants the answer to 1 d.p. so he needs to work out the answer to 2 d.p. then round to 1 d.p.

77

Number

To **divide by a decimal** we do an **equivalent calculation** that has a whole number as the **divisor**.

The divisor is the number you are dividing by.

Worked Example
Calculate   352 ÷ 2·6.

Answer
352 ÷ 2·6 is approximately 360 ÷ 3 = 120.
352 ÷ 2·6 is equivalent to 3520 ÷ 26.

$$\frac{352 \times 10}{2 \cdot 6 \times 10} = \frac{3520}{26}$$

```
26 ) 3520
   – 2600      26 × 100
      920
    – 780      26 × 30
      140
    – 130      26 × 5
       10·0
      – 7·8    26 × 0·3
        2·20
      – 2·08   26 × 0·08
        0·12
```

Answer   135·38 R 0·12
         135·4 (1 d.p.)

Remember
to **check your answer** using one or more of these ways.

See page 7 for examples of each of these.

1 Check the answer is sensible.
2 Estimate to check the answer is the right order of magnitude.
3 Check by working the problem backwards (using inverse operations).
4 Check using an equivalent calculation.
5 Check the last digits.

Exercise 9

1 **a** 530 × 2·4   **b** 640 × 1·2   **c** 386 × 4·6   **d** 68·7 × 2·3   **e** 5·7 × 8·33

2 **a** 240 people paid the entrance fee on Monday.
         How much money is this altogether?
         Show your working.
     b The museum took £600 in entrance fees on Friday.
         How many people paid to visit the museum on Friday?
         Show your working.

[SATs Paper 1 Level 5]

Museum
Entrance fee
£1.20
per person

3 **a** A football club is planning a trip.
         The club hires 234 coaches. Each coach holds 52 passengers.
         How many passengers is that altogether?
     b The club wants to put one first aid kit into each of the 234 coaches.
         The first aid kits are sold in **boxes of 18**.
         How many boxes does the club need?

[SATs Paper 1 Level 5]

78

Calculation

4 Calculate how much a nurse must inject over 24 hours for these body masses. Give the answer to the nearest mℓ.
   a 85 kg   **b** 77 kg   **c** 53·2 kg   **d** 68·7 kg

> **Dose over 24 hours**
> 0·6 mℓ per kilogram of body mass

5 a Mark pays £16·80 to travel to school each week.
He goes to school 38 weeks each year.
How much does he pay to travel to school each year?
Show your working.
  b Mark could buy a season ticket that would let him travel for all 38 weeks.
It would cost £532.
How much is that per week?
  c Show how you could check your answer to **a**.

6 Find the answers to these.
  a 18·2 ÷ 14   **b** 94·5 ÷ 15   **c** 117 ÷ 26   **d** 240 ÷ 32

7 a 68·7 × 2·3   **b** 5·9 × 6·42   **c** 5·7 × 8·33   **d** 72·6 × 0·39   **e** 0·72 ÷ 8·64

8 Oil costs £1·82 per litre. What is the cost of 2·7 litres?
Show a way you could check your answer.

9 Give the answers to these to 1 d.p.
  a 487 ÷ 14   **b** 321 ÷ 17   **c** 843 ÷ 23   **d** 560 ÷ 19   **e** 57·1 ÷ 16

10 What is the cost of 0·45 kg of peanuts at £0·89 per kilogram?

11 Which is the best buy?
       15 pieces of pizza for £12·60
  or 25 pieces of pizza for £20·50
Show how you could check your answer.

12 Which is equivalent to the calculation given?
  a 94 ÷ 0·4   **A** 94 ÷ 4   **B** 940 ÷ 4   **C** 940 ÷ 0·4   **D** 9400 ÷ 0·4
  b 386 ÷ 0·6   **A** 386 ÷ 6   **B** 3860 ÷ 60   **C** 3860 ÷ 6   **D** 38 600 ÷ 6
  c 472 ÷ 4·6   **A** 4720 ÷ 46   **B** 472 ÷ 46   **C** 47 200 ÷ 46   **D** 4720 ÷ 4·6
  d 842·6 ÷ 0·9   **A** 84·26 ÷ 9   **B** 8426 ÷ 9   **C** 8426 ÷ 90   **D** 84 260 ÷ 9
  e 364·2 ÷ 0·06   **A** 3642 ÷ 6   **B** 3642 ÷ 60   **C** 36 420 ÷ 6   **D** 364 000 ÷ 6
  f 0·058 ÷ 0·0045   **A** 5·8 ÷ 45   **B** 5800 ÷ 45   **C** 58 ÷ 45   **D** 580 ÷ 45
  g 0·872 ÷ 7·3   **A** 8·72 ÷ 73   **B** 872 ÷ 73   **C** 8720 ÷ 73   **D** 87 200 ÷ 73

13 a 378 ÷ 4·2   **b** 481 ÷ 7·4   **c** 234 ÷ 2·6   **d** 195 ÷ 3·9   **e** 425 ÷ 1·7

> Think about whether the answer should be bigger or smaller than the dividend.

14 Give the answers to these to 1 d.p.
  a 524 ÷ 0·6   **b** 388 ÷ 0·7   **c** 298·3 ÷ 0·3   **d** 426·3 ÷ 0·09
  e 342 ÷ 2·6   **f** 47·9 ÷ 3·1   **g** 46·3 ÷ 2·7   **h** 683 ÷ 3·5
 *i 0·87 ÷ 0·69   ***j** 0·874 ÷ 0·0045

Number

*15 This plan shows some areas in Andrea's bedroom.
What are the missing measurements?
Give them to the nearest cm.

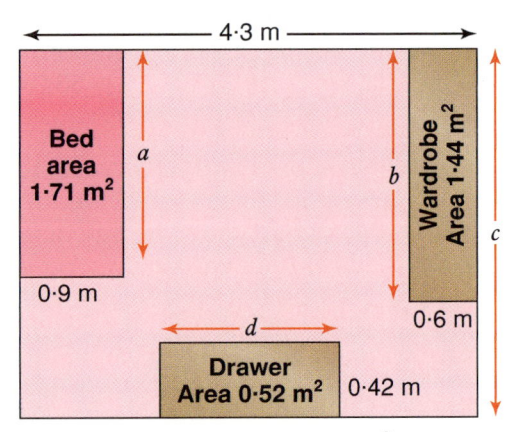

- Bed area 1·71 m², 0·9 m
- Wardrobe Area 1·44 m², 0·6 m
- Drawer Area 0·52 m², 0·42 m
- 4·3 m
- Area of bedroom 15·2 m²

*16 Without using a calculator, pick a possible answer to the calculation.
Explain your choice.

a 426 × 1·4   A 5964   B 382·4   C 596·4
b 52²   A 2809   B 2704   C 27 004
c 61·92 ÷ 0·72 A 0·86   B 8·6   C 86

Review 1

A		A								A				
476	3·91	476	3·91	21·7	3·91	1071	21·7	1·85	18·3	476	5·04	11	4·07	33·85

			A						A				
1071	1·2	21·7	476	0·8	4·07	1·2	21·7	18·3	476	33·85		3·91	11

		A		
56	1·2	476	4·25	3·91

Use a copy of this box.
Answer each question. Put the letter beside each question above its answer in the box.

A 340 × 1·4 = **476**   B 840 ÷ 15   C 238 × 4·5
E 586·8 ÷ 27 (answer to 1 d.p.)   H 32·7 × 0·56 (answer to 1 d.p.)
I If 15 items cost £63·75, what does one cost?
L What is the cost of 1·6 kg of apples at £3·15 per kilogram?
N If bacon costs £8·69 per kilogram, how much will 0·45 kg cost?
O Ann buys 1·7 kg of ham and it costs her £18·70.
   How much does ham cost per kilogram?
R Amy runs 8 laps in 9·6 minutes. How long does she take to run one lap (in minutes)?
S John's take-home pay is £245·62 a week. He pays £75 on rent, £76·77 on food and bus fares
   and he saves £60 each week. How much does he have to spend on other things?
T What is the width of this rectangle in metres?
U What is the cost, to the nearest penny, of 0·72 kg of nuts at
   £5·65 per kilogram?
P A weekly ticket on the bus costs
   £7·50. If Harry buys a return ticket
   each day (5 days) it will cost him
   £1·75 more. How much does a
   return ticket cost?

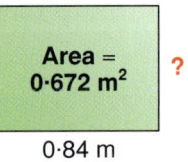

Area = 0·672 m²
0·84 m

Review 2 A gym is selling package deals.

12 visits for £41
or   25 visits for £79

Which package is the better value for money?

Review 3 Which statements are true?
a 72·3 ÷ 0·04 is equivalent to 723 ÷ 4.
b 124·7 ÷ 1·23 is equivalent to 12470 ÷ 1·23.
c 0·72 ÷ 0·058 is equivalent to 7200 ÷ 58.
d 0·046 ÷ 2·3 is equivalent to 46 ÷ 23.
e 9·86 ÷ 14·3 is equivalent to 98·6 ÷ 143.

Review 4 Calculate these. Give your answer to 1 d.p. if rounding is needed.
a 275 ÷ 2·5   b 46·4 ÷ 0·8   c 244 ÷ 0·6   d 89·43 ÷ 3·2

Review 5 Without using your calculator, pick a possible answer to each calculation. Explain.
a 32·5 × 8·6 =   **A** 2795   **B** 279·5   **C** 486·5
b 25·11 ÷ 0·54 =   **A** 4·65   **B** 0·465   **C** 46·5

Puzzle

Find the value of each letter.

a A·B × B·A = B·CB   b L·M × L·L = ML·LM

Investigation

Dividing by zero

Start with the number 200 on your screen.
Divide 200 by 10, 9, 8, 7, ... 1
Now divide it by 0·9, 0·8, 0·7, 0·6, ...
Now divide it by 0·09, 0·08, 0·07, 0·06, ...
Now divide ...
What happens to the answer as the divisor gets smaller and smaller? **Investigate**.
Does dividing by zero have any meaning?

Start with 200 again for each division.

The number you divide by is the divisor.

Choosing a strategy for calculation

Discussion

Discuss whether it is best to use a mental, written or calculator method to find the answers to these.

a £1 = A$2·50
   i How many Australian dollars would you get for £50?
   ii How many pounds would you get for A$45?

Number

b 492 people live in an area of 18 square miles.
What is the mean number of people per square mile?
c What is the area of this rectangle? ⟶ 4·63 m, 12·4 m
d What is the volume of a cuboid of dimensions 8·64 m by 3·27 m by 5·68 m?

Exercise 10

Only use a calculator if you need to.

Choose a mental, written or calculator method to do each of these questions.
Explain why you chose the method you did.

1. For a design and technology project, Jack bought 5 kg of vegetables at £1·95 per kg and a sauce for £2·86.
How much change did he get from £20?

2. In a sale a £45 shirt is reduced by £8·95.
What is the sale price of the shirt?

3. Seadown Youth Club hired a bus for a day outing. The total cost of this hire was £124·20, which consisted of a fixed charge of £45 and 45p per kilometre travelled. How many kilometres did the Seadown Youth Club travel on this outing?

4. Sandya put 56·5 ℓ of petrol in her car. It cost 68p per litre.
How much did this petrol cost altogether?

5. A drink from a machine costs 55p.   [SATs Paper 2 Level 6]

   The table shows the coins that were put into the machine one day.

Coins	Number of coins
50p	31
20p	22
10p	41
5p	59

   How many cans of drink were sold that day?
   Show your working.

6. A company sells and processes films of two different sizes.
The tables show how much the company charges.   [SATs Paper 2 Level 6]

   Film size: 24 photos
   - Cost to **buy** each film — £2·15
   - Postage — free
   - Cost to **print** each film — £0·99
   - **Postage** for each film — 60p

   Film size: 36 photos
   - Cost to **buy** each film — £2·65
   - Postage — free
   - Cost to **print** each film — £2·89
   - **Postage** for each film — 60p

Calculation

I want to take **360** photos.
I need to buy the film, pay for the film to be printed, and pay for the postage.
Is it cheaper to use all films of size 24 photos, or all films of size 36 photos?
How much cheaper is it? Show your working.

7 Hannah went on a cycling holiday. [SATs Paper 2 Level 6]
The table shows how far she cycled each day.

Monday	Tuesday	Wednesday	Thursday
32·3 km	38·7 km	43·5 km	45·1 km

Hannah says: 'On average I cycled **over 40 km** a day'.
Show that Hannah is wrong.

8 The petrol consumption rate for Ailsa's car is 13·3 km per litre.
   a Ailsa travelled a distance of 711 kilometres. How many litres of petrol did her car use on this journey?
   b Ailsa used the conversion rate '1 mile is about 1·609 km' to work out the distance she had travelled in miles. To the nearest mile, she calculated this distance to be 442 miles. Is she correct?
   c What distance could Ailsa travel on 28 litres of petrol?
   *__d__ On a 113 km section of the journey, Ailsa travelled at a constant speed. This section of the journey took Ailsa 1 hour 21 minutes. About how many kilometres did Ailsa travel each 15 minutes?

9

Stir-fry vegetables for one
0·35 kg   carrots
0·25 kg   broccoli
0·55 kg   cauliflower

Cost of vegetables
carrots   £0·89 per kg
broccoli   £1·06 per kg
cauliflower   £1·89 per kg

How much do the vegetables for 'Stir-Fry Vegetables for one' cost in total?

10 One day, a factory made 73 skirts and 22 jackets. The sizes made and the material used for each size are given in the table.

	Size	Material (metres)	Number
Skirt	10	1·2	18
Skirt	12	1·3	32
Skirt	14	1·5	23
Jacket	10–12	2·5	10
Jacket	12–14	2·9	12

   a How much material was used on this day?
   b The next day, the same amount of material was used to make a quantity of size 14 skirts. How many skirts were made?
   c On the day that 73 skirts were made, one person did all the finishing work on them. This person was paid a daily wage of £30 with an extra 75p for every skirt in excess of 50 that were finished. How much did this person earn on this day?
   *__d__ One of the tailors was paid an hourly rate of £6·20 for the first $7\frac{1}{2}$ hours worked, then £9·30 per hour after that. How many hours did this tailor work on a day in which he earned £60·45?

Number

∗11 Two families went to a concert.
The Baileys paid £38 for one adult and four children.
The Thompsons paid £34 for two adults and two children.
What is the cost of an adult ticket?

∗12 This calculation uses the digits 2, 3, 4, 5 and 6.
$$23 \times 45 \times 6$$
What multiplication, using these same digits, has the smallest answer?
Explain your answer.

∗13 Three bananas and two oranges cost £3·99.
Two bananas and three oranges cost £3·81.
How much does a banana cost?

∗14 A book gives this information:

[SATs Paper 2 Level 7]

> A baby giraffe was born that was 1·58 metres high.
> It grew at a rate of 1·3 centimetres **every hour**.

Suppose the baby giraffe continued to grow at this rate.
About how many days old would it be when it was **6 metres** high?
Show your working.

∗15 a The sum of two numbers is 19.
What is the greatest product they can have?
 b What if there are three numbers?
 c What if there are four numbers?

Review 1 Five pieces of string of length 135 cm, 30·7 cm, 12·2 cm, 15·6 cm and 26·7 cm are knotted together to make one length. How long is the completed string if each knot uses up 3·71 cm of string altogether?

Review 2 The account for 15 copies of a book, including postage is £117·55. If postage is £16·30, how much does each book cost?

Review 3 Keung measured the length of his desk as 60 cm. How many desks of this length could be placed side by side along a classroom wall that is 26 feet long?

(Use 1 foot = 0·3048 metres.)

∗ Puzzle

At a Bring and Buy sale table, slices of apple pie were priced at 40p per slice. When none had been sold at this price, a decision was made to reduce them to less than half price. Once this had been done, they all sold quickly for a total of £3·91.

By how much was the price of each slice reduced?

Calculation

Using a calculator

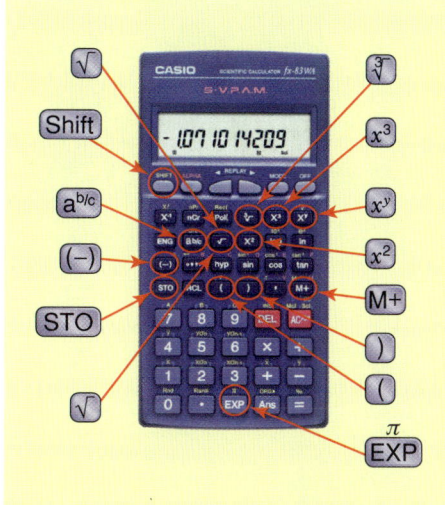

On a calculator we use $\boxed{\text{Shift}}\ \boxed{\text{EXP}}^{\pi}$ for π

$\boxed{(-)}$ to enter a negative number

$\boxed{x^2}$ to square a number

$\boxed{x^3}$ to cube a number

$\boxed{x^y}$ to enter numbers with indices

$\boxed{\sqrt{\ }}$ to find the square root

$\boxed{\sqrt[3]{\ }}$ to find the cube root

$\boxed{a^{b/c}}$ to enter fractions

$\boxed{(}$ and $\boxed{)}$ for brackets

$\boxed{\text{STO}}\ \boxed{\text{M+}}$ to store a number in memory

$\boxed{0}\ \boxed{\text{STO}}\ \boxed{\text{M+}}$ to clear the memory.

Examples $^-8{\cdot}642 \div 0{\cdot}38$ is keyed as $\boxed{(-)}\ \boxed{8{\cdot}642}\ \boxed{\div}\ \boxed{0{\cdot}38}\ \boxed{=}$ to get $^-22{\cdot}74$ (2 d.p.).

$\sqrt{79+83}$ is keyed as $\boxed{\sqrt{\ }}\ \boxed{(}\ \boxed{79}\ \boxed{+}\ \boxed{83}\ \boxed{)}\ \boxed{=}$ to get $12{\cdot}73$ (2 d.p.).

The brackets are needed so that we find the square root of the total of 79 + 83.

$7{\cdot}3^4 \times 1{\cdot}36^5$ is keyed as $\boxed{7{\cdot}3}\ \boxed{x^y}\ \boxed{4}\ \boxed{\times}\ \boxed{1{\cdot}36}\ \boxed{x^y}\ \boxed{5}\ \boxed{=}$ to get $13\ 212{\cdot}5$ (1 d.p.).

$1\frac{3}{4} + \frac{5}{6}$ is keyed as $\boxed{1}\ \boxed{a^{b/c}}\ \boxed{3}\ \boxed{a^{b/c}}\ \boxed{4}\ \boxed{+}\ \boxed{5}\ \boxed{a^{b/c}}\ \boxed{6}\ \boxed{=}$

to get $\boxed{2\lrcorner 7\lrcorner 12}$ which is $2\frac{7}{12}$.

Worked Example

Find $\dfrac{(5{\cdot}8 - 4{\cdot}3)^3 - 2}{3 \times 6 \div (3{\cdot}5 - 0{\cdot}5)^2}$ using a calculator.

The whole numerator must be divided by the whole denominator.
To find the denominator, key this.

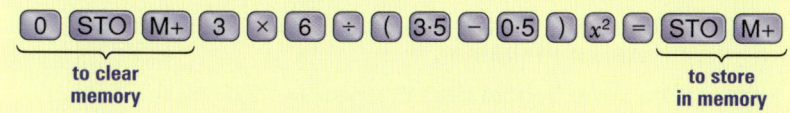

$\underbrace{\boxed{0}\ \boxed{\text{STO}}\ \boxed{\text{M+}}}_{\text{to clear memory}}\ \boxed{3}\ \boxed{\times}\ \boxed{6}\ \boxed{\div}\ \boxed{(}\ \boxed{3{\cdot}5}\ \boxed{-}\ \boxed{0{\cdot}5}\ \boxed{)}\ \boxed{x^2}\ \boxed{=}\ \underbrace{\boxed{\text{STO}}\ \boxed{\text{M+}}}_{\text{to store in memory}}$

To find the numerator and then divide it by the denominator, key

$\boxed{(}\ \boxed{5{\cdot}8}\ \boxed{-}\ \boxed{4{\cdot}3}\ \boxed{)}\ \boxed{x^3}\ \boxed{-}\ \boxed{2}\ \boxed{=}\ \boxed{\div}\ \boxed{\text{RCL}}\ \boxed{\text{M+}}\ \boxed{=}$ to get **0·6875**.

Note There are other possible keying sequences.

Number

Exercise 11

1 a Kiran keyed $\frac{15 \times 10 + 12}{4 \times 2}$ as

(15 × 10 + 12) ÷ 4 × 2 =

What is wrong with his keying sequence?

*b Michaela keyed $\frac{15 + 64 - 2 \times 4}{3(2 + 5) - 1}$ as

15 + 64 − 2 × 4 = ÷ (3 × (2 + 5)) − 1 =

What is wrong with her keying sequence?

2 Use your calculator to find the answers to these.
Give the answers to 2 d.p. if you need to round.

  a $\frac{91 - 17}{54}$ **b** $\frac{69}{5 \times 4}$ **c** $\frac{4 \cdot 6 + 2 \cdot 3}{5 \cdot 8}$ **d** $\frac{8 + 6}{2 \times 3}$

  e $\frac{3 \times 7 \cdot 2}{4 + 3}$ **f** $\frac{1 \cdot 4 + 3 \times 8}{6}$ **g** $\sqrt{16^2 - 5^2}$ **h** $\sqrt{25^2 - 24^2}$

  *i $\frac{(3 \cdot 6 - 2 \cdot 1)^2 - 3}{4 \times 5 \div (8 \cdot 7 - 6 \cdot 2) - 2^2}$ ***j** $^-(231 \times 3 + 432) + 4 \times 268 - (3 - 56)$

  *k $\frac{(17 - 10)^2 (18 - 16)^2}{3(17 - 12)^3}$ ***l** $\frac{(5 \cdot 2 - 3 \cdot 6)^2 (4 \cdot 1 - 2 \cdot 3)^3}{18 - (3 \cdot 2 - 1 \cdot 4)^2}$

You will need to put brackets in some places.

3 Find the answer to these using your calculator.
Round the answers to **b** to **g** and **l** to 2 d.p.

  a $^-4 \cdot 32 + 8 \cdot 74 - \,^-3 \cdot 86$ **b** $^-3 \cdot 42 \times 5 \cdot 37$ **c** $86 \cdot 47 \div \,^-3 \cdot 28$ **d** $8 \cdot 3^2 \times 0 \cdot 21^3$ **e** $\frac{3 \cdot 65^4}{2 \cdot 16^3}$

  f $\sqrt{8 \cdot 4^4 + 3 \cdot 1^2}$ **g** $\sqrt{7 \cdot 1^4 - 8 \cdot 3^3}$ **h** $5\frac{1}{2} + 3\frac{2}{7}$ **i** $8\frac{3}{11} - 5\frac{7}{8}$ **j** $4\frac{1}{2} \times 3\frac{3}{4}$

  k $8\frac{1}{3} \div 2\frac{3}{4}$ **l** $\sqrt{\frac{82 \cdot 3}{\pi}}$ **m** $\sqrt[4]{1296}$

Review 1 Use your calculator to evaluate these. Give your answer to 2 d.p. where rounding is necessary.

  a $\frac{13 \cdot 5 - 1 \cdot 5 \times 8 \cdot 4}{2 \cdot 4}$ **b** $\frac{(\sqrt{41 \cdot 3} - 2 \cdot 75)^2}{13 \cdot 5 \times 3 \cdot 2}$ **c** $\sqrt{7 \cdot 5^3 - 1 \cdot 5 \times 79 \cdot 41}$

Review 2 Use your calculator for these questions. Round answers to 2 d.p. where appropriate.

  a $2\frac{3}{4} \div 1\frac{7}{8}$ **b** $^-6 \cdot 82 \times 4 \cdot 37$ **c** $2 \cdot 8^3 \div 1 \cdot 5^4$ **d** $\sqrt{6 \cdot 1^2 - 2 \cdot 7^3}$

  e $\frac{(^-1 \cdot 78)^5}{\sqrt{5 \cdot 64}}$ **f** $6\frac{2}{3} \times \,^-1\frac{3}{4}$

Summary of key points

A When we **multiply a positive number, a, by a number between 0 and 1**, the answer is **smaller** than a.

When we **divide a positive number, b, by a number between 0 and 1**, the answer is **larger** than b.

Examples $1 \cdot 56 \times 0 \cdot 7 = 1 \cdot 092$ The answer is less than 1·56 because we are multiplying by a number between 0 and 1.

               $1 \cdot 56 \div 0 \cdot 4 = 3 \cdot 9$ The answer is greater than 1·56 because we are dividing by a number between 0 and 1.

B The **order of operations** is   **B**rackets

                                   Indices

                                   Division and **M**ultiplication

                                   Addition and **S**ubtraction.

Remember BIDMAS.

We can work out simple calculations mentally and more difficult ones using a calculator.

Example
$$\frac{(10-4)^2+8}{4\times 2-2^2} = \frac{6^2+8}{4\times 2-2^2}$$ work out the brackets first
$$= \frac{36+8}{4\times 2-4}$$ work out the indices
$$= \frac{44}{8-4}$$
$$= \frac{44}{4}$$
$$= 11$$

Work out the whole numerator and the whole denominator first.

C **Mental calculation**

We can **add and subtract mentally** using

- complements
- partitioning
- counting up
- nearly numbers
- compensation
- facts we already know.

We can **multiply and divide mentally** using

- place value
- partitioning
- factors
- near tens
- known facts
- doubling and halving.

D We can **convert between fractions, decimals and percentages mentally**.
We can also do simple fraction, decimal and percentage calculations mentally.
You need to know
$\frac{1}{8} = 0\cdot125 = 12\frac{1}{2}\%$ $\qquad$ $\frac{1}{3} = 0\cdot\dot{3} = 33\frac{1}{3}\%$ $\qquad$ $\frac{2}{3} = 0\cdot\dot{6} = 66\frac{2}{3}\%$

Examples
$\frac{3}{8} = 3 \times \frac{1}{8}$ $\qquad\qquad\qquad\qquad$ $\frac{2}{3}$ of $45\cdot3 = \frac{2}{3} \times 45\cdot3$
$\phantom{\frac{3}{8}} = 3 \times 0\cdot125$ $\qquad\qquad\qquad\qquad$ $\frac{1}{3} \times 45\cdot3 = 45\cdot3 \div 3$
$\phantom{\frac{3}{8}} = 0\cdot375$ as a decimal $\qquad\qquad\quad$ $= 15\cdot1$
$\phantom{\frac{3}{8}} = 37\frac{1}{2}\%$ as a % $\qquad\qquad\qquad$ $\frac{2}{3} \times 45\cdot3 = 2 \times 15\cdot1$
$\qquad\qquad\qquad\qquad\qquad\qquad\qquad$ $= \mathbf{30\cdot2}$

Example To find 17·5% of 120:
$\qquad$ 10% of 120 = 12
$\qquad$ 5% of 120 = 6
$\qquad$ 2·5% of 120 = 3
$\qquad$ so 17·5% of 120 = 12 + 6 + 3
$\qquad\qquad\qquad\qquad\quad = \mathbf{21}$

E We can solve word problems mentally.

Number

F **Estimating**

Use these guidelines when estimating answers.

1 Approximate to **'nice' numbers** that are easy to work with.
   Example $61.7 \div 7 \approx 63 \div 7 = 9$ rather than $60 \div 7$.

2 Approximate to **numbers that will cancel**.
   Example $\dfrac{9.6 \times 27}{4.12} \approx \dfrac{10 \times 28^7}{1_4} = 70$

3 When **multiplying**, try to **round one number up and one number down**.
   Example $12.5 \times 6.5 \approx 12 \times 7 = 84$

4 When **dividing**, try to **round both numbers up or both numbers down**.
   Example $\dfrac{47.2}{5.6} \approx \dfrac{48}{6} = 8$

> 48 is a nice number too.

G We use written methods with the four operations and with whole numbers and decimals.

To **divide by a decimal** we do an equivalent calculation so that we divide by a whole number.

Worked Example

Calculate $248 \div 3.2$.

Answer

$248 \div 3.2 \approx 240 \div 3 = 80$ 240 is a 'nice' number

$248 \div 3.2$ is equivalent to $2480 \div 32$ $\dfrac{248 \times 10}{3.2 \times 10} = \dfrac{2480}{32}$

```
32 ) 2480
     2240      32 × 70
      240
      224      32 × 7
       16
       16      32 × 0·5
```

Answer **77·5**

With written calculations we **check our answers** by

1 checking the answer is sensible
2 estimating first then checking the order of magnitude of the answer is the same as the estimate
3 working the problem backwards (using inverse operations)
4 doing an equivalent calculation
5 checking the last digits.

H We can choose **a mental, written or calculator** method to do calculations.

Calculation

> **1** On a calculator we use
>
> $\boxed{\text{Shift}}$ $\boxed{\text{EXP}}$ for π
>
> $\boxed{(-)}$ to enter a negative number
>
> $\boxed{x^2}$ to square a number
>
> $\boxed{x^3}$ to cube a number
>
> $\boxed{x^y}$ to enter numbers with indices
>
> $\boxed{\sqrt{}}$ to find the square root
>
> $\boxed{a^{b/c}}$ to enter fractions
>
> $\boxed{(}$ and $\boxed{)}$ for brackets
>
> $\boxed{\text{STO}}$ $\boxed{\text{M+}}$ to store a number in memory
>
> $\boxed{0}$ $\boxed{\text{STO}}$ $\boxed{\text{M+}}$ to clear the memory.
>
> *Examples* To find $4.62^4 \times 3.1^5$
>
> key $\boxed{4.62}$ $\boxed{x^y}$ $\boxed{4}$ $\boxed{\times}$ $\boxed{3.1}$ $\boxed{x^y}$ $\boxed{5}$ $\boxed{=}$ to get 130 429·66 (2 d.p.).
>
> To find $2\frac{1}{3} + 4\frac{5}{8}$
>
> key $\boxed{2}$ $\boxed{a^{b/c}}$ $\boxed{1}$ $\boxed{a^{b/c}}$ $\boxed{3}$ $\boxed{+}$ $\boxed{4}$ $\boxed{a^{b/c}}$ $\boxed{5}$ $\boxed{a^{b/c}}$ $\boxed{8}$ $\boxed{=}$ to get $6\frac{23}{24}$.

Test yourself

Except for questions 6, 7, 21 and 24.

1 Jamie owed Susan 75p.
He had one 50p coin, four 20p coins, five 10p coins and three 5p coins.
Write down all the different ways Jamie could pay Susan. **A**

2 Which of the following calculations will have an answer greater than 0·34? **A**
  a $0.34 \div 1.5$ **b** 0.34×0.04 **c** 0.34×12.76 **d** $\frac{0.34}{0.76}$

3 Find the answer to these mentally. **B**
  a $5 \times (3 + 1)$ **b** $3(4 \times 3 + 2)$ **c** $\frac{3 + 4 \times 8}{5}$ **d** $\frac{3 \times 4^2}{6 \times {}^-2}$
  e $\frac{4 - 5^2}{3 + 2^2}$ **f** $\frac{(2+4)^2}{(5-3)^2}$ **g** $\sqrt{54 - 18}$ **h** $\sqrt[3]{6^2 - 9}$

4 Here are some number cards. **C**

$\boxed{1}$ $\boxed{2}$ $\boxed{3}$ $\boxed{4}$ $\boxed{5}$ $\boxed{6}$

Arrange the six cards to make these calculations.
  a $939 = \boxed{}\boxed{}\boxed{} + \boxed{}\boxed{}\boxed{}$
  b $258 = \boxed{}\boxed{}\boxed{} - \boxed{}\boxed{}\boxed{}$

5 Susie's beaker in science had a mass of 51·2 g.
She needed to add 0·65 g of one chemical and 5·078 g of another to the beaker.
What total mass would she get? **G**

Number

6 Shirley buys 6 tapes at £4·55 each, 3 CDs at £9·60 each and 2 magazines at £1·35 each.
How much change would she get from £60?

7 A water bottle holds 700 ml.
An adult needs about 12·6 litres of water a week to stay healthy.
How many water bottles is that?
Show your working.

8 Use a copy of this.
Work these out mentally.
Shade the answers in the diagram.
  a 20 × 40   b 0·2 × 40   c 300 × 40
  d 3 × 0·4   e 0·04 ÷ 2   f 0·054 ÷ 6
  g 0·054 ÷ 0·1   h 120 × 0·5   i 600 × 0·4
  j 40 ÷ 0·08   k 72 ÷ 0·8   l 0·54 × 0·6
What letter does the shading give?

12	0·324	60	1·2	24
5·4	8	3·24	0·54	80
62	0·009	0·8	90	50
9	240	0·9	800	0·12
1200	12 000	500	0·02	0·2

9 Find the length of wire in this wire frame.
3·6 cm
1·7 cm
7·4 cm

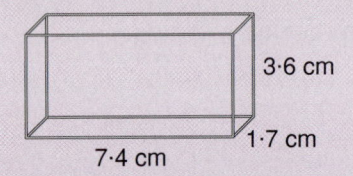

10 Answer these mentally.
  a Write $\frac{3}{4}$ as a decimal.
  b Write $\frac{2}{5}$ as a percentage.
  c Write 0·6 as a fraction.
  d Convert $6\frac{3}{5}$ to an improper fraction.
  e Convert $\frac{47}{8}$ to a mixed number.
  f Write 0·375 as a percentage.
  g Simplify $\frac{65}{100}$.

11 Choose two numbers out of the box so that
  a they multiply to give the biggest answer
  b they divide to give the biggest answer
  c they multiply to give the answer closest to 1.

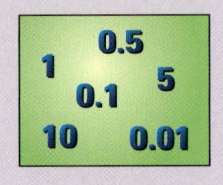

  1   0·5
      0·1   5
  10   0·01

12 Entry to a pool is £1·50 per person.
  a 360 people paid £1·50 on Saturday.
     How much money is that altogether?
  b The pool took £561 one weekend.
     How many people paid to go to the pool that weekend?
  c A ticket for the pool slide costs 45p.
     If 125 people bought slide tickets on Saturday, how much did they pay altogether?

13 Two numbers are added to get the number above.
Find out a possible way to fill in this diagram.

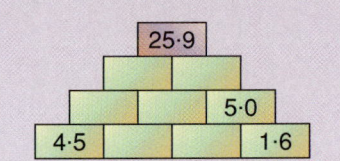

25·9
        5·0
4·5   1·6

14 The number 8 is halfway between 5·6 and 10·4.
What goes in the gaps?
  a The number 8 is halfway between 1 and ____.
  b The number 8 is halfway between 5·7 and ____.
  c The number 8 is halfway between ⁻4 and ____.

90

Calculation

15 Caleb keyed $\frac{16+5\times7}{3\times4}$ as (16 + 5 × 7) ÷ 3 × 4 =
What is wrong with his keying sequence?

16 Find the answer mentally.
Shonagh makes silver necklaces.
A market stall sells them for Shonagh.
The necklaces sell for £6·20 each.
The stall keeps 25% of the sale.
How much does Shonagh get for each necklace sold?

17 Answer these mentally.
   a Increase 60 by 10%.   **b** Decrease 200 ml by 30%.   **c** Find $\frac{3}{5}$ of 45.
   d Find 70% of 20.   **e** Find $2\frac{1}{4}$ of 24.   **f** Find 120% of 40.
 * **g** Find 35% of 25.

18 Find x and y.
   a The sum of x and y is 13.   **b** The difference between x and y is 10.
      Their product is 42.   The quotient is 3.

19 Find three consecutive even numbers with a sum of 84.

20 Without using a calculator, pick out the best estimate for these calculations.
   a $(246)^2$ **A** 6050   **B** 60 500   **C** 605 000
   b 374 ÷ 0·75   **A** 500   **B** 50   **C** 5000
   c 78 ÷ 0·042   **A** 186   **B** 18·6   **C** 1860

21 **a** Estimate the area and perimeter of this rectangle.
    b Calculate the area and perimeter, using your estimates as a check.

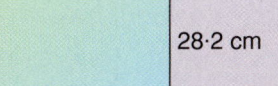

41·4 cm
28·2 cm

22 Give a calculation which would be equivalent to the one given.
The divisor should not be a decimal number.
   a 452 ÷ 0·8   **b** 0·694 ÷ 0·07

23 Give the answers to these to 1 d.p.
   a 587 ÷ 16   **b** 429 ÷ 2·8

24 Use your calculator to find the answer to these.
Round the answer to 2 d.p. if you need to round. Estimate first.
   a $\frac{78}{3\times6}$ **b** $\pi\times4\cdot7^2$ **c** $^{-}4\cdot67+{}^{-}3\cdot81-{}^{-}7\cdot32$ **d** $\sqrt{14^2-6^2}$
   e $(^{-}5\cdot1)^3+6\cdot1^2$ **f** $4\frac{2}{5}+3\frac{6}{7}$ **g** $6\frac{2}{3}\div3\frac{1}{4}$ **h** $\frac{6\cdot24^4}{3\cdot7^3}$ **i** $\frac{(7-4)^2+2\cdot4^3}{6\times2-3\cdot6}$

25 Mrs Martin wants to order 108 marker pens to be delivered to school.
They come in two different sized boxes.

12 pens	
Cost per box	£27
Delivery per box	£1·50

18 pens	
Cost per box	£39
Delivery per box	£2·10

Is it cheaper for Mrs Martin to order all the pens in boxes of 12 or in boxes of 18?
How much cheaper is it?

91

4 Fractions, Decimals and Percentages

You need to know

✓ fractions — page 7
✓ converting between fractions, decimals and percentages — page 8
✓ comparing and ordering fractions — page 10
✓ finding fraction of and percentage of — page 10

Key vocabulary
⩽ less than or equal to, ⩾ greater than or equal to

▶▶ Line up

This is called a **nomogram**.
It converts fractions to percentages.
To use it

1. Join the numerator and denominator of the fraction with a line.
2. Extend the line to the percentage scale.
3. Where the line crosses the percentage scale gives the percentage equivalent to the fraction.

Example $\frac{40}{50}$ = 80% is shown with the purple line.

Use the nomogram to answer these questions.

1. Write these as percentages.
   a $\frac{5}{20}$ b $\frac{27}{50}$ c $\frac{53}{92}$
2. What score out of 60 is needed to get 75%?

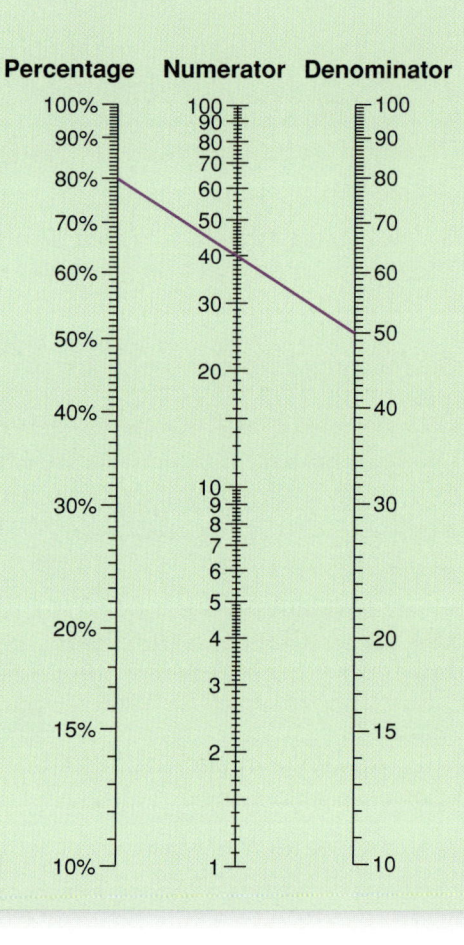

92

Fractions, Decimals and Percentages

Fractions, decimals and percentages

Fractions, decimals and percentages are all ways of expressing **proportions**.

We can **convert** between them.

Remember
To write a **fraction as a percentage**,

either   **a**   write with denominator of 100

Example
$$\frac{9}{25} \xrightarrow{\times 4} \frac{36}{100} = 36\%$$

For notes and practice at converting between fractions, decimals and percentages see pages 8, 9 and 10 in the support chapter.

or   **b**   multiply by 100%

Example $\frac{450}{784} = \frac{450}{784} \times 100\%$ Key [450] [÷] [784] [×] [100] to get 57·39795918

             = 57% to the nearest per cent

All fractions convert to either a terminating decimal or a **recurring decimal**.

Example $\frac{2}{5} = 0\cdot 4$ ← terminating decimal $\frac{1}{3} = 0\cdot 33333333\ldots$ ← recurring decimal with repeating digits

All **recurring decimals are exact fractions**.
Some you should recognise are

    $0\cdot 333333333\ldots = \frac{1}{3}\ (\frac{3}{9})$ $0\cdot 666666666\ldots = \frac{2}{3}\ (\frac{6}{9})$ $0\cdot 111111111\ldots = \frac{1}{9}$

    $0\cdot 222222222\ldots = \frac{2}{9}$ $0\cdot 777777777\ldots = \frac{7}{9}$ $0\cdot 999999999\ldots = \frac{9}{9} = 1$

Discussion

Discuss how to find the answers to these.

    What fraction of 80 is 60?
    What fraction of 60 is 80?
    What fraction of 2 metres is 340 cm?

Hint: The number after 'of' is the denominator.

Worked Example

This frequency diagram shows the sunshine hours for UK weather stations one day in May.
The sunshine hours were put into class intervals, $0 \leq s < 1$, $1 \leq s < 2$, etc.

a What fraction of stations had 2 or more but less than 4 hours of sunshine recorded?

b What percentage of stations had 4 or more hours of sunshine?

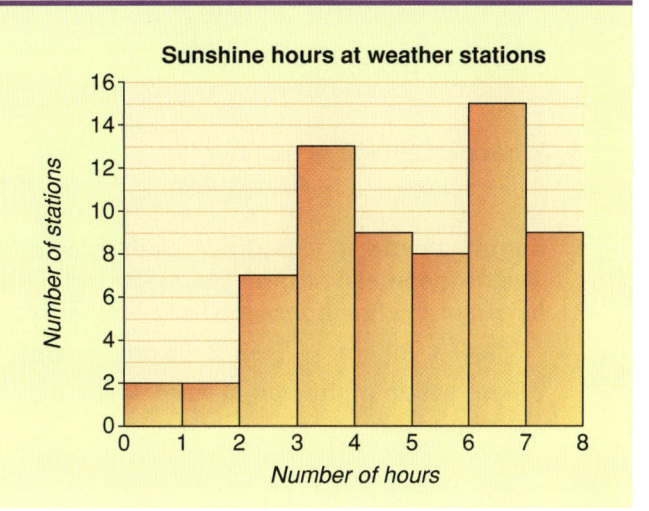

Sunshine hours at weather stations (frequency diagram: Number of stations vs Number of hours; bars at 2, 2, 7, 13, 9, 8, 15, 9)

Number

Answer

a We must add the number of stations that had between 2 and 3, and 3 and 4 hours of sunshine.

$7 + 13 = 20$

20 stations had 2 or more but less than 4 hours of sunshine.
We must also add up the heights of the bars to find the total number of stations.

$2 + 2 + 7 + 13 + 9 + 8 + 15 + 9 = 65$

Fraction of stations that had between 2 and 4 hours of sunshine = $\frac{20}{65} = \frac{4}{13}$

b We must add the number of stations that had between 4 and 5, 5 and 6, 6 and 7 and 7 and 8 hours of sunshine.

$9 + 8 + 15 + 9 = 41$

Fraction of stations that had 4 or more hours = $\frac{41}{65}$

Percentage of stations that had 4 or more hours = $\frac{41}{65} \times 100\%$

= **63%** (nearest per cent)

Always simplify the answer to its lowest terms.

Worked Example
Find the proportion of this square that is shaded.

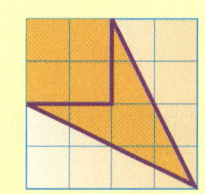

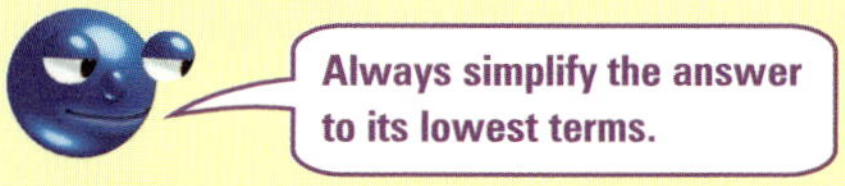

Answer
Count the whole squares shaded, 5.
Fit shaded pieces together to make whole squares.

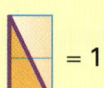

= 1 shaded square. 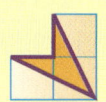   = 1 shaded square.   = 1 shaded square.

Altogether 8 whole squares out of 16 are shaded.
So $\frac{1}{2}$ or **50%** or **0·5** of the square is shaded.

Exercise 1 Except for questions 9b and 10b.

1 What fraction of
 a 3 is 2 **b** 6 is 5 **c** 30 is 28 **d** 150 is 120 *__e__ 6 is 10 *__f__ 150 is 200?

2 What fraction of 10 m is
 a 100 cm **b** 150 cm **c** 125 cm *__d__ 2500 cm?

3 What percentage of an hour is
 a 6 minutes **b** 40 minutes *__c__ 84 minutes?

4 Bernadette did an experiment with three different balls. She dropped each from a height of 1 m. She measured the height of the first bounce. These are her results.

 Ball 1 80 cm   **Ball 2** 55 cm   **Ball 3** 35 cm

 What fraction of the height from which they were dropped did each bounce?

94

Fractions, Decimals and Percentages

5 Each diagram below is drawn on a square grid.
  a Write what percentage of each diagram is shaded.
  i   **ii**

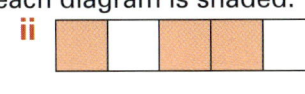

  b Explain how you know that $12\frac{1}{2}\%$ of the diagram below is shaded.

  c Copy this diagram.
  Shade $37\frac{1}{2}\%$ of it.

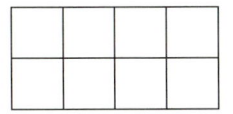

6 A 120 MByte file is downloading onto Meg's computer.
75 MByte have downloaded.
What percentage is this?

7 Write the answers to these as decimals.
  a James added enough water to 375 mℓ of a copper sulphate solution to make it up to 500 mℓ.
  What proportion of the 500 mℓ solution was the 375 mℓ solution?
  b A pendulum swings 50 mm high on its first swing.
  On its second it swings 38 mm.
  What proportion of the first swing height did it reach on its second swing?

8 Write these as fractions.
  a 0·333333333 ... **b** 0·888888888 ... **c** 0·555555555 ... **d** 0·999999999 ...

9 In an experiment a mixture was made by adding
    540 mg iron filings
    320 mg sulphur
    340 mg sand
  a About what fraction of the mixture is sulphur?
  b About what percentage of the mixture is iron filings?

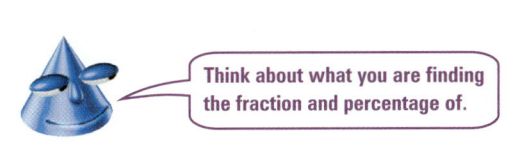

Think about what you are finding the fraction and percentage of.

10 This frequency diagram shows the lengths of the vehicles parked in one section of a supermarket car park.
  a What fraction of vehicles were
    i 3·5 m or longer but less than 4·5 m
    ii 5 m or longer?
  b What percentage of vehicles were shorter than 4 m?
  Give your answer to the nearest per cent.

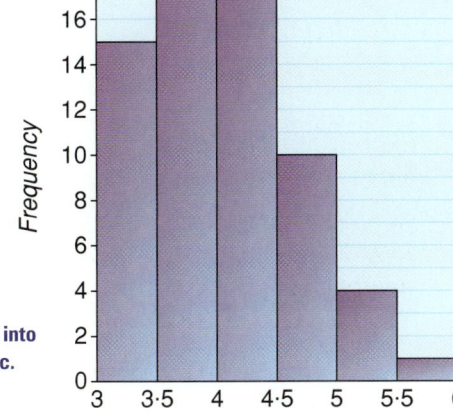

Note The lengths were put into class intervals $3 \leq \ell < 3.5$, etc.

Length of vehicles

95

Number

11 What percentage of the small shape is the large one?
  a
  b

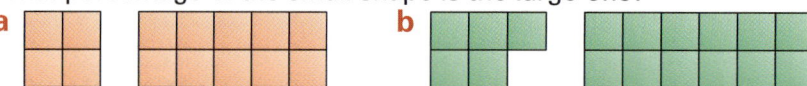

12 Estimate the fraction of each shape that is red.
  a
  b
  c

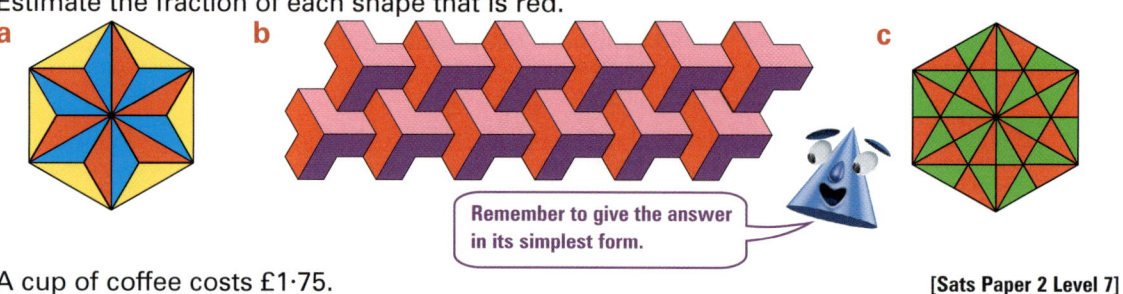

Remember to give the answer in its simplest form.

[Sats Paper 2 Level 7]

***13** A cup of coffee costs £1·75.
The diagram shows how much money different people get when you buy a cup of coffee.

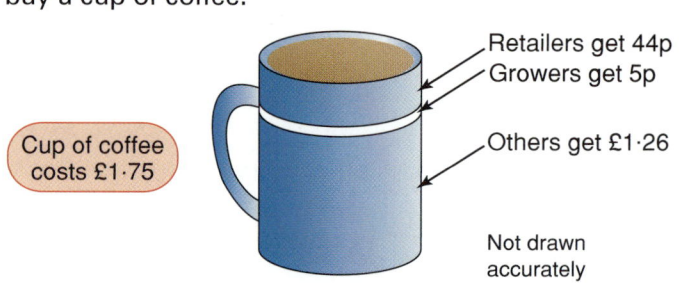

- Retailers get 44p
- Growers get 5p
- Others get £1·26

Cup of coffee costs £1·75

Not drawn accurately

Use a copy of the table.
Complete the table to show what **percentage** of the cost of a cup of coffee goes to retailers, growers and others.
Show your working.

Retailers	%
Growers	%
Others	%

***14** This diagram shows a circle and a square.
The circle touches the edges of the square.
What percentage of the diagram is purple?

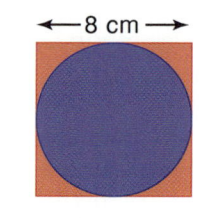

← 8 cm →

See page 343 for finding the area of a circle.

***15** Find the percentage of each large square that is coloured.
  a
  b
  c

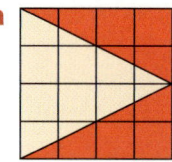

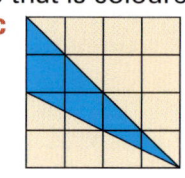

***16** Express the shaded shape as a fraction of the large rectangle.
Note The curves are all semi-circles or quarter-circles.

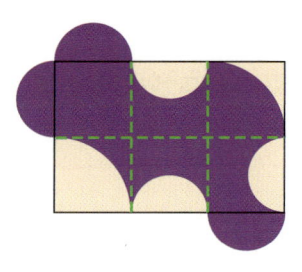

Review 1 Mary had 3 hours for an exam. She began at 9:15 am and finished at 11:45 a.m. What fraction of the time allowed did she use?

Fractions, Decimals and Percentages

Review 2 This frequency diagram shows the distance of the longest tee-shot taken by students in a golf tournament.
  a What fraction of students had a tee-shot.
    i 140 m or longer but less than 170 m
    ii less than 150 m?
  b What percentage had a tee-shot 160 m or greater?
  Note The distances were put into class intervals of $120 \leqslant d < 130$, etc.

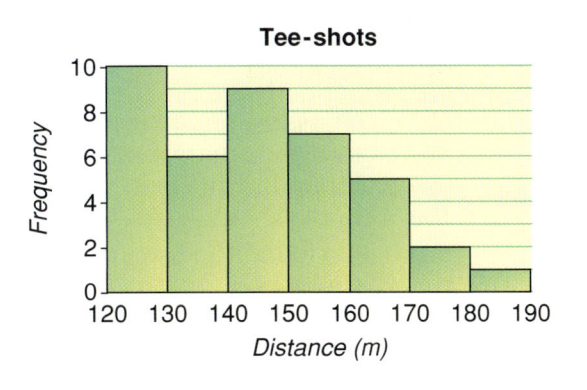

Review 3 Draw a 4 by 6 rectangle.

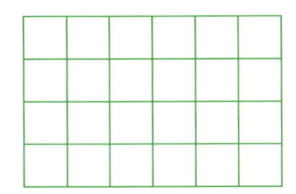

Shade four parts that are $\frac{1}{3}, \frac{1}{4}, \frac{1}{6}$ and $\frac{1}{8}$ of the whole rectangle. The four parts must not overlap. What percentage of the rectangle is left unshaded?

*** Review 4** Find the fraction of each shape that is shaded purple.
  a   **b**

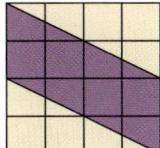

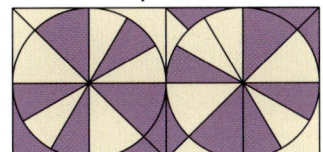

? Puzzle

What fraction am I?

  a I am a unit fraction.
    My denominator is a multiple of 3.
    My denominator is double the number of factors it has.
    I am between $\frac{1}{8}$ and $\frac{1}{20}$.

  *** b** If 1 is added to my numerator I am equivalent to $\frac{1}{3}$.
    If 1 is added to my denominator I am equivalent to $\frac{1}{4}$.

Comparing proportions

Remember
We can compare fractions by
1 converting them to decimals *Example* $\frac{2}{3} > \frac{5}{8}$ because $0 \cdot \dot{6} \dot{6} > 0 \cdot 625$.
2 writing them with a common denominator. *Example* $\frac{3}{4} > \frac{2}{3}$ because $\frac{9}{12} > \frac{8}{12}$.

Number

Discussion

- Maddison used a graphing method to compare fractions. She plotted the denominator on one axis and the numerator on the other.
  This example shows $\frac{3}{4}$ and $\frac{4}{5}$.
  How could Maddison use the graph to tell if $\frac{3}{4}$ or $\frac{4}{5}$ is larger? **Discuss**.

  Use Maddison's method to decide which is larger
  $\frac{2}{3}$ or $\frac{3}{4}$ $\frac{5}{6}$ or $\frac{3}{5}$.
  Discuss.

- **Discuss** how to compare these.
  a $\frac{7}{20}$ and $\frac{3}{10}$
  b 6 out of 13 and 13 out of 28
  c 135 muffins cost £116·10 and 35 scones cost £29·75.
  d 0·3̇3̇ and $\frac{1}{3}$ and 33%

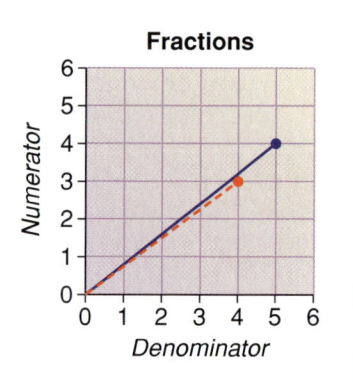

Worked Example
This table shows the colour girls and boys like best for the school crest.

Colour	Boys	Girls
red	3	8
green	4	4
blue	7	14
purple	6	14
Total	20	40

a What percentage of boys like red best?
b Which colour do 20% of boys like best?
c Which colour do 20% of girls like best?
d Selma says that green is liked equally much by both boys and girls. Explain why Selma is wrong.
e Which colour is liked equally much by boys and girls?

Answer

a $\frac{3}{20}$ like red best.

$\frac{3}{20} \xrightarrow{\times 5} \frac{15}{100} = 15\%$

b There are 20 boys.
20% of 20 = 4
4 boys like **green** best.

10% of 20 = 2
20% of 20 = 2 × 2
           = 4

c There are 40 girls.
20% of 40 = 8
8 girls like **red** best.

10% of 40 = 4
20% of 40 = 2 × 4
           = 8

d $\frac{4}{20} \xrightarrow{\times 5} \frac{20}{100} = 20\%$

20% of boys like green best.

$\frac{4}{40} = \frac{1}{10} = 10\%$
10% of girls like green best.
The proportions are different.
The percentage of boys who like green best is higher.

98

Fractions, Decimals and Percentages

e There are twice as many girls as boys.
So we must look for a colour that twice as many girls like as boys like. This will mean the same *proportion* like that colour. **Blue** is liked by the same proportion of boys as girls.

Exercise 2   Except for questions 5d, 6, 9, 10, 11, 13 and Review 3.

1 a What **fraction** of this shape is shaded? [SATs Paper 1 Level 5]
      Write your fraction as simply as possible.
   b What **percentage** of this shape is shaded?

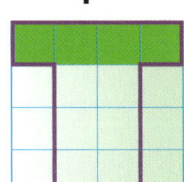

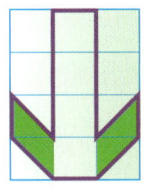

   c Which shape has the **greater percentage** shaded?

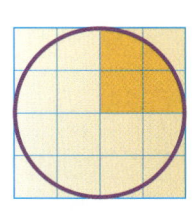

   Shape A   **Shape B**

   Explain how you know.

2 Which of < or > goes in the box?
   a $\frac{1}{4} \square \frac{1}{3}$
   b $\frac{2}{5} \square \frac{1}{2}$
   c $\frac{3}{4} \square \frac{16}{20}$
   d $\frac{2}{3} \square \frac{5}{8}$
   e $\frac{5}{6} \square 0.8$
   f $80\% \square \frac{15}{20}$
   g $3\frac{1}{2} \square 320\%$
   h $66\% \square \frac{2}{3}$
   *i $62\frac{1}{2}\% \square \frac{17}{25}$
   *j $55\% \square \frac{5}{9}$

3 Three boys, Patrick, Brad and Harry, are in different classes for design and technology.
   They were given these marks.

Patrick	Brad	Harry
$\frac{16}{20}$	78%	$\frac{7}{10}$
D and T	D and T	D and T

   Who got the best score? Explain how you know.

4 Which is larger?
   a $1\frac{2}{3}$ or $11 \div 5$
   b $\frac{59}{8}$ or $6\frac{5}{12}$

5 Draw a set of axes with denominator and numerator from 0 to 20.
   Plot these fractions on your graph. Use your graph to put them in order from largest to smallest.

   Use Maddison's method from the Discussion on page 98.

   $\frac{7}{8}$ $\frac{3}{4}$ $\frac{13}{20}$ $\frac{9}{13}$ $\frac{7}{12}$

99

Number

6 Put these in order from smallest to largest.
Use your calculator for part **d** only.

a $\frac{1}{3}$, $\frac{3}{4}$, $\frac{5}{12}$, $\frac{5}{6}$

b 0·25, $\frac{2}{5}$, 35%, $\frac{1}{2}$

c 0·66, $\frac{2}{3}$, 65%, $\frac{7}{9}$

d $\frac{19}{24}$, 0·79, 80%, $\frac{29}{36}$

7 In their last three netball games, Amanda got 38 shots out of 45 shots taken and Mylene got 23 out of 31 shots taken.
Who was the better goal shooter? Explain your answer.

8 Hakan asked 30 pupils which subject they liked best. [SATs Paper 1 Level 5]

Subject	Number of Boys	Number of Girls
Maths	4	7
English	2	4
Science	3	3
History	0	1
French	1	5
	Total 10	Total 20

a Which subject did **20%** of **boys** choose?
b Which subject did **35%** of **girls** choose?
c Hakan said:
   'In my survey, **science** was equally popular with boys and girls'.
   Explain why Hakan was **wrong**.
d Which subject **was** equally popular with boys and girls?

9 There are 60 dogs at the RSPCA.
6 of these are black.
Exactly half of the dogs are female.
From this information, what percentage of female dogs are black?
Choose the correct answer.
A 5%   B 6%   C 10%   D 20%   E 50%
F not possible to tell

10 A garden centre sells plants for hedges. [SATs Paper 2 Level 6]
The table shows what they sold in one week.

Plants	Number of plants sold	Takings
Beech	125	£212·50
Leylandii	650	£2437·50
Privet	35	£45·50
Hawthorn	18	£23·40
Laurel	5	£32·25
Total	833	£2751·15

a What percentage of the total number of plants sold was **Leylandii**?
   Show your working.
b What percentage of the **total takings** was for Leylandii?
   Show your working.
c Which is the **cheaper** plant, Beech or Privet?
   Show working to explain how you know.

Fractions, Decimals and Percentages

11 Brass is made from copper and zinc.
This table gives the amount of copper and zinc in three different grades of brass.
Work out the percentage of copper in each grade.
Which grade has the highest percentage of copper?

Brass	copper	zinc
grade 1	325 g	175 g
grade 2	480 g	320 g
grade 3	620 g	380 g

*12 The table shows the average weekly earnings for men and women in 1956 and 1998. [SATs Paper 2 Level 7]

	1956	1998
Men	£11·89	£420·30
Women	£6·16	£303·70

    a For **1956**, calculate the average weekly earnings for women as a percentage of the average weekly earnings for men.
Show your working and give your answer to 1 decimal place.
    b For **1998**, show that the average weekly earnings for women were a **greater proportion** of the average weekly earnings for men than they were in 1956.

*13 $\frac{3}{4} > \frac{x}{5}$
What is the largest whole number x can be?

*14 x is a decimal with one decimal place. Write down some values x might be if both of these are true.
$\frac{1}{3} < x < \frac{3}{4}$ **and** $\frac{1}{4} < x < \frac{5}{8}$

Review 1
a What fraction of this shape is shaded?

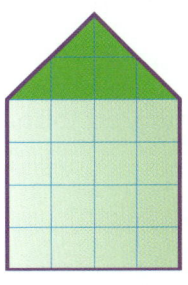

b What percentage of this shape is shaded?

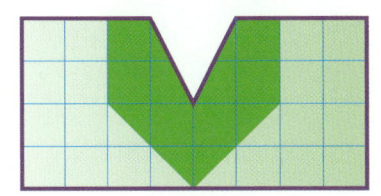

Review 2 In her last three Maths tests, Hazel's marks were $\frac{14}{20}$, 73% and $\frac{18}{25}$.
Rank her results from highest to lowest. Show your working.

Review 3 The table shows the hours of sunshine during July and August for 2 years. It also gives the total sunshine hours for each year.
    a What percentage of the total sunshine hours for year 1 were in
        i July   **ii** August?
    b Answer part **a** for year 2.
    c Which month of which year had the biggest proportion of sunshine hours?

Month	Year 1	Year 2
July	145·7	187
August	179	182·9
Total for year	1350	1423

Number

Adding and subtracting fractions

Remember
To find **equivalent fractions** we multiply or divide both the numerator and denominator by the same number.

Examples

$\frac{3}{4} \xrightarrow{\times 3} \frac{9}{12}$ $\frac{28}{40} \xrightarrow{\div 4} \frac{7}{10}$

Fractions can be added and subtracted easily when they have the same denominator.

Example

$\frac{8}{15} + \frac{13}{15} = \frac{8 + 13}{15}$ add the numerators

$= \frac{21}{15}$

$= 1\frac{6}{15}$ write improper fractions as mixed numbers

$= 1\frac{2}{5}$ write fractions in their simplest form

To **add and subtract fractions with different denominators** we use equivalent fractions.

1. Find the LCM of the denominators.

   Example $\frac{3}{5} + \frac{5}{8}$

   LCM of 5 and 8 is 40.

2. Write equivalent fractions with this LCM.

   $\frac{3}{5} \xrightarrow{\times 8} \frac{24}{40}$ $\frac{5}{8} \xrightarrow{\times 5} \frac{25}{40}$

3. Add or subtract the fractions (they now have the same denominator). Give the answer in its simplest form.

   $\frac{24}{40} + \frac{25}{40} = \frac{24 + 25}{40}$

   $= \frac{49}{40}$

   $= 1\frac{9}{40}$

You could use diagrams to help.

Example $\frac{3}{8} + \frac{5}{24}$

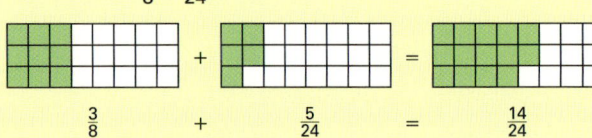

$\frac{3}{8} + \frac{5}{24} = \frac{14}{24}$

$\frac{3}{8} \xrightarrow{\times 3} \frac{9}{24}$

We can add and subtract fractions using the $\boxed{a^{b/c}}$ button on a calculator.

Example $\frac{7}{15} + \frac{19}{24}$ is found by keying

$\boxed{7}\ \boxed{a^{b/c}}\ \boxed{15}\ \boxed{+}\ \boxed{19}\ \boxed{a^{b/c}}\ \boxed{24}$ to get $\boxed{1 \lrcorner 31 \lrcorner 120.}$.

We read this as $1\frac{31}{120}$.

Fractions, Decimals and Percentages

Exercise 3

Except for question 4.

1 Calculate these.
  a $\frac{3}{5} + \frac{4}{5}$ **b** $\frac{5}{8} + \frac{7}{8}$ **c** $1\frac{11}{12} - \frac{7}{12}$ **d** $2 - \frac{2}{3}$ **e** $3\frac{3}{8} + \frac{7}{8}$

2 Calculate these.
  a $\frac{3}{8} + \frac{1}{4}$ **b** $\frac{5}{7} + \frac{3}{14}$ **c** $\frac{3}{4} - \frac{3}{8}$ **d** $\frac{11}{12} - \frac{1}{6}$ **e** $\frac{3}{5} + \frac{6}{10}$
  f $\frac{7}{12} + \frac{5}{6}$ **g** $\frac{9}{10} - \frac{4}{5}$ **h** $\frac{3}{8} + \frac{2}{5}$ **i** $\frac{7}{9} - \frac{4}{7}$ **j** $\frac{4}{5} + \frac{3}{7}$
  k $\frac{2}{5} + \frac{7}{8}$ **l** $\frac{9}{10} - \frac{2}{5} - \frac{1}{2}$ **m** $\frac{7}{8} + \frac{3}{4} - \frac{1}{2}$ **n** $\frac{7}{24} + \frac{7}{12} - \frac{5}{6}$
  *__o__ $\frac{5}{18} + \frac{5}{27}$ *__p__ $\frac{7}{18} + \frac{9}{24}$ *__q__ $\frac{7}{12} + \frac{15}{18} + \frac{19}{36}$

T 3 Calculate these and show the answer on a copy of the number line.
  a $\frac{6}{10} + \frac{6}{5}$

  b $\frac{7}{12} + \frac{7}{6}$

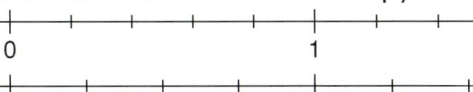

4 Use your calculator to find the answers to these.
  a $\frac{8}{13} + \frac{1}{4}$ **b** $\frac{9}{15} - \frac{7}{25}$ **c** $\frac{1}{6} - \frac{3}{12}$ **d** $\frac{18}{27} + \frac{5}{19} - \frac{3}{8}$

5 Jake's football team won $\frac{1}{3}$ of their games and drew $\frac{1}{2}$ of them.
  a What fraction did they win or draw?
  b What fraction did they lose?

6 Rani took a $\frac{1}{2}$ ℓ bottle of juice to school.
  She drank $\frac{2}{5}$ ℓ.
  a How much juice was left?
  b Did she drink more or less than half the juice she took to school?

7 Find the next term in this sequence.
  $\frac{5}{8}$, $1\frac{1}{8}$, $1\frac{5}{8}$, $2\frac{1}{8}$, ...

8 $\frac{1}{3}$, $\frac{1}{8}$, $\frac{1}{5}$ are all examples of unit fractions.   [SATs Paper 1 Level 6]

> All unit fractions must have
> $\frac{1}{3}$ — a numerator that is 1
> — a denominator that is an integer greater than 1

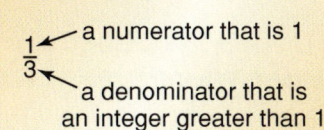

The ancient Egyptians used only unit fractions.
For $\frac{3}{4}$, they wrote the sum $\frac{1}{2} + \frac{1}{4}$.
  a For what fraction did they write the sum $\frac{1}{2} + \frac{1}{5}$?
    Show your working.
  b They wrote $\frac{9}{20}$ as the sum of two unit fractions.
    One of them was $\frac{1}{4}$.
    What was the other?
    Show your working.
  *__c__ What is the biggest fraction you can make by adding two **different** unit fractions?   [Level 7]
    Show your working.

Number

9 These are fraction cards. $\boxed{\frac{1}{2}}$ $\boxed{\frac{1}{3}}$ $\boxed{\frac{1}{4}}$ $\boxed{\frac{1}{5}}$

    a Which two cards make this true? $\Box + \Box = \frac{7}{12}$

    b Which two cards make this true? $\Box - \Box = \frac{1}{6}$

    c Which three cards make this true? $\Box + \Box - \Box = \frac{7}{12}$

   *d Which three cards make the biggest answer for this? What is this answer? $\Box + \Box - \Box = \underline{}$

*10 The numbers $\frac{1}{2}, p, q, \frac{3}{4}$ form an ascending sequence with a constant difference. What are the values of p and q?

*11 What digits could * stand for to make these true?
    a $\frac{*}{5} + \frac{*}{*} = \frac{3}{*}$ **b** $\frac{*}{**} + \frac{*}{6} = \frac{9}{**}$
    Is there more than one way for each?

[T] **Review 1**
Use a copy of this box. Write the letter beside each calculation above its answer in the box.

$\frac{8}{15}$	**A** $\frac{9}{40}$	$\frac{8}{15}$	$\frac{7}{12}$	$2\frac{1}{3}$		$\frac{3}{8}$	$\frac{5}{24}$	$\frac{7}{8}$	$\frac{7}{12}$	$\frac{3}{20}$		$\frac{13}{20}$	**A** $\frac{9}{40}$	$\frac{3}{4}$
$\frac{2}{3}$	$\frac{9}{20}$	$2\frac{1}{3}$	$\frac{3}{4}$	$\frac{1}{30}$		$\frac{1}{16}$	$\frac{3}{4}$	$\frac{7}{12}$	$\frac{7}{20}$		$\frac{9}{20}$	$\frac{7}{8}$		$\frac{11}{12}$	$\frac{3}{5}$	$\frac{9}{20}$	$\frac{7}{8}$	**A** $\frac{9}{40}$

A $\frac{5}{8} - \frac{2}{5} = \frac{9}{40}$ **C** $\frac{3}{4} + \frac{1}{6}$ **F** $\frac{5}{12} + \frac{1}{4}$ **N** $\frac{5}{8} - \frac{1}{2} + \frac{3}{4}$ **R** $3 - \frac{2}{3}$ **T** $\frac{1}{2} - \frac{2}{3} + \frac{1}{5}$

D Jack was counting the candles on a birthday cake. $\frac{2}{5}$ of the candles were red and $\frac{1}{4}$ were blue. The rest were white. What fraction were white?

E Mrs Brown was doing the family budget. She calculated the family spent $\frac{1}{3}$ of their money on groceries and $\frac{1}{4}$ on paying bills. What fraction of their income was spent on bills and groceries?

Katie saves $\frac{2}{5}$ of her allowance.

H What fraction does Katie spend?

I Katie spends $\frac{3}{20}$ of her allowance on entertainment, and the rest on clothes. What fraction does she spend on clothes?

W $\frac{2}{5}$ of a cake is eaten on the day it is made. The next day $\frac{1}{4}$ is eaten. What fraction is eaten?

Y On day 3 another $\frac{1}{5}$ of the cake is eaten. What fraction is left?

The beach is not safe for bathing when the tide is too high or too low.
The tide is too high $\frac{1}{6}$ of the time.

M If the beach is safe for bathing $\frac{5}{8}$ of the time, what fraction of the time is the beach not safe?

O What fraction of the time is the tide too low?

P Mrs Smith's class has a lot of pupils away. $\frac{1}{5}$ of the class are sick and $\frac{1}{3}$ of the class are on a sports exchange. What fraction are absent?

4 is added to both the numerator and denominator of the fraction $\frac{11}{16}$.

S What is the new fraction?

U How much greater is the new fraction than the original?

Fractions, Decimals and Percentages

Review 2 Copy this number line. Calculate and show your answer on the number line.
$\frac{3}{8} + \frac{3}{4}$

Review 3 Use these fraction cards. $\boxed{\frac{1}{2}}$ $\boxed{\frac{1}{4}}$ $\boxed{\frac{1}{6}}$ $\boxed{\frac{1}{8}}$

a Which two cards make each of these true?

☐ + ☐ = $\frac{5}{12}$

☐ − ☐ = $\frac{1}{3}$

b Which three cards make this true?

☐ + ☐ − ☐ = $\frac{5}{24}$

*__c__ Which three cards make the smallest positive answer?

☐ + ☐ − ☐ = ___

What is the answer?

? Puzzle

A tub was $\frac{1}{4}$ full of water. Another 5 ℓ was added. Then the tub was $\frac{1}{3}$ full. How much does the tub hold altogether?

To **add or subtract mixed numbers**, write each as an improper fraction.
When **adding** you can add the whole numbers first.

Examples
$3\frac{2}{3} + 1\frac{3}{4} = \frac{11}{3} + \frac{7}{4}$ **or** $3\frac{2}{3} + 1\frac{3}{4} = 3\frac{8}{12} + 1\frac{9}{12}$ $3\frac{1}{6} - 1\frac{1}{2} = \frac{19}{6} - \frac{3}{2}$
$= \frac{44}{12} + \frac{21}{12}$ $ = 4\frac{17}{12}$ $ = \frac{19}{6} - \frac{9}{6}$
$= \frac{65}{12}$ $ = 5\frac{5}{12}$ $ = \frac{10}{6}$
$= 5\frac{5}{12}$ $ = \frac{5}{3}$
$ = 1\frac{2}{3}$

On a calculator we would key $3\frac{2}{3} + 1\frac{3}{4}$ as

③ [a^b/c] ② [a^b/c] ③ + ① [a^b/c] ③ [a^b/c] ④ = to get ⟦ 5⌐5⌐12 ⟧.

Discussion

Discuss the advantages and disadvantages of both of the above **written** methods for adding $3\frac{2}{3} + 1\frac{3}{4}$.

Discuss how you could find these.

$3\frac{2}{3} + 1\frac{3}{4}$ $15\frac{1}{2} + 23\frac{3}{8}$ $14\frac{3}{5} - 7\frac{3}{10}$ $3\frac{1}{6} - 1\frac{1}{2}$ $14\frac{3}{10} - 7\frac{3}{5}$

Discuss what to do if you subtracted the whole numbers in $3\frac{1}{6} - 1\frac{1}{2}$.

105

Number

Exercise 4 🚫🧮 Except for question 2 and Review 2.

1. a $1\frac{1}{2} + 2\frac{1}{4}$ b $3\frac{2}{3} + 1\frac{1}{4}$ c $2\frac{4}{5} - 1\frac{1}{2}$ d $5\frac{1}{2} + \frac{7}{10}$
   e $4\frac{5}{8} - 2\frac{1}{4}$ f $2\frac{1}{3} - \frac{4}{5}$ g $2\frac{1}{3} - 1\frac{1}{2}$

2. Use your calculator to find these.
   a $3\frac{5}{8} + 2\frac{4}{9}$ b $5\frac{1}{4} - 2\frac{7}{12}$ c $8\frac{3}{4} + 3\frac{7}{15} - 2\frac{1}{8}$ d $5\frac{1}{6} + 7\frac{4}{7} - 3\frac{5}{8}$

   $5\frac{1}{4}$ inches

   $7\frac{5}{8}$ inches

3. A photograph is $5\frac{1}{4}$ inches wide and $7\frac{5}{8}$ inches long. What is the perimeter of the photograph?

4. The last 8 pages of a magazine are for advertisements.
   Two days before publication, $6\frac{7}{8}$ pages of advertising had been sold. Then $2\frac{1}{4}$ pages were cancelled. What fraction of pages still has to be sold?

*5. Find the next term in the sequence. $\frac{2}{3}, 2\frac{1}{2}, 4\frac{1}{3}, 6\frac{1}{6}, \ldots$

*6. What might ■ and ● be in each of the following?
   a ■ + ● = $3\frac{5}{6}$ b ■ − $2\frac{1}{2}$ = ●

   ■ and ● can be different in **a** and **b**.

[T] *7. Use a copy of these magic squares.
   Remember The numbers in each row, column and diagonal must add to the same total.

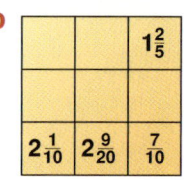

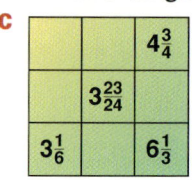

   a
$\frac{1}{2}$		
$1\frac{2}{3}$	1	
$\frac{5}{6}$		

   b
	$1\frac{2}{5}$	
$2\frac{1}{10}$	$2\frac{9}{20}$	$\frac{7}{10}$

   c
		$4\frac{3}{4}$
	$3\frac{23}{24}$	
$3\frac{1}{6}$		$6\frac{1}{3}$

Review 1   Find the answers to these.
a $3\frac{1}{4} + 1\frac{7}{10}$ b $2\frac{2}{3} - 1\frac{1}{4}$ c $2\frac{3}{8} - 1\frac{2}{3}$

Review 2   Use your calculator to find these.
a $3\frac{7}{8} + 8\frac{5}{12}$ b $5\frac{5}{6} - 2\frac{3}{4} + 4\frac{3}{7}$

Review 3   Liz made plum sauce. She filled these two bottles to the top.
a How much plum sauce did Liz make altogether?
b How much more did Liz pour into the large bottle than into the small bottle?

106

Fractions, Decimals and Percentages

Fraction and percentage of

Remember
In mathematics 'of' means multiply.
We can often find a **fraction of a quantity** mentally.

Example   To find $\frac{2}{3}$ of 27, find $\frac{1}{3}$ of 27 first.
$\frac{1}{3}$ of 27 = 9
$\frac{2}{3}$ of 27 = 2 × 9
       = 18

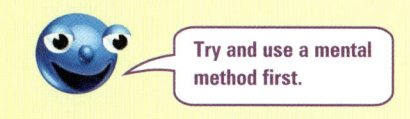

Try and use a mental method first.

Worked Example
About 35% of Mr Health's 300 g burger is protein.
About $\frac{2}{5}$ of Home Burger's 275 g burger is protein.
Which burger has more protein?

Answer
10% of 300 g = 30 g
5% of 300 g = 15 g $\frac{1}{2}$ of 10%
30% of 300 g = 3 × 30 g
          = 90 g
35% of 300 g = 90 g + 15 g
          = **105 g**

$\frac{2}{5}$ of 275 = $\frac{2}{5}$ × 275
       = 2 × $\frac{1}{5}$ × 275
       = 2 × 55 g
       = **110 g**

$5 \overline{)275}^{\,55}$

There is more protein in a Home Burger burger.

Sometimes we get **fractional answers**.

Example $\frac{2}{5}$ of 17 = $\frac{2}{5}$ × 17
        = 2 × $\frac{1}{5}$ × 17
        = 2 × 17 × $\frac{1}{5}$
        = $\frac{34}{5}$
        = **6$\frac{4}{5}$**

$\frac{7}{25}$ of 34 = 7 × $\frac{1}{25}$ × 34
         = 7 × 34 × $\frac{1}{25}$
         = $\frac{238}{25}$
         = **9$\frac{13}{25}$**

25 | 238
    225   9 × 25

     13

Sometimes we use the calculator to find fraction and percentage of amounts.

Example $12\frac{1}{2}$% of 114

   either   key [12·5] [÷] [100] [×] [114] [=]   ← using fractions
   or   key [0·125] [×] [114] [=]   ← using decimals
   or   key [12·5] [×] [1·14] [=]   ← multiplying by 1%
                                    ↑
                                  1% of 114

Exercise 5

Except for questions 5, 8 and Reviews 3 and 4.

1 Find the answers to these mentally.
  a $\frac{1}{5}$ of 35
  b $\frac{2}{5}$ of 35
  c $\frac{3}{5}$ of 35
  d $\frac{4}{5}$ of 35
  e $\frac{2}{5}$ of 40 m
  f 80% of 70 ml
  g $\frac{5}{9}$ of 45 g
  h 30% of £150
  i $\frac{3}{4}$ of 84
  j $\frac{7}{8}$ of 96
  k 45% of 120 l
  l 65% of 3000
  m $\frac{5}{6}$ of 720
  n 11% of 200
  o $\frac{4}{9}$ of 108
  p 29% of 600
  q $1\frac{1}{2}$ of 12 l
  r 85% of 80 cm
  s 35% of 140 g
  t $1\frac{3}{4}$ of 60 m

There are more mental calculations like these in Chapter 3.

107

Number

2 Find the answers to these mentally.
Which is greater?
  a 75% of 16 or $\frac{1}{3}$ of 33
  b $\frac{5}{8}$ of 56 or $\frac{2}{3}$ of 54
  c 70% of 190 or $\frac{13}{20}$ of 200

3 A dog weighs 40 kg.
60% of its total mass is water.
What is the mass of this water?

4 This table shows some percentages of amounts of money. [SATs Paper 1 Level 5]
You can use the table to help you work out the missing numbers.

15% of £30 = £ ☐
£6·75 = 15% of £ ☐
£3·50 = ___% of £10
25p = 5% of £ ___

	£10	£30	£45
5%	50p	£1·50	£2·25
10%	£1	£3	£4·50

5 Use your calculator to find these. Give the answers to **d** and **e** to the nearest penny.
  a 8% of £28·50
  b $12\frac{1}{2}$% of £108
  c $17\frac{1}{2}$% of £118
  d 7% of £0·84
  ***e** 18·75% of £1·75
  f $33\frac{1}{3}$% of £26·85

6 What goes in the gaps? [SATs Paper 1 Level 5]
  a $\frac{1}{2}$ of 20 = $\frac{1}{4}$ of ___
  b $\frac{3}{4}$ of 100 = $\frac{1}{2}$ of ___
  c $\frac{1}{3}$ of 60 = $\frac{2}{3}$ of ___

7 160 women gave birth at a hospital in July.
30% had twins.
The rest had just one baby.
How many babies were born in July at the hospital?

TWIN EXPLOSION
30% of women at local hospital had twins in july.

8 Use your calculator to find which is larger.
  a 24% of 65 or $\frac{4}{7}$ of 45
  b 68% of 120 or $\frac{2}{3}$ of 116

9 Give the answers to these as a fraction.
  a $\frac{2}{5}$ of 13
  b $\frac{2}{3}$ of 16
  c $\frac{3}{4}$ of 15
  d $\frac{2}{3}$ of 140
  e $\frac{3}{25}$ of 36

10 A test took 120 minutes. Josie took $\frac{1}{3}$ of the time for the multi-choice section, 25% of the time for an essay and $\frac{3}{8}$ for a problem solving section. She spent the rest of the time on the short answers. How much time did she spend on the short answers?

11 In a science laboratory, Arshad's group used $\frac{1}{5}$ of a 750 ml bottle of copper sulphate solution. Bea's group used $\frac{2}{3}$ of the solution that was left. How many millilitres were left in the bottle?

***12** In a bag of 24 sweets, $\frac{1}{8}$ are red, $\frac{1}{4}$ are green, $\frac{1}{3}$ are yellow, 4 are blue and the rest are orange.
What fraction are orange?

This is linked to mutually exclusive events – see page 417.

***13** Ben spent $\frac{3}{4}$ of his money.
Half of what he had left was 40p.
How much did he have to start with?

***14** Half a number and twice half the number is two more than twice half the number.
What is the number?

108

Fractions, Decimals and Percentages

*15 Jamilah spent one third of her savings on her plane fare and one quarter of the remainder on her accommodation. She then had £120 left for spending money.
What was Jamilah's plane fare?

Review 1
a Find   i $\frac{2}{3}$ of 27   ii 60% of 45   iii 55% of 120.
b 48% of the pupils in the school are girls. How many girls are there if there are 350 pupils in the school?

Review 2

	£20	£75	£120
5%	£1	£3·75	£6
20%	£4	£15	£24

Use this table to help you work out the missing numbers.
a 25% of £75 = ___   b £9·75 = 5% of ___   c £7·50 = 5% of ___

Review 3   Use your calculator to find which is larger.
a $\frac{4}{7}$ of 42 or $\frac{3}{8}$ of 40   b $\frac{5}{16}$ of 64 or $\frac{7}{8}$ of 24

Review 4   [SATs Paper 2 Level 5]
a 8% of £26·50 = £ ☐
b $12\frac{1}{2}$% of £98 = £ ☐

Review 5   A country exported £48 million worth of produce. Of this, $\frac{1}{3}$ was meat exports, $\frac{1}{6}$ was dairy produce, $12\frac{1}{2}$% was timber, £5 million worth was wool and the rest was other products. What fraction was other products?

*Review 6   The head of a fish is 4 cm long.
The body is as long as the head and tail together.
The tail is as long as the head and half the body.
How long is the fish?

*Puzzle

To escape, a spy has to cross three borders.
The spy agrees to pay one half of her money to someone at each border in order to be escorted to the next border.
The spy needs to have at least £200 left after crossing the last border.
What is the least amount of money this spy needs in order to escape?

109

Number

Multiplying fractions

Discussion

- This diagram can be used to find the answer to $\frac{1}{4} \times \frac{1}{3}$.
  Discuss.

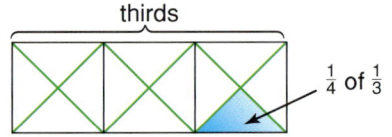

- Draw diagrams to find the answers to $\frac{1}{2} \times \frac{1}{5}$, $\frac{3}{4} \times \frac{1}{3}$, $\frac{1}{4} \times \frac{2}{3}$, $\frac{5}{8} \times \frac{3}{4}$, $\frac{3}{8} \times \frac{4}{5}$ and $\frac{3}{4} \times \frac{2}{3}$.
  Discuss how the answers could be found without using diagrams.

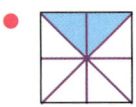

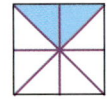

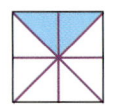

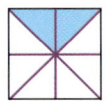

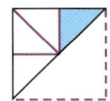

- This diagram shows that the answer to $\frac{1}{4} \times 5\frac{1}{2}$ is $\frac{11}{8}$ or $1\frac{3}{8}$.

  Discuss how to draw diagrams to find the answers to
  $\frac{1}{2} \times 3\frac{1}{4}$, $\frac{3}{4} \times 2\frac{1}{2}$, $\frac{2}{3} \times 3\frac{3}{4}$ and $\frac{3}{5} \times 4\frac{1}{3}$.

  Discuss how to find the answers without drawing diagrams.

Fraction multiplications are made easier by **cancelling** first.

Examples $\frac{3}{4} \times \frac{6}{5} = \frac{3}{{}_2 4} \times \frac{{}^3 6}{5}$ $\frac{5}{8} \times \frac{2}{15} = \frac{{}^1 5}{{}_4 8} \times \frac{{}^1 2}{{}_3 15}$
            $= \frac{9}{10}$ $= \frac{1}{12}$

> You can cancel any numerator and any denominator by dividing both by the HCF.

Note   You can **not** cancel horizontally.

Example $\frac{{}^1 2}{5} \times \frac{{}^2 4}{9}$ is **wrong**.

To multiply fractions:

Step 1 Write whole numbers or mixed numbers as improper fractions.
Step 2 Cancel if possible.
Step 3 Multiply the numerators;
            multiply the denominators.

Examples $\frac{5}{8} \times \frac{16}{25} \times \frac{15}{8} = \frac{{}^1 5}{{}_1 8} \times \frac{{}^2 16}{{}_5 25} \times \frac{15}{8}$
            $= \frac{1}{1} \times \frac{{}^1 2}{{}_1 5} \times \frac{{}^3 15}{{}_4 8}$
            $= \frac{3}{4}$

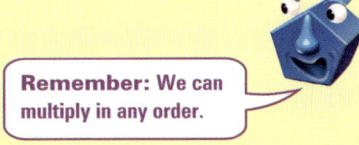

> Remember: We can multiply in any order.

$3\frac{3}{4} \times 1\frac{1}{5} = \frac{{}^3 15}{{}_2 4} \times \frac{{}^3 6}{{}_1 5}$
$= \frac{9}{2}$
$= 4\frac{1}{2}$

$(1\frac{1}{2})^2 = 1\frac{1}{2} \times 1\frac{1}{2}$
$= \frac{3}{2} \times \frac{3}{2}$
$= \frac{9}{4}$
$= 2\frac{1}{4}$

> Write the answer as a mixed number.

110

Fractions, Decimals and Percentages

Exercise 6 Except for questions 7, 8 and Review 4.

1 Copy and finish these.

a $\frac{3}{8} \times \frac{4}{6} = \frac{1\cancel{3}}{_2\cancel{8}} \times \frac{\cancel{4}^1}{\cancel{6}_2}$

$= \frac{\_\_ \times \_\_}{\_\_ \times \_\_}$

$= \frac{\_\_}{\_\_}$

b $\frac{2}{5} \times \frac{3}{10} = \frac{\_\_2}{5} \times \frac{3}{10}$

$= \frac{\_\_ \times \_\_}{\_\_ \times \_\_}$

$= \frac{\_\_}{\_\_}$

2 Find the answers to these.

a $\frac{2}{5} \times \frac{2}{7}$ b $\frac{2}{3} \times \frac{4}{5}$ c $\frac{5}{12} \times \frac{8}{9}$ d $\frac{2}{3} \times \frac{3}{5}$ e $\frac{5}{6} \times \frac{9}{11}$

f $\frac{3}{4} \times \frac{10}{9}$ g $\frac{3}{5} \times \frac{20}{33}$ h $\frac{7}{9} \times \frac{27}{14}$ i $(\frac{2}{3})^2$ *j $(\frac{4}{3})^2$

3 a Susan claims that three-fifths of one-quarter is the same as three-quarters of one-fifth.
Is she correct?

b Is $\frac{a}{b} \times \frac{c}{d} = \frac{a}{d} \times \frac{c}{b}$?

4 Two-fifths of a garden is used to grow vegetables. One-quarter of this is planted in potatoes.
What fraction of the garden is planted in potatoes?

5 Calculate.

a $2\frac{1}{4} \times 3\frac{1}{3}$ b $2\frac{3}{5} \times 1\frac{2}{3}$ c $3\frac{3}{4} \times 1\frac{3}{5}$ *d $(1\frac{1}{2})^2$ *e $(1\frac{3}{4})^2$

6 A train travels at an average speed of 96 mph.
How far does it travel in $2\frac{1}{4}$ hours?

7 David's bedroom floor measures $3\frac{1}{4}$ metres by $3\frac{1}{2}$ metres.
What is the area of this floor?

8 A frame for a picture is $5\frac{1}{4}$ inches by $9\frac{5}{8}$ inches. Calculate its area.

***9** Find the answers to these.

a $\frac{4}{5} \times \frac{20}{25} \times \frac{15}{12}$ b $\frac{3}{5} \times \frac{20}{33} \times \frac{22}{16}$ c $\frac{22}{7} \times 21 \times 21$ d $\frac{22}{7} \times 14 \times 14$

e $\frac{1}{3}(1 - \frac{1}{4})$ f $\frac{1}{5}(2 - \frac{1}{3})$ *g $(1\frac{1}{2})^3$ *h $(2\frac{1}{4})^3$

***10 a** Find three different pairs of fractions which multiply to $\frac{25}{32}$.

b $\frac{a}{3} \times \frac{2}{b} = \frac{8}{15}$ What values could *a* and *b* have?
Is there more than one answer?

***11** What number is halfway between $\frac{1}{3}$ and $\frac{5}{12}$?

***12** Use three of these four fractions to make each statement true. $\frac{1}{4}, \frac{1}{3}, \frac{1}{5}, \frac{1}{8}$.

a $\Box + \Box \times \Box = \frac{7}{24}$ b $\Box \times \Box + \Box = \frac{23}{60}$ c $\Box - \Box \times \Box = \frac{17}{60}$

***13** Look at this diagram.
It is a square with sides of 1 metre.
The largest triangle has area $\frac{1}{2}$ m².
What are the areas of the next two largest triangles?

Review 1 Find the answers.

a $\frac{2}{3} \times \frac{4}{7}$ b $\frac{7}{8} \times \frac{4}{5}$ c $\frac{5}{6} \times \frac{9}{20}$ d $(\frac{3}{5})^2$

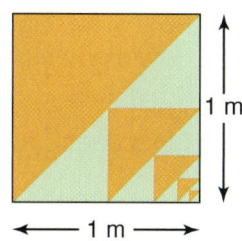

Review 2

a Jane gave John half of her cake. He ate $\frac{1}{3}$ of what she gave him. What fraction did he eat?

b In a test Susan did $\frac{7}{8}$ of the questions. She generally gets $\frac{2}{3}$ of her answers correct. What fraction of the questions does she expect to get correct?

111

Number

Review 3 Calculate these.
a $2\frac{1}{2} \times 1\frac{3}{5}$ b $6\frac{1}{4} \times 2\frac{1}{10}$ c $(1\frac{3}{5})^2$

Review 4
a A picture frame is $4\frac{1}{2}$ inches by $6\frac{3}{4}$ inches. What is the area of the frame?
* b A picture $3\frac{1}{2}$ inches by $5\frac{1}{2}$ inches is put in the frame. What is the area of the shaded region?

Review 5 Find the area of the top of this square table.

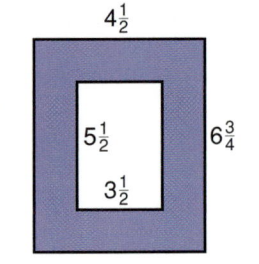

Dividing fractions

Discussion

● Sirah drew this number line.

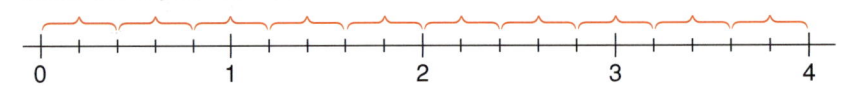

How could she use this to find the answer to $4 \div \frac{2}{5}$? **Discuss**.

● $8 \times \frac{1}{2}$ is the same as $8 \div 2$.
Multiplying by $\frac{1}{2}$ is the same as dividing by 2.
Is $8 \div \frac{1}{2}$ the same as 8×2? **Discuss**. $\frac{1}{2}$ and $\frac{2}{1}$ are inverses.

Is $9 \div \frac{3}{4}$ the same as $9 \times \frac{4}{3}$? Use your calculator to check. $\frac{3}{4}$ and $\frac{4}{3}$ are inverses.

Does dividing by a fraction give the same answer as multiplying by the inverse? **Discuss**.
Do these using a calculator to help you decide.

$3 \div \frac{1}{7}$ and 3×7 $6 \div \frac{3}{5}$ and $6 \times \frac{5}{3}$ $\frac{4}{5} \div \frac{2}{15}$ and $\frac{4}{5} \times \frac{15}{2}$

● How many eighths are there in the whole diagram?
How many eighths are there in one half of the diagram?
What does $\frac{1}{2} \div \frac{1}{8}$ equal? **Discuss**.
What does $\frac{1}{2} \times \frac{8}{1}$ equal? **Discuss**.

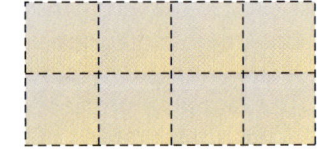

Use diagrams to find these.
$\frac{1}{2} \div \frac{1}{3}$ $\frac{1}{4} \div \frac{1}{5}$

Does $\frac{1}{2} \div \frac{1}{3} = \frac{1}{2} \times \frac{3}{1}$?
Does $\frac{1}{4} \div \frac{1}{5} = \frac{1}{4} \times \frac{5}{1}$? **Discuss**.

Fractions, Decimals and Percentages

We use the **inverse rule** to **divide by fractions**.
To divide by a fraction, multiply by the inverse.

Example $\frac{3}{4} \div 6 = \frac{3}{4} \div \frac{6}{1}$ $\frac{6}{1}$ is 6 written as a fraction.

$= \frac{{}^1 3}{4} \times \frac{1}{{}_2 6}$ multiply by the inverse, $\frac{1}{6}$.

$= \frac{1}{8}$

Cancel once you've got the multiplication written down.

Example $\frac{3}{4} \div \frac{5}{12} = \frac{3}{{}_1 4} \times \frac{12^{\,3}}{5}$ $\frac{12}{5}$ is the inverse of $\frac{5}{12}$.

$= \frac{9}{5}$

$= 1\frac{4}{5}$

Example $6 \div \frac{3}{4} = \frac{6}{1} \div \frac{3}{4}$

$= \frac{{}^2 6}{1} \times \frac{4}{{}_1 3}$ $\frac{4}{3}$ is the inverse of $\frac{3}{4}$.

$= 8$

Turn the fraction you are dividing by upside down to get the inverse then multiply.

Example $1\frac{2}{3} \div 4\frac{1}{6} = \frac{5}{3} \div \frac{25}{6}$

$= \frac{{}^1 5}{{}_1 3} \times \frac{{}^2 6}{25_{\,5}}$ $\frac{6}{25}$ is the inverse of $\frac{25}{6}$.

$= \frac{2}{5}$

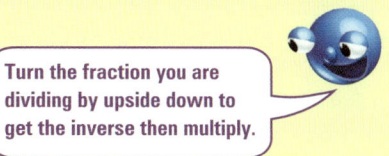

Exercise 7

1. a $\frac{3}{4} \div 3$
    b $6 \div \frac{2}{5}$
    c $\frac{9}{10} \div 5$
    d $12 \div \frac{2}{3}$
    e $\frac{7}{10} \div 3$
    f $8 \div \frac{3}{4}$
    g $2 \div \frac{4}{5}$
    h $9 \div \frac{3}{10}$
    i $7 \div \frac{2}{3}$
    j $3 \div \frac{2}{5}$
    k $\frac{2}{3} \div \frac{1}{2}$
    l $\frac{7}{10} \div \frac{4}{5}$
    m $\frac{9}{10} \div \frac{3}{4}$
    n $\frac{5}{6} \div \frac{2}{3}$

2. a $3\frac{1}{2} \div \frac{3}{4}$
    b $2\frac{3}{4} \div \frac{5}{8}$
    c $1\frac{2}{3} \div \frac{1}{3}$
    d $1\frac{1}{3} \div \frac{5}{9}$
    e $2\frac{3}{8} \div \frac{3}{4}$
    f $10 \div 1\frac{2}{3}$
    g $8 \div 2\frac{2}{3}$
    h $4\frac{1}{2} \div 3$
    *i $\frac{1 - \frac{1}{3}}{1 - \frac{2}{5}}$
    *j $\frac{1 - \frac{2}{3}}{1 - \frac{5}{8}}$

3. a How many **sixths** are there in $3\frac{1}{3}$?
    b Work out $3\frac{1}{3} \div \frac{5}{6}$.
       Show your working.

4. A recipe for a Christmas cake needs $\frac{1}{4}$ kg of flour.
    How many of these cakes can be made from a $2\frac{1}{2}$ kg bag of flour?

5. There are about $4\frac{1}{2}$ litres in 8 pints.
    About how many pints are there in 1 litre?

6. A yacht needs to travel 60 km to get home.
    It travels $7\frac{1}{2}$ kilometres in 1 hour.
    How long will it take to travel the 60 km?

7. If $2\frac{1}{2}$ kg of fruit costs £3, what is the cost per kg?

8. A hovercraft completes one crossing in three-quarters of an hour.
    What is the greatest number of crossings that it could make in 18 hours?

Number

*9 **a** Find three different pairs of fractions which give the answer $\frac{4}{9}$ when they are divided.
   b $\frac{4}{a} \div \frac{b}{3} = \frac{6}{7}$
   What values could *a* and *b* have? Is there more than one answer?

Review 1
a $\frac{3}{5} \div \frac{9}{10}$ **b** $6\frac{1}{2} \div \frac{2}{3}$ **c** $3\frac{1}{8} \div 1\frac{2}{3}$

Review 2
a How many **eighths** are in $5\frac{1}{4}$?
b Work out $5\frac{1}{4} \div \frac{7}{8}$. Show your working.

Review 3
It takes Saad $1\frac{1}{2}$ minutes to make a milkshake.
How many could he make in 12 minutes?

Review 4
A short skirt can be made from $\frac{3}{4}$ m of fabric.
How many of these skirts could be made from $10\frac{1}{2}$ m of this fabric?

Summary of key points

A We can express **proportions** using **fractions, decimals and percentages**.
We can convert between fractions, decimals and percentages.
All fractions convert to either a **terminating** or **recurring decimal**.

Examples $\frac{3}{5} = 0.6$ (terminating decimal) $\frac{4}{9} = 0.44444444...$ (recurring decimal)

All recurring decimals are **exact fractions**.
You should know these.

$0.333333333... = \frac{1}{3} (\frac{3}{9})$ $0.666666666... = \frac{2}{3} (\frac{6}{9})$ $0.111111111... = \frac{1}{9}$

$0.222222222... = \frac{2}{9}$ $0.777777777... = \frac{7}{9}$ $0.999999999... = \frac{9}{9} = 1$

B We can **compare proportions**.
When comparing fractions we either

1 convert them to decimals or
2 write them with a common denominator.

Example Compare $\frac{3}{4}$ and $\frac{4}{7}$.

$\frac{3}{4} \stackrel{\times 7}{=} \frac{21}{28}$ $\frac{4}{7} \stackrel{\times 4}{=} \frac{16}{28}$ or $\frac{3}{4} = 0.75$
$\frac{4}{7} = 0.56$ (2 d.p.)
$\frac{21}{28} > \frac{16}{28}$
so $\frac{3}{4} > \frac{4}{7}$ (28 is the LCM of 4 and 7.) $0.75 > 0.56$
so $\frac{3}{4} > \frac{4}{7}$

114

Fractions, Decimals and Percentages

C To **add and subtract fractions with different denominators** we use equivalent fractions. We find the LCM of the denominators then write both fractions with this as the denominator.

Examples $\frac{3}{8} + \frac{2}{3} = \frac{9}{24} + \frac{16}{24}$

$= \frac{9 + 16}{24}$

$= \frac{25}{24}$

$= 1\frac{1}{24}$

$\frac{3}{8} = \frac{9}{24}$ and $\frac{2}{3} = \frac{16}{24}$

$\frac{5}{8} - \frac{2}{5} = \frac{25}{40} - \frac{16}{40}$

$= \frac{9}{40}$

To **add or subtract mixed numbers**, we write each as an improper fraction first.

Examples $2\frac{3}{4} + 1\frac{1}{3} = \frac{11}{4} + \frac{4}{3}$

$= \frac{33}{12} + \frac{16}{12}$

$= \frac{49}{12}$

$= 4\frac{1}{12}$

or $2\frac{3}{4} + 1\frac{1}{3} = 2 + 1 + \frac{3}{4} + \frac{1}{3}$

$= 3 + \frac{9}{12} + \frac{4}{12}$

$= 3 + \frac{13}{12}$

$= 3 + 1\frac{1}{12}$

$= 4\frac{1}{12}$

When adding, we can add the whole numbers first.

Example $4\frac{1}{5} - 2\frac{1}{2} = \frac{21}{5} - \frac{5}{2}$

$= \frac{42}{10} - \frac{25}{10}$

$= \frac{17}{10}$

$= 1\frac{7}{10}$

We can add and subtract fractions using the $a^{b/c}$ key on a calculator.

Example $2\frac{3}{8} + 3\frac{1}{3}$ key

2 [a^b/c] 3 [a^b/c] 8 [+] 3 [a^b/c] 1 [a^b/c] 3 [=]

to get $5\lrcorner 17\lrcorner 24$. We read this as $5\frac{17}{24}$.

D We can find **fractions or percentages of quantities**.
Try to use a mental method first.

Examples $\frac{3}{5}$ of 45

$\frac{1}{5}$ of 45 = 9

$\frac{3}{5}$ of 45 = 3 × 9

= **27**

35% of 80

10% of 80 = 8

30% of 80 = 24

5% of 80 = 4

35% of 80 = 24 + 4 = **28**

For harder calculations we sometimes **use a calculator**.

Example $17\frac{1}{2}$% of 125

either key [17·5] [÷] [100] [×] [125] [=] to get 21·875   using fractions

or key [0·175] [×] [125] [=] to get 21·875   using decimals

or key [17·5] [×] [1·25] [=] to get 21·875   multiplying by 1%

Number

E When **multiplying fractions** we
1. write whole numbers or mixed numbers as improper fractions
2. cancel if possible
3. multiply the numerators
multiply the denominators.

Example $1\frac{1}{2} \times 2\frac{2}{3} = \frac{3^1}{2_1} \times \frac{8^4}{3_1}$
$= \frac{4}{1}$
$= 4$

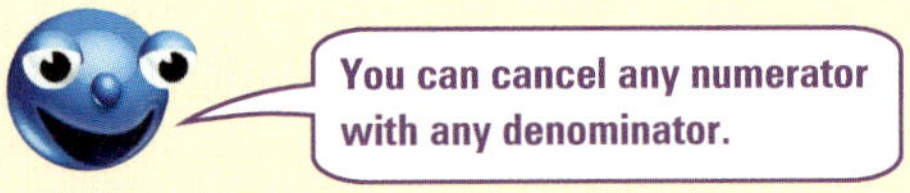

You can cancel any numerator with any denominator.

F When we **divide fractions** we use the **inverse rule**.
To divide by a fraction, multiply by the inverse.

Example $\frac{2}{3} \div \frac{5}{9} = \frac{2}{3_1} \times \frac{9^3}{5}$ $1\frac{3}{4} \div \frac{5}{8} = \frac{7}{4_1} \times \frac{8^2}{5}$
$= \frac{6}{5}$ $= \frac{14}{5}$
$= 1\frac{1}{5}$ $= 2\frac{4}{5}$

$\frac{9}{5}$ is the inverse of $\frac{5}{9}$. $\frac{8}{5}$ is the inverse of $\frac{5}{8}$.

Test yourself

Except for questions 10, 17, 22 and 23.

1. What fraction of
   a 48 is 36
   b 120 is 80
   c 240 is 360
   d 1 hour is 20 minutes
   e 2 m is 50 cm
   f 1 hour is 35 minutes?

2. Convert these to exact fractions.
   a 0·4444 ...
   b 0·6666 ...

3. Each diagram below was drawn on a square grid.
   a Write what percentage of each diagram is shaded.
      i   ii   iii 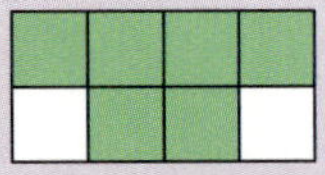
   b Explain how you know that $33\frac{1}{3}$% of the diagram below is shaded.

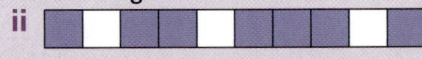

4. A ball bounced 150 cm high on its first bounce.
   On its second bounce, it bounced 60 cm.
   What proportion of the first bounce height was the second bounce?

5. This frequency diagram shows the heights of Mr Yin's piano pupils.
   He put the heights into class intervals of $150 \leq h < 155$, ...
   What fraction of Mr Yin's pupils were
   a 160 cm or taller but less than 175 cm
   b shorter than 160 cm?

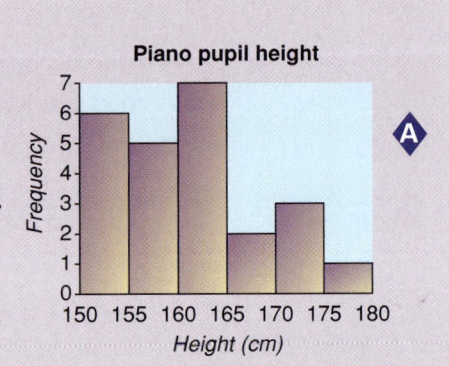

Piano pupil height

Fractions, Decimals and Percentages

6 Which shape has the greater percentage shaded?

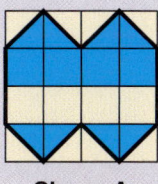

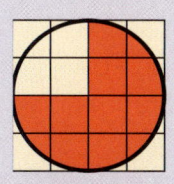

Shape A   Shape B

7 Put these in order from smallest to largest.
   a $\frac{1}{2}, \frac{2}{5}, \frac{7}{25}, \frac{17}{50}, \frac{3}{10}$ b $\frac{12}{20}$, 130%, $\frac{35}{25}$, 0·9

8 7 out of 16 pupils from the lunchtime computer club went on a camp. 19 out of 48 from the after school computer club also went. Which computer club had the greater fraction of pupils that went?

9 Sam asked 30 pupils what after school activity they liked doing most.

Activity	Number of girls	Number of boys
Music	3	3
Sport	4	8
Drama	2	5
Craft	1	3
	Total 10	Total 20

   a Which activity did 40% of the girls choose?
   b Which activity did 25% of the boys choose?
   c Sam said 'Music was equally popular with girls and boys.'
      Explain why Sam is wrong.
   d Which activity is equally popular with girls and boys?

10 This table shows the average rainfall in mm for a city in January and June in 2002 and 2004.

	2002	2004
January	116	142
June	54	62

   a For 2002 find the rainfall in June as a percentage of the rainfall in January.
      Give your answer to 1 decimal place.
   b Show whether the rainfall in June as a percentage of the rainfall in January was greater in 2004 or in 2002.

11 Calculate these.
   a $\frac{2}{5} + \frac{3}{5}$ b $\frac{5}{12} + \frac{2}{3}$ c $\frac{5}{8} + \frac{7}{10}$ d $\frac{5}{12} - \frac{3}{8}$
   e $\frac{7}{12} + \frac{1}{6} - \frac{5}{8}$ f $3\frac{1}{8} + \frac{5}{8}$ g $2\frac{2}{3} + 1\frac{4}{5}$ h $3\frac{5}{8} - 1\frac{2}{5}$

12 Find these using your calculator.
   a $\frac{3}{7} + \frac{4}{9} - \frac{2}{3}$ b $\frac{5}{8} - \frac{3}{20} + \frac{4}{5}$

13 In a 240 g bag of mixed nuts, $\frac{1}{3}$ are brazil nuts, $\frac{1}{4}$ are almonds, $\frac{1}{8}$ are cashews, 30 g are peanuts and the rest are other sorts of nuts. What fraction are other sorts of nuts?

117

Number

14 On a farm 80 sheep gave birth.
30% of the sheep gave birth to two lambs.
The rest of the sheep gave birth to just one lamb.
In total, how many lambs were born?
Show your working.

[SATs Paper 1 Level 6] **D**

15 In a science class, Amelia's group used $\frac{1}{6}$ of a 60 g jar of sodium carbonate.
Simon used $\frac{3}{5}$ of what was left. How many grams were left in the bottle after this?

D

16 Find the answer to these mentally.
   a $\frac{3}{5}$ of 60 ℓ   **b** $\frac{7}{8}$ of 64 km   **c** $1\frac{1}{2}$ of £180   **d** $2\frac{1}{4}$ of £160
   e 15% of 40 m   **f** 30% of 65 ℓ   **g** 85% of 150 km   **h** $12\frac{1}{2}$% of 48 m

D

17 Use your calculator to find these. Give the answers to the nearest penny.
   a 17% of £60   **b** 36% of £45   **c** 87% of £132

D

18 **a** $\frac{3}{4} \times \frac{2}{15}$ **b** $8 \times 3\frac{3}{4}$ **c** $2\frac{2}{5} \times 3\frac{1}{8}$ **d** $\frac{5}{6} \times \frac{1}{4} \times \frac{12}{25}$
   e $\frac{2}{5} \times \frac{3}{4} \times \frac{1}{2}$ **f** $1\frac{1}{3} \times 3\frac{2}{5}$ **g** $(1\frac{1}{2})^2$

E

19 Jenny's bedroom measures $3\frac{1}{2}$ m by $3\frac{1}{4}$ m.
What is the area of the floor?

E

20 Work these out.
   a $\frac{4}{9} \div \frac{2}{3}$ **b** $8 \div \frac{2}{5}$ **c** $\frac{3}{10} \div 5$ **d** $\frac{3}{4} \div \frac{1}{2}$
   e $\frac{5}{6} \div \frac{2}{3}$ **f** $3\frac{1}{4} \div \frac{5}{6}$ **g** $3\frac{1}{3} \div \frac{2}{5}$ **h** $\frac{1-\frac{1}{4}}{1-\frac{2}{5}}$

F

21 How many twelfths in $1\frac{5}{6}$?

F

22 A train takes $1\frac{1}{4}$ hours to complete its journey.
How many journeys could it make in 25 hours?

F

23 $5\frac{1}{2}$ kg of apples costs £8.
What is the cost per kg?

F

∗24 The diagram shows a square and a circle.
The circle touches the edges of the square.

[SATs Paper 2 Level 7] **A**

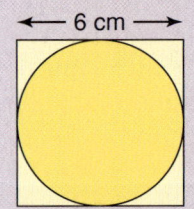

← 6 cm →

What **percentage** of the diagram is shaded?
Show your working.

118

5 Percentage and Proportional Changes

You need to know

✓ finding fraction of and percentage of   page 10
✓ ratio and proportion   page 10

Key vocabulary
proportional to (∝), proportionality

▶▶ Golden wonder

Measure the length and width of this rectangle.

Find the ratio   length : width   or $\frac{\text{length}}{\text{width}}$.

It should be very close to 1·6 : 1.

This is called the *golden ratio* (1·618 : 1).

Rectangles with this ratio are golden rectangles and said to be 'appealing to the eye'.
Buildings such as The Parthenon in Greece are built to this ratio.

Construct a golden rectangle as follows.

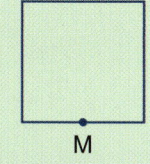

M — Draw a square (any size). Mark the mid-point of the base.

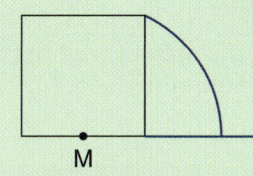

M — Extend the base. Place your compass point on M and draw an arc as shown.

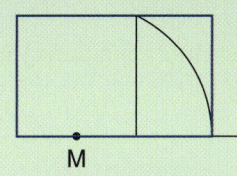

M — Draw the rectangle so that it just encloses the arc.

Number

Percentage change

Percentage increase or decrease

We can calculate a **percentage increase or decrease** using a single calculation.

Example A 10 cm long drawing is enlarged by 44%.
The final length of the drawing = 144% of 10 cm
= 1·44 × 10 cm
= 14·4 cm

144% = 100% + 44%

Example Mary bought a bike for £140 and sold it at a loss of 15%.
Selling price = 85% of £140
= 0·85 × £140
= £119

85% = 100% − 15%

Exercise 1

Except for questions 6, 11 and 12 and Review 5.

1
a Increase 60 g by 10%.
b Decrease 12 ml by 50%.
c Increase £120 by 30%.
d Decrease 200 g by 80%.
e Increase 800 l by 20%.
f Increase £140 by 15%.
g Decrease 160 l by $12\frac{1}{2}$%.
h Decrease 70 mm by 4%.
*i Increase £2000 by 2%.
j Decrease £9 by 33%.

Remember: $17\frac{1}{2}$% = 0·175.

2 A shop increased all prices by 10%.
Use a copy of this table and fill it in.

Item	Old price	New price
Clock	£29	
Table	£232	
CD rack	£45	
Duvet cover	£26·50	

3 Chandra bought a digital camera in a 20% off sale.
The original price of the camera was £1650.
a How much did Chandra pay for the camera?
b Chandra sold the camera 3 months later and made a 15% loss.
How much did she sell it for?

4
a How much, including VAT, did the stereo cost before the sale?
b How much did the stereo cost during the sale?

Price **£120** + VAT ($17\frac{1}{2}$%)

SALE this week only 15% off

120

Percentage and Proportional Changes

5 At both Direct Lighting and Lamplighter a lava lamp was originally £89.
   a Which shop is cheaper now and by how much?
   b Lamplighter then reduce their prices by a **further** 15%. How much is the lava lamp then?

6 The population of London in 1901 was 6 506 889.
Over the next 100 years, the population increased by 10·22%.
What was the population of London in 2001?

7 Bridget owns a boutique. She prices all the clothes so she makes a 40% profit. When her friend Anna bought a dress from her, she gave Anna a 40% discount. Did Bridget make any profit on this dress? Explain.

*8 Neil claims that an increase of 10% followed by a decrease of 10% is less than an increase of 20% followed by a decrease of 20%. Is Neil correct?

*9 Emalia sold her bike to Anna and made 25% profit. Anna sold the bike to Tara for a further 5% profit. Anna told Emalia that the bike had been sold to Tara for 30% more than Emalia had paid for it. Is Anna correct? Explain.

*10 A manufacturer adds 60% to the cost of materials to cover labour. She then adds a further 25% to get the selling price. At what price would she sell an article made from materials which cost 75p?

*11 Kimberley's had a sale on all jumpers. The marked price of all jumpers was reduced by 25% and a cash customer was given a further 5% off. What price would a cash customer pay for a jumper originally marked at £26?

*12 Didier enlarged a drawing in a book by setting the photocopier to 130%. He decided this was too large. He put the enlarged drawing on the photocopier and set it to 90%. If the original drawing was 14 cm by 18 cm, what are the dimensions of the final copy?

*13 A shop reduces its prices by 15% for a sale. On the last day of the sale, the prices are reduced by a further 20%. Show that the prices on this last day were reduced by 32% in total.

Review 1
a Increase 40 by 20%.
b Decrease 320 by 30%
c Increase £64 by $12\frac{1}{2}$%.
d Decrease 400 cm by 35%.

Review 2
a Find the cost, including VAT, of a TV costing £240 + VAT of $17\frac{1}{2}$%.
b The store offers a cash discount of 8% on the TV.
How much did Tom pay for it if he paid cash?

Review 3
a A school bought calculators at a bulk price of £18 each. It sold them to pupils, making a profit of 15%. How much did pupils pay for their calculators?
b A new model is coming out so the school discounts the price of the old model by 10%. What will the price of the calculator be now?
*c Tara said that increasing the price by 15% then reducing it by 10% was the same as increasing it by 5%. Is Tara correct? Explain.

Number

Review 4 A box of 12 pens cost £16. Jo sold them to make a profit of 35%. How much would she charge for each pen?

∗Review 5 The population in a town increased 20% in the last 5 years. It is predicted to increase a further 25% in the next 5 years. If the population 5 years ago was 18 420, what is it predicted to be in 5 years time?

Increase or decrease as a percentage

Discussion

- James scored 2 goals in last week's match.
  In this week's match he scored 4 goals.

  Did James get 50% more goals this week than last week?
  Did James get 100% more goals this week than last week? **Discuss**.

  The school roll increased from 250 in 2000 to 750 in 2004.
  Is this an increase of 200% or 300%? **Discuss**.

- Think of other situations where increases in numbers might be given as a % increase. **Discuss**.

  Think of situations where decreases in numbers might be described as % decreases. **Discuss**.

Noah's trainer told him to increase his exercise time by 20%.
Noah increased his daily exercise time from 40 to 48 minutes.
He checked to see what percentage increase this is.

Fractional increase $= \frac{8}{40}$ ← actual increase / original amount

Percentage increase $= \frac{8}{40} \times 100\%$
$= 20\%$

$$\% \text{ increase} = \frac{\text{actual increase}}{\text{original amount}} \times 100\%$$
$$\% \text{ decrease} = \frac{\text{actual decrease}}{\text{original amount}} \times 100\%$$

Worked Example
In an experiment, 39 g of powder decreased to 28 g.
What percentage decrease is this?

Answer
Actual decrease in mass = 39 g − 28 g
$\qquad\qquad\qquad\quad$ = 11 g

% decrease $= \frac{\text{actual decrease}}{\text{original amount}} \times 100\%$
$\qquad\quad = \frac{11}{39} \times 100\%$
$\qquad\quad = \mathbf{28\%}$ **(nearest per cent)**

key 11 ÷ 39 × 100 =

Percentage and Proportional Changes

Exercise 2 — Round your answers sensibly.

1. Over a two year period, a town population increased from 145 000 to 205 000.
   a. What actual increase is this?
   b. What percentage increase is this?

   Use the formulae on the previous page.

2. Rebecca increased her scoring rate from 20 runs per match last season to 25 runs per match this season.
   a. What was the actual increase?
   b. What was the percentage increase in Rebecca's scoring rate?

3. A newborn baby dropped in weight from 4500 g to 3200 g.
   What percentage weight loss is this?

4. A car appreciated in value from £17 500 to £25 800.
   What percentage appreciation is this?

5. Dale bought some shares for £50 and later sold them for £177.
   What percentage profit did Dale make on these shares?

6. The prices of five items P, Q, R, S and T five years ago and this year are shown on these scales.

   Price (£) five years ago

   Price (£) this year

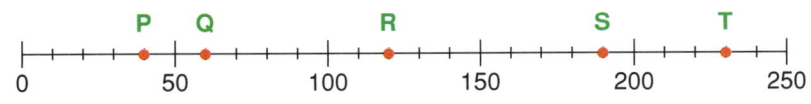

   a. What is the percentage increase of each item?
   b. Which item showed the greatest percentage increase over five years?

7. Thomas was studying expansion in science. He heated a metal bar and noticed it increased in length from 1·16 m to 1·173 m.
   Calculate the percentage increase to one decimal place.

8. This table shows the membership numbers in 1960 and 2000 for four tennis clubs.
   a. In 1960, for every member Champs had, how many did Central have?
   b. Patrick thinks that from 1960 to 2000 Country membership increased by 100%. Is Patrick right? Explain your answer.

Club	Membership 1960	Membership 2000
Reds	222	642
Central	1558	3402
Country	13	26
Champs	166	276

*9. The Atkinsons thought their living room was too small.
   The dashed lines show how they extended it.
   Calculate the percentage increase in the area of the living room.

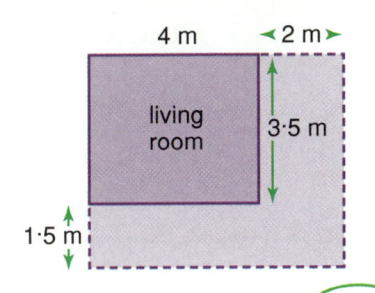

Number

*10

Energy: oil production			
Rank	Country	Barrels produced daily 1990	Barrels produced daily 2000
1.	Saudi Arabia	7 105 000	9 145 000
2.	USA	8 915 000	7 745 000
3.	Russian Federation	10 405 000	6 535 000
4.	Iran	3 255 000	3 770 000
5.	Mexico	2 975 000	3 450 000
6.	Norway	1 740 000	3 365 000
7.	China	2 775 000	3 245 000
8.	Venezuela	2 245 000	3 235 000
9.	Canada	1 965 000	2 710 000
10.	United Kingdom	1 915 000	2 660 000

a Which countries given in the table had an increase in the number of barrels produced daily from 1990 to 2000?
b Which country had the greatest **actual** increase in barrels produced daily?
c Which country had the greatest **percentage** increase in barrels produced daily? What was the percentage increase?
d Which country had the greatest **percentage decrease** in barrels produced daily? What was the percentage decrease?

Review 1
a Stuart paid £7500 for his car. Two years later he sold it for £6300. What percentage loss did he make?
b The school roll has increased from 1080 to 1150 over the last two years. What percentage increase is this? (Answer to 1 d.p.)

Review 2   Marriages in United Kingdom

Year	1979	1989	1999
Number	369 000	345 000	264 000

This table gives the number of marriages, to the nearest thousand. Find the percentage decrease
a between 1979 and 1989   **b** between 1989 and 1999   **c** between 1979 and 1999.

Review 3   Calculate the percentage increase in these prices.
a £1·65 to £1·85   **b** £1560 to £3425.

Practical

You will need a spreadsheet package.

Compare the percentage savings on ten or more items that are on special offer. Use a spreadsheet to help. Ask your teacher for the Savings ICT sheet.

Percentage and Proportional Changes

Calculating the original amount

Discussion

- Look at the newspaper heading.
  Blake wanted to know what the population was a year ago.
  He said
  'The old population must have been *multiplied* by 110% or 1·1 to get the new population. If I *divide* the new population by 110% or 1·1 I will get the old population.'
  Is Blake correct? **Discuss**.

  Town population has increased by 10% to 8635 in the last year.

- Jasmine wanted to know the original price of the shirt.
  She wrote
  £65   represents 85% (100% – 15%)
  £65 ÷ 85   represents 1%
  £65 ÷ 85 × 100   represents 100%

  Is Jasmine correct? **Discuss**.
  What is the original price of a shirt?

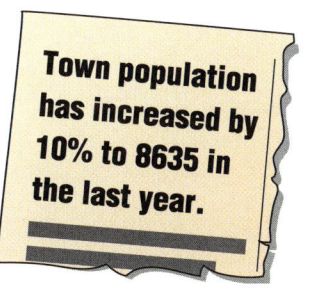

  SHIRT 15% off NOW £65

Worked Example
This year Wolver Farm has 345 sheep.
This is 15% more than last year.
How many did they have last year?

Answer
Three different ways to find the answer are shown.

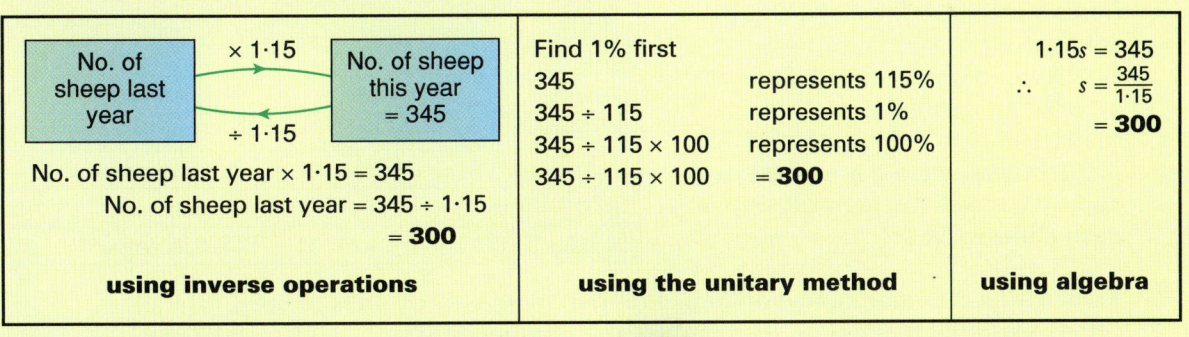

No. of sheep last year ×1·15 → No. of sheep this year = 345 ÷1·15 ← No. of sheep last year × 1·15 = 345 No. of sheep last year = 345 ÷ 1·15 = 300	Find 1% first 345 represents 115% 345 ÷ 115 represents 1% 345 ÷ 115 × 100 represents 100% 345 ÷ 115 × 100 = 300	$1·15s = 345$ $\therefore s = \dfrac{345}{1·15}$ $= 300$
using inverse operations	**using the unitary method**	**using algebra**

Note The **original** amount is always **100%**.

You could use a letter, like s, to represent the unknown no. of sheep last year.

* **Exercise 3**   Only use a calculator if you need to.

1 Find the answers to these mentally.
   a 25% of a number is 8. What is the number?
   b 30% of a number is 3. What is the number?
   c 75% of a number is 15. What is the number?

There are more mental percentage calculations on page 67.

125

Number

2 A coat is on sale for £100, which is 80% of its original price.
Becky started working out the original price like this.
Copy and finish it.

£100 = 80% of original price
     = 0.8 × original price
original price = £100 / ___
               = ___

3 This year 1650 people visited the school on open day.
This was an increase of 20% from the previous year.
How many visitors were there the previous year?
Copy and complete this to help.

Previous open day visitors → [× 1.2] → 1650
___ ← [ ] ← ___

4 Mrs Schmidt's salary was increased by 6% to £47 700. What was her salary before the increase?

5 Find the original price of a painting that sold for £1729 at a 5% loss.

6 This special packet of P + Ps contains 80 sweets.
How many sweets does a normal packet contain?

7 A two-month-old puppy weighs 3·6 kg.
It has increased in mass by 450% since birth.
How much did the puppy weigh at birth?

8 Denise surveyed the clubs at her school.
She worked out the percentage increase or decrease in membership in the last year, giving the percentages to the nearest per cent. What was the membership of each club last year?

Club	Current membership	Increase or decrease	
Drama	62	Increase	17%
Chess	18	Decrease	14%
Painting	67	Decrease	3%
Cricket	70	Increase	23%
Craft	101	Increase	1%
Athletics	45	Decrease	8%

*9 Tandia read that the population of a town had increased by 10% to 8950.
She worked out that before the increase the population was $\frac{8950}{1 \cdot 1} = 8136 \cdot \dot{3}\dot{6}$.
In fact the population before the increase was 8136.
Why is Tandia's answer different?

Review 1 Mel bought a plant. The height of the plant increased 75% to 14 cm in the first month. How high was the plant when Mel bought it?

Review 2 'Bags Us' had 25% off all handbags. The new price was rounded to the nearest penny. In the sale Julia bought a handbag for £26·25. What was the original price of the handbag?

Review 3 The number of telephone calls Tait Electronics made this month increased on last month by $12\frac{1}{2}$%. This month Tait Electronics made 765 calls. How many calls did the company make last month?

Percentage and Proportional Changes

Mixed percentage calculations

This exercise will give you practice at solving percentage problems.

Exercise 4   Only use a calculator if you need to.

1. A brass plate weighs 80 g.
   60% of the brass is copper.
   What is the mass of this copper?

2. 120 pupils are at a camp for the disabled.
   30% of the pupils have a caregiver with them.
   The rest are attending by themselves.
   In total, how many disabled pupils and caregivers are at the camp?

3. A country earned £833 billion from timber exports.
   This pie chart shows the amount from each type of timber.
   a What percentage of the timber exports were from Pine?
   b What percentage were from Beech?

   Other £58 billion
   Beech £125 billion
   Pine £650 billion

4. This table shows what was sold at the school fair.

Stall	Number of items sold	Takings
Cake	84	£231·50
Clothing	186	£927·80
Craft	51	£464·50
Second-hand	364	£1242·25
Total	685	£2866·05

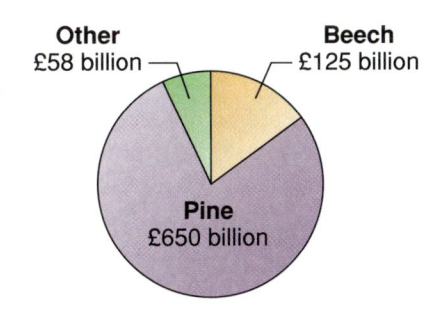

   a What percentage of items sold were second-hand?
   b What percentage of the takings were from the second-hand stall?
   c Was the average price of items sold at the craft stall or at the second-hand stall cheaper?

5. Joel used some scales to weigh powder for a science experiment.
   He was told the scales might have up to a 20% error.
   The powder weighed 65 g on the scales.
   What is the greatest and smallest mass the powder might be?

6. A new bottle of shampoo is advertised containing 25% more than the old bottle for the same price. If the old bottle contained 200 ml, how much does the new bottle contain?

7. A clothing shop advertised 35% off all stock. What would each of the following items be reduced to?
   a a coat priced at £112   b a skirt priced at £99
   c a suit priced at £235

8. How much cheaper is it to pay cash?

   Cash Price £560 +VAT 17.5%
   or
   Deposit of £50 plus 12 payments of £58

Number

9 Which is the better buy?
  a A 600 g block of cheese for £3·40 or a 500 g block plus 20% extra free for £3·45.
  b

  TRENTS — 200 g pasta plus **20% extra** for **£2·64**

  Pasta Plus — 250 g pasta plus **25% extra** for **£3·75**

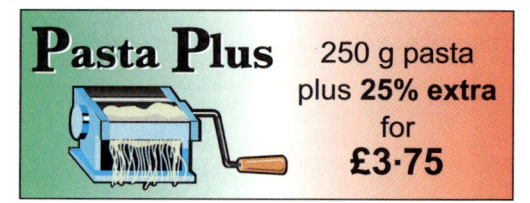

10 a One calculation below gives the answer to the question [SATs Paper 2 Level 7]
  What is 70 increased by 9%?
  Write down the correct one.

  (70 × 0·9)   (70 × 1·9)   (70 × 0·09)   (70 × 1·09)

  b Choose one of the other calculations.
  Write a question **about percentages** that this calculation represents.
  c Now do the same for one of the remaining two calculations.
  d Copy and fill in the missing decimal number.
  To decrease by 14%, multiply by ___.

*__11__ **a** Paul wants to buy a pair of trousers that were £89·70 before the sale.
  He estimated that he would save about £14 in the sale.
  How might he have estimated this?
  b How much will the trousers cost in the sale? Show your working.

  SALE **15% off** all goods

*__12__ VAT of $17\frac{1}{2}$% was added to a bill.
  What percentage of the total bill is VAT?

*__13__ A company spent £860 on advertising.
  As a direct result, the company's profits rose 15% to £6500.
  Was the advertising worthwhile from a financial point of view?
  Justify your answer.

*__14__ A baby octopus increases its mass by about 8% each day.
  It began life with a mass of 220 g.
  a How much will it weigh after a day?
  b How much will it weigh after 3 days?

*__15__ Mel sold her beach yacht for £1500 at a 20% profit.
  What did she pay for the yacht?

*__16__ When 9% interest was added to Julia's savings she had £163·50
  How much did Julia have originally?

*__17__ An antique was sold for £720. This was a loss of 40%.
  What price was paid for the antique originally?

*__18__ A shop had a sale. All prices were reduced by 15%.
  A pair of shoes cost £46·75 in the sale.
  What price were the shoes before the sale?

  SALE 15% off

*__19__ A dog at the RSPCA weighs 18·4 kg.
  This is 180% of its mass when it first arrived.
  How much did the dog weigh when it first arrived at the RSPCA?

Percentage and Proportional Changes

*20 This diagram shows two overlapping identical rectangles.
20% of each rectangle is shaded.
What fraction of the whole diagram is shaded?

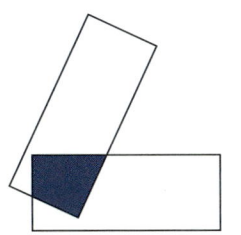

*21 Kayla made 10 ℓ of orange drink. It was 50% water.
How much water must she add to it to make it 75% water?

*22 a The sides of this square are increased by 20%.
What is the percentage increase in the area of the square?
b The area of the square shown increases by 21%.
The new shape is still a square.
What is the length of each side?

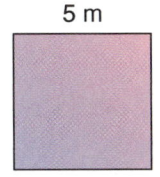

5 m

Review 1
a On holiday Barry was travelling at 90 km/h when he approached a village with a 70 km/h speed limit. He reduced his speed by 20%.
At what speed did he travel through the village?
b The road accident toll in February was 420.   35% of the fatal road accidents were caused by 'driving too fast for conditions'.
How many people died in February as a result of this?

Review 2
This table shows the number of students playing different winter sports at two local schools.
a What percentage of students played hockey at school A?
b What percentage of students at school B played netball?
c Did a greater proportion of students from school A or school B play football?
d What percentage of students in total played football?

Sport	School A	School B
Football	82	95
Rugby	28	25
Hockey	36	50
Netball	45	32
Total	191	202

Review 3 Which is better value?

ACE Shampoo 200 mℓ + 50 mℓ extra FREE £5·25

Silky Shine Shampoo 250 mℓ + 15% extra FREE £5·50

Review 4 One calculation below gives the answer to this question.
'What is 120 decreased by 12%?'
a Which question is it?
A 120 × 1·12   B 120 × 0·12   C 120 × 0·88   D 120 × 1·88
b Choose one of the other calculations. Write a question about percentages that this calculation represents.
c Do the same for one other calculation.
d Copy and fill in the missing decimal number.
To increase by 8% multiply by ___.

129

Number

*** Review 5**
- **a** In 2000 the population of Townsville was 90 160. This is an increase of 12% since 1990. What was the population in 1990?
- **b** All employees in Dick's Discounter received the same percentage increase in salary.
    - **i** Jane's salary went up from £16 000 to £16 800.
      What percentage increase is this?
    - **ii** Peter's salary went up to £25 200. What was his salary before the rise?

Practical

Percentages are all around us. We find them on food labels, clothing labels, in government statistics, in finance, in geographical data, ...

Either
- Make a poster displaying as many examples of the use of percentages as possible.

or
- Choose one topic where percentages are used and make a poster about this.

Examples

Matthew chose food.
On his poster he displayed ten biscuit labels.
He compared the percentages of fat and sugar in each.

Melissa chose the weather.
On her poster she displayed 12 pie charts, one for each month of last year.
Each pie chart showed the percentage of rainy, cloudy and sunny days.
She got the information from the Internet.

Javed chose Africa.
On his poster he displayed percentages for crops, land use, minerals, ethnic groups, ...

Proportionality

There is 5 g of fat for every 8 g of a carbohydrate.

This table shows the amount of fat in different amounts of carbohydrate.

Carbohydrate	8 g	16 g	24 g	32 g
Fat	5 g	10 g	15 g	20 g

The ratio   *amount of fat* : *amount of carbohydrate*   is always 5 : 8.
We say the amount of fat is **proportional** to the amount of carbohydrate or amount of fat ∝ amount of carbohydrate.

A graph of amount of fat and amount of carbohydrate would be a straight line through the origin.

This links to page 172 in algebra.

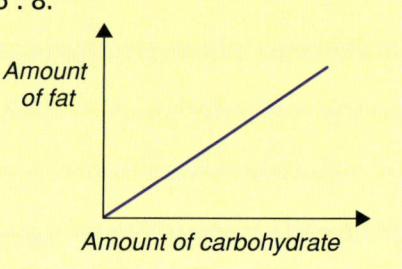

Amount of fat

Amount of carbohydrate

Percentage and Proportional Changes

We can find the amount of fat for other amounts of carbohydrate.

Example Find the amount of fat if there is 20 g of carbohydrate.

Unitary method – find how much fat there is for **1 g** first.
Amount of fat for **1 g** of carbohydrate = $\frac{5}{8}$
Amount of fat for 20 g of carbohydrate = amount in 1 g × 20
$$= \frac{5}{8} \times 20$$
$$= \textbf{12·5 g}$$

Constant multiplier method
Note The constant multiplier method is the same as the unitary method done in one step.

To find the **constant multiplier**, we can use a diagram like this.
The constant multiplier for this example is $\frac{20}{8}$.

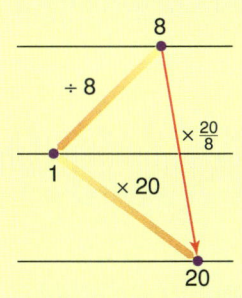

The constant multiplier can also be found from the **ratio**.
Amount required : Amount given = 20 : 8
$$= \frac{20}{8}$$
Amount of fat for 20 g carbohydrate = $\frac{20}{8}$ × amount of fat for 8 g carbohydrate
$$= \frac{20}{8} \times 5$$
$$= \textbf{12·5 g}$$

This method is sometimes called 'scaling'.

Discussion

In the **constant multiplier method** shown above, what would the constant multiplier be for finding the amount of fat if there is x grams of carbohydrate? **Discuss**.

Worked Example
The ratio of red paint to yellow paint in orange paint is 5 : 3.
How much red paint is needed to mix with 400 mℓ of yellow paint?

Answer
Unitary method
Red paint needed for 1 mℓ of yellow paint = $\frac{5}{3}$
Red paint needed for 400 mℓ of yellow paint = $\frac{5}{3} \times 400$
$$= \textbf{666·7 mℓ (1 d.p.)}$$

Constant multiplier
Amount required : Amount given = 400 : 3
Constant multiplier = $\frac{400}{3}$
Red paint required for 400 mℓ yellow paint = $\frac{400}{3} \times 5$
$$= \textbf{666·7 mℓ (1 d.p.)}$$

5 : 3
÷3 ↓ ↓ ÷3
$\frac{5}{3}$: 1

Number

Exercise 5

Use a method of your choice to do these.

1 a 5 miles is approximately equal to 8 km.
About how many kilometres are equal to 40 miles?
  b 10 pieces of fish cost £8·60.
How much do 30 pieces cost?
  c 6 filled baps cost £9.
How much do 9 filled baps cost?
  d 7 posters cost £15·75.
How much would 12 cost?
  e 12 apples cost £5·64.
How much will 15 apples cost?

2 This shows the prices of some sweets.

300 g white stars £1·20
500 g black cats £1·50
200 g red hearts £1·80

How much would Mel pay for
  a 800 g of white stars
  b 800 g of black cats
  *__c__ 500 g of red hearts and 1·2 kg of black cats
  *__d__ 0·4 kg of white stars and 0·3 kg of red hearts?

3 For £5 you would get about US $9·00.
How many US dollars would you get for these amounts?
  a £8   **b** £12   **c** £160   **d** £2750

4 Adapt this recipe to feed 10 people.

Apple crumble
for 4 people
4 large apples
50 g butter
100 g sugar
200 g flour

5 a The label on yoghurt A shows this information.

How many grams of **protein** does **100 g** of yoghurt provide?

Show your working.

Yoghurt A 125 g

Each 125 g provides	
Energy	430 kJ
Protein	4·5 g
Carbohydrate	11·1 g
Fat	4·5 g

[SATs Paper 2 Level 6]

Percentage and Proportional Changes

b The label on yoghurt B shows different information.

A boy eats the same amount of yoghurt A and yoghurt B.

Which yoghurt provides him with more **carbohydrate**?

Show your working.

Yoghurt B 150 g	
Each 150 g provides	
Energy	339 kJ
Protein	6·6 g
Carbohydrate	13·1 g
Fat	0·2 g

Egg Foo Yung for 6 people
8 eggs
200 g broccoli
100 g cauliflower
150 g peas
50 ml soya sauce

6 Sandy wanted to make this recipe for 10 people.
  a Write the recipe Sandy should use.
  *b Gracie used 75 ml of soya sauce for the same recipe. How many people was this enough for?

7 The ratio of flour to sugar in a pastry mix is 3 : 2.
How much sugar is needed to mix with these amounts of flour?
  a 300 g   **b** 1·2 kg   *c 500 g

8 Marcia wants to make a scale drawing of a box.
The ratio to be used is 2 : 25.
One edge of the box is measured as 125 mm.
How long should this edge be on the scale drawing?

Review 1
a 120 g butter is needed in a recipe to make 24 cookies. How much butter will be needed if the recipe is changed to make 40 cookies?
b 4 medium pizzas will feed 14 people. How many pizzas will you need to buy to feed 35 people?
c A wordprocessor types 407 words in 11 minutes. How long will she take to type 925 words?

Review 2 Two packets of breakfast flakes give the following information.

Great Flakes	
Each 250 g provides	
Energy	3882 kJ
Protein	17·8 g
Carbohydrate	203·6 g

Flake Up	
Each 150 g provides	
Energy	2478 kJ
Protein	10·8 g
Carbohydrate	132·2 g

a How much energy would 100 g of Flake Up provide?
b Jade eats the same amount of each cereal.
Which provides more carbohydrate?
Show your working.

Review 3
a Adapt this recipe to feed 16 people.
*b Tina used 1·25 kg of baked beans for the same recipe. How many people was this enough for?

Chilli Con Carne (for 12 people)
3 kg mince
6 small onions
600 g tomatoes
750 g baked beans
chilli powder to taste
3 bay leaves

Number

> **Practical**
>
> **You will need** a spreadsheet package.
>
> Ask your teacher for the Constant Multiplier ICT sheet.

Ratio

Remember

We can **simplify a ratio** by cancelling.

Examples

9 : 12   ÷3 ↓ ↓ ÷3   = 3 : 4

4 : 12 : 20   ÷4 ↓ ÷4 ↓ ÷4   = 1 : 3 : 5

All parts of the ratio have been divided by 4.

A ratio in its simplest form does not have fractions or decimals.

Examples

$1\frac{2}{3}$: 2   ×3 ↓ ↓ ×3   = 5 : 6

Multiply by the denominator of the fraction.

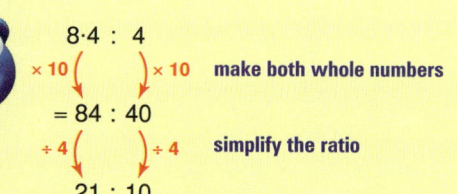

8·4 : 4   ×10 ↓ ↓ ×10   make both whole numbers
= 84 : 40   ÷4 ↓ ↓ ÷4   simplify the ratio
21 : 10

Example   Chandler won £10 in a raffle and Kofi won £25.
The ratio of their winnings is 10 : 25 or 2 : 5.
Chandler won $\frac{2}{5}$ or 40% or 0·4 as much as Kofi.
Kofi won $\frac{5}{2}$ or 250% or 2·5 as much as Chandler.

10 : 25   ÷5 ↓ ↓ ÷5   = 2 : 5

We can **compare ratios** by putting them both into the form 1 : *m* or *m* : 1.

Example   The ratio of goals scored to shots at goal for two netball players is given.

	goals scored : shots at goal
Julie	8 : 12
Darlene	15 : 24

We can compare these by putting them both in the form 1 : *m*.

Julie scored 1 goal for every 1·5 shots.
Darlene scored 1 goal for every 1·6 shots.

Julie
8 : 12   ÷8 ↓ ↓ ÷8   = 1 : 1·5

Darlene
15 : 24   ÷15 ↓ ↓ ÷15   = 1 : 1·6

1 out of 1·5 is a greater success than 1 out of 1·6.

Julie is a better goal shooter.

Percentage and Proportional Changes

Exercise 6

1 Write each ratio in its simplest form.
  a 20 : 25   **b** 16 : 48   **c** 4 : 16 : 28   **d** 7 : 14 : 63   **e** 180 : 120 : 240

2 a Write *grams of fat : grams of carbohydrate* as a ratio in its simplest form.
  b What goes in the gaps?
  i There is ____ as much fat as carbohydrate.
  ii There is ____ as much carbohydrate as fat.

Choco Bar	
Fat	22 g
Carbohydrate	88 g

3 An alloy is made from 35 g nickel and 175 g of copper.
  a Write the ratio of nickel to copper as a ratio in its simplest form.
  b What goes in the gap?
     There is ____ as much nickel as copper in the alloy.

4 Write each ratio in its simplest form.
  a $1\frac{1}{2} : 2$ **b** 3·5 : 3   **c** $\frac{1}{4} : 1\frac{1}{4}$ **d** 4·5 : 2·5   *__e__ $1\frac{3}{4} : 1\frac{1}{2}$

5 Write each of these as a ratio in its simplest form.
  a 3 mm : 1 cm   **b** 15 min : 1 hour   **c** 350 mℓ : 1 litre

6 Petria used 1·2 ℓ of red paint and 500 mℓ of blue paint to make purple paint.
Write the ratio of red to blue paint as a ratio in its simplest form.

7 A recipe uses 1·2 kg of flour and 400 g of sugar.
Write in its simplest form, the ratio of flour to sugar.

8 Two parts of this square design are shaded black.
Two parts are shaded grey.

[SATs Paper 1 Level 6]

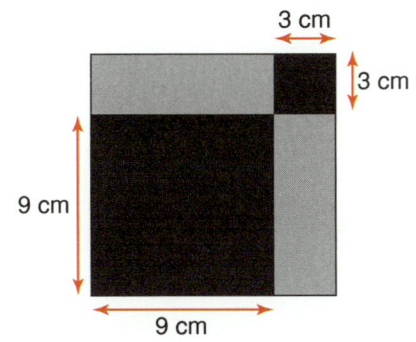

Show that the ratio of black to grey is 5 : 3.

*__9__ Find the ratio $x : y$ if
  a $x = 12$ and $y = 28$ **b** $x = z^2$ and $y = 3z$ **c** $x = 12z$ and $y = 20z^2$

*__10__ Write these ratios in the form $m : 1$. Round to 1 d.p. if you need to round.
  a 8 : 3   **b** 17 : 3   **c** 40 : 19   **d** 83 : 25   **e** 124 : 87

*__11__ Write these ratios in the form $1 : m$. Round to 1 d.p. if you need to round.
  a 5 : 12   **b** 7 : 41   **c** 8 : 23   **d** 18 : 53   **e** 23 : 85

135

Number

∗12 Sanjay wanted to know which pair of trousers has the greater proportion of wool.
He started by writing both ratios in the form $m : 1$

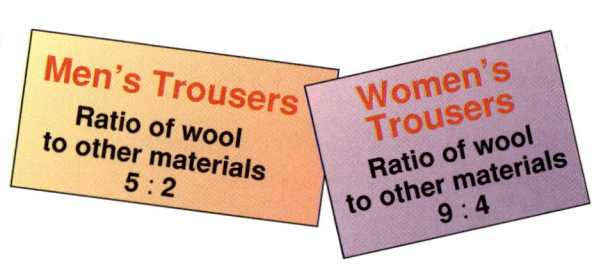

```
    5 : 2              9 : 4
÷2 (    ) ÷2       ÷4 (    ) ÷4
  = __ : __          = __ : __
```

Men's Trousers Ratio of wool to other materials 5 : 2

Women's Trousers Ratio of wool to other materials 9 : 4

Which pair of trousers has the greater proportion of wool? Explain.

∗13 The ratio of bread to meat in two brands of sausages is given.

Meat 4U Sausages 25 : 36

Meat Today Sausages 40 : 72

By changing each ratio to the form $1 : m$, decide which brand has the higher proportion of meat. Explain.

∗14 The ratio of tries converted to tries scored but not converted by two rugby teams, A and B, are respectively 18 : 5 and 15 : 4. By changing each ratio to the form $m : 1$, say which team has the better goal kicker. Explain.

Review 1 Write each ratio in its simplest form.
a 15 : 42   **b** 8 : 12 : 28   **c** 24 : 72 : 120   **d** $2 : 3\frac{1}{2}$ **e** 7·5 : 8
f $1\frac{1}{2} : 2\frac{1}{2}$ **g** 7 g : 1 kg   **h** 20 mins : 1 hour   **i** 15 cm : 1 metre

Review 2 A punch recipe needs 375 mℓ grape juice and 1·5 ℓ of ginger ale.
a Write *amount grape juice : amount of ginger ale* as a ratio in its simplest form.
b What goes in the gaps?
    There is ____ as much ginger ale as grape juice.
    There is ____ as much grape juice as ginger ale.

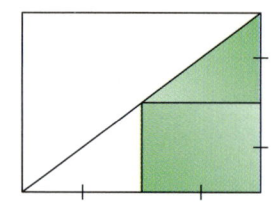

Review 3 Find the ratio
shaded area : unshaded area
in its simplest form.

Review 4 The ratios of other material to elastine in two fabrics, A and B, are 26 : 3 and 39 : 4 respectively. We want to find which has the greater proportion of elastine.
a Write 26 : 3 in the ratio $m : 1$.
```
    26 : 3
÷3 (    ) ÷3
  = __ : 1
```

b Write 39 : 4 in the ratio $m : 1$.
```
    39 : 4
÷4 (    ) ÷4
  = __ : 1
```

c Explain how you know which fabric has the greater proportion of elastine.

Percentage and Proportional Changes

Solving ratio and proportion problems

Remember

We can **divide an amount in a given ratio**.

Example   Jane's aunt Daisy died and left Jane and her brother John £8650 to share in the ratio 3 : 2.

Total number of shares = 3 + 2 = 5
Jane gets $\frac{3}{5}$ and John gets $\frac{2}{5}$.
$\frac{1}{5}$ of £8650 = £1730
$\frac{3}{5}$ of £8650 = 3 × £1730 = £5190
$\frac{2}{5}$ of £8650 = 2 × £1730 = £3460
Jane gets £5190 and John gets £3460.   5190 + 3460 = 8650

In this type of problem you are given a total amount and a ratio.

Worked Example

In a photo a 1·8 m tall man is 3 cm tall.
In the same photo, a child is 2·1 cm tall.
How tall is the child in real life?

You could use the constant multiplier method.

Answer

In real life the man is 1·8 m or 180 cm tall and in the photo he is 3 cm.

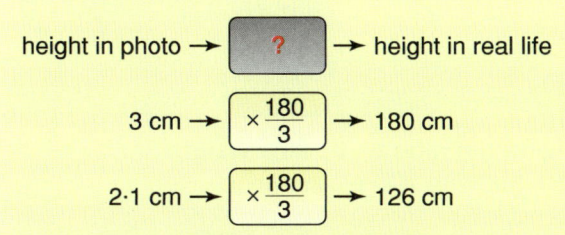

height in photo → [?] → height in real life

3 cm → [× $\frac{180}{3}$] → 180 cm

2·1 cm → [× $\frac{180}{3}$] → 126 cm

The child is **1·26** m tall in real life.

The following exercise gives you practice at **solving ratio and proportion problems**.

Exercise 7

1 Adults normally have 32 teeth.
  8 incisors   4 canines
  8 bicuspids   12 molars
  a Write each of these as a ratio in its simplest form.
   i incisors to molars   **ii** bicuspids to canines   **iii** molars to all teeth
  b What proportion of adult teeth are
   i incisors   **ii** canines   **iii** molars?
   Give each answer as a fraction, decimal and percentage.

Remember: Ratio compares part to part and proportion compares part to whole.

2 Shortcrust pastry is made from flour and butter in the ratio 2 : 1.
  How much flour will make 300 g of pastry?

3 Ross makes a potting mix for his plants from loam, peat and sand in the ratio 7 : 3 : 2 respectively.
  a He uses $1\frac{1}{2}$ kg of peat to make the compost.
   How much loam and sand does he use?
  b How much of each does he use to make 24 kg of compost?

137

Number

4 The angles in a triangle are in the ratio 1 : 2 : 3.
Find the sizes of the three angles.

5 Screenwash is used to clean car windows. [SATs Paper 2 Level 5]
To use Screenwash you mix it with water.

Winter mixture
Mix 1 part Screenwash with 4 parts water

Summer mixture
Mix 1 part Screenwash with 9 parts water

  a In **winter**, how much water should I mix with **150 mℓ of Screenwash**?
  b In **summer**, how much Screenwash should I mix with **450 mℓ of water**?
  c Is this statement correct? Explain your answer.

    25% of **winter** mixture is **Screenwash**

6 Scott uses 12 onions to make $1\frac{1}{2}$ ℓ of chutney.
  a How much chutney can be made with 48 onions?
  b How many onions are needed to make $4\frac{1}{2}$ ℓ of chutney?

7 This is a recipe for 6 people.
How much of each ingredient would you need for 9 people?

Pancakes
3 cups flour
2 tsp baking powder
1 cup milk

8 Eight bars of chocolate cost £5·60.
  a How much do twenty cost?
  b Mick has £16. How many can he buy for this?

9 Flaky pastry is made by using flour, butter and fat in the ratio 8 : 3 : 2 by weight.
How many grams of butter and fat are needed to mix with 200 g of flour?

10 In a game Khalid scored 12, Nicole scored 16 and Paige scored 20.
The ratio of their scores is 12 : 16 : 20 or 3 : 4 : 5.
  a What proportion of Nicole's score did Khalid score?
  b What proportion of the total did Khalid score?
  c What proportion of Khalid's score did Paige score?

11 P and Q are two wheels.
For every 3 complete turns that wheel P makes, wheel Q makes 5 complete turns.
Wheel P makes 225 turns.
How many turns does wheel Q make?

12 A recipe for pickle uses 550 g of tomatoes for every 1000 g of pickle made.
I want to make ten 454 g jars of pickle.
How many grams of tomatoes do I need?

13 The ratio of the dimensions of the picture shown are 7 : 3.
Find the length, ℓ, of the picture.

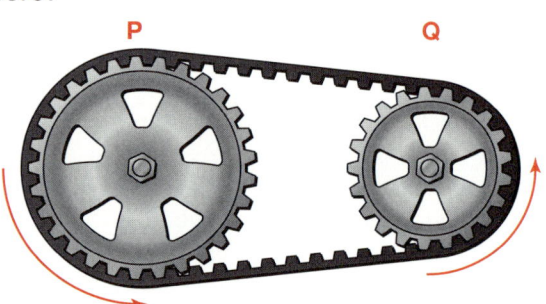

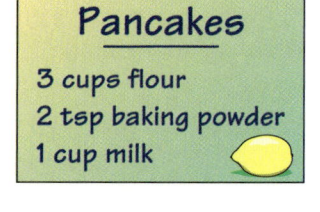

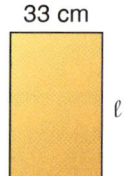

33 cm

138

Percentage and Proportional Changes

14 The tins in a full box weighed 20 kg in total.
Each tin was identical.
Eight tins are eaten.
The tins left weigh 15 kg altogether.
How many tins were in the original box?

15 Logan was growing a plant for a science experiment.
On 1 August, he measured the height as 10 cm.
On 1 September, the height had increased by 30%.
What was the ratio of the height of the plant on 1 August to height on 1 September?

16 A 20 m high tree casts a 15 m shadow.
At the same time a flagpole casts a 12 m shadow.
How high is the flagpole?

*__17__ 2 parts yellow paint mixed with 3 parts blue paint makes green paint.
   a How much of each is needed to make a litre of paint?
   b Henry has 100 mℓ of yellow paint and 200 mℓ of blue paint.
      What is the maximum amount of green paint he can make?
   c Lindy has $1\frac{1}{2}$ ℓ of yellow paint and 1125 mℓ of blue paint.
      What is the maximum amount of green paint she can make?

*__18__ A regular packet of mints weighs 750 g. A special pack weighs 30% more.
What is the ratio of the masses of a special pack to a regular pack?

*__19__ These two pentagonal-based prisms have the same shape for the base.
Prism A is 8 cm high and has a volume of 400 cm^3.
What is the volume of Prism B?

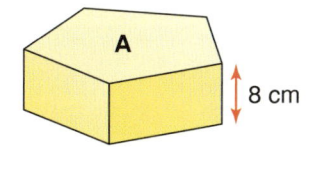

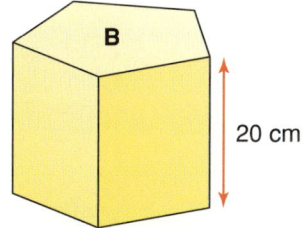

*__20__ Olivia's group played a game of 'Guess my length'.
This table shows the results.
They divided each guess by the actual length to get an accuracy ratio.

Name	Guess	Actual length
Olivia	6 cm	7·2 cm
Grace	40 cm	29 cm
Ryan	2 m	3 m
Keith	20 cm	25 cm

Example
Olivia's accuracy ratio = 0·83 : 1 (2 d.p.)
   a Find the accuracy ratio for each of the others.
   b Which guess was most accurate? Explain your answer.
   c Which guess was least accurate?

Review 1
a At a party, the ratio of smokers to non-smokers was 2 : 7. There were 6 smokers.
How many were at the party?
b Eighty lettuce seeds are planted. The ratio of the number that germinate to the number that do not germinate is 13 : 7. How many seeds germinate?

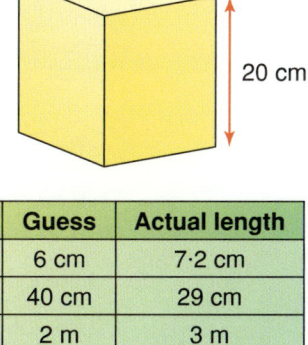

Number

Review 2 Janet and John bought a National Lottery ticket. Janet spent £15 and John £27. They agreed to share any winnings in the ratio of what they spent. They won a total of £1589. What was Janet's share of the winnings?

Review 3
a Gold sovereigns are made of a mixture of gold and copper in the ratio 11 : 1.
   What is the mass of gold in 25 kg of sovereigns (1 d.p.)?
b Pennies are made of copper, tin and zinc in the ratio 91 : 4 : 1.
   How much copper is there in 250 kg of pennies?
c What mass of pennies will contain 50 kg of tin?

Review 4 To make 16 muffins I need 250 g flour and 100 g sultanas.
a How much flour will I need to make 28 muffins?
b I have 180 g sultanas. How many muffins can I make? Round your answer sensibly.

*** Review 5**
a There is a tall tree in the garden. The tree's shadow is 12 m long. My shadow is 1·5 m.
   How tall is the tree if I am 1·85 m tall?
b This rectangle has perimeter 80 cm.
   What is the length of the rectangle if the ratio   *length : width* = 3 : 2?

Puzzle

If the front chain wheel (the wheel the chain goes around) on the bike has 40 teeth and the back cog has 10 teeth, the cog will go around 4 times faster than the chain wheel. The gear ratio is 4 : 1.

Front chain wheels		Rear cogs	
Big	48 teeth	1	28 teeth
Medium	38 teeth	2	24 teeth
Small	28 teeth	3	21 teeth
		4	18 teeth
		5	16 teeth
		6	14 teeth

This chart gives the number of teeth on the three front chain wheels and six rear cogs of an 18-speed bike.

1 Write down the 18 gear ratios possible.

2 One of the gear ratios is 28 : 21 or 4 : 3. This means for every 3 times the front chain wheel rotates, the back cog rotates 4 times.
   Notice that the ratio of the number of turns is the opposite way round to the ratio of the number of teeth.
   Work these out.
   i How many turns does the big front chain wheel make when it is attached to cog 5 and cog 5 makes 288 turns?
   ii How many turns does the rear cog 2 make if the small front chain wheel is attached to it and turns 1440 times?

*3 Each time the rear cog turns, the back wheel of the bike travels 210 cm. How many turns does the medium front chain wheel make if it is attached to cog 4 and the bike travels 4 km?

Percentage and Proportional Changes

Summary of key points

A We often need to find the percentage of an amount or find a proportion to solve a problem.

B We can calculate a **percentage increase or decrease**.
To **increase an amount** by 35% we multiply by 135% or 1·35 (100% + 35%).
To **decrease an amount** by 20% we multiply by 80% or 0·8 (100% − 20%).

Example   Increase 45 by 30%.
$$45 \times 1 \cdot 3 = 58 \cdot 5$$
100% + 30% = 130% = 1·3

C We can give an **increase or decrease as a percentage increase or decrease**.

$$\% \text{ increase} = \frac{\text{actual increase}}{\text{original amount}} \times 100\%$$

$$\% \text{ decrease} = \frac{\text{actual decrease}}{\text{original amount}} \times 100\%$$

Example   The price of a braid increased from 69p to 98p per metre over a one year period.

$$\% \text{ increase} = \frac{\text{actual increase}}{\text{original amount}} \times 100\%$$
$$= \frac{29}{69} \times 100\% \qquad 98 - 69 = 29$$
$$= \mathbf{42\% \text{ to the nearest per cent}}$$

D We can find the original amount if we know the amount after the percentage change. We use **inverse operations** or the **unitary method** or **algebra**.

Example   After a 25% increase, a box of chocolates was £3·40.
We can find the original price in one of these ways.

Unitary method	Inverse operations	Algebra

Find 1% first.
£3·40 represents 125%.
£3·40 ÷ 125 represents 1%.
£3·40 ÷ 125 × 100
    represents 100%.
£3·40 ÷ 125 × 100 = **£2·72**
	Original price of chocolates ×1·25 / ÷1·25 → New price £3·40
	Price of chocolates originally × 1·25
	   = £3·40
	Price of chocolates last year = $\frac{£3 \cdot 40}{1 \cdot 25}$
	   = **£2·72**
		$1 \cdot 25 \times c = £3 \cdot 40$ where c represents original price of chocolates
		
		$c = \frac{£3 \cdot 40}{1 \cdot 25}$
		   = **£2·72**

141

Number

E **Proportional reasoning** can be used to solve problems.
The **unitary method** or **constant multiplier method** can be used.
Example If 8 muffins cost £6·75 we can find the cost of 12 muffins like this.

Unitary method
Cost of 1 muffin = $\frac{£6·75}{8}$
Cost of 12 muffins = $12 \times \frac{£6·75}{8}$ = **£10·13 (nearest penny)**

Constant multiplier method
Ratio of number of muffins required to number given = 12 : 8
The constant multiplier is $\frac{12}{8}$.
Cost of 12 muffins = $\frac{12}{8} \times £6·75$
= **£10·13 (nearest penny)**

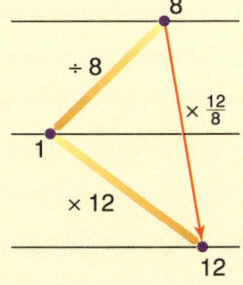

F We **simplify ratios by cancelling**.
Example   12 : 16
                ÷4   ÷4
          =   3 : 4

To **compare ratios** we write each in the form 1 : m or m : 1.
Example The ratios of butter to sugar in recipe A and recipe B are 2 : 3 and 7 : 11.
To compare these we write both in the form 1 : m.

Recipe A	**Recipe B**
2 : 3	7 : 11
÷2 ÷2	÷7 ÷7
1 : 1·5	1 : 1·6 (1 d.p.)

There is a greater proportion of butter in recipe A because $\frac{1}{1·5} > \frac{1}{1·6}$.

G We can solve **ratio and proportion** problems.
Ratio compares part to part.
Proportion compares part to whole.

Test yourself

1 About 48% of calcium carbonate is oxygen.
   If a sample of calcium carbonate weighs 6·5 g, what is the mass of oxygen in it?   **A**

2 a Write the ratio of the length of this photo to its width
      in its simplest form.   **B F**
   b The photo is to be enlarged by 15%.
      What will the length of the enlargement be?

   12 cm
   8 cm

142

Percentage and Proportional Changes

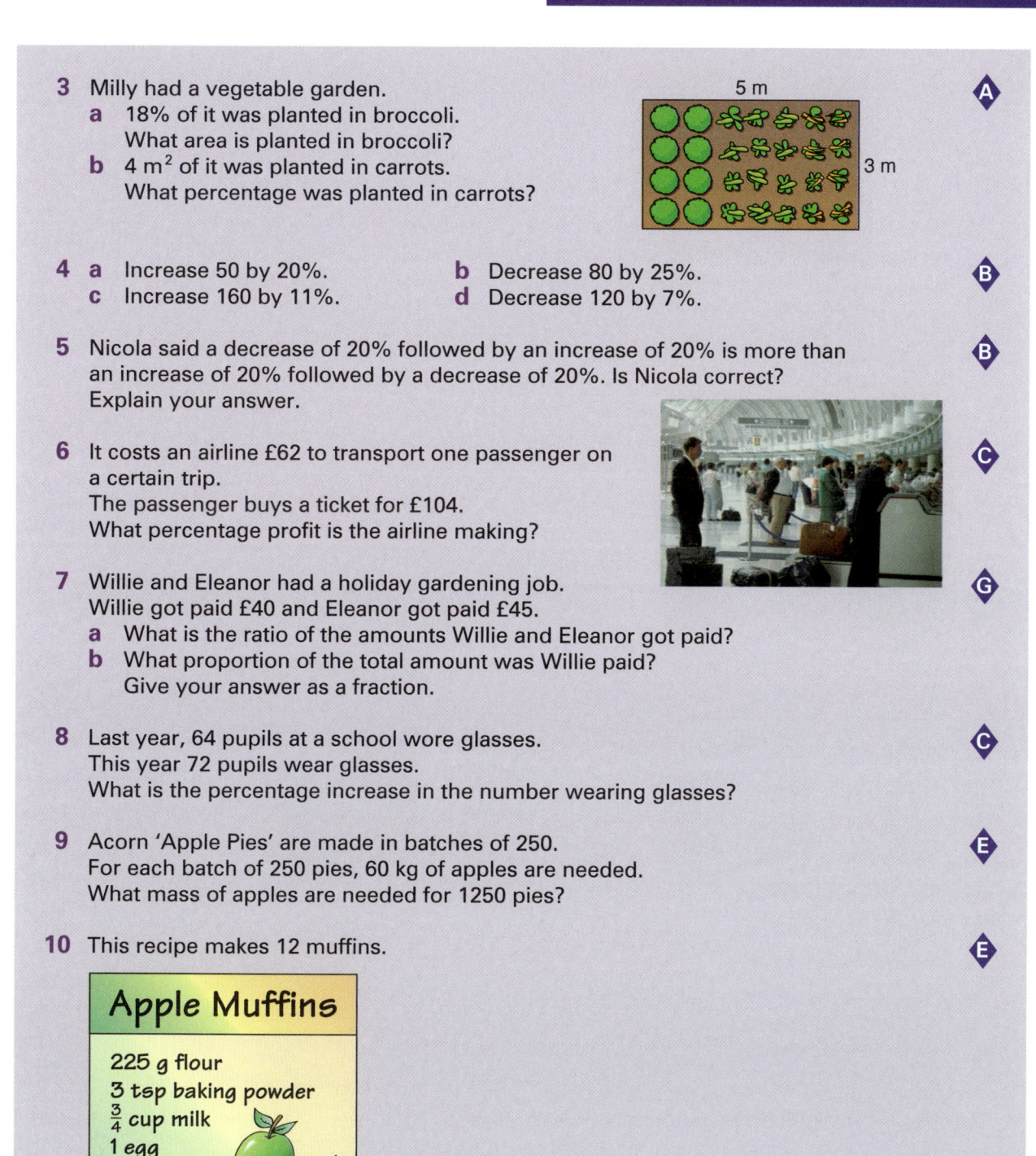

3 Milly had a vegetable garden.
   a 18% of it was planted in broccoli.
      What area is planted in broccoli?
   b 4 m² of it was planted in carrots.
      What percentage was planted in carrots?

5 m
3 m

4 **a** Increase 50 by 20%.   **b** Decrease 80 by 25%.
    c Increase 160 by 11%.   **d** Decrease 120 by 7%.

5 Nicola said a decrease of 20% followed by an increase of 20% is more than an increase of 20% followed by a decrease of 20%. Is Nicola correct? Explain your answer.

6 It costs an airline £62 to transport one passenger on a certain trip.
The passenger buys a ticket for £104.
What percentage profit is the airline making?

7 Willie and Eleanor had a holiday gardening job.
Willie got paid £40 and Eleanor got paid £45.
   a What is the ratio of the amounts Willie and Eleanor got paid?
   b What proportion of the total amount was Willie paid?
      Give your answer as a fraction.

8 Last year, 64 pupils at a school wore glasses.
This year 72 pupils wear glasses.
What is the percentage increase in the number wearing glasses?

9 Acorn 'Apple Pies' are made in batches of 250.
For each batch of 250 pies, 60 kg of apples are needed.
What mass of apples are needed for 1250 pies?

10 This recipe makes 12 muffins.

Apple Muffins
225 g flour
3 tsp baking powder
$\frac{3}{4}$ cup milk
1 egg
120 g sugar
1 chopped apple
45 g butter

Adapt the recipe to make 16 muffins. Round sensibly.

Number

11 This table shows what was sold at a stall at a school fair.

Item	Number sold	Takings
Cakes	32	£170·50
Packets of 6 muffins	27	£148·50
Packets of 6 cookies	22	£116·00
Bagged sweets	45	£ 98·00
Total	126	£533·00

   a What percentage of the total number of items sold was bagged sweets? Show your working.
   b What percentage of the total takings was for bagged sweets? Show your working.
   c Which is cheaper, a packet of muffins or a packet of cookies? Show your working to explain how you know.

12 These are the labels on two snack bars.
   a How many grams of fat would a 120 g Tandem bar provide? Show your working.
   b If both bars are 120 g, which bar would provide more carbohydrate?

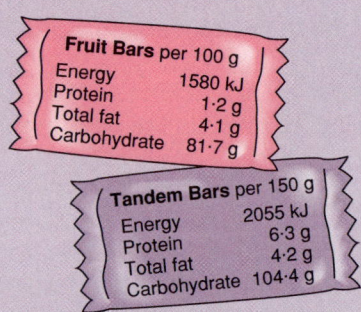

Fruit Bars per 100 g
Energy 1580 kJ
Protein 1·2 g
Total fat 4·1 g
Carbohydrate 81·7 g

Tandem Bars per 150 g
Energy 2055 kJ
Protein 6·3 g
Total fat 4·2 g
Carbohydrate 104·4 g

13 Which is the better buy? By how much?

Cash price **£240** +VAT of $17\frac{1}{2}$%

Deposit of **£30** plus 6 payments of **£45**

14 Write each ratio in its simplest form.
   a 30 : 45   **b** 18 : 54   **c** 3 : 15 : 27   **d** $1\frac{1}{2}$: 4
   e 2·5 : 6   **f** 20 min : 1 hour   **g** 75 cm : 1 m   *__h__ 45 mm : 1 cm
   *__i__ $1\frac{1}{4}$: $2\frac{3}{4}$

15 Juice is mixed in the ratio shown.
Sam has 50 mℓ of concentrate.
What is the biggest amount of juice he can make?

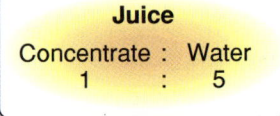

Juice
Concentrate : Water
     1   :   5

16 Last year, the amounts Mr Tan spent on road tax, petrol and car insurance were in the ratio 1 : 8 : 3. He spent a total of £1452 on these three things.
How much did he spend on petrol?

17 Susie and Michelle bought a £10 raffle ticket.
Susie paid £4 and Michelle paid £6.
They won a prize of £240.
How much of the prize should Michelle get?

18 In 2000, a junior tennis club subscription was £80 and a senior subscription was £200.
Tanya thinks that the senior subscription was 150% more than the junior subscription.
Is she correct?

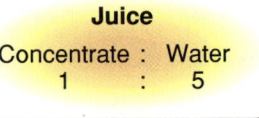

144

Percentage and Proportional Changes

19 Part of this rectangle is shaded red and part blue.
Show that the ratio of red to blue is 7 : 11.

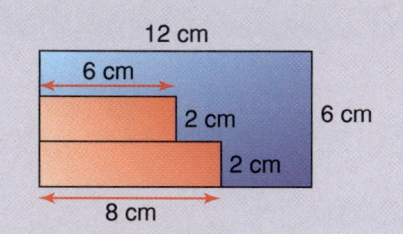

20 Alex is 12 years old.
His sister, Olivia, is exactly 4 years older.
The ratio of Alex's age to Olivia's is 12 : 16.
This can be written as 3 : 4.
  a When Alex is 20, what will be the ratio of Alex's age to Olivia's age?
  Write the ratio as simply as possible.
  b When Olivia is 42, what will be the ratio of Alex's age to Olivia's?
  Write the ratio as simply as possible.
  c Could the ratio of Alex to Olivia's age ever be 7 : 5? Explain how you know.

21 After a 20% increase, a television sold for £228.
Isobel started working out the price of the television before the increase like this.

  Price before increase × 1·2 = £228

  so price before increase = £228 ___ ___

Finish Isobel's working to find the price before the increase.

22 This carton of juice contains 20% more juice.
How much juice does an ordinary carton contain?

20% more juice — 600 ml

23 The ratio of netball goals scored to goals attempted by Rebecca
and Katie one season were 15 : 21 and 19 : 23 respectively.
By changing each ratio to m : 1, decide who is the better goal shooter.
Explain your answer.

145

Algebra Support

In algebra **letters stand for numbers**.

Equations

$m + 6 = 14$ is an **equation**. m has a particular value.

We can **solve equations** using **inverse operations** or by **transforming both sides**.

Example $2p + 5 = 11$

Inverse operations
$2p + 5 = 11$
$2p = 11 - 5$ The inverse of adding 5 is subtracting 5.
$2p = 6$
$p = \frac{6}{2}$ The inverse of multiplying by 2 is dividing by 2.
$p = 3$

Transforming both sides
$2p + 5 = 11$
$2p + 5 - 5 = 11 - 5$ Subtract 5 from both sides.
$2p = 6$
$\frac{2p}{2} = \frac{6}{2}$ Divide both sides by 2.
$p = 3$

Practice Questions 2, 18, 19, 28, 29

Expressions

Algebraic operations follow the same rules as **arithmetic operations**.

arithmetic	algebra
$3 + 4 = 4 + 3$	$a + b = b + a$
$2 + 4 + 6 = 4 + 6 + 2$	$p + q + r = q + r + p$
$4 \times 7 = 7 \times 4$	$xy = yx$
$5 \times 6 \times 2 = 6 \times 2 \times 5$	$cde = dec$

Writing expressions
Alex has m model cars. He is given 4 more.
Alex now has $m + 4$ model cars.

$m + 4$ is an **expression**.

We **write expressions without multiplication or division signs**.

add 2 to a number	$n + 2$
subtract 6 from a number	$n - 6$
multiply a number by 3	$n \times 3$ is written as $3n$
divide a number by 5	$n \div 5$ is written as $\frac{n}{5}$
multiply a number by 3 then add 4	$n \times 3 + 4$ is written as $3n + 4$
add 6 to a number then multiply by 3	$(n + 6) \times 3$ is written as $3(n + 6)$
multiply a number by itself	n^2
multiply a number by itself then double the answer	$2n^2$

Practice Questions 1, 11, 12, 20, 27

Algebra Support

Simplifying expressions

We can simplify expressions by **cancelling**.

Examples $\quad \dfrac{{}^1 m}{{}_1 m} = 1 \qquad \dfrac{2n^1}{n_1} = 2 \qquad \dfrac{{}^1 3p}{{}_1 3} = p$

> We divide the numerator and the denominator by the same thing.

We can simplify expressions by **collecting like terms**.

Examples $\quad 3b + 2b - 4 = 5b - 4$

$\qquad\qquad 6a + 4b - 2a = 6a - 2a + 4b \quad$ We write like terms together.
$\qquad\qquad\qquad\qquad\qquad\;\, = 4a + 4b$

> a and b are *not* like terms.

When there are **brackets** we multiply all the terms inside the bracket by the term outside the bracket.

Examples $\quad 5(x - 2) = 5 \times x + 5 \times {}^-2 \qquad 7(2x + 3) = 7 \times 2x + 7 \times 3$
$\qquad\qquad\qquad\quad\;\, = 5x - 10 \qquad\qquad\qquad\qquad\quad\; = 14x + 21$

Practice Questions 4, 5, 6, 21, 33

Substituting into expressions

We can **find the value of an expression** by **substituting** values for the unknown.
We follow the **order of operations** rules.

Examples If $n = 3$ then
$\quad 2n + 4 = 2 \times 3 + 4 \qquad\qquad \dfrac{16n}{9} = \dfrac{16 \times 3^1}{9_3}$
$\qquad\qquad\;\; = 6 + 4 \qquad\qquad\qquad\qquad\;\; = \dfrac{16}{3}$
$\qquad\qquad\;\; = 10 \qquad\qquad\qquad\qquad\qquad = 5\tfrac{1}{3}$

> See page 7 for the order of operations rules.

Practice Question 13

Formulae

A **formula** is a rule for working something out.

Example Pete the plumber works out his charges using this formula:

charge = call out fee + £8 × number of hours worked

If the call out fee is £32 and he works for 5 hours, then
$\quad$ charge = £32 + £8 × 5
$\qquad\qquad\;\, = £72$

Example $V = IR$ is a formula for working out voltage, V, given current, I, and resistance, R.
If I is 5 amps and R is 1·5 ohms, then
$\quad V = 5 \times 1·5$
$\qquad = 7·5$ volts

Practice Questions 3, 41

Sequences

A **sequence** is a set of numbers in a given order.
Each number is called a **term**.

Example 2, 6, 10, 14, 18, ... ← The dots mean the sequence continues forever. It is infinite.
$\qquad\quad\;\;\uparrow\qquad\;\;\uparrow$
$\qquad\;\,$ 1st term $\;$ 4th term

147

Algebra

We can write a sequence by **counting on** or **counting back**.

Examples   Starting at 3 and counting on in steps of 4 gives   3, 7, 11, 15, …

Starting at 7 and counting back in steps of 3 gives   7, 4, 1, ⁻2, …

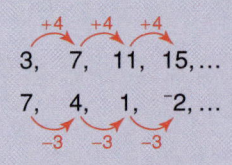

We can write a sequence by **multiplying** or **dividing** each term by the same number.

Examples   Starting at 1 and multiplying each term by 2 gives   1, 2, 4, 8, …

Starting at 10 000 and dividing each term by 10 gives   10 000, 1000, 100, 10, …

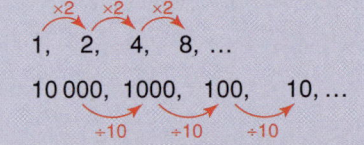

We can write a sequence if we are given the first term and the rule for finding the next term.

Example   **1st term** 5,   **rule** add 7   gives   5, 12, 19, 26, 33, …

We can generate a sequence by **adding a constant term**. The sequence will always be linear (go up in equal steps).
Linear sequences are called **arithmetic sequences** and are generated by starting with a number, a, and adding a constant number, d.

Example   If $a = 5$ and $d = 3$ the sequence is 5, 8, 11, 14, 17, …

We can write a sequence if we know the **rule for the nth term**.

Example   If the rule for the nth term is $n + 3$ the sequence is   4, 5, 6, 7, 8, 9, …

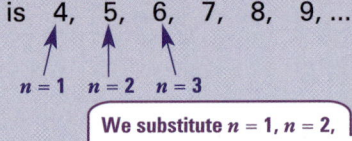

$n = 1$ $n = 2$ $n = 3$

We substitute $n = 1$, $n = 2$, $n = 3$, … to find the terms.

Sequences in practical situations
We can find the rule for the nth shape in a sequence of diagrams.

Example

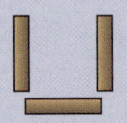

shape 1
3 rods

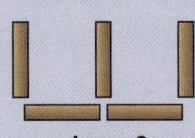

shape 2
5 rods

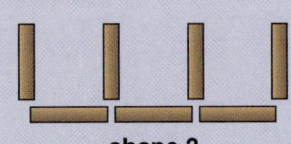

shape 3
7 rods

The sequence for the number of rods is 3, 5, 7, …
Two rods are added to get the next shape.
The first shape needs one extra rod.
For n shapes there will be $2n$ rods plus 1 extra for the first shape.
The rule is $2n + 1$.

Practice Questions 7, 8, 16, 17, 22, 23, 38, 39

Functions

This is a **function machine**.

$x \rightarrow$ multiply by 3 $\rightarrow$ add 1 $\rightarrow y$
   ×3   +1

The rule for the function machine is written as
$y \rightarrow 3x + 1$ or $x \rightarrow 3x + 1$.

Algebra Support

If we are given the input we can find the output.

Example

2, 0, 5, 4 → [add 1] → [multiply by 2] → 6, 2, 12, 10

$(2 + 1) \times 2 = 6$
$(0 + 1) \times 2 = 2$
$(5 + 1) \times 2 = 12$
$(4 + 1) \times 2 = 10$

We can show the input and output in a **table** or on a **mapping diagram**.

Input	Output
2	6
0	2
5	12
4	10

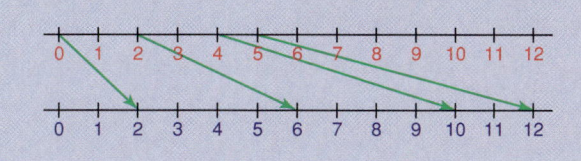

Practice Questions 9, 24, 30, 31, 32, 34, 36

Graphs

(2, 5) is a **coordinate pair**.

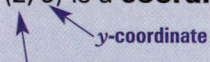

y-coordinate
x-coordinate

Each of these **coordinate pairs** satisfies the rule $y = x - 2$.
(0, −2), (1, −1), (2, 0), (3, 1)
Each *y*-coordinate is found by subtracting 2 from the *x*-coordinate.

To draw the **straight-line graph** of $y = x - 1$:

i Find 2 or more coordinate pairs that satisfy the equation $y = x - 1$.

Examples
$x = 1, y = x - 1$
$= 1 - 1$
$= 0$

$x = 3, y = x - 1$
$= 3 - 1$
$= 2$

$x = -2, y = x - 1$
$= -2 - 1$
$= -3$

x	1	3	−2
y	0	2	−3

ii Plot the coordinate pairs.
Draw a straight line through the points.
Label your line.

The **equation of the line** shown is $y = x - 1$.
The coordinate pairs of **all** points on the line satisfy the equation of the line.

$y = mx$ is the equation of a straight line through (0, 0).
m can have any value.
The greater the value of *m*, the steeper the slope.

Lines **parallel to the *x*-axis** have equation $y = a$ where *a* is any number.

Examples $y = 3$ $y = -2$

Lines **parallel to the *y*-axis** have equation $x = b$ where *b* is any number.

Examples $x = 2$ $x = -2\frac{1}{2}$

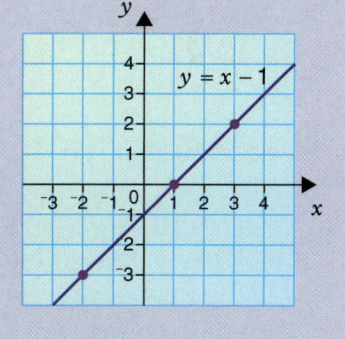

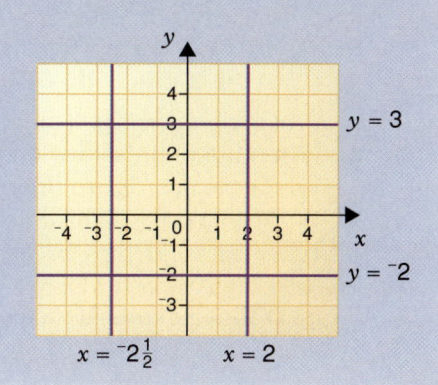

149

Algebra

Graphs of real-life situations

Example The graph shows the charges to hire a car. The points (0, £10), (2, £40), (4, £70) have been plotted and a straight line has been drawn through them.

We can estimate other values from the graph.

Example If I hire a car for 3 days the charge is about £55.

Practice Questions 10, 14, 15, 25, 26, 35, 37, 40, 42, 43

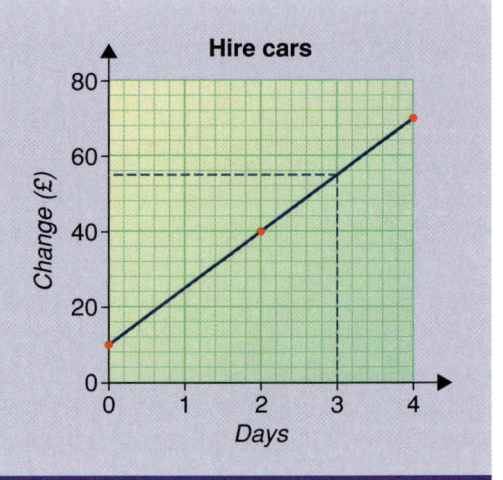

Practice Questions

1 Write true or false for these.
  a $p + q = q + p$ **b** $4c = 4 + c$ **c** $4xy = \frac{xy}{4}$ **d** $ab = ba$

2 Solve these equations.
  a $a + 5 = 12$ **b** $k - 7 = 8$ **c** $4p = 20$ **d** $\frac{x}{5} = 8$
  e $2p + 3 = 7$ **f** $3k - 1 = 5$ **g** $4p + 3 = 15$ **h** $5w - 2 = 8$

3 Bob's Bin Collections used this formula to work out what to charge.
  charge = hire of bin + £4 × number of times bin collected
  If the charge for the hire of the bin is £50 per year, and Mr Martin has his bin collected 26 times a year, how much does Mr Martin pay each year to Bob's Bin Collections?

4 Simplify these.
  a $2a + 3a$ **b** $6p + 2p$ **c** $4m - m$ **d** $3a + a + 2a$
  e $4p + 2p - p$ **f** $4x + 3 + 3x$ **g** $2a + 4b + 2a - 2b$

5 Here are some algebra cards.

  $n + 3$ $2n + 2$ $2n - 1$ $3n$ $4n + 3$

  $3n + n$ $n \div 3$ $n + n + n$ n^2 $3n + 3$

  a Which card will always give the same answer as each of these?
    i $\frac{n}{3}$ **ii** $3 + n$ **iii** $4n - n + 3$ **iv** $6n - 2n + 3$ **v** $n \times n$
  b Which two cards will always give the same answer as $3 \times n$?
  c When the expressions on two cards are added, they can be simplified to give $6n + 2$. Which two cards are they?
  d Write a new card that will always give the same answer as
    i $3n + 5n$ **ii** $5n - 2n$ **iii** $2n^2$.

6 Simplify these expressions by cancelling.
  a $\frac{x}{x}$ **b** $\frac{p}{p}$ **c** $\frac{3a}{a}$ **d** $\frac{4y}{4}$ **e** $\frac{7q}{q}$

Algebra Support

7 Write down the first six terms of these sequences.
  a Start at 1 and count on in steps of 4.
  b Start at 8 and count back in steps of 2.
  c Start at 5 and count on in steps of 1.5.

8 Write down the first five terms of these sequences.
  a **1st term** 2, **rule** add 3
  b **1st term** 1, **rule** multiply by 2
  c **1st term** 40, **rule** subtract 4
  d **1st term** 3, **rule** add 0·5
  e **1st term** 2500, **rule** divide by 5

9 Find the output for these.
  a 3 → [add 5] → ?
   0 → [add 5] → ?
   7 → [add 5] → ?
  b 4 → [subtract 1] → [multiply by 3] → ?
   10 → [subtract 1] → [multiply by 3] → ?
   $1\frac{1}{2}$ → [subtract 1] → [multiply by 3] → ?

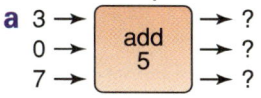

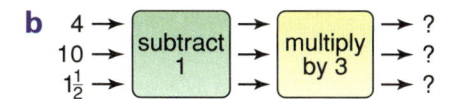

10 Look at this diagram.
  a The point T is halfway between P and S. What are the coordinates of T?
  b PQRS is a rectangle. What are the coordinates of R?

P (2, 5)   Q (6, 5)
S (2, 2)   R

11 Write these without a multiplication sign.
  a $5 \times n$ **b** $y \times 6$ **c** $2 \times (x + 1)$
  d $x \times x$ **e** $(m - 2) \times 6$ **f** $2 \times 3n$
  g $x \times x \times 2$ **h** $5 \times b \times b$

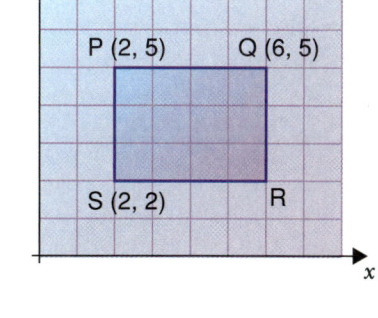

12 Write an expression for these.
Let the unknown number be n.
  a add 7 to a number
  b subtract 4 from a number
  c divide a number by 3
  d multiply a number by 6
  e multiply a number by 2 then add 6
  f add 2 to a number then multiply by 5
  g multiply a number by itself
  h divide a number by 2 then subtract 5

13 a If $x = 2$ and $y = 4$ find the value of these.
  i xy **ii** $y + x$ **iii** $3(y - x)$ **iv** $\frac{y+4}{x}$ **v** $2x + y$
  b If $a = 0.5$ and $b = 6$ find the value of these.
  i $a + b$ **ii** $b - a$ **iii** $2ab$ **iv** $4a + b$ *__v__ $\frac{b}{a}$

14 Copy and complete these coordinate pairs so they satisfy the given function.
  a $y = 3x$ (2, ___), (1, ___), (0, ___), (⁻1, ___), (⁻2, ___)
  b $y = x + 1$ (2, ___), (1, ___), (0, ___), (⁻1, ___), (⁻2, ___)
  c $y = 3x + 4$ (2, ___), (1, ___), (0, ___), (⁻1, ___), (⁻2, ___)

15 Which of these coordinate points lie on the line $y = x - 4$?
  a (1, 5)   **b** (6, 2)   **c** (1, ⁻3)

Remember $y = x - 4$ means the y coordinate is 4 less than the x coordinate.

16 The nth term of a sequence is given.
Write the first 5 terms.
  a $n + 1$ **b** $2n$ **c** $2n - 1$ **d** $n - 2$ **e** $10 - n$

17 Match the descriptions with the sequences given in the box.
  a the sequence starts at 4 and increases in steps of 3
  b the odd numbers from 3 to 13
  c the sequence starts at 18 and decreases in steps of 5
  d each term is one less than a multiple of 6

A 18, 13, 8, 3, ⁻2, ⁻7, …
B 4, 7, 10, 13, 16, 19, …
C 5, 11, 17, 23, 29, 35, …
D 3, 5, 7, 9, 11, 13, …
E 18, 23, 28, 33, 38, …

151

Algebra

18 a A vegetable garden is 4 m wide.
A wooden border of 20 m is needed to go right round the edge of the garden.
If l is the length of the garden, which of these is correct?
   A $4 + l = 20$ **B** $8 + 2l = 16$ **C** $8 + 2l = 20$ **D** $l = 20 - 8$
b Solve the correct equation to find the length of the garden.

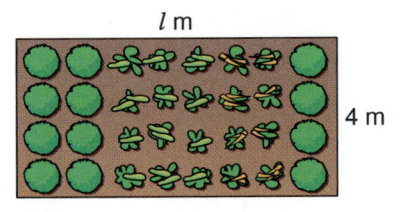

19 Write an equation for each of these.
Solve the equations.
a I think of a number. I add 2. The answer is 6.
b When 7 is subtracted from a number, the answer is 5.
c If a number is multiplied by 3, then 4 is added, the answer is 19.
d Find the value of x in the triangle.
e Susie has £25. She bought 3 magazines, all the same price, and had £10 left over. What was the cost, c, of each magazine?

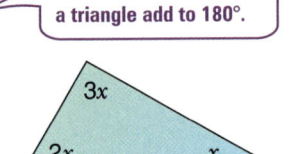

Remember the angles in a triangle add to 180°.

20 Tom has n pounds saved.
These expressions show what some friends have saved compared to Tom.
a Write in words how much Nick, Katie and Emily have saved compared to Tom.
b The friends won a raffle and got 25 pounds each.
Write expressions to show how much they each have then.
Simplify your expressions.

Nick	$n + 20$
Katie	$n - 15$
Emily	$2n$

21 Multiply out these brackets.
a $2(x + 1)$ **b** $3(k + 2)$ **c** $5(n + 4)$ **d** $6(p + 5)$
e $5(n - 2)$ **f** $3(x - 4)$ **g** $7(p - 1)$ **h** $6(k - 5)$
i $4(2a + 3)$ **j** $3(2y - 3x)$ **k** $5(2p - 7)$ ***l** $^{-}2(2m + 3)$

22 Write down the terms generated by this flow chart.

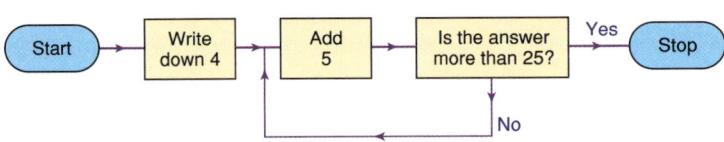

Start → Write down 4 → Add 5 → Is the answer more than 25? — Yes → Stop
                                                              No (loop back)

23 Predict the next three terms of these sequences.
a 3, 6, 9, 12, 15, ...   **b** 43, 39, 35, 31, 27, ...   **c** 1, 2, 4, 8, 16, ...   **d** 243, 81, 27, 9, ...

T 24 Use a copy of this.

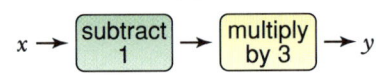

x → subtract 1 → multiply by 3 → y

This is a function machine.
a Fill in the table for the function machine.
b Fill in this mapping diagram for the function machine.
Use $x = 0, 1, 2, 3, 4, 5$.

Input	Output
3	
1	
5	
0	

c Write the rule for the function machine as $y = $ _____ and $x \to$ _____.

Algebra Support

25 Use a copy of this.

x	2	0	⁻2
y			

  a Complete the table for $y = x + 3$.
  b Write down the coordinate pairs for the points.
  c On the grid plot these points.
  Draw and label the line with the equation $y = x + 3$.
  d Does the point (22, 25) lie on the line?
  e Write down the coordinates of another point that lies on the line $y = x + 3$

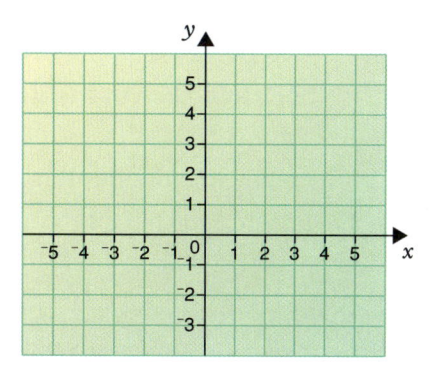

26 Which of these are equations for a line parallel to the *y*-axis?
  a $x = 2$ **b** $y = 5$ **c** $x = {}^-4$ **d** $y = {}^-10$

27 Explain the difference between these.
  a $4k$ and $k + 4$ **b** a^2 and $2a$ **c** $2(n + 3)$ and $2n + 3$

28 Write and solve an equation to find the value of *x*. Use this to find the missing numbers.
  a has been started for you.

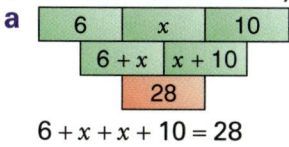

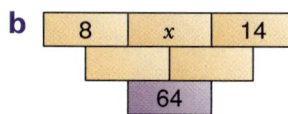

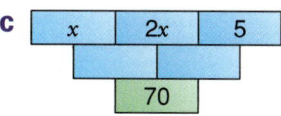

  a | 6 | x | 10 |
         | 6 + x | x + 10 |
         | 28 |

   $6 + x + x + 10 = 28$

  b | 8 | x | 14 |
         | 64 |

  c | x | 2x | 5 |
         | 70 |

29 There are two large tins and one small tin on these scales.
  The two large tins each have the same mass.
  The mass of the small tin is 1·4 kg.
  What is the mass of one large tin?
  Show your working.

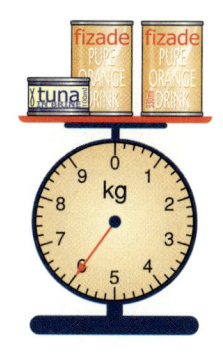

30 Write down the missing operation for each of these.
  a 4, 0, 7, ⁻1 → ? → 8, 0, 14, ⁻2

  b 48, 20, 63, 101 → ? → 42, 14, 57, 95

31 5, 1, 7, 4 → ? → ? → 8, 4, 10, 7

  Jamie was asked to fill in the missing operations.
  He wrote

  5, 1, 7, 4 → add 4 → subtract 1 → 8, 4, 10, 7

  Simon said the two operations could be replaced with one.

  5, 1, 7, 4 → add 3 → 8, 4, 10, 7

  Is Simon correct?

Algebra

32 a $x \rightarrow$ [multiply by 3] $\rightarrow$ [add 2] $\rightarrow y$

Copy and fill in this table.

x	1	2	3	4	5
y					

Write a function for this function machine.

b The order of the operations is changed.

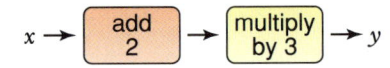

$x \rightarrow$ [add 2] $\rightarrow$ [multiply by 3] $\rightarrow y$

Copy and fill in this table.

x	1	2	3	4	5
y					

Write a function for this function machine.

c What happens when the order of operations is changed?

33 Write an expression for the perimeter of these courtyards. Simplify your expression.

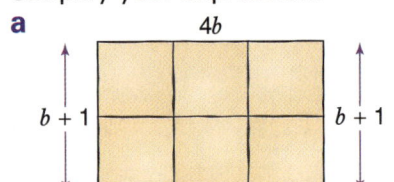

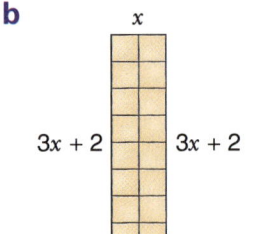

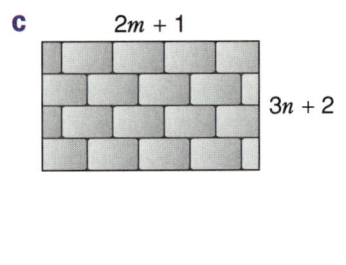

a sides $4b$ and $b+1$

b sides x and $3x+2$

c sides $2m+1$ and $3n+2$

34 These are some function machines.
Write their rules in the form $y = \_\_\_$ or $x \rightarrow \_\_\_$.

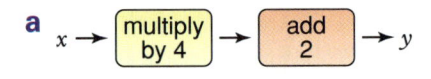

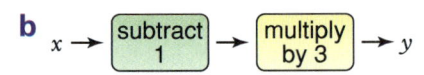

a $x \rightarrow$ [multiply by 4] $\rightarrow$ [add 2] $\rightarrow y$

b $x \rightarrow$ [subtract 1] $\rightarrow$ [multiply by 3] $\rightarrow y$

c $x \rightarrow$ [divide by 2] $\rightarrow$ [add 6] $\rightarrow y$

d $x \rightarrow$ [subtract 3] $\rightarrow$ [divide by 3] $\rightarrow y$

35 Explain these graphs.
For each, say how the variable on the vertical axis is related to the variable on the horizontal axis. For example, as time increases the height of a skier in a chair lift _____.

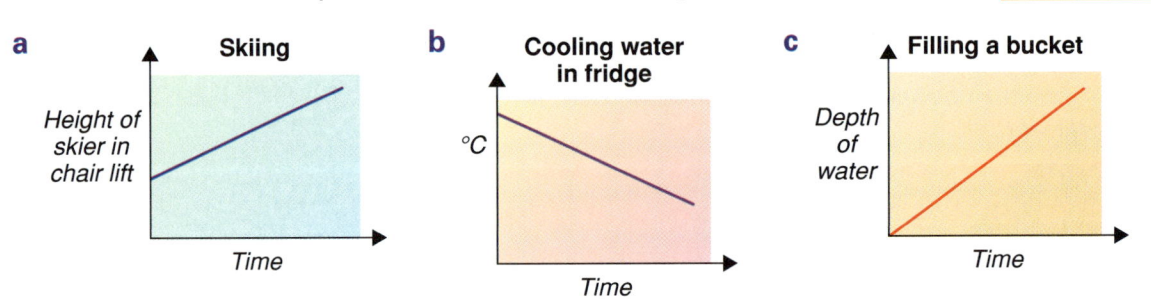

a Skiing — Height of skier in chair lift vs Time

b Cooling water in fridge — °C vs Time

c Filling a bucket — Depth of water vs Time

36 A function machine changes n to the number $3n - 1$.

$n \rightarrow 3n - 1$

What number will it change these to?
a 2 **b** 10 **c** 1 **d** 6 **e** 0

Algebra Support

37 a How many miles does each small square on the horizontal axis represent?
  b How many kilometres does each small square on the vertical axis represent?
  c Convert these to kilometres.
    i 500 miles   **ii** 125 miles
  d Convert these to miles.
    i 400 km   **ii** 160 km
  e Deb's friend lives 600 km away. About how many miles is this?
  f Joe travelled 120 miles in the morning and 80 miles in the afternoon. About how many kilometres did he travel altogether?
  g Simon travelled 400 miles on his holiday altogether. About how many kilometres is this?

Distance conversion (graph: Kilometres vs Miles, straight line from origin passing through approximately (600, 960))

38 ___ , ___ , ___ , 12

What might the missing terms be? Explain your rule.

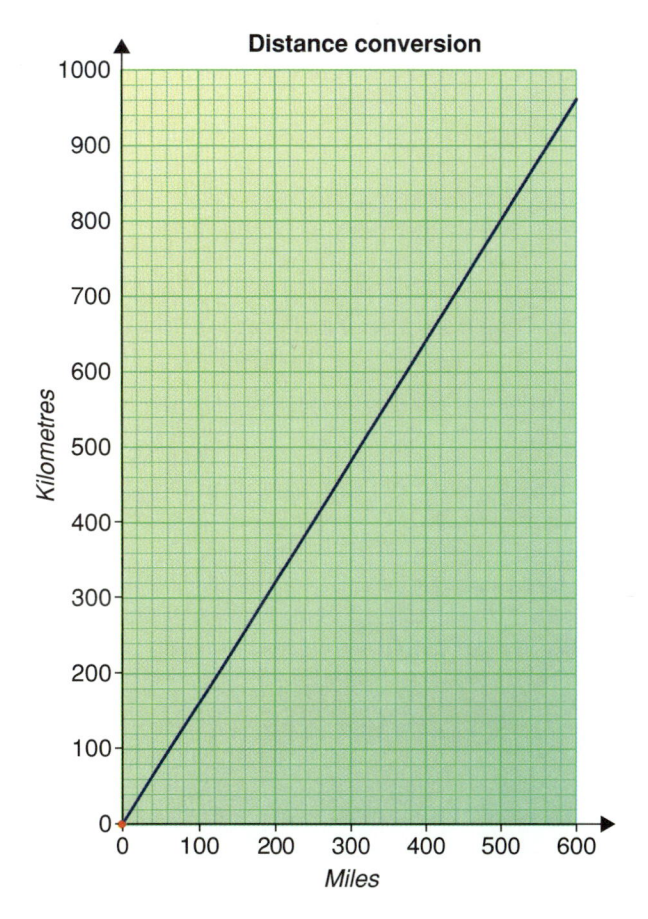

39 a Barbara makes a sequence of patterns with hexagonal tiles.   [SATs Paper 2 Level 5]

pattern number 1
pattern number 2
pattern number 3

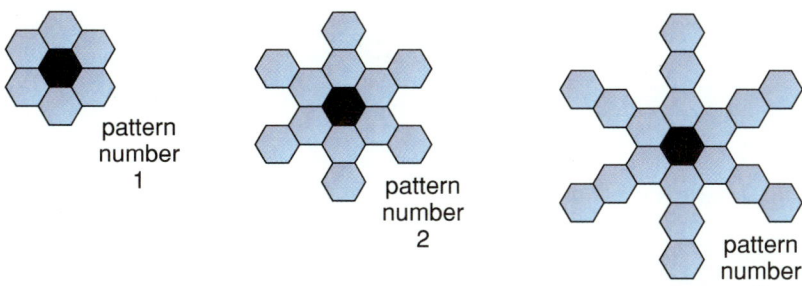

Each pattern in Barbara's sequence has **1 black** tile in the middle.
Each new pattern has **6 more grey** tiles than the pattern before.
Copy and finish the rule for finding the number of tiles in pattern number N in Barbara's sequence.

number of tiles = _____ + _____

  b Gwenno uses some tiles to make a **different** sequence of patterns.
The rule for finding the number of tiles in pattern number N in Gwenno's sequence is:

number of tiles = **1 + 4N**

Draw what you think the first 3 patterns in Gwenno's sequence could be.

155

Algebra

40 The *n*th term of a sequence is given by $T(n) = 2n + 1$.

  a Copy and complete this table for the sequence.

Term number	1	2	3	4	5
T(n)					

  b Plot the sequence on a grid.

x	1	3	5
y			

  c Is 15 a term of the sequence? Explain how you know.
  d Copy and complete this table for the equation $y = 2x + 1$.
  e Draw and label the graph of $y = 2x + 1$.
  f Explain why we do not draw a line through the points in **b** but we do for the points plotted in **e**.

41 The formula for changing °F to °C is °C = $\frac{5}{9}$(°F – 32°).
  Use the formula to find °C if °F is
  a 82   **b** 160   *__c__ 0.

T 42 Use a copy of this.

  a You pay £2·40 each time you go swimming.
  Complete the table.

Number of swims	0	10	20	30
Total cost (£)	0	24		

  b Now show this information on the graph. Join the points with a straight line.
  c A different way of paying is to pay a yearly fee of £22.
  Then you pay £1·40 each time you go swimming.
  Complete the table.

Number of swims	0	10	20	30
Total cost (£)	22	36		

  d Now show this information on the same graph.
  Join these points with a straight line.
  e For how many swims does the graph show that the cost is the same for both ways of paying?

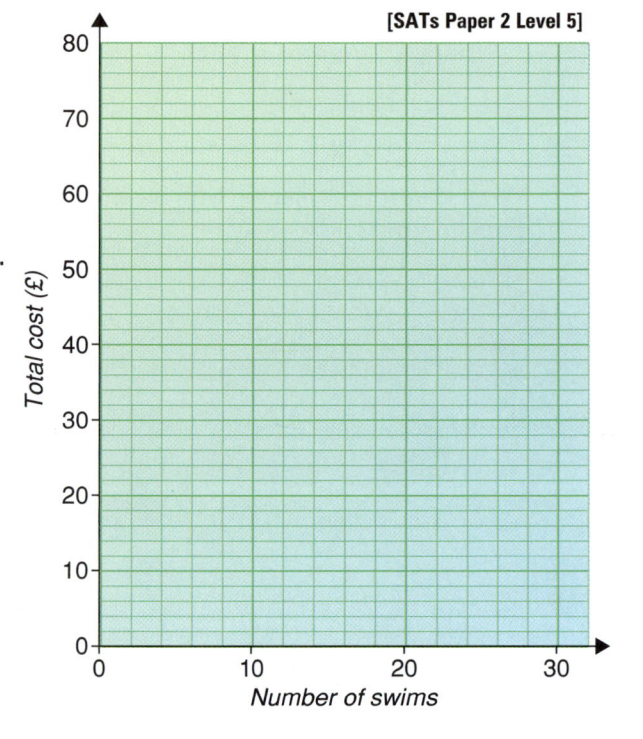

[SATs Paper 2 Level 5]

T 43 Use a copy of this. Helen took her toddler to the shops to buy an ice cream. They walked 800 m to the shop in 10 minutes, then stopped and talked to the shopkeeper for 5 minutes. They walked 400 m towards home in 5 minutes, then stopped at the park for 10 minutes, then walked home in 5 minutes.
Finish drawing the graph.

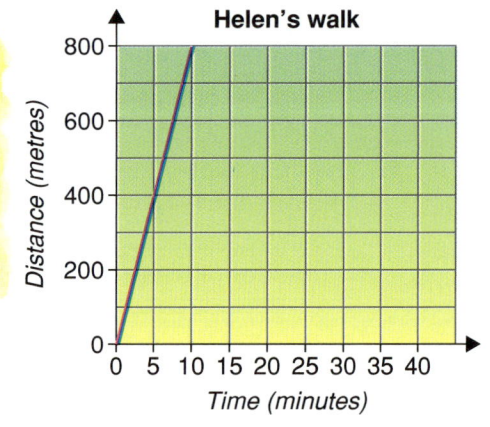

156

6 Algebra and Equations

You need to know
✓ equations   page 146

Key vocabulary
evaluate, identically equal to (≡), identity, inequality, solution, unknown, variable

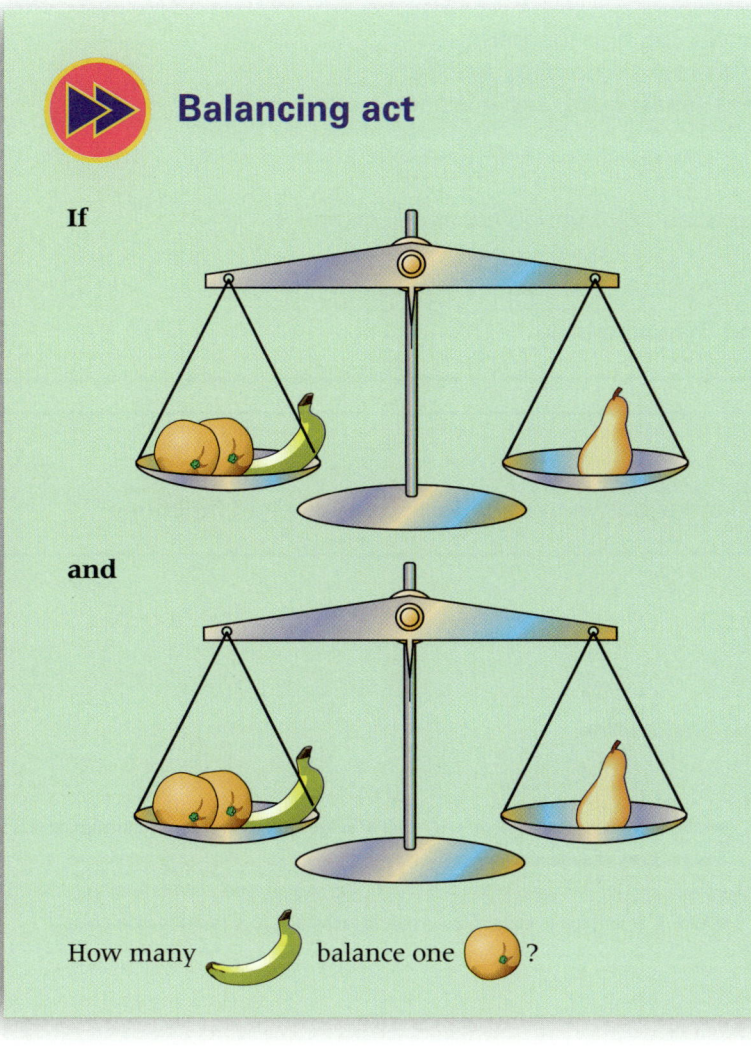

▶▶ Balancing act

If

and

How many 🍌 balance one 🍊?

Algebra

Understanding algebra

Remember
In **algebra** letters stand for numbers.
We use letters in **equations, formulae, functions** and **identities**.

Equations

Here are some examples of **equations**.

$5x + 3 = 2$ $\frac{a+3}{4} = 7$ $4(b - 2) = 36$ $5n + 3 = 2n + 27$

Each has an equals sign.
The unknown has a particular value.

Some equations have more than one unknown.
   $a + b = 7$ $3a + b = 7$
a and b can take many different values, but the value of one will depend on the value of the other.

Formulae

A **formula** gives the relationship between variables.

Example $F = ma$ has three variables F, m and a.

If we know the value of two of them we can find the third.
The variables in a formula always stand for something specific.
In $F = ma$, F is force, in Newtons, m is mass, in kg, and a is acceleration, in $\frac{m}{s^2}$.

Functions

A **function** gives the relationship between two variables, usually x and y.

Example $y = 3x + 4$

$x \rightarrow$ [multiply by 3] $\rightarrow$ [add 4] $\rightarrow y$

If we know the value of x we can find the value of y.

Discussion

Discuss the differences and similarities between equations, formulae and functions.

Exercise 1

T

1 Use a copy of this.
Match these statements with the best name.
The first one is done.

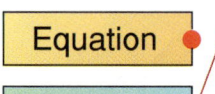

- Equation — $y = 7x + 8$
- $v = u + at$ where v is final velocity in m/s, u is initial velocity in m/s, a is acceleration in m/s² and t is time in seconds
- $3x + 8 = 4x - 7$
- Function — $V = IR$ where V is voltage in volts, I is current in amps and R is resistance in ohms
- $y = \frac{x}{4} - 2$
- Formula — $\frac{2x+4}{7} = x - 3$

2 Write your own example of
   a a formula   **b** an equation   **c** a function.

Review   Write equation, formula or function for each of these.
a $4x - 2 = x + 5$
b $y = 2x - 1$
c $I = \frac{PRT}{100}$ where I = simple interest, P = principal, R = rate of interest and T = time in years
d $y = \frac{3x - 1}{4}$
e $3x - 1 = 5(x + 1)$
f $V = \pi r^2 h$ where V = volume of cylinder, r = radius of base and h = height of cylinder

Identities

An **identity** is true for **all** values of the unknown.

Example $3(x + 2) \equiv 3x + 6$

$\equiv$ means 'is identically equal to'.

= means 'is equal to'.

It doesn't matter what value we substitute for x, $3(x + 2)$ will **always** have the same value as $3x + 6$.

Example $5(x - 1) \equiv 5x - 5$
Choose $x = 3$

$5(\mathbf{3} - 1) = 5(2)$ and $5x - 5 = 5 \times \mathbf{3} - 5$
$\qquad\quad = 10$ $\qquad\quad = 10$

Choose $x = {}^-2$

Check some more yourself.

$5({}^-\mathbf{2} - 1) = 5({}^-3)$ and $5x - 5 = 5 \times {}^-\mathbf{2} - 5$
$\qquad\quad\; = {}^-15$ $\qquad\quad\; = {}^-10 - 5$
$\qquad\qquad\qquad\qquad\qquad\qquad\qquad = {}^-15$

The left-hand side equals the right-hand side for any chosen value of x.

Exercise 2

1 Show that $3x + 7x + 2x - 5 \equiv 12x - 5$ is true for
   a $x = 2$ **b** $x = 10$ **c** $x = {}^-3$.

2 Show that $7(x + 4) \equiv 7x + 28$ is an identity.

Review   Check if these statements really are identities by substituting values for x. You could try $x = 0, 4$ and ${}^-3$.
a $2x + 6 \equiv 2(x + 3)$ **b** $4(x - 3) \equiv 3x - 9$ **c** $3(2x + 1) \equiv 6x + 3$

Algebra

Inequalities

$n > {}^-5$ means 'n is greater than $^-5$'
$n \geqslant {}^-5$ means 'n is greater than or equal to $^-5$'
$n < 3$ means 'n is less than 3'
$n \leqslant 3$ means 'n is less than or equal to 3'
$^-4 < n < 7$ means 'n is between $^-4$ and 7'
or   'n is greater than $^-4$ but less than 7'
$^-4 \leqslant n \leqslant 7$ means 'n is greater than or equal to $^-4$ but less than or equal to 7'
$^-4 \leqslant n < 7$ means 'n is greater than or equal to $^-4$ but less than 7'
$^-4 < n \leqslant 7$ means 'n is greater than $^-4$ but less than or equal to 7'

These are called 'inequalities'.

Discussion

$2 < 8$ is true.

$2 + 3 < 8 + 3$

When we add 3 to both sides, is the inequality still true? **Discuss**.
What if we added 5, subtracted 4, added 7, subtracted 9, ... to both sides?

$2 \times 3 < 8 \times 3$

When we multiply both sides of the inequality by 3, is it still true? **Discuss**.
What if we multiplied both sides by 4, divided both sides by 2, multiplied both sides by 1·5, divided both sides by 0·5, ... ? **Discuss**.

What if we multiplied both sides by $^-1$? What happens?
What if we divided both sides by $^-1$?
Discuss.

If we start with an **inequality** that is true, it will stay true if we

   add or subtract the same number to both sides
   multiply or divide both sides by the same **positive** number.

If we multiply or divide both sides by the same **negative** number, the inequality sign must be reversed.

Examples

$^-4 > {}^-8$
$^-4 + \mathbf{6} > {}^-8 + \mathbf{6}$ adding a positive number
$2 > {}^-2$

$^-3 < 4$
$^-3 \times \mathbf{6} < 4 \times \mathbf{6}$ multiplying by a positive number
$^-18 < 24$

$8 > {}^-4$
$8 \times \mathbf{^-1} < {}^-4 \times \mathbf{^-1}$ reverse the inequality when multiplying or dividing by a negative number
$^-8 < 4$

160

Algebra and Equations

Exercise 3

1 Decide which inequality best describes the statement.
  a More than 250 mm of rain fell yesterday.
     A $r < 250$ **B** $r \leqslant 250$ **C** $r > 250$ **D** $r \geqslant 250$
  b The speed limit through a village is 60 km/h.
     A $s < 60$ **B** $s \leqslant 60$ **C** $s > 60$ **D** $s \geqslant 60$
  c T-bone steaks weigh between 100 g and 200 g.
     A $100 < w < 200$ **B** $100 \leqslant w < 200$ **C** $100 < w \leqslant 200$ **D** $100 \leqslant w \leqslant 200$
  d Hans never arrives at school earlier than 8:30 a.m.
     A $t \leqslant 8:30$ **B** $t < 8:30$ **C** $t \geqslant 8:30$ **D** $t > 8:30$
  e The typing speeds of the students in a class were all greater than 35 words per minute.
     A $t < 35$ **B** $t \leqslant 35$ **C** $t > 35$ **D** $t \geqslant 35$
  f In a test, every student gained at least 70%.
     A $m < 70\%$ **B** $m \leqslant 70\%$ **C** $m > 70\%$ **D** $m \geqslant 70\%$
  g Shane takes from 3 to 4 minutes to iron a shirt.
     A $3 < t < 4$ **B** $3 \leqslant t < 4$ **C** $3 < t \leqslant 4$ **D** $3 \leqslant t \leqslant 4$

2 Write down some other statements that could be described by inequalities. Use inequalities to describe them.

3 a n is a prime number.
  Write down all the values of n that make $n < 30$ true.
  *b m is a fraction.
  Write down a value of m that makes $\frac{1}{3} < m < \frac{1}{2}$ true.

4 Lucy started with the inequality $^-3 < 3$.
  a She added 3 to both sides. $^-3 + 3 < 3 + 3$
  Is it still true?
  b Check to see if the inequality is still true if you do these to both sides.
     i add 10   **ii** subtract 2   **iii** add 1·5   **iv** multiply by 2
     v divide by 2   **vi** multiply by $^-2$ **vii** divide by $^-3$

5 Copy and finish this sentence.
  When we multiply or divide both sides of an inequality by the same negative number it will only remain true if _____.

*6 The perimeter of a triangle is 36 cm.
  The shortest side is p cm long.
  One of the other sides is $2p$ cm long.
  a What **must** the length of the third side be less than?
  b What **must** the length of the third side be greater than?
  c Prove that $6 < p < 9$.

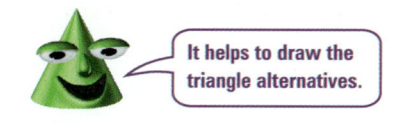

It helps to draw the triangle alternatives.

Review 1 Decide which inequality best describes the statement.
  a 18 is the smallest number, and 27 is the greatest number of students in the classes in a school.
     A $18 < s < 27$ **B** $18 \leqslant s < 27$ **C** $18 < s \leqslant 27$ **D** $18 \leqslant s \leqslant 27$
  b Joanne never arrives at school later than 8:30 a.m.
     A $t \leqslant 8:30$ **B** $t < 8:30$ **C** $t \geqslant 8:30$ **D** $t > 8:30$

Algebra

Review 2 Start with the inequality $^-1 < 2$.

Do the following operations to *each* side of the inequality.

Which must have the inequality sign changed to >, to remain true?
- **a** add 5
- **b** subtract 2
- **c** multiply by 3
- **d** divide by 4
- **e** multiply by $^-3$
- **f** divide by $^-2$

Solving equations

We can **solve equations** using **inverse operations** or by **transforming both sides**.

Discussion

- Rachel and Jude were given this 'I think of a number' problem.

   I think of a number, add 3 then multiply by 4.
   I then add 7 and the answer is 63.
   What was the number I thought of?

  Rachel wrote this.

  number thought of → n → [add 3] → $n + 3$ → [multiply by 4] → $4(n + 3)$ → [add 7] → $4(n + 3) + 7$

  ← [subtract 3] ← 14 ← [divide by 4] ← 56 ← [subtract 7] ← 63

  This shows how Rachel and Jude solved the equation.

  Rachel

  $4(n + 3) + 7 = 63$
  $\therefore \ 4(n + 3) = 63 - 7$
  $\therefore \ n + 3 = \frac{56}{4}$
  $\therefore \ n = 14 - 3$
  $\therefore \ n = 11$

  Jude

  $4(n + 3) + 7 = 63$
  $\therefore \ 4n + 12 + 7 = 63$
  $\therefore \ 4n + 19 = 63$
  $\therefore \ 4n + 19 - 19 = 63 - 19$
  $\therefore \ 4n = 44$
  $\therefore \ \frac{4n}{4} = \frac{44}{4}$
  $\therefore \ n = 11$

  $\therefore$ means 'therefore'.

  Rachel used inverse operations and Jude used transforming both sides.

  Which way do you think is better? **Discuss**.

- **Discuss** the most efficient way to solve these equations.

  $\frac{3(2y - 8)}{7} = 21$ $3(n - 4) + 2n - 3 = 55$ $\frac{2}{5} = \frac{3}{p}$

  Does a bracket always have to be multiplied out first?

Algebra and Equations

When **writing an equation** we must choose a suitable unknown.

Worked Example
Annabel is 3 years older than Derek.
Together their ages add to 17.
Write an equation for this.

Answer
We can use any letter we like to stand for Derek's age.
Let d be Derek's age.
Then Annabel's age is $d + 3$.

$$d + d + 3 = 17$$

Derek's age   Annabel's age

The equation is $2a + 3 = 17$.

Collect like terms if you can – see page 147.

Exercise 4

Except for questions 2m, n, o, 5d, g, Review 1h.

1 Look at this table.
Write in words the meaning of each equation below.
The first one is done for you.   [SATs Paper 1 Level 5]

	Age (in years)
Ann	a
Ben	b
Cindy	c

  a $b = 30$ **Ben is 30 years old.**
  b $a + b = 69$
  c $b = 2c$
  d $\frac{a+b+c}{3} = 28$

2 Solve these equations.
Show your working.
  a $8y - 1 = 15$
  b $2p + 5 = 10$
  c $5m + 2 = 13$
  d $20 = 2x + 8$
  e $\frac{x}{2} = 3$
  f $\frac{m}{7} = 8$
  g $\frac{y}{4} + 7 = 11$
  h $\frac{p}{9} + 6 = 13$
  i $4 = \frac{12}{n}$
  j $8 = \frac{56}{m}$
  k $\frac{n+7}{12} = 4$
  l $\frac{3a+6}{5} = 2$
  m $2.4w + 5.9 = 14.3$
  n $6.3m - 2.7 = 12.42$
  o $4.6b - 2.7 = 11.56$

3 Write and solve equations for these.
  a I think of a number, I multiply it by 4 and add 2.
      The answer is 82.
      What number did I think of?
  b I think of a number.
      I add 3 and then multiply by 2.
      The answer is 8·4.
      What number did I think of?

4 a The number in each rectangle is found by adding the two numbers above it.
Write and solve an equation to find the number, n, in the red rectangle.

18	n	23
	?	?
	56	

  b Use a copy of this.
Fill in the missing expressions.
Write and solve an equation to find the value of x.

$3x + 2$		$x - 3$
	$4x + 5$	
	35	

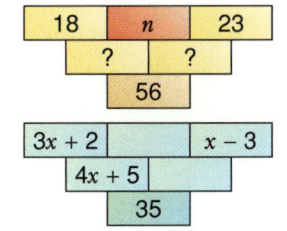

5 Solve these equations.
  a $4(n + 1) = 12$
  b $3(m - 2) = 9$
  c $3(n - 4) + 6 = 30$
  d $6(4a - 3) = 14.4$
  e $6x + 8 + 3x - 4 = 22$
  f $6p + 9 - 3p + 2 = 26$
  *g $6(m - 2) - 3(m + 2) = 12.6$

163

6 Find m

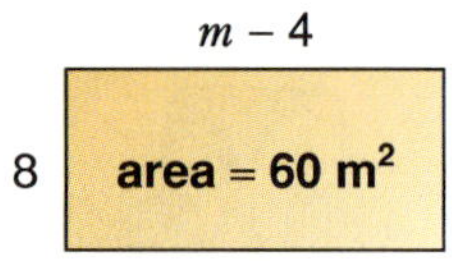
m − 4
8
area = 60 m²

7 Find the values of t and r. **[SATs Paper 2 Level 6]**

$\frac{2}{3} = \frac{t}{6}$

$\frac{2}{3} = \frac{5}{r}$

8 Look at the equations. **[SATs Paper 2 Level 6]**

$3a + 6b = 24$

$2c - d = 3$

a Use the equations to work out the value of the expressions below.
The first one is done for you.

$8c - 4d = \underline{12}$

$a + 2b = ___$

$d - 2c = ___$

b Use one or both of the equations to write an expression that has a value of 21.

____________ = 21

9 Each diagonal of this diagram adds to 33.

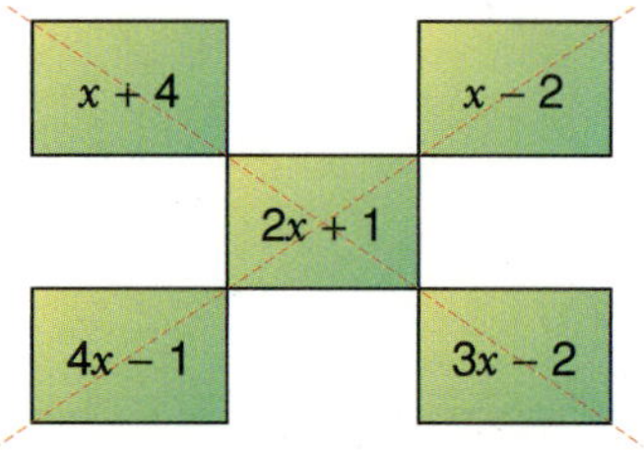
x + 4
x − 2
2x + 1
4x − 1
3x − 2

Write and solve an equation to find x.
Check that both diagonals add to 33.

10 The perimeter of these cross-country courses is given.
Find a and b.

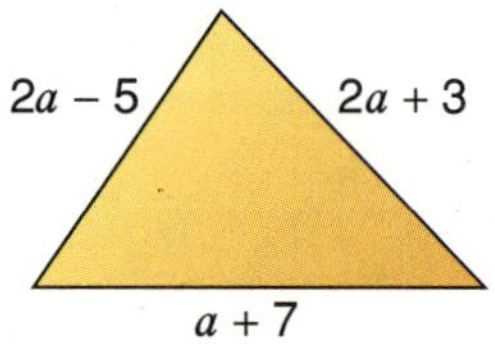
2a − 5
2a + 3
a + 7

Perimeter = 20 km

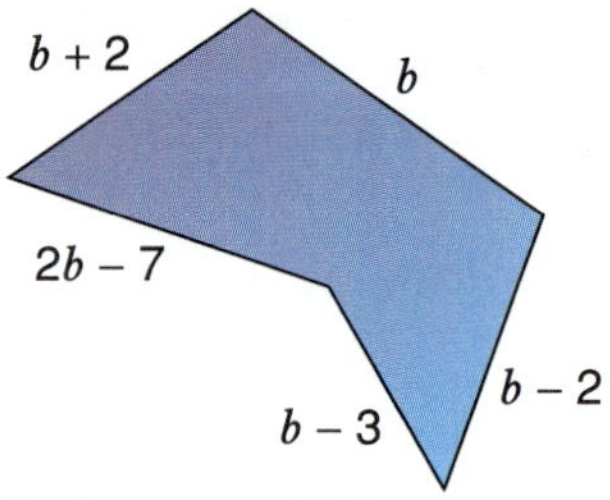
b + 2
b
2b − 7
b − 3
b − 2

Perimeter = 38 km

Algebra and Equations

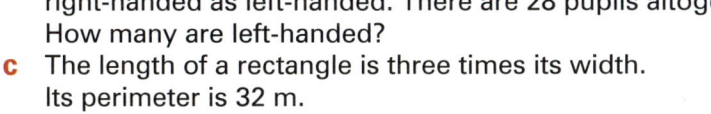

11 Write and solve an equation for these. Choose a suitable unknown.
  a I think of a number, add 7, multiply by 3, subtract 3, divide by 6, then multiply by 12.
  The answer is 72.
  What was the number I thought of?
  b In Kent's class there are three times as many pupils who are right-handed as left-handed. There are 28 pupils altogether. How many are left-handed?
  c The length of a rectangle is three times its width.
  Its perimeter is 32 m.
  Find its area. 
  *__d__ In PQR, ∠Q is half of ∠P and ∠R is three-quarters of ∠P. Find the size of all the angles in the triangle.

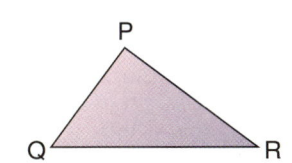

*__12__ Solve these equations.
  a $5d - 8 = {}^-28$ **b** $4x - 8 = {}^-12$ **c** $5m + 6 = {}^-9$
  d ${}^-17 = 8a + 5$ **e** $\frac{x+2}{2} = {}^-4$ **f** $\frac{{}^-4x+2}{2} - 3 = {}^-10$

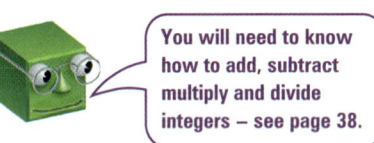

You will need to know how to add, subtract, multiply and divide integers – see page 38.

*__13__ Kade solved the equation $12 - 4x = 4$ like this.

  $12 - 4x = 4$
  $12 = 4 + 4x$ add 4x to both sides to get 4x positive
  $12 - 4 = 4x$ subtract 4 from both sides
  $8 = 4x$
  $\frac{8}{4} = x$ divide both sides by 4
  $2 = x$

  Use Kade's method or another method to solve these.
  a $8 - 2x = 3$ **b** $20 - 4x = 8$ **c** $12 - 9x = 24$ **d** ${}^-3x - 8 = {}^-11$

*__14__ Work out a way to solve these.
  a $\frac{6}{x} + 4 = 7$ **b** $\frac{9}{b} - 3 = 7$ **c** $\frac{20}{r+4} = 4$

*__15__ The solutions to $3x + 5 = {}^-4$ and $5x + 20 = 5$ are both ${}^-3$.
  Write some more equations that have a solution of ${}^-3$.

*__16__ Find a pair of numbers that satisfy $7x - 2y = 38$ if one of the numbers is three times the other.
  Is there more than one answer?

*__17__ Jeanna used this diagram to find two consecutive even numbers with a difference of 100 between their squares.
  She let one number be y and the other be $y + 2$.

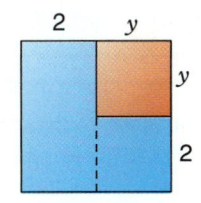

  The red shaded square is y^2.
  The large square is $(y+2)^2$.
  Difference = large square – red shaded square
              = blue shaded region
  Blue shaded region = $2(y+2) + 2y$
  $2(y+2) + 2y = 100$

  Finish Jeanna's working to find the two numbers.

*__18__ Show that if $x(y - 2) = 0$ then either $x = 0$ or $y = 2$.

Review 1 Solve these equations. Show your working.
  a $3a - 2 = 7$ **b** $19 = 3b + 1$ **c** $3 = \frac{21}{c}$ **d** $\frac{d-2}{5} = 10$
  e $2 \cdot 4e - 1 \cdot 3 = 3 \cdot 5$ **f** $3(x-1) + 4 = 16$ **g** $2(x+1) + 3x = 32$ **h** $8(h-2) + 2(h+4) = 27$

165

Algebra

Review 2 $2a - 4b = 20$ and $x + 3y = 5$.
a Evaluate these.   i $6x + 18y$ ii $a - 2b$
b Write an expression that has a value of 25.

'Evaluate' means 'find the value of'.

Review 3 Write and solve equations for these.
a Mary is 3 years older than her sister. The sum of their ages is 21. How old is Mary?
b Kate's grandmother is 4 times as old as Kate. If the sum of their ages is 70, how old is Kate's grandmother?
c The perimeter of this rectangle is 70 cm. What is x?
d A regular pizza costs £4 less than a large one. Lizzie buys 2 large and 3 regular pizzas and spends £45·50. How much does a large pizza cost?

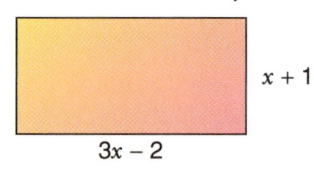

$x + 1$
$3x - 2$

* **Review 4** Solve
a $7a - 3 = {}^-24$ b $\frac{-2b + 4}{3} = {}^-8$

Equations with unknowns on both sides

Discussion

● Kayla solved the equation $8m + 14 = 6m + 15$ like this.

$8m + 14 = 6m + 15$
$8m - 6m + 14 = 6m - 6m + 15$ subtract $6m$ from both sides
$2m + 14 = 15$
$2m + 14 - 14 = 15 - 14$ subtract 14 from both sides
$2m = 1$
$\frac{2m}{2} = \frac{1}{2}$ divide both sides by 2
$m = \frac{1}{2}$

Kayla has used 'transforming both sides' rather than inverse operations.
Could she have used 'inverse operations'? **Discuss.**
As part of your discussion, try to solve the equation using inverse operations.

● **Discuss** how to write and solve an equation for this.
Is it possible to solve the equation using inverse operations?
  Multiplying a number by 3 and then adding 2 gives the same answer as subtracting the number from 30 and adding 4.

To **solve equations with unknowns on both sides** we 'transform both sides' to get all the unknowns on one side.

Worked Example
Solve $5t + 6 = 7t - 3$.

Subtract $5t$ rather than $7t$ from both sides because $5t$ is smaller.

Answer
$5t + 6 = 7t - 3$
$5t - 5t + 6 = 7t - 5t - 3$ subtract $5t$ from both sides
$6 = 2t - 3$
$6 + 3 = 2t - 3 + 3$ add 3 to both sides
$9 = 2t$
$\frac{9}{2} = \frac{2t}{2}$ divide both sides by 2
$4\frac{1}{2} = t$

166

Algebra and Equations

Exercise 5   Only use a calculator if you need to.

1 Solve these equations.
  a $3n + 4 = n + 13$
  b $7 + 5m = 8m + 1$
  c $8y + 17 = 4y + 19$
  d $9b + 3 = 5b + 13$
  e $12 + x = 5x - 2$
  f $8 + 3p = 9p + 4$
  g $25 - 2y = 6y + 5$
  h $14 + 10k = 15k + 5$
  i $5 - 2b = 3b + 25$

2 a Solve this equation.   [SATs Paper 1 Level 6]
    $7 + 5k = 8k + 1$
  b Solve these equations. Show your working.
    i $10y + 23 = 4y + 26$
    ii $\frac{3(2y + 4)}{14} = 1$

3 Sanjay and Niki have the same number of CDs.
    They both store some of their CDs in cases that hold n CDs.
    Sanjay has two full cases of CDs plus eighteen loose CDs.
    Niki has three full cases of CDs plus six loose CDs.
    Write and solve an equation to find how many CDs each case holds.

4 Write and solve an equation to find x.
  a $2x + 9$, $3x + 4$
  b $5x + 12$, $8x - 9$

5 Three times a number plus 6 is equal to twice the number plus 15. What is the number?

6 Multiplying a number by 3 and then adding 4 gives the same answer as subtracting the number from 20. Find the number.

7 Solve these equations.
  a $3(x + 4) = x + 16$
  b $2(m + 3) = 4(m - 1)$
  c $3p - (p + 1) = p - 2$
  d $a + 3(a - 1) = 2a$
  *__e__ $3(2b - 1) = 5(4b - 1) - 4(3b - 2)$
  *__f__ $4(y - 0.6) - 3(y - 2.1) = 3(3y + 3.1)$

8 a Pupils started to solve the equation **$6x + 8 = 4x + 11$**   [SATs Paper 1 Level 7]
    in different ways.
    For each statement below, write true or false.
    i $6x + 8 = 4x + 11$
       so $14x = 15x$
    ii $6x + 8 = 4x + 11$
       so $6x + 4x = 11 + 8$
    iii $6x + 8 = 4x + 11$
       so $6x = 4x + 3$
    iv $6x + 8 = 4x + 11$
       so $2x + 8 = 11$
    v $6x + 8 = 4x + 11$
       so $2x = 3$
    vi $6x + 8 = 4x + 11$
       so $^-3 = ^-2x$
  b A different pupil used trial and improvement to solve the equation $6x + 8 = 4x + 11$.
    Explain why trial and improvement is not a good method to use.

*__9__ Solve these.   **a** $\frac{12}{n+1} = \frac{21}{n+4}$ **b** $\frac{5}{n+3} = \frac{4}{n+5}$

*__10__ Meggie buys 4 ice creams and a drink and this costs the same as 2 ice creams and 4 drinks. If a drink costs 80p, how much does an ice cream cost?

167

Algebra

*11 For each of these, calculate the value of *a* and then use it to find the perimeter of the rectangle.

a area = 115 mm²

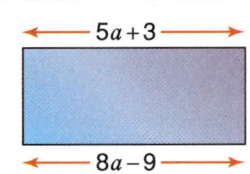

5a + 3
8a − 9

b area = 7100 cm²

4a − 57
2a + 7

*12 Write and solve an equation to find the answers to these.
   a Ben and Maddy are given the same amount of money for Christmas. Before Christmas, Ben had £205 and Maddy had £25. Now Ben has four times as much as Maddy. How much were they each given for Christmas?
   b Marshall and Gretchen have 200 tropical fish between them. Marshall gave Gretchen 10 of his fish. Now Gretchen has three times as many as Marshall. How many fish does Marshall have now?

Review 1 Solve these equations.
a $8x + 2 = 5x + 14$ **b** $5a + 2 = 7a + 1$ **c** $5m + 8 = 12 − 3m$
d $9p − 2 = 11 − 4p$ **e** $5(t − 4) = t + 2$ *f $11 − 4x = 9 + 2x$

Review 2 Write and solve an equation to find *y*.

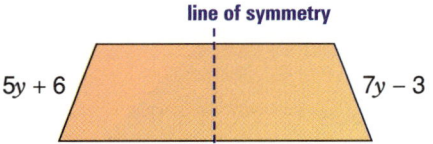

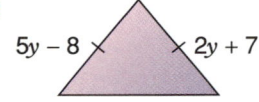

a   line of symmetry
5y + 6   7y − 3

b 5y − 8   2y + 7

Review 3 Jess and Jack were solving the equation $2(2x − 3) = 9 − 2x$. Both made **one** mistake.
a Write down the number of the line in which each made this mistake.
b Solve the equation to find the correct answer.

Jess's working
$2(2x − 3) = 9 − 2x$
1 ∴ $4x − 6 = 9 − 2x$
2 ∴ $4x − 2x = 9 + 6$
3 ∴ $2x = 15$
4 ∴ $x = 7\frac{1}{2}$

Jack's working
$2(2x − 3) = 9 − 2x$
1 ∴ $4x − 3 = 9 − 2x$
2 ∴ $4x + 2x = 9 + 3$
3 ∴ $6x = 12$
4 ∴ $x = 2$

Review 4
a I think of a number, multiply it by 4 and add 7. This gives the same answer as multiplying the number by 6 and subtracting 5. Write an equation to show this and solve it to find the number I thought of.

Solving non-linear equations

A **non-linear equation** has terms with indices greater than 1, such as x^2, x^3, ...
We can solve some non-linear equations to get an exact answer.

Algebra and Equations

Discussion

Jakob solved the equation $37x^2 = 29.97$ using inverse operations.

$37x^2 = 29.97$
$\therefore x^2 = \frac{29.97}{37}$
$\therefore x^2 = 0.81$
$\therefore x = \pm\sqrt{0.81}$
$= {}^+0.9 \text{ or } {}^-0.9$

$x \rightarrow \boxed{\text{square}} \rightarrow x^2 \rightarrow \boxed{\text{multiply by 37}} \rightarrow 37x^2$

$\boxed{\text{square root}} \leftarrow 0.81 \leftarrow \boxed{\text{divide by 37}} \leftarrow 29.97$

Discuss Jakob's method. Is there any other way he could have done it? Did he need to take the positive *and* negative square root of $\sqrt{0.81}$?

Worked Example

Solve these. **a** $x^2 - 10 = 246$ **b** $5 = \frac{125}{x^2}$

Answers

a $x^2 - 10 = 246$
$x^2 = 246 + 10$
$x^2 = 256$
$\sqrt{x^2} = \sqrt[+]{256}$
$x = 16 \text{ or } {}^-16$

Whenever you find the square root when solving an equation, you must give the positive and negative solutions.

b $5 = \frac{125}{x^2}$
$5x^2 = 125$
$x^2 = \frac{125}{5}$
$x^2 = 25$
$\sqrt{x^2} = \sqrt[+]{25}$
$x = 5 \text{ or } {}^-5$

Exercise 6

1 Solve these to find the exact solutions.
  a $m^2 + 20 = 84$ **b** $y^2 - 24 = 97$ **c** $p^2 - 124 = 200$ **d** $4 = \frac{100}{x^2}$ *****e** $\frac{25}{a+3} = a + 3$

Review Solve these.
  a $a^2 + 16 = 52$ **b** $n^2 - 35 = 365$ **c** $8 = \frac{288}{b^2}$ *****d** $\frac{81}{p-4} = p - 4$

We can solve harder non-linear equations using **trial and improvement**, or using **a calculator, spreadsheet** or **graph plotting software**. The answer we get is usually not exact.

Using a calculator

Example $m^2 + 3 = 53$
$m^2 = 50$ subtracting 3 from both sides
$\sqrt[3]{m} = \sqrt[3]{50}$
key $\boxed{\sqrt[3]{}}$ $\boxed{50}$ $\boxed{=}$ to get 3·68 (2 d.p.)

50 is not a cube number so the answer will not be exact.

169

Algebra

Using trial and improvement and a calculator

When using trial and improvement it is important to be systematic.

Example Solve $x^2 + x = 40$ giving the answer to 2 d.p.

> It is no good trying 4 because $4^3 = 64$ so $4^3 + 4$ is going to be much too big.

Guess what x might be

Try $x = 3$	If $x = 3$,	$x^3 + x = 30$	too small
Try $x = 3.5$	If $x = 3.5$,	$x^3 + x = 46.375$	too big
Try $x = 3.3$	If $x = 3.3$,	$x^3 + x = 39.237$	too small but close
Try $x = 3.4$	If $x = 3.4$,	$x^3 + x = 42.704$	too big but close

We can see that the answer is between 3·3 and 3·4. It is closer to 3·3 since 39·237 is closer to 40 than is 42·704.

| Try $x = 3.33$ | If $x = 3.33$, | $x^3 + x = 40.256037$ | too big but close |
| Try $x = 3.32$ | If $x = 3.32$, | $x^3 + x = 39.914368$ | too small but close |

The answer is between 3·33 and 3·32.
Because 39·914368 is closer to 40 than is 40·256037, the answer is closer to 3·32.
The answer to 2 decimal places is **3·32**.

Using a spreadsheet

Example Solve $x^3 + x = 40$.

	A	B
1	x	x³+x
2	3	=A2*A2*A2+A2
3	=A2+0.1	=A3*A3*A3+A3
4	=A3+0.1	=A4*A4*A4+A4
5	=A4+0.1	=A5*A5*A5+A5

Increase the number by 0·1 each time.

	A	B
1	x	x³+x
2	3	30
3	3.1	32.891
4	3.2	35.968
5	3.3	39.237
6	3.4	42.704

Using this we can see that the solution is between 3·3 and 3·4.
Then we can change column A so that it starts at 3·3 and increases by 0·01 each time.

	A	B
1	x	x³+x
2	3.30	=A2*A2*A2+A2
3	=A2+0.01	=A3*A3*A3+A3
4	=A3+0.01	=A4*A4*A4+A4
5	=A4+0.01	=A5*A5*A5+A5

Increase the number by 0·01 each time.

	A	B
1	x	x³+x
2	3.30	39.237
3	3.31	39.575
4	3.32	39.914
5	3.33	40.256
6	3.34	40.600

Using this we can see that the solution is between 3·32 and 3·33.
Because 39·914 is closer to 40 than is 40·256, the answer is 3·32.

Exercise 7

1 Use a calculator to find the solutions to these.
Give the answers to 2 d.p. if you need to round.

a $6.3a^2 = 14.175$
b $3.2m^2 = 20$
c $1.4b^2 = 24.696$
d $a^3 = 50$
e $b^3 = 80$
f $x^3 = 110$
g $3a^3 = 50$
h $1.2x^3 = 8.4$

Algebra and Equations

2 Use a calculator and trial and improvement to find an approximate solution to each of these. Give your answers to 2 d.p.
   a $m^3 - m = 80$ **b** $x^3 + x = 97$ **c** $2y^3 + y = 6$

3 The area of this rectangle is 84·32 cm².
   a Write an equation for the area of the rectangle.
   b Find the value of a to 2 d.p. Show your working. You could use a table like this one.

a	$a + 3$	$a(a + 3)$	too big or too small

*4 The product of three consecutive odd numbers is 68 757.
Use the solution to $x^3 = 68\ 757$ to help you find the numbers.
Explain how you did this.

*5 This cuboid has a square base of side x cm.
It has height 30 cm.
The total surface area of the cuboid is 600 cm².
Write an equation for the surface area of the cuboid.
Solve it to find x, correct to one decimal place.
Use trial and improvement using a calculator or spread sheet.

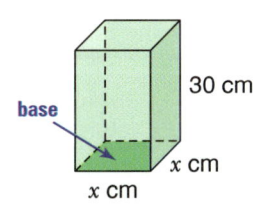

T

*6 Use a copy of the tables.
Fill in the table for the equation and values of x given.
Then continue and find the value of x, to 1 d.p., that gives the value of y closest to 0.
Use trial and improvement.
   a $y = x^3 - x - 4$

x	0	1	2	3	4
y					

   b $y = 2x^3 + 5x - 10$

x	0	1	2	3	4
y					

Review 1 Use a calculator to find the solutions to these to 1 d.p.
a $b^3 = 75$ **b** $4y^3 = 24$ **c** $7·2a^3 = 16·72$

Review 2 Use trial and improvement and a calculator to find a solution to 2 d.p.
a $p^3 - p = 10$ **b** $x^3 + x = 47$

Review 3 The area of this rectangle is 59 m².
a Write an equation for the area of the rectangle.
b Find the value of x to 2 d.p. Show your working.

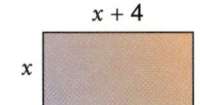

Practical

You will need a spreadsheet package.

Ask your teacher for the ICT worksheet 'Open Boxes'.

Algebra

> **? Puzzle**
>
> **1** A number plus its square equals 30.
> What might the number be?
> Is there more than one answer?
>
> **2 What if** a number plus its cube equals 30?

Algebra and proportion

A recipe for 4 people uses 20 g baking powder.
We can draw a table like this.

Number of people	1	2	3	4	5	6	...
Baking powder (g)	5	10	15	20	25	30	...

The amount of baking powder is **directly proportional** to the number of people.

This is linked to proportion, page 130.

The ratio   *number of people : amount of baking powder*   is constant.

$$\frac{1}{5} = \frac{2}{10} = \frac{3}{15} = \frac{4}{20} = \frac{5}{25} = \frac{6}{30} \ldots$$

We can plot the information in the table above on a graph.

The relationship between number of people, p, and amount of baking powder, b, is given by

$b = 5p$

The graph is a straight line with equation $b = 5p$.

Variables which are in **direct proportion** always give a **straight-line graph** which goes through the origin.

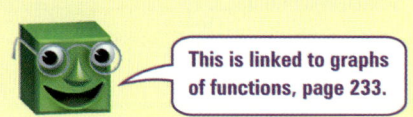

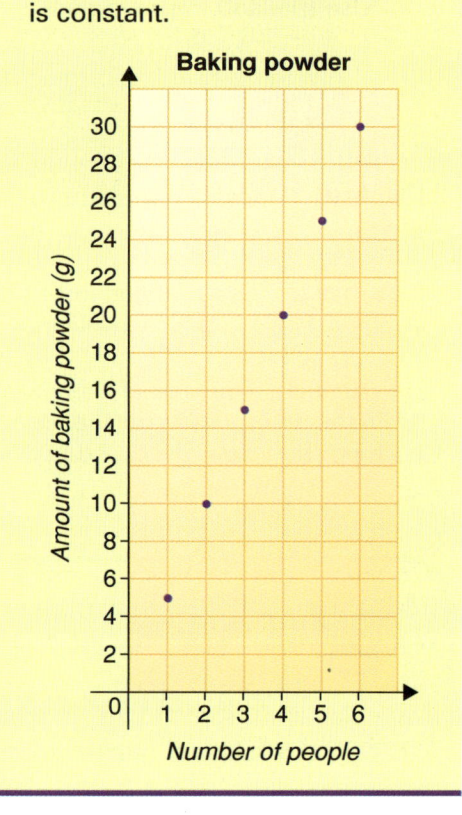

This is linked to graphs of functions, page 233.

Baking powder

Discussion

Bron did an experiment in science to test if the voltage in a circuit was directly proportional to the current in the circuit.
This table shows her results.

Voltage (volts)	3	6	9	12	15	18	21
Current (amps)	0·14	0·32	0·45	0·64	0·74	1·2	1·16

She plotted these results on a graph.

Do the points lie in an exact straight line?
Do the points lie in an approximate straight line?
Why might this be? **Discuss**.

Do you think that voltage and current **are** directly proportional? **Discuss**.

What might explain the point at (18, 1·2)? **Discuss**.

If the current in the same circuit is 2 amps, how could you work out the voltage? **Discuss**.

Write a formula for the relationship between voltage (v) and current (A).

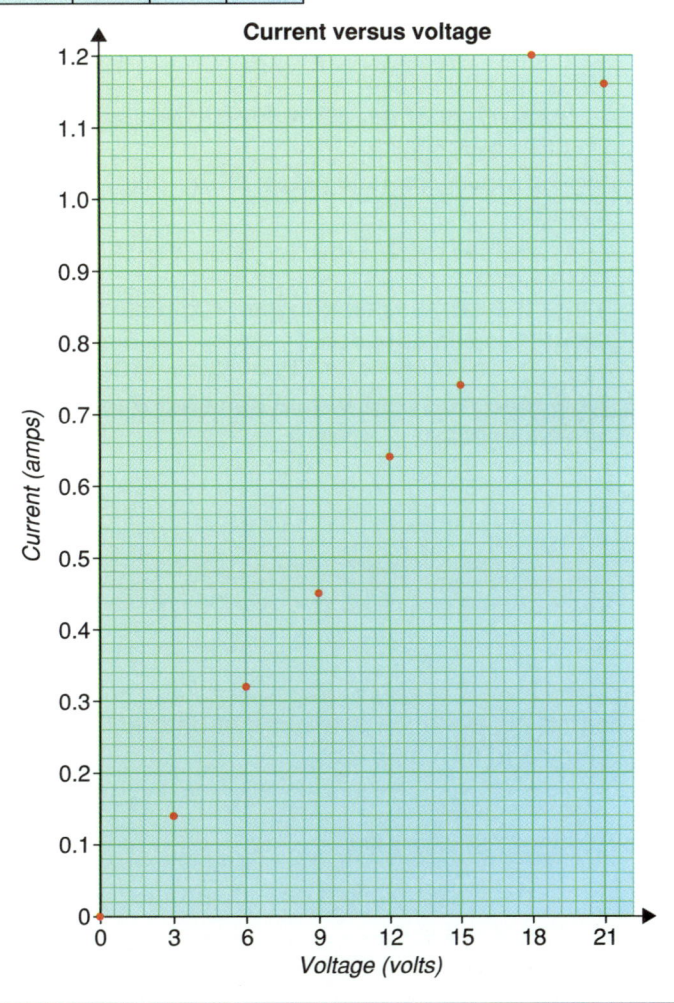

Current versus voltage

Worked Example
A mobile phone company charges in direct proportion to time for off-peak minutes.
Basil got a bill of £11 for 40 off-peak minutes.
Use algebra to find the cost of 70 off-peak minutes.

Answer
The ratio **cost : time** ($\frac{cost}{time}$) is constant.
Let c be the cost for 70 minutes of off-peak time.

$(\frac{cost}{time})$ $\frac{c}{70} = \frac{11}{40}$

$c = \frac{11}{40} \times 70$ **multiplying both sides by 70**

$c = 19{\cdot}25$

The cost of 70 off-peak minutes is **£19·25**.

Algebra

Exercise 8

T

1 Use a copy of this.
Orange paint is made by mixing 5 parts yellow and 3 parts red.
  a Fill in this table for the amounts of red paint.

Yellow (ℓ)	5	10	15	20	25
Red (ℓ)	3				

  b Work out the ratio   red : yellow   for each set of values given in the table. What do you notice?
  c Is the amount of red paint directly proportional to the amount of yellow paint? Justify your answer.
  d Would you expect the graph of red paint versus yellow paint to be a straight line? Explain.
  e Draw a graph of red paint versus yellow paint on a copy of this grid.
  f Write the relationship between red paint (r) and yellow paint (y) as an equation.
   r = _____
  g How much red paint would be needed to mix with 42 ℓ of yellow paint?

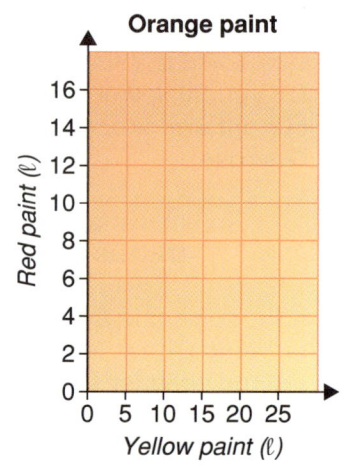

2 A car travels 10 km on every litre of petrol.
  a Copy and fill in this table.

Number of litres	1	2	3	4	5
Distance travelled (km)					

  b Is the distance travelled directly proportional to the number of litres used? Justify your answer using ratio.
  c Draw a graph of distance travelled versus number of litres used.
  d Explain why your graph is or isn't a straight line.
  e Write the relationship between distance travelled (d) and litres used (l) as an equation.
  f How much petrol would be needed to travel 88 km?

3 Use algebra to find the answers.
  a For every 180 mℓ of juice in a fruit punch, there is 120 mℓ of lemonade.
    How much juice is needed to mix with 800 mℓ of lemonade?
  b Green paint is made by mixing 9 parts of blue with 4 parts of yellow paint.
    How many litres of blue paint would be needed to mix with 50 litres of yellow paint?
  c A solution is made of 5 parts ethanol and 12 parts water.
    How much ethanol is needed to mix with 1·2 ℓ of water?
  d The council decides that for every 5000 people in a town they will plant 250 trees.
    If the population of the town is 45 500, how many trees will be planted?

See the worked example on page 173 to help.

Algebra and Equations

4 Jasmine did an experiment in science to work out the acceleration of an object when different forces were applied to it.
This table shows her results.

F (newtons)	2	4	6	8	10	12	14	16	18	20
Acceleration (m/s²)	0·5	0·9	1·4	2·1	3·2	3	3·4	4·1	4·5	4·9

a Use a copy of this grid.
Draw a graph of acceleration versus force.
b Give a possible reason why the points don't lie in an exact straight line.
c Do you think that force and acceleration are directly proportional? Explain.
d Jasmine made an experimental error when collecting data for one of the points. Which point do you think it was?

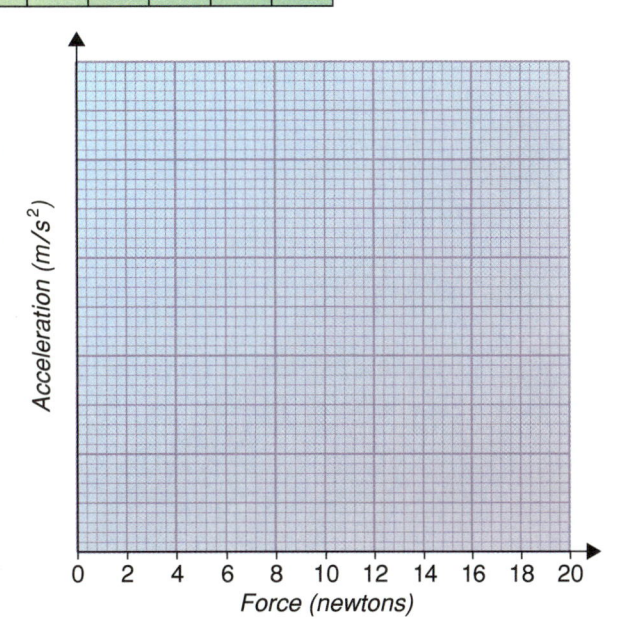

Review 1 Jake is trying to improve his fitness by running each day. The first day he runs steadily at 4 m each second.
a Copy and complete this table for the total distance he has run after each second.

Time (secs)	1	2	3	4	5
Total distance (m)	4				

b Is the total distance directly proportional to the time taken?
Justify your answer using ratios.
c Draw a graph of distance run versus time taken.
d Is your graph a straight line? Explain why or why not.
e Write the relationship between time taken (t) and distance run (d) as an equation.
f How long will he take to run 100 m assuming he continues to run at the same rate?

Review 2 Use algebra to find these answers.
a To make a drink the instructions say 'to every 1 part of juice add 4 parts of water'.
  i Write this as a ratio *juice : water*.
  ii How much water will I need to add to 20 mℓ of juice?
  iii How much drink will I then have?
*** b** On my map the distance from Wakefield to Pontefract is 6 cm.
I know the real distance is approximately 10 miles.
If the distance between Rotherham and Doncaster on the same map is 7 cm, how far apart (in miles) are Rotherham and Doncaster?

175

Algebra

Summary of key points

A $2x - 3 = 7$ $\frac{5p - 3}{2} = 6$ $4(x + 2) = 24$ $5x + 3 = 2x + 9$ are all **linear equations**.
The unknown has a particular value.

A **formula** gives the relationship between variables.
$s = \frac{D}{T}$ is the speed, s, found from distance, D, and time taken, T.
The variables stand for something specific.

A **function** is a special sort of equation. It gives the relationship between two variables, usually x and y.
$y = 2x - 3$ is a function.

$x \rightarrow$ [multiply by 2] $\rightarrow$ [subtract 3] $\rightarrow y$

If we know the value of x we can find the value of y.

B   An **identity** is true for **all** values of the unknown.
Example $2(4x - 3) \equiv 8x - 6$

$\equiv$ is 'identically equal to'

Whatever value of x we choose, the left-hand side will always equal the right-hand side.

Example $4(x + 2) = 4x + 8$

Choose $x = \mathbf{3}$

$4(x + 2) = 4(\mathbf{3} + 2)$ and $4x + 8 = 4 \times \mathbf{3} + 8$
$ = 4 \times 5$ $ = 12 + 8$
$ = 20$ $ = 20$

left-hand side = right-hand side

C   **Inequalities**

$<$ means 'is less than'.
$>$ means 'is greater than'.
$\leqslant$ means 'is less than or equal to'.
$\geqslant$ means 'is greater than or equal to'.

Examples $x \leqslant 7$ $2 \leqslant y < 4$
            x is less than y is greater than or equal
            or equal to 7   to 2 but less than 4

If we start with an inequality, this will stay true if we

     add or subtract the same number to both sides
     multiply or divide both sides by the same **positive** number.

If we multiply or divide both sides by the same **negative** number, the inequality sign must be **reversed**.

Examples $^-2 > {^-5}$ $^-4 < 2$
            $^-2 - \mathbf{3} > {^-5} - \mathbf{3}$ $^-4 \times {^-\mathbf{3}} > 2 \times {^-\mathbf{3}}$ multiply by a negative number
            $^-5 > {^-8}$ $12 > {^-6}$ **inequality sign reversed**

Algebra and Equations

D When we write an equation we must choose a suitable unknown.

We can **solve equations** using **inverse operations** or by **transforming both sides**.

Example $3(n + 2) + 4 = 25$

Inverse operations

$3(n + 2) + 4 = 25$
$3(n + 2) = 25 - 4$
$n + 2 = \frac{21}{3}$
$n = 7 - 2$
$= 5$

Transforming both sides

$3(n + 2) + 4 = 25$
$3n + 6 + 4 = 25$
$3n + 10 = 25$
$3n + 10 - 10 = 25 - 10$
$3n = 15$
$\frac{3n}{3} = \frac{15}{3}$
$= 5$

Use **transforming both sides** when there is an unknown on both sides.

Example

$7p - 3 = 4p + 12$
$7p - 4p - 3 = 4p - 4p + 12$
$3p - 3 = 12$
$3p - 3 + 3 = 12 + 3$
$3p = 15$
$\frac{3p}{3} = \frac{15}{3}$
$= 5$

> Subtract the smaller number of unknowns from each side.

E **Non-linear equations** have terms with indices greater than 1, such as $x^2, x^3, \ldots$

We can solve some non-linear equations to get an exact answer.

Example $x^2 - 10 = 39$
$x^2 = 39 + 10$
$x^2 = 49$
$x = \sqrt[\pm]{49}$
$= {}^+7 \text{ or } {}^-7$

> When you find the square root, give the positive **and** negative solutions.

Harder non-linear equations are solved using **trial and improvement** or using a calculator, spreadsheet or graph plotting software. The answer is not usually exact.

Example $m^2 + 5 = 27$
$m^2 = 27 - 5$
$= 22$
$m = \sqrt[\pm]{22}$
$= {}^+4 \cdot 69 \text{ or } {}^-4 \cdot 69$

See page 170 for the trial and improvement examples.

F **Algebra and proportion**

When two variables are directly proportional, the ratio of corresponding values is always the same.

p	1	2	3	4	5
q	2	4	6	8	10

$\frac{q}{p} = \frac{2}{1} = \frac{4}{2} = \frac{6}{3} = \frac{8}{4} = \frac{10}{5}$
$q = 2p$

This information can be plotted on a graph.
If the variables are directly proportional the points will lie in a straight line through the origin.

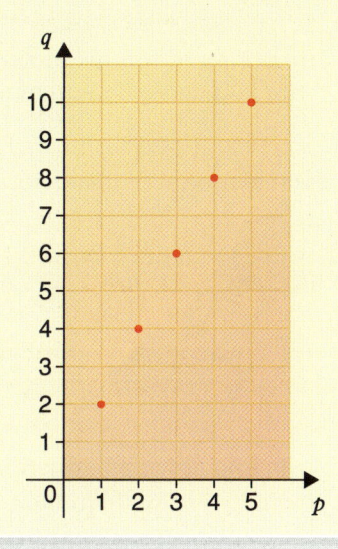

177

Algebra

Test yourself

1 Which of these are equations, which are formulae, which are functions?
  a $y = 2x + 3$
  b $A = \pi r^2$ where r is the radius and A is the area of a circle
  c $a + 7 = 15$
  d $s = \dfrac{D}{T}$ where s is speed, D is distance, T is time
  e $6(x + 5) = 20$
  f $2y - x = 7$

2 Look at this table.

Pocket money (£)

Tim	p
Lisa	q
Kit	r

$p = 3$	Tim gets £3 pocket money
$p + q = 11$	
$q = 2r$	
$\dfrac{p + q + r}{3} = 5$	

Write in words the meaning of each equation in the blue box.
The first one is done for you.

3 Use a copy of this.
Solve these equations.
Show your working.
Shade your answer in the box.
What letter do you get?

  a $2n + 3 = 9$
  b $12n - 2 - 6n = 10$
  c $\dfrac{n}{4} = 3$
  d $\dfrac{n}{5} = 4$
  e $3(n + 2) = 9$
  f $4(n - 2) = 12$
  g $\dfrac{n + 2}{3} = 6$
  *h $\dfrac{n - 2}{3} = {}^-5$
  *i ${}^-n + 7 - 2n = {}^-5$

5	⁻13	12
27	3	17
6	16	13
21	20	⁻3
1	4	2
⁻4	⁻1	$1\tfrac{1}{2}$

4 a Show that $4(x - 3) \equiv 4x - 12$ is true for these.
  i $x = 2$ ii $x = 7$ iii $x = {}^-1$
  b What is the special name we give $4(x - 3) \equiv 4x - 12$?

5 Decide which inequality best describes the statement.
  a A school always has 30 or fewer pupils in its classes.
  A $p \geqslant 30$ B $p > 30$ C $p < 30$ D $p \leqslant 30$
  b Russell takes between 2 and 4 minutes to have a shower.
  A $2 < s \leqslant 4$ B $2 < s < 4$ C $2 \leqslant s < 4$ D $2 \leqslant s \leqslant 4$

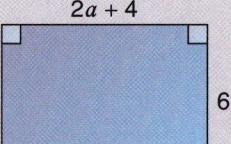

6 The perimeter of this rectangle is 48.
Write and solve an equation to find a.

Rectangle with sides $2a + 4$ and 6.

7 Each diagonal of this diagram adds to 32.

Diagram with circles: $x + 2$, $2x + 7$, $3x + 1$ (centre), $x - 6$, $2x - 1$.

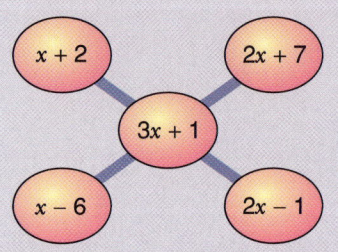

Write and solve an equation to find x.
Check that both diagonals add to 32.

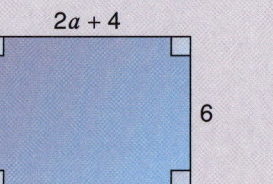

178

Algebra and Equations

8 This is a parallelogram.
Write an equation then solve it to find the value of x

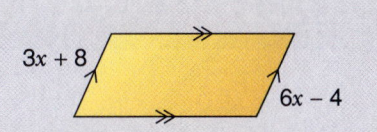

$3x + 8$
$6x - 4$

9 Sam started with $5 > {}^-5$ **True**
She added 4 to both sides. $5 + 4 > {}^-5 + 4$
                                $9 > {}^-1$ **Still true**
Start with $5 > {}^-5$. Do each of these to both sides.
For which do you have to change > to < for the inequality to remain true?
 a subtract 4   **b** add 5   **c** multiply by $^-1$
 d divide by 5   **e** divide by $^-2$ **f** add $^-4$

10 Find the values of a and b.
$\frac{3}{4} = \frac{a}{12}$ $\frac{2}{3} = \frac{3}{b}$

11 Solve these equations.
Show your working.
 a $9t - 2 = 16 + 3t$ **b** $7y + 2 = 4y + 10$ **c** $7y - 15 = 4(y - 3)$
 d $3(4m + 5) = {}^-3$ ***e** $\frac{3(2x + 3)}{8} = 3$ ***f** $2(5k - 3) + 8 = 3k - 5$

12 Solve these to find an exact answer.
 a $3x^2 = 75$ **b** $k^2 - 15 = 129$ ***c** $3 = \frac{108}{n^2}$

13 Use a calculator to find the solutions to these.
Give the answers to 1 d.p.
 a $p^3 = 75$ **b** $2.2m^2 = 18$

14 Use a calculator and trial and improvement to answer these.
 a The length of one side of a rectangle is y.
    This equation shows the area of the rectangle.
    $y(y + 2) = 67.89$
    Find the value of y. Show your working.
    You may find the table helpful.

y	$y + 2$	$y(y + 2)$	
8	10	80	too large

 b Find an approximate solution to $w^3 + w = 94$ to 2 d.p.

15 A chocolate shop sold single chocolates for 20p.
 a Copy and fill in this table.

Number of chocolates (n)	1	2	3	4	5	6
Money earned (p)	20	40				

 b Is the money earned directly proportional to the number of chocolates sold? Justify your answer using ratio.
 c Would you expect the graph of money earned versus number of chocolates sold to be a straight line? Explain.
 d Use a copy of this grid.
    Draw a graph of money earned versus number of chocolates.
 e Write the relationship between number of chocolates, n, and money earned, p.
 f How many chocolates have been sold if 200p is earned?

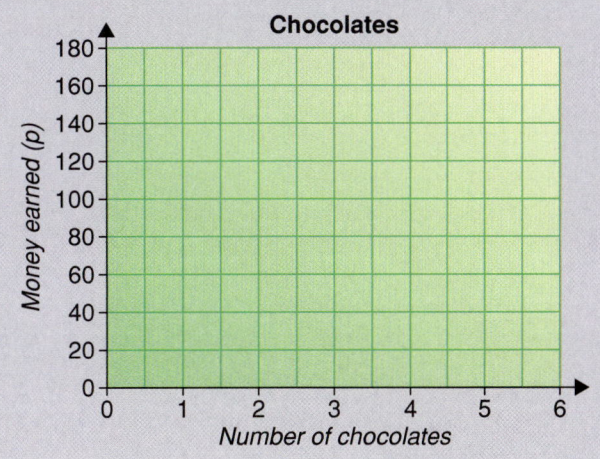

179

7 Expressions and Formulae

You need to know

✓ expressions — page 146
✓ simplifying expressions — page 147
✓ substituting into expressions — page 147
✓ formulae — page 147

> **Key vocabulary**
> algebraic expression, collect like terms, common factor,
> expand the product, factorise, formula, formulae, index law,
> region, simplest form, subject of the formula,
> take out common factors

▶▶ There's a skeleton in the cupboard

When a skeleton is found, forensic scientists can estimate the height this person was from the length of various bones.

For **males**, the formulae are

$H = 3.08h + 70.45$
$H = 3.7u + 70.45$
$H = 2.52t + 75.79$

For **females**, the formulae are

$H = 3.36h + 57.97$
$H = 4.27u + 57.76$
$H = 2.90t + 59.24$

H = estimated height in centimetres
h = length of humerus bone (cm)
u = length of ulna bone (cm)
t = length of tibia bone (cm)

1 A forensic scientist found part of a female skeleton with a tibia bone of 39·9 cm. What was her estimated height?
*2 Work out the length your humerus, ulna and tibia should be for your height.

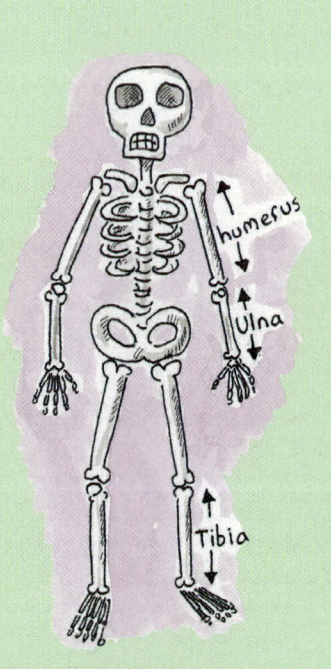

Expressions and Formulae

Simplifying expressions

Collecting like terms

Remember
We can simplify expressions by **collecting like terms**.

Example $2n + 5m - n - 4m = 2n - n + 5m - 4m$
$ = n + m$

like terms like terms

Write like terms next to each other.

The sign **before** the term moves with it.

Example $5x^2 + 3x - 2x^2 + 6 - 8 + 4x = 5x^2 - 2x^2 + 3x + 4x + 6 - 8$
$ = 3x^2 + 7x - 2$

Note: Terms in x and x^2 are **not** like terms so cannot be added or subtracted.

Example $5(x + 3) - 2(x - 1) = (5 \times x) + (5 \times 3) + (^-2 \times x) + (^-2 \times ^-1)$
$ = 5x + 15 - 2x + 2$
$ = 5x - 2x + 15 + 2$
$ = 3x + 17$

For more practice at multiplying out brackets see page 147 of the support chapter.

Example $3p - (^-p) = 3p - 1(^-p)$
$ = 3p + ^-1 \times ^-p$
$ = 3p + p$
$ = 4p$

A negative sign in front of a bracket can be written as $^-1 \times (....)$.

Note Sometimes expanding brackets is called **'expanding the product'**.

Exercise 1

1 Write each expression on the green cards in its simplest form. Find the red card that matches it.

$8a + 3a$	$5a + 3 + 4a$	$10a + 8$	$5a + 5$	$a + 3 + a + 6$	$11a$
$4a + 21$	$2a + 9$	$9a + 8 - 4a - 3$	$9a + 3$	$3a - 5 - a + 6$
$8 + 6a + 4a$	$a + 9 + 3a + 12$	$2a + 1$	$5a - 7 - 4a - 3$	$a - 10$

2 Write each expression in its simplest form. **[SATs Paper 1 Level 6]**
  a $7 + 2t + 3t$ **b** $b + 7 + 2b + 10$

3 Show that this is a magic square.
The sum of the first row is
$x + 4 + 4x + 4x + 5 = 9x + 9$

$x + 4$	$4x$	$4x + 5$
$6x + 4$	$3x + 3$	2
$2x + 1$	$2x + 6$	$5x + 2$

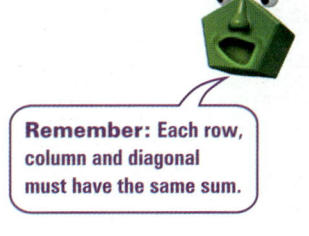

Remember: Each row, column and diagonal must have the same sum.

181

Algebra

4 Write each expression in its simplest form.
  a $3x^2 + 2x + 4x^2 + x$
  b $8x^2 + 9 + 2x^2 - 7$
  c $5x^2 - 3 + 2x^2 + 8$
  d $7x^2 - 3 - 5x^2 + 6$
  e $9x^2 + 3 - 6x^2 - 6$

5 Write an expression in its simplest form for the perimeter of each shape.
  a Triangle with sides $3y - 1$, $3y - 1$, $2y + 3$
  b Rectangle with sides $3a + 4$ and $2a + 1$
  *c Triangle with sides $2m + 7$, $12 - 2m$, $5m - 3$

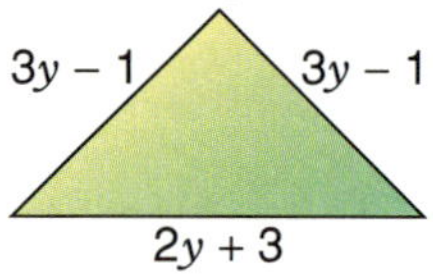

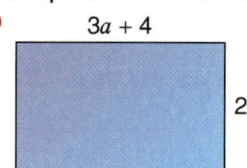

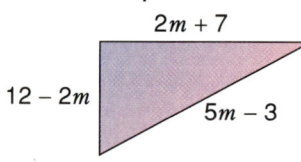

T

6 Use a copy of this.
The expression in the box is the sum of the expressions in the circles on either side of it.
Write the missing expressions as simply as possible.

  a Top circle: $2x + 5$; bottom circles: $5x - 2$ and $4x + 1$
  b Top circle: $6x + 3$; bottom circles: $8 - 4x$ and $2x - 4$
  *c Known boxes/circles: $8x + 7$, $3x + 4$, $6x - 1$

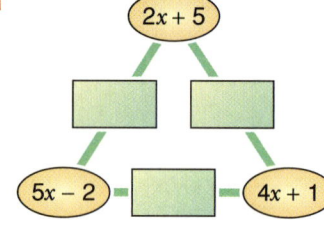

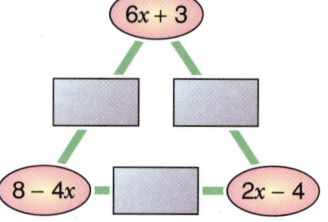

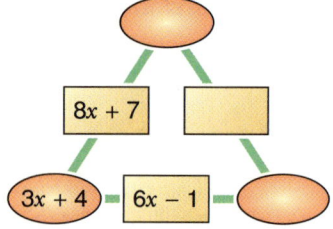

7 Expand these products.
  a $3(x + 4)$
  b $7(y + 2)$
  c $8(b - 2)$
  d $5(k - 3)$
  *e $7(5 - m)$

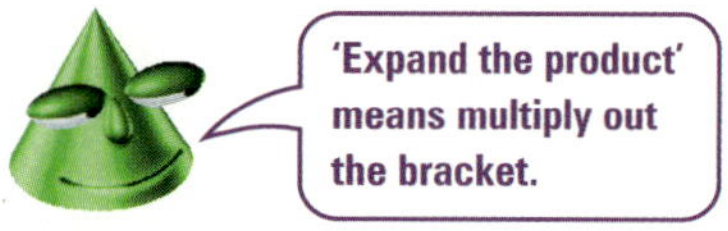

'Expand the product' means multiply out the bracket.

8 Which two of these expressions are equivalent?

$4(3y + 6)$ $4(3y + 24)$ $12(y + 3)$ $3(4y + 8)$

9 Write each expression in its simplest form. [SATs Paper 1 Level 6]
  a $(3d + 5) + (d - 2)$
  b $3m - (^{-}m)$

10 Write these without brackets and then simplify.
  a $(2n + 4) + (n - 3)$
  b $3(p + 2) + (p + 4)$
  c $6(x + 3) + 2(x - 1)$
  d $4(m - 2) + 3(m + 4)$
  *e $7b - (b + 2)$
  *f $5k - (^{-}k)$
  g $4(r + 2) - 3(r - 4)$
  h $5(f - 2) - (3 - f)$
  i $3(n - 2) - 2(4 - 3n)$

*11 Write an expression for the missing lengths.

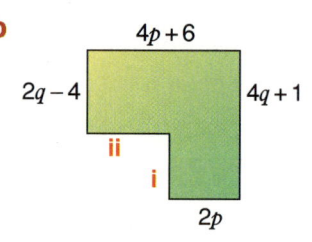

  a Square with top $5b + 2$, side $6a + 4$, marked $3a + 1$ and ii, bottom b and i.
  b L-shape with lengths $4p + 6$, $2q - 4$, $4q + 1$, ii, i, $2p$.
  c L-shape with lengths $2m + 1$, ii, i, $3n - 5$, $2n - 1$, $8m + 7$.

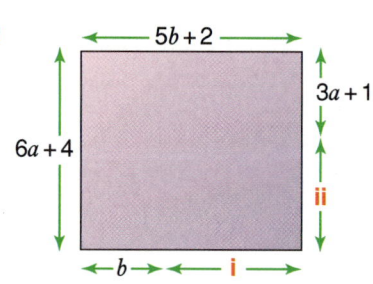

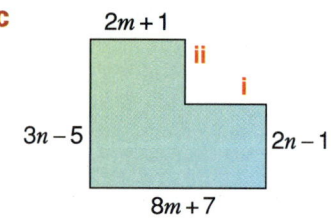

*12 What might the missing lengths be?

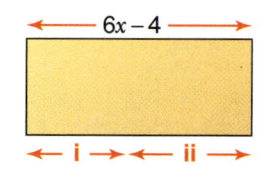

Rectangle with top $6x - 4$ and bottom split into i and ii.

There is more than one possible answer.

Expressions and Formulae

*13 a Use a copy of this.
Fill in the expressions in the squares to make this a magic square.

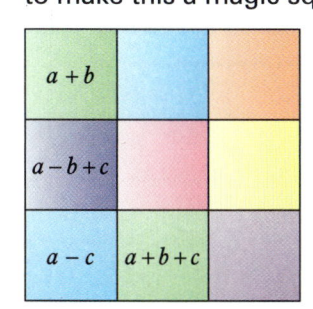

$a+b$		
$a-b+c$		
$a-c$	$a+b+c$	

b Write an expression for each square to make this a magic square with a magic sum of $3x - 3$.

		$x+2$
$x+1$		
		$x-2$

Review 1

						S			
4	3	8	6	2	5	1	7	5	6

Use a copy of the box above. Match your answers to the answers in the red box. Write the letter beside the answer above the question number in your box.

Simplify these expressions.
1 $2x + 3 + x + 4$
2 $5x + 2 - x + 3$
3 $3x^2 + 4 - x^2 - 2$
4 $8x + 5 - 7$
5 $5x^2 + 3x^2 - 6x^2$
6 $7x + 3 - 5x$
7 $4x + 5 - x - 1$
8 $3x - 1 + 2x - 5$

A	$2x^2$
E	$4x + 5$
O	$2x^2 + 2$
R	$2x + 3$
S	$3x + 7$
T	$3x + 4$
U	$5x - 6$
Y	$8x - 2$

Review 2 Use a copy of this diagram.
The number in each box is found by adding the numbers in the two circles on either side.
a Find what goes in the boxes.
b Find the sum of the expressions in the three boxes.

Circles: $2a^2 + a$, $7a^2 + 4a$, $3a^2 - 2a$

Review 3

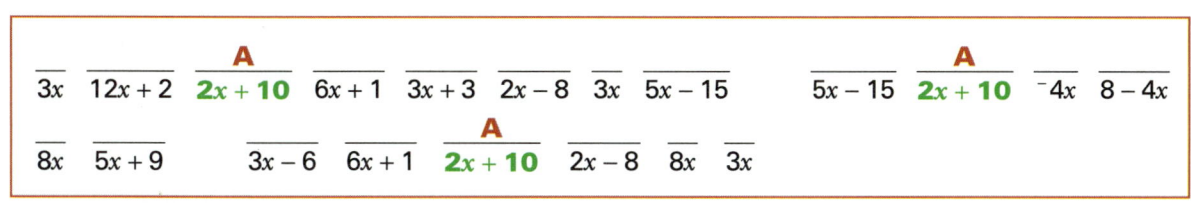

		A							**A**		
$3x$	$12x+2$	$2x+10$	$6x+1$	$3x+3$	$2x-8$	$3x$	$5x-15$	$5x-15$	$2x+10$	^-4x	$8-4x$

				A			
$8x$	$5x+9$	$3x-6$	$6x+1$	$2x+10$	$2x-8$	$8x$	$3x$

Use a copy of this box. Write the letter beside each question above its answer in the box.

Write these without brackets and simplify if possible.
A $2(x + 5) = 2x + 10$
E $4(2 - x)$
F $3(x + 1)$
H $5(x - 3)$
I $2(x - 4)$
B $3(x - 2)$
N $6x - (^-2x)$
O $3(x + 1) + 2(x + 3)$
V $3x + (^-7x)$

Find the perimeters of these shapes.

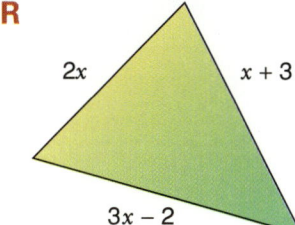

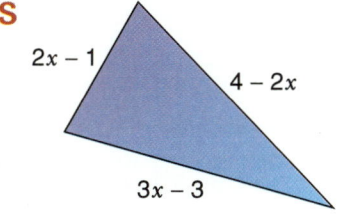

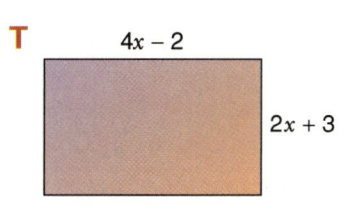

R Triangle with sides $2x$, $x + 3$, $3x - 2$

S Triangle with sides $2x - 1$, $4 - 2x$, $3x - 3$

T Rectangle with sides $4x - 2$ and $2x + 3$

Algebra

Review 4 The number in each box is found by adding the numbers in the two boxes below it.
Write possible expressions for the empty boxes.

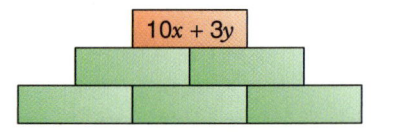

$10x + 3y$

Multiplying and dividing

Remember

$3 \times 2a = 6a$ 3 lots of $2a$

$5m \times 4m = 5 \times m \times 4 \times m$
$\quad\quad\quad\ = 5 \times 4 \times m \times m$ multiply numbers together, then letters together
$\quad\quad\quad\ = 20 \times m^2$
$\quad\quad\quad\ = \mathbf{20m^2}$

$6a \times 4b = 6 \times a \times 4 \times b$
$\quad\quad\quad = 6 \times 4 \times a \times b$
$\quad\quad\quad = \mathbf{24ab}$

$\dfrac{5p^1}{p^1} = 5$ cancel common factors

$\dfrac{12m^2}{4m} = \dfrac{^3\cancel{12} \times \,^1\cancel{m} \times m}{^1\cancel{4} \times \cancel{m}^1}$ cancel common factors
$\quad\quad\ = 3m$

Remember
When multiplying numbers with indices, we **add the indices**.

Example $5^3 \times 5^4 = 5^{3+4}$
$\quad\quad\quad\quad\quad\ = \mathbf{5^7}$

When dividing numbers with indices, we **subtract the indices**.

Example $\dfrac{8^7}{8^3} = 7^{7-3}$
$\quad\quad\quad\ = \mathbf{8^4}$

Discussion
- How could you show that $a^3 \times a^4 = a^{3+4} = a^7$?   **Discuss**.
- How could you show that $n^6 \div n^4 = n^{6-4} = n^2$?   **Discuss**.

Sometimes we use the **index laws** to help **simplify an expression**.

Worked Example
a $3m^3 \times m^2$ **b** $\dfrac{2p^5}{p^2}$

Answers
a $3m^3 \times m^2 = 3 \times m^3 \times m^2$
$\quad\quad\quad\quad\quad\ = 3 \times m^{3+2}$
$\quad\quad\quad\quad\quad\ = \mathbf{3m^5}$

b $\dfrac{2p^5}{p^2} = 2p^{5-2}$
$\quad\quad\ = \mathbf{2p^3}$

There is more about the index laws on page 50.

Remember that $n = n^1$.

Exercise 2

1 Draw a true and a false box.
Put each of these into one of the boxes.

True	False

- $2 \times 5x = 7x$
- $8 \times 2x = 16x$
- $8x + 4x = 12x^2$
- $\dfrac{3x}{3} = x$
- $3x \times 4 = 12x$
- $5a \times 3a = 15a$
- $7p \times 4p = 28p^2$
- $\dfrac{4y^2}{y} = 4$

Expressions and Formulae

2 Simplify these.
  a $2 \times 6x$
  b $3 \times 4m$
  c $2p \times 5$
  d $^-3 \times 2y$
  e $2n \times {}^-4$
  f $3a \times 2a$
  g $6b \times 2b$
  h $3f \times 7f$
  i $5d \times d$
  j $9q \times {}^-3q$
  k $5a \times 6b$
  l $7m \times 3n$
  m $9k \times 5l$
  *n $3a \times 4a^2$
  *o $2n \times 6n^2$

3 Simplify these by cancelling.
  a $\frac{x^2}{x}$
  b $\frac{12y}{4}$
  c $\frac{45n}{27}$
  d $\frac{35b^2}{7b}$
  e $\frac{16p^2}{12p}$

4 Simplify these using the index laws.
  a $m \times m^2$
  b $b^3 \times b^2$
  c $3n \times n^2$
  d $6a^2 \times a^3$
  e $\frac{y^4}{y^2}$
  f $\frac{q^5}{q^3}$
  g $x^4 \div x^3$
  h $k^8 \div k^5$
  i $\frac{15x^4}{5x^2}$
  *j $\frac{12y^{12}}{8y^8}$
  *k $\frac{m^3}{m^5}$
  *l $5x^2 \times 3x^3$

5 Use a copy of these. Fill them in.

  a

×	3n	⁻2n	4a
5			
4n			

  b

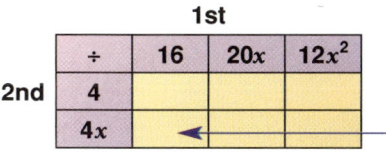

		1st		
	÷	16	20x	12x²
2nd	4			
	4x			

  ← This square is tricky!

6 Write an expression for the area of these.
  a rectangle 3x by 8
  b right triangle with legs 4x and 6x
  *c trapezium with parallel sides 7x and 13x, height 6x

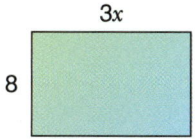

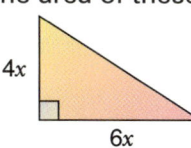

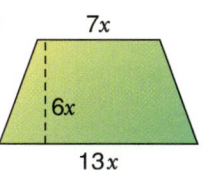

***7** Write an expression for the red length in each of these.
  a rectangle, width 4x, area = 24x²
  b triangle, side 4y, area = 20y²
  c trapezium, top 8a, bottom 12a, area = 40a²

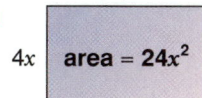

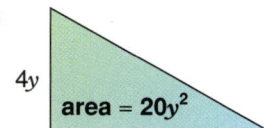

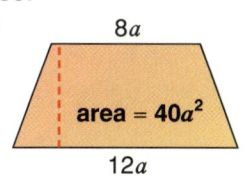

Review 1

| $6a$ | a^5 | $12a^2$ | a^6 | $12a^5$ | $2a$ | a^9 | a^6 | $6a^2$ | **A** $15a$ | a^4 | $2a$ |

| $12a^2$ | $6a$ | $12a^3$ | $2a$ | $12a^2$ | $6a$ | a^5 | a^5 | $12a$ |

Use a copy of this box.
Simplify by multiplying, cancelling or using the index laws.
Put the letter beside each question above its answer in the box.

  A $3 \times 5a = \mathbf{15a}$
  B $3a \times 4a$
  O $a^2 \times a^3$
  E $\frac{16a}{8}$
  R $a \times a^8$
  L $\frac{12ab}{2b}$
  D $^-4 \times {}^-3a$
  H $\frac{24a^3}{4a}$
  S $a^8 \div a^2$
  T $3a^2 \times 4a^3$
  V $a^9 \div a^5$
  U $\frac{24a^5}{2a^2}$

Review 2 Use a copy of these. Fill them in.

×	6m	⁻3p	2p²
3			
5p			

		1st		
	÷	6x²	12x	⁻18x³
2nd	3			
	6x²			

185

Algebra

T

? Puzzle

Use a copy of this.
Simplify these.
Shade the answer on your diagram.

a $5(2x - 7)$ b $3(x - 4) - (x + 2)$
c $5(x - 4) - (x - 2)$ d $4 \times 2x$
e $3x \times 2x$ f $3x \times 5x^2$
g $x(x + 3)$ h $\frac{36xy}{18x}$
i $\frac{5x^3}{15x}$ j $\frac{12x^4}{10x^2}$

What does the shading make?

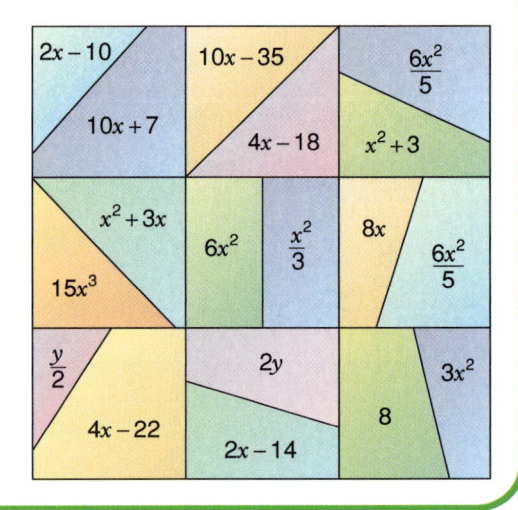

Writing expressions

Worked Example
Chelsea cut a rectangle like this in half.
Allanah cut a rectangle like this in half a different way.
They each joined their two halves to make two new rectangles.

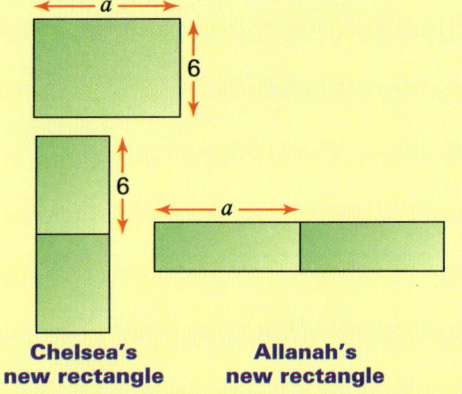

Chelsea's new rectangle   **Allanah's new rectangle**

a   Write and simplify an expression for the perimeter of each new rectangle.
b   What value of a would make the perimeters of Chelsea's and Allanah's new rectangles the same?

Answer
a   Perimeter of Chelsea's rectangle $= 6 + 6 + \frac{a}{2} + 6 + 6 + \frac{a}{2}$
                                    $= \mathbf{24 + a}$
    Perimeter of Allanah's rectangle $= a + a + 3 + a + a + 3$
                                     $= \mathbf{4a + 6}$

b $24 + a = 4a + 6$
        $24 + a - a = 4a + 6 - a$ subtracting a from both sides
        $24 = 3a + 6$
        $24 - \mathbf{6} = 3a + 6 - \mathbf{6}$ subtracting 6 from both sides
        $18 = 3a$
        $a = 6$

186

Expressions and Formulae

Exercise 3

1 It is Imogen's birthday and she is n years old.
This table gives the ages of Imogen's brother and sisters.

	Expression	Words
Teagan	$n + 2$	two years older than Imogen
Greta	$n - 3$	a
Matthew	$2n$	b

a What would be written for **a** in the table?
b What would be written for **b** in the table?
c In two years time Imogen will be $n + 2$ years old.
Write a simplified expression for the age of her brother and each of her sisters in two years time.

2 A teacher has a large pile of cards.
An expression for the **total** number of cards is **$6n + 8$**

[SATs Paper 2 Level 5]

a The teacher puts the cards in two piles.
The number of cards in the first pile is **$2n + 3$**.

first pile   second pile

Write an expression to show the number of cards in the second pile.

b The teacher puts all the cards together.
Then he uses them to make **two equal piles**.

Write an expression to show the number of cards in one of the piles.

c The teacher puts all the cards together again, then he uses them to make two piles.
There are **23** cards in the first pile.

23 cards   ? cards
$n + 3$ $5n + 5$
first pile   second pile

How many cards are in the second pile?
Show your working.

187

Algebra

T

3 Use a copy of this. [SATs Paper 1 Level 6]
You can often use algebra to show why a number puzzle works.
Fill in the missing expressions.

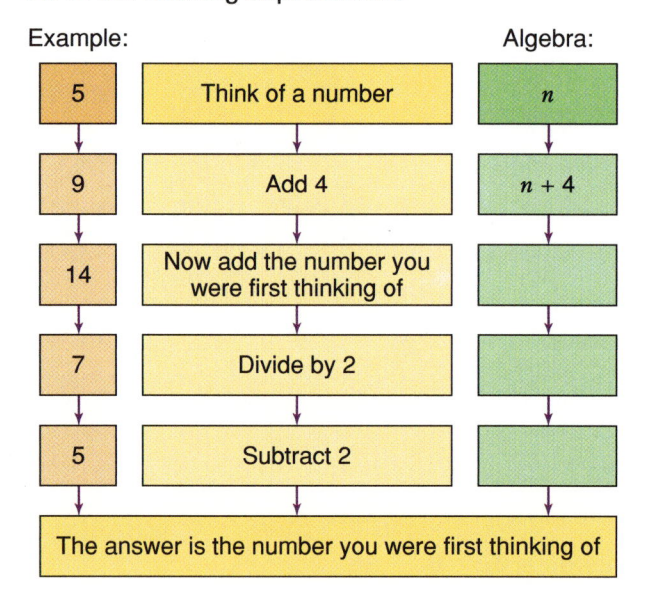

Example: Algebra:

5	Think of a number	n
9	Add 4	$n + 4$
14	Now add the number you were first thinking of	
7	Divide by 2	
5	Subtract 2	

The answer is the number you were first thinking of

4 Jesse and Sam each have this rectangle made out of paper.
   a They write an expression for the perimeter of the rectangle.

   Jesse writes $2m + 16$.
   Sam writes $2(m + 8)$.

   *They could **both** be correct.*

   Who is correct?

   b They each cut the rectangle in half in a different way and join the two halves.
   This is what each ends up with.

   Jesse's new rectangle   **Sam's new rectangle**

   What is the perimeter of each of the new rectangles?
   Write the expressions as simply as possible.

   c What value of m would make the perimeter of Jesse's new rectangle the same as the perimeter of Sam's new rectangle?

5 James, Jenni and Wayne each have a bag of sweets.
They do not know how many are in each bag.
They know that:

   • Jenni has two more sweets than James.
   • Wayne has four times as many sweets as James.

   a If James has x sweets, write an expression, using x, for the number of sweets in Jenni's and Wayne's bags.
   b If Jenni has y sweets, write an expression, using y, for the number of sweets in James's and Wayne's bags.
   c If Wayne has w sweets, which of these expressions gives the number of sweets in Jenni's bag?

   A $4w + 2$ **B** $4w - 2$ **C** $\frac{w}{4} + 2$ **D** $\frac{w}{4} - 2$ **E** $\frac{w+2}{4}$ **F** $\frac{w-2}{4}$

Expressions and Formulae

6 You will need some square dot paper.
On square dot paper you can join dots with two different length lines, a and b.

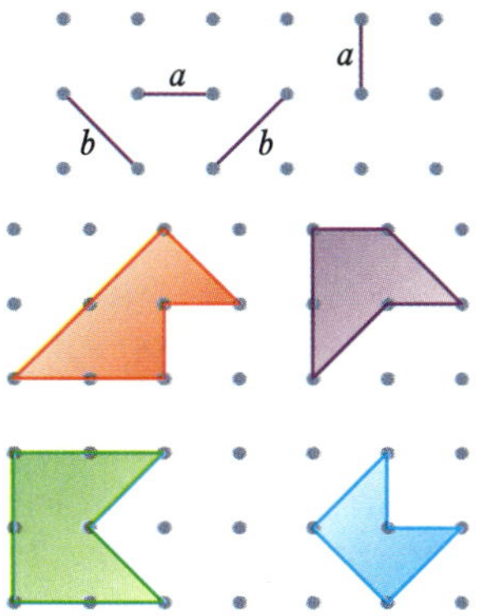

The perimeter of the red shape is $4a + 3b$.
  a Write an expression for the perimeter of these shapes.
   i purple **ii** green **iii** blue
  b On square dot paper, draw shapes with these perimeters.
   i $4a + b$ **ii** $2(2a + b)$

  *__c__ What is the area of this triangle?
   Write it in terms of a.

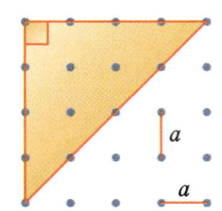

  *__d__ This is the same triangle and grid.
   What is the area of the triangle?
   Write it in terms of b.
  *__e__ Use your answers to **c** and **d** to explain why $2a^2 = b^2$. 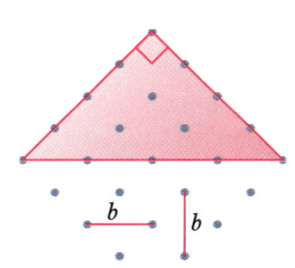

7 To cook roast lamb, allow 30 minutes per $\frac{1}{2}$ kg and then 25 minutes extra.
A leg of lamb weighs x kg.
Write an expression for the time needed to cook lamb.

8 a Write simplified expressions for the area and perimeter of this rectangle.

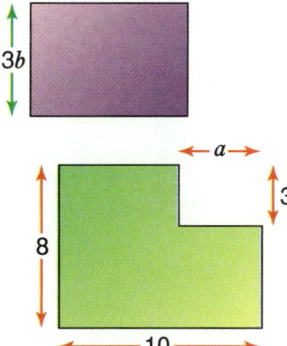

  *__b__ A different rectangle has area $15a^2$ and perimeter $16a$.
   What are the dimensions of this rectangle?

  *__c__ Chiraq and Isra both wrote expressions for the area of this shape.

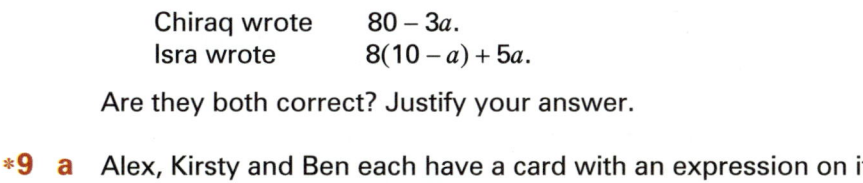

   Chiraq wrote $80 - 3a$.
   Isra wrote $8(10 - a) + 5a$.

   Are they both correct? Justify your answer.

*__9__ **a** Alex, Kirsty and Ben each have a card with an expression on it.
Ben's card is turned so we can't see the expression.

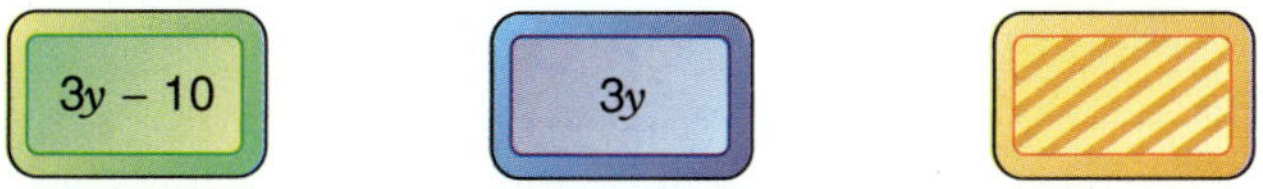

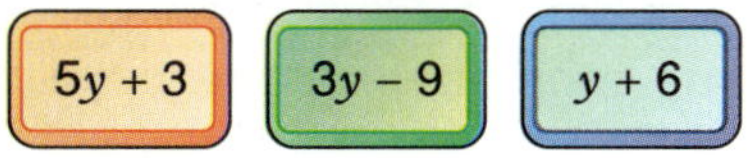

  Alex's card: $3y - 10$
  Kirsty's card: $3y$
  Ben's card

  The mean of the three expressions is $3y$.
  What is written on Ben's card?
  b Write three expressions which have a mean of $4y$.
  c What is the mean of these three expressions?
  Write your expression as simply as possible.

  $5y + 3$ $3y - 9$ $y + 6$

Algebra

*10 Two cube-shaped tanks are filled with water.
    a Write an expression for the volume of the larger tank.
    b Write an expression for the volume of the smaller tank.
    c How much more water will the larger tank hold than the smaller one?

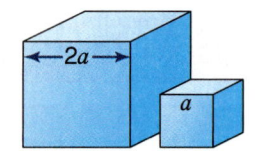

*11 **a** Write an expression for the area of the smaller square.
    b Write an expression for the area of the larger square by dividing it into rectangles as shown.
    c Write an expression for the difference between the larger square and the smaller square.
    d If the difference in the areas is 37, what is the value of x?

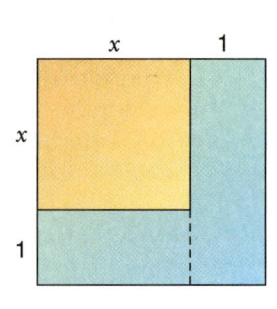

Review 1 Mary earns £p each week.
This table gives the weekly earnings of Mary's friends, in terms of p.

	Expression	Words
John	$p + 3$	£3 more than Mary
Peter	$p - 5$	
Sara	$3p$	

a Write in words what Peter and Sara earn.
b If one week they all get a bonus of £10, what will each earn in terms of p? (Simplify your answers).

Review 2 If the area of **A** (in cm^2) is a and the shaded area of **B** is b then the shaded area of **C** is $a + b$.

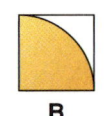

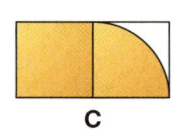

    A   B   C

Here are some tile patterns. They are drawn on the same size grid.
Find the shaded area of each one in terms of a and b.

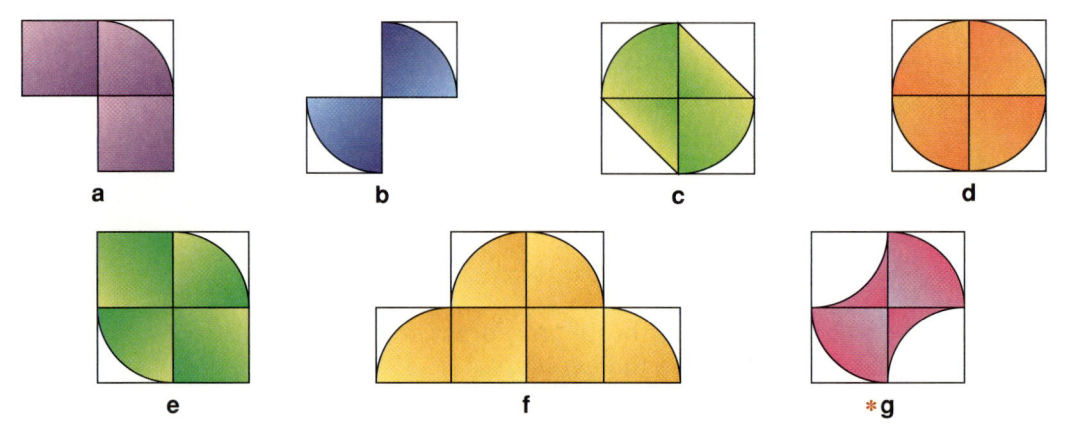

    a   b   c   d

    e   f   *g

Review 3
a Find a simplified expression for the perimeter and area of each of these rectangles.

    A: $4x$ by x
    B: $2x + 3$ by $2x$

b If the perimeters are the same, find the value of x.

190

Expressions and Formulae

Factorising

Factorising an expression is the inverse of multiplying out a bracket.

Example $2(x + 3) = 2x + 6$
If we are asked to factorise $2x + 6$, we get $2(x + 3)$.

We factorise $2x + 6$ by finding the common factor of $2x$ and 6, which is 2. This is then put outside the bracket.

$2x + 6 = 2(x + 3)$

> This is linked to expanding brackets, page 147.

Discussion

- Karen factorised $12x - 8$ like this.

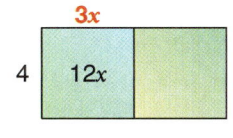

  | 12x | ⁻8 |

  4 | 12x | ⁻8 | 4 is a common factor of $12x$ and $⁻8$.

  3x
  4 | 12x | $4 \times 3x = 12x$ or $\frac{12x}{4} = 3x$

  3x   ⁻2
  4 | 12x | ⁻8 | $4 \times ⁻2 = ⁻8$ or $\frac{⁻8}{4} = ⁻2$

  So $12x - 8 = 4(3x - 2)$

  Discuss Karen's method.

- Saad factorised $12x - 8$ like this.

  $12x - 8 = 4(\quad)$
  $\quad\quad\quad = 4(3x\quad)$ because $4 \times 3x = 12x$
  $\quad\quad\quad = 4(3x - 2)$ because $4 \times ⁻2 = ⁻8$

  Discuss Saad's method.

Always take out the **highest common factor** possible.

Example $16x - 12$ could be factorised as
$16x - 12 = 2(8x - 6)$
or $16x - 12 = 4(4x - 3)$

> Check to see if what you have in the brackets has any common factors.

$4(4x - 3)$ is factorised completely because 4 is the HCF of $16x$ and $⁻12$.

> 4 is the highest number that will divide into $16x$ and 12 so it is the HCF.

Always check your answer by multiplying out the brackets.

$4(4x - 3) = 4 \times 4x + 4 \times ⁻3 = 16x - 12$

Worked Example
Factorise these.   **a** $12n + 6m$ **b** $y^3 + y^2 + 5y$

Answers
a $12n + 6m = \mathbf{6(2n + m)}$

check $6(2n + m) = 6 \times 2n + 6 \times m$
$\quad\quad\quad\quad\quad = 12n + 6m$ ✓

	2n	m
6	12n	6m

b $y^3 + y^2 + 5y = y(y^2 + y + \mathbf{5})$

check $y(y^2 + y + 5) = y \times y^2 + y \times y + y \times 5$
$\quad\quad\quad\quad\quad\quad\quad = y^3 + y^2 + 5y$ ✓

	y²	y	5
y	y³	y²	5y

191

Algebra

Exercise 4

1 Factorise these. Use a copy of the diagrams to help.
  a $2x + 4$

	2x	4
2		

  b $3y + 9$

	3y	9
3		

  c $16p + 24$

	16p	24
8		

  d $8a - 16$

	8a	⁻16
8		

  e $14n - 28$

	14n	⁻28
14		

  f $5a + 5b$

	5a	5b
5		

  g $2n + 4m$

	2n	4m
2		

  h $12x + 8y$

	12x	8y
4		

  i $x^2 + x$

	x^2	x
x		

  j $p^3 + p$

	p^3	p
p		

Remember to check your answers.

2 Copy and complete.
  a $3x + 6 = 3(\_\_ + \_\_)$
  b $5a - 10 = 5(\_\_ - \_\_)$
  c $14x + 4 = 2(\_\_ + \_\_)$
  d $16n - 12 = 4(\_\_ - \_\_)$
  e $4x + 4 = 4(\_\_ + \_\_)$
  f $12n - 4 = \_\_(3n - 1)$
  g $15d - 25 = \_\_(3d - 5)$
  h $18 + 3n = \_\_(6 + n)$
  i $6 - 3a = \_\_(\_\_ - a)$
  j $6 + 9x = \_\_(2 + \_\_)$
  k $15x - 10 = \_\_(\_\_ - 2)$

3 Factorise these.
  a $2n + 2$
  b $4x + 12$
  c $14y - 7$
  d $12y - 8$
  e $8n + 4$
  f $10 + 15n$
  g $9 - 21x$
  h $40 - 15n$
  i $20n + 16$
  j $18 - 6a$
  k $12 + 16n$
  l $6x - 20$

4 Copy and complete.
  a $2a + 2b = 2(\_\_ + \_\_)$
  b $5x + 10y = 5(\_\_ + \_\_)$
  c $4a + 8b = \_\_(a + \_\_)$
  d $2n^2 + n = n(\_\_ + \_\_)$
  e $a^2 + 4a = a(\_\_ + \_\_)$

5 a $y^2 - 2y = y(\_\_ - \_\_)$
  b $x^3 + x^2 = x^2(\_\_ + \_\_)$
  c $a^2 + 4a = a(\_\_ + \_\_)$
  d $8y^2 - 2y = \_\_(4y - \_\_)$
  e $p^3 + p^2 + 6p = p(\_\_ + \_\_ + \_\_)$
  ***f** $15m^2 - 5m = \_\_(\_\_ - \_\_)$
  ***g** $5x^3 - x^2 = \_\_(\_\_ - \_\_)$
  ***h** $12m^3 + 4m^2 = \_\_(\_\_ + \_\_)$

6 a One of these expressions is **not** a correct factorisation of $12a + 24$.
  Which one is it?
  A $12(a + 2)$ **B** $3(4a + 8)$ **C** $2(6a + 12)$ **D** $12(a + 24)$ **E** $6(2a + 4)$
  b Factorise $8y + 16$.
  ***c** Factorise this expression as fully as possible. $8y^3 - 2y^2$

***7 a** The perimeter of a rectangle is $8x^2 + 16x$.
  What might the lengths of its sides be?
  b The area of a rectangle is $8x^2 + 16x$.
  What might the lengths of its sides be?

***8 a** Prove that the sum of three consecutive integers is always a multiple of 3.
  b Prove that the sum of five consecutive integers is always a multiple of 5.

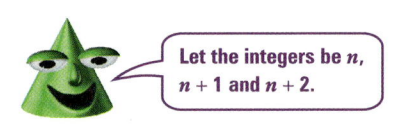

Let the integers be n, $n + 1$ and $n + 2$.

Expressions and Formulae

*9 I think of a number.
I multiply it by 4, add 20, divide by 4, subtract 5.
Try this for several starting numbers. What do you notice?
Use algebra to prove the result.

Review 1 Factorise these. Use a copy of the diagrams to help.
a $20p - 15$

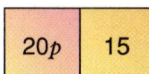

b $5x^2 + x$

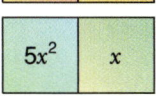

Review 2 Factorise these.
a $5y + 10$ b $20p - 10$ c $3n + 18$ d $20 - 5m$ e $4n + 12m$
f $8q - 16p$ g $3n^2 + n$ h $10a^2 + 5$ i $x^3 + x^2 + 4x$

Review 3
a One of these expressions is **not** a correct factorisation of $36x - 24$. Which one is it?
   A $12(3x - 2)$ B $6(6x - 4)$ C $4(9x - 24)$ D $3(12x - 8)$ E $4(9x - 6)$
b Factorise $12x - 18$.
c Factorise as fully as possible $12a^2b - 6a^2$.

* Adding and subtracting algebraic fractions

Discussion

One way of finding $\frac{2}{3} + \frac{4}{5}$ is like this.

$\frac{2}{3} + \frac{4}{5} = \frac{}{15} + \frac{}{15}$ ← Find a common denominator   3, 6, 9, 12, ⑮
$= \frac{10}{15} + \frac{12}{15}$ ← make equivalent fractions   5, 10, ⑮
$= \frac{22}{15}$

$\frac{2}{3} \xrightarrow{\times 5} \frac{2 \times 5}{3 \times 5}$ and $\frac{4}{5} \xrightarrow{\times 3} \frac{4 \times 3}{5 \times 3}$

How could we use the same method to find $\frac{n}{m} + \frac{\ell}{q}$? **Discuss**.

$\frac{n}{m} + \frac{\ell}{q} = \frac{}{} + \frac{}{}$ ← Find a common denominator

$= \frac{}{} + \frac{}{}$ ← make equivalent fractions

$= \frac{}{}$

Example $\frac{x}{2} + \frac{y}{3} = \frac{3x}{6} + \frac{2y}{6}$ make equivalent fractions with a common denominator of 6 $\frac{x}{2} \xrightarrow{\times 3} \frac{3x}{6}$ and $\frac{y}{3} \xrightarrow{\times 2} \frac{2y}{6}$
$= \frac{3x + 2y}{6}$

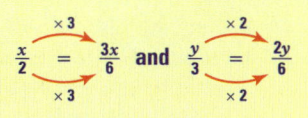

Example $\frac{3}{a} + \frac{b}{c} = \frac{3c}{ac} + \frac{ab}{ac}$ $\frac{3}{a} \xrightarrow{\times c} \frac{3c}{ac}$ and $\frac{b}{c} \xrightarrow{\times a} \frac{ab}{ac}$
$= \frac{3c + ab}{ac}$

Link to adding and subtracting fractions, page 102.

Algebra

Exercise 5

1 a $\frac{2}{3} + \frac{1}{4}$ b $\frac{2}{3} - \frac{1}{2}$ c $\frac{5}{6} + \frac{3}{4}$ d $\frac{3}{8} - \frac{1}{5}$ e $\frac{5}{8} + \frac{3}{7}$

2 Copy these and fill in the gaps.

  a $\frac{2}{p} + \frac{4}{q} = \frac{}{pq} + \frac{}{pq}$
  $\phantom{\frac{2}{p} + \frac{4}{q}} = \frac{}{pq}$

  b $\frac{a}{3} - \frac{b}{2} = \frac{}{} - \frac{}{}$
  $\phantom{\frac{a}{3} - \frac{b}{2}} = \frac{}{}$

  c $\frac{c}{d} + \frac{e}{f} = \frac{}{} + \frac{}{}$
  $\phantom{\frac{c}{d} + \frac{e}{f}} = \frac{}{}$

  d $\frac{3y}{4} - \frac{y}{3} = \frac{}{} - \frac{}{}$
  $\phantom{\frac{3y}{4} - \frac{y}{3}} = \frac{}{}$

3 Simplify these.

  a $\frac{3}{x} + \frac{2}{x}$ b $\frac{y}{3} + \frac{2y}{3}$ c $\frac{5}{y} - \frac{3}{y}$ d $\frac{a}{4} + \frac{a}{3}$ e $\frac{2}{x} - \frac{3}{y}$

  f $\frac{7}{m} + \frac{3}{n}$ g $\frac{1}{p} + \frac{2}{q}$ h $\frac{p}{q} + \frac{r}{s}$ i $\frac{2x}{5} - \frac{x}{4}$ j $\frac{3x}{y} - \frac{2w}{z}$

4 Meryl wrote this.

  For all values of n and m
  $\frac{1}{n} + \frac{1}{m} = \frac{2}{n+m}$

  Show that Meryl is wrong.

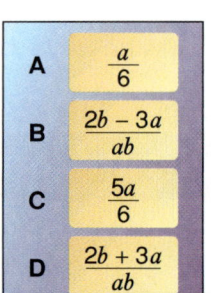

5 Find a fraction in the box that matches each of these.
  a $\frac{a}{2} + \frac{a}{3}$ b $\frac{2}{a} + \frac{3}{b}$ c $\frac{a}{2} - \frac{a}{3}$ d $\frac{2}{a} - \frac{3}{b}$

A	$\frac{a}{6}$
B	$\frac{2b - 3a}{ab}$
C	$\frac{5a}{6}$
D	$\frac{2b + 3a}{ab}$

6 Find two pairs of matching expressions.

$\frac{x}{3} - \frac{y}{4}$ $\frac{3}{x} + \frac{4}{x}$ $\frac{7}{x}$ $\frac{7}{x^2}$ $\frac{4x - 3y}{12}$

*7 Use a copy of this.
Add the expressions in two circles to find the expression in the square in between.

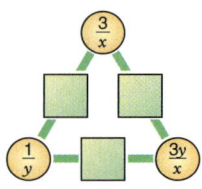

(Triangle diagram with circles: $\frac{3}{x}$ at top, $\frac{1}{y}$ bottom-left, $\frac{3y}{x}$ bottom-right)

Review

| $\frac{5b - 2a}{ab}$ | $\overset{A}{\frac{7}{a}}$ | $\frac{4}{a}$ | $\frac{5a + 4b}{20}$ | $\frac{5b - 2a}{ab}$ | $\overset{A}{\frac{7}{a}}$ | $\frac{2a + 8b}{ab}$ | $\frac{4}{a}$ |
| $\frac{4}{a}$ | $\overset{A}{\frac{7}{a}}$ | $\frac{5a + 4b}{20}$ | $\frac{4}{a}$ | $\frac{b^2 - 3a^2}{ab}$ | $\frac{5a + 4b}{20}$ | $\frac{3a^2 + 2b^2}{ab}$ | $\frac{7a}{12}$ | $\overset{A}{\frac{7}{a}}$ | $\frac{13a}{10}$ |

Use a copy of this box. Write the letter beside each, above its answer in the box.

A $\frac{4}{a} + \frac{3}{a} = \frac{7}{a}$ **G** $\frac{a}{4} + \frac{a}{3}$ **R** $\frac{3a}{2} - \frac{a}{5}$ **T** $\frac{6}{a} - \frac{2}{a}$

C $\frac{5}{a} - \frac{2}{b}$ **N** $\frac{8}{a} + \frac{2}{b}$ **S** $\frac{a}{4} + \frac{b}{5}$ **U** $\frac{3a}{b} + \frac{2b}{a}$

E $\frac{b}{a} - \frac{3a}{b}$

Expressions and Formulae

Substituting into expressions

Examples

When $x = {}^-2$
$3x^2 + 4 = 3({}^-2)^2 + 4$
$= 3(4) + 4$
$= 12 + 4$
$= 16$

When $y = 8$
$4(y - 2)^2 = 4(8 - 2)^2$
$= 4(6)^2$
$= 4 \times 36$
$= 144$

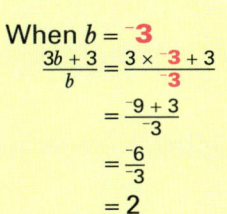

Use BIDMAS – see page 61.

When $m = 0{\cdot}2$
$2 - 4m = 2 - 4 \times 0{\cdot}2$
$= 2 - 0{\cdot}8$
$= 1{\cdot}2$

When $b = {}^-3$
$\frac{3b + 3}{b} = \frac{3 \times {}^-3 + 3}{{}^-3}$
$= \frac{{}^-9 + 3}{{}^-3}$
$= \frac{{}^-6}{{}^-3}$
$= 2$

When $a = 4$
$\frac{1}{2}(a^2 + 4) = \frac{1}{2}(4^2 + 4)$
$= \frac{1}{2}(16 + 4)$
$= \frac{1}{2}(20)$
$= 10$

Exercise 6

Except for questions 7, 8 and Review 3.

1 When $a = 20$ find the value of these.
   a $3a$ **b** $2a - 4$ **c** $3(a - 10)$ **d** $5(a - 10)^2$ **e** $\frac{a^2}{2}$

2 **a** When $n = 30$, find the value of $2n + 1$ [SATs Paper 2 Level 5]
   b When $n = 30$, find the value of $2(n + 1)$.

3 **a** When $x = 5$, work out the values of the expressions below.   [SATs Paper 2 Level 5]
      $2x + 13$ $5x - 5$ $3 + 6x$
   b When $2y + 11 = 17$ work out the value of y. Show your working.

4 **a** Use a copy of this.   [SATs Paper 2 Level 5]
      Join pairs of algebraic expressions that have the **same value** when $a = 3$, $b = 2$ and $c = 6$.
      One pair is joined for you.
   b Repeat **a** when $a = b = c$

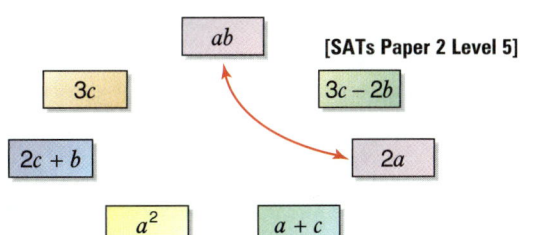

Boxes: ab, $3c$, $3c - 2b$, $2c + b$, $2a$, a^2, $a + c$

5 Work out the value of the expression $2y^2 - 3$ when
   a $y = 2$ **b** $y = 10$ **c** $y = {}^-1$ **d** $y = {}^-3$ *__e__ $y = 0{\cdot}1$ *__f__ $y = 0{\cdot}5$.

6 Use a copy of this.

Start

$\frac{p^2}{2}$	$\frac{p^2}{4} + 50$	$\frac{3p^2}{2}$	$p^2 - 100$	$5p^2(p+1)$
$p^2 - 75$	$\frac{p^2}{5}$	$4p^2 + 4$	$\frac{2p^2(p-3)}{2}$	p^3
$p^2 + 8$	$\frac{(p-8)^2}{2}$	$\frac{(p+2)^2}{24}$	$(p-4)^2$	$\frac{2p^2}{8}$

'Adjacent' means next to.

Work out the value of each expression when $p = 10$.
Start at the red square and always move to an adjacent square with a greater value.
What colour square do you end in?

195

Algebra

T **7** Use a copy of this.
Find the answer to each of **a**, **b** and **c**.
Shade the answers in the grid to get a picture.
  a If $x = 10$ find the value of these expressions.
   i $3x^2$ **ii** $\frac{3x^2}{2}$ **iii** $\sqrt{9x^2}$ **iv** $\sqrt{325 - x^2}$
   v $3(x^2 - 9)$ **vi** $3x^2(x - 5)$ * **vii** $\frac{2x^2(x-3)}{7x}$
  b Find the value of these when $x = {}^-4$.
   i $2x + 12$ **ii** $3x + 2$ **iii** $20 - x$ **iv** $3(x - 2)$
   v $\frac{2x+4}{x}$ **vi** $\frac{x-2}{x+2}$ **vii** $3x^2 + 4$ **viii** $\frac{4x^2 + 0·6}{2}$
  c Repeat **b** for $x = 0·1$.
    Round the answer to **vi** to 1 d.p.

12	21·1	⁻18	20	900	2·3	7
24	15	1	4	450	17·7	⁻3
30	3	1500	52	90	19	⁻5·7
14	16	300	⁻10	150	19·9	0·32
6	2	2·3	4·03	12·2	⁻0·9	273
7·7	$\frac{1}{3}$	32·3	400	14·2	8·6	42

8 Cans of spaghetti are stacked in piles.

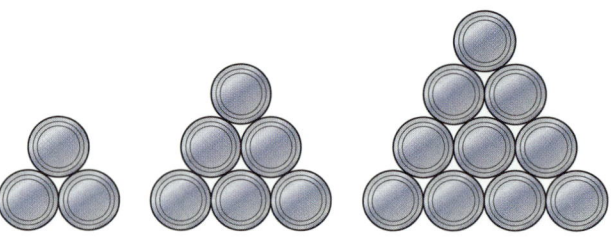

If the pile has p rows, the number of cans stacked is
$\frac{1}{2}(p^2 + p)$
How many cans are stacked in a pile with
  a 12 rows   **b** 16 rows   **c** 24 rows?

* **9 a** y is an odd number.
    Draw an odd and an even box on your page.
    Which of these numbers must be odd and which must be even?
    Put each in one of your boxes.
       $2y$ y^2 $2y - 1$ $3y - 2$ $(y - 1)(y + 1)$

odd	even

  b y is an odd number.
    Is the number $\frac{y+1}{2}$ odd or even or is it not possible to tell? Explain your answer.

* **10** **A** $n - 3$ **B** $2n$ **C** n^2 **D** $\frac{n}{2}$ **E** $\frac{3}{n}$
  a Which of these expressions has the greatest value when n is between 1 and 2?
  b Which expression has the greatest value when n is between 0 and 1?
  c Which expression has the greatest value when n is negative?

* **11** Write true or false for each of these.   [SATs Paper 1 Level 7]
  a i When x is even,   **ii** When x is even,
       $(x - 2)^2$ is even. $(x - 2)^2$ is odd.
     Show how you know it is true for **all** even values of x.
  b i When x is even,   **ii** When x is even,
       $(x - 1)(x + 1)$ is even. $(x - 1)(x + 1)$ is odd.
     Show how you know it is true for **all** even values of x.

Review 1 When $x = 8$, find the values of these.
  a $5x$ **b** $3x - 5$ **c** $4(2x - 5)$ **d** $2(x - 3)^2$ **e** $\frac{5x}{4}$

Expressions and Formulae

Review 2 When $a = 3$, $b = {}^-4$ and $c = 5$, find the values of these.
a $a + b + c$ **b** $2a + b$ **c** abc **d** $\frac{ab}{c}$ **e** $a^2 - c$
f $a(2c + 3)$ **g** $3(b^2 - 5)$ **h** $\frac{bc^2}{10}$ **i** $(2a - b)^2$ **j** $a^2 + b^2 + c^2$

Review 3

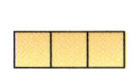

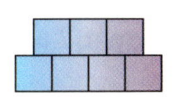

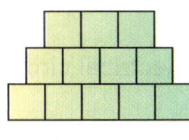

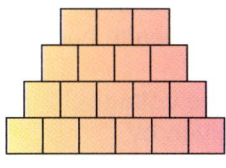

Pattern 1   Pattern 2   Pattern 3   Pattern 4

Amri made these wall patterns.
If the pattern number is n, the number of bricks is $\frac{1}{2}(n^2 + 5n)$.
How many bricks are in pattern
a 12 **b** 20 **c** 28?

Substituting into formulae

The number of diagonals in a polygon with n sides is given by the **formula**
$$D = \frac{n(n-3)}{2}$$
where D is the number of diagonals and n is the number of sides.

To find the number of diagonals in a 12-sided polygon we **substitute** 12 for n.

$D = \frac{n(n-3)}{2}$ Write down the formula first.

$= \frac{12(12-3)}{2}$ Substitute 12 for n.

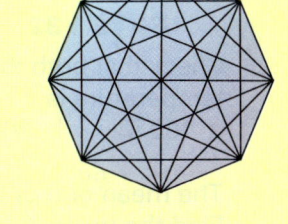

$= \frac{{}^6 12(9)}{{}_1 2}$

$= 54$

Sometimes we have to **solve an equation** once we have substituted for the known values.

Example   The formula for finding the perimeter P of a rectangle is $P = 2(l + w)$ where l and w are the length and width.

Dan wanted to make a large rectangular table in design and technology.
He wanted the perimeter to be 8·5 m and the length to be 2·5 m.
He worked out the width of the table like this.

$p = 2(l + w)$
$8·5 = 2(2·5 + w)$ Substitute the known values.
$8·5 = 5 + 2w$
$8·5 - 5 = 2w$ Solve the equation to find w.
$3·5 = 2w$
$\frac{3·5}{2} = w$
$w = \mathbf{1·75}$ **m**

Remember to put units in the answer.

Algebra

★Review 4 $s = 4t + \frac{1}{2}at^2$ is a formula for finding the distance, s metres, that an object has moved after time, t seconds, and acceleration, a m/s². Find s if
a $t = 4$ seconds, $a = 3$ m/s²   **b** $t = 1.5$ seconds, $a = 10$ m/s²   **c** $t = 1\frac{1}{2}$ seconds, $a = {}^-3$ m/s².

▦Review 5 The circumference of a circle of radius r is given by the formula
$C = 2\pi r$.
Find r to 2 d.p. if $C = 186.4$ cm.

Changing the subject of a formula

Monique is making kites out of two triangular pieces of nylon. She knows the area and the length of the base of each piece. She wants to know the height.

The formula for the area of a triangle is $A = \frac{b \times h}{2}$.
A is the **subject of the formula**.

Monique wants to change the formula so that h is the subject.
She uses inverse operations.

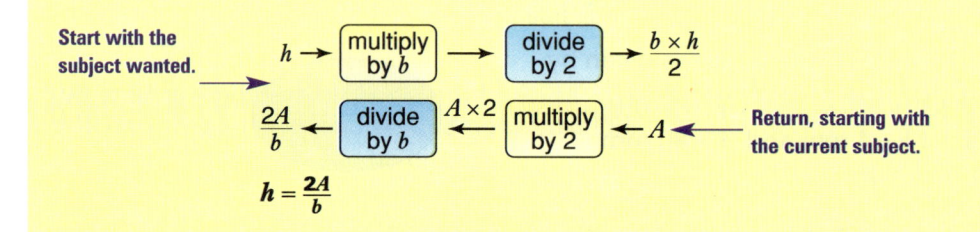

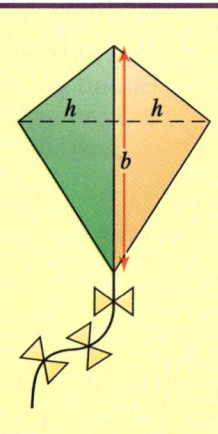

Start with the subject wanted. $h \rightarrow$ [multiply by b] $\rightarrow$ [divide by 2] $\rightarrow \frac{b \times h}{2}$

$\frac{2A}{b} \leftarrow$ [divide by b] $\xleftarrow{A \times 2}$ [multiply by 2] $\leftarrow A \leftarrow$ Return, starting with the current subject.

$h = \frac{2A}{b}$

Worked Example
Make t the subject of $v = u + at$.

Answer

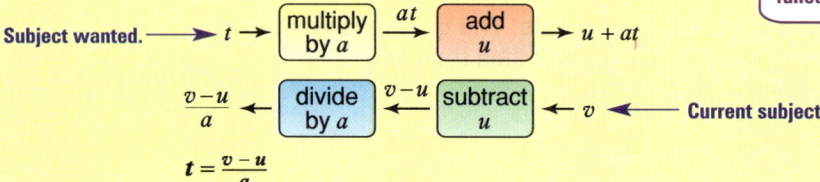

Subject wanted. $\longrightarrow t \rightarrow$ [multiply by a] $\xrightarrow{at}$ [add u] $\rightarrow u + at$

$\frac{v-u}{a} \leftarrow$ [divide by a] $\xleftarrow{v-u}$ [subtract u] $\leftarrow v \leftarrow$ Current subject.

$t = \frac{v-u}{a}$

There is more about inverse functions on page 225.

Discussion
Freya says that she changes the subject of a formula by transforming both sides.

She started to change the subject of $A = \frac{b \times h}{2}$ to b, like this.

$A = \frac{b \times h}{2}$

$A \times 2 = \frac{b \times h}{2} \times 2$

How might she continue? **Discuss**.

How could you use Freya's method to change the subject of these formulae?
$v = u + at$ (subject u) $C = 2\pi r$ (subject r)

Expressions and Formulae

Exercise 8

1 a Make m the subject of $F = ma$. Use the function machines to help.

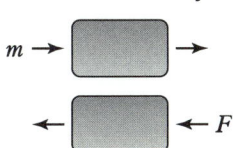

    b Use your new formula to find m if $F = 20$ and $a = 2.5$.

2 a Make a the subject of $F = ma$.

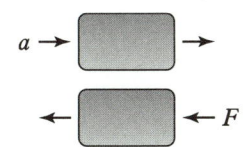

    b Find a if $F = 16$ and $m = 3.2$.

3 a Make l the subject of $A = lb$.
    b Find l if $A = 168$ and $b = 32$.

4 a Make w the subject of $P = 2(l + w)$.

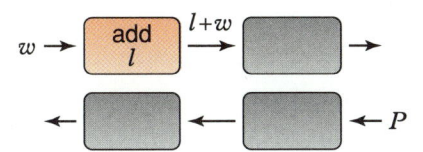

    b Find w if $P = 68$ and $l = 7.4$.

5 Rearrange these formulae to give all the subjects shown.
    a $R =$, $I =$ $V = IR$
    b $h =$, $b =$ $A = \frac{1}{2}bh$
    c $b =$, $h =$, $l =$ $V = lbh$
    d $t =$, $a =$, $u =$ $v = u + at$

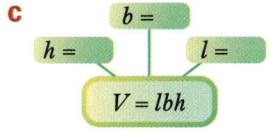

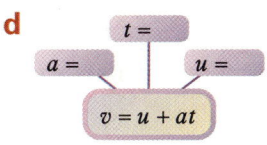

6 a Make l the subject of $P = 2(l + w)$.
    b Find l if $P = 112$ and $w = 16.75$.

7 a Make r the subject of $C = 2\pi r$.
    b Find r to 1 d.p. if $C = 32.4$ cm.

∗8 a The subject of the equation below is p.   [SATs Paper 1 Level 7]
$$p = 2(e + f)$$
Rearrange the equation to make e the subject.
    b Rearrange the equation $r = \frac{1}{2}(c - d)$ to make d the subject.
Show your working.

∗9 a Isobel began to rearrange $A = \pi r^2$ to make r the subject.
$$A = \pi r^2$$
$$\frac{A}{\pi} = r^2$$
$$\underline{} = r$$
What goes in the gap?
    b Rearrange $V = \frac{4}{3}\pi r^3$ to make r the subject.

Algebra

Review 1
a Make l the subject of $V = lbh$.
 Use a copy of these diagrams to help.

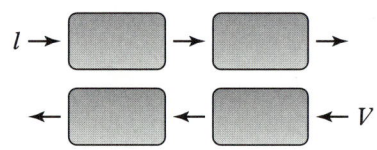

 $l \rightarrow \square \rightarrow \square \rightarrow$
 $\leftarrow \square \leftarrow \square \leftarrow V$

b Find l if $V = 60$, $b = 2 \cdot 5$, $h = 3$.

Review 2
a Make h the subject of $A = \frac{3h}{2}$.
b Find h if $A = 32$ cm^2.

Review 3 Rearrange these formulae to give the subjects asked for.
a $v = \frac{d}{t}$ i $d =$ ___   ii $t =$ ___
b $C = 2\pi r$ i $r =$ ___   ii $\pi =$ ___
c $S = \pi dh$ i $d =$ ___   ii $h =$ ___

Review 4 The formula for converting degrees Celsius to degrees Fahrenheit is $F° = \frac{9C°}{5} + 32°$
a Find the temperature in degrees F when the temperature is 70 °C.
*b Make C° the subject of the formula.
*c Find the temperature in degrees C when the temperature is 176 °F.

Finding formulae

Worked Example
When we put two cubes together, we can count 10 square faces if we pick the shape up and turn it round.

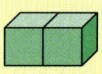

2 cubes

Find a formula for the number of square faces we can count when n cubes are joined in a line.

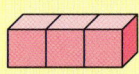

3 cubes 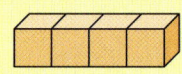   4 cubes

Answer
It is sometimes best to draw a table.

Number of cubes (n)	2	3	4	5	6	...
Number of faces (f)	10	14	18	22	26	...

We can then draw (or make) the shapes, count the faces, and fill in the table.
The number of faces forms the sequence 10, 14, 18, 22, 26, ...
Each number is **4** more than the one before.
The formula will be
    $f = 4 \times n + ?$

We can find what **?** is by looking at the sequence.
1st term $10 = 4 \times 2 + 2$
2nd term $14 = 4 \times 3 + 2$ and so on

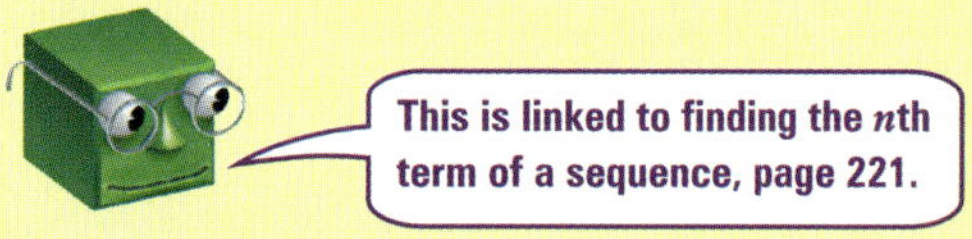

So the formula is $f = 4n + 2$.

This is linked to finding the nth term of a sequence, page 221.

202

Expressions and Formulae

Exercise 9

1 Show, using algebra, that the area of the green part of the diagram is $A = 3ab$.

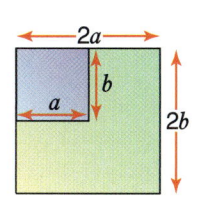

2 Mel wants to put square paving stones in a row.
She wants to plant a shrub along each side of the paving stones.
If she has one paving stone she can plant four plants.
If she has two paving stones she can plant six plants.

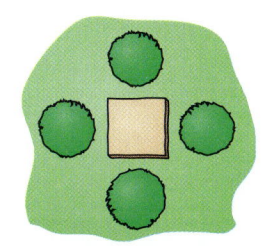

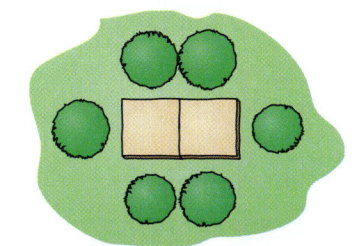

Find a formula for the number of plants (p) that Mel can plant if she puts n paving stones in a row.
A table like this might help.

Number of paving stones (n)				
Number of plants (p)				

3 This network has 3 nodes (•), 5 arcs (⌒) and 4 regions (a, b, c and d – we count the outside as a region).
Look at these networks and count the number of nodes, arcs and regions.
Note: Arcs must not cross.
All nodes do not have to be joined to every other node.

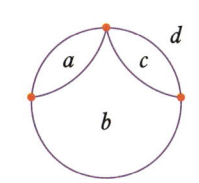

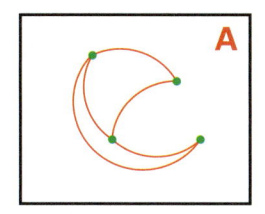

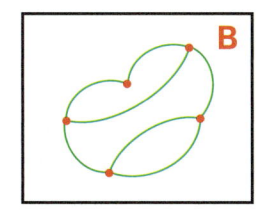

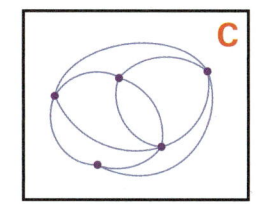

Draw some more diagrams.
Fill in this table.

	example	A	B	C
Number of nodes (n)	3	4		...
Number of regions (r)	4	3		...
Number of arcs (a)	5	5		...

Which of these gives the relationship between n, r and a?

A $n + a - 4 = r$ **B** $r + a = 3n$ **C** $r + a - 4 = n$ **D** $n + r - 2 = a$

203

Algebra

4 a Show, using algebra, that the perimeter P, of a semicircle of radius r is
$$P = r(\pi + 2).$$

b Find a formula for the area of an annulus (ring) with outer radius r_1, and inner radius r_2.

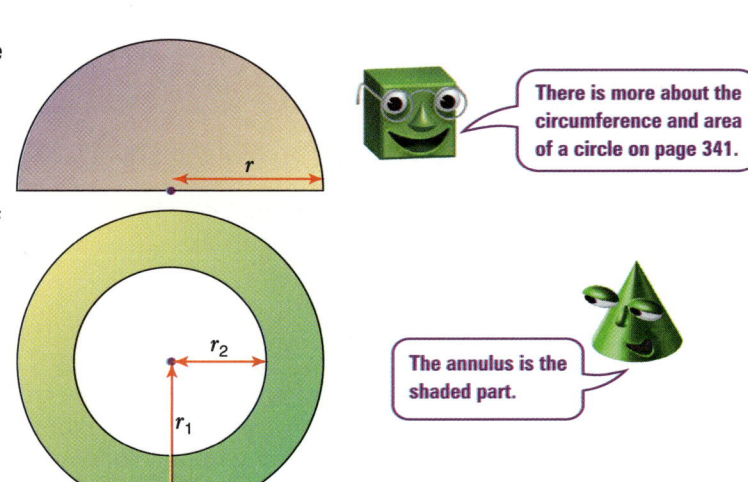

There is more about the circumference and area of a circle on page 341.

The annulus is the shaded part.

*5 The length of one side of a cube is a cm. The surface area of the cube is S cm². Prove, using algebra, that $S^3 = 216\, V^2$ where V is the volume in cm³.

*6 Fill in a table like this for the shapes shown.

Number of dots on perimeter (P)	Number of dots inside shape (I)	Area of shape (units²) (A)

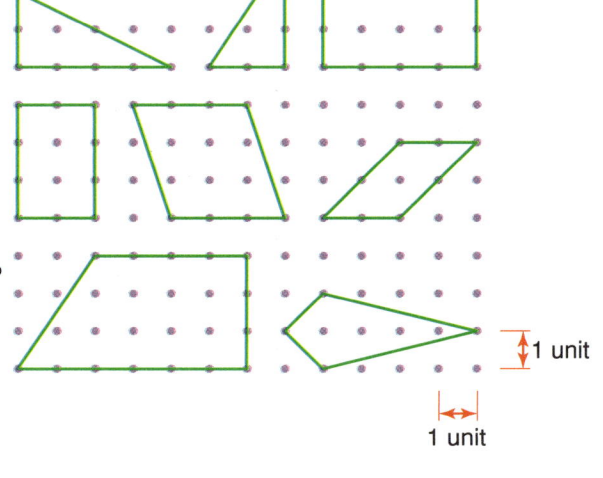

Which of these is the formula for finding A?

A $A = \frac{I}{2} + P + 1$ **B** $A = I + \frac{P}{2} - 1$ **C** $A = I + P$

Draw some other shapes and test if your formula is true for them also.

What if there are no dots inside the shape?
What if there are no dots on the perimeter?
What if ...

1 unit

1 unit

Review This pattern has intersecting circles.

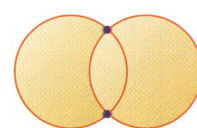

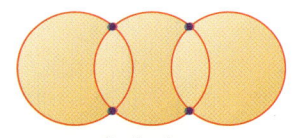

1 circle   2 circles   3 circles

a Copy and complete the table.

Number of circles	1	2	3	4	5	...
Number of intersections	0	2				...

b Find the formula for the number of intersections, N, if there are c circles in the row.

Practical

You will need a spreadsheet package.
Ask your teacher for ICT worksheet '**Modelling with Formulae**'.

Summary of key points

A We can **simplify expressions** by **collecting like terms**.

Examples $8q + 2(p - 3q) = 8q + 2p - 6q$ $\qquad 6x^2 - 2x + 3x^2 + 3x = 6x^2 + 3x^2 - 2x + 3x$
$\qquad\qquad\qquad\quad = 2q + 2p \qquad\qquad\qquad\qquad\qquad\qquad\quad = 9x^2 + x$

B We can simplify expressions by **cancelling**.

Examples $\dfrac{8p^1}{p^1} = 8 \qquad \dfrac{18x^2}{12x} = \dfrac{^3 \cancel{18} \times x \times \cancel{x}^1}{_2 \cancel{12} \times \cancel{x}_1}$
$\qquad\qquad\qquad\qquad\qquad\quad = \dfrac{3x}{2}$

We can also simplify expressions using **the index laws**.

Examples $2x^2 \times x^3 = 2 \times x^2 \times x^3 \qquad \dfrac{3k^5}{k^3} = 3k^{5-3}$
$\qquad\qquad\qquad = 2 \times x^{2+3} \qquad\qquad\qquad = 3k^2$
$\qquad\qquad\qquad = 2x^5$

C We can **write expressions**.

Example An expression for the area of this rectangle is
$2(2a + 6 + a - 1) = 2(3a + 5)$
$\qquad\qquad\qquad\qquad\quad = 6a + 10$

Rectangle with sides $2a + 6$ and $a - 1$.

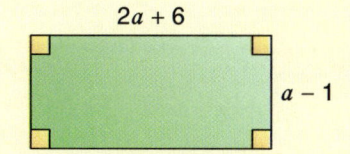

D When we **factorise** an expression we put the highest common factor of the terms outside the bracket.

Examples $12x - 16$ is factorised as $4(3x - 4)$ **4 is the HCF of 12x and 16**
$\qquad\qquad 8y + 24w$ is factorised as $8(y + 3w)$ **8 is the HCF of 8y and 24w**
$\qquad\qquad m^3 + m^2 + 3m$ is factorised as $m(m^2 + m + 3)$ **m is the HCF of m^3, m^2 and 3m**

Always check your factorising by multiplying out the brackets.

E We can **add and subtract algebraic fractions** in the same way that we add and subtract fractions in arithmetic.

Example **Arithmetic**   **Algebra**

$\dfrac{3}{4} + \dfrac{2}{5} = \dfrac{3 \times 5}{20} + \dfrac{2 \times 4}{20}$ find a common denominator $\dfrac{4}{m} + \dfrac{p}{n} = \dfrac{4 \times n}{m \times n} + \dfrac{p \times m}{n \times m}$
$\qquad = \dfrac{15 + 8}{20}$ and make equivalent fractions. $= \dfrac{4n + pm}{mn}$
$\qquad = \dfrac{23}{20}$
$\qquad = 1\dfrac{3}{20}$

F We **find the value of an expression** by substituting values for the unknown. We follow the rules for **order of operations**.

Examples When $p = 5$
$\dfrac{3p^2}{10} = \dfrac{3 \times 5^2}{10} \qquad\qquad 4(p - 2)^2 = 4(5 - 2)^2$
$\qquad = \dfrac{3 \times \cancel{25}^5}{\cancel{10}^2} \qquad\qquad\qquad\qquad = 4(3)^2$
$\qquad = \dfrac{15}{2} \qquad\qquad\qquad\qquad\qquad = 4 \times 9$
$\qquad = 7\dfrac{1}{2} \qquad\qquad\qquad\qquad\qquad = 36$

Algebra

G When we substitute values for unknowns into a **formula** we sometimes need to solve an equation.

Example The formula for finding speed, S, in m/sec, is $S = \frac{D}{T}$ where D is distance in metres and T is time in seconds.

If $S = 22$ m/s and $T = 30$ sec, then
$$22 = \frac{D}{30}$$
$$22 \times 30 = D$$
$$D = \mathbf{660 \text{ m}}$$

H Sometimes we need to **change the subject of a formula**.

Example $C = 2\pi r$ where C is the circumference of a circle
r is the radius

To make r the subject, use inverse operations.

Start with the subject wanted. → r → [multiply by π] → [multiply by 2] → $2\pi r$

$\frac{C}{2\pi}$ ← [divide by π] ← $\frac{C}{2}$ ← [divide by 2] ← C ← Return with the current subject.

$$r = \frac{C}{2\pi}$$

I We can **write formulae** using given information.

Test yourself

1 Simplify these expressions.
  a $6m + 8 + 2m$
  b $n + 2 + n + 6$
  c $5 + 3x + 5x$
  d $k + 5 + 2k + 9$
  e $(2a + 7) + (a - 4)$
  f $4n - (^-n)$
  g $8y^2 - 2 - 6y^2 + 7$
  h $5x^2 + x + 3x^2 + 2x$

2 A teacher has **5 full packets** of mints and **6 single** mints. [SATs Paper 2 Level 5]
The number of mints inside each packet is the same.

The teacher tells the class:

  'Write an expression to show how many mints there are altogether.
  Call the number of mints inside each packet y'

Here are some of the expressions that the pupils write:

$5 + 6 + y$ $5y6$ $5y + 6$ $6 + 5y$ $5 + 6y$ $(5 + 6) \times y$

  a Write down **two** expressions that are correct.
  b A pupil says: 'I think the teacher has a total of **56 mints**'.
    Could the pupil be correct? Explain how you know.

Expressions and Formulae

3 Use a copy of this.
The expression in the box is the sum of the expressions in the circles on either side of it.
Write the missing expressions as simply as possible.

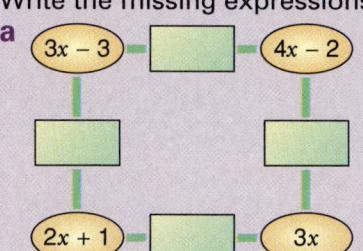

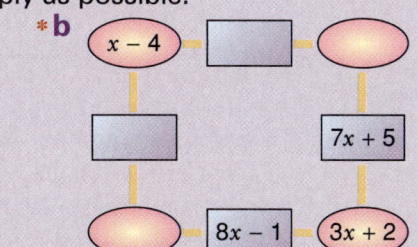

a $3x - 3$ — □ — $4x - 2$
□
$2x + 1$ — □ — $3x$

*b $x - 4$ — □ — ○
□ — $7x + 5$
○ — $8x - 1$ — $3x + 2$

4 Write an expression for perimeter in its simplest form.

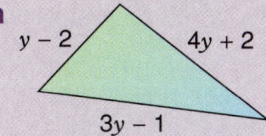

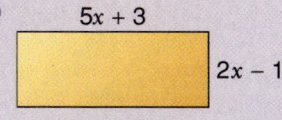

a Triangle with sides $y - 2$, $4y + 2$, $3y - 1$

b Rectangle with sides $5x + 3$ and $2x - 1$

5 Simplify these. Use the index laws for **h**, **i** and **j**.
 a $5 \times 4x$ **b** $3n \times 2$ **c** $5m \times 2m$ **d** $4a \times {}^-3b$ **e** $\frac{n^2}{n}$
 f $\frac{16p}{8}$ **g** $\frac{25k^2}{5k}$ **h** $3b^2 \times b^4$ **i** $\frac{n^8}{n^3}$ ***j** $\frac{24x^5}{18x^2}$

6 a When $x = 20$ find the value of these.
 i $3x - 2$ **ii** $3(x + 2)$ **iii** $2x^2 + 50$
 b Repeat **a** for $x = 0.2$.

7 The charge to hire a van is given by
$$C = 25d + 80$$
where C is the charge, in £ and d is the number of days hired.
 a The Todd family hire a van for 15 days.
 How much did this cost them?
 b The Martins paid £405 to hire the van. For how many days did they hire it?

8 Find an expression on the right which will have the same value as an expression on the left if $p = 3$ and $q = 2r$.

pqr	$6 + q$
$2p + q$	$6r$
$3q$	$6r^2$
q^2	$2(6 - r)$
$4p - q$	$4r^2$

9 A formula for speed is $s = \frac{1}{2}at^2$ where s is distance in metres, a is acceleration, in secs, and t is time in secs.
 a Find distance if $a = 5$ m/s² and $t = 4$ secs.
 b Find distance if $a = 1.5$ m/s² and $t = 5$ secs.

207

Algebra

10 Factorise these expressions.
The first four have been started.
- **a** $9y + 27 = 9(\quad)$
- **b** $15x + 5 = 5(\quad)$
- **c** $8x^2 + 3x = x(\quad)$
- **d** $k^3 + k^2 = k^2(\quad)$
- **e** $8d - 24$
- **f** $27l - 18$
- ∗**g** $2m^3 + m^2$
- ∗**h** $y^3 + 2y^2 - 4y$

11 Only one of the expressions below is a correct factorisation of $16p + 24$.
Which one is it?

$4(2p + 3)$ $8(p + 3)$ $2(8p + 16)$
$8(2p + 3)$ $8(2p + 24)$

12 Rachel collected information about the number of people living in households.
She displayed the information on a frequency chart but then spilt some ink on it.

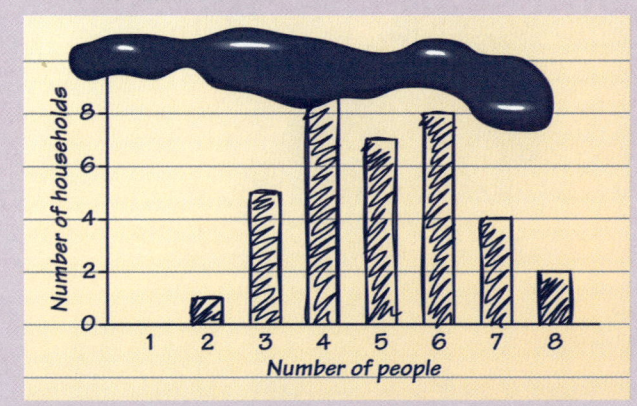

Call the number of households with 4 people x.
- **a** Show that the total number of people in all the households is $144 + 4x$.
- **b** Write an expression for the total number of households.
- ∗**c** The mean number of people per household is 5.
What is the value of x?
Show your working.

13
- **a** Make r the subject of the formula $C = 2\pi r$.
- **b** Make T the subject of the formula $PV = nRT$.
- ∗**c** Make h the subject of the formula $A = \frac{1}{2}(a + b)h$.

14
- **a** What is the mean of these three expressions?

  $2c + 9$ $2c$ $2c - 9$

  Show your working.
- **b** Write two expressions which have a mean value of $5c$.
- **c** The mean of three expressions is $3c$.
Two of the expressions are $3c + 5$ and $3c$.
What is the third expression?

15
- **a** The subject of this equation is y.
$$y = 3(x + z)$$
Rearrange the equation to make z the subject.
- ∗**b** Rearrange the equation $m = \frac{1}{3}(n - p)$ to make p the subject. Show your working.
- ∗**c** Rearrange the equation $y = \frac{3}{5}x^2$ to make x the subject.

Expressions and Formulae

16 Show, using algebra, that the surface area of this prism is
$ab + cd + bd + ad$

17 Copy these and fill in the gaps.

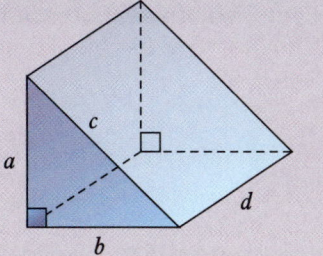

  a $\dfrac{1}{m} + \dfrac{3}{n} = \dfrac{}{mn} + \dfrac{}{mn}$

  $\phantom{\dfrac{1}{m} + \dfrac{3}{n}} = \dfrac{}{mn}$

  b $\dfrac{x}{4} - \dfrac{y}{3} = \dfrac{}{} - \dfrac{}{}$

  $\phantom{\dfrac{x}{4} - \dfrac{y}{3}} = \dfrac{}{}$

18 Simplify these.

  a $\dfrac{2}{y} + \dfrac{5}{y}$ **b** $\dfrac{x}{3} - \dfrac{x}{4}$ **c** $\dfrac{a}{b} + \dfrac{c}{d}$ **d** $\dfrac{2x}{5} - \dfrac{x}{3}$

19 a n is an **even** number.
Which of the numbers below must be even and which must be odd?

$n + 3 \qquad n^2 \qquad 2n - 1 \qquad (n + 1)^2 \qquad (n - 1)(n + 1)$

***b** n is an even number.
Is the number $\dfrac{n+4}{2}$ odd or even or is it not possible to tell? Explain.

8 Sequences and Functions

You need to know

✓ sequences page 147
  – sequences in practical situations
✓ functions page 148

Key vocabulary

flow chart, first/second difference, identity function, inverse function, inverse mapping, quadratic sequence, $T(n)$

▶▶ Don't tell Fibonaccis

The Fibonacci sequence is generated by this rule.
 first terms 1, 1 **rule** add the two previous terms together

 1, 1, 2, 3, 5, 8, 13, …

1 Write down the first 20 terms of the Fibonacci sequence.

2 Look at every third number. What sort of number is it?
 What about every fourth/fifth number?

3 Count the petals on this daisy.
 Is it a Fibonacci number?
 Count the number of petals on some real flowers.

4 Fibonacci numbers occur often in nature.
 To find out more, here is a web site you could look at
 www.mcs.surrey.ac.uk/Personal/R.Knott/Fibonacci

Sequences and Functions

Generating sequences

Sequences can be generated from a **term-to-term** definition and a starting point.

Example **First term** 4   **rule** multiply the previous term by 2
gives   4, 8, 16, 32, 64, ...

Sequences can be generated from an expression for the *n*th term.

Example The *n*th term of a sequence is **3***n* − 1.

The sequence is found by substituting $n = 1, 2, 3, 4, ...$ into $3n - 1$.
The sequence is

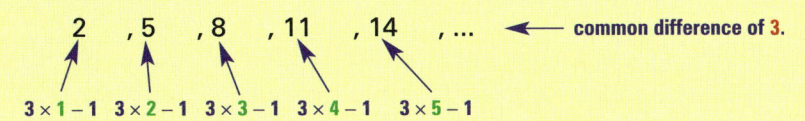

2 , 5 , 8 , 11 , 14 , ...   ← common difference of 3.

3 × 1 − 1   3 × 2 − 1   3 × 3 − 1   3 × 4 − 1   3 × 5 − 1

We can also find it by working out the first term and using the common difference.

$2^{+3}, 5^{+3}, 8^{+3}, 11^{+3}, 14^{+3}, 17, ...$ ← common difference of 3.

↑
first term

> The common difference is 3.
> This is the number multiplying *n*.

Note We call the rule for the *n*th term a **position-to-term** rule.
It is sometimes written as $T(n) = 3n - 1$.

$T(n)$ is *n*th term   position

Linear sequences always have a constant first difference.

Examples $T(n) = 4n - 1$ sequence first difference   3, 7, 11, 15, 19, ...
             $T(n) = 40 - 5n$ sequence first difference   35, 30, 25, 20, 15

Exercise 1

Except for questions 8 and 9.

1 Write down the first six terms of these sequences.

	1st term(s)	term-to-term rule
a	5	multiply by 2
b	3	subtract 2
c	1	add 0·5
d	2	add consecutive numbers 1, 2, 3, 4, ...
e	1, 2	add the two previous terms together
f	1	multiply by ⁻2
*g	1	divide by 2

2 Which of the sequences you found in question **1** are linear?
Explain how you can tell.

Algebra

3 a Write down the terms generated by this flow chart.

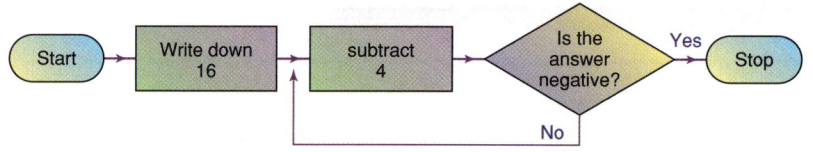

Start → Write down 16 → subtract 4 → Is the answer negative? — Yes → Stop / No (loop back to subtract 4)

  b Design a flow chart that generates this sequence.
    3, 8, 13, 18, 23, 28.

4 Write down the first six terms of the sequences given by these position-to-term rules.
  a $T(n) = 2n + 5$ **b** $T(n) = 3n - 5$ **c** $T(n) = 10 - 2n$ **d** $T(n) = n + \frac{1}{2}$ **e** $T(n) = 0\cdot 1n$

5 Sam bought two goldfish in June. Each following month he bought twice as many goldfish as the month before.
  a How many goldfish did he buy in September that year?
  *b His goal was to have over 125 goldfish in total.
    In which month would he reach his goal?

6 $T(2) = a + T(1),\quad T(3) = a + T(2), \ldots$
  Write down the first six terms of the sequence if
  a $T(1) = 2,\ a = 1$ **b** $T(1) = 4,\ a = {}^-2$ **c* $T(1) = 3,\ a = 0\cdot5$ **d* $T(1) = \frac{1}{2},\ a = \frac{1}{4}$

7 $T(3) = T(1) + T(2),\quad T(4) = T(2) + (T3), \ldots$
  Write down the first eight terms of the sequence if the first two terms are
  a 1, 1   **b** 2, 1   **c* ${}^-2, {}^-1$ **d* $\frac{1}{2}, \frac{1}{4}$ **e* $a, b + 1$.

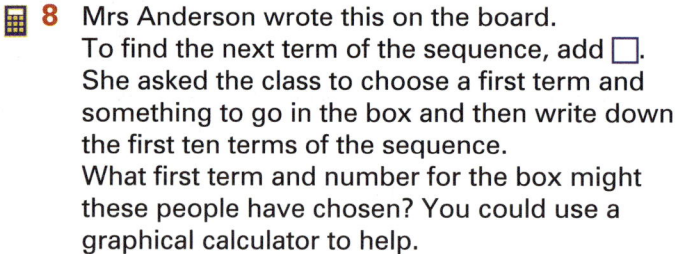

8 Mrs Anderson wrote this on the board.
  To find the next term of the sequence, add ☐.
  She asked the class to choose a first term and something to go in the box and then write down the first ten terms of the sequence.
  What first term and number for the box might these people have chosen? You could use a graphical calculator to help.
  a The terms of Andre's sequence are all odd.
  b The terms of Stefan's sequence are all multiples of 4.
  c Dorothy's sequence has every second number an integer.
  d Zoe's sequence has every fourth number an integer.
  *e Casey's sequence has exactly eight two-digit numbers.
  *f Harim's sequence has every fourth number a multiple of 8.

> You could use a graphical calculator for this question.

*9 Use a graphical calculator to find the 24th term of 5, 8, 11, 14, …

Review 1 Write down the first five terms of these sequences.

	1st term	term-to-term rule			1st term	term-to-term rule
a	5	add 3		c	9	subtract 4
b	2	multiply by 3		**d	36	divide by 3

Review 2
a Write down the first six terms of the sequence given by   **i** $T(n) = 3n - 2$ **ii** $T(n) = 20 - 4n$.

Review 3 $T(3) = T(1) + T(2)\quad T(4) = T(2) + T(3), \ldots$
Write down the first six terms of the sequence if $T(1)$ and $T(2)$ are
a ${}^-1, 2$ **b* $\frac{3}{4}, \frac{1}{2}$ **c* $a, 3$.

Sequences and Functions

Describing and continuing sequences

We can **describe linear sequences** by looking at the rule for the *n*th term.

Example $T(n) = 4n + 1$ gives the sequence 5, 9, 13, 17, 21, ...
Each term is one more than a multiple of 4.
It is **ascending** – the constant difference is **positive**.

Example $T(n) = 40 - 5n$ gives the sequence 35, 30, 25, 20, ...
Each term is a multiple of 5.
It is **descending** – the constant difference is **negative**.

We often predict how a sequence continues if given the first few terms.

Note To be **certain** of how a sequence continues we need to know the term-to-term or position-to-term rule.

Exercise 2

1. Each of these sequences has a well-known name.
   Choose the correct name from the box and write down the next term.

   a 10, 100, 1000, ...   **b** 1, 4, 9, 16, ...   **c** 1, 8, 27, 64, ...
   d 2, 4, 8, 16, ...   **e** 1, 3, 6, 10, 15, ...

   > Square numbers
   > Powers of ten
   > Powers of two
   > Triangular numbers
   > Cube numbers

2. Predict the next three terms of these sequences.

   a 0·3, 0·6, 0·9, 1·2, 1·5, ...   **b** 3, 6, 12, 24, 48, ...   **c** 10 000, 1000, 100, 10, ...
   d 320, 160, 80, 40, ...   ***e** 0, 1, 1, 2, 3, 5, 8, ...   ***f** 1, 2, 4, 7, 11, 16, ...

3. For each of the sequences in question **2**, write down the term-to-term rule.

   > Remember **first term 4 rule add 2** is a term-to-term rule.

4. The sequence which begins 1, 2, 3, ... might continue as

   1, 2, 3, 4, 5, ...   add one to the previous term
   1, 2, 3, 5, 8, 13, ...   add the two previous terms

   Give two ways this sequence might continue.   1, 2, 4, ...
   Explain the rule for each.

5. The sequence $T(n) = 4n - 1$ has terms with a common difference of **4** which are all one less than a multiple of 4.
   It starts at 3 and ascends.
   Describe the terms of the sequence given by each of these.

   a $T(n) = 3n$ **b** $T(n) = 3n + 1$ **c** $T(n) = 3n - 1$ **d** $T(n) = 33 - 3n$

*6 A linear sequence has the formula $T(n) = an + b$.
   a What will the value of *a* be if the sequence
      i increases in 3s   **ii** decreases in 5s?
   b What will the value of *b* be if the sequence
      i is the multiples of 3 starting at 3
      ii has terms all one more than a multiple of 3 and starts at 4?

*7 A linear sequence is given by $T(n) = an + b$.
   Will the sequence be ascending or descending if *a* is
   a positive   **b** negative?

213

Algebra

Review 1
a Predict the next three terms of these sequences.
  i 1·5, 3, 4·5, 6, 7·5, ...   **ii** 16, 8, 4, 2, 1, ...   **i** 7, 14, 28, 56, 112, ...
b Write down the term-to-term rule for the sequences in part **a**.
c Describe these sequences. Write at least two sentences about each.
  i 7, 11, 15, 19, ...   **ii** 80, 71, 62, 53, ...
*__d__ A linear sequence has the formula $T(n) = an + b$.
  i What will the value of a be if the sequence increases in 5s?
  ii What will the value of b be if the sequence has terms all one more than a multiple of 5 and starts at 6?

Review 2
The sequence which begins 1, 3, ... could continue in different ways.
Show two different ways it could continue, giving the first five terms for each way.
Explain the rule for each.

Investigation

Tens and units

Bjorn started with a two-digit number, TU.
He found $2U + T$.
He then found $2U + T$ for the new number.
He kept repeating this to get a number chain.

25 → (12) → 5 → 10 → 1 → 2 → 4 → 8 → 16 → 13
→ 7 → 14 → 9 → 18 → 17 → 15 → 11 → 3 → 6 → (12)

He found that the number chain then repeated.

Investigate which number gives the shortest chain before it repeats.
What about the longest chain?

What if you found $3U + T$?
What if ...

Example
25
$2 \times 5 + 2 = 12$
$2 \times 2 + 1 = 5$
$2 \times 5 + 0 = 10$
$2 \times 0 + 1 = 1$
and so on.

Quadratic sequences

1, 4, 9, 16, 25, ... is the sequence of square numbers.
The rule for this sequence is $T(n) = n^2$.
Sequences that have a rule with a squared term as the highest power are called **quadratic sequences**.

Example $T(n) = 2n^2 + 1$

Position (n)	1	2	3	4	5
Term $T(n)$	$2 \times 1^2 + 1 = 3$	$2 \times 2^2 + 1 = 9$	$2 \times 3^2 + 1 = 19$	$2 \times 4^2 + 1 = 33$	$2 \times 5^2 + 1 = 51$

The sequence is 3, 9, 19, 33, 51, ...

Note Quadratic sequences have a common **second** difference.

```
    3    9    19    33    51
      6    10    14    18      ← 1st difference
        4    4    4             ← 2nd difference
```

Sequences and Functions

Exercise 3

1 Write down the first six terms of the sequences given by these rules.
  a $T(n) = n^2 + 1$ **b** $T(n) = n^2 + 3$ **c** $T(n) = 2n^2 + 2$ **d** $T(n) = n^2 - 3$

2 Which of these sequences are quadratic?
  a 4, 12, 20, 28, 36, ...   **b** 3, 6, 11, 18, 27, ...   **c** 2, 11, 26, 47, 74, ...

Hint: Find the first and second differences.

*__3__ **a** The nth term of a sequence is $\frac{n}{n^2 + 2}$.
   The first term of the sequence is $\frac{1}{3}$.
   Write down the next three terms of the sequence.
   b Write down the first four terms of the sequence $T(n) = \frac{n+1}{n^2+1}$.

Review 1 Write down the first ten terms of the sequence given by these rules.
  a $T(n) = n^2 + 5$ **b** $T(n) = n^2 - 1$ **c** $T(n) = 3n^2 - 2$ **d** $T(n) = n^2 + n$

Review 2 Is 2, 3, 5, 8, 12, 17, ... a quadratic sequence?

*__Review 3__ The first term of the sequence $T(n) = \frac{n}{2n^2 - 1}$ is $\frac{1}{2 - 1} = 1$.
Write down the next four terms. Leave your answer as a fraction.

---

*Practical

A You will need a graphical calculator.

Key this into your graphical calculator.

[25] [EXE]

[Ans] [÷] [2] [+] [3] [EXE]

[EXE] [EXE] [EXE] [EXE] [EXE] ...

```
25
            25
Ans÷2+3
            15.5
            10.75
            8.375
            7.1875
            6.59375
```

What happens if you keep pressing [EXE]?
What value does the sequence get closer and closer to?

What if you start with a different number?
What if you divide by 4 instead of 2?
What if you divide by 5 instead of 2?
What if you divide by 2 and add 5 instead?
What if ...

B You will need a spreadsheet package.
Use a spreadsheet to generate the sequence given by these.
   $T(n) = \frac{n}{n^2}$ $T(n) = \frac{n}{n^2 + 1}$

Ask your teacher for the **Generating Sequences** ICT worksheet.

215

Algebra

Sequences in practical situations

Discussion

This is a tile pattern.

pattern 1   pattern 2   pattern 3

Predict how many tiles you think will be in patterns 4 and 5. **Discuss**.
Draw them to check.
What term-to-term rule would describe this sequence?
What would the expression for the number of tiles in pattern n be?
Discuss and give an explanation for your choice.
Is there any other way of finding the number of tiles in pattern n? **Discuss**.

Worked Example
Jolene made wall hangings.

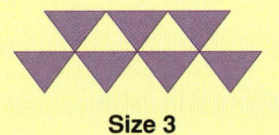

Size 1   Size 2   Size 3

a Draw the next two diagrams.
b Fill in this table.

Size	1	2	3	4	5	...
Number of coloured triangles						...

c Give the term-to-term rule for the number of coloured triangles.
d Predict how the sequence for the coloured triangles might continue.
e Explain the sequence by referring to the diagrams.
f Write an expression for the nth term. Explain how you found it.

Answer
a

b
Size	1	2	3	4	5	...
Number of coloured triangles	3	5	7	9	11	...

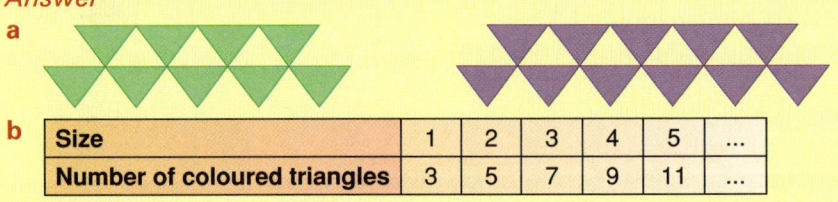

c **first-term** 3   **rule** add 2.
d Each size has two more triangles.
   The sequence might continue as 13, 15, 17, 19, ...
e There are two rows of triangles.
   Each time a new size is drawn, a triangle is added to each row.
f The expression for the nth term is $n + n + 1$ or $2n + 1$.
   In size n there are two rows, one with n and one with
   $n + 1$ triangles. In total there are $2n + 1$ triangles.

Link to finding the nth term of a sequence.

Sequences and Functions

Exercise 4

1 You can make 'huts' with matches.   [SATs Paper 2 Level 5]

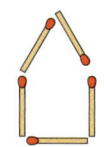

1 hut needs
5 matches

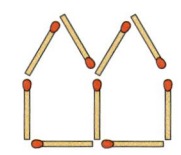

2 huts need
9 matches

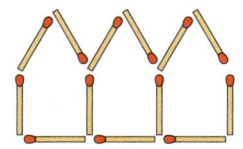

3 huts need
13 matches

A rule to find how many matches you need is

$m = 4h + 1$

m stands for the number of matches.
h stands for the number of huts.

a **Use the rule** to find how many matches you need to make **8** huts.
Show your working.

b I use **81 matches** to make some huts.
How many huts do I make?
Show your working.

c Andy makes different 'huts' with matches.

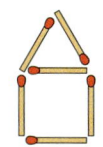

1 hut needs
6 matches

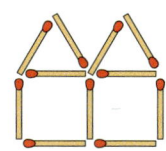

2 huts need
11 matches

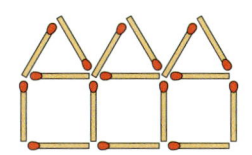

3 huts need
16 matches

Which rule below shows how many matches he needs?
Remember: m stands for the number of matches.
h stands for the number of huts.

$m = h + 5$ $m = 4h + 2$ $m = 4h + 3$

$m = 5h + 1$ $m = 5h + 2$ $m = h + 13$

2 Joey makes a sequence with some purple and blue tiles.

a How many purple tiles will there be in pattern 8?

b How many purple tiles will there be in pattern 15?

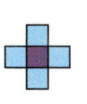

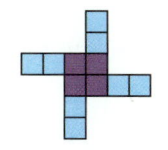

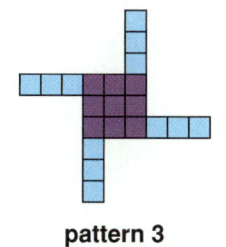

pattern 1   pattern 2   pattern 3

c Predict what numbers go in the gaps for the number of blue tiles.

Pattern number	1	2	3	4	5	...	20
Number of blue tiles	4	8	12	__	__	...	__

d What sequence does the number of blue tiles make?
What is the term-to-term rule for it?

e Write an expression for the number of blue tiles in pattern n.
Justify your expression by referring to the diagrams.

f Check that your expression gives you the numbers you predicted in **c**.

217

Algebra

3 Jordan made paving designs with brown and orange hexagonal pavers.

design 1   design 2   design 3

a Copy and fill in this table.

Design number	1	2	3	4	5	...	16
Number of orange pavers						...	
Number of brown pavers						...	
Total number of pavers						...	

b Describe how the sequence for the number of brown pavers continues, referring to the designs.

c Choose an expression from the box for these.
   i The number of orange pavers in design n.
   ii The number of brown pavers in design n.
   iii The total number of pavers in design n.

d Justify your answers to part **c** by referring to the diagram. Is there more than one way of justifying your answers?

$2n$
$n + 2$
$n + 1$
$2n - 1$
$3n + 1$
$n + 3$

4 Elijah's Fashion made a series of Es from neon lights.

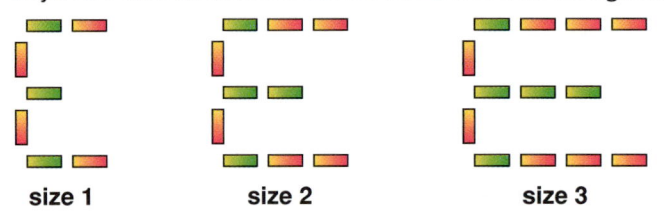

size 1   size 2   size 3

a Predict what numbers go in the gaps.

Size	1	2	3	4	5	...	16
Number of lights	7	10	13	___	___	...	___

b Write down the sequence made by the number of lights. Describe how this sequence continues.

c How could you find the number of neon lights needed for an E of size 14?

d Write an expression for the number of lights needed for size n.
Justify your expression by referring to the diagrams. Is there more than one way of justifying your answer?

*5 Raphael wanted to know the maximum number of times lines crossed. He drew these diagrams.

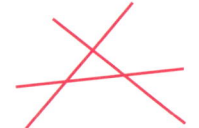

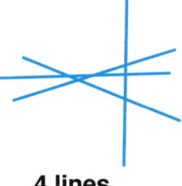

1 line   2 lines   3 lines   4 lines

a Copy and fill in this table.

Number of lines	1	2	3	4	5	...
Maximum crossings						...
Increase						

Sequences and Functions

b Predict how the sequence for maximum crossings might continue.
c Raphael explained the sequence by referring to the diagrams.

> *When we add a new line, it crosses each of the existing lines. This increases the maximum crossings by the number of existing lines.*

Is Raphael correct?
Explain the sequence in your own words.

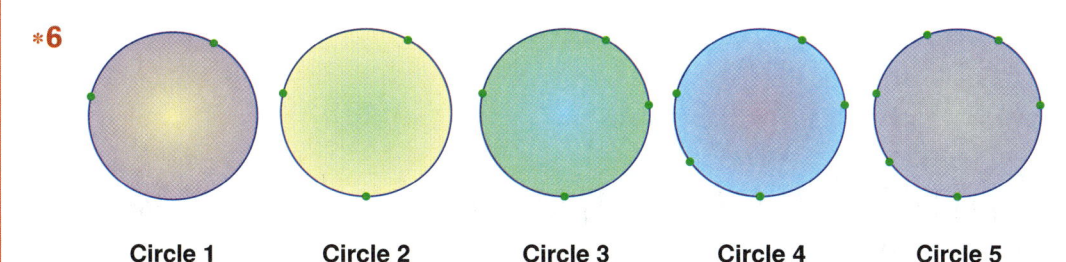

*6

Circle 1   Circle 2   Circle 3   Circle 4   Circle 5

a Draw circles like those shown.
b How many dots are on the next circle?
Draw this circle.
c On each circle, every point is to be joined to every other point with a straight line.
   On Circle 1 there will be 1 line.
   On Circle 2 there will be 3 lines.
   On Circle 3 there will be 6 lines.
Join every point to every other point on each of your 6 circles.
d Copy and complete this sequence for the number of lines on the 6 circles.
1, 3, 6, ..., ..., ...
e Predict how the sequence might continue.
Explain your answer.

*7 At Mr Bradshaw's front door there are four steps.
There are five different ways he can climb them if he can only climb them one or two steps at a time.

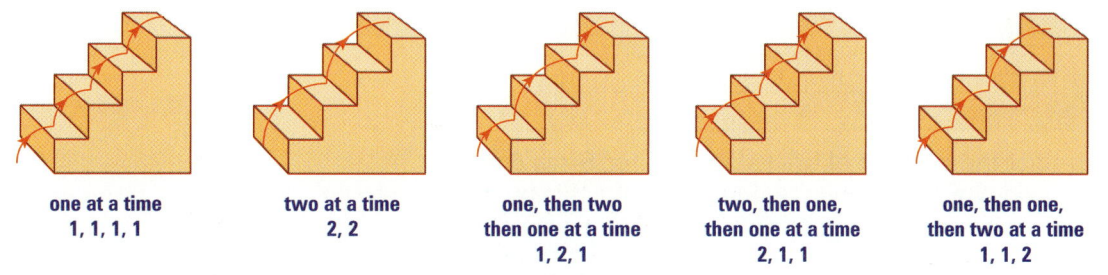

| one at a time | two at a time | one, then two then one at a time | two, then one, then one at a time | one, then one, then two at a time |
| 1, 1, 1, 1 | 2, 2 | 1, 2, 1 | 2, 1, 1 | 1, 1, 2 |

Draw diagrams to work out the number of ways to climb a staircase for different numbers of steps.
Use a table like this to help.

Number of steps	Number of ways to climb
1	1
2	
3	

219

Algebra

Review 1
Hexagonal pavers are put in a pattern as shown with 1 black paver surrounded by 6 brown ones.

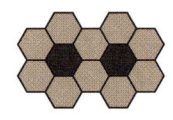

1 black   **2 black**

a   Draw pattern 3.
b   Copy and complete this table.

Black tiles	1	2	3	4	5	...	10
Brown tiles	6	10					

c   If I have 20 black tiles, predict how many brown tiles I will need if the pattern remains the same.
d   Which of these is an expression for the number of brown tiles if there are n black tiles?
    A $n + 5$ **B** $4n$ **C** $4n + 2$ **D** $5n - 2$
e   Check that your expression gives you the numbers you predicted in **c**.

*** Review 2**   Trent makes miniature fountains from bricks.

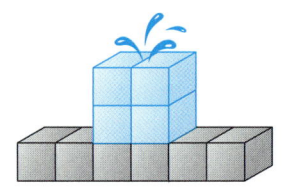

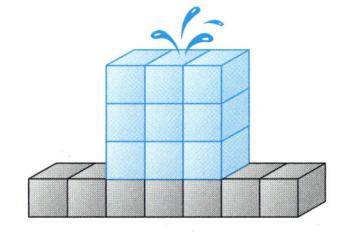

Size 1   **Size 2**   **Size 3**

a   Draw Size 4 and Size 5 fountains.
b   Copy and fill in this table.

Size	1	2	3	4	5	...
Number of bricks	6	10				...
Increase		4				

c   Predict the number of bricks needed for Sizes 6 and 7.
   *Explain why the sequence continues like this by referring to the diagrams. Is there more than one way of doing this?

? Puzzle

1   This diagram shows the top 3 rows of a 'tower' that has been built from building blocks. Each row has one block less than the row below. If a total of 276 blocks was used, find the number of rows in this tower.

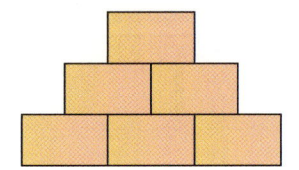

2   Jake has a 6 metre long stick which he cuts into 25 pieces. Each piece that he cuts off is 1 cm longer than the preceding piece. What was the length of the first piece that Jake cut off?

Sequences and Functions

Finding the rule for the *n*th term

To find the **rule for the *n*th term** of a linear sequence, find the **constant difference** between consecutive terms.

Worked Example
Find the *n*th term of the sequence   46, 39, 32, 25, ...

Answer

Term	46	39	32	25
Difference		⁻7	⁻7	⁻7

The difference between consecutive terms is ⁻7, so the *n*th term is of the form $T(n) = {}^-7n + b$ or $b - 7n$

$T(1) = 46$ $\qquad b - 7 \times 1 = 46$
$\qquad$ so $\qquad b - 7 = 46$
$\qquad\qquad\qquad b = 53$

$T(n) = 53 - 7n$

Check by testing a few more terms

$n = 2 \quad 53 - 7n = 53 - 7 \times 2 \qquad n = 3 \quad 53 - 7n = 53 - 7 \times 3 \qquad n = 4 \quad 53 - 7n = 53 - 7 \times 4$
$\qquad\qquad\qquad = 39 \checkmark \qquad\qquad\qquad\qquad = 32 \checkmark \qquad\qquad\qquad\qquad = 25 \checkmark$

Exercise 5

1 Find the *n*th term of these sequences. Draw a difference table like this for each.

Term	30	34	38	42
Difference		4	4	4

Remember: The common difference tells you the number that multiplies *n*.

a 5, 7, 9, 11, 13, ...
b 2, 5, 8, 11, 14, ...
c 3, 8, 13, 18, 23, ...
d 30, 34, 38, 42, ...
e 28, 37, 46, 55, ...
f 58, 66, 74, 82, ...
g 80, 72, 64, 56, ...
h 66, 59, 52, 45, 38, ...
i 1·1, 1·2, 1·3, 1·4, 1·5, ...
j 3·3, 3·5, 3·7, 3·9, 4·1, ...
k ⁻7, ⁻17, ⁻27, ⁻37, ...
l ⁻3, ⁻12, ⁻21, ⁻30, ⁻39, ...

*2 Write a rule for each of the following sequences as $T(n) = \underline{\quad}$. Then find the required term.

a Which term of 4, 7, 10, 13, ... is equal to 100?
b Which term of 2, 7, 12, 17, ... is equal to 197?
c Which term of 7, 5, 3, 1, ... is equal to ⁻15?
d Which term of 60, 56, 52, 48, ... is equal to ⁻20?

Review Find the *n*th term.
a 3, 5, 7, 9, 11, ...
b 88, 81, 74, 67, 60, ...
c 2·2, 2·5, 2·8, 3·1, 3·4, ...
d ⁻7, ⁻13, ⁻19, ⁻25, ⁻31, ...

Algebra

Functions

Remember
We can find the **output** of a **function** machine if we are given the input.

Example $x \to$ [multiply by 2] $\to$ [subtract 4] $\to y$

The function is $x \times 2 \to x \times 2 - 4 \to 2x - 4$
We write this as $y = 2x - 4$ or $x \to 2x - 4$.

We can show the inputs and outputs on a table.
We can also show a function using a mapping diagram.

Example $x \to \frac{x}{2} + 1$

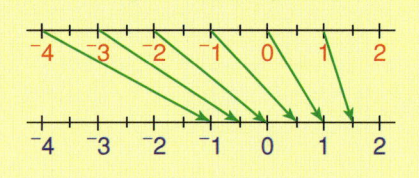

Input	Output

If $x \to x$ the function is called the **identity function**, because it maps every number onto itself. The number is unchanged.

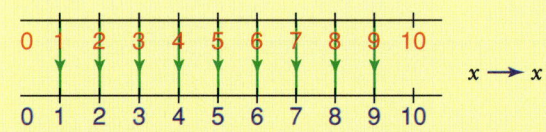

$x \to x$

To find the input given the output we work backwards doing the **inverse operations** in the reverse order.

Example   ? $\to$ [add 4] $\to$ [multiply by 2] $\to$ 14

To find the input, start with 14.

3 $\leftarrow$ [subtract 4] $\leftarrow$ [divide by 2] $\leftarrow$ 14   *Start with the output and work backwards.*

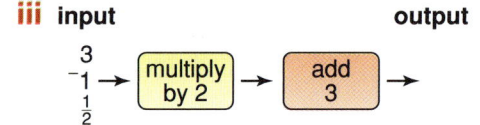

The input was **3**.

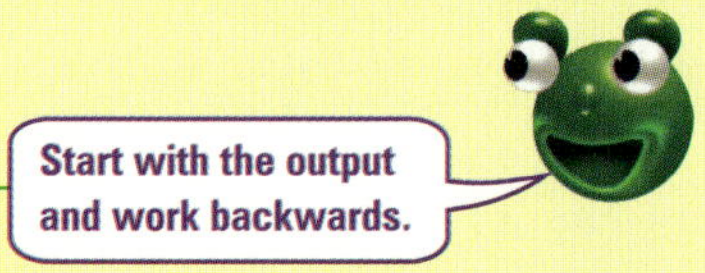

Exercise 6

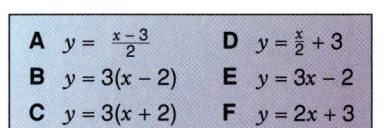

A $y = \frac{x-3}{2}$	D $y = \frac{x}{2} + 3$
B $y = 3(x - 2)$	E $y = 3x - 2$
C $y = 3(x + 2)$	F $y = 2x + 3$

1 a Write down the output for each of these function machines.
   b Match each function machine with a function from the box.

i input → output

1, 2, 3 → [multiply by 3] → [subtract 2] →

ii input → output

2, 4, 6 → [divide by 2] → [add 3] →

iii input → output

3, ⁻1, $1\frac{1}{2}$ → [multiply by 2] → [add 3] →

iv input → output

0·5, 78, ⁻4 → [add 2] → [multiply by 3] →

v input → output

1, 1·5, ⁻2 → [subtract 3] → [divide by 2] →

vi input → output

1·5, $2\frac{1}{2}$, 3·6 → [subtract 2] → [multiply by 3] →

222

Sequences and Functions

2 Use a copy of this.
Fill in the missing input and output numbers.

a $x \rightarrow$ [multiply by 2] $\rightarrow$ [add 4] $\rightarrow y$

Input	Output
5	
17	
	8

b $x \rightarrow$ [divide by 3] $\rightarrow$ [add 2] $\rightarrow y$

Input	Output
12	
⁻3	
	4

c input(x)

?, 3, ?, 0·5 → [add 2] → [multiply by 3] → 6, ?, 21, ?

d __5, __, ½ → [subtract 1] → [multiply by 2] → 4, __, 30, __

3 Use a copy of these mapping diagrams.
Fill them in for the function given.

a $y = 2x + 1$ for $x = 0, 1, 2, 3, 4$

b $x \rightarrow 2(x + 1)$ for $x = 0, 1, 2, 3, 4$

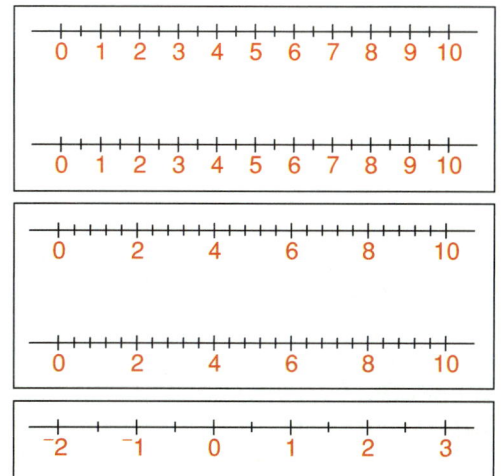

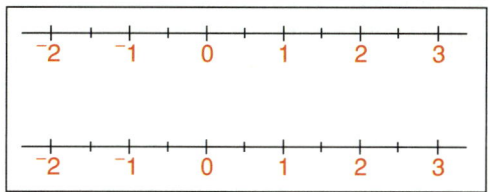

c $x \rightarrow \frac{x}{2} + 1$ for $x = ⁻2, ⁻1, 0, 1, 2$

4 Draw a function machine for each of these.
a $y = 2x - 1$ **b** $y = \frac{x}{4} + 3$ **c** $y = 2(x - 1)$

5 a Draw a mapping diagram for $x \rightarrow x$ for $x = ⁻2, 0, 3, 4·5$.
b What special name does this function have?
c What would ⁻37·6 map onto?

6 Each of these function machines can be replaced with a single-operation machine. Write down the single operation.

a $x \rightarrow$ [+4] $\rightarrow$ [+6] $\rightarrow y$

b $x \rightarrow$ [×2] $\rightarrow$ [×4] $\rightarrow y$

c $x \rightarrow$ [+6] $\rightarrow$ [−3] $\rightarrow y$

d $x \rightarrow$ [×4] $\rightarrow$ [÷2] $\rightarrow y$

Algebra

7 Find a function from the box that would give the same output as each of these.

a 8, 6, 2, 4 → [multiply by 3] → [add 3] →

b 3, 6, 9, 12 → [subtract 2] → [divide by 2] →

A $x \to \frac{x}{2} - 1$
B $x \to 3(x + 3)$
C $x \to 3(x + 1)$
D $x \to \frac{x}{2} - 2$

*__8__ Sajid thought of a number.
He carried out these operations on the number.

[multiply by 6]   [add 5]

When he did them in one order he got 89.
When he did them in the other order he got 114.
a Draw a function machine for each of Sajid's calculations.
b Write a function for each of the function machines.
c What is the number Sajid thought of?
d Explain why doing the operations in a different order gives a different result.
*e The difference between the answers is 25.
   Prove that the difference will **always** be 25, no matter what the number is.

Review 1

a Find the output for these.

i input   output
   3
   5 → [add 4] → [multiply by 3] →

ii input   output
    ⁻1
    ½ → [multiply by 4] → [subtract 3] →
    1·2

b Write the rule for each of the function machines in part **a** as $y = $ ___.

Review 2 Use a copy of each table. Fill in the missing input and output values.

a x → [multiply by 3] → [subtract 1] → y

b x → [add 3] → [divide by 2] → y

Input	Output
6	
	2
	11

Input	Output
⁻2	
	3
	12

c ___, 5·4, ___, ½ → [subtract 3] → [multiply by 2] → 4, ___, 24, ___

Review 3

a Use a copy of the mapping diagram.
   Fill it in for $y = 3x - 2$ and $x = 0, 1, 2, 3$.

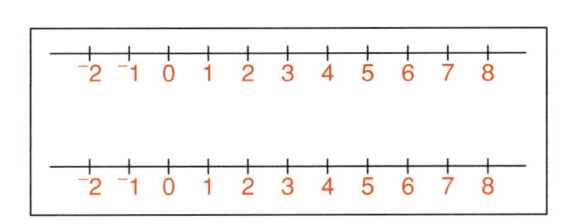

⁻2 ⁻1 0 1 2 3 4 5 6 7 8

⁻2 ⁻1 0 1 2 3 4 5 6 7 8

Sequences and Functions

b Write down the functions for the mapping diagrams.

  i

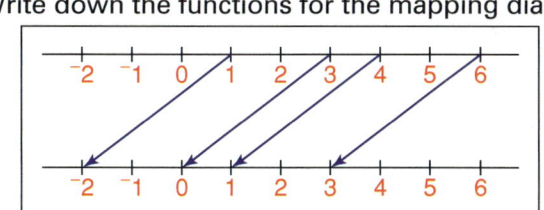

  -2 -1 0 1 2 3 4 5 6
  -2 -1 0 1 2 3 4 5 6

  ii

  -2 -1 0 1 2 3 4 5
  -2 -1 0 1 2 3 4 5

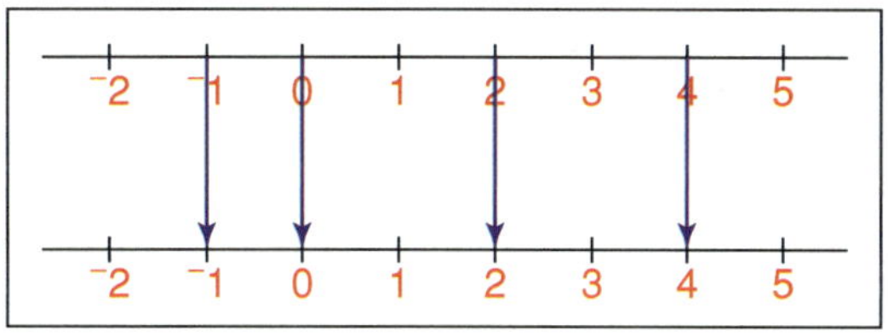

c i What is the special name of the function in **b ii**?
  ii In **b ii** what would 45·2 map onto?

Review 4 Replace the two operations in the function machine with a single operation.

a $x \to [+2] \to [+4] \to y$

b $x \to [\times 6] \to [\div 2] \to y$

Review 5 This shows the input and output guesses Matthew made in a game of 'what is my rule?'

If the guess was correct it has a tick. If wrong, a cross.

Find the rule for each game.

Game 1

Input	Output	
3	6	✓
7	10	✓
12	14	✗
5	8	✓
6	12	✗
11	14	✓

Game 2

Input	Output	
5	17	✓
1	5	✓
3	9	✗
7	11	✗
3	11	✓
10	32	✓

Inverse of a function

We can find the **inverse of a function** by doing the inverse operations in the reverse order.
On a mapping diagram the inverse function maps the function back to itself.

Example

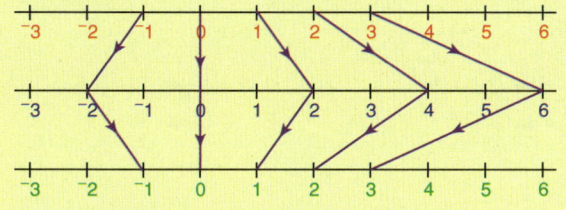

-3 -2 -1 0 1 2 3 4 5 6
-3 -2 -1 0 1 2 3 4 5 6
-3 -2 -1 0 1 2 3 4 5 6

$x \to 2x$ function

$x \to \frac{x}{2}$ inverse function

The inverse of multiplying by 2 is dividing by 2.

The inverse of $x \to 2x$ is $x \to \frac{x}{2}$.

Example

We can use an inverse function machine to find the inverse of a function.

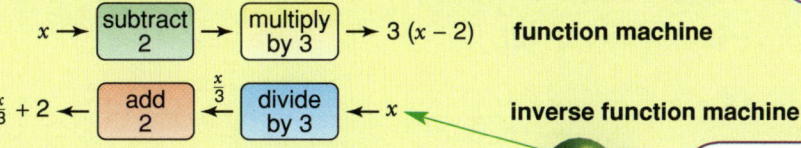

Example

$x \to [\text{subtract } 2] \to [\text{multiply by 3}] \to 3(x-2)$ **function machine**

$\frac{x}{3} + 2 \leftarrow [\text{add } 2] \leftarrow \frac{x}{3} [\text{divide by 3}] \leftarrow x$ **inverse function machine**

The inverse of $x \to 3(x-2)$ is $x \to \frac{x}{3} + 2$.

This is linked to changing the subject of a formula, see page 200.

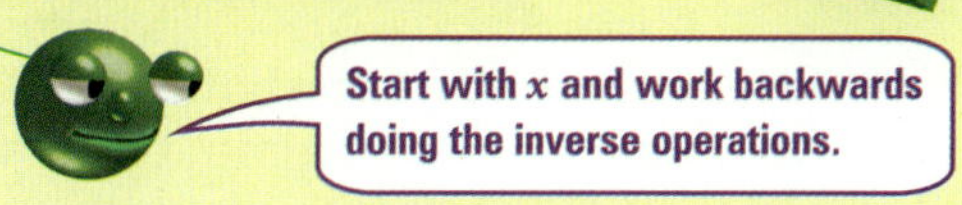

Start with x and work backwards doing the inverse operations.

225

Algebra

Exercise 7

1 Use a copy of these mapping diagrams.
   Fill each in to show the function and its inverse.
   Write down the inverse function.

   a $x \longrightarrow x+3$ for $x = ^-3, ^-2, ^-1, 0$

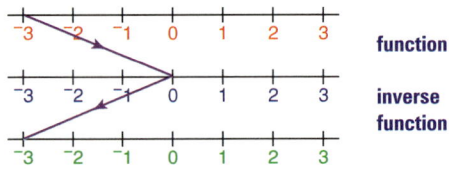

   b $x \longrightarrow 3x$ for $x = ^-1, 0, 1$

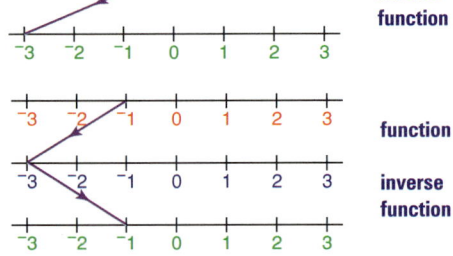

2 Use a copy of this.
   Fill in the inverse function machine to find the inverse function.

   a $x \to$ [multiply by 3] $\to$ [add 2] $\to 3x + 2$ **function**

   $\longleftarrow$ [ ] $\longleftarrow$ [subtract 2] $\longleftarrow x$ **inverse function**

   b $x \to$ [divide by 3] $\to$ [subtract 3] $\to \frac{x}{3} - 3$ **function**

   $\longleftarrow$ [ ] $\longleftarrow$ [ ] $\longleftarrow x$ **inverse function**

   c $x \to$ [add 2] $\to$ [multiply by 4] $\to 4(x + 2)$ **function**

   $\longleftarrow$ [ ] $\longleftarrow$ [ ] $\longleftarrow x$ **inverse function**

3 Find the inverse function for these.

   a $x \longrightarrow 2x + 1$ **b** $x \longrightarrow 3x - 2$ **c** $x \longrightarrow 2(x - 5)$
   d $x \longrightarrow \frac{x+4}{8}$ **e** $x \longrightarrow \frac{x}{2} + 4$ **f** $x \longrightarrow \frac{1}{3}x - 1$
   g $x \longrightarrow \frac{1}{2}x + 15$

*4 **a** Start with the values $x = 1, 2, 3, 4$.
         Use the rule $x \longrightarrow 3x - 2$ to find the output values.
   b Use these new values as the input values for
         i $x \longrightarrow \frac{1}{3}x + 2$ and   **ii** $x \longrightarrow \frac{1}{3}(x + 2)$.
   c Is **i** or **ii** the inverse of $x \longrightarrow 3x - 2$?

*5 **a** Find the inverse function of these.
         $x \longrightarrow 8 - x$ $x \longrightarrow 12 - x$ $x \longrightarrow 4 - x$
   b What do you notice about your answers to **a**.
   c Draw a mapping diagram to show that $x \longrightarrow 5 - x$ is the inverse of $x \longrightarrow 5 - x$.

Sequences and Functions

Review 1 Use a copy of these mapping diagrams.

Fill in each to show the function and its inverse.

Write down the inverse function.

a $x \rightarrow x-2$ for $x = {}^-1, 0, 1, 2, 3$

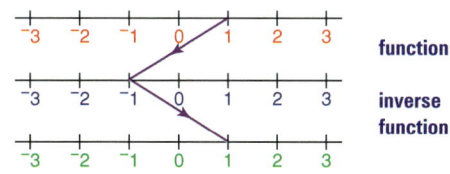

b $x \rightarrow 2x+1$ for $x = {}^-1, 0, 1, 2, 3$

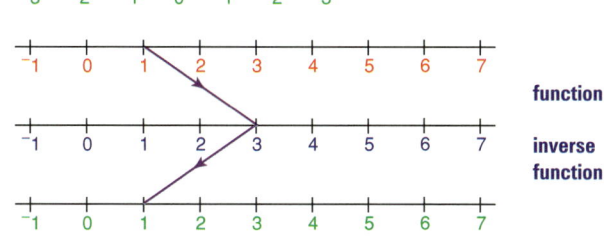

Review 2 Use a copy of this. Fill in the inverse function machine to find the inverse function.

$x \rightarrow$ [divide by 2] $\rightarrow$ [add 3] $\rightarrow \frac{x}{2}+3$

___ ← [ ] ← [ ] ← x

Review 3 Find the inverse functions for these.

a $x \rightarrow 4x-3$ **b** $x \rightarrow 3(x+2)$ **c** $x \rightarrow \frac{1}{4}x+10$

Summary of key points

A Sequences can be generated from a **term-to-term** rule.

Example **First term** 3 **Rule** add 5   generates 3, 8, 13, 18, 23, ...

Sequences can also be generated from an expression for the nth term.

We call this a **position-to-term** rule.

This is sometimes written as $T(n)$.

Example The rule for the nth term of a sequence is $T(n) = 2n - 3$.

This generates the sequence

$^-1, \quad 1, \quad 3, \quad 5 ...$
$n=1 \;\; n=2 \;\; n=3 \;\; n=4$

$T(n)$ is the nth term.

To find the sequence substitute $n = 1, 2, 3, 4,$ into $2n - 3$.

The difference between terms is 2, which is the number multiplying n.

Linear sequences always have a constant difference between terms.

We can **describe linear sequences** by looking at the rule for the nth term.

Example $T(n) = 3n + 1$ gives the sequence   4, 7, 10, 13, ...

Each term is one more than a multiple of 3.

It is ascending with a common difference of 3.

Algebra

B **Quadratic sequences** have a rule with a squared term as its highest power.
Example $T(n) = n^2 + 1$

Position	1	2	3	4	5	...
Term $T(n)$	$1^2 + 1 = 2$	$2^2 + 1 = 5$	$3^2 + 1 = 10$	$4^2 + 1 = 17$	$5^2 + 1 = 26$	...

The quadratic sequence is   2, 5, 10, 17, 26.
          3 5 7 9 ← 1st difference
           2 2 2   ← 2nd difference is constant for a quadratic sequence

C Sequences can be generated from **practical situations**.
Example

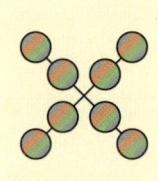

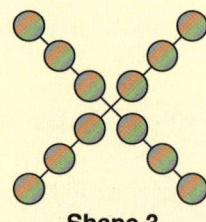

Shape 1   **Shape 2**   **Shape 3**

The expression for the number of circles in the *n*th shape is 4*n*.
Each time a new shape is drawn 4 new circles are added.
There are *n* lots of 4 where *n* is the shape number.

D We can find a **rule for the *n*th** term by finding the difference between consecutive terms.
Example

Term	13	19	25	31	37
Difference		6	6	6	6

The difference between consecutive terms is **6** so the *n*th term is of the form $T(n) = \mathbf{6}n + b$

$T(\mathbf{1}) = 13$ $6 \times \mathbf{1} + 7 = 13$

$T(n) = 6n + 7$

Check by testing some more terms.

E If the **output in a function machine** is 11, we work backwards to find the input.

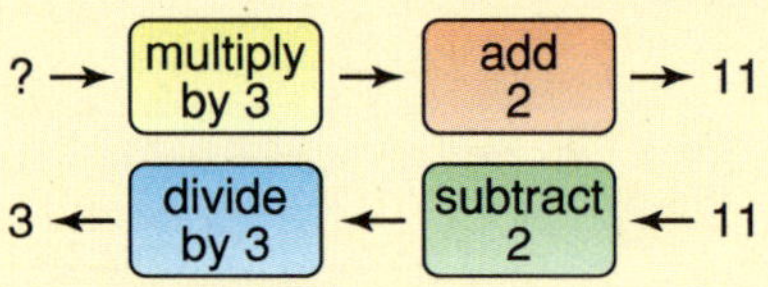

? → [multiply by 3] → [add 2] → 11

3 ← [divide by 3] ← [subtract 2] ← 11

The input was 3.

The **identity function** is $x \to x$. It maps every number onto itself.

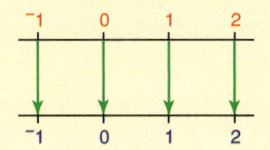

228

Sequences and Functions

F The **inverse of a function** can be found by doing the inverse operations in the reverse order.

Example

$x \to$ [add 4] $\to$ [multiply by 3] $\to 3(x+4)$ **function machine**

$\frac{x}{3} - 4 \leftarrow$ [subtract 4] $\leftarrow \frac{x}{3} \leftarrow$ [divide by 3] $\leftarrow x$ **inverse function machine**

The inverse of $3(x+4)$ is $\frac{x}{3} - 4$

Test yourself

1 Write down the first five terms of these sequences. **A**
  a **1st term** 10   **rule** subtract 0·5
  b **1st terms** 2, 2   **rule** add the two previous terms together

2 Predict the next three terms of these sequences. **A**
  a 0·2, 0·5, 0·8, 1·1 ... **b** 2, 4, 8, 16, ... **c** 3, 4, 6, 9, 13, ... **d** 1, 1, 2, 3, 5, ...

3 For each of the sequences in question **2**, write down the term-to-term rule. **A**

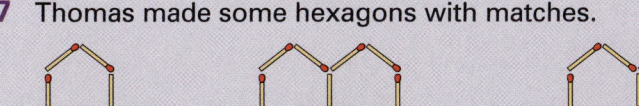

4 The *n*th term of a sequence is given. Write down the first six terms. **A**
  a $T(n) = 4n - 2$ **b** $T(n) = 2n - 0.5$ **c** $T(n) = 0.2n$ **d** $T(n) = 36 - 4n$

5 In $T(n) = 2n + 1$, the sequence starts at 3 and ascends. It has terms with a common difference of 2 which are all one more or less than a multiple of 2. Describe the terms of the sequences in **4a** and **4d** like this. **A**

6 Write down the first six terms of these sequences. **B**
  a $T(n) = n^2 + 2$ **b** $T(n) = 2n^2 - 3$

7 Thomas made some hexagons with matches. **C**

1 hexagon   2 hexagons   3 hexagons
6 matches   11 matches   16 matches

A rule to find the number of matches is $m = 5h + 1$ where m is the number of matches and h the number of hexagons.
  a Use the rule to find how many matches Thomas needed to make 12 hexagons.
  b Thomas used 76 matches to make some hexagons.
     How many hexagons did he make? Show your working.
  c Nicholas made some different hexagons with matches.

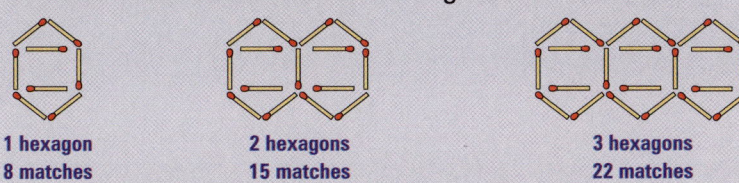

1 hexagon   2 hexagons   3 hexagons
8 matches   15 matches   22 matches

Which rule shows how many matches he needs?
    $m = h + 7$ $m = 7h - 1$ $m = 6h + 2$ $m = h + 8$
                $m = 7h + 1$ $m = 6h - 2$

Algebra

8 Find the *n*th term of these sequences.
If you need to, draw a difference table like this for each.

Term	5	7	9	11
Difference		2	2	2

  a 5, 7, 9, 11, ...   **b** 32, 40, 48, 56, ...   **c** 3, ⁻1, ⁻5, ⁻9, ...

9 A sequence has the rule 'to find the next number subtract ☐'.
What could the first term and rule be for a sequence in which every fifth number is an integer?

10 Use a copy of this.
Fill in the missing input and output numbers.

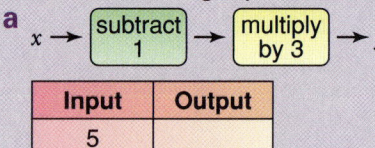

a $x \rightarrow$ subtract 1 $\rightarrow$ multiply by 3 $\rightarrow y$

Input	Output
5	
	18
10	

b $x \rightarrow$ divide by 2 $\rightarrow$ add 3 $\rightarrow y$

Input	Output
12	
20	
	15

11 Use a copy of this mapping diagram.
Fill it in for $y = 3(x + 1)$ for $x = $ ⁻1, 0, 1, 2, 3.

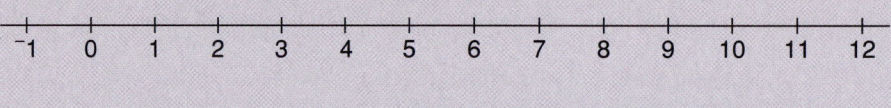

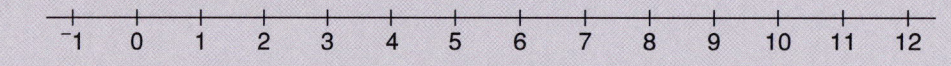

⁻1 0 1 2 3 4 5 6 7 8 9 10 11 12

⁻1 0 1 2 3 4 5 6 7 8 9 10 11 12

12 Draw a function machine for each of these.
  a $y = 2x + 5$ **b** $y = \frac{x}{2} - 4$ **c** $y = 3(x - 2)$

13 What single operation could replace the two given?
  a $x \rightarrow$ add 3 $\rightarrow$ subtract 2 $\rightarrow y$
  b $x \rightarrow$ divide by 2 $\rightarrow$ multiply by 8 $\rightarrow y$

14 a I think of a number then I carry out these operations on my number.

  multiply by 3   add 5

  When I carry out the operations in one order the answer is 42.
  When I carry out the operations in the other order, the answer is 32.
  What is my number?
  Show your working.
  *b The difference between my two answers is 10.
  Prove that the difference will always be 10, no matter what my number is.

230

Sequences and Functions

15 Find the inverse function for these.
The first one is started.

a $x \rightarrow$ [multiply by 2] $\rightarrow$ [add 3] $\rightarrow 2x + 3$ function

___ $\leftarrow$ [ ] $\leftarrow$ [ ] $\leftarrow x$ inverse function

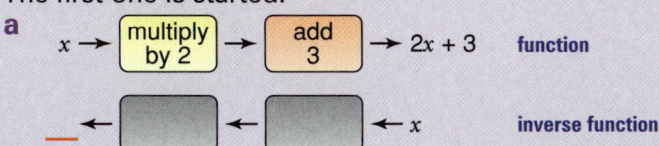

b $x \rightarrow 2(x-1)$

c $x \rightarrow \frac{1}{2}x - 3$

16

| 4 sides | 5 sides | 6 sides |
| 2 diagonals | 5 diagonals | 9 diagonals |

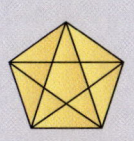

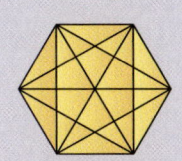

Use the explanation below to complete this formula for the number of diagonals, d, in an n-sided polygon.

$d =$ _____

Each vertex is joined to all the other vertices, except the two next to it.
This gives $n - 3$ diagonals.
For n vertices this gives $n \times (n - 3)$ diagonals.
But each diagonal is only drawn from one end and $n \times (n - 3)$ counts each diagonal twice.

9 Graphs of Functions

You need to know
✓ graphs
    – graphs of real-life situations   page 149

Key vocabulary
gradient, intercept, linear function

▶▶ Dealing in Dollars

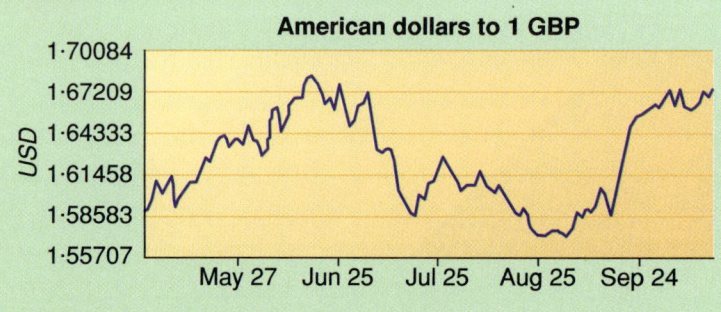

American dollars to 1 GBP

This graph of how many American dollars you got for £1 versus time, came from the Internet.
Find some other real-life graphs in newspapers, magazines or the Internet.
Make a poster of your graphs explaining what each is about.
Are any of them misleading?

Graphs of Functions

Graphing functions

Remember

$y = 3x + 7$ $y = \frac{x}{2} - 4$ $y = 8 - 5x$ are all **linear functions**.

If we draw a graph of y against x for a linear function we get a **straight line**.

A linear function has no terms with powers > 1.

To draw the graph of a function, make a table of values, plot the coordinates, then draw a straight line through them.

Example   To draw $y = \frac{x}{2} + 5$ choose three or four values for x and draw a table.

($\frac{x}{2}$ is $\frac{1}{2}x$)

x	0	2	4	⁻2
y	5	6	7	4

$x = 0$ $x = 2$ $x = 4$ $x = {}^-2$
$y = \frac{0}{2} + 5$ $y = \frac{2}{2} + 5$ $y = \frac{4}{2} + 5$ $y = \frac{-2}{2} + 5$
$= 0 + 5$ $= 1 + 5$ $= 2 + 5$ $= {}^-1 + 5$
$= 5$ $= 6$ $= 7$ $= 4$

Note We chose even numbers for x because $\frac{x}{2}$ is then a whole number answer.

Plot the coordinates (0, 5), (2, 6), (4, 7) and (⁻2, 4).
Draw a straight line through them.
Label the line.

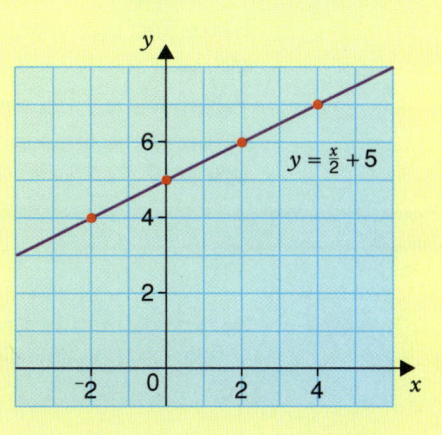

A point will lie on the line if it satisfies the equation.

Example   (2, 13) lies on $y = 3x + 7$ because $13 = 3 \times 2 + 7$ is true.

↑ *y-coordinate*   ↑ *x-coordinate*

★ Practical

You will need graph paper, a graph plotting software package or a graphical calculator.

- Graph these lines.
  $y = x + 2$
  $y = 2x + 2$
  $y = 3x + 2$
  $y = {}^-x + 2$
  $y = {}^-2x + 2$
  $y = {}^-3x + 2$

  Try to draw some graphs on paper, some using a software package and some using a graphical calculator.

  Describe the similarities and differences.

  Make and test a statement about the position of the line $y = 4x + 2$.

  What if the lines were
  $y = 3x - 3$
  $y = 2x - 3$
  $y = x - 3$
  $y = {}^-x - 3$
  $y = {}^-2x - 3$?

  What if the lines were
  $y = 3x - 1$
  $y = 2x - 1$
  $y = x - 1$
  $y = {}^-x - 1$
  $y = {}^-2x - 1$
  $y = \frac{1}{2}x - 1$?

233

Algebra

What if the lines were
$y = 3x$
$y = 2x$
$y = x$
$y = \frac{1}{2}x$
$y = {}^-x$
$y = {}^-2x$
$y = {}^-3x$?

- Graph these lines.
$y = 2x + 2$
$y = 2x + 1$
$y = 2x$
$y = 2x - 1$
$y = 2x - 2$

Describe the similarities and differences.

Make and test a statement about the position of the lines $y = 2x + 3$ and $y = 2x - 3$.
What if the lines were $y = 3x + 2$, $y = 3x + 1$, $y = 3x$, $y = 3x - 1$, $y = 3x - 2$?
What if the lines were $y = x + 2$, $y = x + 1$, $y = x$, $y = x - 1$, $y = x - 2$?
What if the lines were $y = {}^-2x + 2$, $y = {}^-2x + 1$, $y = {}^-2x$, $y = {}^-2x - 1$, $y = {}^-2x - 2$?
What if ...

Remember
In $y = mx + c$ m represents the **gradient** or slope.
c tells us the **y-intercept**.

> The gradient is the steepness of the line.
> The y-intercept is where it cuts the y-axis.

$y = 3x - 4$ and $y = 3x + 6$ have the same slope because m is the same for both.
$y = {}^-3x + 2$ and $y = 5x + 2$ cross the y-axis at the same place because c is the same.
$y = 4x + 2$ has a steeper positive gradient than $y = 2x + 3$ because 4 is greater than 2.

If m is positive the line slopes ╱.
If m is negative the line slopes ╲.

Sometimes the equation of a straight line is not given in the form $y = mx + c$.
If we want to find m and c we must **rearrange it into the form** $y = mx + c$.

Worked Example
Rearrange each of the following into the form $y = mx + c$.
a $x + y - 3 = 0$ *__b__ $2y = 5x - 4$

Answer
We need to make y the subject of each. One way of doing this is to use inverse operations.

a Begin with y.

$y \rightarrow \boxed{\text{add } x} \rightarrow x + y \rightarrow \boxed{\text{subtract } 3} \rightarrow x + y - 3$

$3 - x \leftarrow \boxed{\text{subtract } x} \leftarrow 3 \leftarrow \boxed{\text{add } 3} \leftarrow 0$

$y = 3 - x$

> Link to changing the subject of a formula (page 200) and finding inverse functions (page 225).

> Begin with the right-hand side of the equation.

*__b__
$y \rightarrow \boxed{\text{multiply by 2}} \rightarrow 2y$

$\frac{5x - 4}{2} \leftarrow \boxed{\text{divide by 2}} \leftarrow 5x - 4$

$y = \frac{5x - 4}{2}$

$y = \frac{5x}{2} - 2$

> We can write this as $\frac{5x}{2} - \frac{4}{2}$ because 2 is the common denominator.

Graphs of Functions

Discussion

Tracy used 'transforming both sides' rather than inverse operations to rearrange $2y = 5x - 4$ into the form $y = mx + c$.

$$2y = 5x - 4$$
$$\frac{2y}{2} = \frac{5x - 4}{2} \quad \text{dividing both sides by 2}$$
$$y = \frac{5x - 4}{2}$$

Compare Tracy's method with the method using inverse operations.
Use Tracy's method to rewrite $x + y - 3 = 0$, $2y - 2x = 4$ and $x + 2y = {}^-3$ in the form $y = mx + c$.

Discuss the advantages and disadvantages of each method.

Exercise 1

1 Write true or false for these.
  a The graph of $y = 2x - 3$ will have a steeper slope than the graph of $y = x + 4$.
  b The graph of $y = x + 2$ crosses the y-axis at (0, 2).
  c The graph of $y = {}^-3x + 2$ has a negative gradient which slopes ╲.
  d The graph of $x = 5$ is a horizontal line.
  e The graph of $y = {}^-2$ is a horizontal line.
  f The graph of $y = \frac{x}{2} + 4$ has a steeper gradient than the graph of $y = {}^-2x + 3$.

> See page 149 for graphs of horizontal and vertical lines.

2 Some equations are given in the box.
If the graph of each is drawn, which will
  a have the steepest gradient
  b cut the y-axis at (0, $^-2$)
  c have the same gradient
  d cut the y-axis at the same point?

A	$y = 3x + 4$
B	$y = x + 3$
C	$y = x - 3$
D	$y = 2x - 2$
E	$y = {}^-2x - 3$

3 a Draw axes with both x- and y-values from $^-6$ to 6.
  On these axes draw and clearly label these lines.
  $y = 2x - 1 \quad y = {}^-x + 2$
  b Will $y = 2x - 1$ go through the point (8, 15)? Explain how you can tell.
  c Will the point $(8\frac{1}{2}, 10\frac{1}{2})$ lie on the line $y = {}^-x + 2$? Explain how you can tell.
  d The point ($^-7$, ___) lies on the line $y = {}^-x + 2$.
  What is the missing y-coordinate?

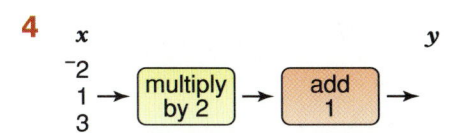

> You could use a graphical calculator or graph plotter.

4
x → [multiply by 2] → [add 1] → y
$^-2$
1
3

  a Write down the coordinate pairs made with the input given. ($^-2$, ___), (1, ___), (3, ___).
  b Draw a straight-line graph for the function given and label it with an equation.

5 Rachel plotted these points on a grid.

Term number	1	2	3	4	5	6	7
Term $T(n)$	1	3	5	7	9	11	13

> $T(n)$ means the nth term.

If she joins them with a straight line will the intermediate points have meaning? Explain.

235

Algebra

6 These straight-line graphs all pass through the point (10, 10). [SATs Paper 1 Level 6]

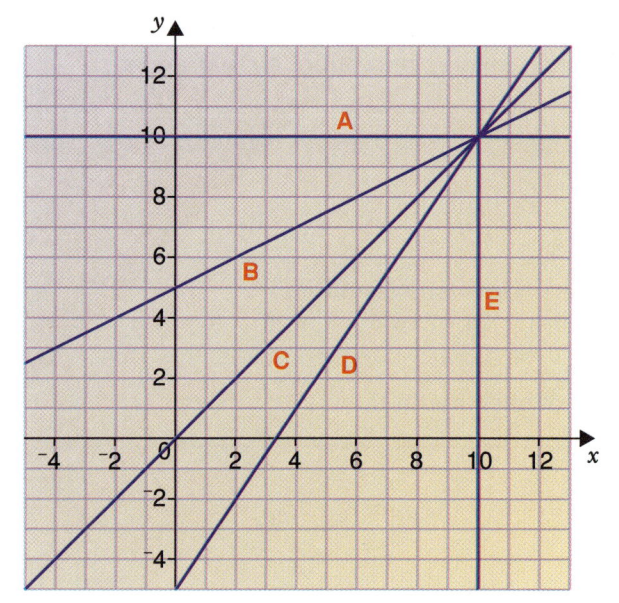

    a What goes in the gaps to show which line has which equation?
       i   line ___ has equation $x = 10$.
       ii line ___ has equation $y = 10$.
       iii line ___ has equation $y = x$.
       iv line ___ has equation $y = \frac{3}{2}x - 5$.
       v line ___ has equation $y = \frac{1}{2}x + 5$.
    b Does the line that has equation $y = 2x - 5$ pass through the point (10, 10)?
       Explain how you know.
  ***c** I want a line with equation $y = mx + 9$ to pass through the point (10, 10).   [Level 7]
       What is the value of m?

7 Write each of the following linear equations in the form $y = mx + c$.
    a $y - x = 3$

    $y \rightarrow$ [subtract x] $\rightarrow y - x$
    ___ $\leftarrow$ [add x] $\leftarrow 3$

    b $y + x = 6$

    $y \rightarrow$ [add x] $\rightarrow y + x$
    ___ $\leftarrow$ [ ] $\leftarrow 6$

    c $x + y = {}^-7$

    $y \rightarrow$ [ ] $\rightarrow x + y$
    ___ $\leftarrow$ [ ] $\leftarrow {}^-7$

    d $x + y = {}^-2$

    $y \rightarrow$ [ ] $\rightarrow$ ___
    ___ $\leftarrow$ [ ] $\leftarrow {}^-2$

    e $3y = 2x + 6$ **f** $2y = x - 4$ **g** $4y = x + 8$ **h** $x + 2y = 2$

8 Does the point (25, 28) lie on the line $x + y = 3$?
    Explain how you can tell.

9 The diagram shows a square drawn on a square grid.   [SATs Paper 1 Level 6]

a Use a copy of this.
The points A, B, C and D are at the vertices of the square.
Match the correct line to each equation.
One is done for you.

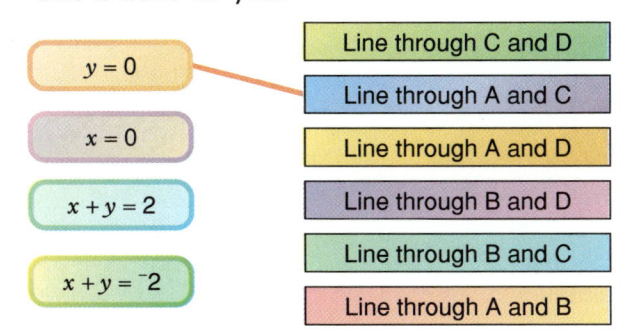

- $y = 0$ — Line through C and D
- $x = 0$ — Line through A and C
- $x + y = 2$ — Line through A and D
- $x + y = {}^-2$ — Line through B and D
- Line through B and C
- Line through A and B

The mid-points of each side, E, F, G and H, join to make a different square.

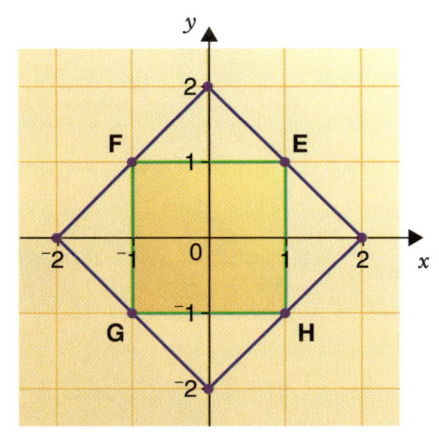

b Write the equation of the straight line through E and H.
c Is $y = {}^-x$ the equation of the straight line through E and G?
Explain how you know.

10 Draw axes with both x- and y-values from $^-5$ to 5. On these axes draw and clearly label the following lines.

$2x + y = 5$ $2y = 3x$ $y = 3x - 2$ $x + 2y = 8$

Choose some x-values and substitute them into the equation to find y.

∗11 a Write down the coordinates of the point that lies on both the straight lines $y = 3x + 1$ and $y = 5x - 3$.
Show your working.
b Explain how you can tell there is no point that lies on both straight lines $y = \frac{1}{2}x + 4$ and $y = \frac{1}{2}x + 6$.

∗12 Here are six different equations.

| A $y = 2x - 3$ | B $y = 5$ | C $x = {}^-3$ | D $x + y = 13$ | E $y = 3x + 1$ | F $y = x^2$ |

I draw the graphs of these equations.
a Which graph goes through the point (0, 1)?
b Which graph is parallel to the y-axis?
c Which graph is not a straight line?
d Which two graphs pass through the point (3, 10)?

Algebra

T ***13** Use a copy of this. [SATs Paper 2 Level 6]
   a Each point on the straight line $x + y = 12$ has an x-coordinate and a y-coordinate that **add together** to make 12.
   Draw the straight line $x + y = 12$.

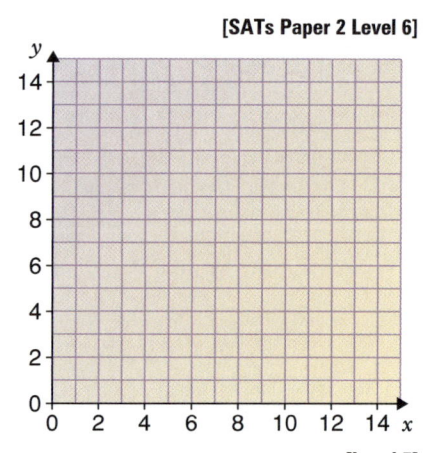

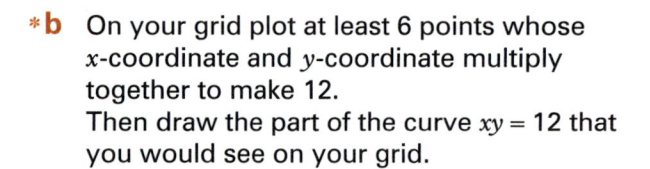

   *b On your grid plot at least 6 points whose x-coordinate and y-coordinate multiply together to make 12.
   Then draw the part of the curve $xy = 12$ that you would see on your grid. [Level 7]

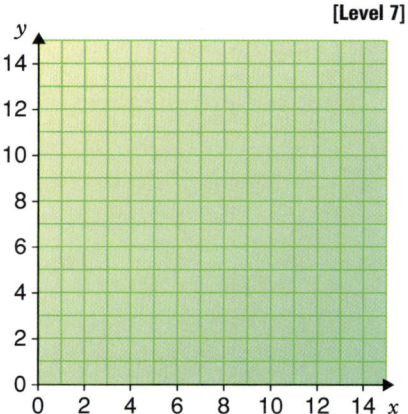

*14 Explain why the graph you drew in **13b**, $xy = 12$, is not a straight line.

Review 1 Draw axes with both x- and y-values from $^-6$ to 6.
   a On these axes draw and clearly label the lines
   A $y = 2x + 1$ **B** $y = ^-x + 5$ and   **C** $y = 2x - 4$.
   b Will the point (10, 5) lie on line B? Explain how you can tell.
   c Will the point (3·5, 8) lie on line A? Explain how you can tell.
   d The point (4, ___) lies on line C. What is the missing y-coordinate?
   e Make a comment about the similarities between your graphs of $y = 2x + 1$ and $y = 2x - 4$.

Review 2 These straight-line graphs all pass through the point (8, 8).
   a What goes in the gaps to show which line has which equation?
   i Line ___ has equation $x = 8$.
   ii Line ___ has equation $y = 8$.
   iii Line ___ has equation $y = \frac{5}{4}x - 2$.
   iv Line ___ has equation $y = \frac{1}{2}x + 4$.
   v Line ___ has equation $y = x$.
   *b The line with equation $y = mx + 6$ is to pass through (8, 8). What is the value of m?

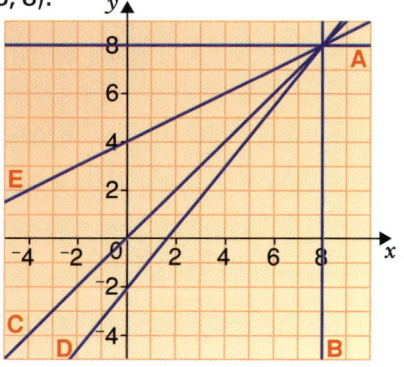

Review 3
   a Write all the equations in the form $y = mx + c$.
   A $y + 3 = 2x$ **B** $2y = x + 4$ **C** $4x - 2y = 7$ **D** $6x + 3y = 2$ **E** $\frac{1}{2}y = x - 5$
   b Which of the equations in **a** have gradient 2?
   c Which of these lines cut the y-axis at the same point?
   A $y = 3x + 2$ **B** $x + 2y = 4$ **C** $x + y + 2 = 0$ **D** $6x - y + 2 = 0$ **E** $3x + 2y = 6$
   d Does the point (2, 3) lie on the line $2y = x + 4$?
   e Draw the graph of $4x - 2y = 8$.

Graphs of Functions

Gradient of a straight line

Discussion

- James drew this table for $y = 2x + 1$.

x	0	1	2	3	4	5	6
y	1	3	5	7	9	11	13
Difference in y values		2	2	2	2	2	2

He drew the graph of $y = 2x + 1$.
He noticed that when x changed by 1, y changed by 2; when x changed by 2, y changed by 4; when x changed by 3, y changed by 6.

He drew these triangles to show this.

What do you notice about this ratio?
$$\frac{\text{change in } y}{\text{change in } x} = \frac{6}{3} = \frac{4}{2} = \frac{2}{1}$$
Is the ratio the same for all corresponding changes in y and changes in x? **Discuss**.

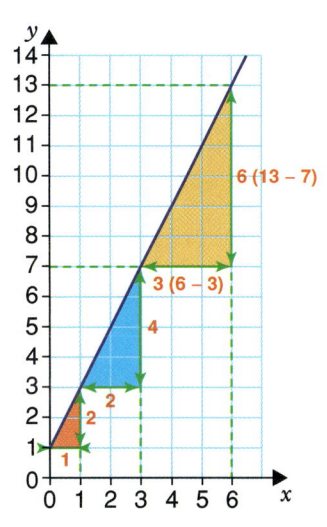

- **Discuss** these questions.

    Is the change in y proportional to the change in x? i.e. Is $\frac{\text{change in } y}{\text{change in } x}$ always the same?
    What can you say about the triangles James drew on his graph?
    Hint think about enlargement.
    How are the equation $y = 2x + 1$ and the ratio $\frac{\text{change in } y}{\text{change in } x}$ related?

- Draw the graph of $y = 3x + 1$. Draw some triangles on your grid like James did.
    Find $\frac{\text{change in } y}{\text{change in } x}$ for each triangle.
    What do you notice?

- **What if** you drew the graph of $\quad y = {}^-2x + 1 \quad$ or $\quad y = {}^-3x + 1$?

$y = mx + c$ is a **linear function**.
The change in y is proportional to the change in x.
So if you change x by 1, the change in y is always the same.

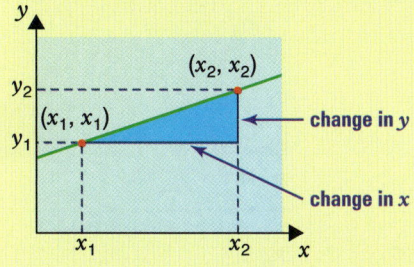

The gradient, m, of a straight line joining (x_1, y_1) to (x_2, y_2) is

$$m = \frac{y_2 - y_1}{x_2 - x_1} = \frac{\text{change in } y}{\text{change in } x}$$

We call $\frac{\text{change in } y}{\text{change in } x}$ the **constant of proportionality**.

For a positive gradient, y increases as x increases.
For a negative gradient, y decreases as x increases.

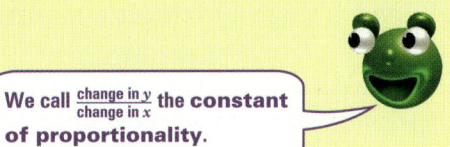

Algebra

Worked Example
Find the gradient of each of these lines.

Always check that a positive slope has a positive value and a negative slope has a negative value for the gradient.

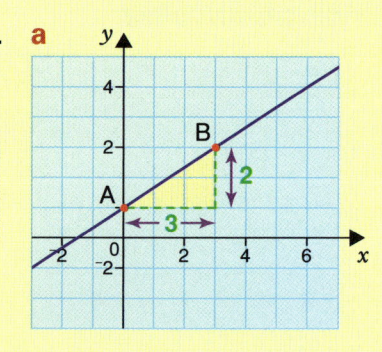

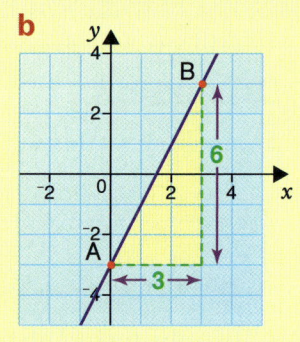

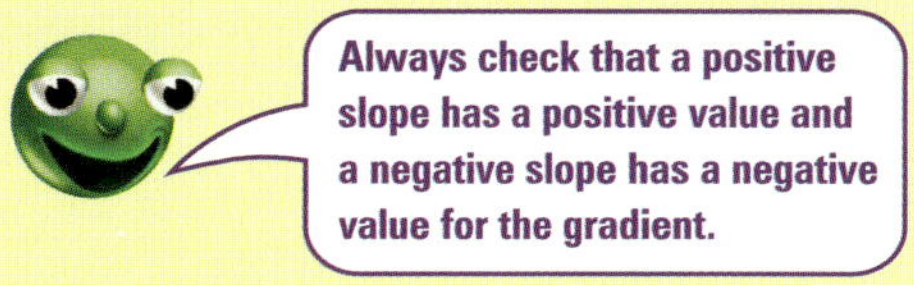

Answer

a $(x_1, y_1) = (0, 1)$ and $(x_2, y_2) = (3, 3)$

gradient $= \dfrac{\text{change in } y}{\text{change in } x}$

$= \dfrac{y_2 - y_1}{x_2 - x_1}$

$= \dfrac{3 - 1}{3 - 0}$

$= \dfrac{2}{3}$

b $(x_1, y_1) = (0, {}^-3)$ and $(x_2, y_2) = (3, 3)$

gradient $= \dfrac{\text{change in } y}{\text{change in } x}$

$= \dfrac{y_2 - y_1}{x_2 - x_1}$

$= \dfrac{3 - {}^-3}{3 - 0}$ ← difference in y-coordinates
← difference in x-coordinates

$= \dfrac{6}{3}$

$= 2$

To find the **equation of a line**, find the gradient, m, and the y-intercept, c. Then substitute these into $y = mx + c$ to give the equation.

Example The equation of this line is $y = 2x + 1$ because the gradient is 2 and it crosses the y-axis at 1.

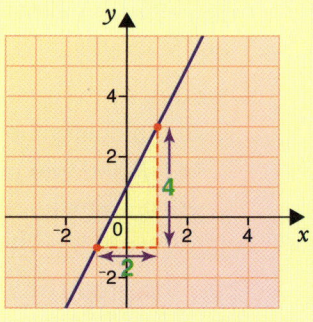

gradient $= \dfrac{\text{change in } y}{\text{change in } x} = \dfrac{4}{2}$

$= 2$

Exercise 2

1

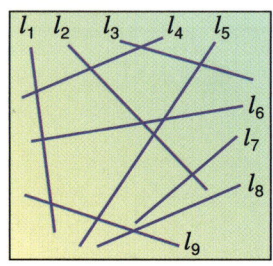

a Name the lines that have a positive gradient.
b Name the lines that have a negative gradient.

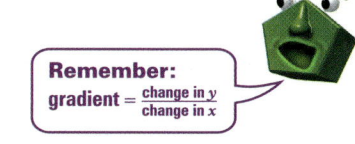

Remember:
gradient $= \dfrac{\text{change in } y}{\text{change in } x}$

2 Find the gradients of these.

a

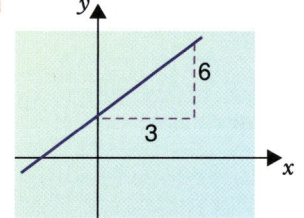

b

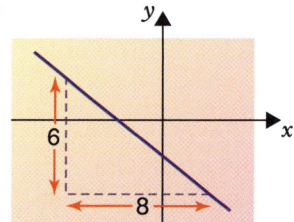

c

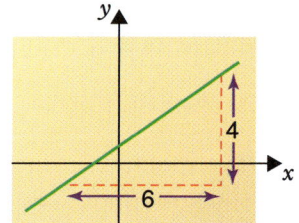

240

Graphs of Functions

3 Find the gradient of these lines.

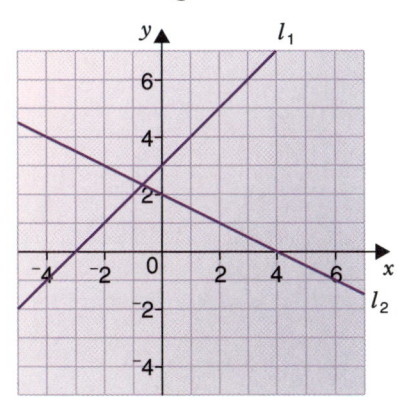

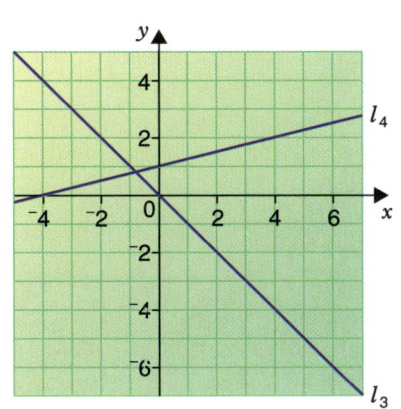

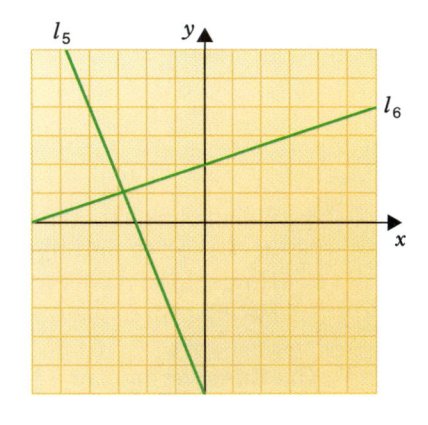

4 If the value of y decreases as x increases, will the gradient, m, be negative or positive?

5 Match these sketches with an equation from the box.

a   b 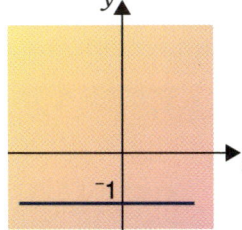   c

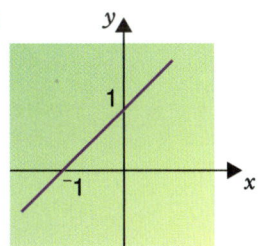

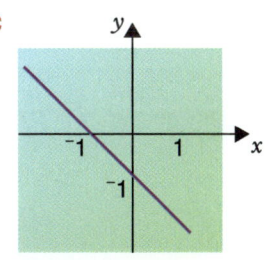

d 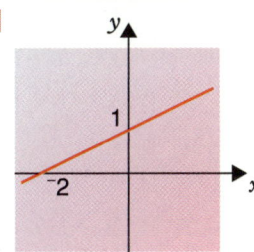   e

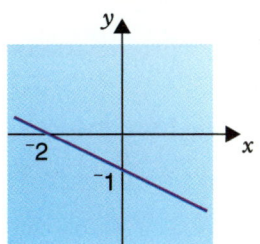

A $y = ^-1$
B $y = ^-x - 1$
C $y = \frac{1}{2}x + 1$
D $y = x + 1$
E $y = ^-\frac{1}{2}x - 1$

6 Write down the equations of lines **a** to **f**.

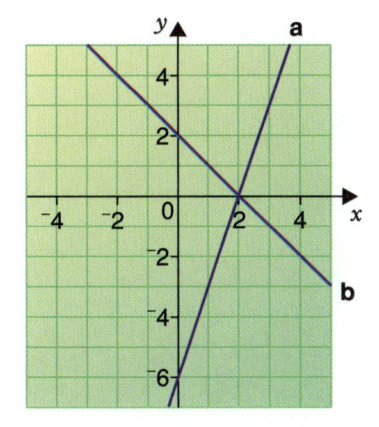

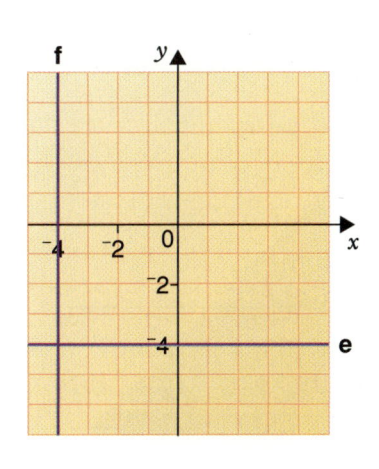

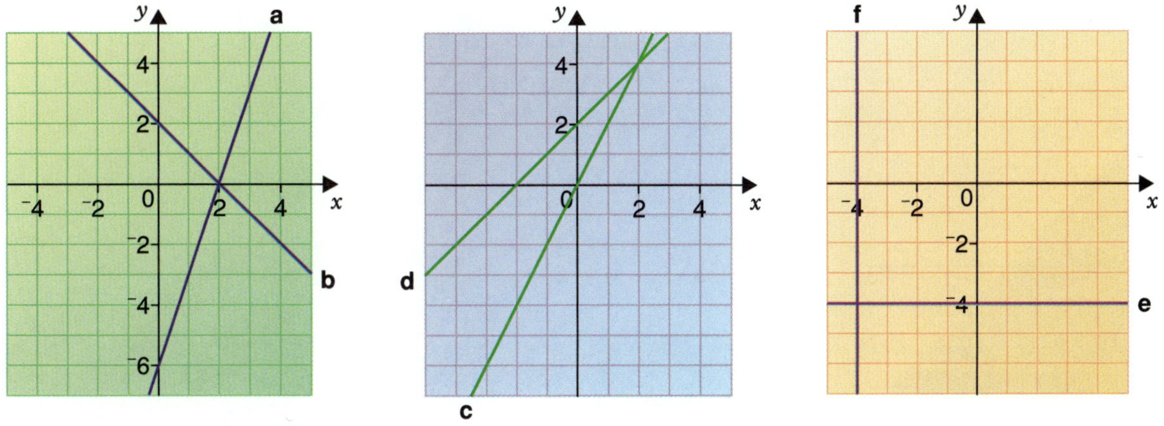

7 Write true or false for these.
   a A parallelogram will have two pairs of lines with equal gradient.
   b A trapezium will have a pair of lines with equal gradient.
   c A rhombus will have four sides of equal gradient.
   d A kite will have one pair of sides with equal gradient.

Draw sketches if you need to.

241

Algebra

*8 **a** Jack wanted to know the gradient of the line $y = 3$.
He wrote
$$m = \frac{y_2 - y_1}{x_2 - x_1}$$
$$= \frac{}{}$$
$$= \frac{}{}$$

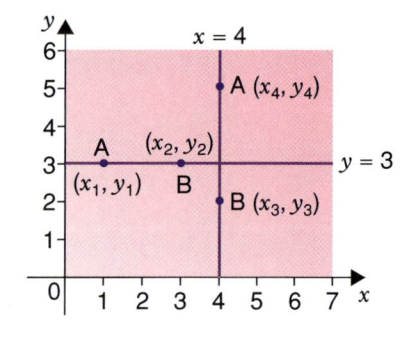

Finish Jack's working to find the gradient of $y = 3$.

b Jack tried to find the gradient of $x = 4$.
He decided it was not possible to give a gradient for $x = 4$.
He is right. Explain why you think this is.

*9 The three vertices of a triangle are   P(2, 1),   Q(4, ⁻3),   R(7, 0).
Find the gradient of each side of this triangle.

Review 1   Find the gradient of each line on this graph.

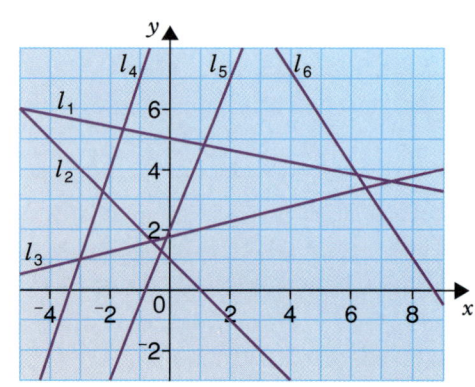

Review 2   Match each line with an equation from the box.

a   b 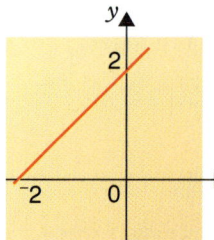   c

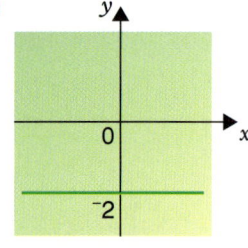

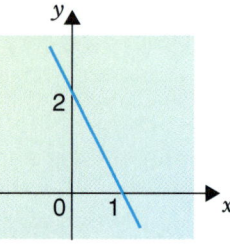

d 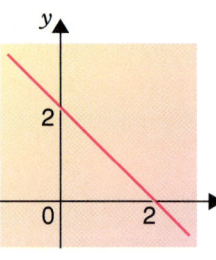   e 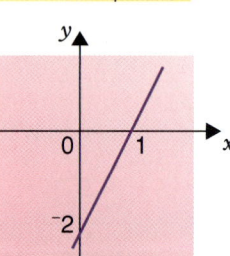   f

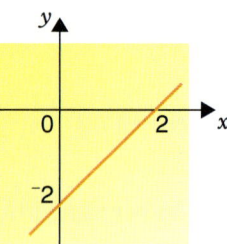

g

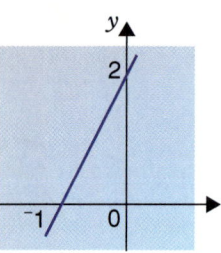

A $y = {}^-2$
B $y = x - 2$
C $y = {}^-2x$
D $y = 2x + 2$
E $y = 2x - 2$
F $y = {}^-2x + 2$
G $y = x + 2$
H $y = {}^-x + 2$

242

Graphs of Functions

Review 3 Write down the equations of lines A to E.

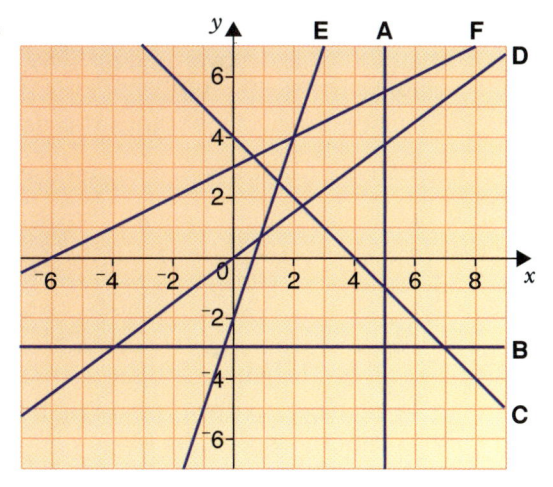

*****Review 4** The vertices of a quadrilateral are
A(⁻3, 2),   B(1, 5),   C(7, 4),   D(3, ⁻1).
Find the gradient of the diagonals of this quadrilateral.

Distance–time graphs

We can tell some things about how an object is moving by looking at its **distance–time graph**.

Example   Adriana drew a distance–time graph for this.
She drove out of the drive and down the road. After 200 m she realised that she had forgotten something and so she stopped and then drove back home.

A straight sloping line means the car is moving at a constant speed.

A horizontal line means the car has stopped.

A negative slope means the car is moving in the opposite direction.

A curve means the car is not moving at a constant speed.

Note The gradient of a distance–time graph tells us the speed.
A steeper slope represents a faster speed.

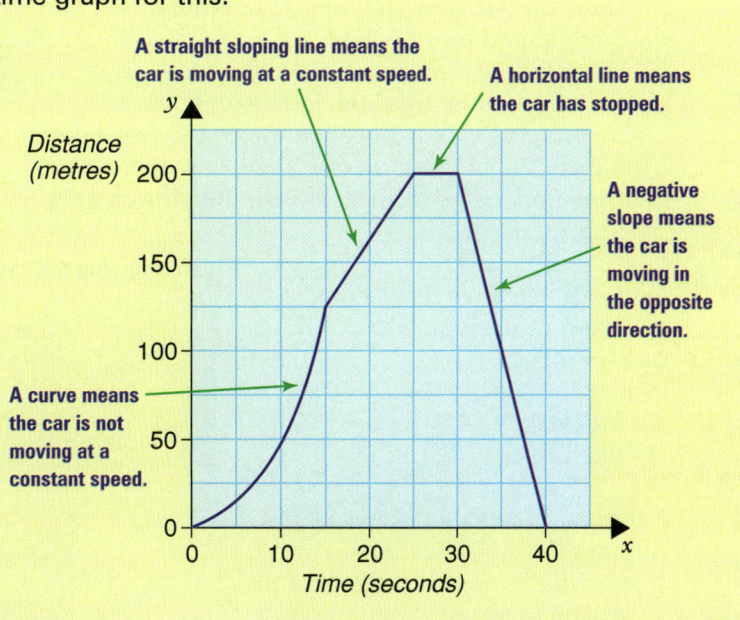

Discussion

•

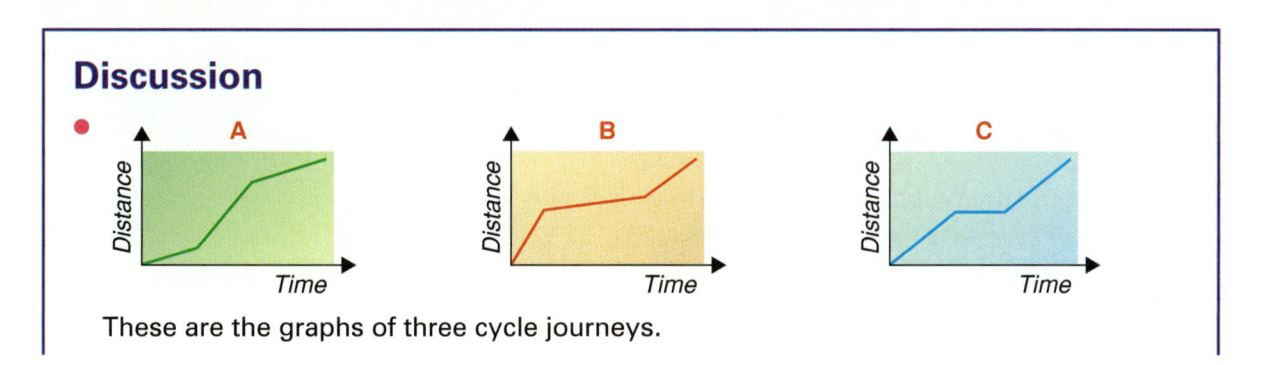

These are the graphs of three cycle journeys.

243

Algebra

Graph A shows that at first the speed was quite slow, then the speed was quite fast, then the cyclist slowed down. The speed in the last section of the journey was not as slow as in the first part.
Describe the cycle journeys represented by graphs B and C. **Discuss**.

- Match the graphs with the statements. **Discuss**.

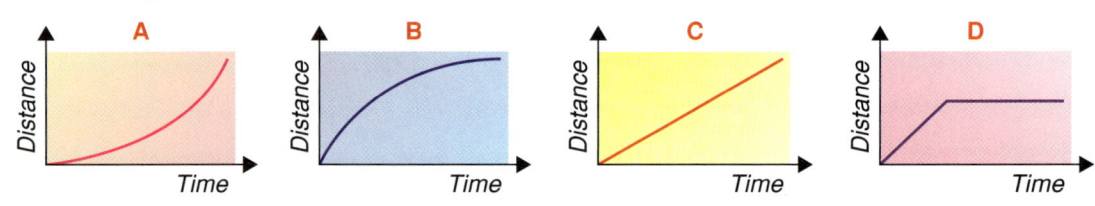

A Distance / Time
B Distance / Time
C Distance / Time
D Distance / Time

1 A car slowing down going up a hill.
2 A car cruising on the M4.
3 A car hitting a concrete wall.
4 A car rolling down a hill.

Exercise 3

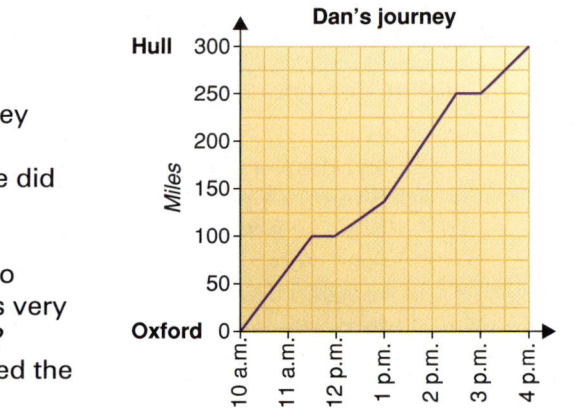

1 This is a distance–time graph for Dan's journey from Oxford to Hull.
  a Dan stopped after 100 miles. At what time did he stop and for how long?
  b What time did he arrive at Hull?
  c For about an hour of the journey he had to travel quite slowly because the traffic was very heavy. Which hour do you think this was?
  d How far was he from Hull when he stopped the second time?

Dan's journey

2 One of these lines represents a walker, one a jogger and one a cyclist.
Which shows
  a the walker
  b the jogger?

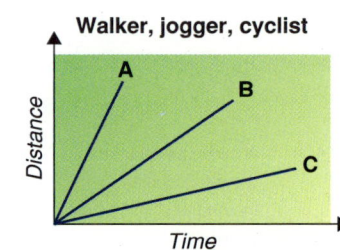

Walker, jogger, cyclist

3 Karen and Susan were two of the runners in a 400 m race.
  a At what times were Karen and Susan level with each other?
  b Who finished first, Karen or Susan?
  c Who had the faster speed during the first 10 seconds?
  d Who was leading after 40 seconds? About how far ahead was she?
  e How might an announcer have spoken about Karen's and Susan's progress during this race? Write a short report on this.

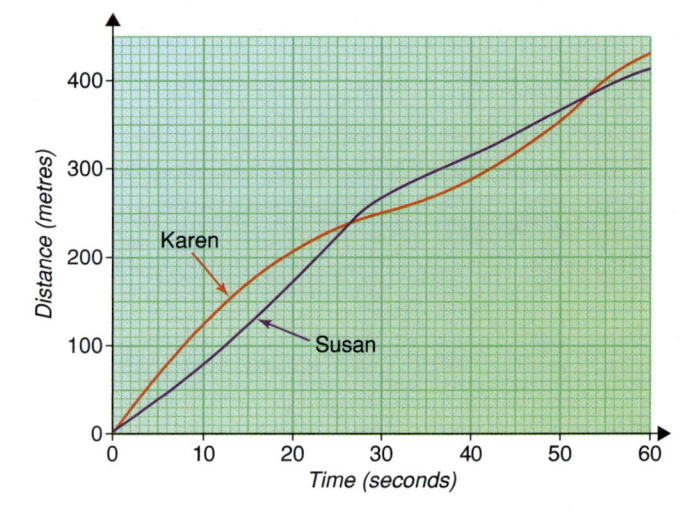

Graphs of Functions

4 I went for a walk.
The distance–time graph shows information about my walk.
Which of these best describes my walk?
  A I was walking faster and faster.
  B I was walking slower and slower.
  C I was walking north-east.
  D I was walking at a steady speed.
  E I was walking uphill.

[SATs Paper 2 Level 6]

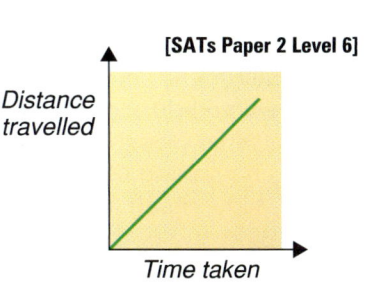

5

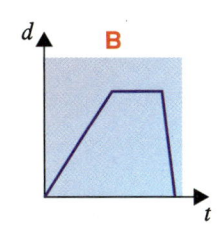

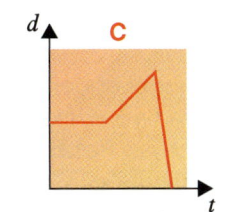

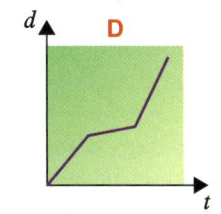

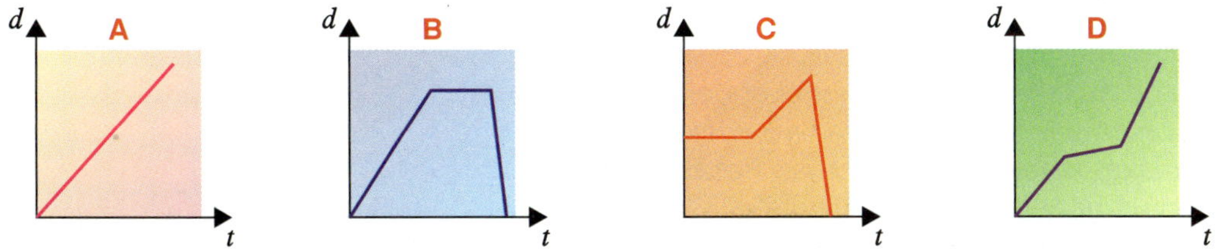

Jake cycles along a flat road at a steady speed, then up a hill more slowly, then down the other side. Which graph best describes Jake's cycle journey?

6 The graph shows my journey in a lift.
I got into the lift at floor number 10.
  a The lift stopped at two different floors before I got to floor number 22. What floors were they?
  b For how long was I in the lift while it was moving?
  c After I got out of the lift at floor number 22, the lift went directly to the ground floor.
  It took 45 seconds.
  Use a copy of the graph.
  Show the journey of the lift from floor 22 to the ground floor.

[SATs Paper 2 Level 6]

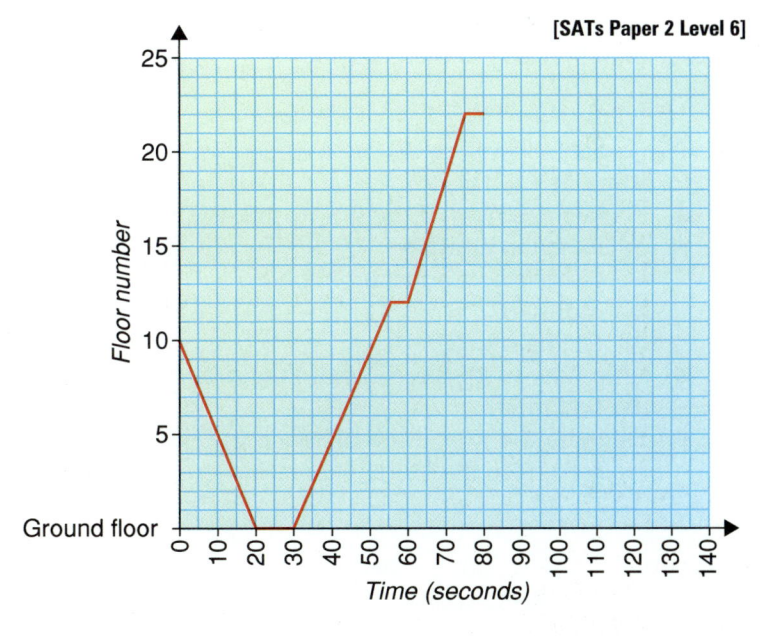

7 Use a copy of this grid.
Plot a distance–time graph for two sisters' car journeys.
  1. Ellie left home at 9 a.m. She travelled to her aunt's at a constant speed for 30 km. She arrived there at 9:30 a.m. She stayed for 30 minutes then travelled home, arriving at 11 a.m.
  2. Vicki left home at 9:30 a.m. She travelled at a constant speed till 10 a.m. She was then 35 km from home. She then slowed down and travelled the next 20 km in 45 minutes. She stopped for an hour.

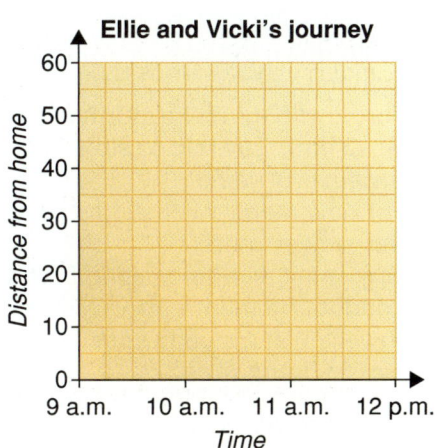

245

Algebra

8 A beaker of liquid was used as part of an experiment. This graph shows the level of the liquid during this experiment.
  a What was the depth of liquid at the beginning of this 6-minute experiment?
  b How much liquid was in the container at the end of the 6 minutes?
  c Describe what was happening to the depth of liquid during these 6 minutes.

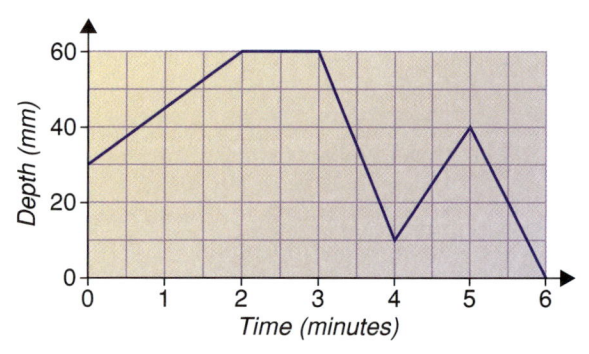

*9 Robbie and Julie both threw a cricket ball up into the air. This graph shows how high the two cricket balls went. Julie's cricket ball went higher than Robbie's.
  a Estimate how much higher Julie's cricket ball went than Robbie's.
  b Estimate the time after which their cricket balls were the same height.
  c Estimate the number of seconds that Julie's cricket ball spent more than 8 m above the ground.

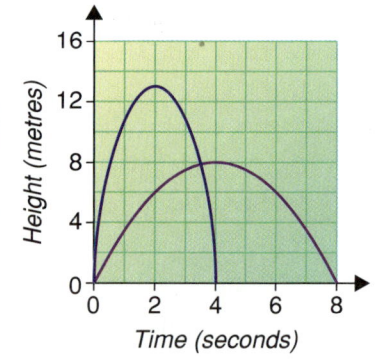

*10 This graph shows the distance–time graph for a ride at a fun park.
  a In which section of the graph, AB, BC, CD or DE, is the carriage
    i travelling at constant speed
    ii stopped
    *iii accelerating?
  b After how many seconds did the ride stop the first time?
  c Estimate the maximum distance the ride reached from the start.

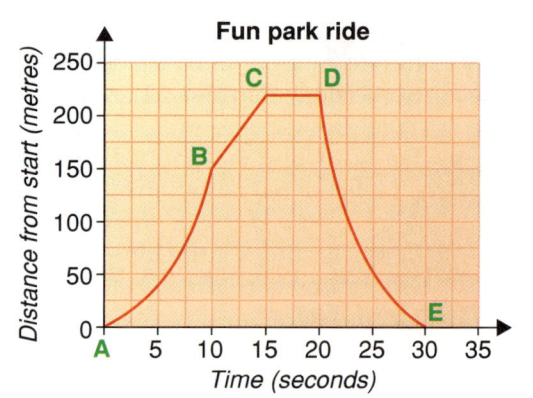

T Review 1 Use a copy of this.
The graph represents Guy's journey from home to London.
Guy stopped for coffee on the way.
  a Write down the time at which he stopped.
  b For how long did he stop?
  c At 12 p.m. Guy had to slow down because of traffic.
    For how many miles did he travel at this slower speed?
  d Guy spent an hour visiting friends in London. He then returned home, travelling at a steady speed. It took him $2\frac{1}{2}$ hours.
    Use this information to complete the graph of his journey.
  e Between which times did Guy travel fastest?

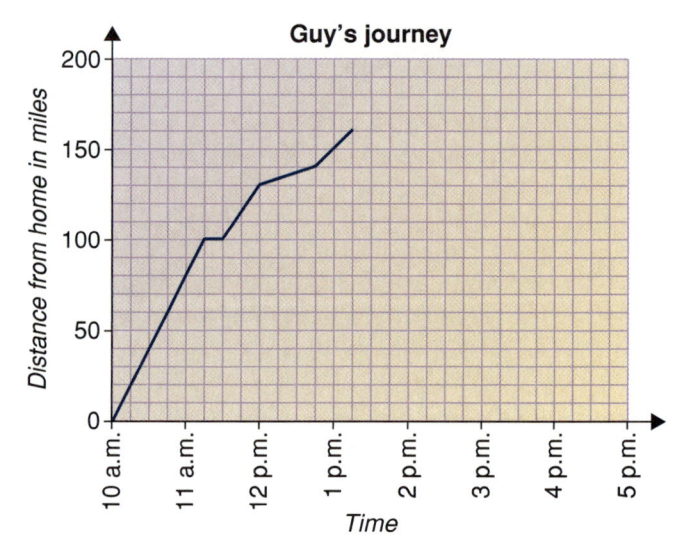

Review 2 Which of these best describes the coach trip?

A The coach travelled at a constant speed for the first half-hour then stopped for 15 minutes. It then travelled at a constant speed then it slowed down and then got faster again.

B The coach travelled at a constant speed for the first half-hour then stopped for 15 minutes. It travelled for another $\frac{1}{2}$ an hour then stopped for $\frac{1}{2}$ an hour then travelled at a faster, constant speed for 30 minutes.

Review 3 Use a grid with distances of 10, 20, 30, 40 miles and times from 10 a.m. to 3 p.m.
Draw a graph for these journeys.

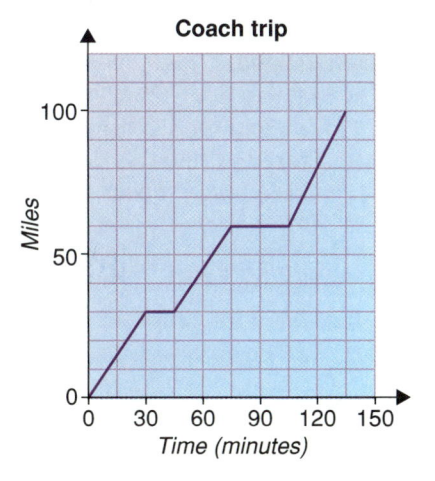

Janet
Janet left home at 10:30 and cycled for 1 hour at a constant speed, covering 6 miles. She took a rest for 15 minutes then rode for another 30 minutes at the same speed. After a $\frac{1}{2}$-hour break for lunch she decided to cycle home. She took 2 hours to cycle home.

Vic
Vic left home at 10 a.m. and stopped $1\frac{1}{4}$ hours later after travelling 16 miles. He stopped for 15 minutes then travelled a further 12 miles in the next hour. He stopped for 45 minutes then travelled the last 12 miles in $1\frac{1}{4}$ hours.

Drawing, sketching and interpreting graphs

Remember
If we are asked to **draw** a real-life graph we must
- construct a table of values using a formula or relationship
- choose suitable scales for the axes
- plot the points accurately
- draw a line through the points if it is sensible to do so
- give the graph a title and label the axes.

A sketch shows the **relationship between variables**.

Examples

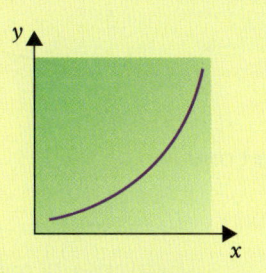

When x is large y is large.
As x increases in equal steps y increases by increasing amounts.

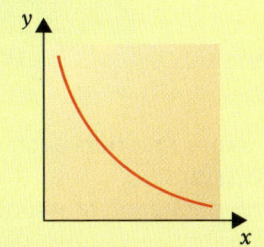

When x is large y is moving to 0.
As x increases in equal steps y decreases by decreasing amounts.

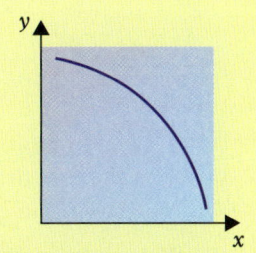

When x is large y becomes 0.
As x increases in equal steps y decreases by increasing amounts.

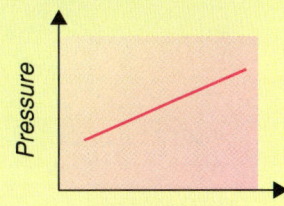

Example When the temperature of a closed can is increased the pressure inside the can increases also.
This sketch shows the relationship,
    as temperature increases so does pressure.

Algebra

Exercise 4

1 Temperatures given in °C can be changed to °F by using the relationship $F = 1.8C + 32$.
   a Debbie drew the graph of this relationship. Debbie chose $C = 40$ as one of her values. Choose two other values for C between 0 and 100.
   b Copy and complete these coordinates.
   (___, ___), (40, ___), (___, ___).
   Plot the three points. Draw the line that goes through these.
   c Use your graph to change 75 °C to °F.
   d Use your graph to change 75 °F to °C.

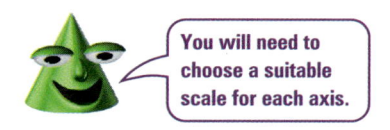

You will need to choose a suitable scale for each axis.

2 A video store gives customers a choice of two deals. In deal A customers pay a certain price for each video. In deal B they pay a joining fee and then a cheaper price for each video.
   a Which line represents deal B?
   b How much was the joining fee for deal B?
   c How many videos must be hired for the cost to be the same for both deals.
   d How much do customers who choose deal B pay per video?

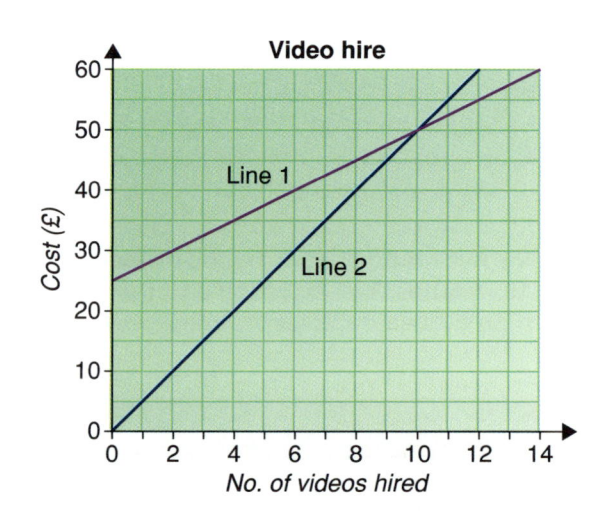

3 Write down a possible explanation for the shape of each of these graphs.

   a Amount of cereal in a packet
   b Water in a bath
   c Thawing and cooking a pie

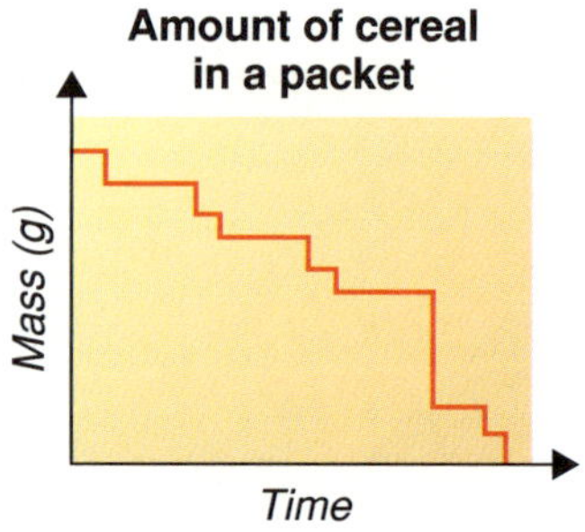

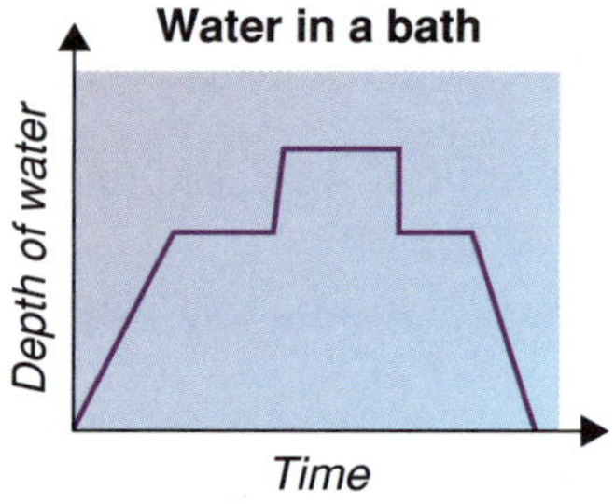

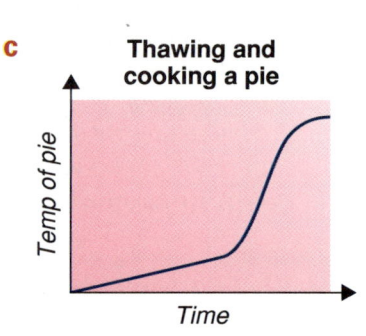

4 Water flowed steadily at the same rate into each of these containers.
A depth against time graph was drawn.
Which line on the graph represents each container? Explain your answer.

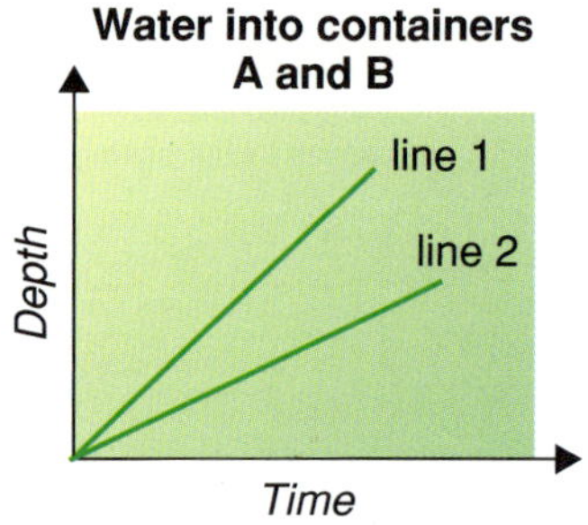

248

Graphs of Functions

*5 Match these graphs with the statements below.

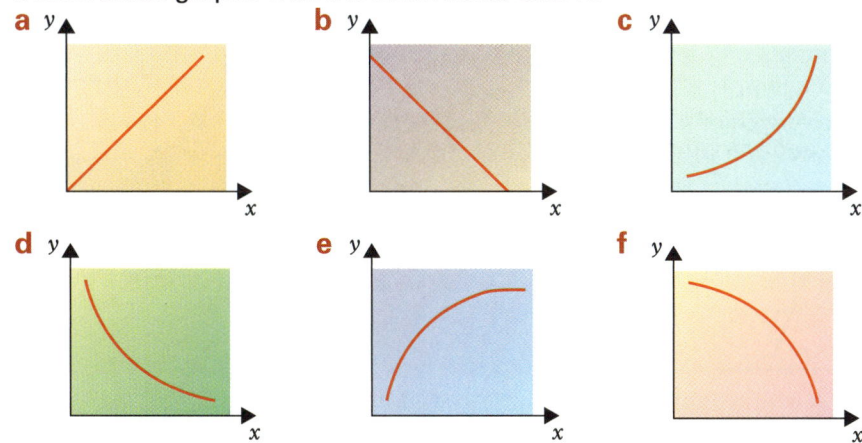

a, **b**, **c**, **d**, **e**, **f** (graphs)

As x increases by equal amounts
- **A** y increases by equal amounts.
- **B** y increases by increasing amounts
- **C** y increases by decreasing amounts
- **D** y decreases by equal amounts
- **E** y decreases by increasing amounts
- **F** y decreases by decreasing amounts.

*6 For each of the graphs given in question **5**, choose *one* of these statements. Each graph has a different statement.
- **A** the distance (y) plotted against time (x) travelled by a train moving at constant speed
- **B** the number (y) of flies left in a room as fly spray begins to work slowly at first and then more rapidly, plotted against time (x)
- **C** the volume of water (y) left in a bath being emptied at a constant rate, plotted against time (x)
- **D** the temperature (y) of a hot water bottle left on the floor to cool, plotted against time (x)
- **E** the distance (y) plotted against time (x), of a car which accelerates away from the lights then gradually slows down and stops
- **F** the number of bacteria cells (y) in a piece of rotting meat, plotted against time (x)

*7 The graph of depth of water against time when a steady flow of water pours into this container is shown.

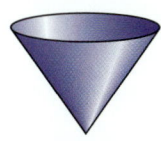

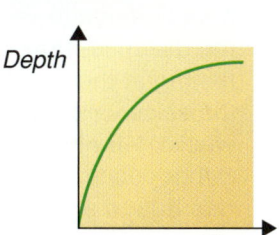

Sketch the graph of depth against time for water poured at a steady rate into these containers.

a   **b** 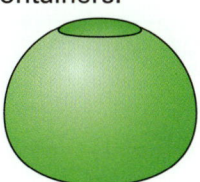   **c**

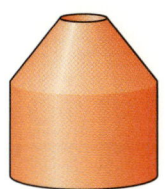

249

Algebra

*8 Rosalie did three experiments as part of her science project.
Sketch a graph of y against x for each of these situations.
   a She suspended a mass of x grams from a piece of rubber which stretches to a length of y cm. 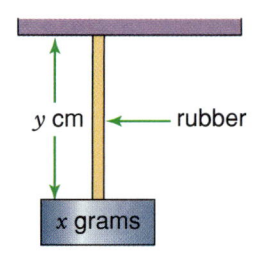
   b She put two equal masses on a see-saw. One mass is x cm above the ground and the other is y cm above the ground. 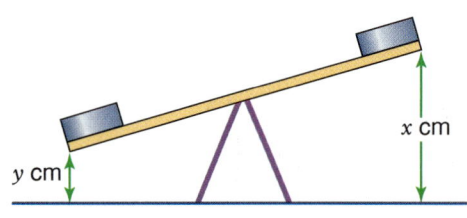
   c Rosalie modelled a swimmer on a straight hydroslide by rolling a ball down a piece of sloping pipe onto a table. The angle between the pipe and the table is $x°$. The horizontal distance the ball rolls is y cm.

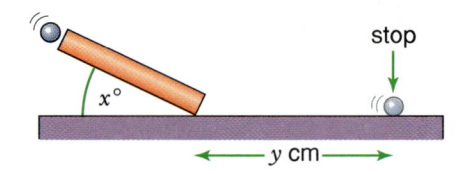

Review 1 Two rental car companies advertise these daily rental rates.

Rentadent	Hireakar
£20 basic charge plus £3 per 10 miles	£25 basic charge plus £5 per 20 miles

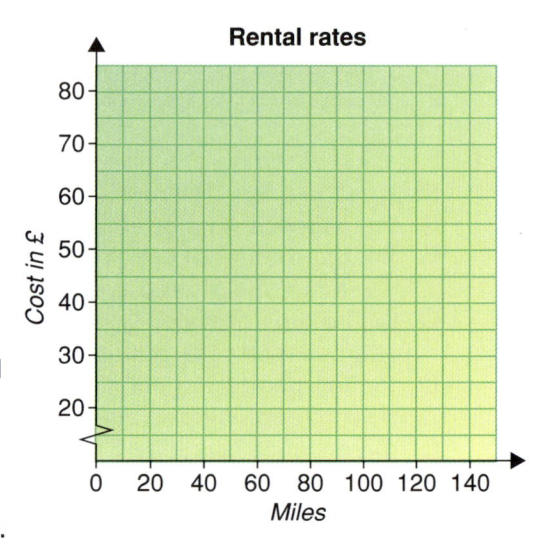

   a Use a copy of this grid.
      Use £c as the charge and d miles as the distance travelled to graph each rate on the same axes.
   b Which company would you use if you want to travel
      i 50 miles   ii 130 miles?
   c For what mileage will the cost be the same?

Review 2 Here are four statements, and four graphs.
Match the statements to the graphs.
  A the depth of water versus time graph for water being poured into a kettle from a tap, boiled then allowed to cool down
  B the distance–time graph for someone cycling up a steep hill, going slower and slower, resting at the top then cycling faster and faster downhill
  C the sales versus time graph for the sales of a new magazine which is advertised on TV from weeks 4–8 after it is first published
  D the population versus time graph for the Pacific Island population decreasing at a constant rate due to emigration

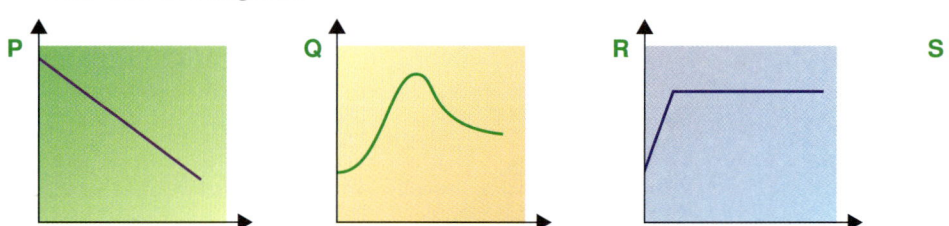

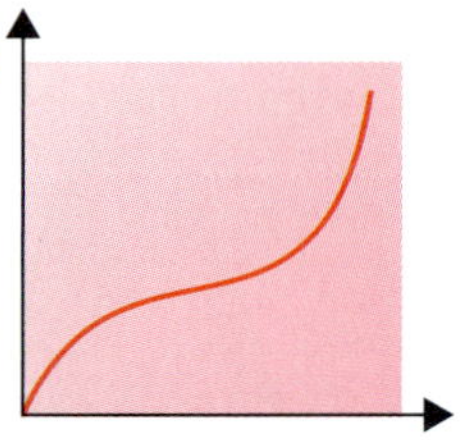

Graphs of Functions

> ⭐ **Practical**
>
> **You will need** a motion detector and a graphical calculator.
> Use a motion detector and graphical calculator to display the motion of a bouncing ball.

Summary of key points

A $y = mx + c$ is the equation of a straight line.

m is the **gradient** or steepness of the line.

c is the **y-intercept** (where the line cuts the y-axis).

B We can **rearrange equations in the form** $y = mx + c$.

Example $y - 2x + 3 = 0$

Start with y. $y \rightarrow$ [subtract $2x$] $\rightarrow$ [add 3] $\rightarrow y - 2x + 3$

$2x - 3 \leftarrow$ [add $2x$] $\leftarrow$ [subtract 3] $\leftarrow 0$ **Start with the right-hand side of the equation.**

$y = 2x - 3$

Once the equation is in the form $y = mx + c$ we can plot the graph by constructing a table of values.

Example $y = 2x - 3$

Choose 2 or 3 x-values.

x	0	1	3
y	⁻3	⁻1	3

C

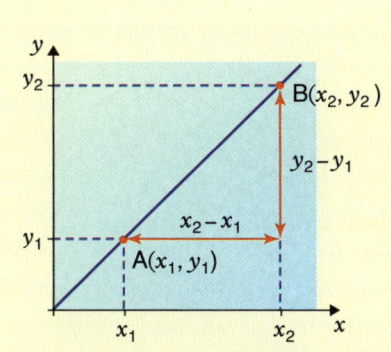

For a straight line, the change in y is **proportional** to the change in x.

$\frac{\text{change in } y}{\text{change in } x} = m$, the gradient of the line

$m = \frac{y_2 - y_1}{x_2 - x_1}$ for any two points on the line.

> We also call this the constant of proportionality.

We can find the equation of a line by substituting the gradient and y-intercept into $y = mx + c$.

251

Algebra

D This shows a **distance–time graph**.
Laura cycled at a steady pace.
She cycled 10 km in 30 mins. She stopped for 15 mins then cycled more slowly at a steady pace back to the start in 45 minutes.
She drew this graph.
We can use the graph to estimate how far she had cycled after 15 mins.
She had cycled about 5 km.

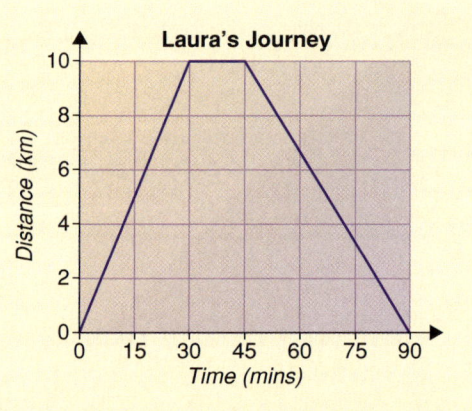

Laura's Journey (Distance (km) vs Time (mins))

E Sometimes we **sketch** a graph for a real-life situation, or interpret a sketch.
Example This graph shows the height of a ball above the ground when Todd threw it.

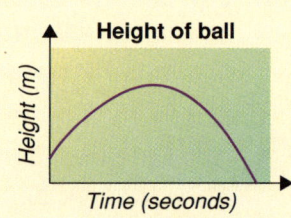

Height of ball (Height (m) vs Time (seconds))

Test yourself

1 Some equations are given in the box.
If the graphs are drawn, which will
  a have the steepest slope
  b cut the y-axis at (0, 3)
  c have a negative gradient
  d be a vertical line
  e have the same gradient?

  A $x = 4$
  B $y = {}^-2x + 1$
  C $y = 3x + 2$
  D $y = 2x + 3$
  E $y = 2x + 5$

2

x : 2, 0, $^-3$ → multiply by 3 → subtract 2 → y

  a Write down the coordinate pairs made with the given input.
    (2, ___), (0, ___), ($^-$3, ___)
  b Draw a straight-line graph for the function and label it with an equation.

3 a Which of the straight-line graphs shown have these equations?
   i   Line ___ has equation $y = 6$.
   ii Line ___ has equation $y = {}^-x$.
   iii Line ___ has equation $y = 3x - 2$.
   iv Line ___ has equation $y = {}^-3x + 2$.
  b Does the point (4, 8) lie on the line with equation $y = 3x - 4$?
    Explain how you know.
  *__c__ The line with equation $y = mx + 5$ passes through (3, 17).
    What is the value of m?

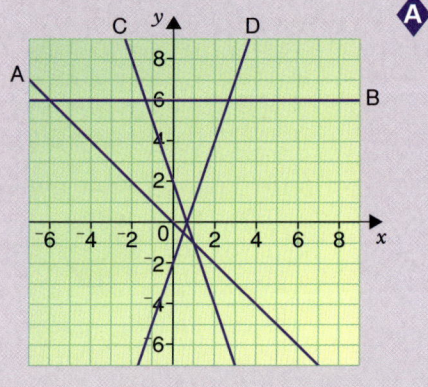

4 a Draw axes with x- and y-values from 5 to $^-5$.
On these axes draw and label
$y = x - 3$ $y = 2x + 1$ $y = {}^-x + 4$.
b Will $y = 2x + 1$ go through the point (2, 5)? Explain how you can tell.
c The point (3, ___) lies on $y = x - 3$. What is the missing y-coordinate?
d Which has a negative gradient?

5 Find the gradient of each of these lines.

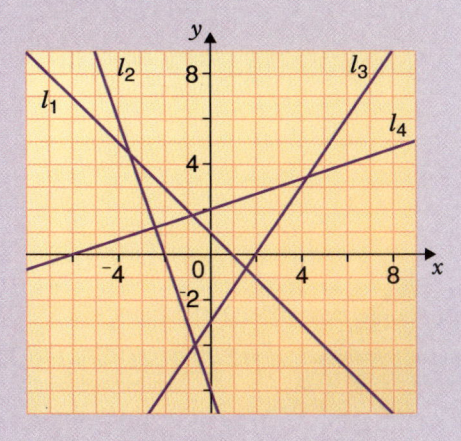

6 Match these lines with the equations.

A $y = {}^-x + 3$
B $y = -\frac{1}{2}x + 3$
C $y = x$
D $y = \frac{1}{3}x - 1$
E $y = {}^-2x + 6$

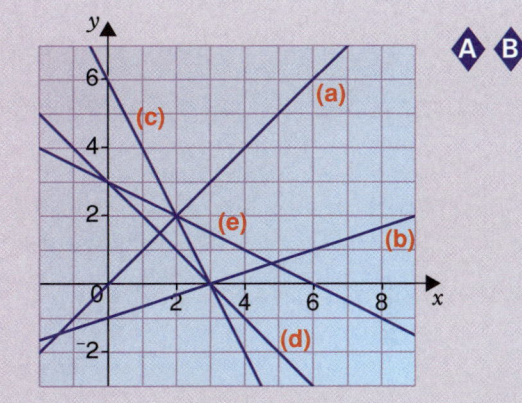

7 Rearrange these line equations into the form $y = mx + c$.
a $2x + y = 3$ **b** $x + 2y - 6 = 0$ **c** $3x - y = 1$

8 Amy and her brother Alan set off from their home in separate cars to go to a disco. Alan left home before Amy.
a How many times did Amy stop on her way to the disco?
b What does the section of Alan's graph that has a negative slope tell us?
c Who got to the disco first?
d After Alan left home the second time, did he travel at a constant speed until he stopped? How can you tell?

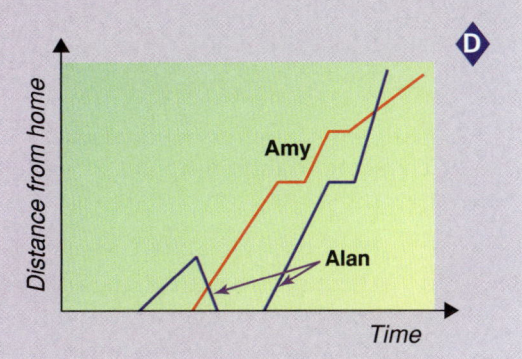

Algebra

9 This graph shows how high two fireworks went during a display. Firework A didn't reach as high as firework B.
  a Estimate how much higher firework B went than firework A.
  b Estimate the time at which the fireworks were at the same height.
  c Estimate the time that firework B was more than 250 m above the ground.
  d In the first 50 seconds, as time increases in equal steps, is the height of firework B
  A increasing in equal steps
  B increasing in increasing amounts
  C increasing in decreasing amounts?

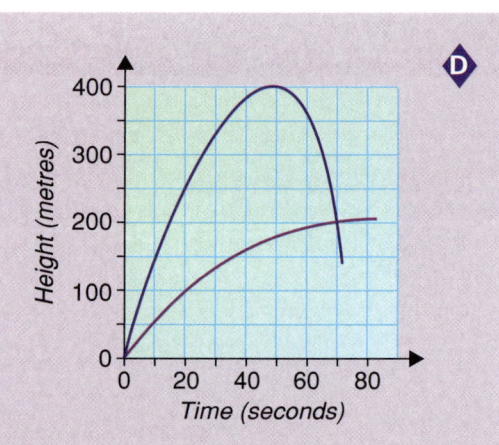

10 Write a possible explanation of each of these graphs.
  a Height of skier above lodge vs Time
  b Depth of water in kettle vs Time
  c Weight of newborn baby vs Time

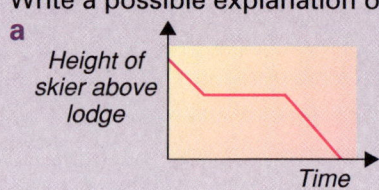

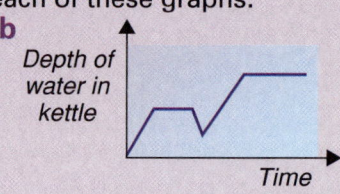

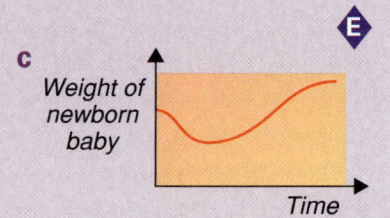

*__11__ The graph shows a straight line. The equation of the line is $y = 2x$.
  a Does the point (35, 70) lie on the straight line $y = 2x$?
  Explain how you know.
  b Write down the coordinates of the point that lies on both the straight lines $y = 3x - 1$ and $y = 5x - 5$.
  You must show your working.
  c Explain how you can tell that no point lies on both $y = {}^-2x + 4$ and $y = {}^-2x - 3$.

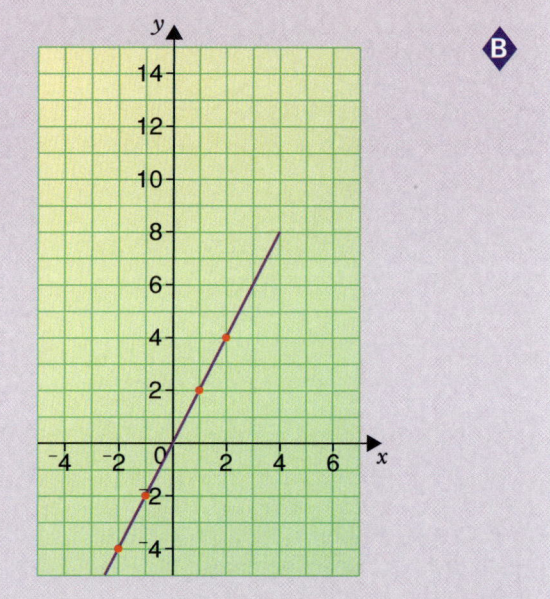

*__12__ Here are six different equations.
Think about their graphs.

$y = 2x + 4$ $y = 5x$ $x = 5$
$y = x^2 + 1$ $y = {}^-2$ $y = x - 2$

  a Which of the graphs goes through the point (0, 0)?
  b Which graph is parallel to the x-axis?
  c Which graph is **not** a straight line?
  d Which graph passes through (6, 4)?
  e Which graph has the steepest slope?
  f Write down the coordinates of the point that lies on both the straight lines $y = 2x + 4$ and $y = x - 2$.

254

Shape, Space and Measures Support

Lines and angles

MN is a **line segment**.
It has **finite** length.

M ———————— N

A **line** has infinite length.

⟵——————⟶

We name this angle

1. using the letter at the vertex, ∠Q
or 2. using three letters, the middle letter being the vertex, ∠PQR or ∠RQP or PQ̂R or RQ̂P.

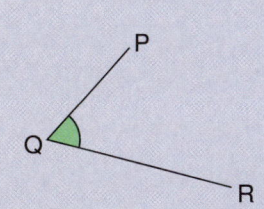

If there is more than one angle at the vertex use three letters to name an angle.

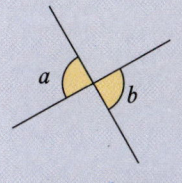

$a = b$
Vertically opposite angles are equal.

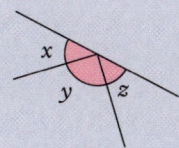

$x + y + z = 180°$
Angles on a straight line add to 180°.

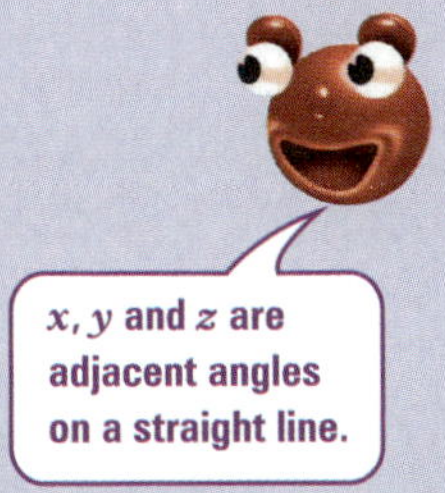

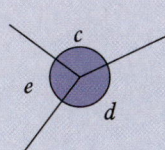

x, y and z are adjacent angles on a straight line.

$c + d + e = 360°$
Angles at a point add to 360°.

Angles made with parallel lines

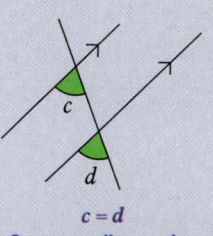

$c = d$
Corresponding angles are equal.

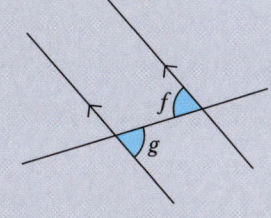

$f = g$
Alternate angles are equal.

Parallel lines are usually marked with arrows

Complementary angles add to 90°
Supplementary angles add to 180°.

The interior angles of a triangle add to 180°

Example $m + 57° + 64° = 180°$
$m = 180° - 57° - 64°$
$= 59°$

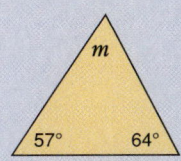

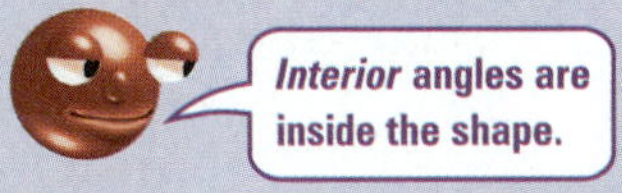

Interior angles are inside the shape.

The exterior angle of a triangle is equal to the sum of the two opposite interior angles.

Example $f = 47° + 58°$
$= 105°$

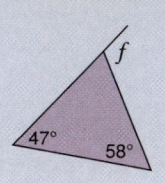

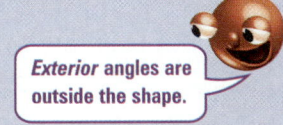

Exterior angles are outside the shape.

Practice Questions 4, 5, 17, 40

255

Shape, Space and Measures

2-D shapes

A **triangle is named** using the capital letters at the vertices. This triangle could be named as △PQR or △QRP or △RPQ or ... The side opposite each vertex is named with the lower-case letter of the vertex.

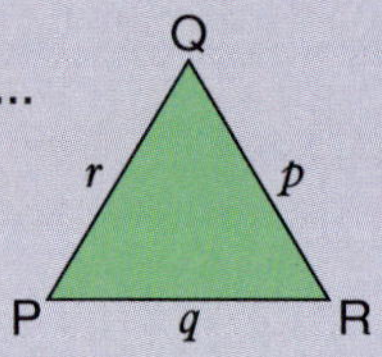

Start with one letter and go round in order or .

Properties of triangles A triangle is a 3-sided polygon.

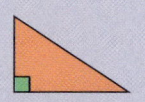

right-angled
one angle is a right angle

isosceles
2 equal sides
2 base angles equal

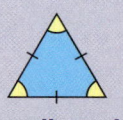

equilateral
3 equal sides
3 equal angles

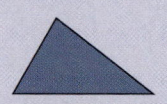

scalene
no 2 sides are equal
no 2 angles are equal

Properties of quadrilaterals A quadrilateral is a 4-sided polygon.

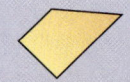

These are the **special quadrilaterals**.

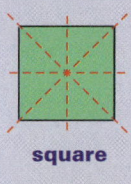

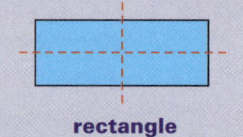

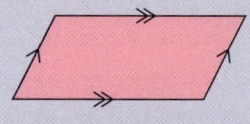

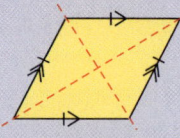

square   rectangle   parallelogram   rhombus

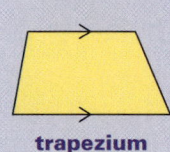

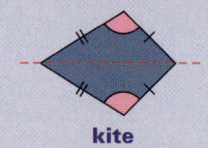

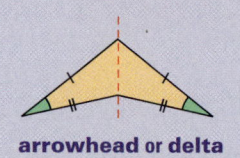

trapezium   kite   arrowhead or delta

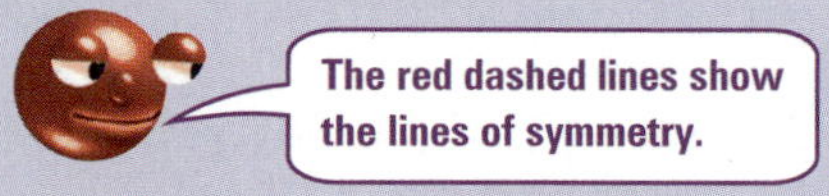

The red dashed lines show the lines of symmetry.

Some of the properties of these special quadrilaterals are shown in the following table.

	Square	Rhombus	Rectangle	Parallelogram	Kite	Trapezium	Arrowhead
one pair of opposite sides parallel	✓	✓	✓	✓		✓	
two pairs of opposite sides parallel	✓	✓	✓	✓			
all sides equal	✓	✓					
opposite sides equal	✓	✓	✓	✓			
all angles equal	✓		✓				
opposite angles equal	✓	✓	✓	✓	1 pair		
diagonals equal	✓		✓				
diagonals bisect each other	✓	✓	✓	✓			
diagonals perpendicular	✓	✓			✓		✓
diagonals bisect the angles	✓	✓					

Polygons

A **polygon** is a closed 2-D shape made from line segments.

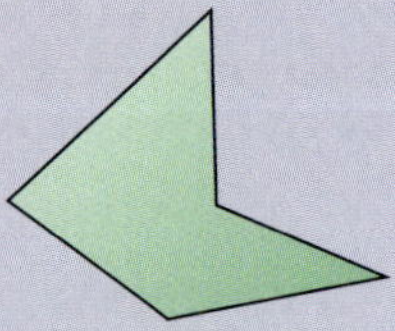

A 3-sided polygon is a triangle.   A 4-sided polygon is a quadrilateral.
A 5-sided polygon is a pentagon.   A 6-sided polygon is a hexagon.
A 7-sided polygon is a heptagon.   An 8-sided polygon is an octagon.

A **regular polygon** has all its sides equal and all its angles equal.
A **convex** polygon has no reflex angles.
A **concave** polygon has at least one reflex angle.

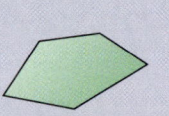

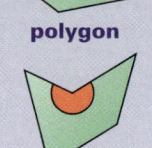

Practice Questions 2, 23, 24, 33, 44, 45

polygon

convex   concave

Shape, Space and Measures Support

Constructions

We use compasses and a ruler to construct the **perpendicular bisector** of a line segment, BC.

Open the compasses to a little more than half the length of BC. With compass point first on B and then on C, draw arcs to meet at P and Q.

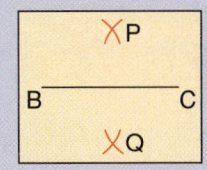

Draw the line through P and Q. R is the point which bisects BC.

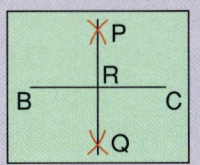

We use compasses and a ruler to construct the **bisector of an angle P**.

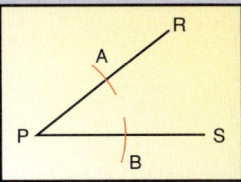

Open out the compasses to a length less than PR or PS. With compass point on P, draw arcs as shown.

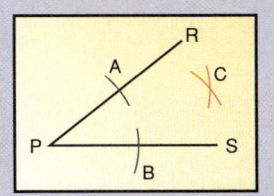

With compass point first on A, then B, draw arcs to meet at C.

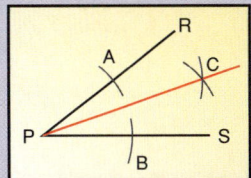

Draw the line from P through C. This line, PC, is the bisector of angle P.

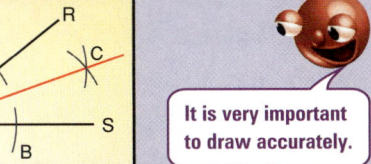

It is very important to draw accurately.

This shows the **construction of the perpendicular from A to the line segment BC**.

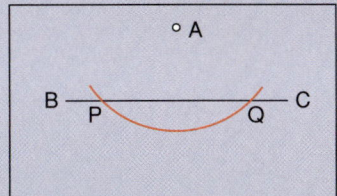

Open out the compasses. With the point on A, draw an arc to cross BC at P and Q.

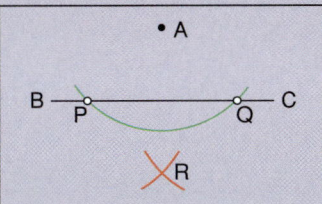

With the point first on P, then on Q, draw two arcs to meet at R.

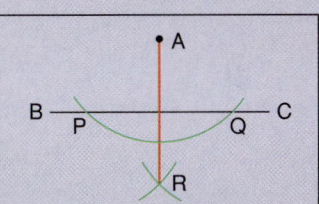

Join A and R. AR is the perpendicular from A to the line segment BC.

This shows the construction of the **perpendicular from a point P on a line segment BC**.

Keep the same length on your compasses.

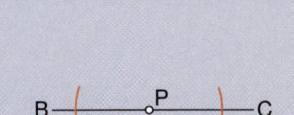

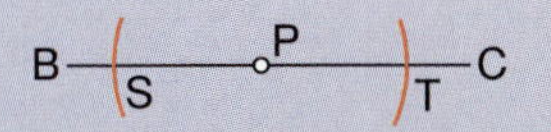

Open out the compasses to less than half the length of BC. With the point on P, draw arcs, one on each side of P. Label where they cross BC as S and T.

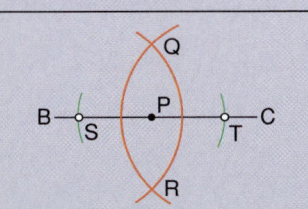

Open out the compasses a little more. With the point first on S and then on T, draw arcs so they cut at Q and R.

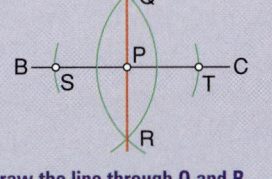

Draw the line through Q and R. QR is the perpendicular from P on the line segment BC.

We can **construct triangles and quadrilaterals** using a set square and ruler or compasses and ruler.

Examples

To construct this triangle:
1 Draw PR 2·6 cm long.
2 Draw an angle of 85° at R.
3 Draw RQ 2·8 cm long.
4 Join P to Q.

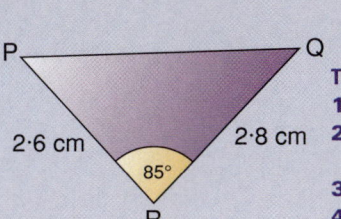

To construct this triangle:
1 Draw AB 2·8 cm long.
2 Open compasses to 2·5 cm and with point on A draw an arc.
3 Draw an arc from B, 2 cm long.
4 Complete the triangle.

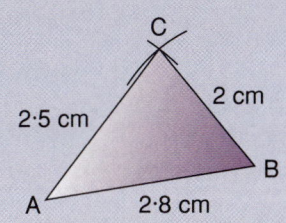

Practice Questions 20, 31, 42, 55

Shape, Space and Measures

Locus

A **locus** is a set of points that satisfies a rule or set of rules.

Example
The locus of a ball tied to the end of a string and being swung round so it is always the same distance from the person swinging it is a circle.

Practice Question 60

3-D shapes

3-D stands for three-dimensional. 3-D shapes have length, width and height.

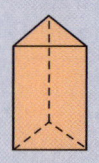

Triangular prism   **Pyramid** (pentagonal base)   **Tetrahedron** (triangular-based pyramid)   **Hemisphere**   **Octahedron**   **Dodecahedron**

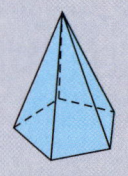

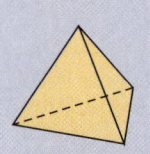

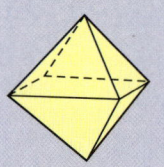

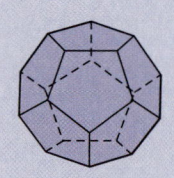

A 2-D shape that can be folded to make a 3-D shape is called a **net**.

Example This net folds to make a tetrahedron.

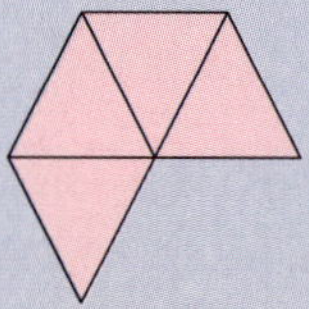

Practice Questions 1, 12, 28, 29, 30, 34, 35, 39, 43, 51

Coordinates

We use **coordinates** to give the position of a point on a grid.
The coordinates of A are ($^-$2, 1).
We always give the *x*-coordinate first.
The coordinates of the **origin** are (0, 0).
The *x*- and *y*-axes make four quadrants as shown.

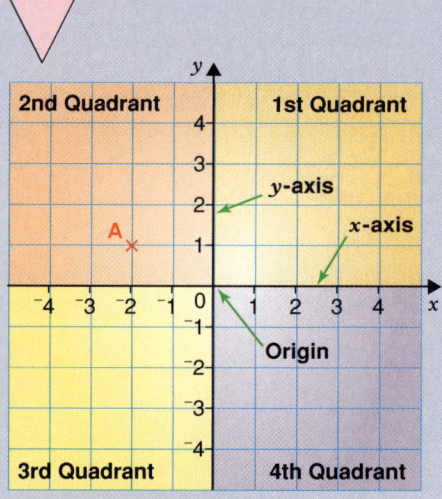

Practice Questions 22, 52

Symmetry

A shape has **reflection symmetry** if one half of the shape can be reflected in a line to the other half. The line is a **line of symmetry**.
A shape has **rotation symmetry** if it fits onto itself **more than once** during a complete turn.
The **order of rotation symmetry** is the number of times a shape fits exactly onto itself during one complete turn.
If a shape has rotation symmetry of order 1, we say it does not have rotation symmetry.

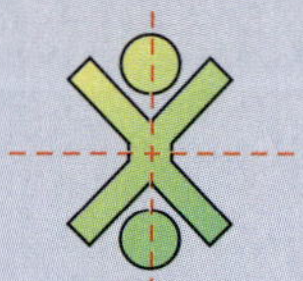

2 lines of symmetry

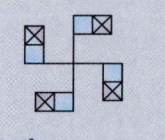

rotation symmetry of order 4

Practice Questions 26, 36, 54

258

Shape, Space and Measures Support

Congruence

Congruent shapes are exactly the same size and shape.

In congruent shapes
corresponding sides are equal
corresponding angles are equal.

Example   ABC and DEF are congruent.

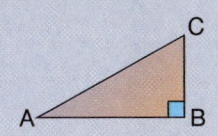

AB = DE   ∠A = ∠D
AC = DF   ∠B = ∠E
BC = EF   ∠C = ∠F

Practice Questions 8, 56

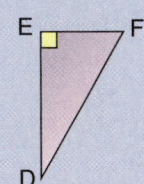

Transformations

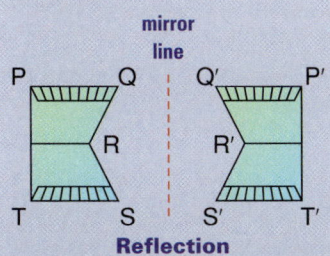

Reflection
Corresponding points are equidistant from the mirror line.
If you reflect the image in the mirror line you get back to the original shape (**self-inverse**)

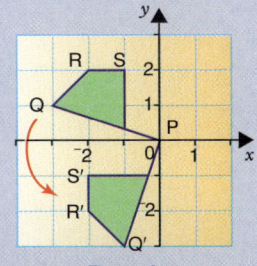

Rotation
To rotate we need
- the angle of rotation
- the centre of rotation.

PQRS has been rotated 90° about the origin. 90° means 90° **anticlockwise**.
The **inverse** rotation is 90° clockwise about the origin or 270° anticlockwise.

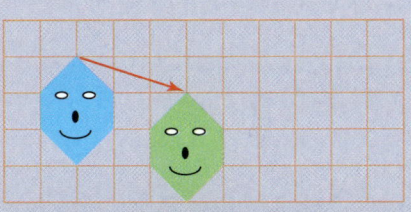

Translation
To translate we slide the shape without turning. The blue shape has been translated 3 units to the right and 1 unit down. The **inverse** translation is the same number of units in the opposite directions.

To **enlarge** a shape we need to know
- the scale factor
- the centre of enlargement.

PQR has been enlarged to P'Q'R' by a scale factor 2, centre of enlargement O.
Each point on P'Q'R' is two times as far from O as the corresponding point on PQR.

Practice Questions 11, 19, 37, 38, 47, 53, 57, 62

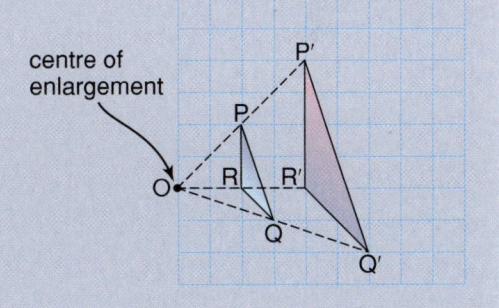

Measures

Metric conversations
You need to know these **metric conversions**.

length	mass	capacity (volume)	area	time
1 km = 1000 m	1 kg = 1000 g	1 ℓ = 1000 mℓ	1 ha = 10 000 m^2	1 minute = 60 seconds
1 m = 100 cm	1 tonne = 1000 kg	1 ℓ = 100 cℓ	(hectare)	1 hour = 60 minutes
1 m = 1000 mm		1 cℓ = 10 mℓ		1 day = 24 hours
1 cm = 10 mm		1 ℓ = 1000 cm^3		1 year = 12 months or
		1 mℓ = 1 cm^3		52 weeks and 1 day
		1 m^3 = 1000 ℓ		1 year = 365 days or
				366 in a leap year
				1 decade = 10 years

259

Shape, Space and Measures

Examples

$0.6 \ell = (0.6 \times 1000)$ mℓ
$\quad\quad = $ **600 mℓ**

500 cm$^3 = (500 \div 1000) \ell$
$\quad\quad\quad = $ **0.5 ℓ**

65 cm $= (65 \div 100)$ m
$\quad\quad = $ **0.65 m**

$54\,000$ m$^2 = (54\,000 \div 10\,000)$ ha
$\quad\quad\quad = $ **5.4 ha**

8000 cm$^3 = $ **8000 mℓ**

Example Steph stacked 7 shoe boxes, which were each 150 mm high, on top of each other.
The height of the pile in mm $= 7 \times 150$ mm
$\quad\quad\quad\quad\quad\quad\quad\quad\quad\quad = 1050$ mm
The height of the pile in m $= (1050 \div 1000)$ m
$\quad\quad\quad\quad\quad\quad\quad\quad\quad = $ **1.05 m**

Metric and imperial equivalents

These are some rough **metric and imperial equivalents**.

length	mass	capacity
5 miles ≈ 8 km	1 kg ≈ 2.2 lb	1 pint ≈ 600 mℓ
1 yard = 3 feet ≈ 1 m	1 oz ≈ 30 g	1 gallon ≈ 4.5 ℓ
1 inch ≈ 2.5 cm		1 litre ≈ 1.75 pints

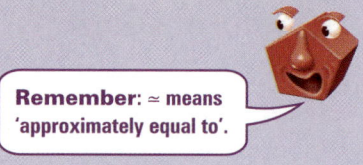

Remember: ≈ means 'approximately equal to'.

Reading scales

When **reading scales** you need to work out the value of each small division.

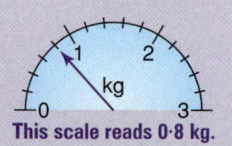

This scale reads 0.8 kg.

When measuring we must choose the **degree of accuracy**, the **unit** and a suitable **measuring instrument**.

Example When measuring the length of a book we could measure it to the nearest centimetre using a ruler.

Practice Questions 3, 6, 9, 14, 15, 16, 21, 25, 32, 41, 46

Bearings

A direction from one place to another may be given as a **bearing**. 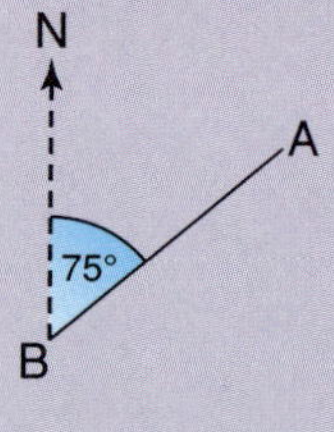
Bearings from North are always given as three digits.
To find the bearing of A from B:

1. Join AB.
2. Draw a North line at B.
3. Measure the angle in a **clockwise** direction between the North line and the line AB.

Always draw the North line at the point you are measuring **from**.

In this diagram the bearing of A from B is 075°.

Practice Question 61

Perimeter, area and volume

Perimeter is the distance around the outside of a shape.

Area is the amount of space covered by a shape.
Area is measured in km^2, m^2, cm^2, mm^2 or hectares.

Area of a triangle $= \frac{1}{2}$ area of rectangle
$\quad\quad\quad\quad\quad\quad\quad = \frac{1}{2} \times$ base $\times$ height
$\quad\quad\quad\quad\quad\quad\quad = \frac{1}{2} bh$

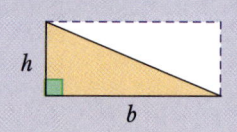

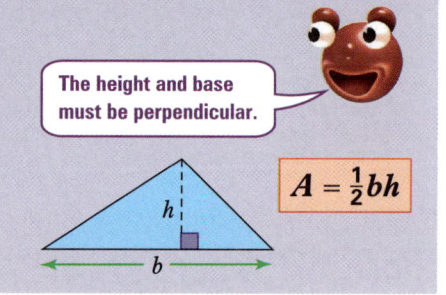

The height and base must be perpendicular.

$A = \frac{1}{2} bh$

260

Shape, Space and Measures Support

Area of a parallelogram = bh

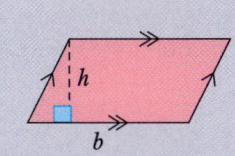

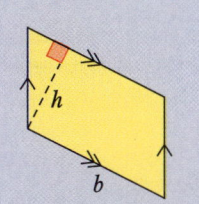

$$A = bh$$

Area of a trapezium = $\frac{1}{2}(a+b)h$.

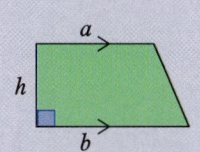

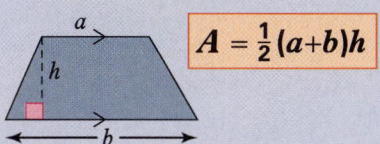

$$A = \frac{1}{2}(a+b)h$$

Example Sophie dug this triangular garden to plant herbs.
Area of triangular garden = $\frac{1}{2} \times$ base $\times$ height
$= \frac{1}{2} \times 2 \times 3$
$= \frac{1}{2} \times 6$
$= 3$ m²

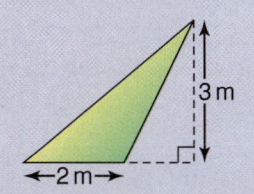

The **surface area of a cuboid** = 2(length × width) + 2(length × height) + 2(height × width)
= $2lw + 2lh + 2hw$

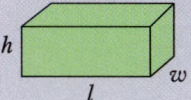

Example Surface area = $2lw + 2lh + 2hw$
= (2 × 10 × 4) + (2 × 10 × 5) + (2 × 4 × 5)
= 80 + 100 + 40
= **220 cm²**

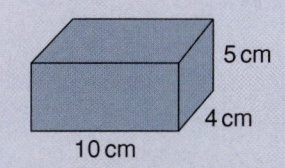

Volume is the amount of space taken up by a solid.
Volume is measured in mm³, cm³, m³ or ℓ, pints or gallons.

Volume of a cuboid = length × width × height
= lwh

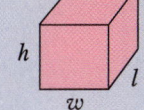

Practice Questions 7, 10, 13, 18, 27, 48, 49, 50, 58, 59

Practice Questions

1 a I slice a cuboid in half like this.
       How many faces does each piece have?
    b I then slice another cuboid in half like this.
       How many faces does each piece have?
    c I slice another cuboid in half through its corners like this.
       How many faces does each piece have?

T 2 Look at this quadrilateral. 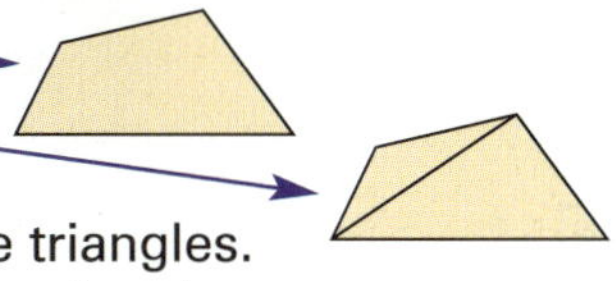
      You can draw one line on the quadrilateral to make two triangles.
      Use a copy of the quadrilateral.
       a Use a ruler to draw two lines on the quadrilateral to make three triangles.
       b Draw one line on the quadrilateral to make a quadrilateral and a triangle.
       c Draw two lines on the quadrilateral to make three quadrilaterals.
          Use a copy of this rectangle. 
       d Draw two lines on the rectangle to make four isosceles triangles.
       e Draw two lines on the rectangle to make four rectangles all the same size.
          Use a ruler and draw the rectangles accurately.

Shape, Space and Measures

3 What times go in the gaps?
  a 07:10 + 45 minutes → ____
  b 14:26 + __ minutes → 15:10
  c ____ + 35 minutes → 17:00

4 Label these angles as acute, obtuse, right-angled or reflex.
  a   b   c   d   e   f

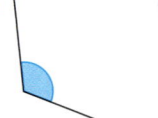

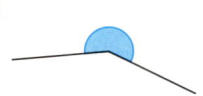

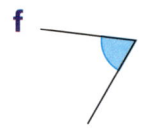

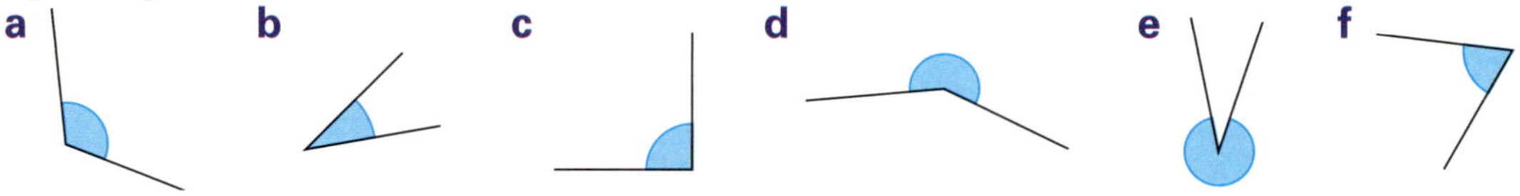

5 An angle is 35°.
  a What is its complementary angle?
  b What is its supplementary angle?

6

| km | m | cm | mm | tonne | kg | g | ℓ | mℓ |

State which unit of measurement the following are most likely to be measured in. Choose from the units in the box.
  a the depth of water in a bath
  b the length of a sports ground
  c the amount of water in a bath
  d the mass of a ship
  e the mass of a mouse
  f the distance between two villages

7 a What is the **area** of this rectangle?

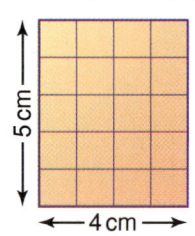

  5 cm
  4 cm

  b Sam uses the rectangle to make four triangles of the same size.

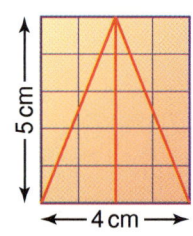

  5 cm
  4 cm

  What is the area of one of the triangles?
  c Sam then uses the four triangles to make a parallelogram. What is the area of the parallelogram?

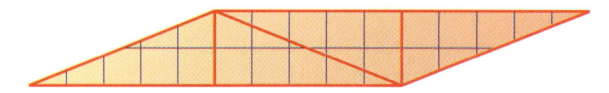

8 Look at these shapes.
  Which ones are congruent to each other?

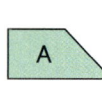

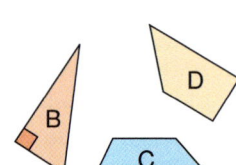

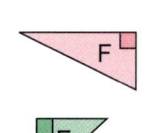

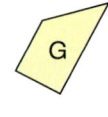

  A   B   C   D   E   F   G

262

Shape, Space and Measures Support

9 a Steven's height is 0·9 m.
  Holly is 0·4 m taller than Steven.
  How tall is Holly?
 b Andrew's height is 1·35 m.
  Mardee is 0·2 m shorter than Andrew.
  How tall is Mardee?
 c Zoe's height is 1·6 m.
  How tall is Zoe in centimetres?

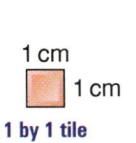

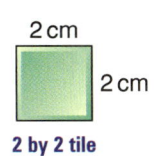

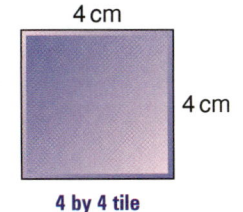

10 Aiisha has three different sized tiles.

1 by 1 tile   2 by 2 tile   4 by 4 tile

She has a mat that is 8 cm by 4 cm.
32 of the 1 by 1 tiles will cover the mat.
 a How many of the 2 by 2 tiles will cover the mat?
 b How many of the 4 by 4 tiles will cover the mat?

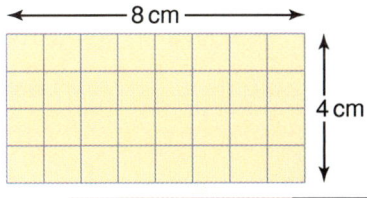

 c Aiisha puts two tiles on her mat like this.
  What would go in the gaps?
    She could cover the rest of the mat using ___ 2 by 2 tiles.
  or She could cover the rest of the mat using a 4 by 4 tile
    and another ___ 1 by 1 tiles.

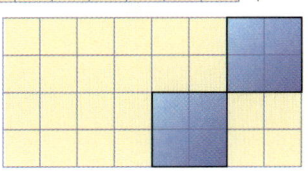

11 Which blue shape is
 a a translation of the
  red shape
 b a rotation of the
  red shape
 c a reflection of the
  red shape?

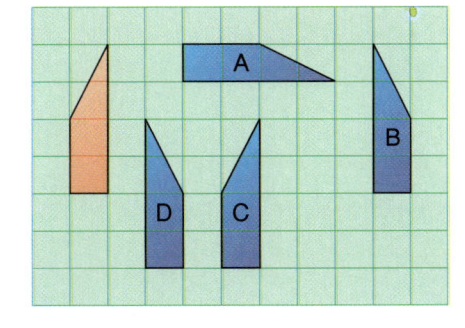

12 Look at these pictures.
 Sketch the view from the top for each picture.
 a   **b**

13 Look at the quadrilateral and the pentagon.
 a Do the quadrilateral and pentagon have the same area?
  Explain your answer.
 b Do the quadrilateral and pentagon have the same
  perimeter?
  Explain your answer.

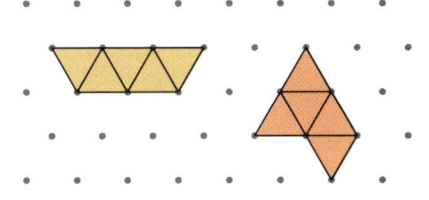

Shape, Space and Measures

14 a Winstone travelled 25 miles from Andover to Newbury. About how many kilometres is this?
  b Winstone had a suitcase with him. It was 65 cm long and weighed 13·2 lb. About how long was this case, in inches? About how heavy was it, in kilograms?
  c In the suitcase, Winstone had a 3-litre bottle of juice. About how many pints is this?

15 Find the missing numbers.
  a 39 mm = ___ cm
  b 2800 m = ___ km
  c 340 cm = ___ m
  d 580 mm = ___ m
  e 960 mℓ = ___ ℓ
  f 57 g = ___ kg
  g 6152 mℓ = ___ ℓ
  h 4900 kg = ___ tonne
  i 0·07 kg = ___ g
  j 5·26 cℓ = ___ ℓ
  k 72 kg = ___ tonne
  l 90 mℓ = ___ cm^3
  m 3·6 ℓ = ___ cm^3
  n 5720 ℓ = ___ m^3
  o 43 000 m^2 = ___ ha

16 Choose the best range.
  a A 50 g ⩽ mass of a calculator ⩽ 200 g
       B 1 kg ⩽ mass of a calculator ⩽ 1·5 kg
       C 500 g ⩽ mass of a calculator ⩽ 1 kg
  b A 0·5 m ⩽ length of a bike ⩽ 1 m
       B 1 m ⩽ length of a bike ⩽ 2 m
       C 1·5 m ⩽ length of a bike ⩽ 2·5 m

17 Find the angles marked with letters.

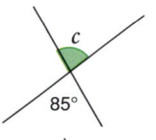

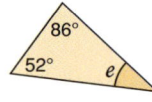

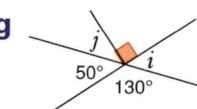

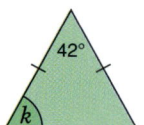

a 106°, a
b b, 42° (right angle)
c c, 85°
d 86°, 52°, e
e 88°, f, g, 136°
f 116°, h, 48°
g j, i, 50°, 130° (right angle)
h 42°, k
i l, 52° (isosceles triangle)
j m, n, 122° (parallelogram)
k o, p, 60° (regular hexagon)

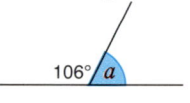

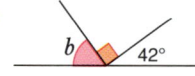

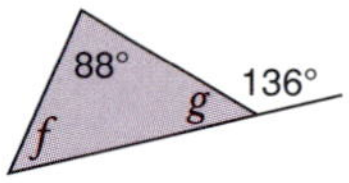

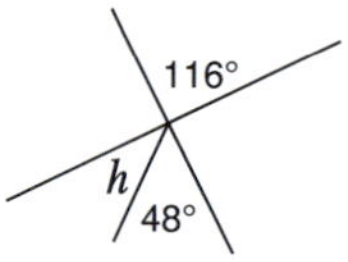

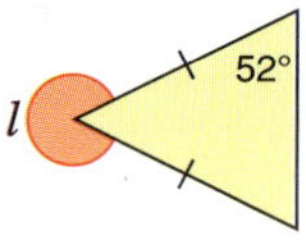

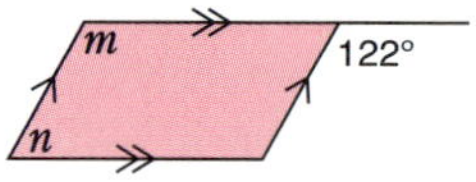

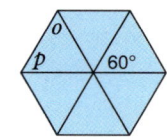

T **18 a** Look at the T-shape. What is the perimeter and area of the T-shape? 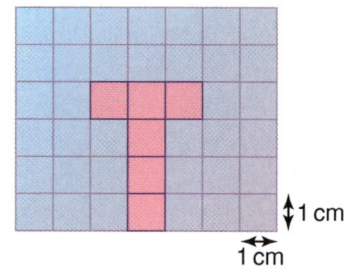
  b Use a copy of this grid. Draw a shape with an area of 8 cm^2. 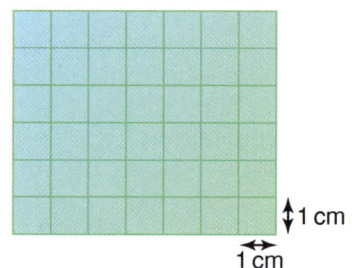
  c What is the perimeter of your shape?
  d Look at this shape. What is the area of the shape?
  e Explain how you know that the perimeter of the shape is more than 12 cm.

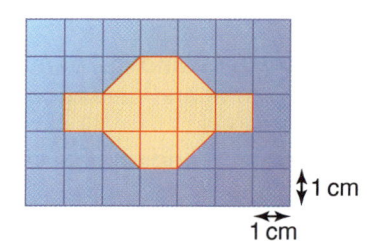

264

Shape, Space and Measures Support

19 The shape A has been enlarged to the shape A'. What is the scale factor for this enlargement?

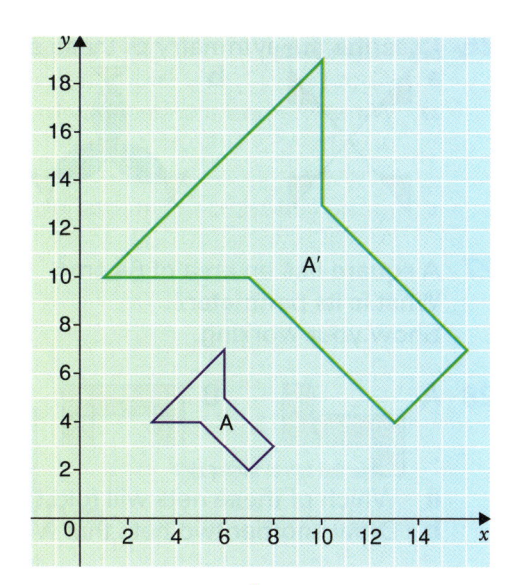

20 Use ruler and protractor to construct this triangle accurately. Measure the length of the red side on your diagram.

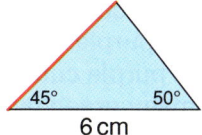

21 a The thickness of a ruler could be
  A 1 cm **B** 1 mm **C** 0·1 mm.
  b The mass of a train could be
  A 1 tonne **B** 100 tonne **C** 100 kg.
  c The capacity of a small tank could be
  A 100 tonne **B** 100 mℓ **C** 100 ℓ.

22 This diagram shows a rectangle.
  a What are the coordinates of C?
  b Give the coordinates of the mid-point of AB.
  c What are the coordinates of the mid-point of BD?

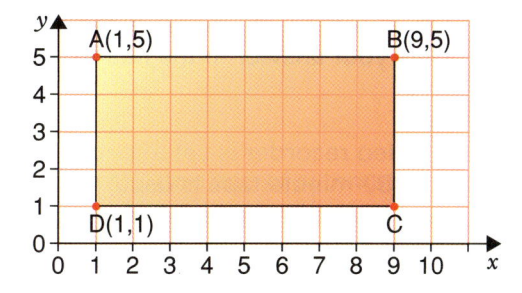

23 a Explain why it is possible for a quadrilateral to have a reflex angle whereas it is not possible for a triangle to have a reflex angle.
  b Why is it always possible to make a kite from two identical isosceles triangles?

24 On triangle dotty paper, tessellate this shape.

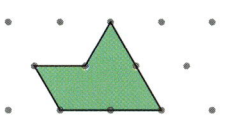

25 Find the measurements given by pointers A, B and C. In part **d** you will need to estimate.

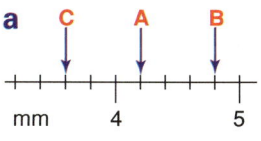

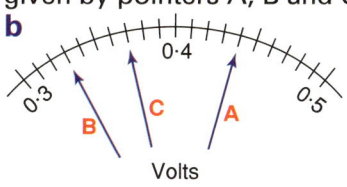

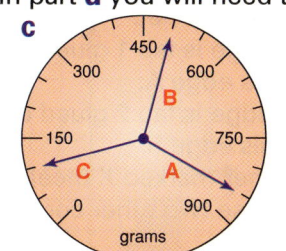

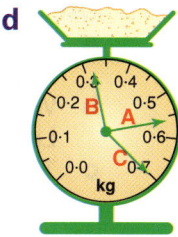

265

Shape, Space and Measures

38 What translation is the inverse of the translation given in question **37**?

39 a I have a paper circle.
Then I cut a sector from the circle. It makes this net.
Which 3-D shape below could I make with my net?

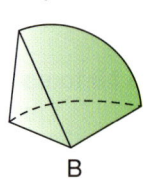

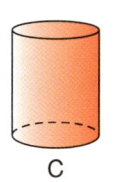

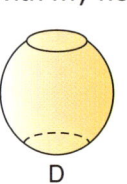

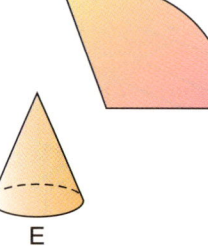

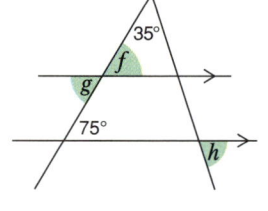

[SATs Paper 2 Level 5]

A   B   C   D   E

b Here is a sketch of my net.
Make an **accurate drawing** of my net.

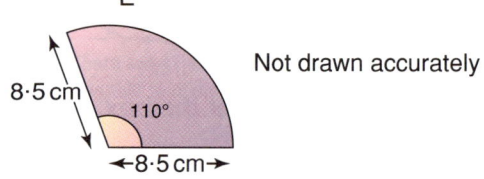

8·5 cm   110°   ←8·5 cm→   Not drawn accurately

40 Find the angles marked with letters.

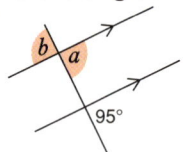

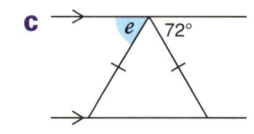

a   95°, b, a

b   50°, c, d

c   72°, e

d   35°, f, g, 75°, h

41 How many miles is 16 kilometres?

Cliffdon 16 kilometres

42 Use a copy of this.
BC is a line segment.

X

B — Y — C

a Construct a perpendicular from X to BC.
b Construct a line from Y which is perpendicular to BC.
Leave your construction lines.

43 Use some triangle dotty paper.
Draw these two shapes on your dotty paper.

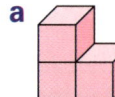

a   b

44 a Imagine joining adjacent mid-points of the sides of a rectangle.
What shape is formed by the new lines? Explain why.
b Imagine a rhombus with its diagonals drawn in.
Remove two of the triangles. What shapes could be left?
How do you know?

268

Shape, Space and Measures Support

45 Write true or false for these.
  a An arrowhead has one line of symmetry and two equal angles.
  b A parallelogram has diagonals that bisect the angles.
  c A rhombus has two lines of symmetry.
  d An equilateral triangle has three angles of 60° each.
  e A right-angled triangle can never have a line of symmetry.

46 This scale measures in grams and in ounces.

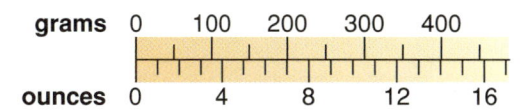

Use the scale to answer these questions.
  a About how many ounces is 400 grams?
  b About how many grams is 15 ounces?
  c About how many ounces is 3 kilograms?
       Explain your answer.

T **47** Use a copy of this.

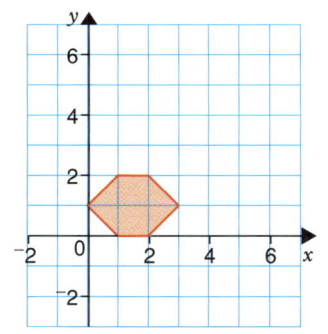

Enlarge this shape by a scale factor of 2, centre of enlargement (0, 0).
Write down the coordinates of the image.

48 Find the perimeter of each of these.
  a 3 m, 2 m
  b 8 cm, 6 cm
  c 5 mm, 13 mm, 12 mm
  d 5 m, 4 m, 6 m
  e 9 cm, 5 cm, 12 cm, 4 cm

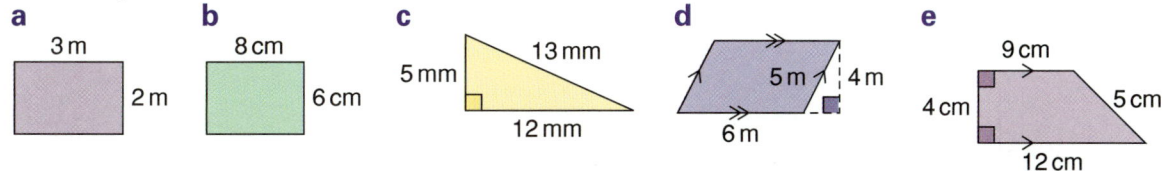

49 Find the area of each of the shapes in question **48**.

50 William folded this net of centimetre squares to make a box 3 cm high and 2 cm wide.
  a How long is the box?
  b What is the volume of the box?
  c Sarah made a box which had the same volume as William's.
       Her box was 5 cm wide and 1 cm high.
       How long was Sarah's box?

Not drawn to scale

51 Here are three views of the same cube.
Which shapes are opposite each other?

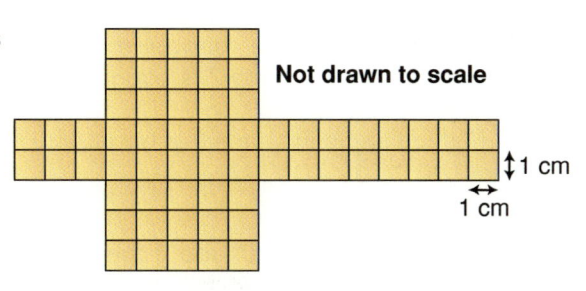

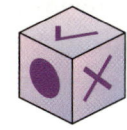

269

Shape, Space and Measures

52 P(−2, 1), Q(1, 2), R(−1, 3), S(?, ?)
Plot P, Q and R.
Find the coordinates of S so that PQRS is
a a parallelogram **b** a kite.

T **53** Use a copy of these shapes.
The centre of rotation and angle of rotation are given.
Draw the image shapes.
a (0, 0), 90°   *b (1, 1), 180°

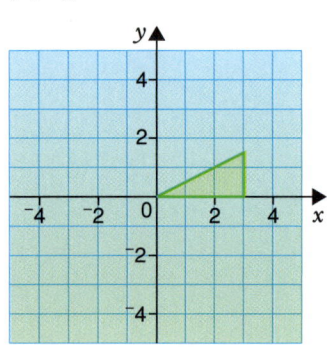

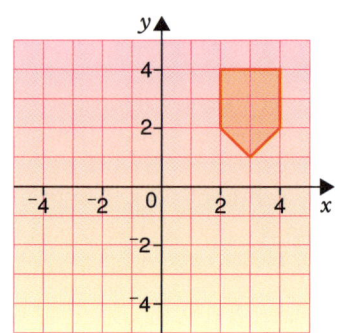

54 Combine these shapes to make a single shape with order of rotation symmetry 2.

T **55** Use a copy of this diagram.
a Name the shaded angle.
b Construct the bisector of the shaded angle.
c Construct the perpendicular bisector of the line segment MN. Label the point where it crosses the line segment MP as X.
d Measure MX on your diagram.

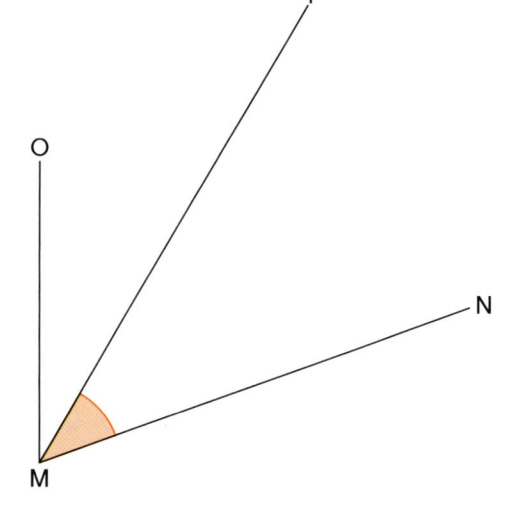

56 These two shapes are congruent.
a Which side in shape 2 is equal to
i AB   **ii** BC?
b Which angle in shape 2 is equal to
i ∠C   **ii** ∠D

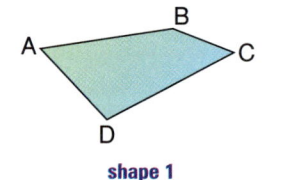

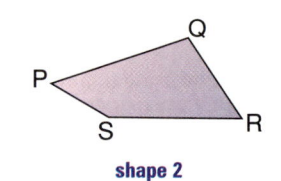

57 A rotation through 270° about the origin maps A onto A′.
Which of these maps A′ onto A? There are two correct answers.
A a rotation through 270° about (0, 0)
B a rotation through 90° clockwise about (0, 0)
C a rotation through 90° about (0, 0)
D a rotation 270° clockwise about (0, 0)

Shape, Space and Measures Support

58 a What is the total surface area of this cuboid?
   b Jasmine wants to cover the sides and bottom with silver glitter and the top and ends with red glitter to make a Christmas decoration. What area of the decoration will be
   i silver glitter   **ii** red glitter?
   c What is the volume of the cuboid?

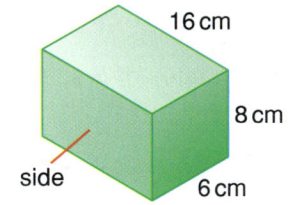

59 Toby wraps a box.
It measures 20 cm × 3 cm × 4 cm.
He has a rectangular sheet of paper measuring 25 cm by 30 cm.
Is the paper big enough to cover all the box?
Show your working.

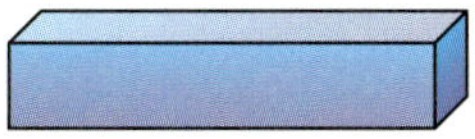

60 Abbie went to a horse-riding camp.
   a She rode her horse so she was always the same distance from a pole in the middle of a field. Describe Abbie's locus in words.

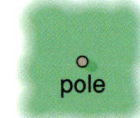

   b She rode from the corner of the field so she was always the same distance from two fences which are at right angles to each other. Describe and sketch Abbie's locus.

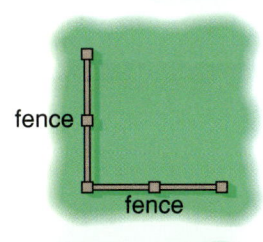

   c Abbie then rode between two marker posts so she was always the same distance from them. Sketch Abbie's locus. Describe this locus in words.

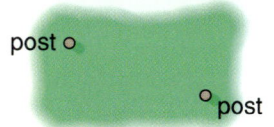

61 This diagram shows the position of three moored yachts, X, Y and Z. Measure and write down the bearing of these.
   a Y from X   **b** Z from X
   c Z from Y   **d** X from Y

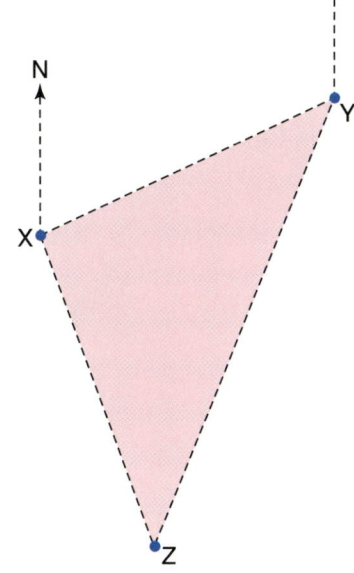

62 Triangles A, B, C and D are drawn on a grid.

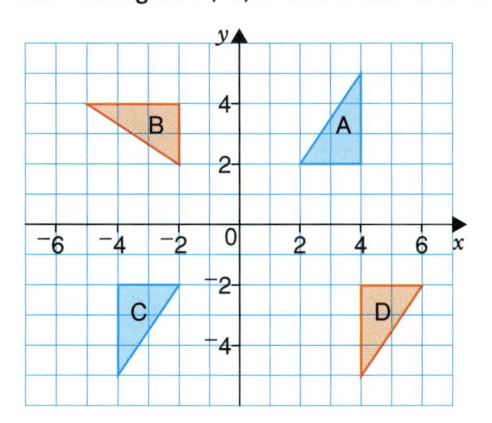

Find a single transformation that will map
   a A onto C   **b** C onto D.

10 Lines and Angles

You need to know
✓ lines and angles   page 255

Key vocabulary
alternate angles,   convention,   corresponding angles,   definition,
derived property,   exterior angle,   interior angle

▶▶ Snap it!

Interesting photos often contain interesting lines and angles.

Find some interesting photos. You could look at home, in magazines, newspapers, on the Internet or on a CD-Rom.

Make a poster or collage of your photos.

Lines and angles

Conventions, definitions and derived properties

Discussion

- **Arrows are used to show parallel lines**.
  This is a **convention** that was chosen so that everyone easily recognises parallel lines.
  Something different **could** have been chosen to show parallel lines.

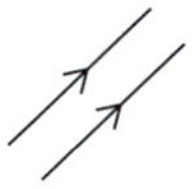

  What are some other mathematical conventions? **Discuss**.

- **A rhombus is a quadrilateral with all sides equal**.
  This is a **definition**. It tells us the minimum amount of information needed to identify a rhombus.
  What might the definition of a square be? **Discuss**.
  What about a rectangle?

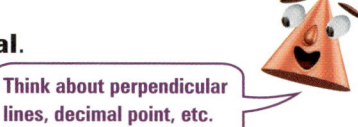

  > Think about perpendicular lines, decimal point, etc.

- **The angles inside a triangle add to 180°**.
  Do we **need** to know this to identify a triangle? **Discuss**.
  A **derived property** is not essential to a definition but it follows as a result of the definition.

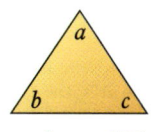

  $a + b + c = 180°$

- What do you think these are, a convention, a definition or a derived property? **Discuss**.
  a We label the vertices of a shape with upper-case letters and the side opposite each vertex with the same lower-case letter.
  b If no direction is given for a rotation we turn anticlockwise.
  c The diagonals of a rectangle are equal. 
  d One complete turn is divided into 360°. A degree is a unit for measuring angle.
  e The diagonals of a kite cross at right angles. 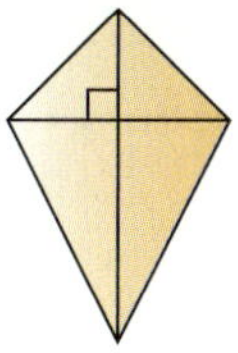
  f A parallelogram has no lines of symmetry.
  g The inverse of a reflection in the mirror line m, is a reflection in mirror line m.
  h A reflection is a transformation that maps P to P′ such that P and P′ are equidistant from the mirror line and PP′ is perpendicular to it.
  i A parallelogram is a quadrilateral with two pairs of parallel sides.
  j A circle is the set of points equidistant from one fixed point.

Finding angles

Remember

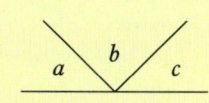

$a + b + c = 180°$
Angles on a straight line add to 180°.

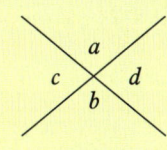

$a = b$
$c = d$
Vertically opposite angles are equal.

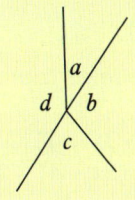

$a + b + c + d = 360°$
Angles at a point add to 360°.

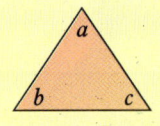

Shape, Space and Measures

$a + b + c = 180°$
Angles in a triangle add to 180°.

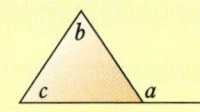

$a = b + c$
The exterior angle of a △ is equal to the sum of the two opposite interior angles.

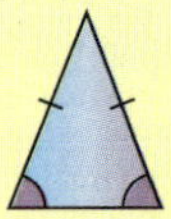

isosceles triangle
2 equal sides
2 base angles equal

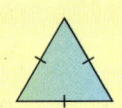

equilateral triangle
all sides equal
all angles equal to 60°.

Angles made with parallel lines

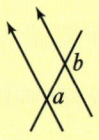

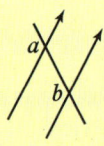

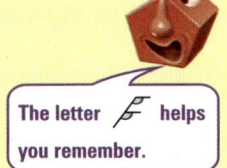

In each of these diagrams we can translate angle a onto angle b.

angle a = angle b.

Angle a and angle b are called **corresponding angles**.

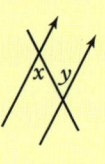

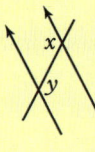

The letter F helps you remember.

In each of these diagrams we can rotate angle x onto angle y.

angle x = angle y.

Angle x and angle y are called **alternate angles**.

The letter Z helps you remember.

We often use **geometrical reasoning** to find an angle.

1. Name any other angles that need naming.
2. Write down what you know.
3. Write down the steps one-by-one that are needed to find the angle you want. Always give reasons.

Worked Example
Find y.

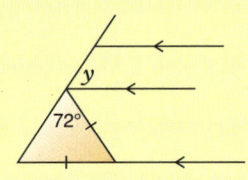

Answer
Name angle x.
$x = 72°$ base angles of an isosceles triangle 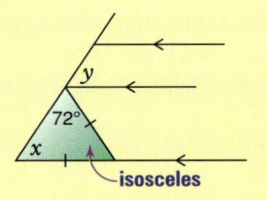
$y = x$ corresponding angles on parallel lines are equal
$y = \mathbf{72°}$ because $x = 72°$

isosceles

Worked Example
Find the value of x.

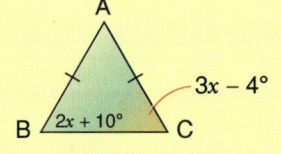

Answer
ABC is an isosceles triangle.
$\angle B = \angle C$
$\quad 2x + 10° = 3x - 4°$
$2x + 10° - 2x = 3x - 4° - 2x$ subtracting $2x$ from both sides
$\quad 10° + 4° = x - 4° + 4°$ adding 4° to each side
$\qquad\quad x = \mathbf{14°}$

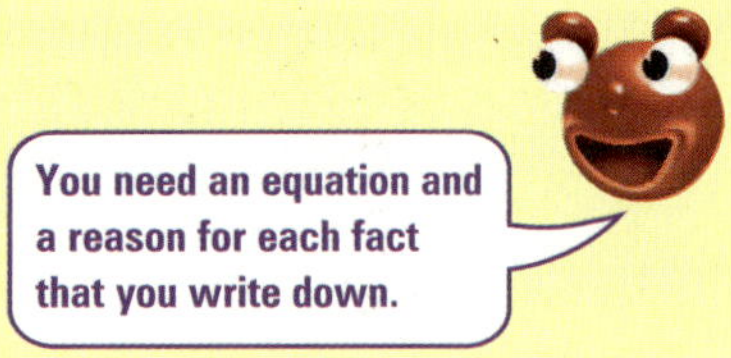

You need an equation and a reason for each fact that you write down.

Lines and Angles

Exercise 1 Only use a calculator if you need to.

1. Find the value of the angles marked with letters.
   a. a, 56°
   b. 119°, 132°, b
   c. c, 78°
   d. 146°, d, f, e, 130°
   e. 40°, g, 92°
   f. i, h, 46°

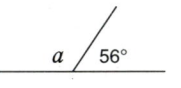

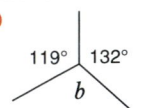

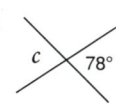

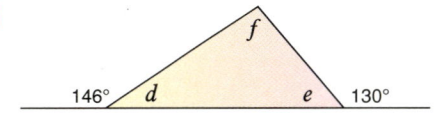

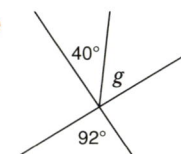

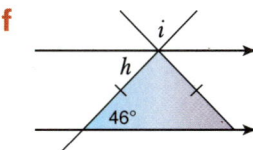

2. Prove that x has the value shown. Show each step clearly and give reasons.
   a. a, 62°, x; $x = 118°$
      Hint: Find a, then x.
   b. a, b, x, 56°; $x = 124°$
      Hint: Find a, then b, then x.
   c. 141°, 78°, x; $x = 63°$
   d. 24°, 68°, x; $x = 32°$

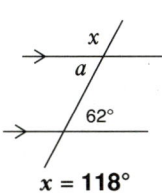

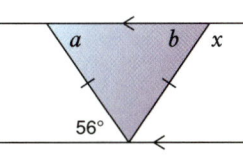

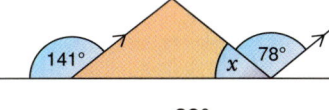

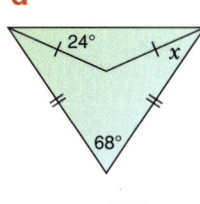

3. ABCD is a rectangle.
   Work out the size of b.
   Show your working clearly.
   (55°, b, 50°)

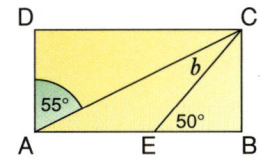

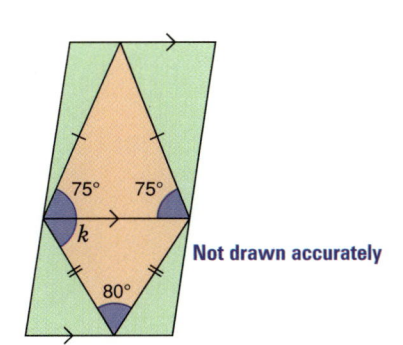

4. Use a copy of this.
   The diagram shows two isosceles triangles inside a parallelogram.
   a. On the diagram, mark another angle that is 75°. Label it 75°.
   b. Calculate the size of the angle marked k.
      Show your working.
   (75°, 75°, k, 80°)
   Not drawn accurately

   [SATs Paper 1 Level 6]

5. Find the sizes of the angles marked with lower-case letters.
   Show your working clearly and give reasons.
   a. c, 42°, d, 81°
   b. A, a, 64°, B, b, C; AB = AC

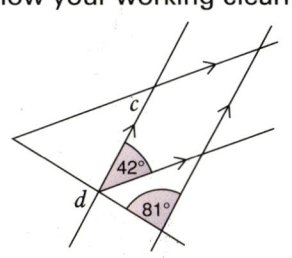

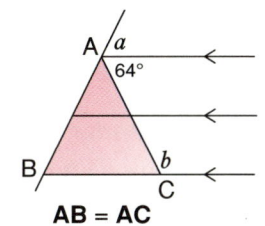

275

Shape, Space and Measures

6 a PQRS is a rectangle.
XYZ is an equilateral triangle.

Find the size of ∠SRY.
Show your working clearly and give reasons.

b ABC is a straight line.
BCD is an equilateral triangle.

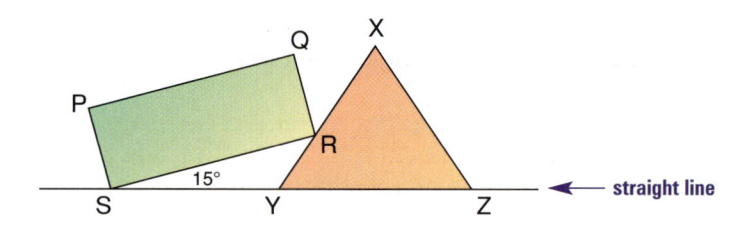

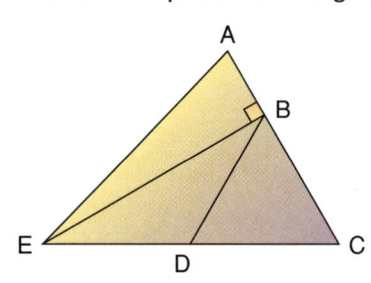

Show that triangle EBD is isosceles.

7 This shape has 3 lines of symmetry.
What is the size of angle y?
Show your working.

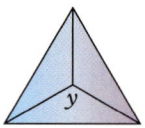

8 This pattern is made from isosceles triangles. It has rotation symmetry of order 8.

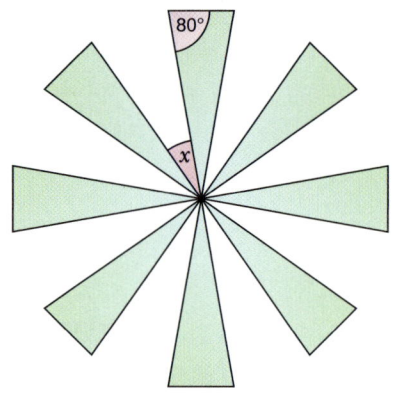

Find the size of angle x.
Show your working.

*__9__ This triangle has been drawn on a straight line ST.
  a Write b in terms of a
  b Write b in terms of d and c.
  c Use your answers to parts **a** and **b** to show that $a = d + c$.

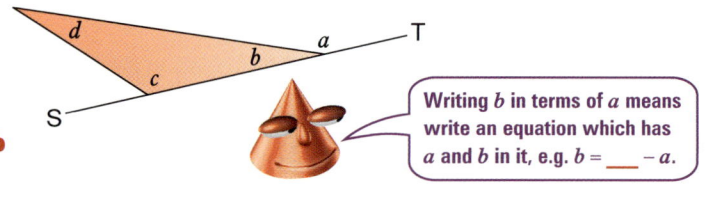

Writing b in terms of a means write an equation which has a and b in it, e.g. $b = \rule{1cm}{0.15mm} - a$.

*__10__ Naseem drew these triangles.
   AB is parallel to CD.
   AB = AC
   BC = BD
Find the size of all the other interior angles.
Show your working clearly and give reasons.

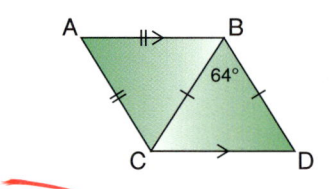

Lines and Angles

*11 Use this diagram to prove that the angles of a triangle add to 180°.
Hint Label the two angles next to a.

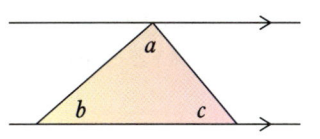

*12 Use the fact that the angles of a triangle add to 180° to prove that the angles in a quadrilateral add to 360°.
Hint Two triangles joined together make a quadrilateral.

*13 Calculate the value of p by writing and solving an equation.
a (2p, p + 30°, 3p, p + 50°)
b triangle with angles $p + 20°$, $2p + 5°$
c $3p + 40°$, $2p − 30°$

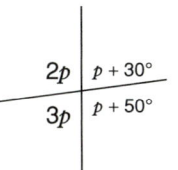

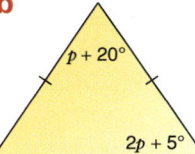

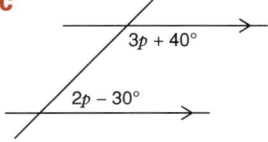

14 a Prove that
  i $a = 60°$
  ii $b = 25°$
  (angles 46°, 74°, 85°)

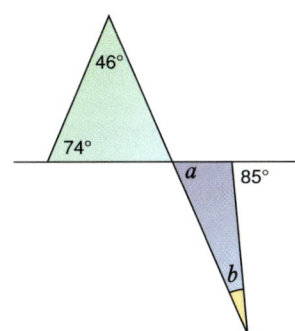

b Prove that
  i $c = 55°$
  ii $d = 50°$
  (angles 75°, 130°)

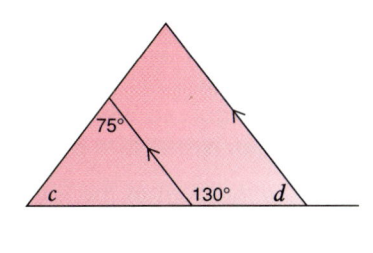

Review 1 Prove that x has the value shown. Show each step clearly and give reasons.
a (75°, 44°, x, a) $x = 61°$
b (125°, 32°, x) $x = 23°$

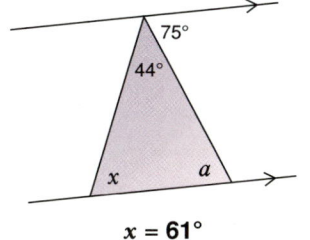

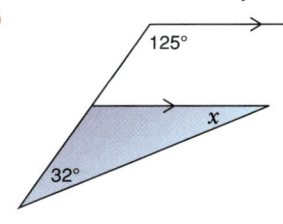

Review 2 Find the sizes of the angles marked with letters. Show your working clearly and give your reasons.
a (28°, 71°, a, b, c)
b (44°, d, e, f)

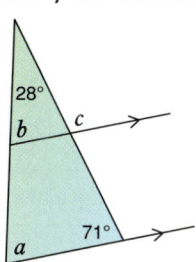

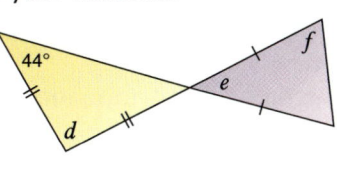

Review 3 This shape has two lines of symmetry. Find the size of angle a. (28°)

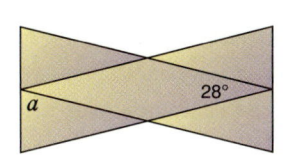

*Review 4 Prove that $x = 57.5°$. (65°)

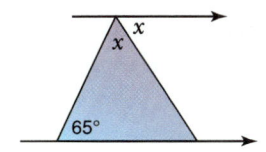

Shape, Space and Measures

Interior and exterior angles of a polygon

Discussion

- This pentagon can be divided into three triangles by drawing all the diagonals from one vertex.

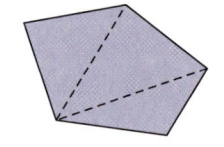

  How many triangles can a hexagon be split into by drawing all the diagonals from one vertex? **Discuss**.

  What if it was a quadrilateral?
  What if it was an octagon?
  What if it was a heptagon?
  What if ...

  What goes in the gap? **Discuss**.
  A polygon with *n* sides can be split into _____ triangles.   ← expression with *n* in it

- The pentagon above is split into three triangles.
  What then is the sum of the interior angles of a pentagon? **Discuss**.

  What is the sum of the interior angles of a hexagon, quadrilateral, ... ?

  What is the sum of the interior angles of an *n*-sided polygon? **Discuss**.

- At *each* vertex of this pentagon, what is the sum of the interior and the exterior angle? **Discuss**.
  Use this answer and the answer to the sum of the interior angles of a pentagon to find the sum of the exterior angles of a pentagon.

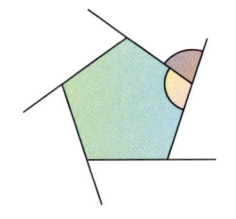

  What is the sum of the exterior angles of a quadrilateral, hexagon, ... ? **Discuss**.

Practical

A Mark a polygon on the floor or pavement.
You could use chalk or string.
Start at one vertex (A).
Walk along one side.
When you get to the next vertex, turn and walk along the next side.
Continue until you are back facing the way you were when you started.
Through what angle have you turned altogether?

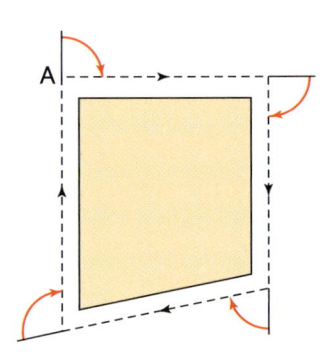

What is the sum of the exterior angles of this quadrilateral?

What if you walked around a pentagon instead?
What if you walked around a hexagon instead?
What if ...

B **You will need** a **LOGO** package.
Ask your teacher for the **Exterior Angles of Polygons** ICT worksheet.

Lines and Angles

The sum of the interior angles of an n-sided polygon is $(n - 2) \times 180°$.

Example This is a pentagon so $n = 5$.
$$p + q + r + s + t = (5 - 2) \times 180°$$
$$= 3 \times 180°$$
$$= 540°$$

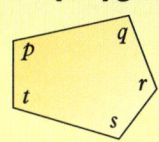

Worked Example
Find the value of n.

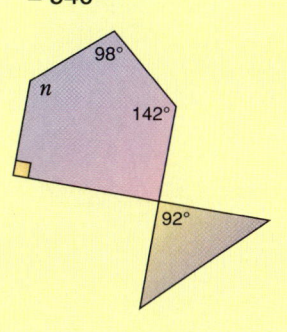

Answer
Name any unknown angles you need to find.

$m = 92°$ vertically opposite angles equal

The larger shape is a pentagon.
Sum of interior angles of a pentagon $= (5 - 2) \times 180°$
$$= 540°$$
$$n + 98° + 142° + 92° + 90° = 540°$$
$$n = 540° - 90° - 92° - 142° - 98°$$
$$= \mathbf{118°}$$

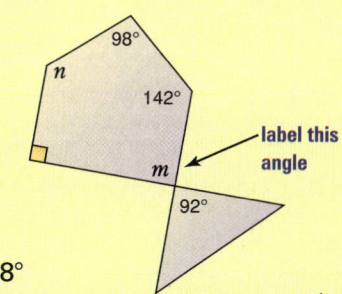

The sum of the exterior angles of any polygon is 360°.

Example $n + 64° + 58° + 82° + 26° + 100° = 360°$
$$n = 360° - 64° - 58° - 82° - 100° - 26°$$
$$n = \mathbf{30°}$$

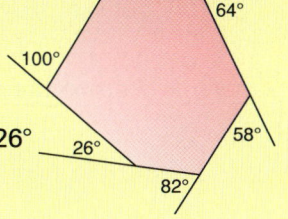

Exercise 2

Only use a calculator if you need to.

1 What goes in the gap?
  a A quadrilateral can be divided into ___ triangles.
  b A pentagon can be divided into ___ triangles.
  c A hexagon can be divided into ___ triangles.
  d An octagon can be divided into ___ triangles.
  e An n-sided polygon can be divided into ___ triangles.

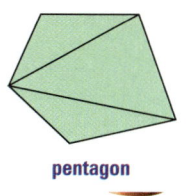

quadrilateral   pentagon

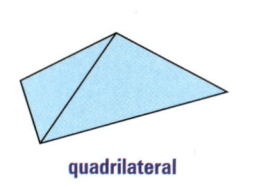

2 a If a 7-sided polygon was divided into triangles by drawing all the diagonals from one vertex, how many triangles would there be?
  b What is the sum of the interior angles of a heptagon?

A heptagon has 7 sides.

3 What is the sum of the exterior angles of
  a a heptagon   **b** a decagon   **c** a 12-sided polygon   **d** an equilateral triangle?

4 Using the formula for the sum of the interior angles of an n-sided polygon, find the sum of the interior angles of
  a a decagon   **b** a 12-sided polygon.

279

Shape, Space and Measures

5 Find the size of the angle marked as *x*.

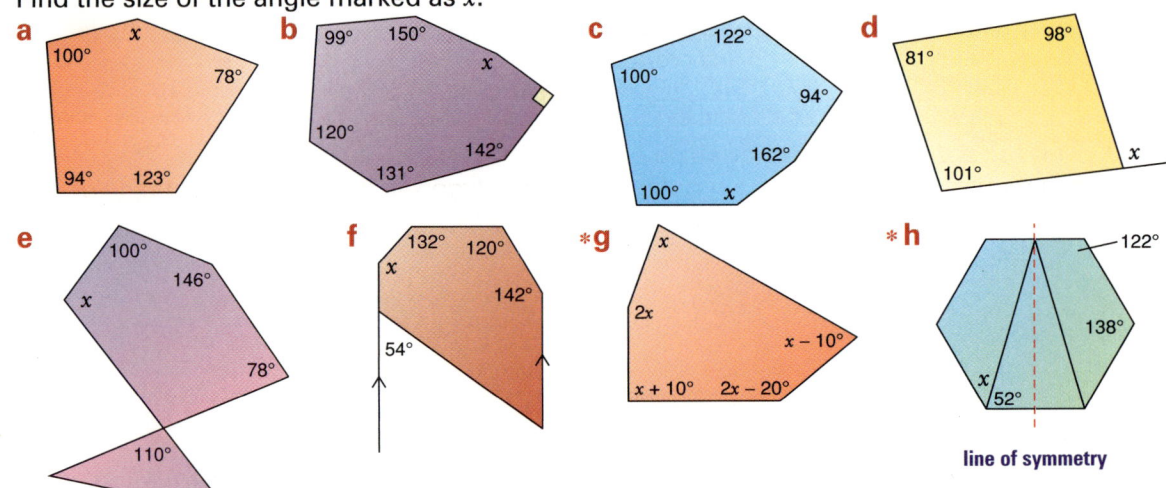

a 100°, *x*, 78°, 94°, 123°

b 99°, 150°, *x*, 120°, 142°, 131° (right angle marked)

c 122°, 100°, 94°, 162°, 100°, *x*

d 81°, 98°, 101°, *x*

e 100°, 146°, *x*, 78°, 110°

f 132°, 120°, *x*, 142°, 54°

*g *x*, 2*x*, *x* + 10°, 2*x* − 20°, *x* − 10°

*h 122°, 138°, *x*, 52° — line of symmetry

6 The drawing shows how shapes A and B fit together to make a **right-angled** triangle.

[SATs Paper 1 Level 6]

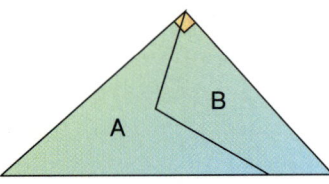

Work out the size of each of the angles in shape B.

Use a copy of the diagram.
Write them in the correct place in shape B.

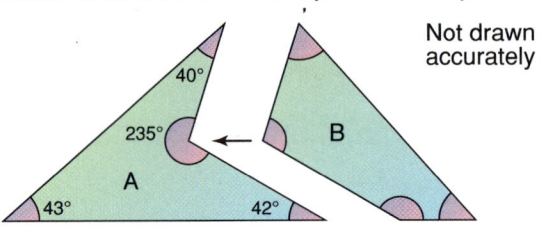

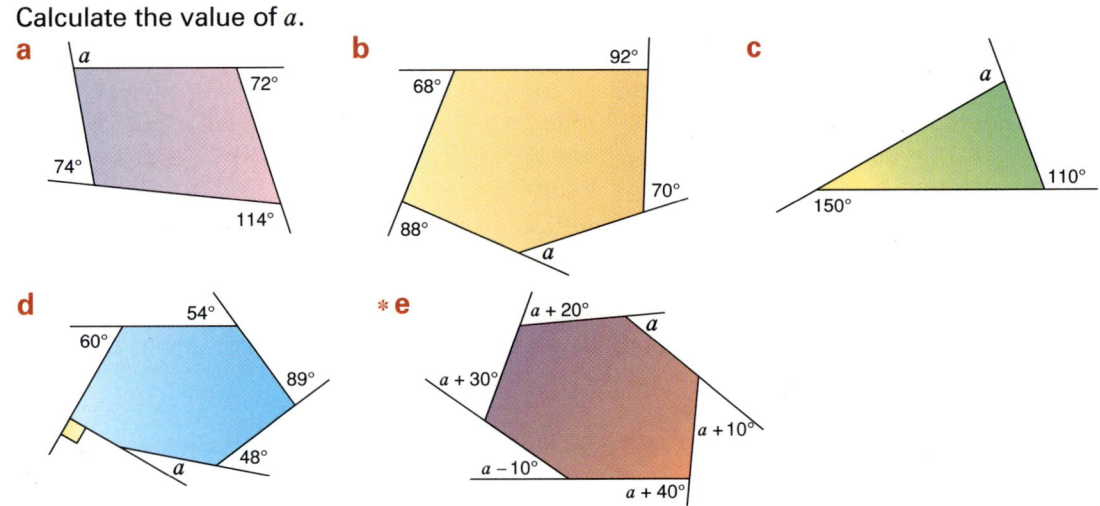

Not drawn accurately

A: 40°, 235°, 43°, 42°

7 Calculate the value of *a*.

a *a*, 72°, 74°, 114°

b 92°, 68°, 70°, 88°, *a*

c *a*, 150°, 110°

d 54°, 60°, 89°, 48°, *a* (right angle marked)

*e *a* + 20°, *a*, *a* + 30°, *a* + 10°, *a* − 10°, *a* + 40°

8 Toby walked right around the outside of a pentagonal pool.
What **total** turn did he make as he did this?

280

Lines and Angles

9 Find the size of each interior angle of a
  a equilateral triangle
  b square
  c regular octagon
  d regular pentagon
  e regular hexagon
  f regular 12-sided polygon.

Remember: A regular shape has all its sides and angles equal.

10 Find the size of each exterior angle of
  a a regular pentagon
  b a regular 20-sided polygon
  c an equilateral triangle.

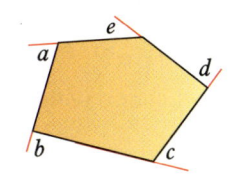

***11 Prove** that $a + b + c + d + e = 360°$.

***12** The ratio of the size of angles a, b and c is $a : b : c = 2 : 3 : 4$.
  a Find the size of each angle a, b and c.
  b Find the ratio of $d : e : f$.

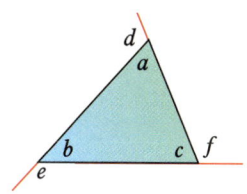

Review 1 Find the value of y.
a (162°, 154°, 98°, y, 150°, 161°, 114°)
b (y, 135°, 78°)
c Regular octagon, y
***d** (108°, 75°, y, 115°, 110°)

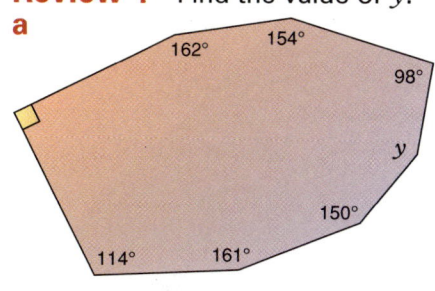

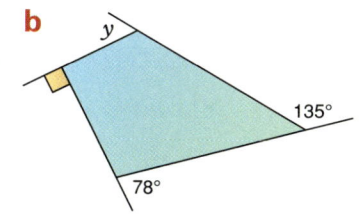

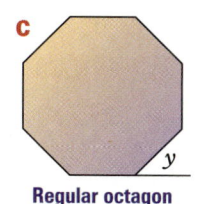

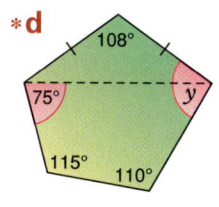

Review 2
a Find the size of each interior angle of a regular decagon.
b Find the size of each exterior angle of a regular 12-sided polygon.

***Review 3** Prove, using diagrams and geometric reasoning, that each of the interior angles of a regular octagon is 135°.

***Review 4** Find the values of x and y. (128°, $2x$, y, x, x)

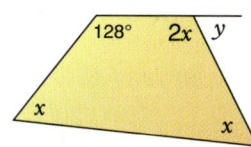

Investigation

Polygons

How many sides has a regular polygon with an exterior angle of 40°?

What if each exterior angle was 72°?
What if each exterior angle was 15°?
What if each exterior angle was 80°?
What if each exterior angle was 50°?
What if ...
Investigate.

Shape, Space and Measures

Summary of key points

A The sides of a triangle are labelled with the lower-case letter of the opposite angle.
This is called a **convention**.

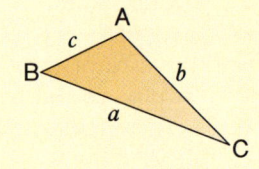

A **definition** is the minimum amount of information needed to specify a geometrical term.
Example A polygon is a closed shape with straight sides.

A **derived property** follows as a result of a definition.
It is not essential to a definition.
Example The angles of a triangle add to 180°.

B We often use **geometrical reasoning** to find an unknown angle or prove something.
Write down the steps clearly, one by one, and give reasons.
Example Prove that $x = 63°$.

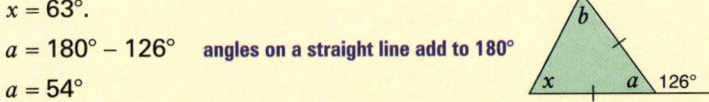

$a = 180° − 126°$ angles on a straight line add to 180°
$a = 54°$

$x = b$ base angles of isosceles △

$x + b = 180° − 54°$ angles of a triangle add to 180°
$2x = 126°$ because $x = b$
$x = \mathbf{63°}$

C The **sum of the interior angles of a polygon with n sides is $(n − 2) \times 180°$**.
Example This is a regular hexagon. 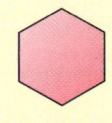
It has **6** sides.
Sum of interior angles = $(\mathbf{6} − 2) \times 180°$
$= 720°$

All interior angles in a regular hexagon are equal.
Each interior angle = $\frac{720°}{6}$
$= \mathbf{120°}$

D The sum of the exterior angles of any polygon is 360°.
Example Exterior angles add to 360°. 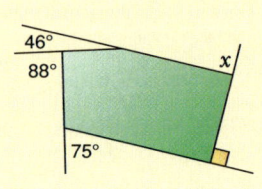
$x + 46° + 88° + 75° + 90° = 360°$
$x = 360° − 46° − 88° − 75° − 90°$
$= \mathbf{61°}$

Lines and Angles

Test yourself

1 State whether each of these is a **convention**, a **definition** or a **derived property**.
  a The vertices of a shape are labelled with upper-case letters.
  b A half-turn is 180°.
  c The equal sides of a shape are indicated with dashes.
  d An isosceles trapezium has one pair of parallel sides and a pair of equal sides.
  e The inverse of a rotation of 90° is a clockwise rotation of 90°.
  f A rhombus is a parallelogram with four equal sides.

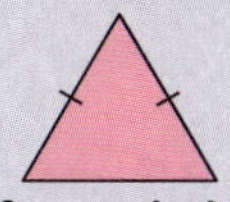

2 Find the sizes of the angles marked with letters.
Show your working clearly and give reasons.

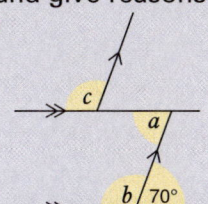

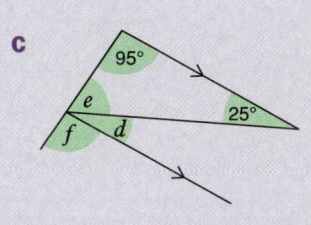

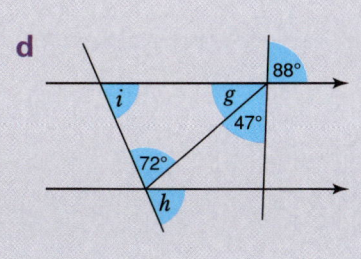

  a (angles y, x with 68°, 135°)
  b (angles a, b, c with 70° and parallel arrows)
  c (angles d, e, f with 95°, 25° and parallel arrows)
  d (angles g, h, i with 88°, 47°, 72°)
  *e arrowhead with angle l and 15°

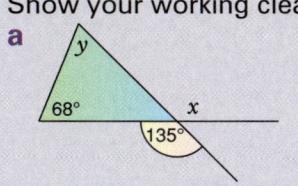

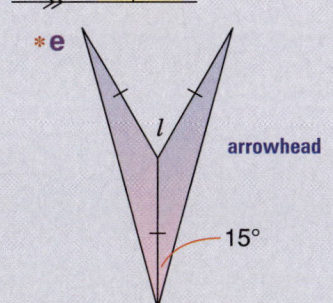

3 Calculate the value of p.

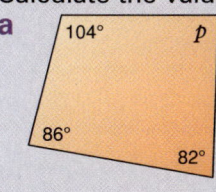

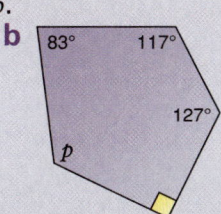

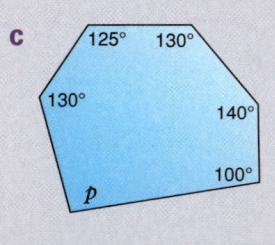

  a quadrilateral with 104°, 86°, 82°, p
  b pentagon with 83°, 117°, 127°, right angle, p
  c pentagon with 125°, 130°, 130°, 140°, 100°, p
  d pentagon with 61°, right angles, 72°, p

  [SATs Paper 2 Level 6]

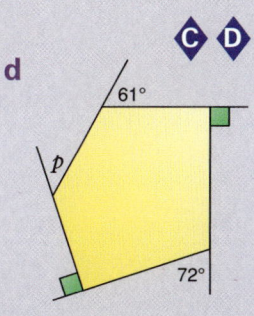

4 a Any quadrilateral can be split into 2 triangles.

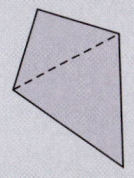

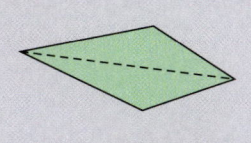

  Explain how you know that the angles inside a **quadrilateral** add up to 360°. 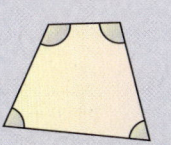

  b What do the angles inside a **pentagon** add up to? 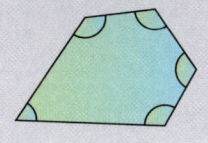

  c What do the angles inside a **heptagon** (7-sided shape) add up to?
  Show your working.

283

Shape, Space and Measures

5 a Calculate the size of an exterior angle of a regular 8-sided polygon.
   b Calculate the size of an interior angle of a regular 8-sided polygon.
  ***c** Can a regular polygon be drawn with each exterior angle equal to 54°?
         Give reasons for your answer.

6 Jody made this pattern with tiles.
   The side lengths of all the tiles are the same.
   What are the four angles in the rhombuses equal to?
   Show your working.

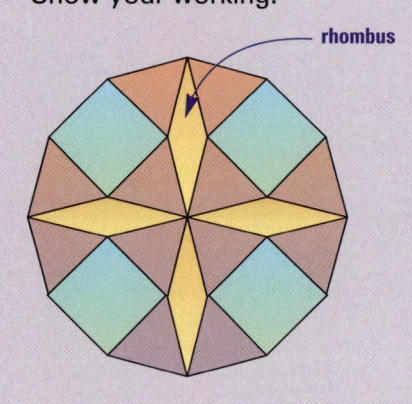

   — rhombus

7 Calculate the value of x. Show your working clearly and give reasons.
   a   3x, 86°, $x + 46°$
   b $x - 30°$, $x + 15°$, $x - 15°$

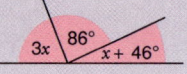

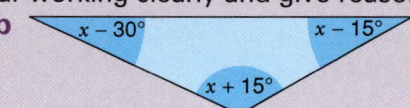

11 Shape, Construction and Loci

You need to know

✓ 2-D shapes   page 256
        – polygons
✓ constructions   page 257
✓ locus   page 258
✓ 3-D shapes   page 258

Key vocabulary

arc, centre (of circle), chord, circumference, cross-section, diameter, plan view, radius, sector, segment, tangent (to a curve), tessellate, tessellation, view

▶▶ Mission impossible

- Maurits Escher drew this picture.
  Look closely at it to see if you can see anything 'impossible'.
  Find other M.C. Escher 'impossible' drawings.

- This rectangle is an 'impossible rectangle'.

  Try to draw an 'impossible triangle'.

285

Shape, Space and Measures

Triangles, quadrilaterals and polygons

Discussion

Asad: I cut a shape into quarters and each quarter is an isosceles triangle.

Irene: I cut a shape into quarters and each quarter is a rhombus.

What shapes might Asad and Irene have started with? **Discuss**.

Remember
The properties of **triangles** and **special quadrilaterals** are given on page 000.

Exercise 1

1 Use a copy of this table. Fill it in.

Shape	Number of lines of symmetry	Order of rotation symmetry
Equilateral △		
Isosceles △		
Square		
Rectangle		
Parallelogram		
Rhombus		
Kite		
Isosceles trapezium		
Trapezium		
Arrowhead		

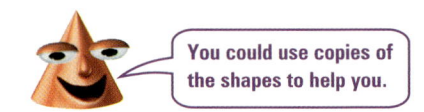

You could use copies of the shapes to help you.

2 Write true or false for each of these.
   a A kite can be split into two congruent triangles.
   b A parallelogram can be split into two congruent triangles.
   c In any triangle, the longest side is opposite the largest angle and the shortest side is opposite the smallest angle.
   d A rhombus can be split into four equilateral triangles.

Remember: 'congruent' means 'exactly the same shape and size'.

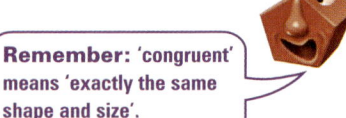

286

Shape, Construction and Loci

3 Use a copy of this.
Four squares join together to make a bigger square.

[SATs Paper 1 Level 5]

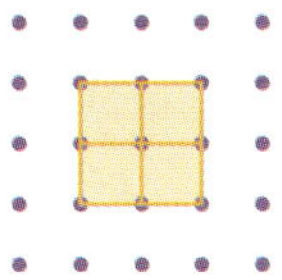

a Four congruent triangles join together to make a bigger triangle.

Draw **two more** triangles to complete the drawing of the bigger triangle.

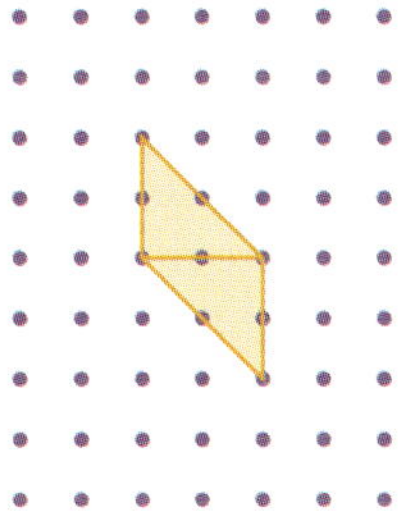

b Four congruent trapeziums join to make a bigger trapezium.

Draw **two more** trapeziums to complete the drawing of the bigger trapezium.

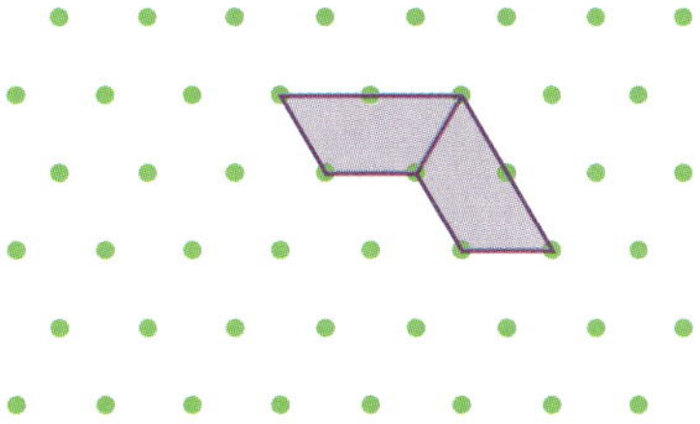

c Four congruent trapeziums join to make a **parallelogram**.

Draw **two more** trapeziums to complete the drawing of the parallelogram.

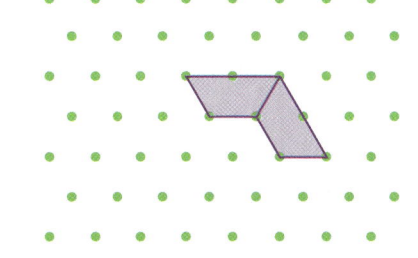

4 This shape has 2 axes of symmetry.
  a Name an angle equal to ∠ABC.
  b Name a line segment equal in length to AD.
  c What triangle is congruent to △ABD?
  d What type of triangle is △ABC?

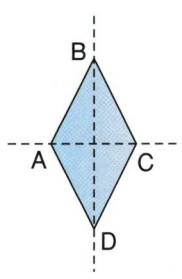

5 Find the red length and the angles marked with letters. Show your reasoning clearly.
See page 274 for how to show reasoning clearly.

a 78°, 14 cm, a

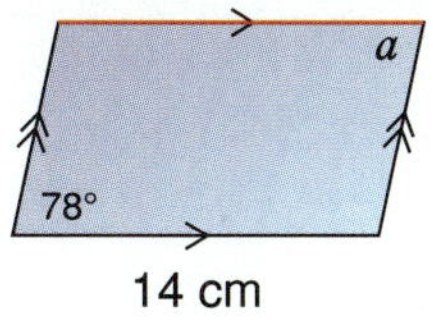

b b, 120°, isosceles trapezium

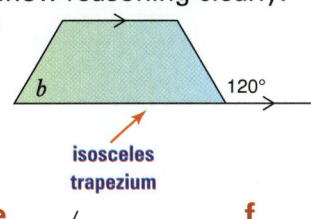

c d, 11·2 cm, 52°, c, rhombus

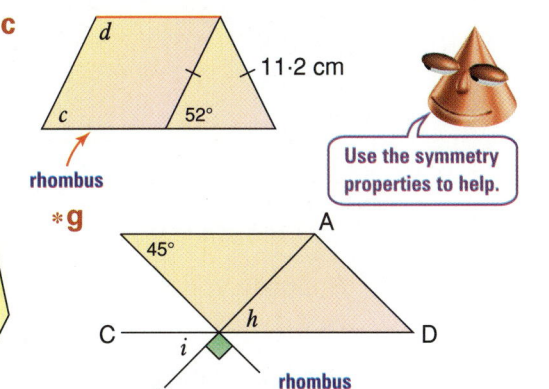

Use the symmetry properties to help.

d e, 100°, 45°, A, arrowhead

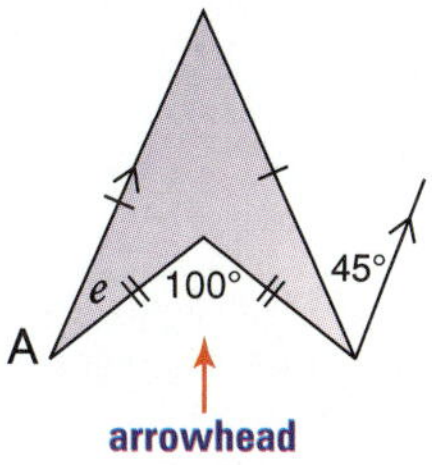

e 82°, f, 8 m, 47°

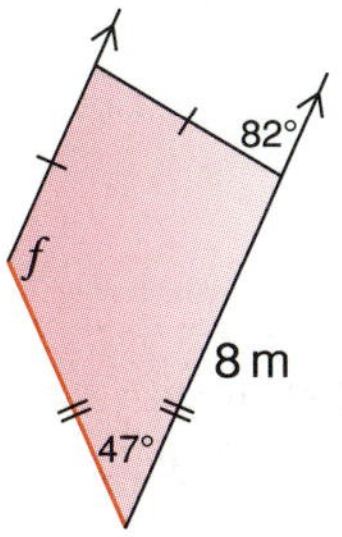

f g, 141°, 26°, kite

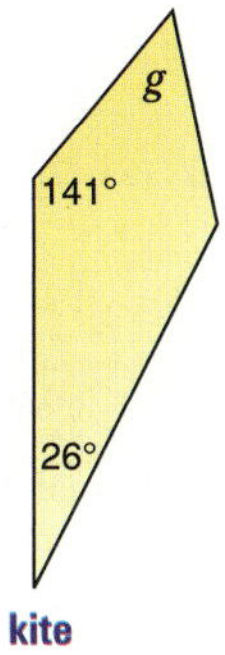

*g 45°, A, C, h, i, B, D, rhombus AB and CD are straight lines.

287

Shape, Space and Measures

6 a Explain why all equilateral triangles are isosceles triangles.
  b Explain why not all parallelograms are rhombuses.

7 Which is the odd one out in this list? Explain why.
    square   rhombus   rectangle   parallelogram   kite
Is there more than one possible answer?

8 Imagine two different isosceles triangles but with the same base length.
What shape is made by joining them together along the base?
Is there more than one answer?
What if they are not joined along their bases?

9 a Think of an equilateral triangle with one side horizontal.
  Call this side the base.
  Think of this base as fixed.
  The opposite vertex of the triangle moves slowly in a straight line perpendicular to the base.
  What happens to the triangle?
  b Think what would happen if the opposite vertex moves parallel to the base.
  Can you get a right-angled triangle?
  What about an obtuse-angled triangle?

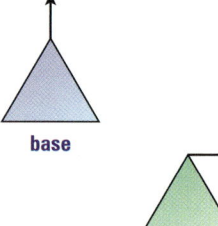

10 Think of a rectangular sheet of paper.
Imagine making a straight symmetrical cut across one corner.
  a What shape is left?
  ***b** What if you made a series of cuts, always parallel to the first cut.
  What shapes is it possible to make?

***11** A famous mathematician, called Pythagoras, discovered that in a right-angled triangle the square of the longest side (hypotenuse) is equal to the sum of the squares on the other two sides.
Find the missing length using *Pythagoras' theorem*.

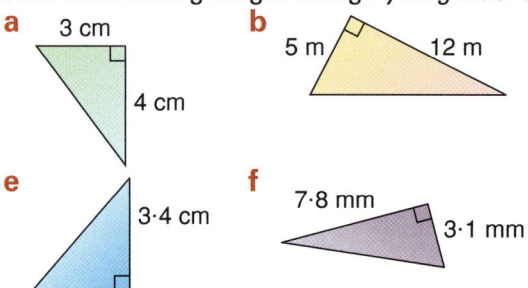

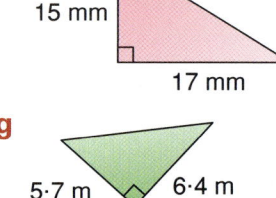

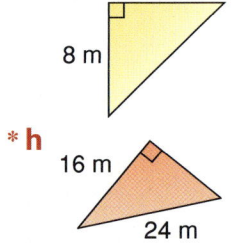

$c^2 = a^2 + b^2$

  a 3 cm, 4 cm
  b 5 m, 12 m
  c 15 mm, 17 mm
  d 9 m, 8 m
  e 3·4 cm, 2·8 cm
  f 7·8 mm, 3·1 mm
  g 5·7 m, 6·4 m
  ***h** 16 m, 24 m

***12** Ann cycles 8 km from A to B, then 5 km from B to C.
She then cycles back to A.
How far did she cycle altogether?

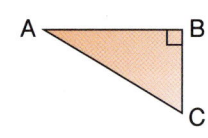

***13 a** Suppose you were to draw a set of parallel lines 4 cm apart on each of two sheets of acetate.
  Imagine placing one set on top of the other so that the two sets are perpendicular.
  What shapes would you see?
  b What happens as you rotate one of the sheets about a fixed point (intersection of two lines)?
  c Repeat **a** and **b** for one set of lines 4 cm apart and the other set 2 cm apart.

You might like to try this.

Shape, Construction and Loci

* **14** Marcy bought tiles which were the shape of a rhombus.
She put three tiles together to make this shape.
  a Find the value of angles a, b, c and d.
  b Write down all the things you know or can deduce about the shape formed by the three tiles.

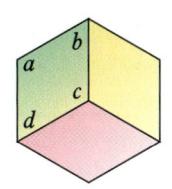

Review 1 Write true or false for these statements.
a A rectangle can be divided into four isosceles triangles.
b An isosceles trapezium has two pairs of equal sides.

Review 2 Use the properties of the shape and other angle properties to find the lengths marked x and the angles marked a, b, c, ...

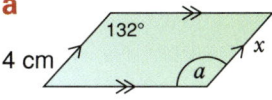

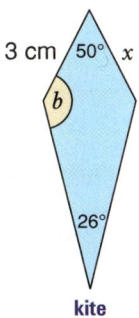

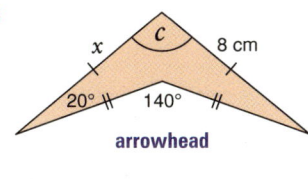

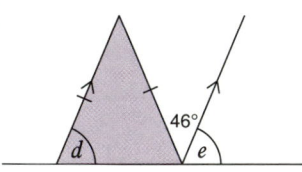

a (parallelogram, 4 cm, 132°, a, x)
b kite (3 cm, 50°, x, b, 26°)
c arrowhead (x, c, 8 cm, 20°, 140°)
d (triangle with 46°, d, e)

Review 3 By finding all the other angles in these triangles, what can you say about triangles ABC and CDE?

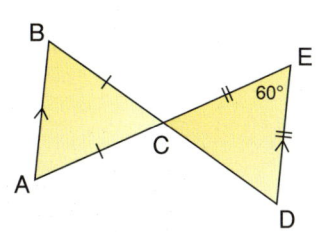

Review 4 Can a parallelogram be split into two isosceles triangles? What about two scalene triangles?

Review 5 ABC is an equilateral triangle. BCDE is a rhombus.
  a Find the length of ED.
  b Find the size of angle BCD.
  c Find the size of angle CBE.

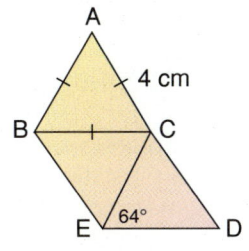

(AC = 4 cm, angle E = 64°)

Practical

You will need a dynamic geometry software package.

Ask your teacher for the **2-D Changes** ICT worksheet.

Shape, Space and Measures

Tessellations

Remember
A shape will **tessellate** if it can be used to completely fill a space with no overlapping and no gaps.

Example

A **tessellation** is made by reflecting, rotating or translating a shape.

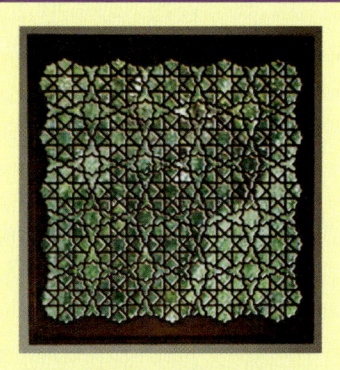

Exercise 2   You will need some squared paper and thin card for this exercise.

1 Make four copies of the small shape.

   Tessellate these to tile the large area.
   Which of reflection, rotation and translation did you use?
   a   b

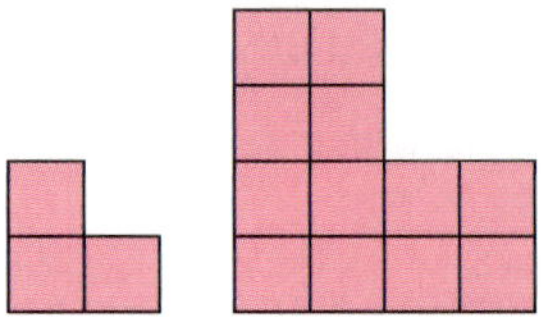

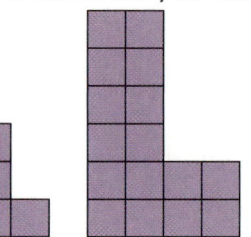

   You could use interlocking cubes to help.

2 Use copies of these shapes.

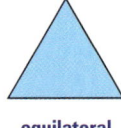

   equilateral triangle   **regular hexagon**   **regular pentagon**

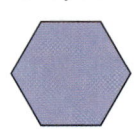

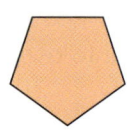

   Which ones will tessellate? Explain why or why not?

3 Tessellate **one** of the quadrilaterals shown below or a quadrilateral of your choice, to tile an area. Which of reflection, rotation and translation did you use to make the tessellation? Colour your design using not more than four colours.

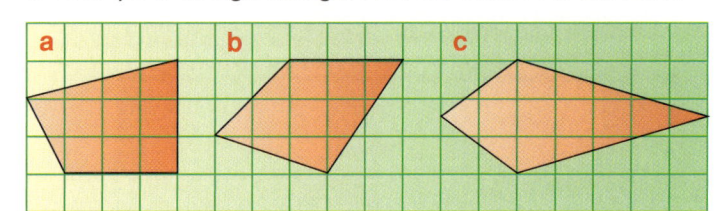

   a   b   c

Review   There are three regular polygons that will tessellate.
Which three are they? Explain why these three will tessellate but the other regular polygons will not.

Shape, Construction and Loci

*Investigation

Tessellating polygons

1. There are eight tessellations that can be made using a combination of two or three regular polygons.
   Two of these are shown.

   regular octagons and squares

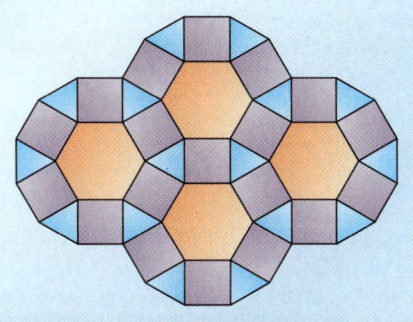

   regular hexagons, squares and equilateral triangles

   What are the other six? **Investigate**. Explain why each will tessellate.

2. A tessellation can be made by overlaying octagons and squares on octagons and squares.

   Examples

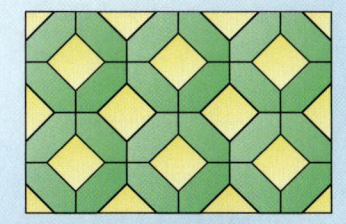

   Explore other tessellations that can be made this way.
   Describe the outcomes.

Circles

A **circle** is a set of points equidistant from its centre.

The circumference is the distance around the outside of the circle (red).

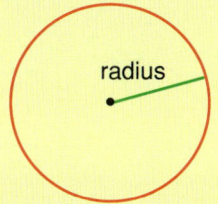

An arc is part of the circumference (blue).

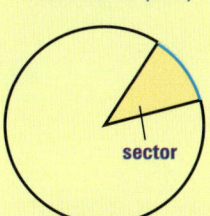

radius

sector

The **radius** is the distance from the centre to the circumference (green).

A **sector** is the area made by an arc and two radii (yellow).

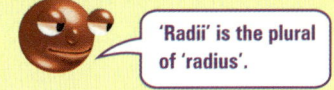

'Radii' is the plural of 'radius'.

291

Shape, Space and Measures

Imagine a line moves towards a circle.

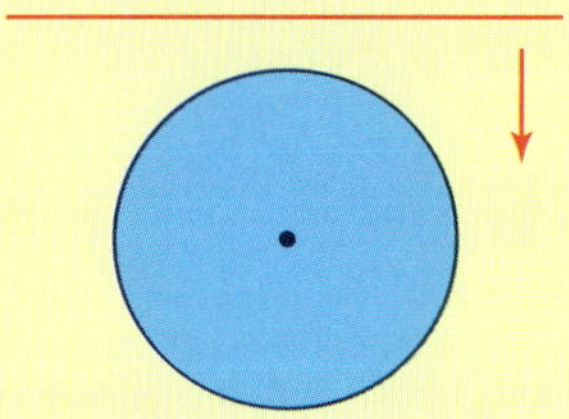

When the line *just touches* the circle at P, it is called a **tangent** to the circle at that point.

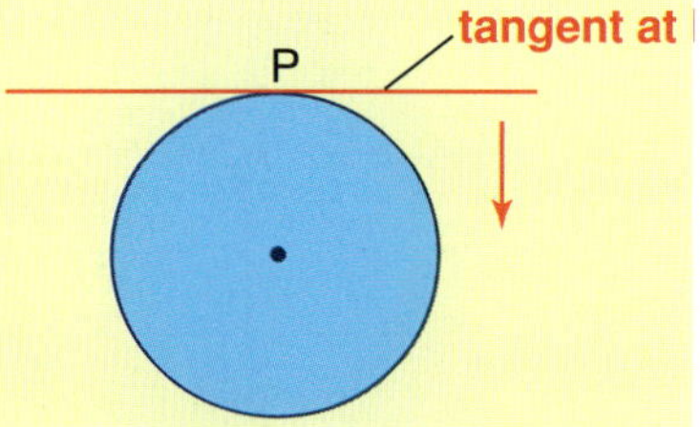

When the line intersects the circle at two points M and N, the line segment MN is called a **chord** of the circle.
The chord divides the area enclosed by the circle into two **segments**.

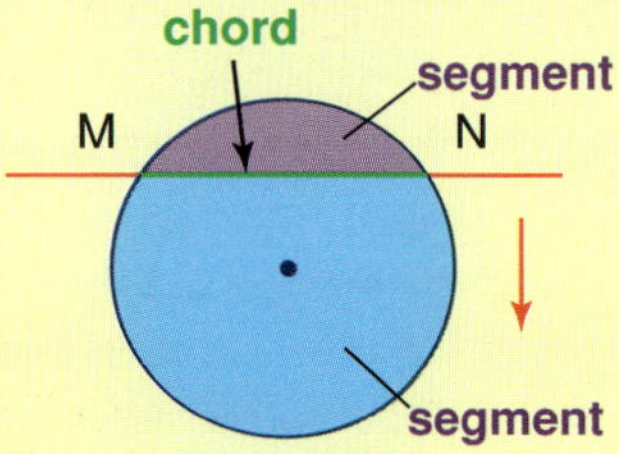

When the line passes through the centre, the line segment CD becomes the **diameter**.
It divides the area enclosed by the circle into two **semicircles**.

The diameter is twice the radius.

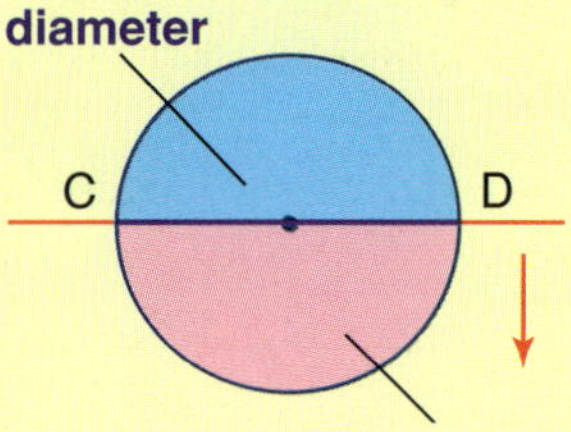

Exercise 3

1 Name the parts of the circle shown in red. The • shows the centre of the circle.

a   b 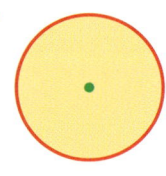   c

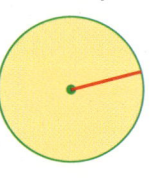

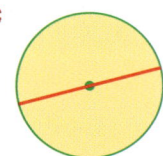

d 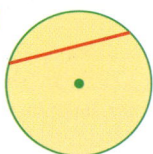   e 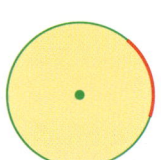   f

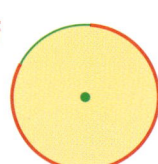

Shape, Construction and Loci

2 Name the regions shaded in green.
a   b   c   d   e

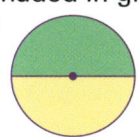

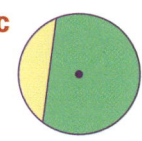

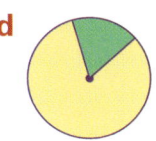

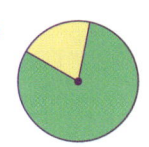

3 a Use a set of compasses to draw a circle with radius 6 cm.
Draw and label these parts of your circle.
   radius   diameter   arc   sector   tangent
b Make another circle and draw and label these parts.
   chord   segment   circumference

4 Match these definitions with the correct name from the box.
a A line that touches the circle at just one point, P.
b A line that joins two points on the circumference and passes through the centre of the circle.
c A region enclosed by a chord and an arc.
d A set of points equidistant from another fixed point.
e The distance around a circle.
f The distance from the centre to the circumference.
g A region enclosed by an arc and two radii.
h The two regions the circle is divided into by the diameter.

A	circle
B	circumference
C	radius
D	arc
E	diameter
F	tangent
G	chord
H	segment
I	semicircle
J	sector

5 Hazel drew a chord on a circle.
She drew two radii to make a triangle.
a What is the special name of this triangle?
She then drew three more chords **exactly** the same length.
By chance, the last chord joined exactly to the first chord.
b Will the four triangles made all be congruent?
c Will angles a, b, c and d be the same?
d What shape do the chords make?
e How could Hazel use what she learnt, to draw a regular pentagon?

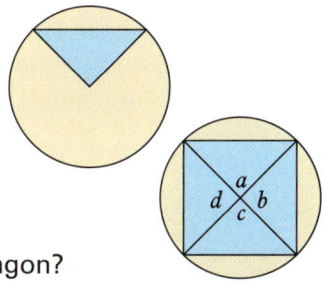

6 Draw a regular hexagon by dividing the circumference of a circle into six equal arcs, using a protractor.
Explain why a regular hexagon can be constructed this way.

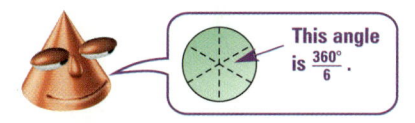

This angle is $\frac{360°}{6}$.

*7 A chord, PQ, of a circle is drawn.
Tangents to the circle are drawn at P and Q.
The tangents intersect at R.
a Imagine PQ moves to the left.
What happens to R?
b Imagine PQ moves to the right.
What happens to R?

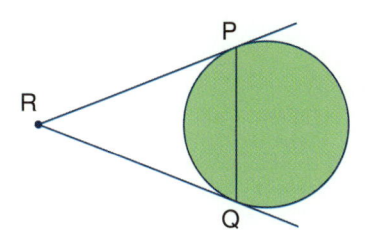

Review 1 Draw a circle.
On your circle label these parts.
a radius   **b** circumference   **c** arc   **d** segment   **e** sector   **f** chord

Review 2 Draw a regular octagon by dividing the circumference of a circle into equal arcs.
Explain why an octagon can be constructed in this way.

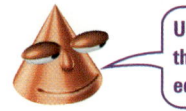

Use a protractor to divide the circumference into equal parts.

293

Shape, Space and Measures

⭐ Practical

1 Use these diagrams to help you draw the interlocking square design.

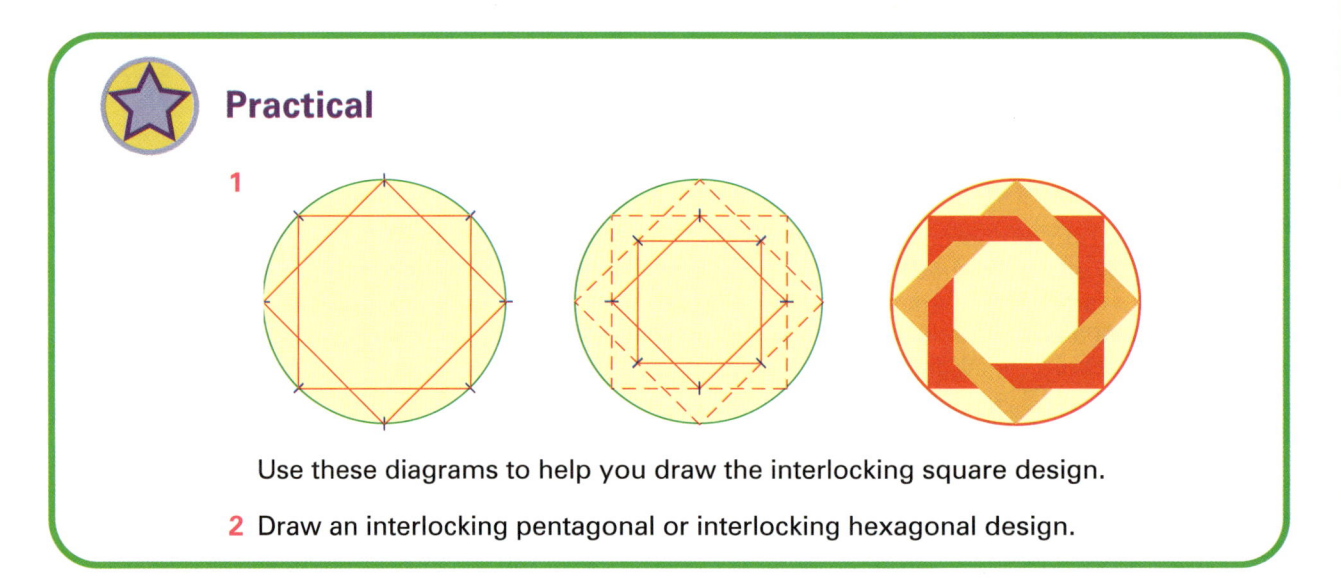

2 Draw an interlocking pentagonal or interlocking hexagonal design.

Constructions

Remember
See page 257 for the following constructions:
- mid-point and perpendicular bisector of a line segment
- bisector of an angle
- perpendicular from a point to a line segment
- perpendicular from a point on a line segment.

See page 257 for how to construct a triangle given
- two sides and the angle between (SAS)
- two angles and the side between (ASA)
- three sides.

We can construct a right-angled triangle given the right angle, the length of the longest side and one other side (RHS).

The longest side is called the **hypotenuse**.

4 cm
3 cm

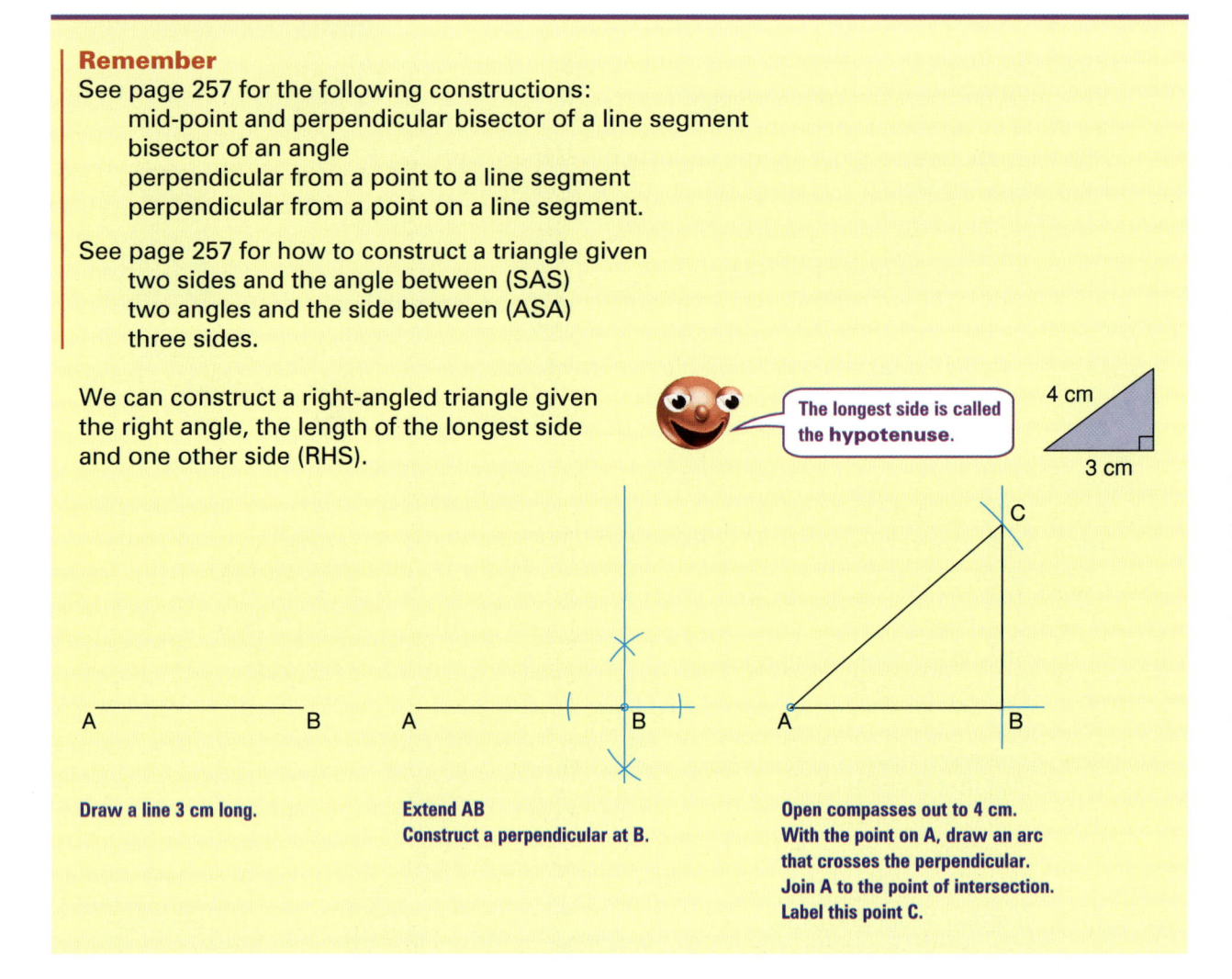

A —————— B

Draw a line 3 cm long.

A —————— B

Extend AB
Construct a perpendicular at B.

A ——————— B
         C

Open compasses out to 4 cm.
With the point on A, draw an arc that crosses the perpendicular.
Join A to the point of intersection. Label this point C.

Shape, Construction and Loci

We sometimes construct a scale drawing of a triangle to help solve a problem.

Example A 20 m high flagpole casts a 6 m shadow.
We can draw a scale drawing to find the angle the sun's rays make with the ground.
Using a scale of 1 mm to represent $\frac{1}{2}$ m, we construct the triangle.
We carefully measure the shaded angle as 73°.

The angle the sun's rays make with the ground is 73°.

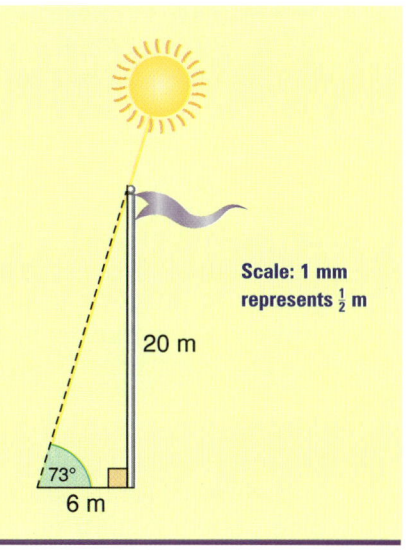

Scale: 1 mm represents $\frac{1}{2}$ m

Exercise 4

1 a Use compasses to construct a triangle that has sides 8 cm, 6 cm and 7 cm. Leave in your construction lines.
   b Use compasses and a ruler to construct this quadrilateral.

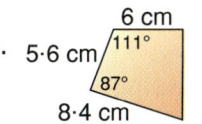

   5·6 cm, 6 cm, 111°, 87°, 8·4 cm

   [SATs Paper 2 Level 5]

2 Here is a plan of a ferry crossing.

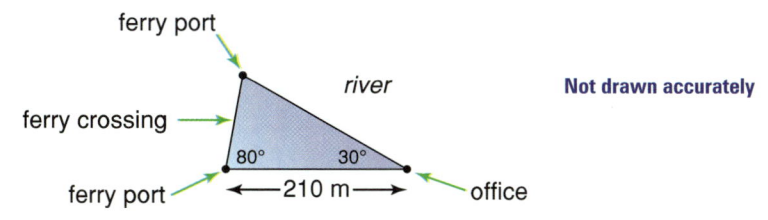

   Not drawn accurately

   ferry port, river, ferry crossing, 80°, 30°, 210 m, ferry port, office

   a Make an accurate scale drawing of the ferry crossing. Draw the line between the ferry port and the office 10·5 cm long.
   b What is the length of the ferry crossing on **your** diagram?
   c The scale is **1 cm** to **20 m**. Work out the length of the real ferry crossing. Show your working, and **write the units with your answer**.

3 In a gale, a tree falls against a house. The top of the tree is 5 m up the wall of the house.
   The foot of the tree is 7 m from the wall of the house.
   Make a scale drawing. Use the scale 1 cm represents 1 m.
   Use a ruler and protractor to find
   a the height of the tree
   b the angle between the tree, after it has fallen, and the ground.

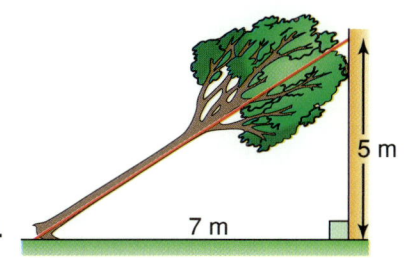

4 A 12-foot ladder is leaned against a wall so that its base is 3·5 feet from the wall. Construct a triangle to scale. Use a ruler and protractor to find
   a how far up the wall the ladder reaches
   b the angle between the ladder and the ground.

5 Explain why it is not possible to draw a triangle ABC such that AB = 10 cm, AC = 5 cm and BC = 3 cm.

Shape, Space and Measures

*6 Is it possible to construct triangle PQR such that
   a P = 60°, Q = 30°, R = 90°
   b P = 60°, Q = 60°, R = 60°
   c PQ = 5 cm, QR = 3 cm, PR = 2 cm
   d PQ = 4 cm, QR = 4 cm, PR = 3 cm
   e PQ = 7 cm, QR = 3 cm, PR = 3 cm
   f QR = 8 cm, PR = 6 cm, R = 50°
   g P = 30°, Q = 45° PR = 6 cm
   h QR = 7 cm, PR = 4·85 cm, Q = 45°?

*7 How many different triangles could be drawn using any three of the following lengths for the sides?
     8 cm   7 cm   6 cm   5 cm   4 cm   3 cm

Review 1 Construct a triangle with sides 5 cm, 6 cm and 8 cm using compasses. Leave your construction lines.

Review 2
a Make an accurate scale drawing of the triangular play area shown. Use the scale 1 cm represents 2 m.
b Find the length of RF on your drawing.
c Find the actual distance between the climbing frame and the roundabout.
Show your working and write the units with your answer.

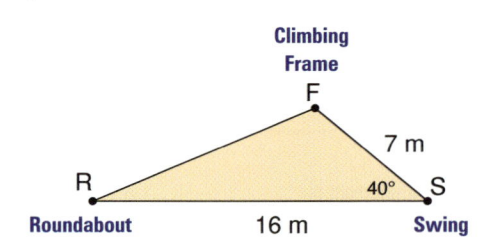

Review 3 At an adventure playground a 12 m slide ends 5 m from the bottom of a rock wall.
Make a scale drawing. Use a ruler and protractor to find
a the height of the wall
b the angle the slide makes with the ground.

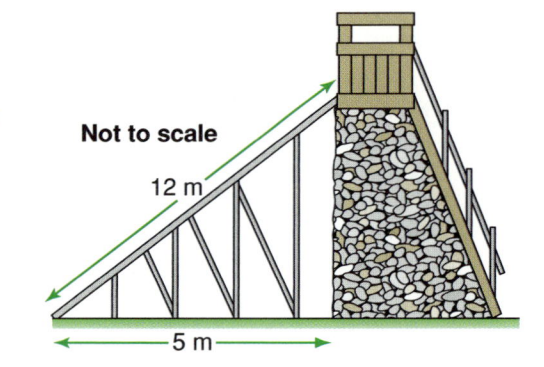

*** Review 4** Is it possible to construct triangle EFG such that
a E = 40°, F = 60°, EF = 5 cm   b FG = 7 cm, EG = 4 cm, F = 45°?
If not, explain why not.

Discussion

This diagram shows two intersecting circles with equal radii.

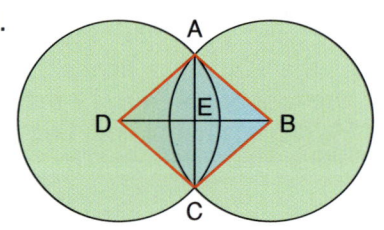

a What can you say about the common chord, AC, of two intersecting circles with equal radii and the line joining their centres? **Discuss**.
b What can you say about the shape formed by the radii joining the centre to the points of intersection? **Discuss**.
*c How could you relate these properties to the construction of the
   ● mid-point and perpendicular bisector of a line segment
   ● bisector of an angle
   ● perpendicular from a point to a line
   ● perpendicular from a point on a line? **Discuss**.

Shape, Construction and Loci

Locus

Remember
A **locus** is a set of points that satisfy a rule or set of rules.
The locus of a moving object is the path that it follows.

Example A fly walks so that it is always the same distance from two spider webs.
The locus is the perpendicular bisector of the line joining the two webs.
We can construct this locus.

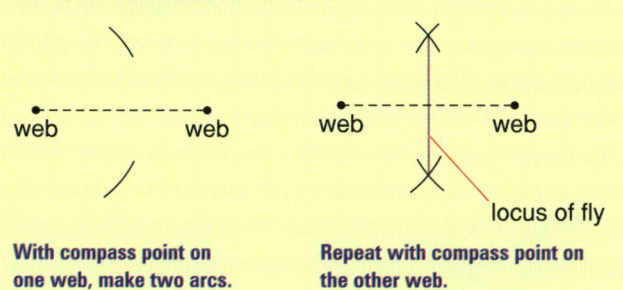

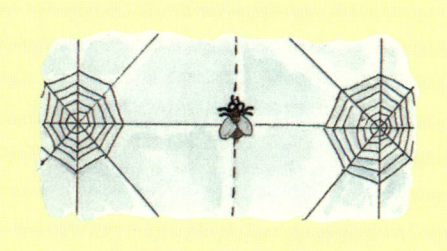

web ——— web

web ——— web
locus of fly

With compass point on one web, make two arcs.

Repeat with compass point on the other web.

For full instructions see page 257.

Discussion

- There are two fences at the dog trials.
  A dog must run so that it is exactly the same distance from both fences.
  Which of these is the locus of the dog? **Discuss**.

  circle
  perpendicular bisector of the line between the fences
  bisector of the angle made by the fences

  How could you construct this locus? **Discuss**.

- Juanita made a spinner by glueing a piece of rectangular card onto a stick.
  She spun the stick between her palms as fast as she could.
  If you were watching, which of these shapes would you appear to see?
  Discuss.
     sphere   cone   cylinder   cuboid

Exercise 5

1 Which of these could be the locus of a ball thrown in the air?

   A   B   C   D

Shape, Space and Measures

2 Draw a possible path for these.
  a the tip of a windscreen wiper
  b the head of a boy on a merry-go-round
  c a car going halfway round a traffic roundabout
  d a horse running parallel to a straight ditch

3 Match these loci and descriptions.
  a A piece of machinery moves so that it is always the same distance from a fixed point.
  b Russ runs so that he is always the same distance from two gates in a park.
  c Russ runs so that he is always the same distance from two dry stone walls that meet at an angle.

  A Perpendicular bisector of the line joining two points

  B a circle

  C bisector of the angle between the lines

T 4 Use a copy of this. [SATs Paper 1 Level 7]
The diagram below shows two points A and B that are 6 cm apart.
Around each point are six circles of radius 1 cm, 2 cm, 3 cm, 4 cm, 5 cm and 6 cm. Each circle has either A or B as its centre.

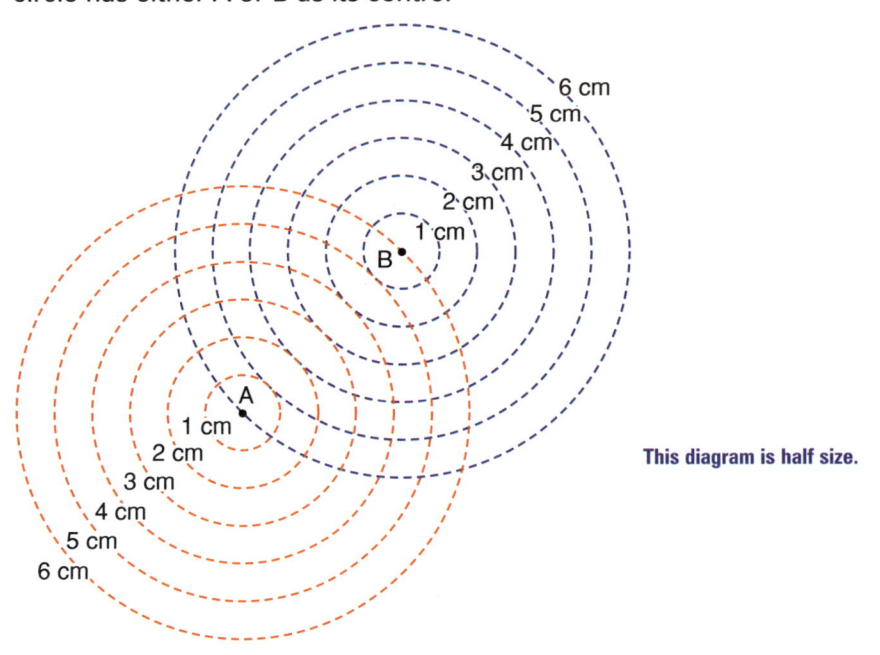

This diagram is half size.

  a On the diagram, mark with a cross any points that are 4 cm away from A **and** 4 cm away from B.
  b Now draw the locus of **all** points that are the **same distance** from A as they are from B.
  c Draw two points C and D, 10 cm apart
Use a straight edge and compasses to draw the locus of all points that are the **same distance** from C as from D.
Leave in your construction lines.

T 5 Use a copy of this.
This is a scale drawing of a field.
The scale is 1 mm = 2 m.
AB, BC, CD and DA are hedgerows.

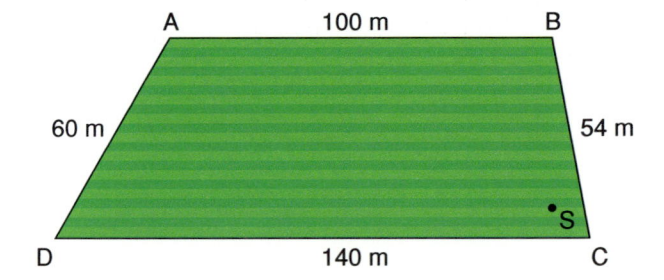

298

Shape, Construction and Loci

Construct the following loci, using compasses and a straight edge.
Leave your construction marks.
  a The locus of a ball kicked by a boy at D so that it is always the same distance from AD and DC.
  b The locus of a dog tethered at S on a 20 m rope.
     Can the dog get to the ball?
  c The locus of a man walking through the field so that he is always the same distance from A and B. Could the ball hit the man?

6 a The locus of all points that are the same distance from (3, 3) as from (⁻1, 3) is a straight line.
  Make a copy of this grid.
  Draw this straight line. Label it with its equation.
  b The locus of all points that are the same distance from the *x*-axis as they are from the *y*-axis is **two** straight lines.
  Draw both straight lines on a set of axes.
  Label these lines with their equations.

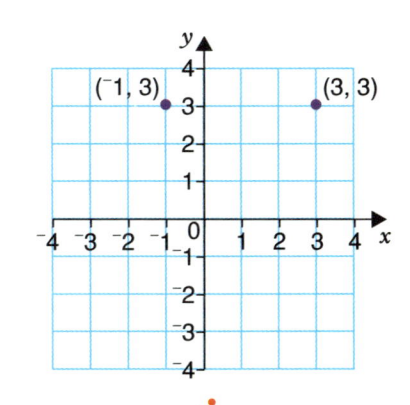

*****7** At a ski field, a box of ski boots is rolled along the floor.
  What path would the point P move along?

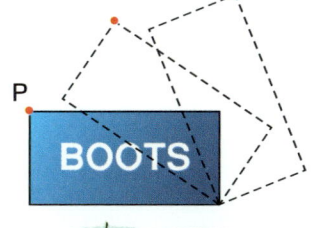

*****8** A spider is hanging on a single web.
  A fly flies so that it is always 10 cm from the spider.
  The spider does not move.
  What is the locus of the fly?

*****9** In a play, a boy is pretending to turn a frog into a handsome prince.
  He has a wand and he moves the tip of his finger so that it is always 7 cm from the wand.
  What is the locus of his finger tip?

Review 1 Draw a possible path for these.
  a a dog tied to a pole in the middle of the garden
  b the top of a ladder sliding down a wall
  c the head of a child on the end of a see-saw

Review 2 Use a copy of this.
Scale 1 cm represents 5 m

This is a triangular piece of land owned by a market gardener.
BA and BC are boundary paths and AC is a fence.

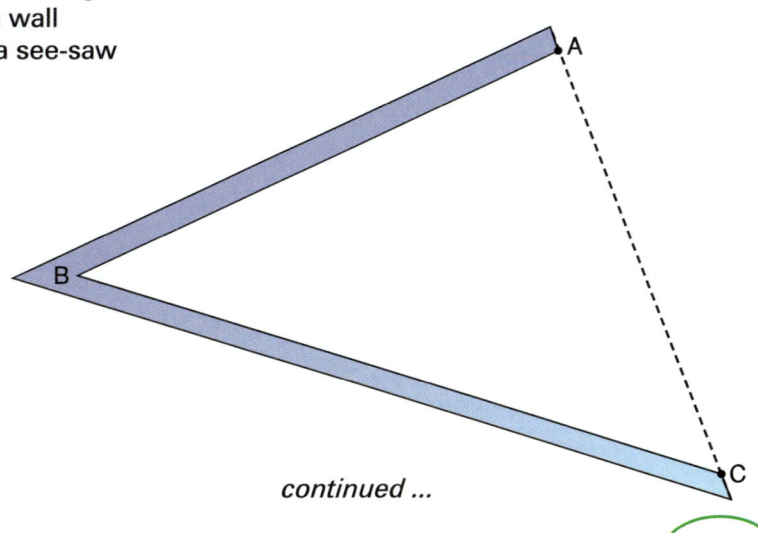

continued ...

Shape, Space and Measures

a   How long is the fence?

Remember to show all your construction lines.

b   The gardener wants to put another path through his property, equidistant from AB and BC. Construct the locus of points equidistant from AB and BC using compasses and a straight edge. This is the new path. Call it BD.

c   He wants to build a shed on this path exactly halfway along the path. Construct the locus of points the same distance from B and D using compasses and a straight edge.
Mark the point where he will build his shed H.

d   He wants to water an area 20 m from C inside his property. Show this area. Will the water spray reach the shed?

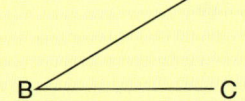

---

* **Worked Example**

Sketch the region in which a point P would be if it is

a   always less than 15 mm from the point A
b   always closer to the line BD than the line BC, and within the acute angle DBC.

Answer

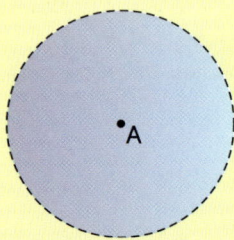

a   Locus is shown shaded.
It is the interior of the circle, centre A, radius 15 mm.

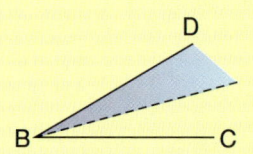

b   Locus is shown shaded.
It is the area between the line BD and the bisector of the angle DBC.

Note A boundary which is not included in the region is dotted.

Exercise 6

1   Draw two points A and B in positions similar to that shown. Sketch the region in which a point P would be if it is always closer to A than to B.

2   Sketch the region in which a point Q would be if it is always less than 2 cm from a fixed point C.

3   Sketch the region in which a point R would be if it is always further from the line AB than from the line CD.

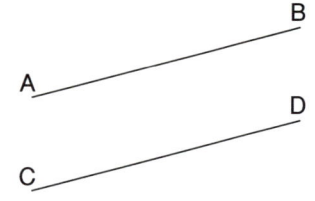

4   Two villages A and B are 20 km apart, B being due south of A.
The fire brigade from A services an area of radius 10 km around A while the brigade from B services an area of radius 12 km around B.
Using the scale 1 cm represents 4 km, shade the area that is serviced by both brigades.

300

5 Use a copy of this.
This diagram shows three towns.
The towns need a mobile phone tower.
It must be nearer to Crocksford than Ramsby and less than 25 km from Raydown.
Construct on the diagram the region where the new tower can be placed.

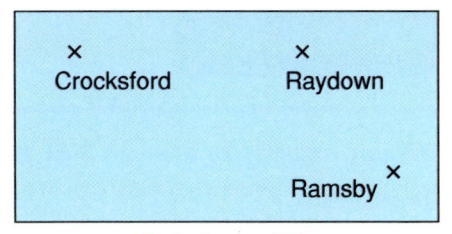

× Crocksford   × Raydown

Ramsby ×

Scale: 1 cm to 10 km

Review

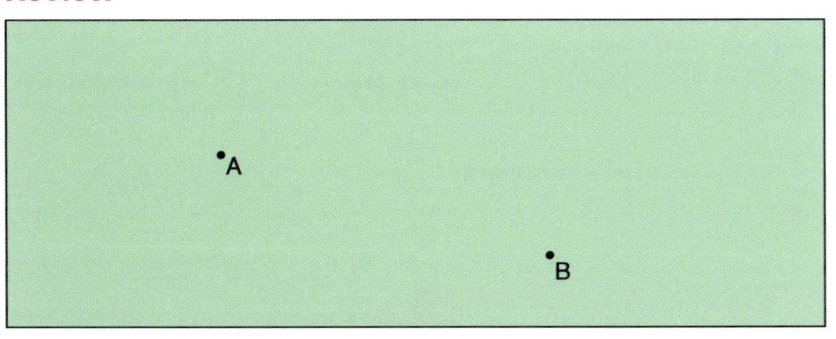

Scale: 1 cm represents 5 km

This diagram represents two towns at A and B. Use a copy of this diagram.
The hospital at A will admit patients who live closer to A than to B. The fire brigades from A and B will travel a maximum of 15 km.
On your diagram, shade the area in which the ambulance from the hospital at A and the fire brigade from either A or B would attend an accident.

Practical

You will need Logo.
Ask your teacher for the **Stars** ICT worksheet.

Investigation

ABCD is a grassed area enclosed by fences. A goat is tethered, as shown, at C.
The goat cannot enter the grassed area.

Investigate the region that the goat can graze, if it is on a 2 m rope.
What if the goat is on a 3 m rope?
What if the goat is on a 5 m, 8 m, 10 m, ... rope?

Shape, Space and Measures

3-D shapes

We can visualise or analyse **3-D shapes** from 2-D drawings, cross-sections or descriptions.

Remember

This is an **isometric drawing of 3 cubes**.

On an isometric drawing
- vertical edges are drawn as vertical lines
- horizontal edges are drawn at 30° to the horizontal.

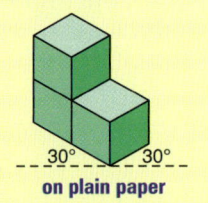

on plain paper

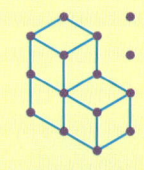

on isometric (triangle dotty) paper

We can represent 3-D shapes using **plans and elevations**.

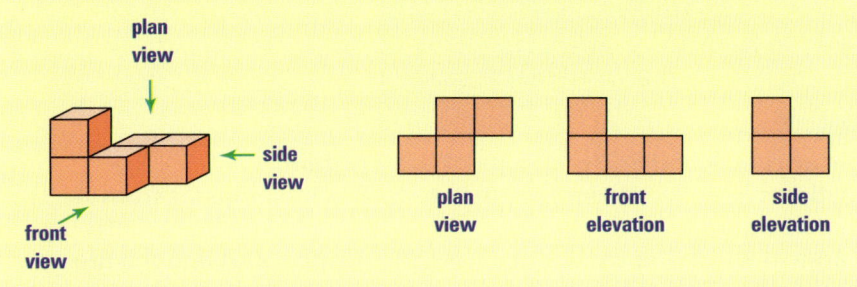

plan view
side view
front view

plan view   front elevation   side elevation

Exercise 7

1. Match each shape with the correct plan, front elevation and side elevation.

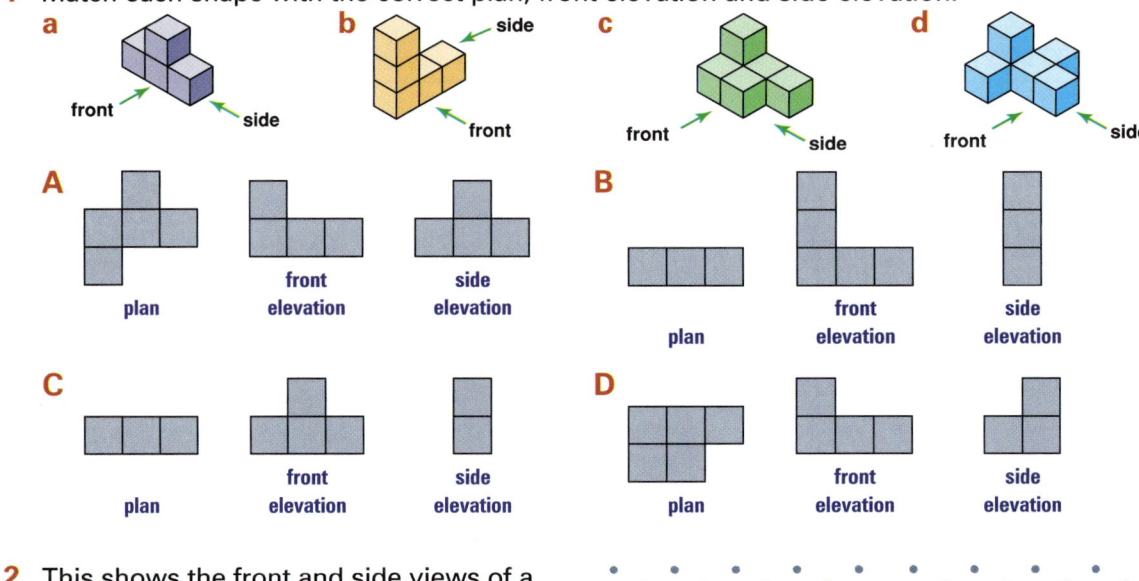

   a front, side
   b side, front
   c front, side
   d front, side

   A plan, front elevation, side elevation
   B plan, front elevation, side elevation
   C plan, front elevation, side elevation
   D plan, front elevation, side elevation

2. This shows the front and side views of a model with six cubes.
   a Draw the plan and front and side elevations of this model.

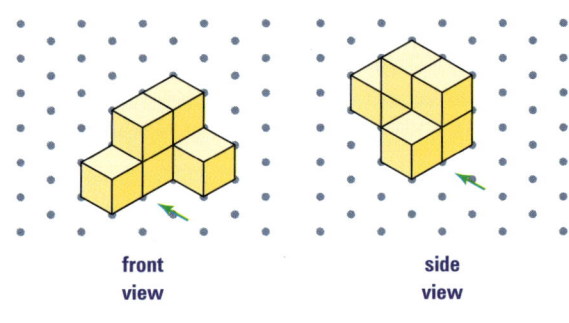

   front view   side view

Shape, Construction and Loci

b One cube is added to the model.
Use a copy of the side view and draw in the new cube.
c Draw the plan and front and side elevations of the new model.

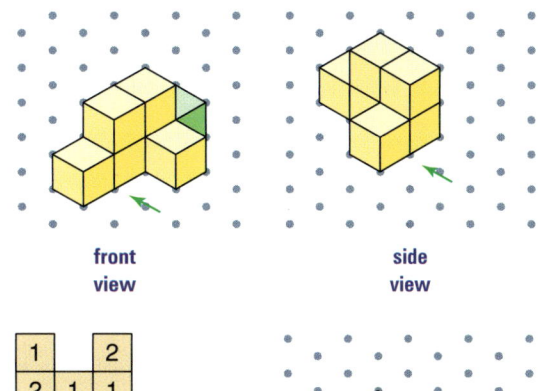

front view

side view

3 This diagram represents the plan view of the model on the right. 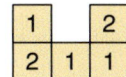 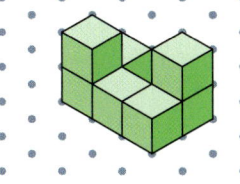
  a How many cubes does the model have?
  b On isometric paper, draw the shapes that these represent.

  i
2	
2	1

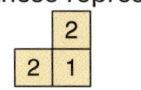

  ii
	1
2	2
1	1

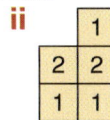

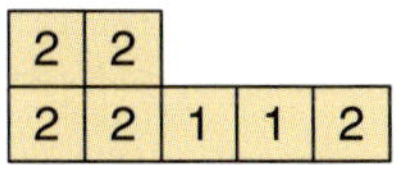

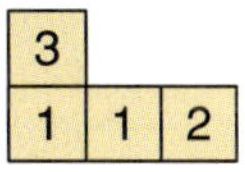

  iii
2	2			
2	2	1	1	2

  iv
3		
1	1	2

4 a Draw two different shapes on isometric paper that have this plan.

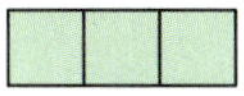

plan

b Draw two different shapes on isometric paper that have this front elevation.

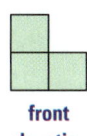

front elevation

5

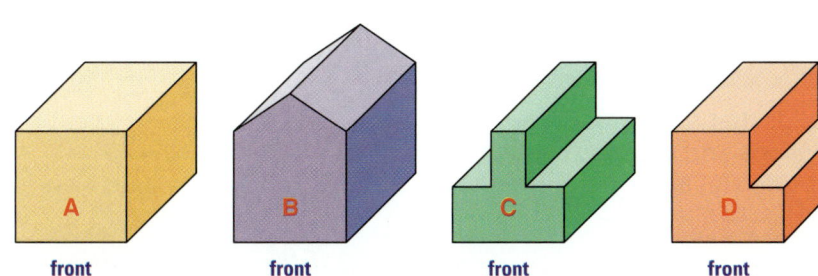

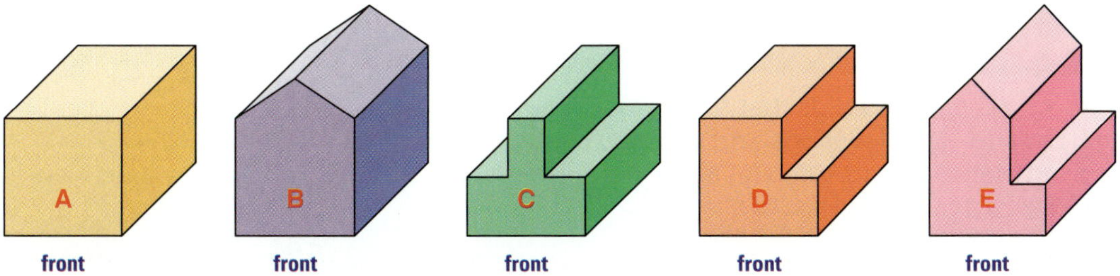

A front B front C front D front E front

  a Which of these shapes have the same plan view?
  b Which have the same front elevation?
  c Which have the same side elevation?

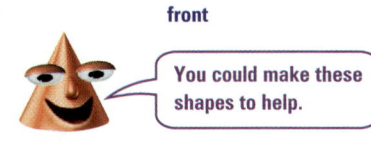

  You could make these shapes to help.

*****6** Sketch the solids that these describe.
  a The front and side elevations are both triangles and the plan view is a square.
  b The front and side elevations are both rectangles and the plan view is a circle.
  c The front elevation is a rectangle, the side elevation is a triangle, and the plan view is a rectangle.
  d The front and side elevations and the plan view are all circles.

*****7** These show the shadows of some solids.
Describe a possible solid for each shadow.
Is there more than one answer?

  a    b    c    d

303

Shape, Space and Measures

*8 Sketch a net for each of these solids.

a front elevation, side elevation, plan view (three squares)

b front elevation (right triangle), side elevation (rectangle), plan view (square)

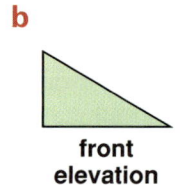

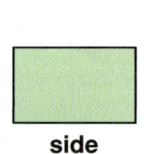

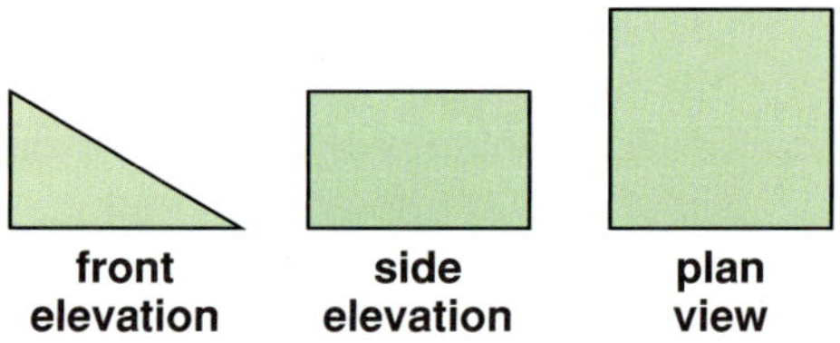

*9 Name some solids that could have each of these as a front elevation.
   a square   **b** rectangle   **c** isosceles triangle

Review 1 This shows the front and side views of a model with six cubes.
a Draw the plan and front and side elevations of this model.

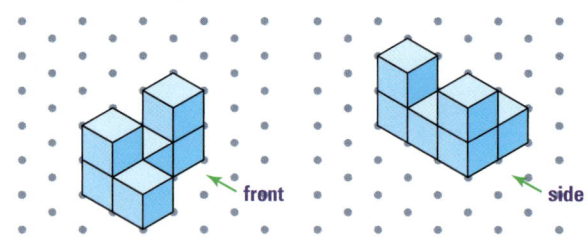

b One cube is added to the model as shown. Use a copy of the side view and draw in the new cube.
c Draw the plan and front and side elevations of the new model.

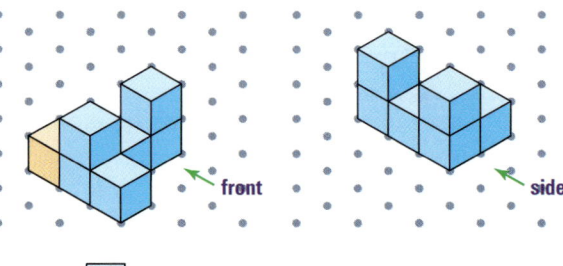

Review 2 Draw two different shapes on isometric paper that have this plan.

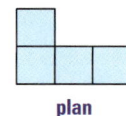

Review 3 Sketch the solids that these describe.
a The front and side elevations and the plan are all triangles.
b The front elevation and side elevation are different sized rectangles and the plan view is oval.

Review 4 Sketch a net for this solid.

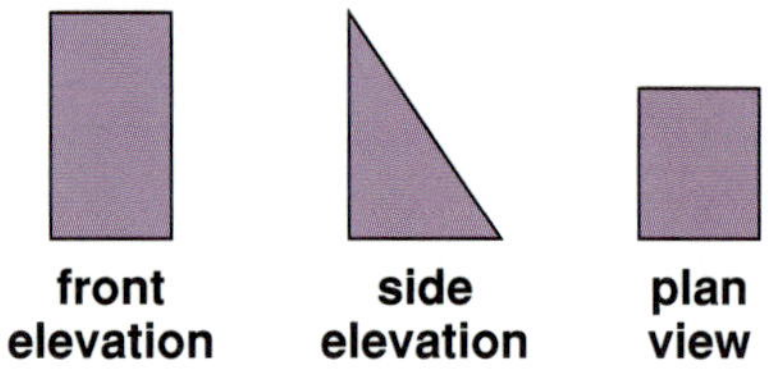

front elevation (rectangle), side elevation (right triangle), plan view (rectangle)

Practical

Work in pairs.
1 Use cubes to build a 3-D shape.
   Draw the front elevation, side elevation and plan view.
   Ask your partner to build the shape from your drawings.

Shape, Construction and Loci

2 Build and then sketch the shapes with plans and elevations as shown below.

a plan view, front elevation, side elevation

b plan view, front elevation, side elevation

c plan view, front elevation, side elevation

d plan view, front elevation, side elevation

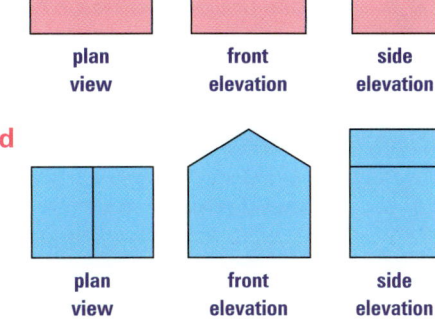

3 Choose a building in the school grounds or a piece of equipment in the gymnasium or workshop.
Draw the plan view, front elevation and side elevation.
See if another pupil can identify the building or object from your drawing.

Cross-sections

When we slice a shape, the face that is made is called a **cross-section**.

Example   If we slice a cuboid as shown the cross-section is a rectangle.

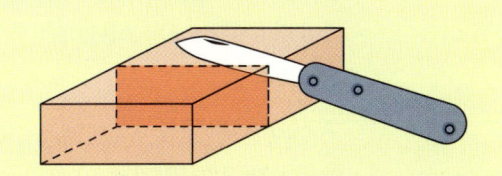

Exercise 8

1 Tonya sliced a square-based pyramid horizontally near the top.
   a What shape will the cross-section be?
   b What if Tonya had sliced closer to the base?
   c What if Tonya had sliced closer to the top?

2 Brittany sliced a cone horizontally.
   a What shape will the cross-section be?
   b What if Brittany had sliced closer to the base?
   c What if Brittany had sliced closer to the top?

3 a If we slice a cube vertically as shown, what shape is the cross-section?
   b Is it possible to slice a cube to get
      i a rectangle   **ii** a triangle   **iii** a pentagon   **iv** a hexagon?
      If so, explain how.

Review
   a If we slice a ball vertically, what shape will the cross-section be?
   b Is it possible to get any other shaped cross-section by slicing a ball?

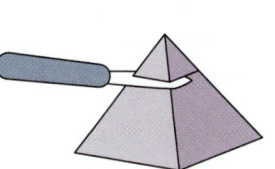

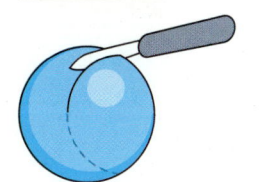

Shape, Space and Measures

Summary of key points

A We use the **properties of 2-D shapes** to solve problems.

Example The shaded angle is 135° because a kite is symmetrical.

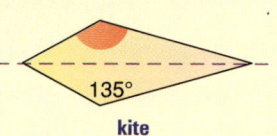

kite

B A **tessellation** is made by reflecting, rotating or translating a shape.

Example

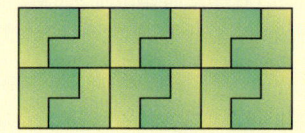

This tessellation could be made by rotating and translating the shape.

C The **parts of a circle** are shown on this diagram. The definitions of circumference, arc, radius and sector are given on page 29.

A **tangent** is a line which just touches a circle at a point, P.

When a line intersects the circle at two points, A and B, the line segment AB is a **chord**.

A chord divides a circle into two **segments**.

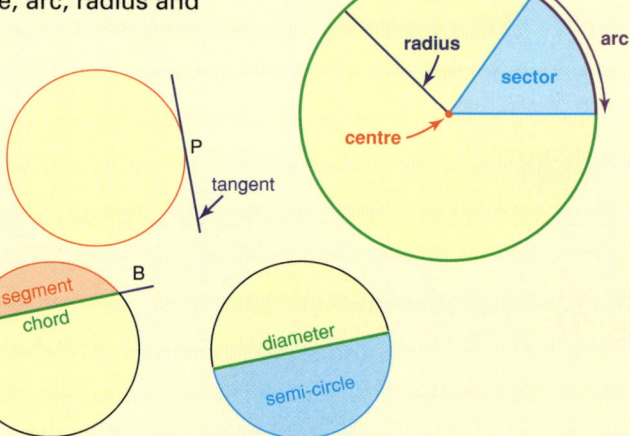

When a chord passes through the centre of a circle it is called a **diameter**. It divides the circle into two **semicircles**.

D We **construct triangles** in different ways depending on the information we are given.

The method for constructing a right-angled triangle given the right angle, the length of the longest side and one other side (RHS) is given on page 294.

E A **locus** is a set of points that satisfy a rule or a set of rules.

Examples The locus of the head of a boy jumping from a tree might look like this.

The locus of a robot moving so that it is always the same distance from a fixed point is a circle.

We can **construct a locus**.

Example Your locus if you walked so that you were always the same distance from two trees would be the perpendicular bisector of the line joining the two trees.

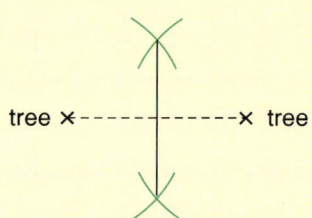

Shape, Construction and Loci

F We can visualise or analyse 3-D shapes from 2-D drawings, such as isometric drawings, or from cross-sections or descriptions.

We can represent 3-D shapes using **plans and elevations**.

The view from the top of a shape is called the **plan view**.

The view from the front is called the **front elevation**.

The view from the side is called the **side elevation**.

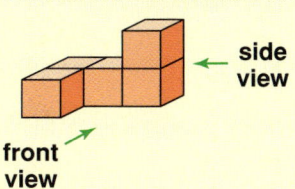

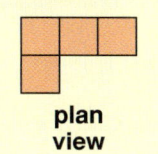

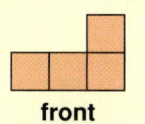

Example

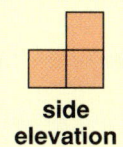

G When we slice a shape, the face that is made is called a **cross-section**.

Example If we slice a square-based pyramid parallel to the base as shown, the cross-section is a square.

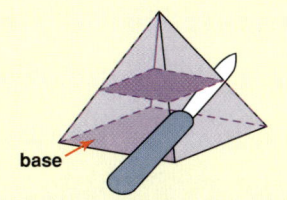

Test yourself

1. Write true or false for each of these.
   a In a right-angled triangle, the shortest side is opposite the right-angle.
   b An arrowhead can be split into two congruent triangles.
   c A rhombus can be split into two isosceles triangles.
   d A rectangle can be split into two equilateral triangles.

2. Use the properties of the shapes to find the length in red and the angles marked with letters. Show your reasoning clearly.

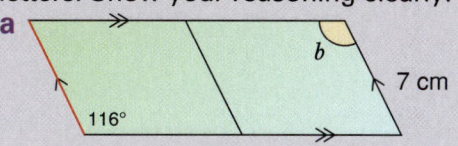

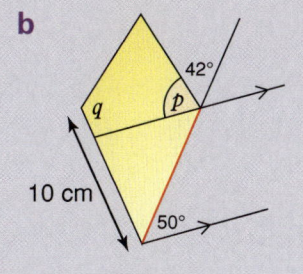

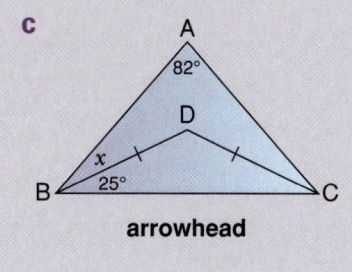

   a (parallelogram, 116°, b, 7 cm)

   b kite (42°, p, q, 10 cm, 50°)

   c arrowhead (A = 82°, x at D, 25°, B, C)

3. a Imagine a special quadrilateral with two lines of symmetry. What could it be?
   b Suppose it also has rotation symmetry of order 2. What could it be now?

307

Shape, Space and Measures

4 a Can a square be cut into two equilateral triangles?
 b What about into two scalene triangles?
 c Can a parallelogram be cut into two equilateral triangles?
 d What about into two scalene triangles?

5 a PQRS is a rhombus.
  $\angle P = 54°$
  Find the size of **i** $\angle PSQ$ **ii** $\angle RQP$.

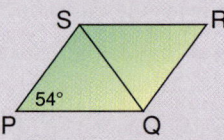

 b ABE is a straight line and ABCD is a parallelogram.
  If $\angle A = 75°$ and $\angle BCE = 30°$ show that $\triangle BCE$ is isosceles.

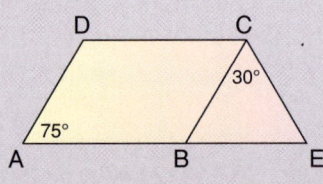

6 Use isometric (triangle dotty) paper to tessellate this shape.
  Describe how you did this using the words reflection, rotation or translation.

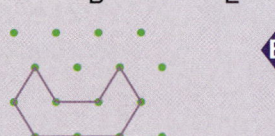

7 Draw a regular pentagon by dividing the circumference of a circle into five equal arcs.
  Explain why a regular pentagon can be constructed in this way.

8 Draw a circle.
  Label these parts on your circle.
     radius   sector   arc   circumference

9 A line and a circle move towards each other.
  Match the description below with a diagram from the box. The line
  a makes a tangent to the circle
  b intersects the circle at two points, making a chord that is not a diameter
  c passes through the centre of the circle, making a diameter
  d divides the area enclosed by the circle into two regions called segments
  e divides the area enclosed by the circle into two regions called semicircles.

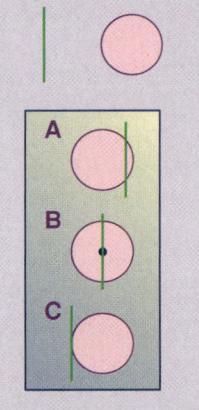

10 Use compasses to construct a right-angled triangle with sides 6 cm, 8 cm and 10 cm.

11 A tree needed bracing.
  A cable was attached to the ground 4 m away from the base of the tree.
  Sam then attached the cable to the trunk 7 m up the tree.
  Make a scale drawing and measure carefully to find
  a the angle, x, the cable makes with the ground
  b the length of cable, l.

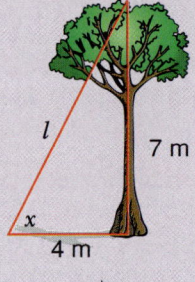

Not drawn to scale

308

Shape, Construction and Loci

12 Is it possible to construct triangle LMN such that
   a LM = 7 cm, ∠L = 50°, ∠M = 45°   **b** LM = 8 cm, MN = 3 cm, LN = 3·5 cm?
   If it isn't, explain why not.

13 Sketch the locus of these.
   a the head of a child diving into a swimming pool
   b the nose of an aeroplane when taxiing then taking off

14 A ski-racer skis to and then past the finish line so that he is the same distance from two poles marking the finish.
   Construct the locus of the skier. Show all your construction lines.

15 Match the shapes with the sketches of their plans and elevations.

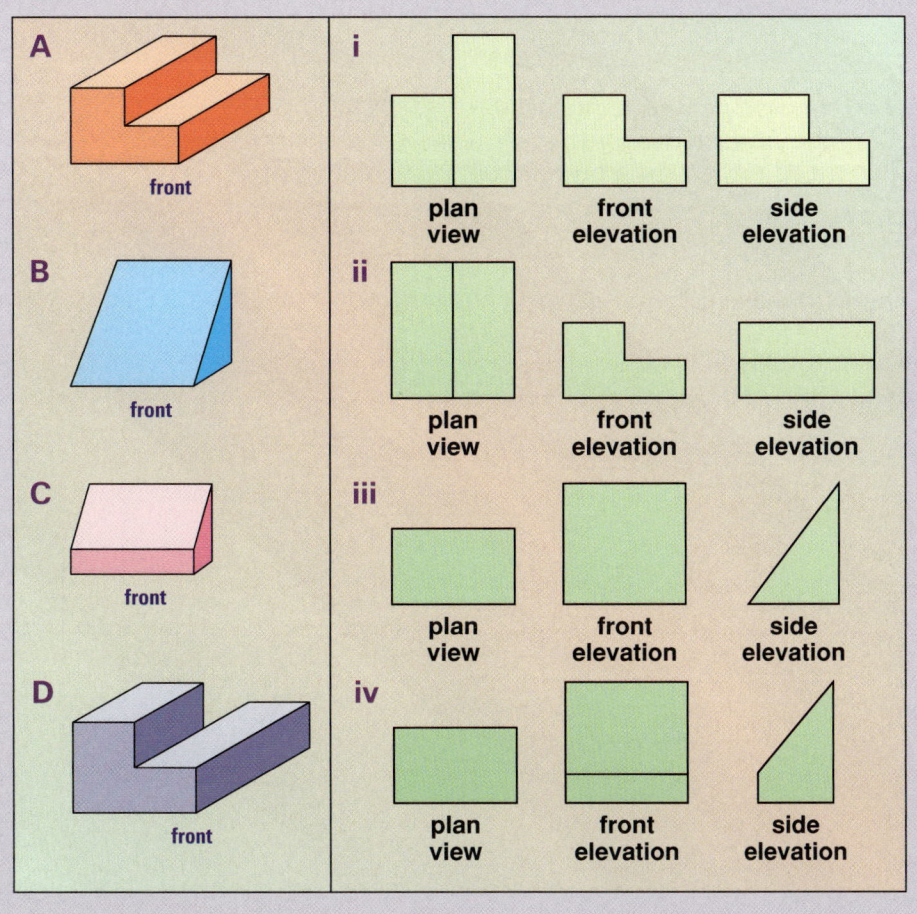

16 This shows a model with nine cubes, four red and five blue.
   a These drawings show the four side views. Which view does each drawing show?

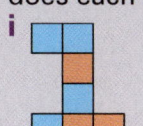

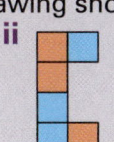

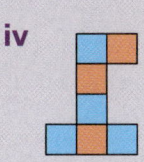

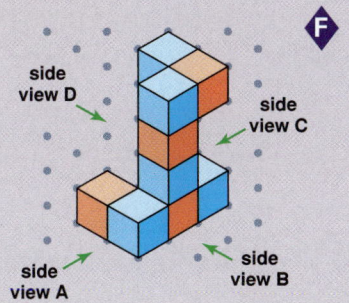

309

Shape, Space and Measures

b Use a copy of this.
Complete the top view of the model by shading the squares which are blue and red.

c Imagine you turn the model upside down.
Complete the top view of the model by shading the squares which are red.

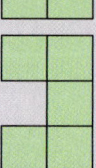

17 On isometric paper, draw the shape that this represents. Draw it from the view given by the red arrow.

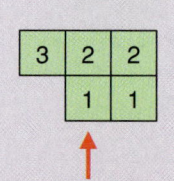

3	2	2
	1	1

18 Marlon sliced a tetrahedron parallel to the base.
   a What shape will the cross-section be?
   b What if Marlon sliced the tetrahedron vertically through the top?

***19** This shape is made from five cubes. Two pairs are joined only by a common edge.
Use isometric paper to draw a different shape made from five cubes in which two pairs are joined by just a common edge.

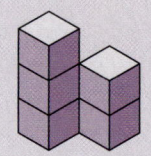

12 Transformations and Scale Drawings

You need to know

✓ coordinates — page 258
✓ symmetry — page 258
✓ congruence — page 259
✓ transformations — page 259

Key vocabulary

centre of enlargement, enlarge, enlargement, map, plan, plane symmetry, plane of symmetry, similar, scale, scale factor, scale drawing

▶▶ Room for improvement

This is a picture of Cassandra's room.

This is the floorplan.

She decides to change her bedroom around.
She
　rotates the bookcase 90°
　translates the desk left
　rotates the bed and table 180°
　and then translates them right
　to the wall
　rotates the chair 180° and then
　translates it left to the wall.

Draw a possible floorplan for Cassandra's new arrangement.

Shape, Space and Measures

Congruence and transformations

Remember

Congruent shapes are exactly the same size and shape.
In congruent shapes
- sides in corresponding positions are equal
- angles in corresponding positions are equal.

One congruent shape is mapped onto another by a translation, reflection or rotation or some combination of these.

Example In the example below, to map ABC onto PQR, the triangle ABC is reflected and then rotated.

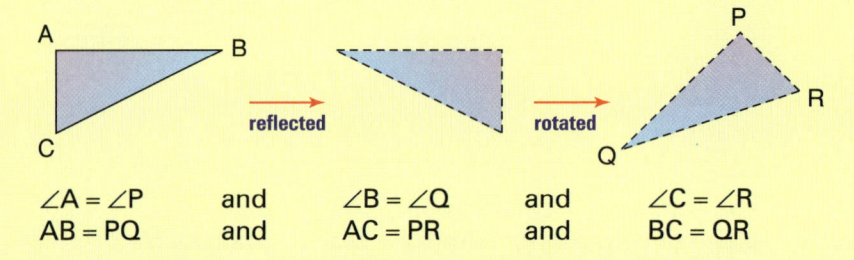

∠A = ∠P and ∠B = ∠Q and ∠C = ∠R
AB = PQ and AC = PR and BC = QR

Practical

You will need some squared paper.

Copy this shape onto grid paper with axes labelled from ⁻12 to 12.

Reflect the shape in the *x*-axis.
Is the image congruent?

Rotate the shape 180° about (0, 0).
Is the image congruent?

Translate the shape 6 units left and 4 units down.
Is the image congruent?

Try some other reflections, rotations and translations.
Are the images always congruent?

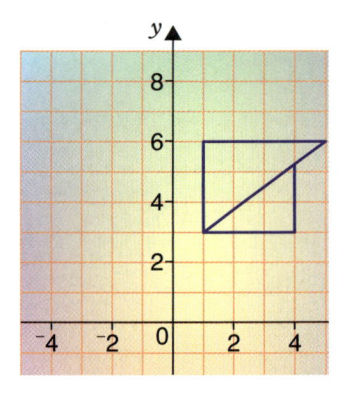

When a shape is **reflected, rotated or translated**, the **image** is always **congruent to the original shape**.

Transformations and Scale Drawings

Exercise 1

1 a Name the triangles which are congruent to triangle ABC.
  b For each of the congruent triangles name the side equal to
    i AB   **ii** BC.
  c For each of the congruent triangles name the angle equal to
    i A   **ii** C   **iii** B.
  d The transformation that maps ABC onto GHI is a
    A rotation of 90°   **B** rotation of 180°
    C reflection   **D** translation.

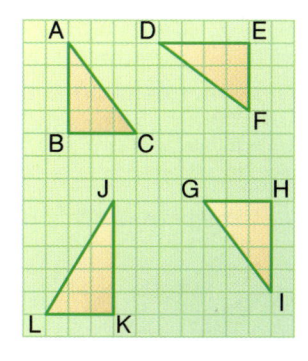

[SATs Paper 2 Level 5]

2 Look at the diagram.
Triangle ABD is the reflection of triangle ABC in the line AB.

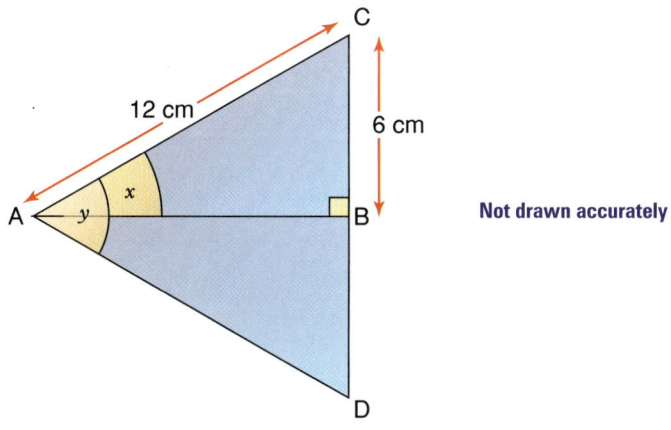

Not drawn accurately

What goes in the gaps to explain how to find angle x?

The length of AC is __12__ cm.

a The length of AD is ____ cm.

b The length of CD is ____ cm.

c ACD is an equilateral triangle because _____

d so angle y is ____° because _____

e so angle x is ____° because _____

3 Ronan drew this shape.
Copy it onto squared paper.
  a Write down the coordinates of A after
    i translation 2 units to the right and 1 unit down
    ii rotation 180° about (0, 0)
    iii reflection in the x-axis.
  b Are all of the image shapes found in part **a** congruent to the shape Ronan drew?
  c When we translate a shape, is the image *always* congruent to the original shape?
  d Answer part **c** again if 'translate' is replaced with 'rotate'.
  e Answer part **c** again if 'translate' is replaced with 'reflect'.

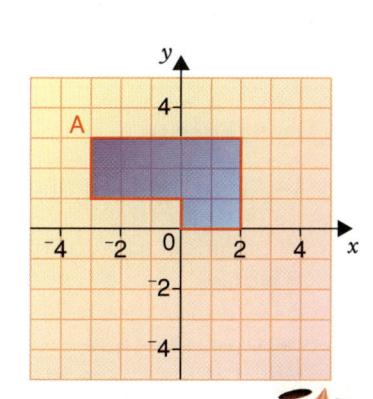

Start with the original shape each time

313

Shape, Space and Measures

4 The points (⁻4, ⁻2), (⁻1, 2) and (2, ⁻1) are the vertices of a triangle.
Plot these points on a grid.
  a Draw the image and write down the coordinates of the vertices after
     i translation 2 units to the left and 4 units down
     ii rotation 90° about the origin
     iii reflection in the line $y = ^-1$.
  b Which of the shapes that you drew in **i**, **ii** and **iii** are congruent to the shape you started with?

Hint: the line $y = ^-1$ is a horizontal line.

[T] *5 Ramsay made this pattern by reflecting and rotating this shape.

Use a copy of this.
Identify all the equal angles and equal lengths.

Review 1 △OAB is rotated through 180° to △OXY.
  a What is the length of XY?
  b What is the size of ∠OYX?
  c What is the size of ∠OXY?
  d △AOB is isosceles. Explain why.

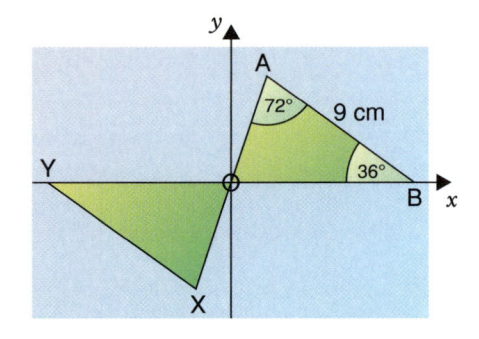

[T] **Review 2** Use three copies of this diagram.
  a Draw the image and write down the coordinates of the vertices after
     i reflection in the y-axis
     ii translation 3 units right and 4 units down
     iii rotation of 90° about the origin.
  b Are all the image shapes congruent to the original shape?

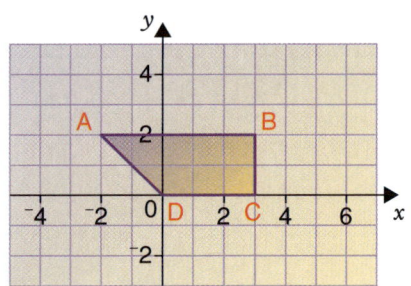

Combinations of transformations

Discussion

- Sajid reflected this shape in the *x*-axis and then he reflected the image in the *y*-axis.
  What single transformation would give the same result?
  Discuss.
- If Sajid did these reflections in the opposite order, what would happen? **Discuss**.
- **What if** the shape is reflected in the line $x = ^-1$, then the image is reflected in the line $y = 1$? **Discuss**.
  What if these reflections are done in the opposite order? **Discuss**.

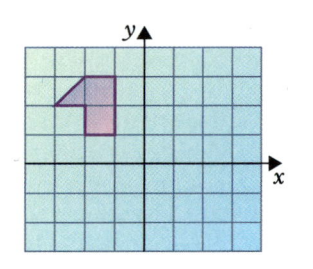

314

Transformations and Scale Drawings

Exercise 2

1 Use a copy of this diagram.
  a Rotate △ABC 90° about C.
  b Reflect △ABC in the mirror line m.
  c What name is given to the quadrilateral formed by the three triangles?

Remember to rotate anticlockwise.

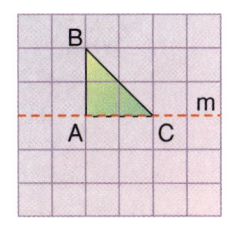

2 Use a copy of this.
  a Reflect ABC in the *x*-axis to give A'B'C'.
  b Reflect A'B'C' in the *y*-axis to give A"B"C".
  c Identify the equal lengths and equal angles in the original and A"B"C".

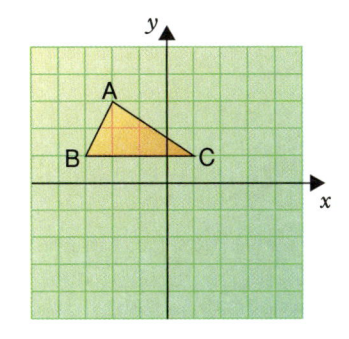

3 *Imagine* these transformations or combinations of transformations. What shape will the **combined** object and image(s) form?
  a A square is reflected along one of its sides.
  b A right-angled triangle is reflected along its longest side.
  *****c** A square is rotated 90° about any one of its corners.
  *****d** A square is rotated twice by 90° about any one of its corners.
  *****e** A square is rotated three times by 90° about any one of its corners.
  *****f** An isosceles triangle is rotated by 180° about the mid-point of its base.
  g A scalene triangle is rotated by 180° about the mid-point of one of its sides.

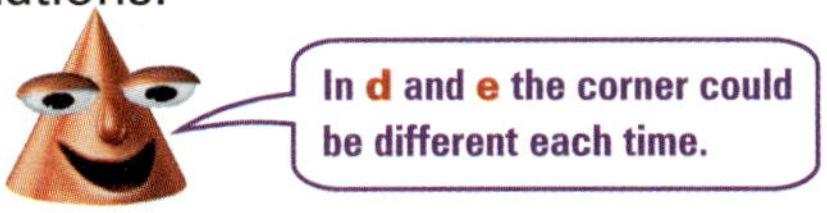

*In **d** and **e** the corner could be different each time.*

4 Jack drew the same triangle in two different positions. Which combination maps A to B?
  A translation and reflection
  B rotation and translation
  C rotation and reflection

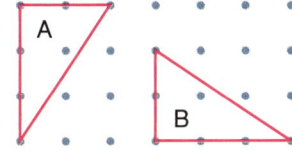

5 P maps onto Q under a combination of
  A translation and enlargement
  B translation and rotation
  C reflection and rotation.

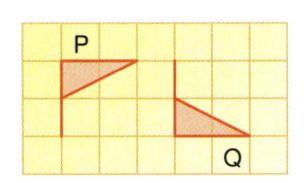

6 Use a copy of this.
  a Reflect ABC in the *x*-axis. Label the image A'B'C'.
  b Rotate A'B'C' about (0, 0), through 270°. Label the image A"B"C".
  c Which single transformation maps △ABC onto △A"B"C"?
    A reflection   **B** rotation
  ***C** translation   **D** enlargement
  d Describe the single transformation fully.

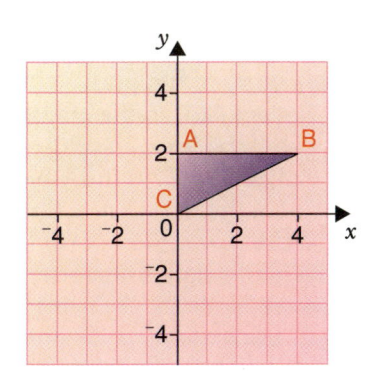

315

Shape, Space and Measures

7 A is reflected in the dashed line, $y = x$, to give A'.
A' is then rotated through 90° about (0, 2) to give A".
   a What combination of reflection and translation maps A onto A"?
  ***b** What other combinations of transformations map A onto A"?

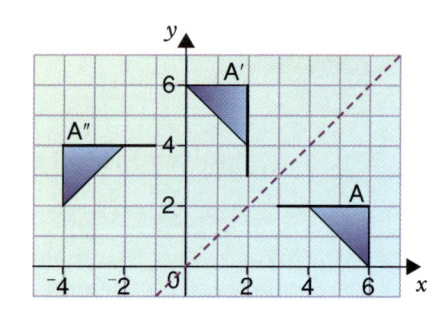

***8** Wasim wrote down two transformations.
  A: reflection in the y-axis
  B: rotation 270° about the origin

Wasim transformed a shape first by A then by B.
Percy transformed the same shape first by B then by A.
Does the order in which these transformations, A and B, are carried out matter?

***9** Some congruent shapes are shown on this grid.
Describe a combination of two transformations that will map A onto each of the other shapes.

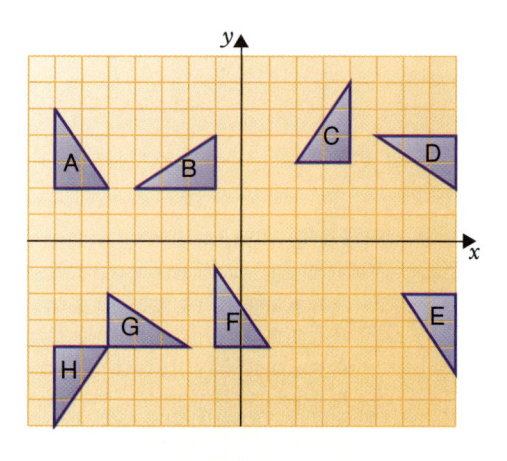

Review 1 ABC is a right-angled triangle.
a ABC is reflected in the line BC.
What shape do the object and image together make?
b This new shape is reflected in the line AC extended.
What shape do all the shapes combined make?

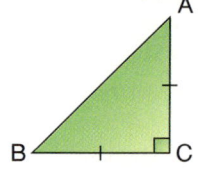

Review 2 PQRS → P'Q'R'S' under a combination of
A translation and reflection
B translation and rotation
C rotation and reflection.

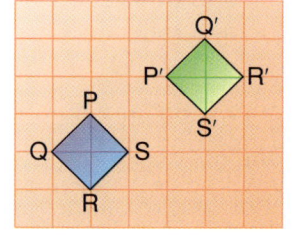

Review 3 Triangle ABC is shown on the grid.
Use a copy of the grid.
a Reflect ABC in the x-axis.
Label the image A'B'C'.
b Reflect A'B'C' in the y-axis.
Label the image A"B"C".
c Write down the coordinates of A", B" and C".
d Which single transformation maps △ABC onto △A"B"C"?
  A reflection   **B** rotation
  C translation **D** enlargement

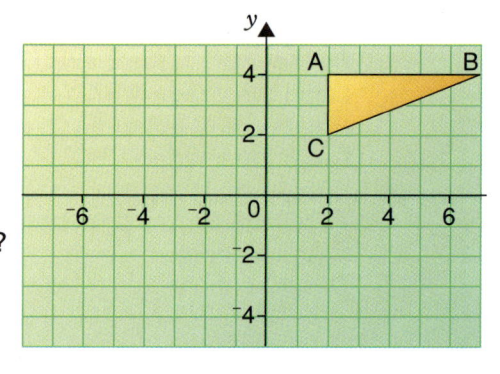

Transformations and Scale Drawings

Practical

You will need a dynamic geometry software package.

Ask your teacher for the **Combinations of Transformations** ICT Worksheet.

Symmetry

Remember
A shape has **line symmetry** or **reflection symmetry** if one or more lines can be found that divide the shape into two congruent shapes where one is the reflection of the other.

A shape has **rotation symmetry** if it fits onto itself **more than once** during a complete turn.

The **order of rotation symmetry** is the number of times a shape looks identical in a complete turn.

See page 258 for more about reflection and rotation symmetry.

Discussion

- Is this shape symmetrical? How do you know? **Discuss**.

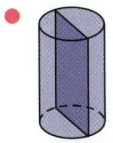

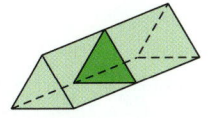

- What is the shaded part called? **Discuss**.

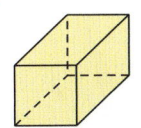

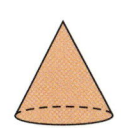

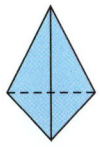

- How can we tell if these shapes are symmetrical? **Discuss** how to draw a shaded part that cuts the shape in half.

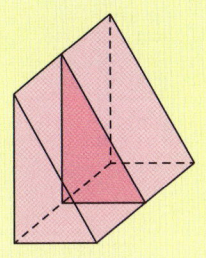

This solid shape is symmetrical.
The darker pink shape is called a **plane of symmetry**.
The plane of symmetry divides a solid shape into two equal parts.

We say this shape has **plane symmetry**.

317

Shape, Space and Measures

Exercise 3

1 Describe the symmetry of these shapes.
   a
   b

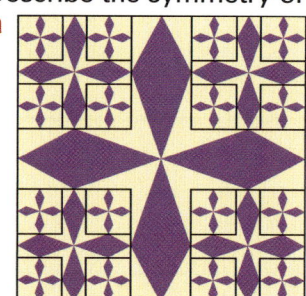

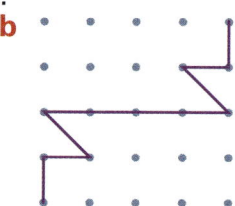

2

Paige: I know that the opposite angles of a parallelogram are equal because it has rotation symmetry of order 2.

Ben: I know that the diagonals of a rhombus bisect each other, because the diagonals are lines of symmetry.

Copy and finish these sentences to explain why these are true.
   a   I know that the base angles of an isosceles triangle are equal because it has ___ line _____.
   b   I know that the diagonals of a parallelogram bisect each other because it has _____ symmetry of _____.
   c   I know that opposite sides of a parallelogram are equal because it has _____.

3 This pattern has rotation symmetry of order 6.   [SATs Paper 2 Level 6]
   a   What is the size of angle w?
       Show your working.
   b   Each quadrilateral in the pattern is made from two congruent isosceles triangles. What is the size of angle y?
       Show your working.

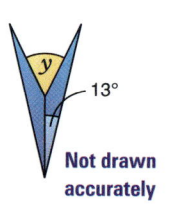

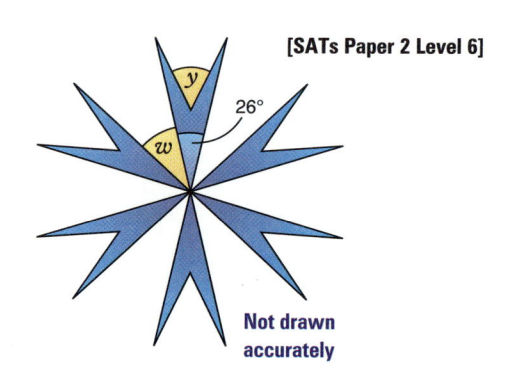

   13°
   26°
   Not drawn accurately
   Not drawn accurately

4 Which of these 3-D shapes are symmetrical?
   a   b   c   d   e

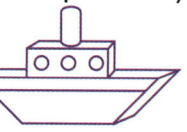

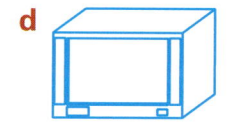

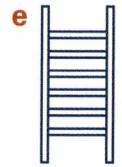

5 Which shapes have
   a   exactly one plane of symmetry
   b   more than two planes of symmetry?

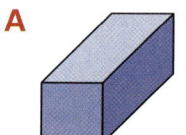

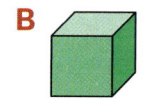

   A   B   C

318

Transformations and Scale Drawings

6 Use some copies of the shapes in question **5**.
Draw all the planes of symmetry for each shape.
Use a separate copy for each plane of symmetry.

> You could draw the shapes on isometric dot paper first and then draw the planes of symmetry.

7 a Imagine a regular tetrahedron.
Describe its planes of symmetry.
b Imagine a regular octahedron.
Describe its planes of symmetry.

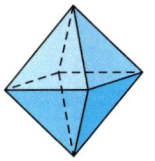

Review 1 This shape is a regular pentagon.
a What is the size of angle x?
b What is the size of angle y?
Use a copy of this shape.
c Draw on all the axes of symmetry.
d What is the order of rotational symmetry?

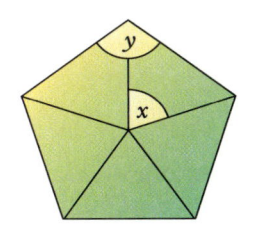

Review 2 This pattern has rotational symmetry of order 8. Each quadrilateral is made from two isosceles triangles.
a What is the size of angle x?
b What is the size of angle y?
Show your working.

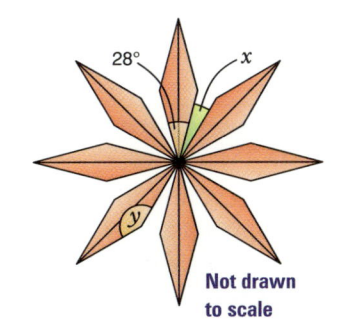

Not drawn to scale

Review 3 Is this shape symmetrical if you ignore the label?

Review 4 Use some copies of this shape.
Draw all the planes of symmetry.
Use a separate copy for each plane of symmetry.

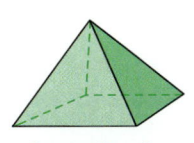

Square-based pyramid

★ Practical

You will need four multilink cubes or centicubes and isometric paper.

Make all the shapes possible with the four cubes.
Draw each on isometric paper.

For each, identify any planes of symmetry.

Investigate the ones which are not symmetrical to see if they will fit together to make a symmetrical pair.

Shape, Space and Measures

Enlargement

Remember
To draw an enlargement you need to know the **scale factor** and the **centre of enlargement**.

When the scale factor is **2**, each distance from O to the image is **2** times the distance from O to the object.

So OA′ = 2 × OA and OB′ = 2 × OB and OC′ = 2 × OC.

Note: The centre of enlargement does not change its position after an enlargement.

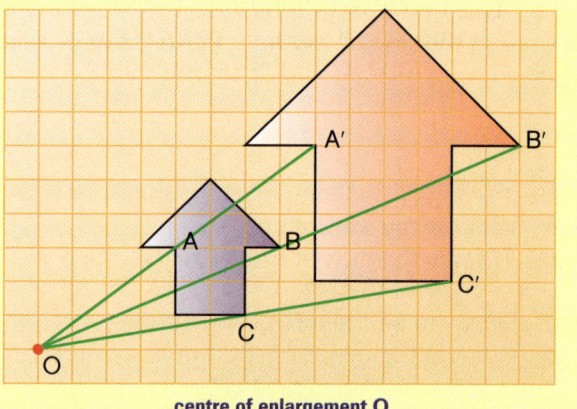

centre of enlargement O
scale factor 2

Discussion

Sita drew this enlargement.
Find the lengths of AB and A′B′.
What is the ratio A′B′ : AB?
What is the ratio C′D′ : CD?
What is the scale factor for this enlargement?
What do you notice? **Discuss**.

Are the shaded angles the same size? **Discuss**.

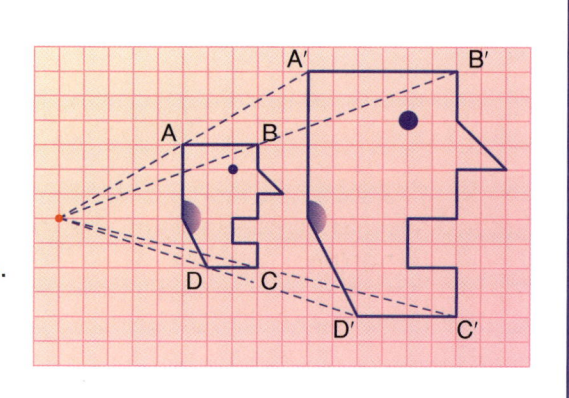

Link to ratio.

For **any enlargement the ratio of all pairs of corresponding line segments is equal to the scale factor**.

Example   ABC has been enlarged to A′B′C′ by scale factor **3**.
So $\frac{A'C'}{AC} = 3$, $\frac{C'B'}{CB} = 3$, $\frac{A'B'}{AB} = 3$.

When the ratio of all pairs of corresponding sides of two shapes is the same, we say the shapes are **similar**.
A′B′C′ and ABC are similar shapes.

Worked Example
The purple shape has been enlarged to the red shape by a scale factor of 2.
Find the length of x.

Answer
$\frac{\text{length of red yacht}}{\text{length of purple yacht}} = 2$

$\frac{x}{4} = 2$

$x =$ **8 cm**

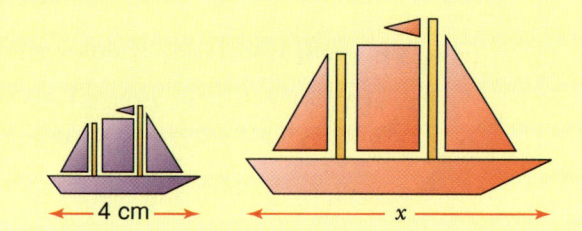

320

Transformations and Scale Drawings

Exercise 4

1 Use a copy of this.
This grid shows a house.
On the grid, draw an enlargement of scale factor 2 of the house.
Use point C as the centre of enlargement.

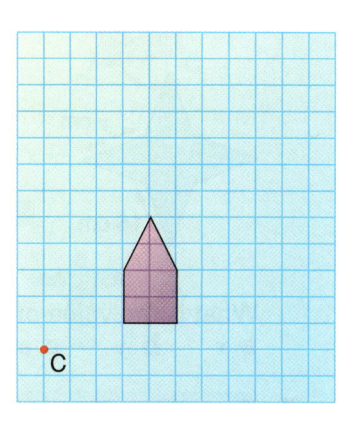

2 Jade drew this enlargement.
What is the scale factor of the enlargement?

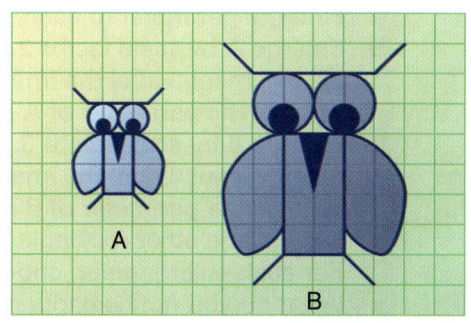

3 a When a shape is enlarged, which of these is **always** the same on the original and the image?
   lengths   **angles**
b Jacinta drew this enlargement of triangle ABC.
What is the size of angle D?

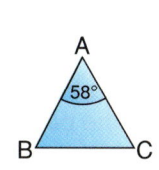

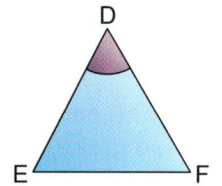

4 In each of these diagrams the smaller shape has been enlarged to the larger shape.
Use the dimensions given to find the scale factor of each of these enlargements.

a   1, 3
b   2, 4
c   4, 16
d   3, 5
e   5, 8   Not to scale

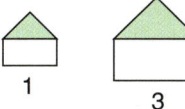

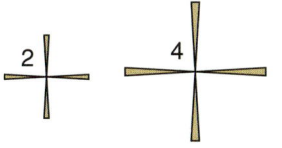

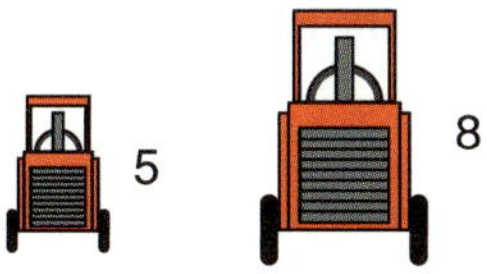

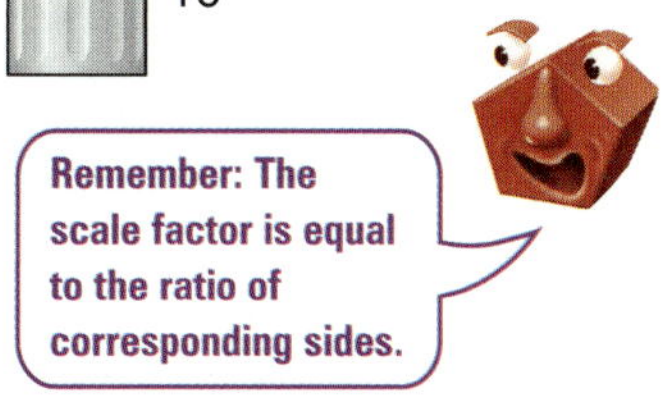

Remember: The scale factor is equal to the ratio of corresponding sides.

5 The red shape has been enlarged to the green shape.
The scale factor for each enlargement is given in green.
Find the length of x.

a x, 4 scale factor 2
b 2·1, x scale factor 3
c x, 3·4 scale factor 4

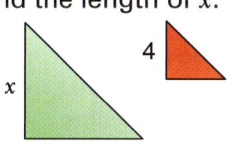

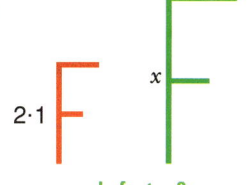

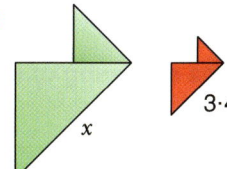

See the worked example for help.

321

Shape, Space and Measures

B We can transform shapes using a **combination of transformations**.

Example A has been reflected in the y-axis and then translated 3 units down.

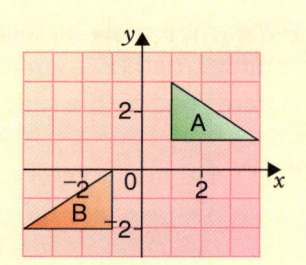

C **Symmetry**

Some 3-D shapes are **symmetrical**.

Example The shaded shape is called a plane of **symmetry**. It divides the shape into two congruent pieces such that one is a reflection of the other.

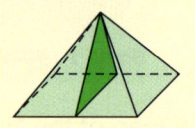

D When a shape is **enlarged, the ratio of any two corresponding line segments is equal to the scale factor**.

Example

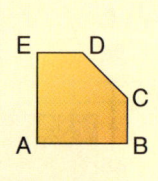

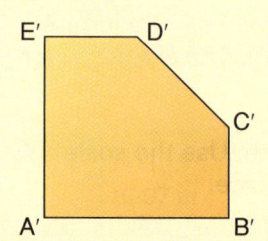

ABCDE has been enlarged to A'B'C'D'E' by scale factor 2.

So $\frac{A'B'}{AB} = 2$ $\frac{B'C'}{BC} = 2$ $\frac{C'D'}{CD} = 2$ $\frac{D'E'}{DE} = 2$ $\frac{E'A'}{EA} = 2$

When a shape is enlarged we say the shapes are **similar**.
ABCDE and A'B'C'D'E' are similar shapes.

When a shape is enlarged, angles stay the same but lengths do not.

If a shape with perimeter, n, is enlarged by scale factor **3**, the perimeter of the image is **3** × n.

E A **scale drawing** represents something in real life. The real-life object is an **enlargement** of the object in the scale drawing.

Example This is a scale drawing of a car.
Each millimetre on the drawing represents 6 cm in real life.
So 1 mm on the drawing represents 60 mm in real life.
The car is 51 mm on the drawing.
In real life it is 51 × 60 = 3060 mm
= 306 cm
= 3·06 m.

Scale: 1 mm represents 6 cm

Transformations and Scale Drawings

Test yourself

1 a When a shape is translated, which of these stay the same?
        lengths   angles
    b What about when a shape is rotated?
    c What about when a shape is reflected?
    d When a shape is translated, rotated or reflected is the image always congruent to the original shape?
    e Will the image remain congruent if a shape is transformed by a combination of translation, rotation and reflection?

2 ABCD and EFGH are congruent.
    a What is the size of angle E?
    b What is the length of HG?
    c Which of these would map ABCD onto EFGH?
        A translation   **B** reflection
        C rotation and translation

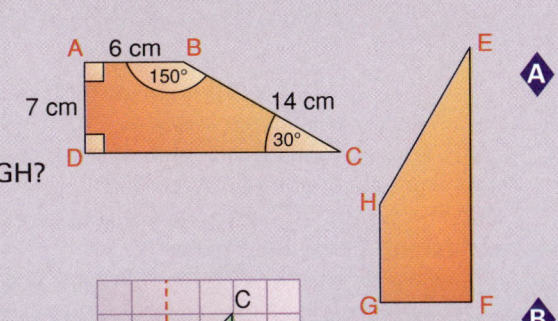

3 Use a copy of this diagram.
    a Rotate △ABC 90° about A to A'B'C'.
    b Reflect △ABC in the mirror line m.
    c Reflect △A'B'C' in the mirror line m.
    d What shape is formed by the four triangles?

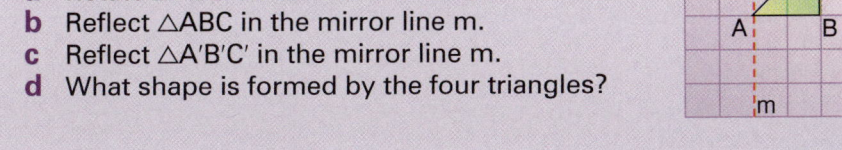

4 a Copy this diagram.
    b R is translated 2 units left and 2 units up to T.
        Draw T.
        Write down the coordinates of the vertices of T.
    c T is rotated 90° clockwise about the point (⁻2, 2) to V.
        Draw V and give its coordinates.
    d Are the images in **b** and **c** congruent to R?

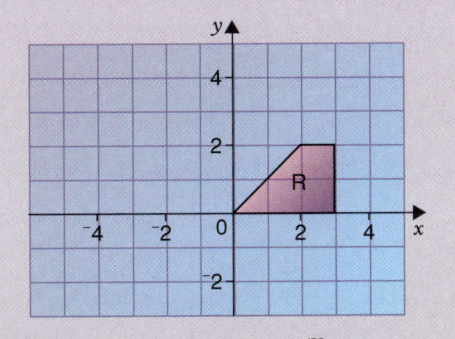

5 Faizeh reflected the blue triangle in the mirror line to the green triangle.
    Use the properties of reflection symmetry to write down the value of
    a x **b** a **c** b

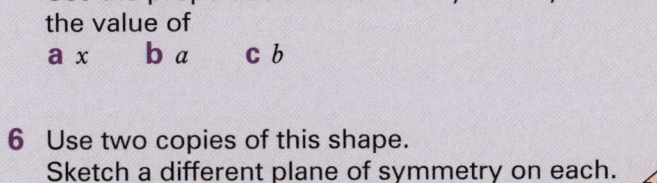

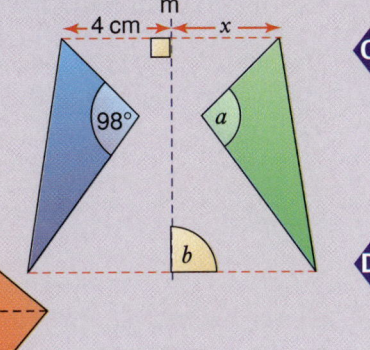

6 Use two copies of this shape.
    Sketch a different plane of symmetry on each.
    Shade your planes.

7 The red shape has been enlarged to the purple shape.
    Find the scale factor for the enlargement.

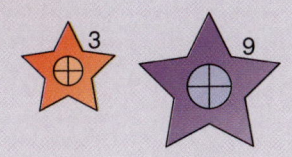

329

Shape, Space and Measures

8 a Use a copy of the grid.

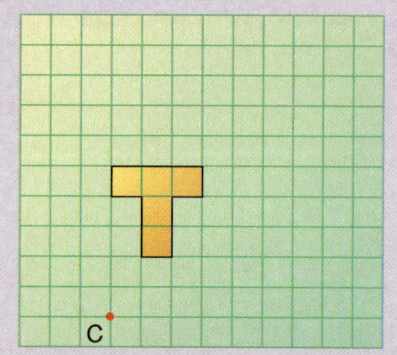

On the grid draw an enlargement of the T-shape with scale factor 2.
Use point C as the centre of enlargement.

*b The sketches show two As.
The bigger A is an enlargement of scale factor 2·5 of the smaller A.
Write down the missing values **i**, **ii** and **iii**.

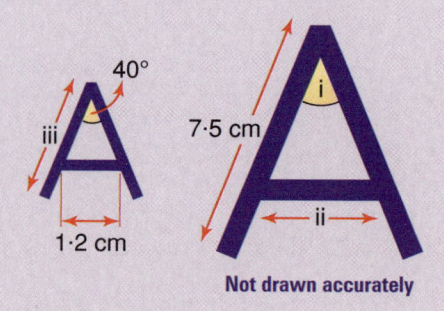

9 a The large triangle, **B**, is an enlargement of the small triangle, **A**.
What is the value of
  i x **ii** the shaded angle?
*b If the perimeter of triangle A is 12 cm, what is the perimeter of triangle B?

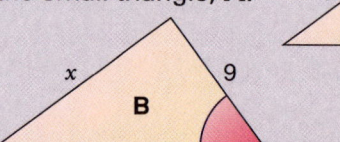

10 Estimate the length of the house in this picture.
The man is about 1·8 m tall.

11 Maryanne is making a scale drawing of the school grounds.
She is using the scale 1 cm represents 10 m. How long in real life is a length that is
  a 4 cm on the scale drawing   **b** 15·5 cm on the scale drawing?

12 This shows the cutting layout for a shirt.
The pattern pieces are as follows:
1 – front
2 – back
3 – front band
8 – collar
9 – sleeve
  a What is the width of the collar at the fold line?
  b What is the length of the back at the fold line?
  c What are the dimensions of the front band?
  d What is the width of the sleeve at its widest point?
  e What is the length of the front at the selvage line?

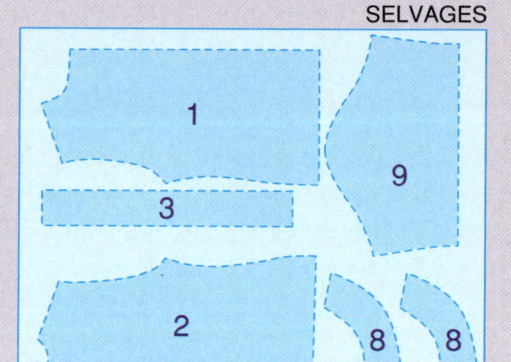

Scale: 1 mm to 2 cm   FOLD LINE

13 Measures, Perimeter, Area and Volume

You need to know

✓ measures — page 259
  – metric conversions
  – metric and imperial equivalents
  – reading scales
✓ bearings — page 260
✓ perimeter, area and volume — page 260

Key vocabulary

bearing, cubic millimetre, cubic centimetre, cubic metre, foot, hectare, miles per hour, speed, yard, tonne, volume

▶▶ Greener than green

Heather has a lawn mowing business.
She is asked to give a quote for mowing this circular park.
Heather doesn't know the formula for finding the area of a circle.
She draws this scale drawing of the park.

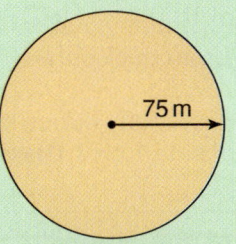

75 m

scale 1 mm = 5 m

Draw a circle on a loose piece of paper with a radius of 15 mm.
Cut it into 'slices'. Rearrange these 'slices' as shown.

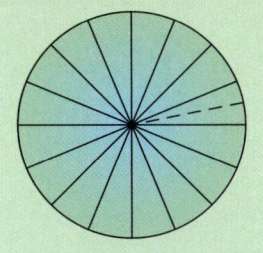

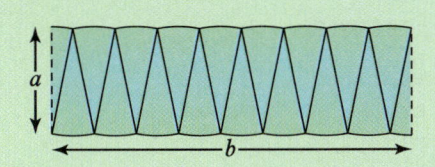

Use a piece of string to measure the circumference of the circle.

Which of a or b is equal to the radius of the circle?
Which is about the same as half the circumference?

How could Heather use what you have found out to find the area of the park?

If Heather charges £10 for every 1000 m² mowed, what should her quote be to the nearest £5?

331

Shape, Space and Measures

Metric conversions, including area, volume and capacity

Remember
Length   1 km = 1000 m   1 m = 100 cm   1 m = 1000 mm   1 cm = 10 mm
Mass   1 tonne = 1000 kg   1 kg = 1000 g
Capacity 1 ℓ = 1000 mℓ 1 ℓ = 100 cℓ 1 cℓ = 10 mℓ 1 ℓ = 1000 cm^3 1 mℓ = 1 cm^3
1000 ℓ = 1 m^3
Area   1 hectare = 10 000 m^2
Time   1 hour = 60 minutes   1 week = 7 days
1 minute = 60 seconds   1 year = 365 days (366 in a leap year)
1 day = 24 hours   1 decade = 10 years

See page 261 for more on metric conversions.

Discussion

● How many squares of side 1 cm will fit along one side of a square of side 1 m? **Discuss**.

How many squares of side 1 mm will fit *on* a square of side 1 cm? **Discuss**.

How many squares of side 1 cm will fit *on* a square of side 1 m? **Discuss**.

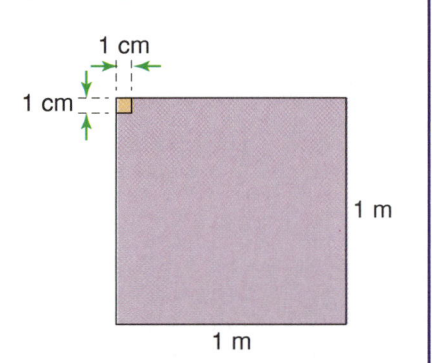

● How many cubes of side 1 mm will fit along one side of a cube of side 1 cm? **Discuss**.

How many cubes of side 1 mm will fit on a layer of 1 mm thick cube?

How many cubes of side 1 mm will fit *inside* a cube of side 1 cm? **Discuss**.

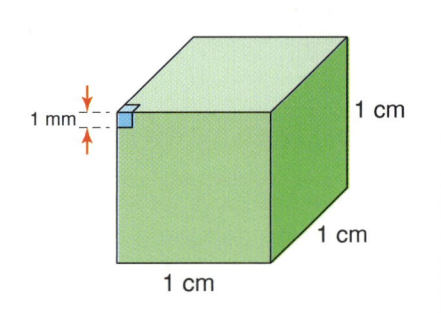

Area and volume conversions

Area
1 m^2 = 10 000 cm^2
1 cm^2 = 100 mm^2

Capacity
1 cm^3 = 1000 mm^3
1 m^3 = 1 000 000 cm^3

Worked Example
What is the volume of this tank in
a m^3 **b** cm^3 **c** mℓ **d** ℓ?

There is more about the volume of a cuboid on page 261.

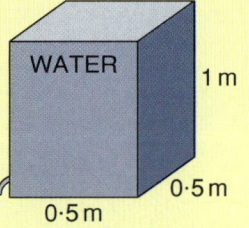

Answer
a Volume of a cuboid = $w \times l \times h$
= 0·5 × 0·5 × 1
= **0·25 m^3**

b 0·25 m^3 = (0·25 × 1 000 000) cm^3
= **250 000 cm^3**

c 1 cm^3 = 1 mℓ
So volume of tank in mℓ = **250 000 mℓ**

d 1 ℓ = 1000 mℓ
So 250 000 mℓ = (250 000 ÷ 1000) ℓ
= **250 ℓ**

Measures, Perimeter, Area and Volume

Exercise 1 — except for question 3.

Questions 1, 2 and 3 are revision of the conversions given under 'Remember' on the previous page.

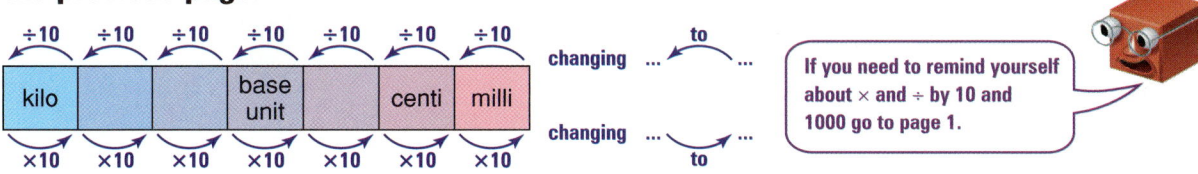

changing ... to ...
changing ... to ...

If you need to remind yourself about × and ÷ by 10 and 1000 go to page 1.

1 Change
 a 4820 mm to m
 b 86 mm to cm
 c 3245 cm to m
 d 832 cm to m
 e 4·6 ℓ to mℓ
 f 1790 g to kg
 g 397 mm to m
 h 520 cℓ to ℓ
 i 5680 g to kg
 j 36 mm to m
 k 0·86 m to cm
 l 50 mℓ to ℓ
 m 49 g to kg
 n 3 mm to m
 o 9 g to kg
 p 7600 kg to tonnes
 q 420 kg to tonnes
 r 8·2 tonnes to kg
 s 0·3 tonnes to kg
 t 85 mℓ to cℓ.

2 Change
 a 5 ha to m^2
 b 3·2 ha to m^2
 c 20 000 m^2 to ha
 d 30 500 m^2 to ha
 e 0·62 ha to m^2
 f 4·6 m^3 to ℓ
 g 43 cm^3 to mℓ
 h 8420 cm^3 to ℓ
 i 3·5 ℓ to cm^3
 j 5682 ℓ to m^3
 k 0·82 ℓ to cm^3
 l 0·28 cm^3 to mℓ
 m 32 cm^3 to ℓ
 n 864 cm^3 to cℓ.

3 a How many minutes in $2\frac{1}{4}$ hours?
 b How many hours and minutes in 165 minutes?
 c How many hours in 562 minutes? Round sensibly.
 d Change 126 months to years and months.

4 Change
 a 5 m^2 to cm^2
 b 9·6 m^2 to cm^2
 c 8 cm^2 to mm^2
 d 5000 mm^2 to cm^2
 e 830 cm^2 to m^2
 f 0·042 m^3 to cm^3
 g 9·872 m^3 to cm^3
 h 92 700 000 cm^3 to m^3
 i 780 000 mm^3 to cm^3
 j 8·4 cm^2 to mm^2
 k 330 000 mm^2 to cm^2
 l 0·421 m^3 to cm^3
 m 48 000 square centimetres to square metres
 n 7·5 cubic centimetres to cubic millimetres
 o 89·62 square centimetres to square millimetres.

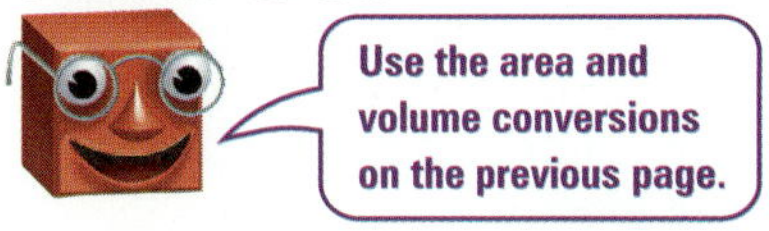

Use the area and volume conversions on the previous page.

5 What is the area of this poster in
 a m^2 b cm^2 c mm^2?

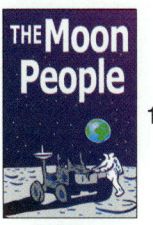

1·2 m
0·75 m

Link to area and volume.

*6 What is the volume of this dish in
 a cm^3 b mm^3 c mℓ d ℓ?

14 cm
28 cm
8 cm

Remember: Volume = lbh.

333

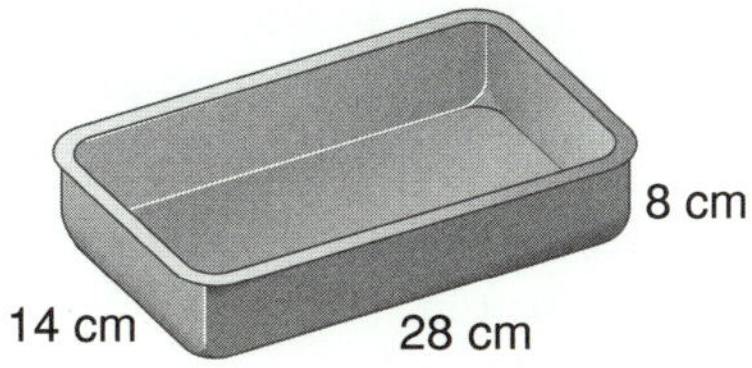

Shape, Space and Measures

T **Review 1**

4·23	5600	84 000	42·3	84 000		0·423	5·6				
			U								
84 000	0·056	56 000	**840**	4·275	5600	0·0056	42 700	42·3	56	56 000	0·056
						U					
0·423	0·056	4·23	5600	84 000	5600	**840**	423	42 700	0·056		
56	56 000	427·5	8400	4·23	56 000	0·84	0·423	0·084	0·084		
						U					
0·056	0·423	0·056	84 000	4·23	5600	56 000	**840**	5·6	42 700	0·056	427·5
42·75	84 000	0·056	0·0056	0·423	0·084	5·6					

Use a copy of this box.
What goes in the gap? Write the letter beside each question above its answer in the box.

- **U** 0·84 tonnes = **840** kg
- **I** 4230 m² = ___ ha
- **G** 4275 ℓ = ___ m³
- **E** 8·4 m² = ___ cm²
- **A** 0·0427 m³ = ___ cm³
- **C** 5600 cm³ = ___ m³
- **L** 840 cm² = ___ m²

- **T** 42·3 mℓ = ___ cℓ
- **H** 5·6 m³ = ___ ℓ
- **Y** 8·4 ℓ = ___ cm³
- **M** 4·23 cm² = ___ mm²
- **F** 840 000 cm³ = ___ m³
- **N** 560 cm² = ___ m²

- **O** 5·6 ha = ___ m²
- **R** 42·3 cm³ = ___ mℓ
- **D** 427 500 cm³ = ___ ℓ
- **B** 560 000 cm² = ___ m²
- **S** 560 mm² = ___ cm²
- **P** 42 750 mm³ = ___ cm³

Review 2 How many
- **a** minutes in 5·4 hours
- **b** hours and minutes in 572 minutes
- **c** hours in 2 weeks 4 days
- **d** years and months in 486 months?

Working with measures

The following exercise gives you practice at **estimating measures** and **solving measures problems**.
You often need to know metric conversions or the rough metric and imperial equivalents to solve problems.

See page 260 for the metric and imperial equivalents.

When estimating, it is useful to compare to something you know well.

Example A door is about 2 m high so the height of a window is about half this height, 1 m.

- When we give a measurement, say 3 m to the nearest m, the **shortest distance** it could be is 2·5 m and the **longest distance** is up to but not including 3·5 m. We work this out by finding **half a unit either side** of the nearest unit.

    Example A javelin is thrown 83 m to the nearest metre.
    The shortest distance this could be is 82·5 m.
    The longest is up to but not including 83·5 m.

- You may need to use this formula.

    average speed = $\frac{\text{distance}}{\text{time}}$

    distance = time × average speed
    time = $\frac{\text{distance}}{\text{average speed}}$

Measures, Perimeter, Area and Volume

Remember
A direction from one place to another may be given as a **bearing**.

Bearings from North are always given as three digits.
To find the bearing of Ailsford from Burke, follow these steps.

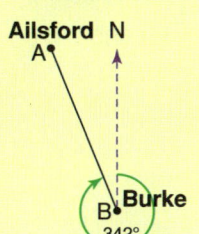

Step 1 Join AB.

Step 2 Draw a North line from B.

Step 3 Measure the angle (in a *clockwise* direction) between this North line and the line AB.

There is more about bearings on page 260.

In this diagram, the bearing of Ailsford from Burke is 342°.

Worked Example
a Use £1 = 16·07 Mexican dollars to work out how much 85p is in Mex$.
b Use 134 Krona = £1 to work out how much 500 Krona is in pounds.

Answer
We can use proportional reasoning.

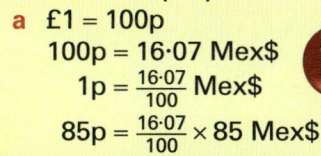

a £1 = 100p
100p = 16·07 Mex$
1p = $\frac{16·07}{100}$ Mex$
85p = $\frac{16·07}{100} \times 85$ Mex$
= **13·66 Mexican dollars** (2 d.p.)

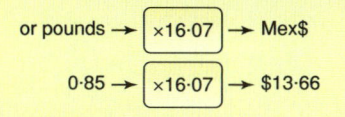

There are other ways of doing these.

b 134 Krona = £1
1 Krona = £$\frac{1}{134}$
500 Krona = £$\frac{1}{134} \times 500$
= **£3·73 to the nearest penny**

This is linked to proportion.

or pounds → ×16·07 → Mex$
0·85 → ×16·07 → $13·66

or pounds → ×134 → Krona
pounds ← ÷134 ← Krona
£3·73 ← ÷134 ← 500

Exercise 2
Only use a calculator if you need to.

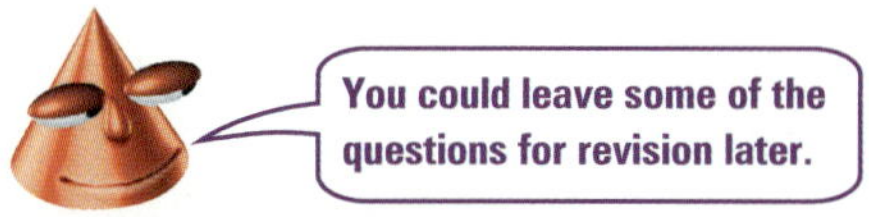

1 Estimate these. Give a range for each.
   Example   0·5 cm < thickness of calculator < 1·5 cm
   a height, in cm, of your school desk
   b capacity, in ℓ, of a bucket
   c area, in cm², of this page
   d mass, in kg, of a school bag

   You could leave some of the questions for revision later.

2 Cartons are to be stacked in a cupboard 1·36 m high.
   Each carton is 14 cm high.
   How many layers will fit in the cupboard?

3 Each afternoon Manzoor catches a train at 4:05 p.m.
   He gets off at 4:40 p.m.
   On Wednesdays, the train takes longer and he doesn't get off until 4:55 p.m.
   How long does Manzoor spend on the train each week (5 days)?

4 'Telephone Tales' make extension cables for telephones.
   Each extension uses 364·5 cm of cable.
   10 000 of these are made each day.
   a How many km of cable are made each day?
   b How many extension cables can be made from 1 km of cable?

335

Shape, Space and Measures

5 Which is the better buy? Explain how you worked it out.

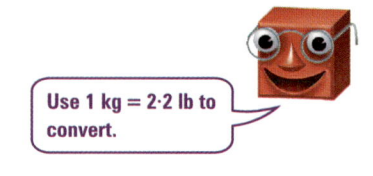

80p per kg. 44p per pound.

Use 1 kg = 2·2 lb to convert.

6 a Do you think this sign gives the distances to the nearest mile, nearest $\frac{1}{2}$ mile or nearest $\frac{1}{4}$ mile?
Use your answer to find
  b the shortest possible distance to Dunston
  c the shortest possible distance between Nocton and Blankney.

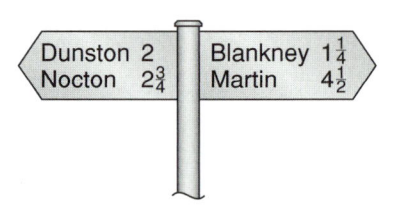

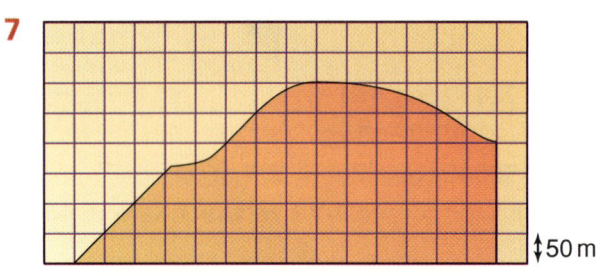

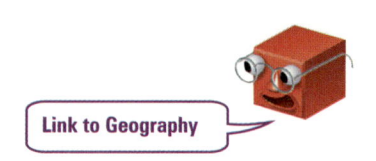

Dunston 2 Blankney $1\frac{1}{4}$
Nocton $2\frac{3}{4}$ Martin $4\frac{1}{2}$

7

$\updownarrow$ 50 m

Link to Geography

Each square has a length of 50 m.
  a What is the area of each square?
  b How many squares make 1 hectare?
  c By counting squares, find the area of land sketched. (Give your answer to the nearest hectare.)

8 This shows two parks with the same area.
  a How many hectares is Park A?
  b What is the width of Park B?

Park A — 1 km × 100 m
Park B — 400 m

9 Use this chart to work out how much
  a £55 is in ringgit
  b £1050 is in euros
  c 1000 yuan is in pounds
  d 5000 Jamaican dollars is in pounds
  e 20 000 rupees is in pounds
  f 95p is in rand.

TODAY'S CONVERSION RATES
for **£1** you get

10·8	rand	13·16	yuan (China)
79·32	Jamaican dollars	6·04	ringgit (Malaysia)
1·57	euro	92·24	rupees

10 a What length of this wallboard, in cm, is needed to replace an 8 foot length?
  b How much will it cost?

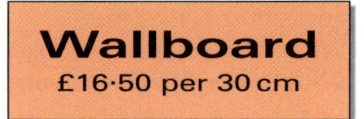

Wallboard
£16·50 per 30 cm

Measures, Perimeter, Area and Volume

11 Pippa's grandmother used this recipe to make custard.
    Change the amounts to metric measures.

    Custard
    ¼ pound flour
    1 pint milk
    2 eggs

12 *(Scale drawing with North arrow, showing W Water Tower and A Apartment block)*

    There is more about bearings on page 260.

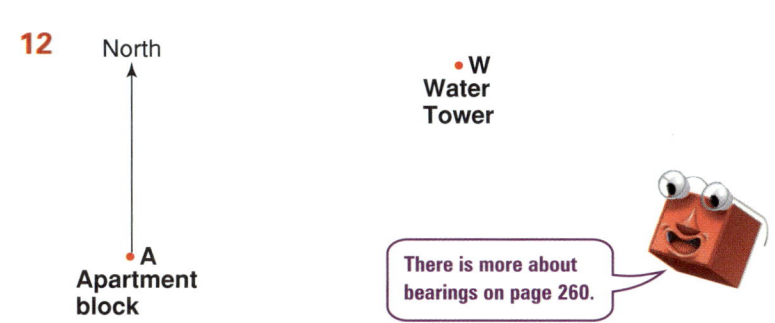

    This scale drawing shows the positions of a water tower, W and an apartment block, A.
    1 cm on the diagram represents 20 m.
    a i   Measure, in centimetres, the distance AW.
       ii Work out the distance, in metres, of the apartment block from the water tower.
    b i   Measure and write down the bearing of the water tower from the apartment block.
       ii Write down the bearing of the apartment block from the water tower.

*13 The diameter of a red blood cell is 0·000714 cm.
    The diameter of a white blood cell is 0·001243 cm. 
    a Work out the difference between these two diameters.
       Give your answer in millimetres.

    Link to Science

    b How many white cells would fit across a needle point which has a diameter of 0·12 mm?

*14 An old knitting pattern uses twenty 1 oz balls of wool.
    How many 25 g balls are needed to make this pattern?

*15 A uniform block of cheese in the shape of a cuboid weighed 1·2 kg.
    5 cm of the cheese was cut off its length.
    The remaining block weighed 0·75 kg.
    What was the length of the original block? Round your answer sensibly.

*16 a An aeroplane travels 2340 miles in 5 hours.
       What is its average speed? 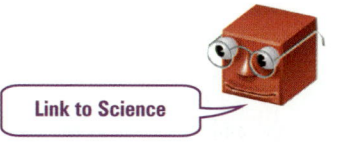
    b A minibus travels 260 miles at an average speed of 40 mph.
       For how many hours does the minibus travel?

    Link to Science

    c A lorry travels for $3\frac{1}{2}$ hours at an average speed of 24 mph.
       How far does the lorry travel?

17 The diagram shows the distance between my home, H, and two towns, A and B.
    It also shows information about journey times.   [SATs Paper 1 Level 7]

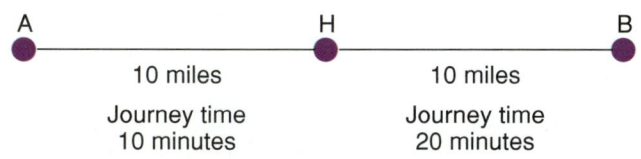

    A ●————————————● H ————————● B
         10 miles   10 miles
         Journey time   Journey time
         10 minutes   20 minutes

    a What is the average speed of the journey from my home to **town A**?
    b What is the average speed of the journey from my home to **town B**?
    c I drive from town A to my home and then to town B.
       The journey time is 30 minutes.
       What is my average speed?
       Show your working.

337

Shape, Space and Measures

*18 Ellsie marked out a basketball court. 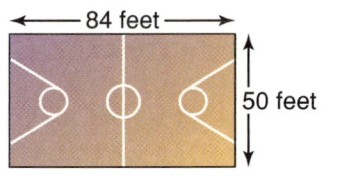
   a She makes it 84 feet long to the nearest foot.
      What is the shortest possible length of the court?
   b She makes the court 50 feet wide to the nearest foot.
      What is the shortest possible width?
   c Ellsie's coach makes her team run around the outside
      of the court to get fit.
      Use your answers to parts **a** and **b** to find how many times they should
      run around the court to be sure of running at least 4 miles.
      1 mile = 5280 feet

*19 Marie cycles a distance of 8 km from F to G on a bearing of 090°. From G she cycles 6 km
    to H. The bearing of H from G is 180°.
    What is Marie's bearing and distance from F once she is at H?
    Make a scale drawing using a scale of 1 cm to 1 km.

Review 1 Write down an approximate measurement for each of these.
Give a range. Use metric units.
a the area, in cm^2, of the top of a filing cabinet
b the volume, in ℓ, of a laundry basket
c the mass, in kg, of a telephone

Review 2 Elle is in training. She swims 53 lengths of her local swimming pool every day.
Each length is 30 m.
a How far does she swim every day in km?
b If she swims five times a week, about how many miles does she swim in a week? Give your
   answer to the nearest mile.

*Review 3** Julie took 50 minutes to cycle to her friend's house. If her friend lives $12\frac{1}{2}$ miles
from Julie's home, what was her average cycling speed in miles per hour?

*Review 4**
a The price of petrol was quoted in an old log book as £1·80 per gallon.
   How much is this per litre?
b If it is now 68p per litre, how much is this per gallon?

Perimeter and area

Remember
The distance right around the outside of a shape is called the **perimeter**.
Perimeter is measured in mm, cm, m or km.

The amount of surface a shape covers is called the **area**.
Area is measured in mm^2, cm^2, m^2 or km^2.

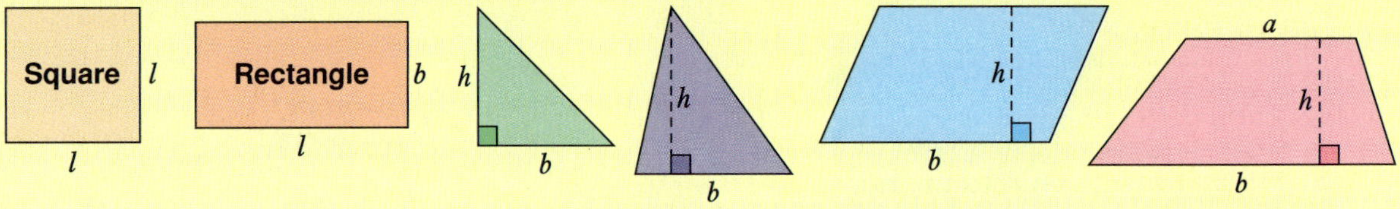

Square	Rectangle	Triangle	Parallelogram	Trapezium
$A = l^2$	$A = lb$	$A = \frac{1}{2}bh$	$A = bh$	$A = \frac{1}{2}(a+b) \times h$

Measures, Perimeter, Area and Volume

Worked Example
Show that these shapes have the same area.

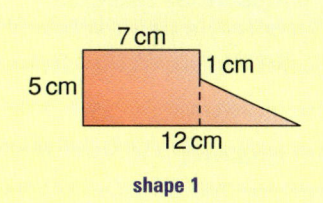

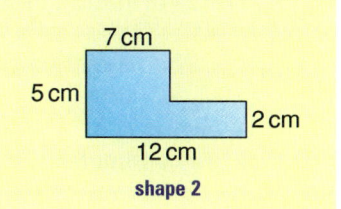

shape 1

shape 2

Answer
Area Shape 1 = area of rectangle + area of triangle
$= 5 \times 7 + \frac{1}{2} \times 5 \times 4$ triangle base = 12 – 7 = 5, triangle height = 5 – 1 = 4
$= 35 + 10$
$= \mathbf{45\ cm^2}$

Area Shape 2 = area of A + area of B
$= 35 + 5 \times 2$
$= 35 + 10$
$= \mathbf{45\ cm^2}$

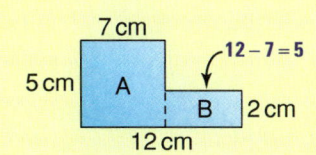

Exercise 3

1 a Draw a rectangle on 1 cm squared paper that has an area of 12 cm².
  b Draw a triangle on 1 cm squared paper that has an area of 6 cm².

2 a Show that the triangle and the rectangle have the same area.

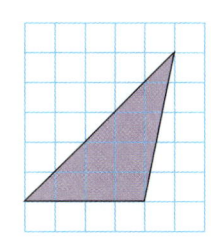

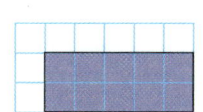

  b Use a copy of this.

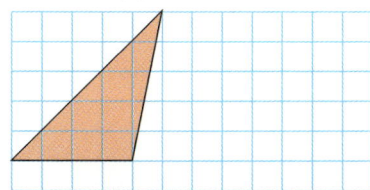

  On your grid, draw a parallelogram which has the same area as the triangle. It must **not** have right angles.

3 Calculate the areas and perimeters of these shapes.
  a 18 cm, 5 cm, 12 cm, 8 cm
  b 10·4 m, 9·2 m, 1·6 m, 8·4 m
  c 21·5 mm, 18·7 mm, 21·6 mm, 10·6 mm

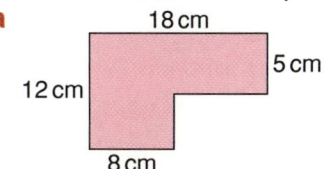

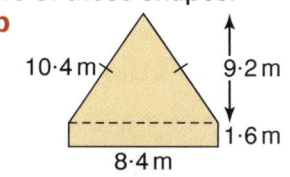

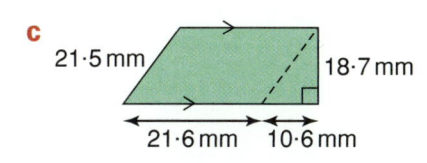

4 Sonal made a design for her art class using identical rectangles and identical triangles.
Find the area of the whole design.

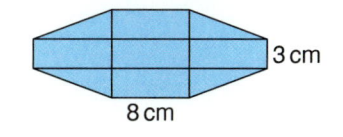

3 cm, 8 cm

***5** The length of a rectangle is 5 cm more than its width. Its area is 414 cm². What is its perimeter?

339

Shape, Space and Measures

6 The information in the box describes three different squares, A, B and C.   [SATs Paper 2 Level 6]

> The **area** of square A is **36 cm²**.
> The **side length** of square B is **36 cm**.
> The **perimeter** of square C is **36 cm**.

Put squares A, B and C in order of size, starting with the smallest.
You **must** show calculations to explain how you work out your answer.

7 Farmer Jones has three fields.

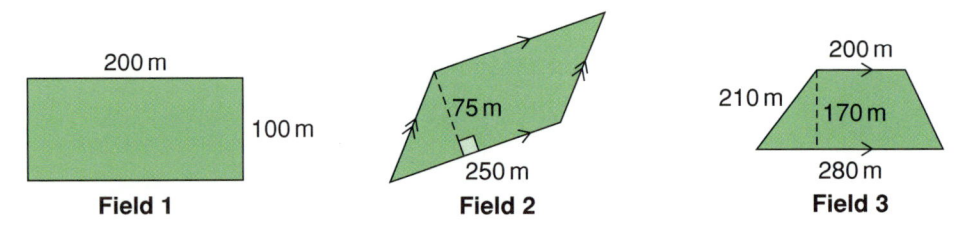

Field 1: 200 m × 100 m rectangle
Field 2: parallelogram, 250 m base, 75 m height
Field 3: trapezium, parallel sides 200 m and 280 m, height 170 m, slant 210 m

 a Find the area of each in hectares.
***b** Farmer Jones has 600 m of fencing.
     What is the area of the largest field he can enclose?

8 Explain how you know that the areas of each of the shaded shapes are equal.

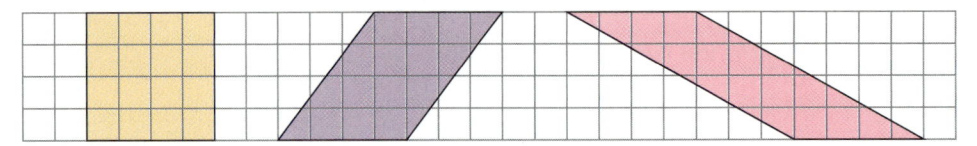

*9 **a** This shows a rectangle and a trapezium.

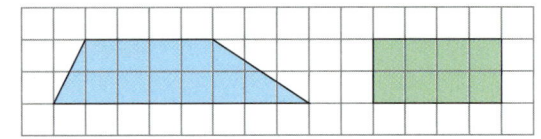

What is the ratio of   area of trapezium : area of rectangle?

 b A square is drawn on the same grid paper so that the ratio
     area of trapezium : area of square   equals 3 : 4.
     What is the area, in square units, of the square?
     How many squares are along each side of the square?
     Show your working.

Review 1

a Calculate the areas of these shapes.

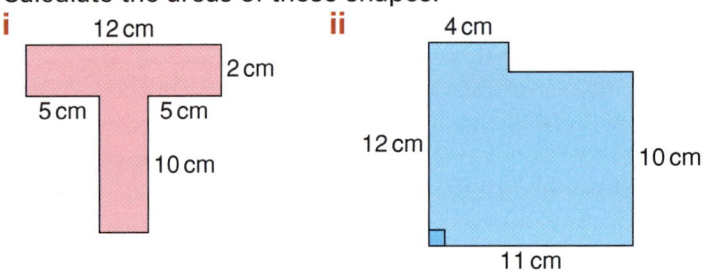

 i T-shape: top 12 cm × 2 cm, stem 5 cm wide × 10 cm tall, flanked by 5 cm segments

 ii L-shape: 4 cm top, 12 cm left side, 11 cm bottom, 10 cm right side

 iii trapezium: 7 cm top, 14 cm bottom, 6 cm left, with 4 cm and 4 cm heights marked

b Find the perimeters of **i** and **ii**.

340

Measures, Perimeter, Area and Volume

Review 2 The perimeter of a rectangle is 266 cm. If its length is 7 cm more than its width, find the area of the rectangle.

Review 3 A photograph in a frame is surrounded by coloured card.
a What is the area of the frame and photograph together?
*b What is the ratio   *photograph* : *card*   in its simplest form?

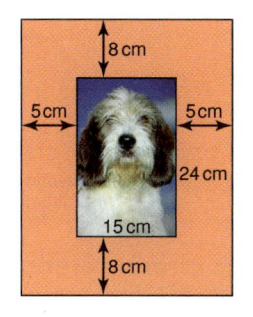

8 cm
5 cm   5 cm
24 cm
15 cm
8 cm

Circumference and area of a circle

Practical

You will need some circular objects such as coins, saucers, ...

1 a The circumference of a circular object, such as a coin or saucer or the top face of a cylinder can be found as follows.

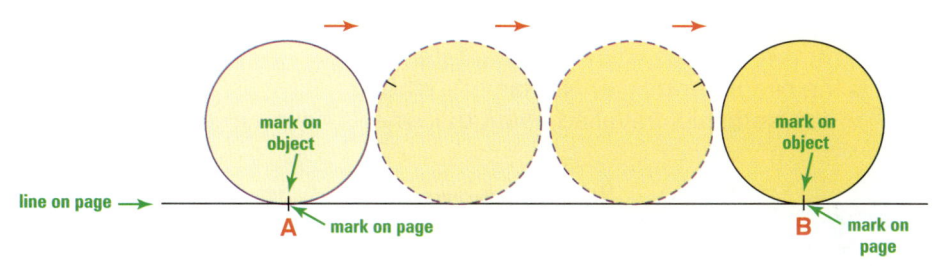

mark on object   mark on object
line on page →
A mark on page   B mark on page

Put a mark on the edge of the object.
Draw a line on your page.
Put a mark, A, on the line.
Line up the two marks.

Roll the object vertically along the line until the mark on the object touches the page again.
Make a mark, B, on the line.

Measure the length of AB, in millimetres.

b Repeat **a** for five or six objects.
c Measure the diameter, in mm, of each object as accurately as possible.
d Fill in your results in a table like this one.
e Calculate $\frac{C}{d}$ for each object.
Give the answer to 1 d.p.
What do you notice?

Object	Circumference, C (in mm)	Diameter, d (in mm)	$\frac{C}{d}$

2 Another way of finding the circumference of a cylindrical object, such as a baked bean tin, is to measure with a tape measure.
Another way is to wind a length of cotton around the tin a number of times. Why do you think the cotton is wound around a number of times, rather than just once?
Use this method to find the ratio $\frac{C}{d}$ for a number of tins of different sizes. What do you notice?

341

Shape, Space and Measures

The meaning of π

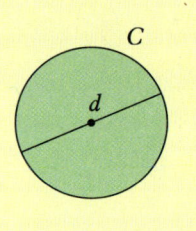

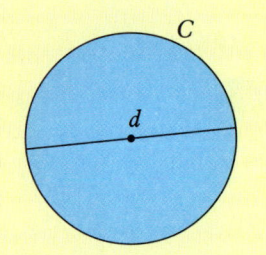

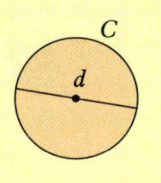

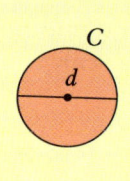

C is the **circumference** of a circle, d is the diameter.
The ratio $\frac{C}{d}$ is the same for any circle, regardless of how big or small the circle is.

Link to circles, page 291.

$\pi \approx 3$. You can use this to estimate answers

The ratio $\frac{C}{d}$ is called π (pronounced 'pi'). To 1 d.p. the value of π is 3·1.

Most calculators have a π key. This gives π to 9 decimal places as 3·141592654.
π has been worked out, accurate to many millions of decimal places, on the computer.

Circumference of a circle

Circumference of a circle = πd
or **Circumference of a circle** = $2\pi r$ because $d = 2r$ and $C = \pi d = \pi(2r) = 2\pi r$

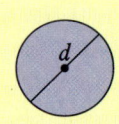

Worked Example

Nathaniel's motorcycle has wheels of diameter 40 cm.
a What is the circumference of Nathaniel's wheel?
b How far has Nathaniel travelled when the wheels have turned 300 times each?

Answer
a $C = \pi d$ We estimate the answer as $3 \times 40 = 120$.
   $= \pi \times 40$
   $= \mathbf{125 \cdot 6637061 \text{ cm}}$

Do not round the intermediate answer.

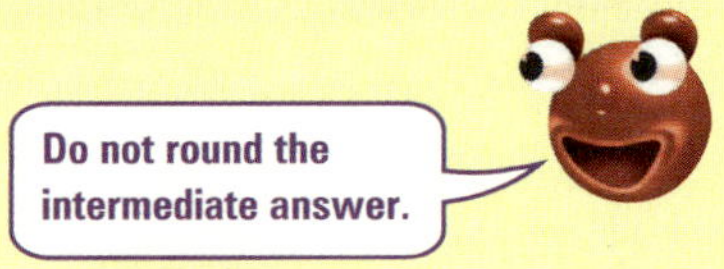

b Distance travelled for 300 turns = $300 \times 125 \cdot 6637061$
                                   = 37 699 cm to the nearest cm
                                   = **376·99 m**

Link to rounding, pages 1 and 31.

Key Shift π × 40 × 300 =

Practical

You will need 1 cm squared paper

Draw circles inside squares up to a 6 by 6 square.
Estimate the areas of the circles by counting squares.
What do you notice about the area of the circles?

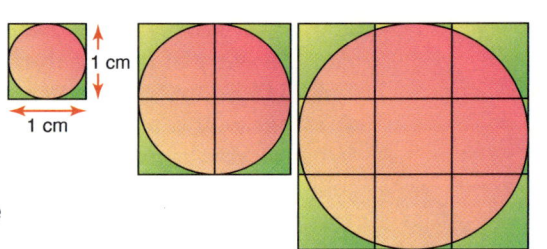

1 cm

1 cm

and so on ...

Measures, Perimeter, Area and Volume

Exercise 4

1. Find the circumference of each of these circles. Use $\pi = 3.14$. Give your answers to 2 d.p.
   a) 8 mm
   b) 12 cm
   c) 3 m
   d) 64 mm

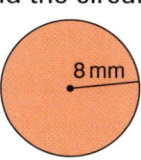

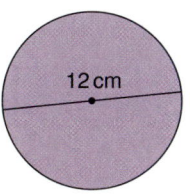

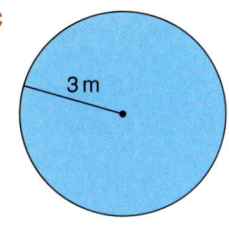

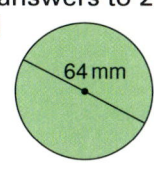

Use the π key on your calculator for questions 2, 3 and 4. Round your answers sensibly.

2. A container Cass used in science has a diameter of 9 cm. What is the distance around the edge of the top of this?

3. A ribbon is tied around a hat, as shown. Find the total length of the ribbon, if the bow needs 30 cm.

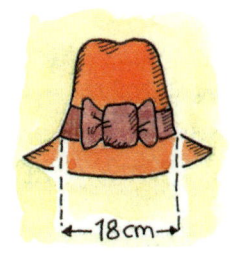

4. Nishi's bicycle has 0·6 m diameter wheels. On the way to school, the front wheel rotates 500 times. How far does Nishi live from school?

←18 cm→

Review Find the circumference of these circles. Use $\pi = 3.14$.
   a) 12 mm
   b) 2·4 m

Area of a circle

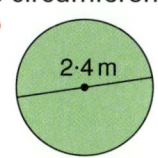

The **area of a circle** can be calculated using the formula $A = \pi r^2$.

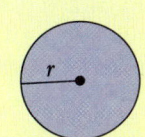

Worked Example
Find the area of these circles.
Use $\pi = 3.14$.
Give the answers to 2 d.p.

a) 4·3 cm   b) 79 mm

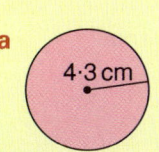

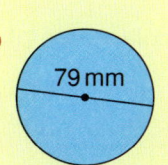

Answer
a) $A = \pi r^2$
   $A = 3.14 \times 4.3^2$ Key [3·14] [×] [4·3] [x²] [=]
   $= 58.06$ (2 d.p.)

b) $d = 79$ mm $r = 39.5$ mm $A = \pi r^2$
   $= 3.14 \times 39.5^2$
   $= 4899.19$ mm² (2 d.p.)

Remember: the radius is half of the diameter.

Exercise 5

Remember: the formula uses radius not diameter.

1. Find the area of each of these circles. Give the answers to 1 d.p.
   a) 9 m
   b) 17 cm
   c) 0·2 m
   d) 18·6 mm

343

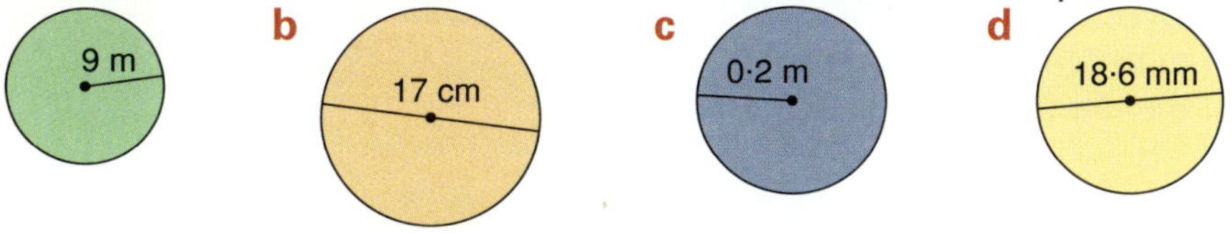

Shape, Space and Measures

2 A plastic cover is made to fit exactly over a circular pool.
The diameter of this pool is 8·4 m.
What is the area of the cover?

3 A circular embroidery, of diameter 39 cm, is covered with glass.
What is the area of the glass?

Review Find the area of each of these to 1 d.p.

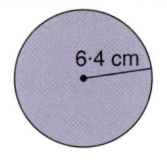

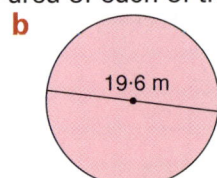

a 6·4 cm

b 19·6 m

Circumference and area of a circle

This exercise gives you practice at choosing the right formula to use.

Worked Example
Ryan's trailer has wheels of diameter 40 cm.
How many turns must each wheel make to travel 5 km?

Answer
The question is asking for a distance not an area so we must find the circumference.

5 km = 5000 m
5000 m = x turns × πd
5000 m = $x \times \pi \times 0\cdot 4$ m
$x = \dfrac{5000}{\pi \times 0\cdot 4}$

$C = \pi d$

40 cm = 0·4 m

x = 3978·9 or about **3979** to the nearest turn

Worked Example
An advertising board is in the shape of a rectangle with a semicircular end.
The rectangular part is 1·2 m long and 0·6 m wide.
Find the area of the board.

0·6 m GOOD FOOD
1·2 m

Answer
Area of board = area of rectangle + area of semicircle

Area of rectangle = lw
= 1·2 × 0·6
= 0·72 m²

Area of semicircle = half of area of circle = $\frac{1}{2}$ of πr^2
= $\frac{1}{2}$ of $\pi \times 0\cdot 3^2$ diameter of circle = 0·6 m so radius = 0·3 m
= 0·5 × $\pi \times 0\cdot 3^2$
= 0·14 m² (2 d.p.)

Area of board = 0·72 m² + 0·14 m²
= **0·86 m² (2 d.p.)**

Exercise 6   Use the π key on your calculator.

1 A circular tablecloth overhangs a circular table, as shown.
Mai-Lin buys 3·4 m of braid to sew around the edge.
Is 3·4 m enough to sew around the outside edge?
Hint Work out the diameter of the tablecloth first.

50 cm
30 cm   30 cm

344

Measures, Perimeter, Area and Volume

2 A trundle wheel is used to measure distances. [SATs Paper 2 Level 6]
   Imran makes a trundle wheel, of **diameter 50 cm**. 
   a Calculate the **circumference** of Imran's trundle wheel.
      Show your working.
   b Imran uses his trundle wheel to measure the length of the
      school car park.
      His trundle wheel rotates **87 times**.
      What is the **length** of the car park, to the **nearest metre**?

3 In the McMath solar telescope, in Arizona, there are two flat round mirrors.
   One has a radius of 1 m and the other a diameter of 122 cm.
   What is the difference in the areas of these mirrors? Give the answer in cm².

4 a The larger wheel on Joshua's wheelchair is 58 cm in diameter.
      Joshua pushes it around exactly 20 times.
      How far, in m, has Joshua moved?
   b Joshua gets a new electronic wheelchair with a large wheel radius of 26 cm.
      How many times must the wheel rotate for him to travel 860 cm?

5 Here is a circle and a square.
   The radius of the circle is 10 mm. 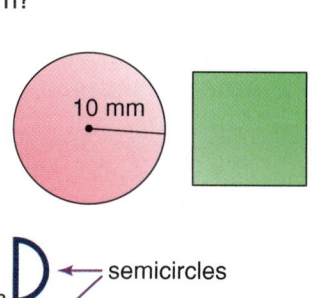
   a Find the area of the circle to the nearest mm².
   b The ratio of the area of the circle to the area of the square
      is 2 : 1. What is the area of the square to the nearest mm?
   c What is the length of the side of the square?

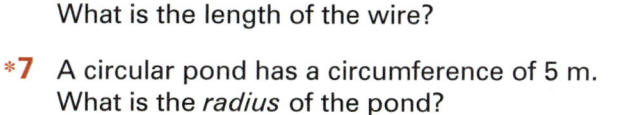

*6 Andrea uses wire to make a 'B' with a straight side and two
    equal semicircles.
    What is the length of the wire?

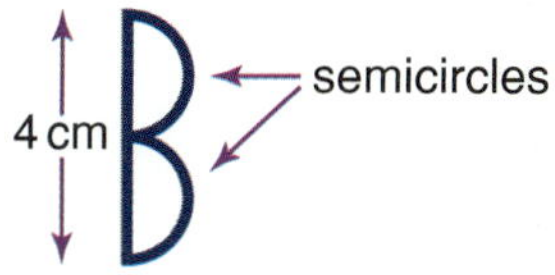

*7 A circular pond has a circumference of 5 m.
    What is the *radius* of the pond?

*8 Calculate the area of each of the shaded shapes.
    a   b

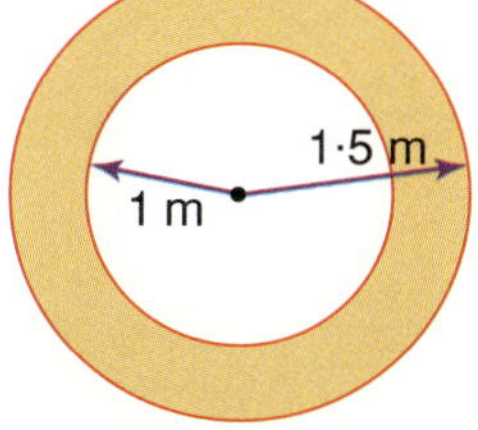

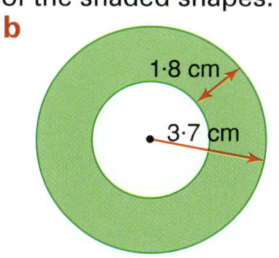

*9 A gate from a courtyard to a garden is in the shape of a rectangle
    with a semicircular arch.
    The rectangular part is 1·6 m wide and 2·4 m high.
    What is the area of the gate?

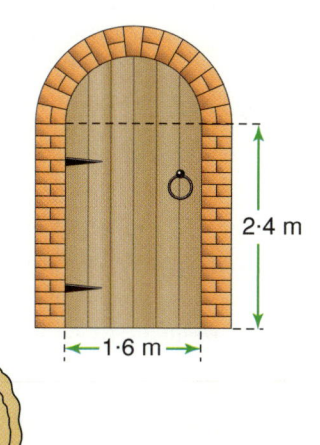

*10 a 'Delicious Pastries' make small and large pies.
       The surface area of the top of the larger pies is
       twice the surface area of the top of the smaller
       ones.
       If the smaller pies have a diameter of 12 cm,
       what is the diameter of the larger pies?
    b Janna eats a 120° sector of a large pie.
       What area of pastry covers the top of this piece?

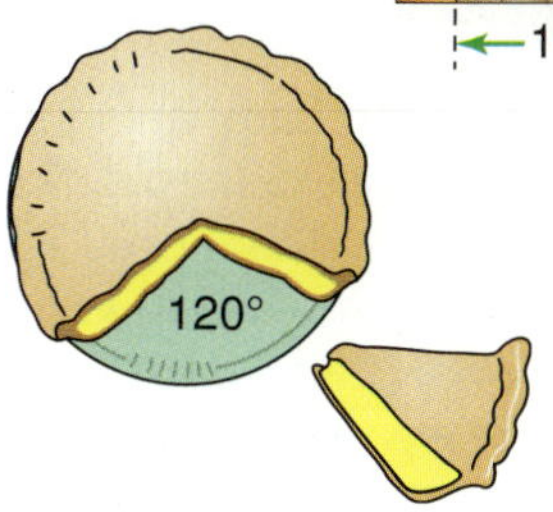

345

Shape, Space and Measures

*11 This diagram shows a circle and a square.
The circle touches the sides of the square.
What percentage of the diagram is shaded yellow?

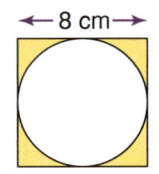

←— 8 cm —→

Review 1 A bakery sells a mini pizza with diameter 14 cm.
Their regular size pizza has diameter 25 cm.
 a What is the area of a mini pizza (to the nearest whole number)?
 b How many people could share a regular pizza if they each eat approximately the same amount of pizza as the mini one?

Review 2
 a The diameter of King Arthur's Round Table is 5·5 m.
If each person needs 45 cm round the circumference of the table, what is the maximum number of people that could be seated around it?
 b If 50 people sat around this table, how much room round the circumference would each have?
Is it possible to sit 50 people around the table?

Review 3 Roger's bicycle has wheels of diameter 68 cm.
How many times do the wheels on Roger's bicycle rotate in 4 km?
 A about 200 times   **B** about 2000 times   **C** about 20 000 times

*Review 4 Mr Green's backyard is 6·5 m by 5 m.
He wants to put a circular pool of diameter 4 m in the ground and
pave the remaining area.
 a What is the area of the pool?
 b What area will be covered with paving stones?
 c If paving stones are 20 cm by 40 cm,
how many paving stones will he need?
(Assume he can use all the cut off bits.)

Remember not to round intermediate calculations.

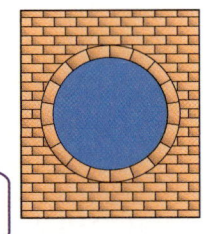

❓ *Puzzles

1 The six equally spaced circles all have the same centre.
Which region has the greater area the pink or the blue area?

Hint: Area of ring = area of outer circle – area of inner circle.

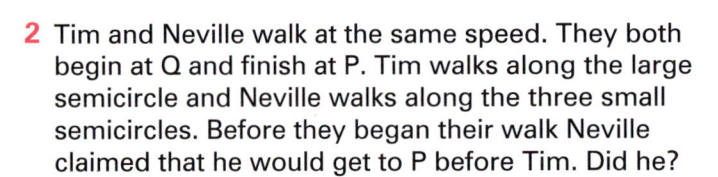

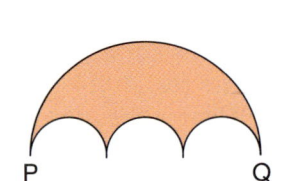

2 Tim and Neville walk at the same speed. They both begin at Q and finish at P. Tim walks along the large semicircle and Neville walks along the three small semicircles. Before they began their walk Neville claimed that he would get to P before Tim. Did he?

3 Lightning Lady and Stirling Monarch set off from the same point on their circular training track, with their jockeys riding them in opposite directions. The first time they meet, Lightning Lady has run 500 m. The next time they meet Stirling Monarch still has 200 m to go to complete his first lap. How far is it around their training track?

Assume they both travel at a constant speed.

Measures, Perimeter, Area and Volume

⭐ Practical

1 You will need a dynamic geometry software package.
  a Draw a circle inside a square.
  b Draw a square inside a circle with the same diameter as the circle in **a**.
  What is the ratio of areas of the squares?

2 Design a running track.

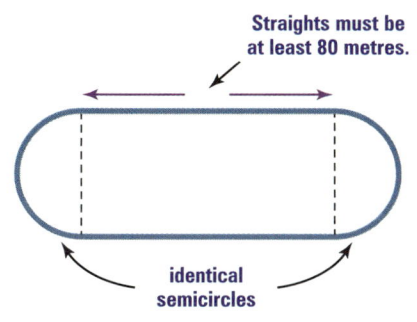

Straights must be at least 80 metres.

Total inside perimeter must be 400 m.

identical semicircles

The inside perimeter must have this shape and dimensions.
What is the greatest area the running track can enclose?
* If the track itself must be 10 m wide, what is the smallest rectangular field needed to contain it?

Surface area and volume of a prism

Discussion

The areas of the cross-sections of these prisms are given.

How could you use these to find the volume of each prism? **Discuss**.

area of cross-section = 20 cm²   8 cm

area of cross-section = 14 cm²   8 cm

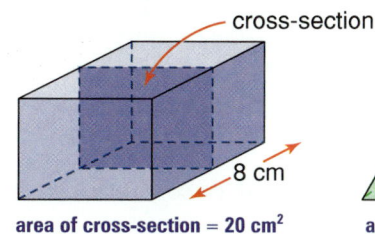

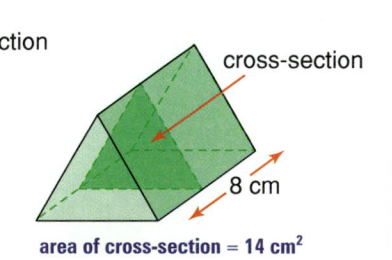

* The volumes of both can be found from the same formula. **Discuss** how to finish this formula.

    Volume = area of cross-section × _____

Could the formula you discussed be used to find the volume of any of these shapes? Which ones? **Discuss**.

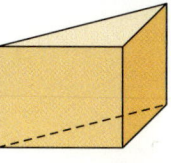

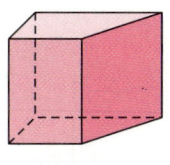

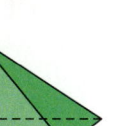

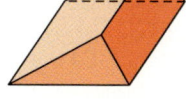

A   B   C

D   E   F

Shape, Space and Measures

Remember
The surface area of a cuboid is given by the formula

surface area = 2lw + 2lh + 2hw

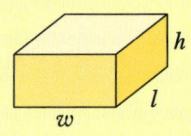

The surface area of other prisms is the sum of the areas of the faces of the prism.

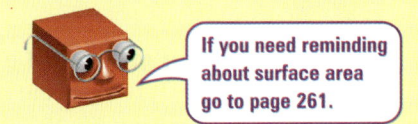

If you need reminding about surface area go to page 261.

A **prism** has a **constant cross-section** throughout its length.
The cross-section is congruent and parallel to the two congruent end faces.

Examples

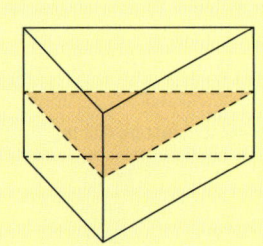

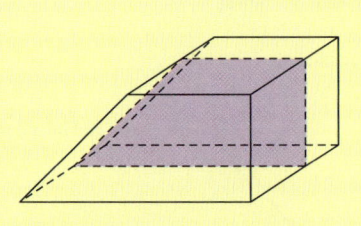

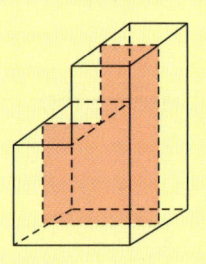

Volume of a prism = area of cross-section × length

Example   Volume of prism = area of cross-section × length

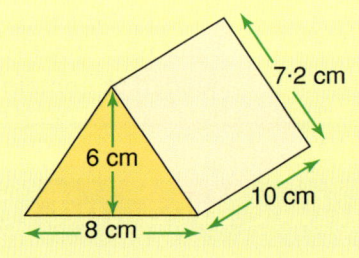

Area of cross-section = $\frac{1}{2}bh$
$= \frac{1}{2} \times 8 \times 6$
$= 24$ cm^2

Volume = 24 × 10
= **240 cm^3**

Surface area of prism = 2 × area of end triangle + 2 × area of side + area of base
= 2 × 24 + 2 × 7·2 × 10 + 10 × 8
= 48 + 144 + 80
= **272 cm^2**

Exercise 7   **Round your answers sensibly.**

1 Find the volume of these shapes. The cross-section is shown shaded.

a) 8 cm, 6 cm, 6 cm

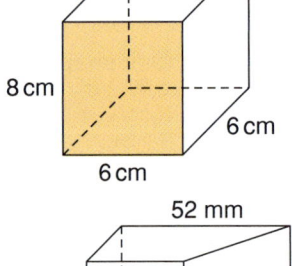

b) 3·2 cm, 3 cm, 2 cm, 4 cm

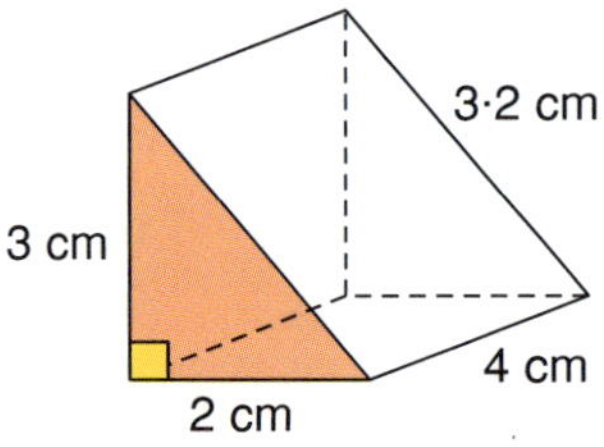

c) 5 cm, 3 cm, 6 cm

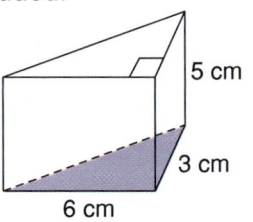

d) 52 mm, 46 mm, 25 mm, 28 mm — The shaded face is a trapezium.

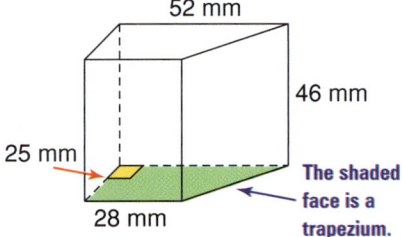

*e) 1·5 m, 1·5 m, 1·5 m, 1·5 m, 3 m, 2 m, 3 m

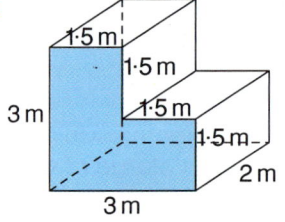

*f) 10, 20, 10, 16, 24, 66 — Dimensions are in cm.

348

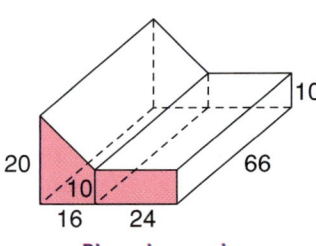

Measures, Perimeter, Area and Volume

2 Find the surface areas of the shapes in questions **1a** and **1b**.

3 The drawing shows two cuboids that have the same volume.

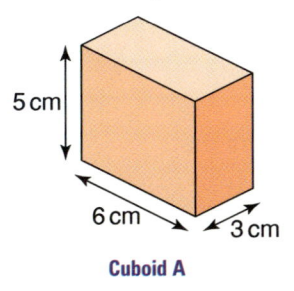

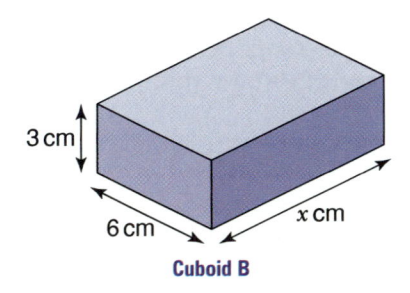

Cuboid A: 5 cm, 6 cm, 3 cm
Cuboid B: 3 cm, 6 cm, x cm

  a What is the volume of cuboid A?
   Remember to state your units.
  b Work out the value of the length marked x.

4 The squared paper shows the nets of cuboid A and cuboid B. [SATs Paper 2 Level 6]

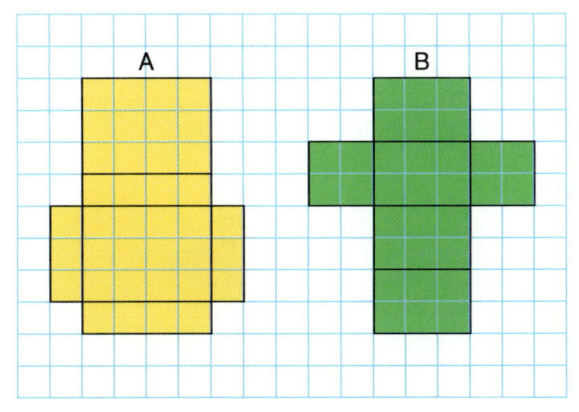

  a Do the cuboids have the **same surface area**?
   Show calculations to explain how you know.
  b Do the cuboids have the **same volume**?
   Show calculations to explain how you know.

5 Write an expression for the volume of this prism.
 It has cross-sectional areas L_1, L_2, L_3 and L_4 all of length p.

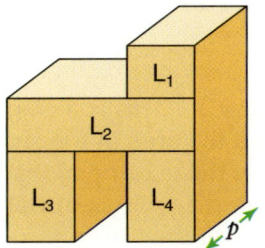

*6 A door stop is in the shape of a prism.
  a The purple shaded end is a trapezium.
   Calculate its area.
  b Calculate the volume of the door stop.
  c The **whole** door stop is to be covered in rubber.
   What area of rubber is needed?

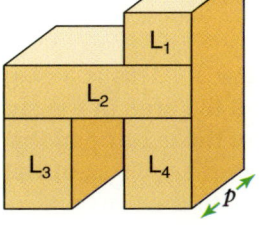

 Dimensions: 2·5 cm, 3·8 cm, 1·4 cm, 2·0 cm, 6·0 cm

*7 Boxes are made using rectangular sheets of card.
 The sheet is marked out using these dimensions.
 Solid lines are cut lines.
 Dotted lines are fold lines.
 If the card is 28 cm long and 16 cm wide and the
 box is 10 cm high, what is the volume of the box?

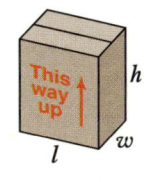

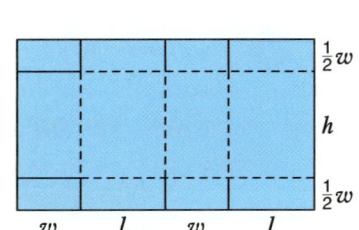

349

Shape, Space and Measures

*8 Contractors are digging a ditch which is to be 30 m long and 1·25 m deep.
    The cross-section is a symmetrical trapezium, as shown in the diagram.
    The ditch must be 1·5 m wide at the bottom and 2·5 m wide at the top.
    a What are the values of a, b and c on the cross-section?
    b Find the area of the cross-section.
    c Calculate how many m^3 of dirt are to be excavated from the ditch.

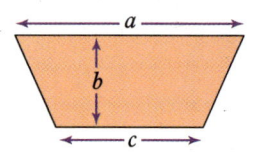

    The contractors use an excavator and the dirt is taken away in lorries that
    can take 12 m^3 at a time.
    d How many full loads of dirt are taken away?
    e The last lorry is only partially filled up. What fraction of a full load does
       the last lorry take?

*9 A pentagonal box is filled with chocolate drops.
    Each of the five triangles in the pentagon are identical.
    a Calculate the area of the pentagon.
    b The box is 12 cm long. Calculate its volume in cm^3.
    c The chocolate drops fill 90% of the box.
       1 cm^3 of chocolate drops are 0·6 grams.
       What mass of chocolate drops are in the box?

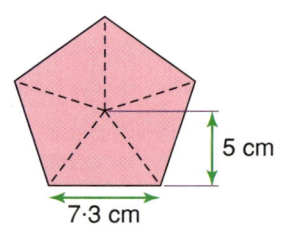

Review 1 Find the volumes of these shapes. The cross-sections are shaded.
a (3 cm, 5 cm, 6 cm)
b (12 cm, 5 cm, 8 cm)
c (4 cm, 4 cm, 12 cm, 6 cm, 14 cm, 5 cm)

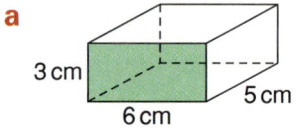

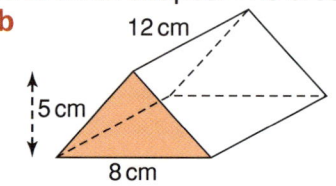

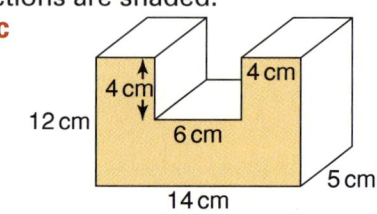

Review 2
a Find the volume of this triangular prism.
*b A cube has the same volume as this triangular prism.
    What is the length of the side of the cube?
(6 mm, 16 mm, 36 mm)

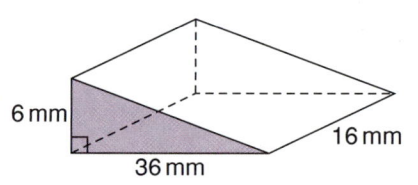

Review 3 This is a diagram of a swimming pool.
a Find the area of the shaded cross-section of the pool.
b Find the volume of the pool in m^3.
*c How many litres of water will be needed to fill the pool
    right to the top?
(10 m, 1·2 m, 2·5 m, 25 m)

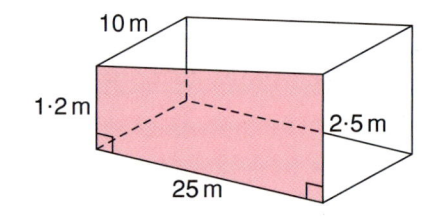

Summary of key points

A You need to know these **area, volume and capacity conversions**.

area
$1 m^2 = 10\,000 cm^2$
$1 cm^2 = 100 mm^2$

capacity
$1 cm^3 = 1000 mm^3$
$1 m^3 = 1\,000\,000 cm^3$

Measures, Perimeter, Area and Volume

B **Solving measures problems**

You often need to convert between metric units or between metric and imperial units to solve problems.

When **estimating measures** it is useful to compare to something you know well.

C **Bearings** are always measured in a clockwise direction from North.
They always have three digits.

Examples

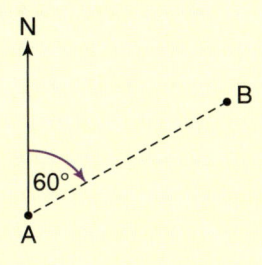

The bearing of B from A is 060°.   The bearing of C from A is 235°.

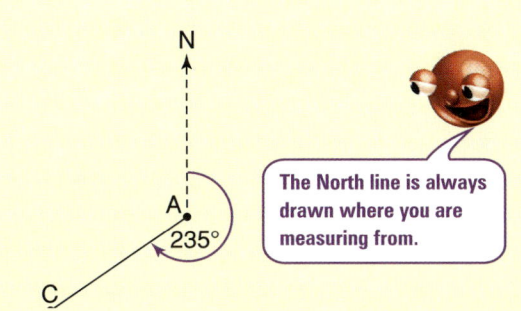

The North line is always drawn where you are measuring from.

D **Perimeters and areas** of complex shapes can be found by dividing into simple areas then adding them.

Example

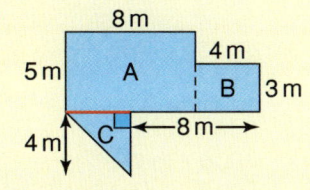

Area = area A + area B + area C
= $8 \times 5 + 4 \times 3 + \frac{1}{2} \times 4 \times 4$ (length red line = 8 + 4 − 8 = 4 m)
= 40 + 12 + 8
= 60 m²

E $C = \pi d$ or $C = 2\pi r$ give the **circumference**, C, **of a circle** of diameter, d and radius, r.

$\pi = 3.14$ (2 d.p.) or you can use the π key on your calculator.

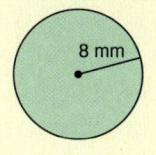

Example $C = 2\pi r$
$= 2 \times \pi \times 8$
$= 50.3$ mm (1 d.p.) using the π key on a calculator

F $A = \pi r^2$ gives the **area**, A, **of a circle** of radius, r.

Example   The area of the circle in **E** is
$A = \pi r^2$
$= \pi \times 8^2$
$= 201.0$ mm² (1 d.p.) using $\pi = 3.14$

351

Shape, Space and Measures

> **G** A **prism** has a constant cross-section throughout its length.
> The cube is a common example of a prism.
>
> **Volume of a prism = area of cross-section × length**
>
> *Example* This is a triangular prism. 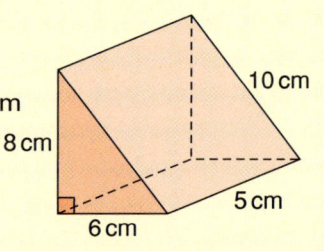
>
> Volume of prism = area of cross-section × length
> = area of triangle × length of prism
> = ($\frac{1}{2}$ × 8 × 6) × 5
> = 24 × 5
> = **120 cm³**
>
> Surface area = sum of areas of all faces
> = 2 × area of triangle + area base + area back + area sloping rectangle
> = 2 × 24 + 6 × 5 + 8 × 5 + 10 × 5   area of △ = $\frac{1}{2}$ × 8 × 6
> = 48 + 30 + 40 + 50   = $\frac{1}{2}$ × 48
> = **168 cm²**   = **24 cm²**

Test yourself

1 Change these.
  a 4 ha to m²
  b 800 m² to ha
  c 5 m³ to ℓ
  d 52 cm³ to mℓ
  e 5800 cm³ to ℓ
  f 4900 ℓ to m³
  g 5 m² to cm²
  h 4 cm³ to mm³
  i 850 000 mm³ to cm³
  j 8 cm² to mm²
  k 0·65 m³ to cm³
  l 52 800 mm² to cm²

2 What is the volume of this petrol can in
  a cm³   **b** mm³   **c** mℓ   **d** ℓ?

3 What is the surface area of the petrol can in question **2** in
  a cm²   **b** mm²?

4 An empty crate weighs 15 kg.
   Simon puts 12 cartons in it and it then weighs 39 000 grams.
   What is the mass, in kilograms, of each carton?

5 A shopping centre has an area of 3 ha.
   If the shopping centre is rectangular and one side is 200 m, what is the length of the other side in metres?

6 a Replace the metric units in this sentence with imperial units.
        Mary cycles 16 km to the nearest station. She takes a 4 kg backpack and a 450 mℓ water bottle.
   b Replace the imperial units in this sentence with metric units.
        Rick went for a 5 mile walk one Saturday. He took with him 2 pints of water and 4 oz of nuts.

Measures, Perimeter, Area and Volume

7 Estimate these using metric units. Give a range for each.
   a the width of your house
   b the mass of 10 apples
   c the capacity of a washing machine

8

1 cm represents 10 m

This scale drawing shows the position of the school library from the school office.
   a i Measure in centimetres, the distance OL.
       ii Work out the distance from the office to the library, in metres.
   b i Measure and write down the bearing of the library from the office.
       ii Write down the bearing of the office from the library.

9 This information describes some shapes.
The **area** of a square, A, is 25 cm².
The **height** of a right-angled triangle, B, is 8 cm and the **base** is 6 cm.
The **perimeter** of a rectangle, C, is **24 cm**. The length is twice as long as the base.
Put the shapes A, B and C in order of size, starting with the smallest.
You must show calculations to explain how you work out your answer.

10 Find the area and circumference of these circular placemats.
Use the π key on your calculator
   a 6 cm   **b** 16 cm   **c** 8·2 cm

11 Kieren had the Irish crest printed on the back of a t-shirt.
The diameter of the circle was 20 cm.
   a Find the area of the design.
   b Find the circumference.

12 The end of this garden is semicircular. Find
   a the area of the garden
   b the perimeter of the garden

24 m, 26 m, 10 m

13 Find the volume of each of these solids.
   a 6 cm, 5·2 cm, 15 cm, 6 cm. The triangular faces are isosceles triangles.
   b 1·4 cm, 0·7 cm, 1·2 cm, 0·8 cm
   c 5 cm, 4 cm, 7 cm, 9 cm

14 Find the surface area of the solid in question **13a**.

Shape, Space and Measures

*15 **a** The capacity of a jug is 2 ℓ to the nearest litre.
What is the smallest capacity it could be?
b The width of the jug is 15 cm to the nearest centimetre.
What is the smallest width it could be?
***c** How many jugs could you be *certain* of fitting side by side in a cupboard 60 cm wide?
Explain.

*16 **a** A van travels 200 miles at an average speed of 50 mph.
For how many hours does the van travel?
b A train travels 415 miles in 5 hours.
What is its average speed?
c A car travels for $3\frac{1}{2}$ hours at an average speed of 21 mph.
How far does the car travel?

Handling Data Support

Planning and collecting data

Use these steps to plan a survey.

Step 1 Decide on the purpose of the survey or specify the problem.
Think of related questions you might want to explore.

Step 2 Decide what data needs to be collected.

Step 3 Decide where to collect data from, and how much to collect.
- You could use a primary source, for example
  a survey of a **sample** of people
  an experiment — observe, count or measure.
- You could use a secondary source, for example reference books, CD-ROMs, websites, books newspapers, ...

The **sample** size should be as large as is sensible.

Once the survey has been planned, a **collection sheet** or a **questionnaire** often has to be designed.

Example Renine mixed some chemicals together in a science lab.
She recorded whether bubbles were given off with and without heating.

	Tally	Frequency
Bubbles with no heat	ⅢⅠ Ⅰ	6
Bubbles only with heat	ⅢⅠ ⅠⅠⅠⅠ	9
No bubbles with and without heat	ⅠⅠⅠ	3

ⅢⅠ is 5.

Link to science.

Discrete or continuous data

When collecting data you need to decide if it is **discrete** data or **continuous** data. Discrete data can only have certain values. It is usually found by counting.

Example The number of people at a concert must be a whole number.

Continuous data can have any values within a certain range. It is usually found by measuring.

Example The temperature of humans usually lies between 35° and 40 °C.
It can have any value within this range.

Grouped data

Sometimes **discrete data** is grouped into **equal class intervals** (groups of equal size).

Rachel drew this frequency table to show the number of points scored by a basketball team one year.

Number of pupils	Tally	Frequency
1–15		0
16–30	Ⅰ	1
31–45	ⅢⅠ Ⅰ	6
46–60	ⅢⅠ ⅢⅠ Ⅰ	11
61–75	ⅢⅠ ⅠⅠ	7
>75	ⅠⅠⅠ	3

Sometimes the last class interval is open.

355

Handling Data

When we collect **continuous data** we usually group it into **equal class intervals** on a **frequency table**.

Example This frequency table shows the length of books in room 7.

equal class intervals

Length in cms	Tally	Frequency
$10 < \ell \leq 15$	|||| |||| |||	13
$15 < \ell \leq 20$	|||| |||| |||| ||	17
$20 < \ell \leq 25$	|||| ||	7
$25 < \ell \leq 30$	||||	4
> 30	||	2

$10 < \ell \leq 15$ means a length greater than 10 but less than or equal to 15.

Practice Questions 10, 11, 12, 20, 33

Mode, median, mean, range

The **range** is the difference between the **highest data value** and the **lowest data value**.

The **mode** is the most commonly occurring data value.
Sometimes a set of data has two modes.

Examples For 16, 17, 9, 11, 13, 11, 16, 14 the modes are 11 and 16.

For the frequency table above the modal class is $15 < \ell \leq 20$.

$$\text{Mean} = \frac{\text{sum of data values}}{\text{number of data values}}$$

Example 10, 13, 16, 18, 15, 14, 15, 11

$$\text{Mean} = \frac{10 + 13 + 16 + 18 + 15 + 14 + 15 + 11}{8}$$
$$= \frac{112}{8}$$
$$= 14$$

Number of sports	0	1	2	3	4
Frequency	4	6	8	5	2
Total number of sports	0	6	16	15	8

Sometimes the data is given in a **frequency table**.

Example Kim collected this data on how many sports her classmates played.

$$\text{Mean} = \frac{\text{sum of data values}}{\text{number of data values}}$$
$$= \frac{0 + 6 + 16 + 15 + 8}{4 + 6 + 8 + 5 + 2}$$ ← sum of total number of sports played
  ← sum of frequencies
$$= \frac{45}{25}$$
$$= 1 \cdot 8$$

The **median** is the middle value when a set of data is arranged in order of size.
When there is an even number of values, the median is the mean of the two middle values.

Example 25, 26, 13, 19, 26, 14, 22, 11
In order these are 11, 13, 14, **19**, **22**, 25, 26, 26.
Median = $\frac{19 + 22}{2}$ **19** and **22** are the two middle values.
       = 20·5

When there are two middle values we find the mean of them.

Practice Questions 3, 7, 9, 13, 26

356

Displaying and interpreting data

These diagrams show some ways of **displaying discrete data**.

Pictogram

Each symbol represents 4 caps	
Red	🧢 🧢
Navy	🧢 🧢
Black	🧢 🧢 🧢
White	🧢 🧢 🧢 🧢

Bar chart
Sometimes bar charts are drawn horizontally.

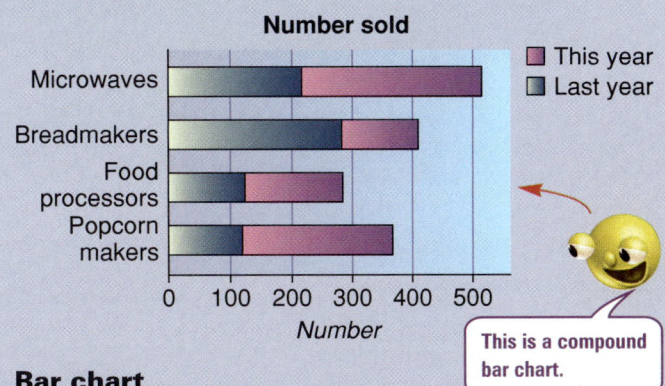

Number sold (Microwaves, Breadmakers, Food processors, Popcorn makers) — This year / Last year

This is a compound bar chart.

Bar-line graph
This bar-line graph shows the number of pets students in a Year 9 class had.

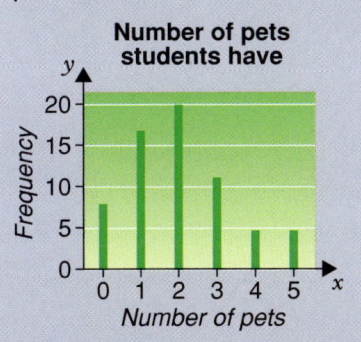

Number of pets students have

Bar chart
Sometimes two sets of data are shown on a bar chart.
Always give a key.

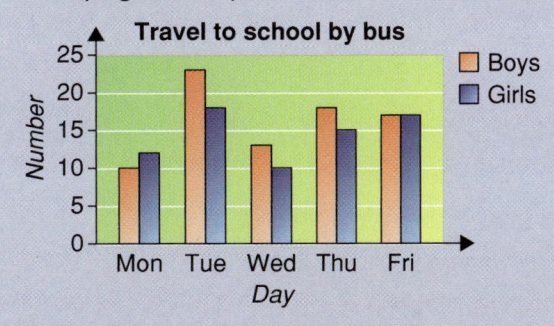

Travel to school by bus — Boys / Girls (Mon, Tue, Wed, Thu, Fri)

Line graph

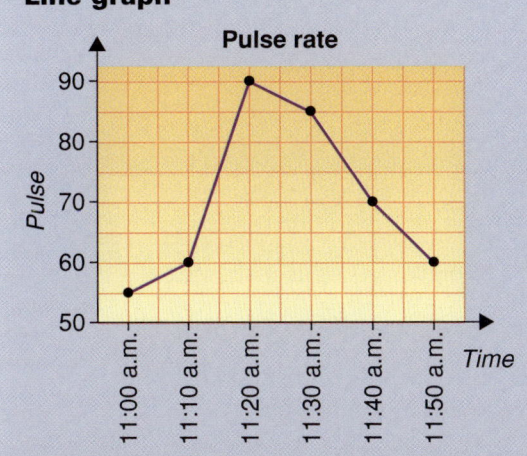

Pulse rate (11:00 a.m. – 11:50 a.m.)

Pie chart
A pie chart shows the **proportion** in each category.

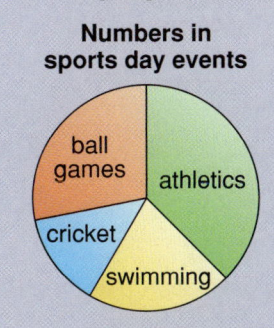

Numbers in sports day events — ball games, athletics, cricket, swimming

Pictograms, bar charts and pie charts are used to show **categorical** data.
Categorical data is non-numerical data.
Line graphs are usually used to show changes over time.

Always — give your graph a **title**
— label any axes
— have values at equal intervals on the axes.

Once we have displayed data on a graph, we can use the graph to help **interpret the data**.

Other ways to display data are in Venn diagrams, two-way tables or databases.

Handling Data

We can use a **bar chart** to show **grouped discrete data**.

Example

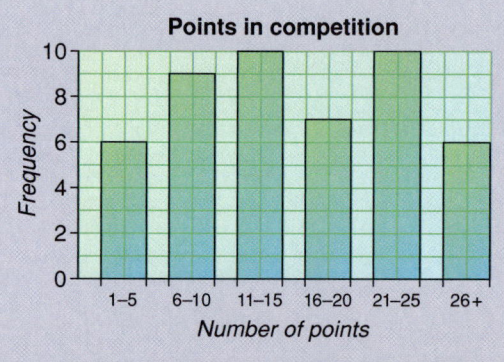

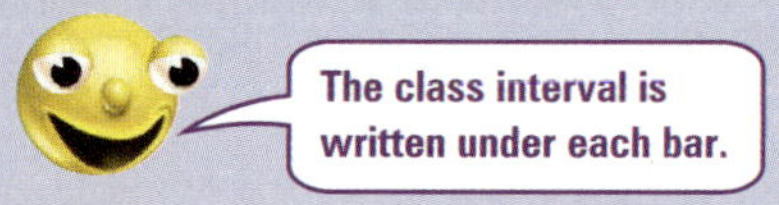

Points in competition

(bar chart with Frequency on y-axis, Number of points on x-axis with intervals 1–5, 6–10, 11–15, 16–20, 21–25, 26+)

The class interval is written under each bar.

For continuous data we draw a **frequency diagram**.

Example This frequency diagram shows the length of books in Abbie's bookcase.

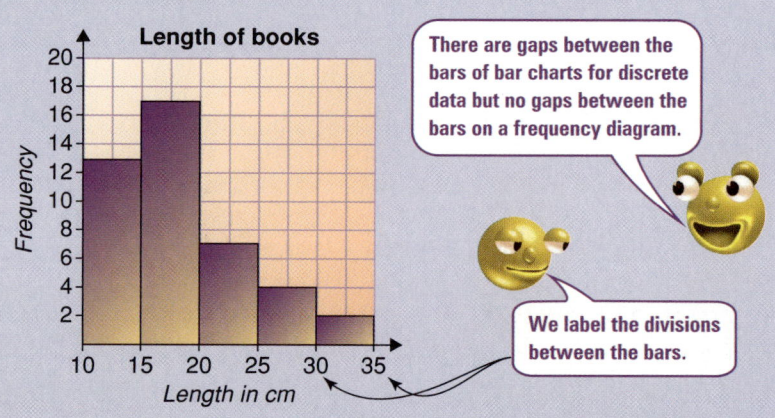

Length of books

(frequency diagram with Frequency on y-axis, Length in cm on x-axis: 10, 15, 20, 25, 30, 35)

There are gaps between the bars of bar charts for discrete data but no gaps between the bars on a frequency diagram.

We label the divisions between the bars.

A **scatter graph** displays two sets of data.

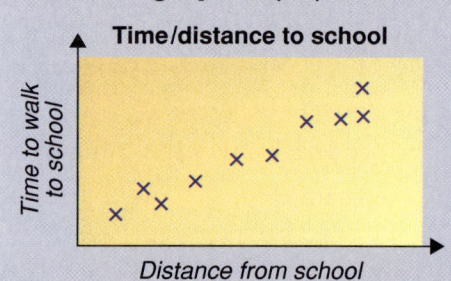

Time/distance to school

(scatter graph with Time to walk to school on y-axis, Distance from school on x-axis)

This scatter graph shows that as distance from school increases, it takes a longer time to walk to school.

Practice Questions 4, 5, 6, 18, 19, 24, 27, 32, 34

Comparing data

To **compare data** we can use the **range** and one of the **mean**, **median** or **mode**.

Example Paula and Melanie both want to be chosen to represent the school in a 15 km run. The mean and range of their last ten races are given in the table.

	Mean	Range
Paula	1 hour 48·62	19 minutes
Melanie	1 hour 49·25	3 minutes

We could choose Paula because her mean time is better or we could choose Melanie because her times are more consistent.

Practice Question 25

Handling Data Support

Probability

We can describe the probability of an event happening using one of these words.

**certain   likely   even chance   unlikely   impossible   better than even chance
less than even chance   very likely   very unlikely**

Examples   It is **certain** that the next pentagon you draw will have 5 sides.
It is **very unlikely** that it will rain every day for the next 6 weeks.
There is a **better than even chance** that you will get a number greater than 2 next time you roll a dice.

Probability is a way of measuring the chance or likelihood of a particular outcome.
We can show probabilities on a probability scale.

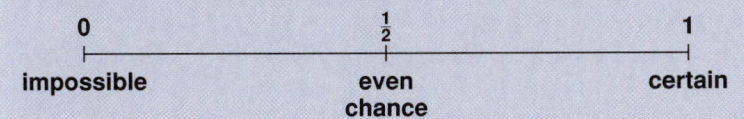

```
0              1/2              1
|───────────────|───────────────|
impossible     even          certain
               chance
```

Example   The probability of drawing a spade from a pack of cards (without jokers) is shown.

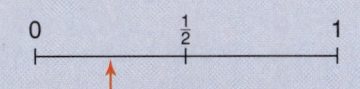

All probabilities lie from 0 to 1.
We can write probability as a decimal, fraction or percentage.

A marble is taken from this bag without looking.
This is called at **random**.
It could be red, green or purple.
These are called the possible **outcomes**.
If one marble is taken at random then put back in the bag, then another is taken at random, the possible outcomes are:

RR   RG   RP   GG   GR   GP   PP   PR   PG.

Equally likely outcomes have an equal chance of happening.

Example   Getting green, red or blue with this spinner are all equally likely outcomes because each colour is the same proportion of the spinner.

For equally likely outcomes:
probability of an event = $\frac{\text{number of favourable outcomes}}{\text{number of possible outcomes}}$

Example   The letters in the word HOBBIT are put in a bag.
One is taken at random.
The probability of getting a T is $\frac{1}{6}$ or 16·7% (1 d.p.) or 0·17 (2 d.p.) (one in six).
The probability of getting a B is $\frac{2}{6}$ or $\frac{1}{3}$ or 33·3% (1 d.p.) or 0·33 (2 d.p.) (one in three).

When a probability experiment is repeated the results are likely to be slightly different each time.

Example   Junita tossed a coin 50 times. She got 28 heads.
She tossed it another 50 times. She got 22 heads.

Practice Questions 1, 2, 8, 14, 15, 16, 17, 21, 22, 23, 28, 29, 30, 31

359

Handling Data

Practice Questions

1 Decide if each of these is **certain**, **very likely**, **likely**, **unlikely**, **very unlikely** or **impossible**.
  a A cylinder has no curved faces.
  b At least half of your class will be away sick all next week.
  c Wednesday will come before Thursday next week.
  d At least six people in your class will watch TV this week.
  e You will receive at least two phone calls tonight.

2 Jenni has 40 marbles altogether in a bag.
They are all either white or blue.
Jenni is going to take a marble without looking.
It is **equally likely** she will take a blue or white marble.
How many blue and how many white marbles are in the bag?

3 Find the mode of each of these data sets.
  a 5, 7, 11, 5, 8, 3, 5, 7, 5, 2
  b 13, 19, 15, 19, 19, 19, 13, 13, 24, 16, 18, 13
  c 2·6, 4·1, 8·3, 5·2, 7·1, 6·4, 3·9

4 The chart shows which factor sun cream is recommended for different places.

[SATs Paper 2 Level 3]

Type of skin	Warm UK first 3 days	Warm UK after the first 3 days	Hot Southern Europe first 3 days	Hot Southern Europe after the first 3 days	Very Hot The Tropics first 3 days	Very Hot The Tropics after the first 3 days
Fair	20	12	20	12	35	20
Medium	16	8	20	12	20	12
Dark	12	6	12	6	12	8

  a Amy says:

  > I have dark skin and I'm going to The Tropics.

  What factor sun cream should she use after the first 3 days?
  b Eric says:

  > The chart shows I must use factor 16 sun cream for my holiday.

  Use the chart to answer the following questions.
  Where might Eric be going on his holiday?
  What type of skin does Eric have?

5 This pie chart shows the colour of cats seen by a vet during one day.
  a Which colour cat was seen most by the vet?
  b Which colour cats were seen in about equal numbers by the vet?
  c The vet said 'This shows that tortoiseshell cats are the healthiest.'
  Explain why he might be wrong.

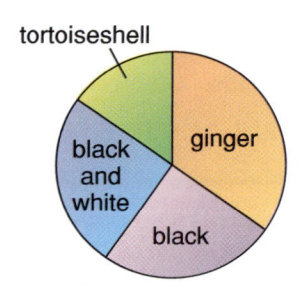

Handling Data Support

6 Danny did a survey.
He asked pupils at his school:
   'Would you like a new uniform?'
This table shows his results.

	Yes	No	Don't know
Year 7	12	31	7
Year 8	23	23	8
Year 9	27	18	4

  a How many Year 9 pupils took part in the survey?
  b Altogether more pupils said 'No' than 'Yes'. How many more?
  c Danny asked the same question of 40 pupils in Year 10. 25% said 'Don't know', 50% said 'No'. The rest said 'Yes'.
  Copy and complete the table to show how many pupils from Year 10 gave each answer.

	Yes	No	Don't know
Year 10			

T **d** Stacey does a different survey with Year 9 pupils.
  She wants to know if more boys than girls have spent a night in hospital.
  She asks 'Have you spent at least one night in hospital since starting school?'
  Use a copy of the table. Fill in the labels Stacey could use.

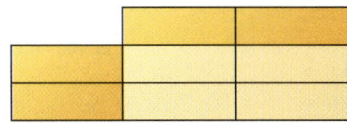

7 Find the mean, median and range of each of these sets of data.
  a 14, 17, 15, 42, 27, 32, 28
  b 144 g, 179 g, 230 g, 98 g, 273 g, 87 g, 135 g, 190 g
  c 11·2 cm, 7·2 cm, 6·9 cm, 14·6 cm, 16·5 cm, 12·6 cm, 5·8 cm, 15·3 cm, 8·7 cm, 4·2 cm

T **8** Tom spins this spinner.
  a Use a copy of the probability scale.

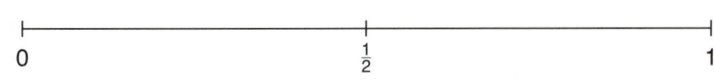

  ├─────────────┼─────────────┤
  0   ½   1

  Show on the probability scale, the probability of spinning each of these.
   i 1   **ii** 3   **iii** an even number   **iv** an odd number
  b Tom now spins the above spinner at the same time as he spins this one.
   i Tom started writing the list of possible outcomes.
     Copy and complete this list.
       R1, R2, R2, R3, R3, ...
   ii Show on the probability scale the probability of getting red and an even number.

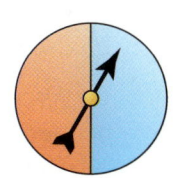

9 Kylie collected data on the number of bikes owned in 45 households. Find the mean of the number of bikes owned.

Number of bikes	1	2	3	4	5
Frequency	10	12	10	9	4

10 Which of the following data is discrete and which is continuous?
  Year of birth   Waist measurements   Time spent watching TV
  Length of babies   Size of families.

  Remember: Discrete data is counting data and continuous data is measurement data.

11 For each of these questions, how would you collect the data?
   A Questionnaire or data collection sheet
   B Experiment
   C Secondary source such as website, book, newspaper, CD-ROM, ...
  a How much does a plant grow over a few weeks?
  b What is the average rainfall of the ten largest cities in the UK?
  c Do boys or girls in your class read more books?

361

Handling Data

12 Sam did a traffic survey.
He counted the number of cars that passed through an intersection in half-hour intervals during the day.
These are his results.

    15 24 93 72 43 29 32 19 17 31 48 56 42
    47 26 32 54 63 56 41 106 97 51 43 25 29

Draw a frequency table with class intervals 1–20, 21–40, 41–60, ... to show Sam's results.

13 Find the median, range and mode from this stem-and-leaf diagram.

Marks out of 60
stem = tens
leaves = units

1 | 0 1 4 8
2 | 3 8 6
3 | 0 1 3 3 4 7 9 9 9
4 | 0 1 4 5 5 6 6 7 7 8 8 9
5 | 0 3 6 7 8

14 I toss a fair coin.
For each statement below, say whether it is true or false and explain your answer.
  a On each toss, the probability of getting a tail is $\frac{1}{2}$.
  b On six tosses, it is certain I will get three heads and three tails.

15 a The diagram shows spinner A and spinner B.   [SATs Paper 1 Level 4]

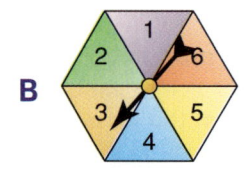

A (pentagon spinner with sections 1, 2, 3, 4, 5)
B (hexagon spinner with sections 1, 2, 3, 4, 5, 6)

Which spinner gives you the better chance to get 1? Explain why you chose that answer.
  b Here are two different spinners.
The spinners are the same shape but different sizes.

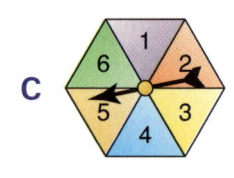

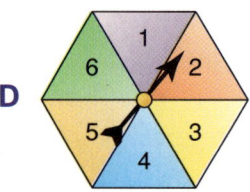

C (hexagon spinner with sections 1, 2, 3, 4, 5, 6)
D (hexagon spinner with sections 1, 2, 3, 4, 5, 6)

Which spinner gives you the better chance to get 3? Explain why you chose that answer.
  c Each section of spinner E is the same size.
Make a copy of spinner E and fill in numbers so that **both** of these statements are true.
    It is **equally likely** that you will spin 3 or 2.
    It is **more likely** that you will spin 4 than 2.

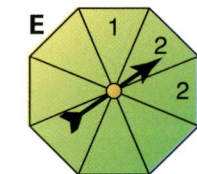

E (octagon spinner showing 1, 2, 2)

16 Andrew has 7 number cards.
He says:
    'I am going to take a card at random.
    Each card shows a different positive whole number.
    It is certain that the card will show a number between 10 and 25.
    It is impossible that the card will show an odd number.'
What numbers are on the cards?

Handling Data Support

17 a A teacher put 4 red counters and 1 blue counter in a box.
Jyoti is going to take one without looking.
She says:
'There are two colours so it is just as likely that I will get a red counter as a blue counter.'
Explain why Jyoti is wrong.
b How many more blue counters should the teacher put in the box so Jyoti is just as likely to get a red as a blue counter?
c Susie has a different box with 10 red and blue counters in it.
It is more likely that Susie will take a red than a blue counter from her box.
How many red counters might there be in Susie's box?

T 18 This table gives the population, to the nearest thousand, of a town and the projected population for future years.

Year	1985	1990	1995	2000	2005	2010	2015	2020
Population	28 000	30 000	31 000	29 000	28 000	26 000	26 000	28 000

a Use a copy of this grid.
Draw a line graph for the data.

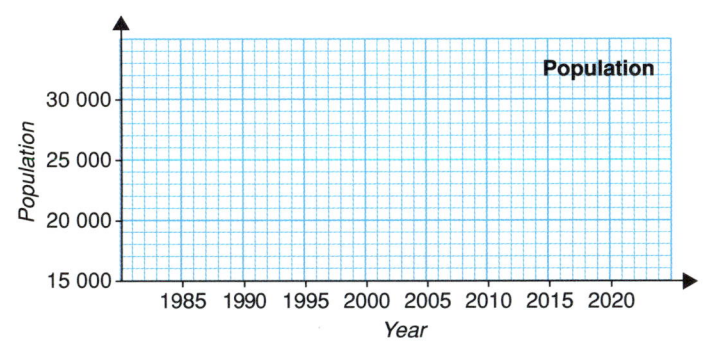

b What was the increase in population between 1985 and 1995?
c What is the expected increase in population between 2010 and 2020?
d It seems that the population in the middle of 1987 was 29 000. Is this necessarily so?
Explain your answer.

T 19 Tara recorded the heights of some pupils in this table.
a Use a copy of the grid below to draw a frequency diagram.
b How many pupils were 135 cm or taller?
c How many were shorter than 155 cm?
d Another pupil is measured. Her height is 140 cm.
Into which class interval should her height be placed?

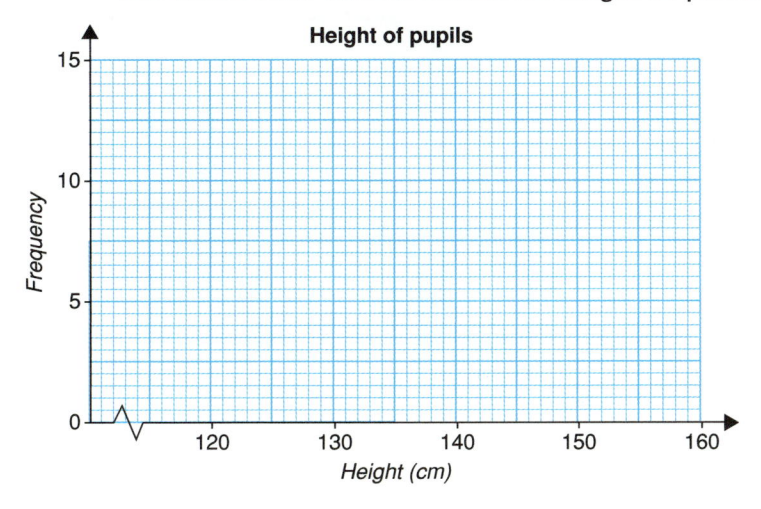

Height h (cm)	Frequency
$120 \leq h < 125$	2
$125 \leq h < 130$	5
$130 \leq h < 135$	8
$135 \leq h < 140$	14
$140 \leq h < 145$	11
$145 \leq h < 150$	9
$150 \leq h < 155$	3
$155 \leq h < 160$	1

363

Handling Data

20 Beryl wanted to know whether Year 9 girls could juggle two or three balls for longer than Year 9 boys.
  a Write down two things Beryl might find out from her survey.
  b What data does Beryl need to collect?
  c Design a collection sheet for this data.
  d How could Beryl collect the data?
  e What does Beryl need to consider when choosing a sample size?

21 In each box of cereal there is a free gift of a card. [SATs Paper 2 Level 5]
You cannot tell which card will be in a box.
Each card is equally likely.
There are four different cards A, B, C or D. 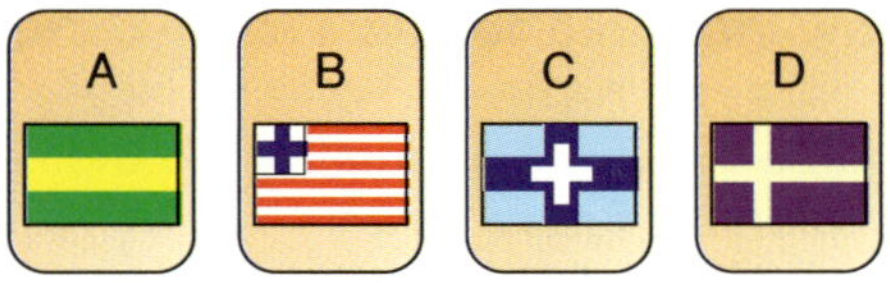
  a Zoe needs card A.
    Her brother Paul needs cards C and D.
    They buy one box of cereal.
    i What is the probability that the card is one that Zoe needs?
    ii What is the probability that the card is one that Paul needs?
  b Then their mother opens the box.
    She tells them that the card **is not** card A.
    i Now what is the probability the card is one that Zoe needs?
    ii What is the probability that the card is one that Paul needs?

22 a A spinner has eight equal sections. [SATs Paper 1 Level 5] 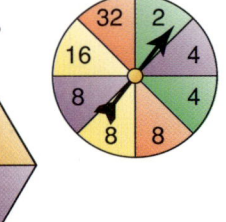
    i What is the probability of scoring 4 on the spinner.
    ii What is the probability of scoring an **even** number on the spinner?
  b A different spinner has six equal sections and **six numbers**.
    On this spinner, the probability of scoring an **even** number is $\frac{2}{3}$.
    The probability of scoring **4** is $\frac{1}{3}$.
    Copy this spinner.
    Write what numbers could be on this spinner.

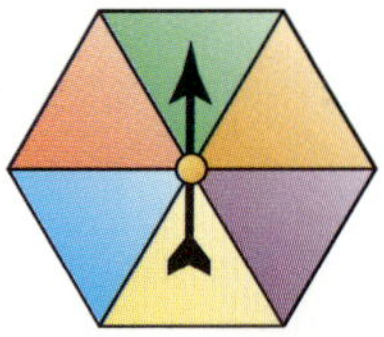

23 At a fair, you pay £1 to take a marble at random from one of these bags.
If you take a red marble you win £1·50.
From which bag is it most likely you will get a red marble? Explain.

Bag A   Bag B   Bag C

T 24 A survey was carried out on vehicle registration.
This table gives the number of cars, lorries and motorcycles without correct registration in three areas.

	Cars	Lorries	Motorcycles
Area 1	58	12	18
Area 2	14	8	15
Area 3	63	7	22

Use a copy of this grid.
Draw a compound bar graph to show this data.

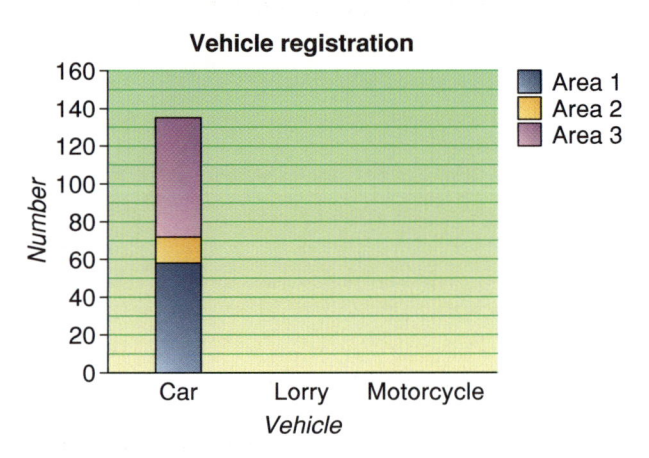

Handling Data Support

25 This table gives the mean and range for times taken by pupils in 9L and 9T to run the cross-country. Write a sentence comparing the speed of the pupils in 9L and 9T.

	Mean (min)	Range (min)
9L	15·5	3
9T	14·6	6

26 Pansy got these marks in three tests: 80, 86, 94.
She has one more test to sit.
She wants a mean of 85 for the four tests.
What mark must she get in her fourth test?

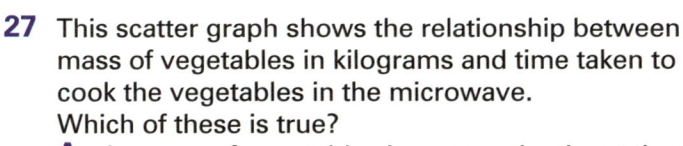

27 This scatter graph shows the relationship between mass of vegetables in kilograms and time taken to cook the vegetables in the microwave.
Which of these is true?
A As mass of vegetables increases the time taken to cook increases.
B As mass of vegetables increases the time taken to cook decreases.

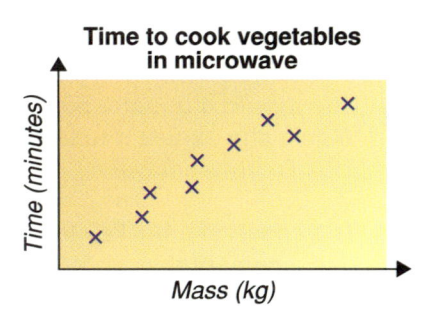

Time to cook vegetables in microwave

28 Mark and Kate each buy a family pack of crisps.
Each family pack contains **ten bags** of crisps.
The table shows how many bags of each flavour are in each family pack.

[SATs Paper 1 Level 5]

a Mark is going to take a bag of crisps at random from his family pack.
Copy and complete these sentences.
  The probability that the flavour will be _____ is $\frac{1}{2}$.
  The probability that the flavour will be **cheese** is _____.

Flavour	Number of bags
Plain	5
Vinegar	2
Chicken	2
Cheese	1

b Kate ate **two bags** of **plain** crisps from her family pack of 10 bags.
Now she is going to take a bag at random from the bags that are left.
What is the probability that the flavour will be cheese?

c A shop sells **12 bags** of crisps in a large pack.
I am going to take a bag at random from the large pack.
The table shows the probability of getting each flavour.
Use the probabilities to work out **how many bags** of each flavour are in this large pack.

Flavour	Probability	Number of bags
Plain	$\frac{7}{12}$	
Vinegar	$\frac{1}{4}$	
Chicken	$\frac{1}{6}$	
Cheese	0	

29 A door has a security lock. To open the door you must press the correct buttons.
The code for the door is one letter followed by a single-digit number.
For example: B6.

[SATs Paper 2 Level 5]

a How many **different** codes are there altogether?
Show your working.
b I know that the correct code begins with D.
I press D, then I guess the single-digit number.
What is the probability that I open the door?

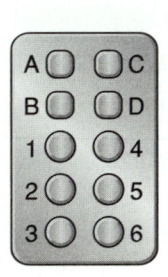

365

Handling Data

30 A school has a new canteen. A special person will be chosen to perform the opening ceremony.
The names of all the pupils, all the teachers and all the canteen staff are put into a box.
One name is taken out at random.
A pupil says:

> There are only three choices.
> It could be a pupil, a teacher or one of the canteen staff.
> The probability of it being a pupil is $\frac{1}{3}$.

[SATs Paper 2 Level 5]

The pupil is **wrong**. Explain why.

31 Julia repeated a probability experiment 50 times.
She tossed a drawing pin 50 times. It landed on its head 32 times.
She tossed it another 50 times.
Would she expect it to land on its head 32 times again?
Explain your answer.

T 32 The coach of a hockey team started a pie chart of the team's 24 results.
Use a copy of this.
Fill in the gaps and complete the pie chart.

Hockey results

		Angle
Won	15	$\frac{15}{24} \times 360° = 225°$
Lost	3	$\frac{3}{24} \times 360° =$ ___
Drawn	$\frac{6}{24}$	$\frac{}{24} \times 360° =$ ___

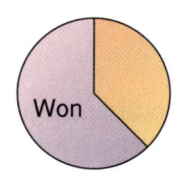

33 This data lists the height, in cm, of some Year 9 pupils.

159 152 136 145 156 172 139 142 147 157
156 157 160 151 149 154 156 152 151 156
165 164 157 156 157 161 160 168 158 165
159 161 161 166 168 162 150 176 166 163

Height h (cm)	Tally	Frequency
$135 < h \leq 140$		
$140 < h \leq 145$		
$145 < h \leq 150$		
$150 < h \leq 155$		
$155 < h \leq 160$		
$160 < h \leq 165$		
$165 < h \leq 170$		
> 170		

a Fill in the frequency table.
b How many pupils were taller than 165 cm?
c How many were 150 cm or shorter?
d How many pupils' heights were recorded altogether?

34 This graph shows the amount spent at a shop on cameras, video cameras and digital cameras.

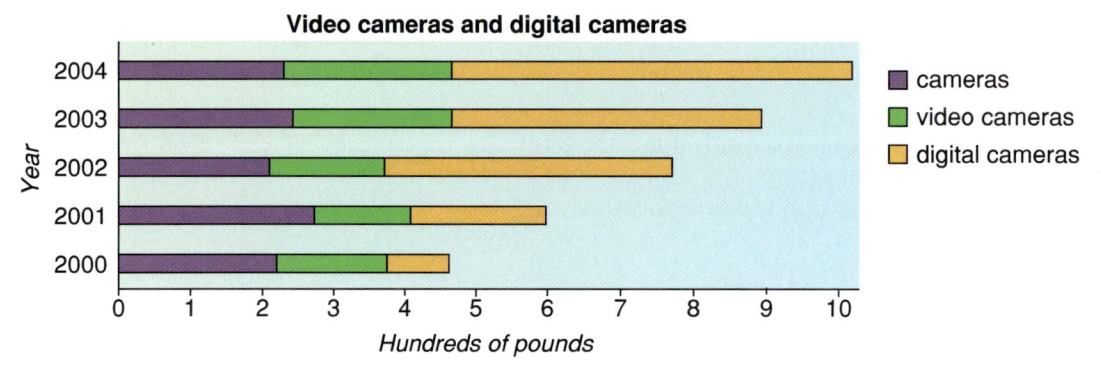

a How did spending change over five years?
b Using the data in the graph, predict what the results might look like this year and in ten years' time.

14 Planning a Survey and Collecting Data

You need to know

✓ planning and collecting data page 355
        – discrete or continuous data
        – grouped data

Key vocabulary

primary source, representative (sample), sample, secondary source, two-way table

▶▶ The customer is always right

BMW    **British Telecom**    **McDonalds**

Big companies often carry out surveys to find out

– what customers want in new products
– if customers are happy with existing products
– market conditions.

What might companies such as BMW, British Telecom and McDonalds want to find out in a survey?

What data might they collect?

Handling Data

Planning a survey

A The problem

The first thing to do when **planning a survey** is to decide on the **problem** you want to explore.

Example 1 The PE teacher wants to explore what factors affect pupil performance on an exercise circuit.

Example 2 A gardener wants to know what factors affect weed growth in lawns.

It is helpful to formulate a **conjecture**.
These could be the conjectures for **Example 1**.

A conjecture is a statement that you want to test the truth of.

1 A pupil's height affects performance on the jumping part of the circuit.
2 Year 9 pupils complete the course faster than Year 7 pupils.
3 The length of the mat given for the standing start jump affects the distance pupils jump.
4 Practice improves performance on the course.

For **Example 2** conjectures might be

1 Weed growth is greater in areas of higher sunlight.
2 Weed growth is less if the lawn is fertilised.

Note There are other possible conjectures for both examples.

Exercise 1

1 For each of these, write two possible conjectures.
   a Jan wants to know if the claim made by this advertisement is true.

   94% of people have contact with someone smoking a cigarette at least once a week.

   b 'The Lettering Company' makes letters for people's surnames to put on post office boxes.
      They want to know which letter to make the most of.
   c 'Dino's' makes take-away dinners.
      They want to know the best three times of the day or evening to advertise the dinners on the radio.

2 Suggest a problem you could explore using a statistical survey.
   Write two possible conjectures for your problem.
   Keep your conjectures for the next exercise.

Review Deepak wants to know if the size of the leaves on a rhododendron bush vary with their position on the bush.
Write two possible conjectures Deepak could explore.

Planning a Survey and Collecting Data

B The data

The next thing to do when planning a survey is to decide **what data** needs to be collected and possible **sources of data**.

Sometimes there are related questions you need to explore.
If so, you may need to collect data for these as well.

Example If you are exploring how height affects pupil performance in the jumping section of an exercise circuit you will need to collect data about pupil height and the score given for the jumping section.
A related question might be 'Is there any difference between performance on the high jump and standing start jump?'
You may need to collect individual data for each jump.

Remember
Data can be gathered from

1 a questionnaire or survey of a sample of people
2 an experiment which may use technology, such as a data logger, graphical calculator or computer
3 **secondary sources** such as reference books, websites, printed tables or lists, CD-ROMS, newspapers, historical records, **interrogating** a database.

*1 and 2 are called **primary sources**.*

When **planning a survey** it is helpful to identify all the possible sources of data. Then you must decide how you are going to collect the data.

Example If you are investigating factors that affect how well a vacuum cleaner sucks up dirt you will need to find published data on tests done or conduct your own tests.

Discussion

For each of these, **discuss** possible conjectures, any related questions and the possible sources of data.
Discuss how you might collect the data.

- What factors affect pupil performance in a football match?
- What effect does power, in watts, have on vacuum cleaner performance?
- What factors affect plant growth in gardens?
- Have rainfall patterns changed in Britain in the last 50 years?
- What do people think of shops with a no return of goods policy?

Handling Data

C How much data and how accurate?

The next thing to decide is the **sample size** and the **degree of accuracy** needed for the data.

A **sample** should be as large as it is sensible to make it.
The results that you get from the sample should be **representative of everyone the survey relates to**.

Example If you wanted to know if the age of a chicken affected what size egg it laid, you would need to survey chickens of all different ages.
It is important that the chickens are similar in all other ways, e.g. living conditions, breed, ...

You need to decide the degree of accuracy for any data you are collecting.

Example The mass of the egg in the example above could be measured to the nearest gram or, using very accurate scales, to the nearest 0·1 g.

Discussion

- How many people do you think you should survey so that the data collected is representative? **Discuss**
  Will it change depending on the survey?

- For each of the questions given in the last Discussion, **discuss** a sensible sample size and a degree of accuracy for any data you need to collect.

Exercise 2

1 For each of the conjectures given in **a** to **d** write these down.
   - **i**   The data that needs to be collected and the degree of accuracy.
   - **ii** Possible sources of data. Whether the source is primary or secondary.
   - **iii** A possible sample size and a reason for your choice.

   a The height of a pupil affects how far he or she can jump.
   b More than 80% of people have contact with a person smoking a cigarette at least once a week.
   c The greater the engine size of a car, the greater its acceleration. (Think carefully about how accurate the engine size needs to be.)
   d More than 50% of people think Britain should have euros as its currency.

2 Use the problem you suggested in question **2** of Exercise 1.
   For each conjecture, write down **i** to **iii** of question **1** above.

Review Deepak wrote this conjecture.
   'The leaves on the sunny side of a bush are longer than those against a fence or wall.'
Write down
   a the data that needs to be collected and the degree of accuracy
   b a possible sample size and a reason for your choice
   c possible sources of data.

D Collecting the data

You must now design a **collection sheet or questionnaire** to collect the data.

> **Remember**
> We group **continuous data** in equal class intervals.

Example   Data collection sheet

Height of plant (mm)	Tally	Frequency
$0 < h \leq 10$		
$10 < h \leq 20$		
$20 < h \leq 30$		
$30 < h \leq 40$		
$40 < h \leq 50$		

Class intervals must be equal width. They must not overlap.

See page 356 for more on grouping continuous data.

Here are some **guidelines for writing a questionnaire**.

1. Allow for any possible answers.
   Example
   not at all ☐
   up to 1 hour ☐
   1 up to 2 hours ☐
   2 up to 3 hours ☐
   more than 3 hours ☐

   rather than:
   up to 1 hour ☐
   1 up to 2 hours ☐
   2 up to 3 hours ☐

2. Give instructions on how you want the questions answered.
   Example   Tick one of these boxes.

3. Do not ask for information that is not needed.
   Example   Name of person.

4. Avoid questions that people may not be willing to answer.

5. If your questions are asking for opinions, word the questions so that *your* opinion is not evident.
   Example   Tick one box to show what you thought of the concert.
   Excellent ☐   Very good ☐   Good ☐   Not very good ☐   Very poor ☐
   rather than
   Do you agree our concert was wonderful?   Yes ☐   No ☐

6. Make the questions clear and concise.

7. Keep the questionnaire as short as possible.
   Example   **Questionnaire on health**

   > How many times have you been to the doctor in the last year?
   > Tick one box.
   > 0 ☐   1 ☐   2 ☐   3 ☐   more than 3 ☐
   >
   > How many days off work or school have you had in the last year?
   > Tick one box.
   > 0 ☐   1–3 ☐   4–6 ☐   7–10 ☐   more than 10 ☐

Once you have written a questionnaire, it is a good idea to **trial** it. Have a few people answer the questionnaire. If any of these people have problems answering any questions you will need to improve them.
Check the wording is clear and all possible responses are covered.

Handling Data

Exercise 3

1 This advert was in a newspaper. [SATs Paper 1 Level 6]

It does not say how the advertisers know that 93% of people drop litter every day.

Some pupils think the percentage of people who drop litter every day is much lower than 93%.

They decide to do a survey.

a Jack says:

'We can ask 10 people if they drop litter every day.'

Give two **different** reasons why Jack's method might not give very good data.

b Lisa says:

'We can go into town on Saturday morning.
We can stand outside a shop and record how many people walk past and how many of those drop litter.'

Give two **different** reasons why Lisa's method might not give very good data.

> 93% of us drop litter every day.
> Gang up on litter
> Do your bit. Use a bin.

2 a Design a data collection sheet for these. Group the data sensibly.
  i Timing of goals scored in FA cup games one weekend.
  ii Price of second hand cars sold privately and at a dealers.
  iii Number of weeds in eight equal sized sections of lawn.
b Give a reason why we group data.

3 Renata gathered information about the times taken to complete the school cross-country.
She initially grouped the data in 15-second intervals, then she regrouped them in 30-second intervals and then in 1-minute intervals.
Here are her three collection sheets.

A

Time (min:sec)	Frequency
$15{:}00 < t \leq 15{:}15$	
$15{:}15 < t \leq 15{:}30$	
$15{:}30 < t \leq 15{:}45$	
$15{:}45 < t \leq 16{:}00$	
$16{:}00 < t \leq 16{:}15$	
$16{:}15 < t \leq 16{:}30$	
$16{:}30 < t \leq 16{:}45$	
$16{:}45 < t \leq 17{:}00$	
$17{:}00 < t \leq 17{:}15$	
$17{:}15 < t \leq 17{:}30$	
$17{:}30 < t \leq 17{:}45$	
$17{:}45 < t \leq 18{:}00$	
$18{:}00 < t \leq 18{:}15$	
$18{:}15 < t \leq 18{:}30$	
$18{:}30 < t \leq 18{:}45$	
$18{:}45 < t \leq 19{:}00$	

B

Time (min:sec)	Frequency
$15{:}00 < t \leq 15{:}30$	
$15{:}30 < t \leq 16{:}00$	
$16{:}00 < t \leq 16{:}30$	
$16{:}30 < t \leq 17{:}00$	
$17{:}00 < t \leq 17{:}30$	
$17{:}30 < t \leq 18{:}00$	
$18{:}00 < t \leq 18{:}30$	
$18{:}30 < t \leq 19{:}00$	

C

Time (min:sec)	Frequency
$15{:}00 < t \leq 16{:}00$	
$16{:}00 < t \leq 17{:}00$	
$17{:}00 < t \leq 18{:}00$	
$18{:}00 < t \leq 19{:}00$	

Which of these do you think is the most useful? Explain.

Planning a Survey and Collecting Data

4 Which of these do you think would be the most suitable class intervals for the age distribution of the population of a country? Justify your answer.
   A 0– , 10– , 20– , 30– , 40– , 50– , 60– , 70– , 80– , 90+
   B 0– , 15– , 30– , 45– , 60– , 75– , 90+
   C 0– , 20– , 40– , 60– , 80+

5 Which of these would be a better question to put in a questionnaire to find out what people think of cats as a pet?
   A Do you like cats?   Yes ☐   No ☐

   B I think a cat is a good pet.   Strongly agree ☐
                                       Agree ☐
                                       Not sure ☐
                                       Disagree ☐
                                       Strongly disagree ☐

6 Nia was doing a survey on how much Year 8 pupils helped at home.
   She wrote this question for her questionnaire.

   | I help at home enough.   Yes ☐   No ☐ |

   a Give a reason why Nia's question may not give very good data.
   b Write a question for Nia's questionnaire that would give better data.

7 Anthony designed this data collection sheet to collect data on the length of run up and height jumped by people in a high jump competition.
   a Give two things about it that could be improved.

Name	Length of run up to nearest 5 m	Height jumped to nearest 10 cm
Greg Bate		1·2 m

   b Design a more suitable data collection sheet.

8 Which of the following statements are likely to get responses that would not be very useful? Explain your answer.

   Rewrite these statements so the responses would give you more useful information.

   a I get 8 hours sleep each night.   Always ☐   Sometimes ☐   Never ☐
   b I do my maths homework.   Always ☐   Sometimes ☐   Never ☐
   c I go out on a Friday night.   Always ☐   Sometimes ☐   Never ☐
   d I play sport.   Always ☐   Sometimes ☐   Never ☐

*9 Design a data collection sheet or questionnaire to collect data for each of these.
   a Joanna wants to know if the number of hours people sleep depends on age.
   b Pablo wants to know if the acceleration of a car depends on engine size.

*10 Write a short questionnaire with three or four questions to find out attitudes on one of these.
         The school report   Fairly-traded goods

Handling Data

*11 Choose a survey topic from these.
   A What factors affect how often people eat take-aways?
   B Are people happy with the local bus service?
   a Write down what questions you want answered.
   b Write down a possible conjecture.
   c Write down what data you need to collect and, if relevant, the accuracy needed.
   d Design a collection sheet or questionnaire to collect the data.
   e Suggest a suitable sample size if this is relevant to the question.

Review 1 Jonathon said 'most pupils in the school don't wear their school tie on most days'. Some pupils decide to do a survey to see if Jonathon is right.
a Natalie says 'we can ask 10 people in our class if they wear their tie'.
   Give two reasons why Natalie's method might not give very good data.
b Kylie says 'we could stand outside the gym at lunchtime and record how many people come out and how many don't have a tie'.
   Give two reasons why Kylie's method might not give very good data.

Review 2
a Sean was investigating the heights of 15-year-olds. He initially grouped the data in 2 cm intervals, then he regrouped them in 4 cm intervals and then in 10 cm intervals. Here are the three collection sheets.

A

Height (cm)	Frequency
$145 < t \leq 147$	
$147 < t \leq 149$	
$149 < t \leq 151$	
$151 < t \leq 153$	
$153 < t \leq 155$	
$155 < t \leq 157$	
$157 < t \leq 159$	
$159 < t \leq 161$	
$161 < t \leq 163$	
$163 < t \leq 165$	
$165 < t \leq 167$	
$167 < t \leq 169$	
$169 < t \leq 171$	
$171 < t \leq 173$	
$173 < t \leq 175$	

B

Height (cm)	Frequency
$145 < t \leq 149$	
$149 < t \leq 153$	
$153 < t \leq 157$	
$157 < t \leq 161$	
$161 < t \leq 165$	
$165 < t \leq 169$	
$169 < t \leq 173$	
$173 < t \leq 177$	

C

Height (cm)	Frequency
$145 < t \leq 155$	8
$155 < t \leq 165$	70
$165 < t \leq 175$	22

Which do you think is the most useful? Give a reason.
b What related question could Sean ask about the heights of the 15-year-olds?
What data would he need to collect?

Review 3 Tony's class is doing a survey on the factors that may affect the distance thrown by people in a discus competition for 500 competitors of all ages.
a Tony decided to ask 10 people what they thought affected the distance they threw.
   Give two reasons why this method may not give very good data.
b Brady designed this collection sheet to gather data.
   Give two ways Brady could improve this collection sheet.

Name	Distance thrown	Feel well?

c Mariana wrote this question for her questionnaire.

   I think I threw well.   Yes ☐   No ☐

   Give a reason why Mariana's question may not give very good data.
   Write a question for Mariana that would give better data.

Planning a Survey and Collecting Data

Practical

Plan a survey.
You could choose one of the surveys already mentioned in this chapter **or** you could use one of the suggestions below **or** you could make up your own.
Check your choice with your teacher.

Follow the steps given on pages 368 to 371.
Design a collection sheet or questionnaire. Remember you may need to group the data. Decide first if it is continuous or discrete data.
Collect the data.

Suggestions
Acceleration of popular cars.
Jumping or throwing distances and the factors that affect these.
Distribution of grass/weeds in different parts of the school.
Estimate the number of grass and weed plants growing in equal sized areas.
Divide a larger area into a grid pattern of equal sized areas before estimating.
Attitudes to the legal driving age.
Attitudes to underage drinking.

Two-way tables

Sometimes **two-way tables** are used to collect data or sometimes data is summarised in a two-way table.

Example This two-way table gives the percentage of each age group working towards the qualification given.

People working towards a qualification by age
United Kingdom — Qualification — Percentages

Age (in years)	Degree or higher and equivalent	Higher education	GCE A Level/ NVQ3 or equivalent	GCSE/ NVQ2 or equivalent	Other qualification	Total working towards any qualification
16–24	58	39	79	72	22	52
25–34	21	26	9	11	30	20
35–44	14	23	7	10	26	16
45–54	6	10	4	7	18	10
55–59/64	1	2	1	..	4	2
	100%	100%	100%	100%	100%	100%

Discussion

Look at the two-way table above and **discuss** the answers to these questions.
   What percentage of those working towards higher education are aged under 35?
   What percentage of those working towards GCSE/NVQ2 or equivalent are aged 35 or older?
   If the numbers in the row 16–24 are added, the total is 322. Does this number have any meaning?

What other questions could you answer using the two-way table?

Handling Data

Exercise 4

1 The drinks males and females had one day at a café are shown in this table.
  a How many males in total had drinks?
  b How many in total had tea?
  c How many females had tea or water?
  d How many had drinks in total?
  e Compare the choices of males and females.

	Male	Female
Tea	4	12
Coffee	14	6
Water	3	7
Fizzy	7	1
Milk	0	2

2 This two-way table shows the number of pupils achieving grades A to E in examinations in maths and science.
  a How many pupils achieved the same grade in both subjects?
  b How many of the pupils who achieved grade B in maths achieved a different grade in science?
  c What does the table suggest about the grades achieved by these pupils in maths and science?

Maths grade

Science grade

	A	B	C	D	E
A	5	3	2	0	0
B	3	4	4	1	0
C	1	5	7	0	1
D	0	1	0	6	5
E	0	0	0	4	6

3 A study on alcohol was done in the Netherlands.
These tables show the percentage of problem drinkers aged 16 years and above in three cities.

Utrecht

Age	Men	Women
16–24	23%	14%
25–34	17%	7%
35–44	14%	7%
45–54	15%	8%
55–69	6%	3%
Total	16%	8%

Rotterdam

Age	Men	Women
16–24	19%	9%
25–34	12%	5%
35–44	16%	5%
45–54	15%	4%
55–69	11%	4%
Total	14%	5%

Parkstad Limburg

Age	Men	Women
16–24	16%	4%
25–34	10%	2%
35–44	8%	3%
45–54	11%	2%
55–69	6%	3%
Total	10%	3%

  a Which city has the greatest proportion of problem drinkers in most age groups?
  b Which city has the greatest proportion of problem female drinkers aged 55–69?
  c Compare male and female problem drinkers.

4 These tables show the percentage of male and female smokers at a factory in 1983, 1993 and 2003.

2003

Age	Male %	Female %
16–19	24	30
20–24	40	38
25–34	36	31
35–49	26	26
50–59	30	31
60+	19	21

1993

Age	Male %	Female %
16–19	31	32
20–24	42	39
25–34	35	32
35–49	38	32
50–59	34	34
60+	27	21

1983

Age	Male %	Female %
16–19	38	36
20–24	49	45
25–34	48	41
35–49	49	44
50–59	50	46
60+	41	40

Write some sentences comparing
  a the trends over time
  b male and female smokers.

Planning a Survey and Collecting Data

5 Use a copy of this.
A retirement home has 59 residents.
  a Complete the two-way table.
  b How many females are there in the home?
  c How many females are 70 or over?

	M	F	Totals
Under 70	12		21
70 and over	16		
Totals			59

6 The price of a ten-year-old second-hand car depends on its condition and mileage.
The table shows what percentage of the original price the second-hand value retains.

	Mileage		
Condition	**High**	**Medium**	**Low**
Excellent	25%	35%	55%
Good	20%	25%	30%
Poor	15%	18%	20%

James thinks that the mileage being low becomes more important as the condition gets better.
Do you think he is right? Explain.

*7 Rob was studying the differences between the learning ability of rats and mice. He tested them by trying to teach them to find their way out of a maze, roll a ball into a hole and retrieve food from a cage. He recorded the results and worked out what percentage of rats and mice achieved the tasks.
Design a two-way table to summarise Rob's results.

Review 1 One lunchtime a café recorded their sales of food items to males and females. The results are shown in this table.

Food	Males	Females
Sandwiches	30	56
Salad rolls	28	45
Chips	52	27
Pies	45	17
Pasties	19	12

  a How many pies were sold?
  b How many items were bought by females?
  c How many items of hot food (pies, pasties or chips) were bought by males?
  d How many rolls or sandwiches were bought by females?
  e How many items were sold in total?
  f Compare the purchases of males and females.

Review 2 Use a copy of this.
Pupils in a play either sang, had a main part or had a minor part.
65 pupils took part in the play altogether.
  a Complete the two-way table.
  b How many Year 8 pupils took part in the play?
  c How many minor parts were there altogether?

	Singing	Main	Minor	Totals
Year 7	12	0		18
Year 8	17		8	
Year 9		4	12	
Totals		6		65

Review 3 Ali did a survey on male and female participation in a science fair. She recorded the percentage of males and females from her school who participated in these five sections:

'animal behaviour'
'plants'
'chemistry at home'
'how does it work?'
'seeing and hearing'

Design a two-way table for her results.

377

Handling Data

Summary of key points

A To **plan a survey** follow these steps.

A conjecture is a statement you want to test the truth of.

1 Decide what **problem** you want to explore.
   To help you, it is useful to formulate a **conjecture**.
   Example 'Girls are better than boys at juggling three balls.'

2 Decide **what data** needs to be collected and the possible sources of the data.
   - You could use a **primary source**, for example
       a survey of a **sample** of people
       an experiment – observe, count or measure.
   - You could use a **secondary source**, for example reference books, CD-ROMs, websites, books, newspapers, ...

3 Decide the **sample size** and the **degree of accuracy** for the data.
   A sample should be as large as it is sensible to make it.
   The results you get from the sample should be representative of everyone the survey relates to.
   Example If you want to know if the height of the father affects the length of a newborn baby, you could measure the lengths of babies to the nearest 0·5 cm, 1 cm or 2 cm.
   You would need a sample size of at least 100 fathers and babies.

4 Design a **questionnaire** or **data collection sheet**.
   It is a good idea to trial your questionnaire or collection sheet on a few people.

For guidelines on writing a questionnaire see page 371.

B A **two-way table** displays two sets of data.
   Example This two-way table shows the ages of students in school sports teams.

	Netball	Football	Hockey
Under 14	16	25	27
14 to 16	36	53	26
Over 16	29	34	28

Test yourself

1 Write two possible conjectures for these.
   a 'The Athletics Trust' wants to know if temperature affects the performance of sprinters.
   b 'The Lawn Seed Company' wants to know what conditions affect the germination and growth of their seeds.

Planning a Survey and Collecting Data

2 For each of the conjectures, A and B, given below, write these down. **A**
  i The data that needs to be collected and the degree of accuracy.
  ii Possible sources of data. Whether the source is primary or secondary.
  iii A possible sample size and a reason for your choice.
  iv A questionnaire or data collection sheet.

  A The wattage of a hairdryer affects efficiency of the hairdryer.
  B Teenagers watch more TV in winter than in summer.

3 Design a data collection sheet for this. **A**
  The price of diamond rings sold by 'Pascoes' jewellers and 'Morten's' jewellers.
  First decide how to group the data.
  Explain why you have chosen your particular class interval size.

4 Mia was doing a survey on attitudes to family. **A**
  She wrote this question for her questionnaire.

  | I like all the people in my family.   Yes ☐   No ☐ |

  a Give a reason why Mia's question may not give very good data.
  b Write a suitable question for Mia's questionnaire.
  c Once Mia's questionnaire had been improved, she gave it to ten of her relatives to fill in.
  Give two reasons why Mia's sample might not give very good data.

*5 Write some questions suitable for a questionnaire to find out what people think about teenage smoking. **A**

*6 Choose a survey topic. **A**
  Plan your survey using the steps given in **A**.
  Design a data collection sheet or questionnaire to collect the data.
  You could choose a topic already mentioned in this chapter or choose one of your own.

7 This two-way table shows the number of pupils in three school clubs. **B**
  a How many boys are in the computer club?
  b How many boys in total are in the three clubs?
  c How many pupils are in the dance club?
  d Compare the number of boys and girls in the three clubs.

	Drama	Computer	Dance
Boys	9	17	4
Girls	9	11	18

8 A charity is doing a survey on the age and gender of people in a retirement home. **B**
  All of the residents are over 60.
  Design a two-way table to collect the data.

9 Use a copy of this. **B**
  The table gives the number of cloudless days and the number of days it rained at some stage, for June and July.
  a Complete the two-way table.
  b How many cloudless days were there altogether?
  c How many days did it rain in June?

	Rained	Cloudless	Total
June		6	15
July	11		
Total			33

379

15 Analysing and Displaying Data

You need to know

✓ mode, median, mean, range — page 356

✓ displaying and interpreting data — page 357

✓ comparing data — page 358

Key vocabulary

continuous, discrete, distribution, estimate of the mean, line graph, line of best fit, population pyramid, raw data, scatter graph

▶▶ Searching ...

Find each of these words in the square.

- DATA
- MEAN
- MEDIAN
- MODE
- RANGE
- CLASS
- TABLE
- FREQUENCY
- MODAL

N	P	O	M	E	D	N	M	O	D	A	L
A	D	M	M	E	D	I	R	N	R	C	S
N	A	E	E	U	R	D	A	A	A	L	S
G	T	A	M	D	E	O	N	C	N	A	T
R	P	N	E	Q	I	A	L	T	R	G	A
L	E	R	D	A	T	A	T	A	B	L	E
O	N	F	E	N	S	C	N	Y	E	D	B
M	A	A	N	S	M	G	M	I	A	N	L
W	E	M	E	A	E	D	O	M	O	C	E
H	M	T	A	F	M	O	D	S	A	L	S
M	E	F	R	E	Q	U	E	N	C	Y	F
A	N	C	L	A	S	S	A	L	C	L	A

380

Analysing and Displaying Data

Mode, median, mean

Remember

range = highest data value − lowest data value

The **mode** is the most commonly occurring data value.

The **modal class** is the class interval with the highest frequency.

The **median** is the middle value of a set of ordered data.
If there is an even number of values, the median is the mean of the two middle values.

Mean = $\dfrac{\text{sum of data values}}{\text{number of data values}}$

We sometimes find the mean using a calculator or spreadsheet.
Sometimes we find the mean using an assumed mean.

See page 356 for more on mode, median and mean.

The median, mean and mode are all ways of summarising the data into a single number.
They are values that **represent** the data set.

Often one of the mean, median or mode summarises or represents the data best.

The mean can be affected by extreme values.

Example Marcia earns £165 000 per year.
All the other people in her office earn about £20 000 per year.
The mean of all their salaries is £32 460.
The mean does not represent this data well because Marcia's salary raises the mean significantly.
All of the salaries except one are below the mean.
The median, for this example, represents the data better.

Example In a class test, twenty people all got between 75 and 85 and the other ten got between 40 and 75.
The mean of the results was 71 and the median was 78.

The difference between the mean and median is greatest when the results are **skewed**.

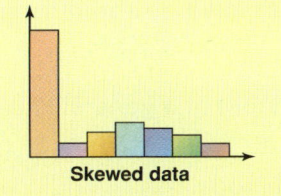

Skewed data

'Skewed' means not evenly spread.

In these cases it is often best if both the mean and median are given when summarising the data.

Exercise 1

1 a There are four people in Sita's family.
Their shoe sizes are 4, 5, 7 and 10.
What is the **median** shoe size?

b There are **three** people in John's family.
The **range** of their shoe sizes is **4**.
Two people in the family wear shoe size 6.
John's shoe size is **not 6** and it is **not 10**.
What is John's shoe size?

[SATs Paper 1 Level 5]

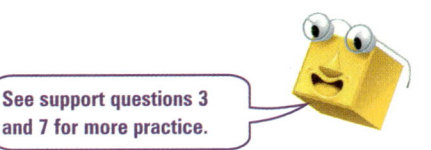

See support questions 3 and 7 for more practice.

Handling Data

2 This table shows the lengths of 100 paperback books.
  a What is the modal class for length?
  b If the shortest length was 22·6 cm and the longest length was 34·6 cm, what is the range?

Length (cm)	Frequency
$22 \leq l < 24$	5
$24 \leq l < 26$	27
$26 \leq l < 28$	26
$28 \leq l < 30$	31
$30 \leq l < 32$	8
$32 \leq l < 34$	2
$34 \leq l < 36$	1

3 a Ikram handed in four computing assignments.
For three of them he got 8 marks each.
In the other he got no marks.
What was Ikram's mean mark for the four assignments?
  b Jessica only handed in two assignments.
Her mean mark was 3.
Her range was 4.
What did Jessica get for each assignment?
  c Sarah handed in three assignments.
Her mean mark was also 3.
Her range was also 4 marks.
What marks might Sarah have got in her three assignments?
Show your working.

4 **Mean age** = 19 years 7 months
Range = 3 years 0 months

This gives the mean age and range of members of a football club.
Damion, who is 20 years 7 months, joins the club.
  a Which of these is correct about the mean age of members?
  A It will increase by exactly 1 year.
  B It will increase by less than 1 year.
  C It will stay the same.
  D It is not possible to tell.
  b Which of **A**, **B**, **C** or **D** in part **a** is true about the range of ages of members once Damion has joined?

5 These are the results of eight pupils in a general knowledge test.
  10   10   10   10   8   10   0   2
  a Find the mean, median and mode.
  b Does the mode represent the data well?
Give a reason for your answer.
  c Does the mean represent the data well?
Give a reason for your answer.

6 Four men and two women were on a minibus tour.
They all received letters while on tour.
The mean number of letters received by the men was 20. The mean number of letters received by the women was 26.
Are these true or false? Explain.
  a The person who received the *most* letters *must* have been a woman.
  b The mean number of letters received by the six people was 23.

Analysing and Displaying Data

7 The cost of the last nine t-shirts sold at 'Just t-shirts' is given.

   £25   £31   £20   £27   £30   £20   £22   £33   £26

   a Find the mean, median and mode.
   b Does the mean represent the data well?
   Give a reason for your answer.

   Hint Is the data evenly spread around the mean?

8 These are the number of hours that 10 batteries lasted.

   100   120   140   142   143   145   145   145   482   498

   a Find the mean and median.
   b Does the median represent the data well?
   Give a reason for your answer.
   c Does the mean represent the data well?
   Give a reason for your answer.

9 Ben measured the heights, in cm, of some of his friends. Their heights in order were

   172, 171, 170, 170, 169, 168, 161, 158.

   a Find the mean, median and mode of these heights.
   b If you were describing the data, which of these would you use?
   Explain.

10 A small business has a manager and eight other staff. These are their salaries in order.

   £70 000   £30 000   £19 000   £17 000   £15 000   £15 000   £12 500   £11 000   £10 000

   a Find the mean, median and mode of these salaries.
   b Which of these statistics would you be more likely to use if you were the manager and one of the other employees came to you wanting a rise in salary?
   c What if you were the employee who earned £11 000 negotiating for a rise in salary with the manager?

11 The median score of three people in a game is 8. The mean is 7 and the range is 7.
What are the three scores?

*12 Five friends got scores in the range 0 to 10 for a car rally.
One of them said, 'The range of our marks is 5, the mean is 6 and the mode is 7.'
Is this possible? If it is, what scores could they have got?

*13 Owls eat small mammals.   [SATs Paper 2 Level 7]
They regurgitate the bones and fur in balls called pellets.
The table shows the contents of **62** pellets from long-eared owls.

Number of mammals found in the pellet	1	2	3	4	5	6
Frequency	9	17	24	6	5	1

See page 356 for how to find the mean from a frequency table.

   a Show that the **total** number of mammals found is **170**.
   b Calculate the **mean** number of mammals found in each pellet.
   Show your working and give your answer correct to 1 decimal place.
   c There are about **10 000** long-eared owls in Britain.
   On average, a long-eared owl regurgitates **1·4 pellets** per day.
   Altogether, how many **mammals** do the 10 000 long-eared owls eat in **one day**?
   Show your working and give your answer to the nearest thousand.

383

Handling Data

Review 1 In the last month Mary and four of her friends read 3, 7, 2, 1 and 3 books.
a What is the median number of books read?
b Three other friends read 5, 6 and 9 books.
   What is the median of the number of books read by the 8 friends?
c What is   **i** the mode and   **ii** the mean of the 8 books read?

Review 2 Owen has three number cards.
The mode of the three numbers is 6.
The mean of the three numbers is 7.
What are the three numbers?

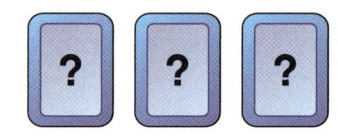

Review 3 This is how long Anita had to wait for a bus each day this week.

   1 min   3 min   3 min   13 min   14 min   4 min   11 min

a Calculate the mean time Anita had to wait.
b Work out the median waiting time.
c What is the mode of the waiting times?
d Does the mean or median represent this data better?
   Give a reason.
e Does the mode represent the data well?

Review 4 Mr Green has thirty steer to sell. These are the masses in kg.

84	85	86	88	88	89	90	90	90	91
94	94	94	95	96	96	97	100	101	101
102	104	124	126	373	382	387	390	392	394

The masses are in order and the total mass is 4623.

a Find the mean, median and mode mass.
b If you were Mr Green and wanted to quote an 'average mass' to a possible buyer, which of the mean, median or mode would you use? **Explain**.
   Would this 'average' be a fair one to quote?

Review 5 Suzie played three games in a competition.
Her mean score was 5 and her range was 8.
What did she score if her median was   **a** 3   **b** 5?

Displaying data

Discussion

- Data that has been collected is usually recorded in a table first.
  Then it is often displayed on a chart, graph or diagram.
  What does the data on a graph show us that a table does not?
  What does a table tell us that a graph does not?
  Discuss.

- Can you always write down the original data that was collected if it is displayed on a chart, graph or diagram? **Discuss**.

- We call the data that is collected in a survey, **raw data**.
  What raw data might have been collected and put on a table before this pie chart could be drawn?

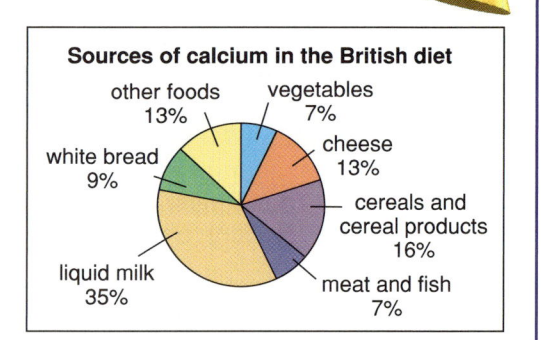

Look at the graphs and questions below and on the next page to help your discussion.

Sources of calcium in the British diet
- other foods 13%
- vegetables 7%
- cheese 13%
- cereals and cereal products 16%
- meat and fish 7%
- liquid milk 35%
- white bread 9%

Analysing and Displaying Data

- What data was collected for this graph? What features does the graph highlight? Would a table of the same data be as good at highlighting the same thing?

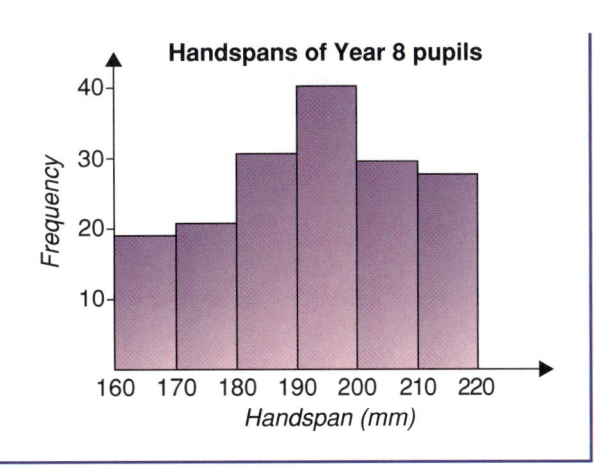

Handspans of Year 8 pupils

A **graph** or **chart** highlights features or trends that a table does not show well.

To display **categorical data** you can use a pictogram, pie chart or bar graph.

Categorical data is non-numerical data.

To display ungrouped **discrete data** you can use a pictogram, pie chart, bar chart or bar-line graph.

There is more about these graphs on page 357.

To display **grouped discrete data** use a bar chart.

To display **continuous data** use a frequency diagram.

Remember: Continuous data is measurement data.

To show **data over time** use a line graph.

More than one set of data can be displayed on compound bar charts, line graphs and frequency diagrams.

Example Robbie collected this information about how males and females travel to work.

	Car	Bus	Train	Walk	Cycle	Other	Total
Males	42	13	36	19	6	4	120
Females	21	27	34	30	4	4	120

He drew these two pie charts after first working out the angles in each sector. For example,

Male   **car** $\frac{42}{120} \times 360° = 126°$,   **bus** $\frac{13}{120} \times 360° = 39°$ ...

↑ fraction who came by car   ↑ fraction who came by bus

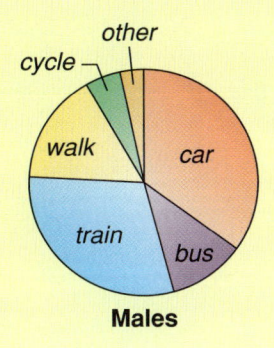

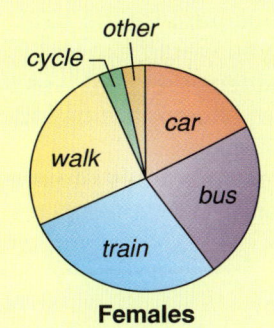

Males   **Females**

385

Handling Data

Line graphs are often used to show trends over time.

Example A study from 1986 to 1996 was carried out to test cigarettes for amounts of tar, nicotine and carbon monoxide.
The graph shows the trend more clearly than the table.

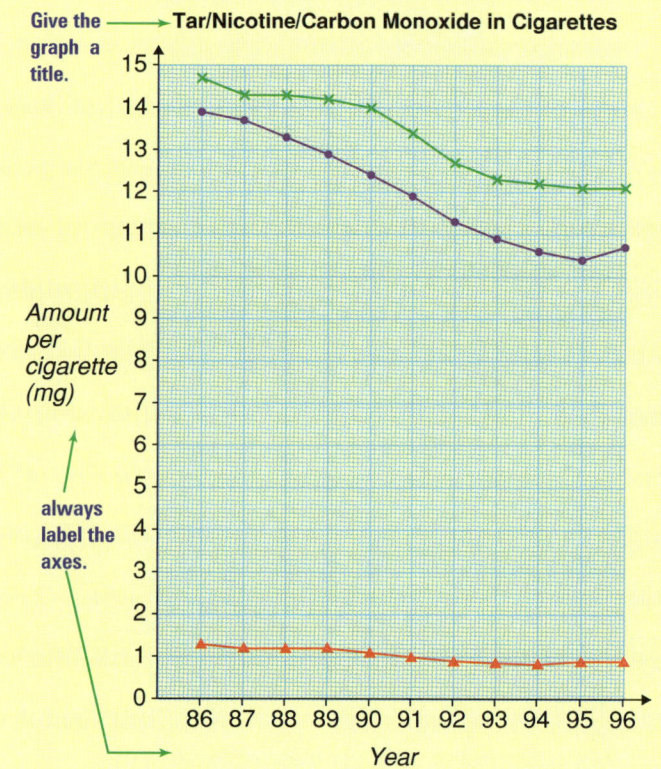

Year	Tar (mg)	Nicotine (mg)	Carbon monoxide (mg)
1986	13·9	1·30	14·7
1987	13·7	1·21	14·3
1988	13·3	1·17	14·3
1989	12·9	1·17	14·2
1990	12·4	1·15	14·0
1991	11·9	1·02	13·4
1992	11·3	0·91	12·7
1993	10·9	0·86	12·3
1994	10·6	0·83	12·2
1995	10·4	0·85	12·1
1996	10·7	0·87	12·1

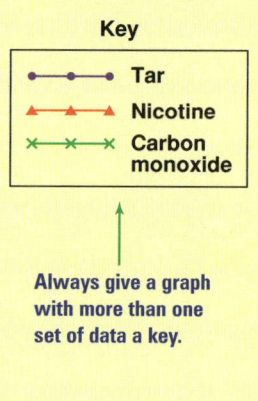

Give the graph a title.

Tar/Nicotine/Carbon Monoxide in Cigarettes

Amount per cigarette (mg) — always label the axes.

Year

Key:
- Tar
- Nicotine
- Carbon monoxide

Always give a graph with more than one set of data a key.

Exercise 2

1 This table shows the masses of 25 newborn kittens.

Mass (g)	75–	100–	125–	150–	175–	200–225
Frequency	7	8	7	4	2	1

a Joel thinks that a frequency diagram is best to display this data. Explain why he is correct.
b Use a copy of this grid. Draw a frequency diagram for the data.
c Is the shape what you would expect? Explain.
d How many of the kittens weighed less than 150 g?
e The next kitten born had a mass of 149·5 g. This was rounded to 150 g. Which class interval should this kitten be put into? Justify your answer.

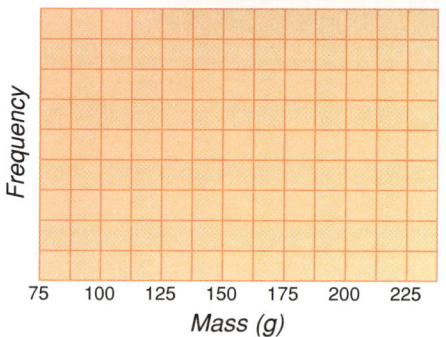

Frequency

Mass (g)

Analysing and Displaying Data

2 This table gives the wind speed at hourly intervals at the top and bottom of a hill.

Time	6 a.m.	7 a.m.	8 a.m.	9 a.m.	10 a.m.	11 a.m.	12 p.m.	1 p.m.	2 p.m.	3 p.m.	4 p.m.	5 p.m.	6 p.m.
Windspeed (knots) Top of hill	4	4	4	8	12	16	22	24	26	27	28	23	8
Windspeed (knots) Bottom of hill	2	2	3	5	7	9	15	16	17	18	18	12	4

a Use a copy of this grid.
Draw a line graph for this data.
Put both sets of data on the same axis. Use ■ for top of hill and ● for bottom of hill.
b Could we use the graph to estimate wind speeds at times in between the times given?
c Compare the wind speeds at the top and bottom of the hill.
*__d__ Explain why a line graph will display this data best.

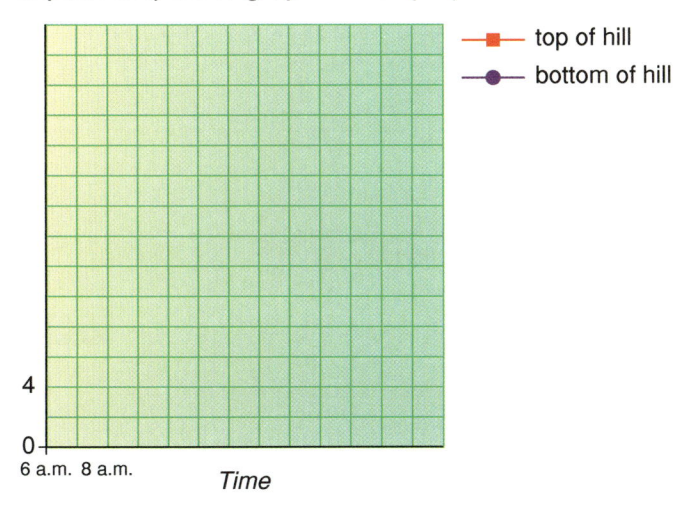

3 A teacher asked two different classes:
'What type of book is your favourite?'

[SATs Paper 2 Level 6]

a Results from **class A** (total 20 pupils):

Type of book	Frequency
Crime	3
Non-fiction	13
Fantasy	4

Use a copy of the diagram.
Complete the pie chart to show this information.
Show your working and draw your angles accurately.

b The pie chart on the right shows the results from all of **class B**.
Each pupil had only one vote.

The sector for **Non-fiction** represents **11 pupils**.
How many pupils are in class B?
Show your working.

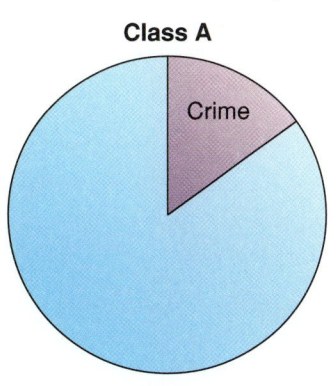

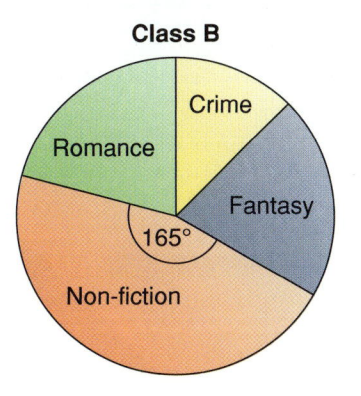

387

Handling Data

4 This table gives the average weekly cigarette consumption by some female smokers aged 16 and over.

	16–19	20–24	25–34	35–49	50–59	60 and over
1976	92	109	106	111	104	74
1986	75	82	98	109	97	83
1996	71	79	89	108	108	86

a Plot this data on a line graph.
b Write true or false for these.
  i The weekly consumption went down from 1976 to 1996 for all age groups except 50–59 and 60 and over.
  ii 25–34 year olds had the greatest drop in weekly consumption from 1976 to 1996.

5 This data gives the number of notifications of infectious diseases in 1990 and 2000.

Year	TB	Whooping Cough	Meningitis	Malaria	Total
1990	5010	14 125	2369	1469	22 973
2000	6379	658	2251	1110	10 398

a Draw two circles of radius 3 cm.
  Find the angle at the centre of each sector for each year.
  Draw two pie charts to show the data in the table.
b Draw a bar chart to show the data. You will need to round the data to the nearest 100 before plotting.
c Which graph do you think gives better information about the data?

*6 Show this data on a suitable graph.
Say why you chose the type of graph you used.

Accidental deaths: by age and gender, 2000
United Kingdom   Numbers

	Males	Females
0–	282	157
15–	943	241
25–	1125	207
35–	985	264
45–	732	289
55–	658	319
65–	755	524
75 and over	2001	3551
All ages	7481	5552

Source: Office for National Statistics; General Register Office for Scotland; Northern Ireland Statistics and Research Agency

T **Review 1** The mass of trucks for sale at a dealers are given in the table.

Mass (kg)	1000–	2000–	3000–	4000–	5000–6000
Frequency	12	16	24	6	2

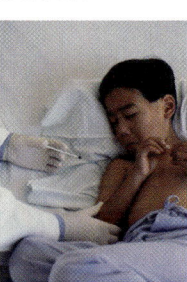

Analysing and Displaying Data

a Use a copy of this grid to draw a frequency diagram for the data.
b Is the shape what you would expect? Explain.
c How many trucks had a mass less than 4000 kg?
d How many trucks had a mass from 1000 up to 3000 kg?
e Into which group would you put a truck with a mass of 3900 kg?

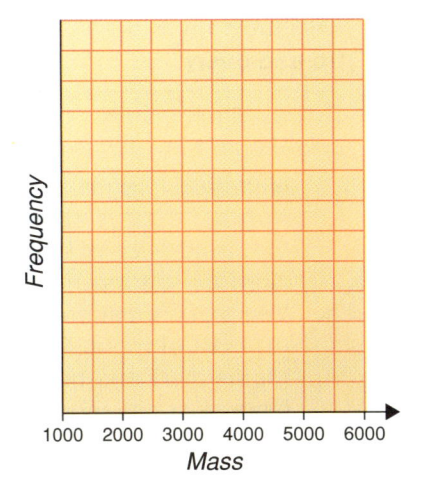

* **Review 2** This table gives the ages of people at a 'Stop Smoking' seminar.
Display this data on a bar chart, a pie chart and a line graph.
Choose which one you would use to put into a report on the seminar. Explain why you chose it.

Age	Number
20–29	4
30–39	6
40–49	9
50–59	10
60+	23

Practical

You will need a motion detector and graphical calculator.

Use a motion detector and a graphical calculator to draw a distance–time graph for a bouncing ball.

Scatter graphs

Remember

A **scatter graph** displays two sets of data.

A scatter graph sometimes show a relationship or **correlation** between the variables.

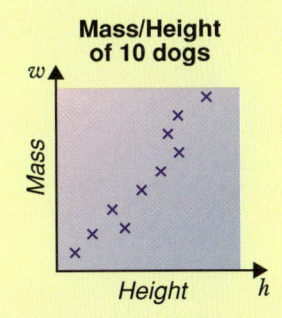

Mass/Height of 10 dogs

This graph shows a **positive correlation** between the height and mass of dogs. It shows that the taller a dog is, the heavier it is likely to be.

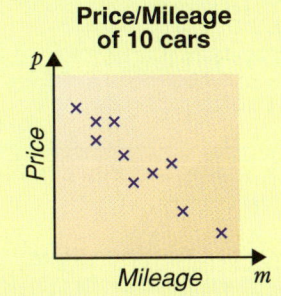

Price/Mileage of 10 cars

This graph shows a **negative correlation** between the price of a second-hand car and mileage. The higher the mileage, the lower the price is likely to be.

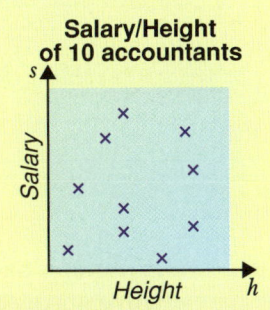

Salary/Height of 10 accountants

This graph shows there is **no correlation** between the height of an accountant and the salary earned. There doesn't seem to be any relationship between these variables.

Handling Data

Discussion

- Do you think there would be a positive correlation or negative correlation or no correlation between the following? **Discuss**.

   Number of pages and number of advertisements in magazines
   Number of days absent from school and marks in tests
   Circumference of head and arm length of 13-year-old students
   Number of supporters of a football team and goals scored by the team
   Years of education and income
   Amount of money people earn and the time they spend watching TV
   Maths mark and height of students from one year group
   Income of households and number of people in the households
   Height and number of leaves on pot plants
   Age and amount of pocket money received
   Length and weight of cats
   Number of rooms and number of windows in houses
   Time spent on homework and time spent watching TV
   Number of boys and number of girls in families

- Think of some pairs of variables that would be likely to have positive correlation, some that would be likely to have negative correlation and some that would be likely to have no correlation. **Discuss**.

If there is a correlation between two variables, we can use a scatter graph to estimate values.

Example
This scatter graph shows the number of worms and birds found in a garden.

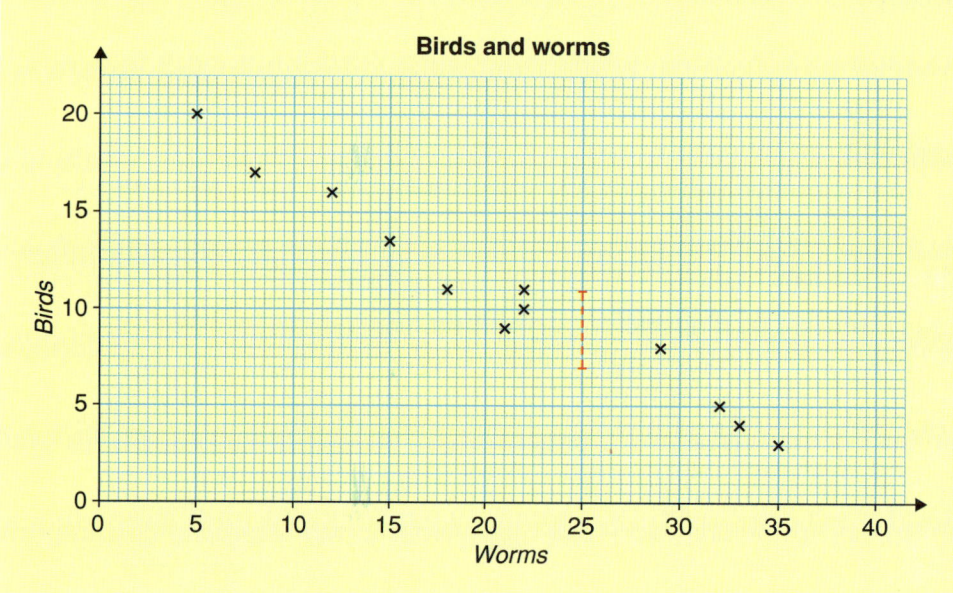

Birds and worms

The greater the number of birds the fewer the number of worms.
There is a negative correlation.
We can estimate how many birds there would be if there were 25 worms. Draw a vertical line from 25 worms. Estimate from this, that between about 7 and 11 birds would be in the garden.

Analysing and Displaying Data

*If the data shows some correlation, we can draw a **line of best fit**.

This line should be as close as possible to the points. There should be about the same number of points above the line as below it.
To find a line of best fit you could stand your ruler on its edge and move it until it seems to be in the best place.

We can use the line of best fit to estimate one measurement, given another. The more closely the points are clustered around the line of best fit, the better the estimate.

Example
We can draw a line of best fit on the graph given above.

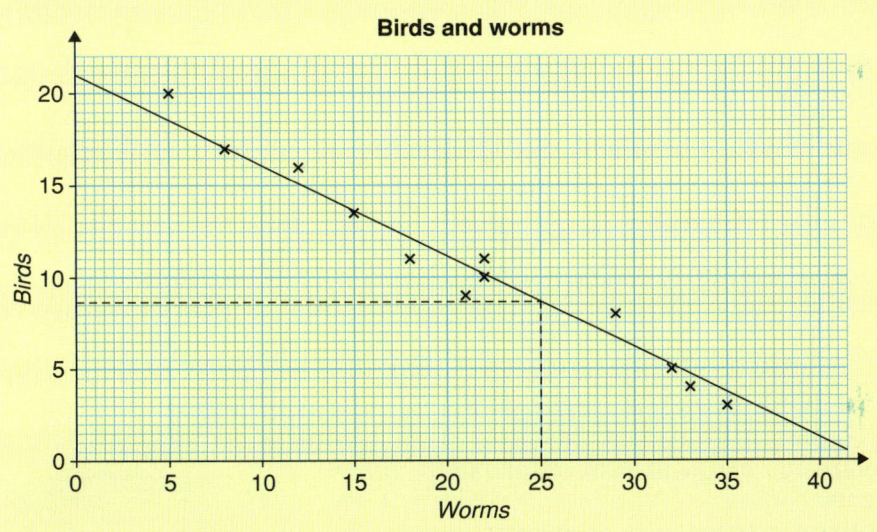

Birds and worms

We can use this to more accurately estimate how many birds there would be if there were 25 worms.
An estimate is 8·5 birds (8 or 9 birds).
This estimate is fairly reliable as the plotted points are clustered quite closely around the line of best fit.

Exercise 3

1 Look at these three scatter graphs.

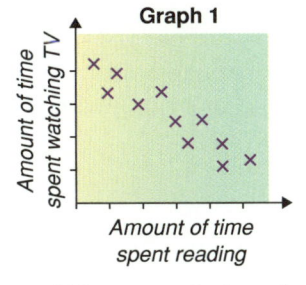

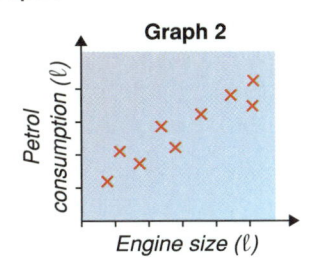

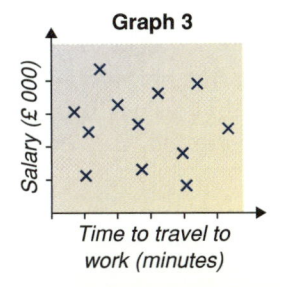

Graph 1: Amount of time spent watching TV vs Amount of time spent reading

Graph 2: Petrol consumption (ℓ) vs Engine size (ℓ)

Graph 3: Salary (£ 000) vs Time to travel to work (minutes)

a What correlation does each show?
Choose from the box.

b Write a sentence about the relationship between the variables for each graph.
Your sentence will be of the form,
  As ____ increases ____ decreases/increases.
or There is no relationship between the variables.

> negative correlation
> positive correlation
> no correlation

391

Handling Data

T 2 The following data gives the golf scores of 14 people on two consecutive days.

Friday	74	79	71	68	81	75	72	69	78	70	81	77	82	75
Saturday	72	76	73	69	77	75	70	71	77	72	79	75	78	74

a Use a copy of the grid.
Draw a scatter graph for the data.
The scales have been started for you.
b Does the scatter graph show that there is positive, negative or no correlation between the scores on the two days?
c Grace scored 68 on Friday.
Estimate her Saturday score.
d Hal scored 79 on Saturday.
Estimate his Friday score.

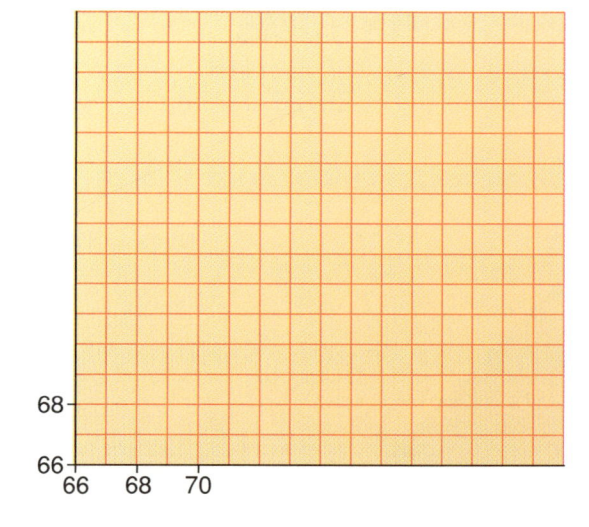

3

Long jump (m)	4·90	4·30	5·85	5·98	5·02	5·52	4·53	6·03	5·45	4·67	5·28
High jump (m)	1·55	1·60	1·86	2·03	1·83	1·74	1·54	1·30	1·88	1·78	1·73

This table gives the long jump and high jump results of the pupils who entered both events.
a Would you expect there to be positive correlation between these results?
b Plot the data on a scatter graph. (Have long jump on the horizontal axis.)
c Describe the correlation between long jump and high jump results.
*d If you were drawing a line of best fit, which point would you ignore?

4

Height (m) of pupil	1·64	1·70	1·58	1·65	1·81	1·67	1·62	1·73	1·71	1·77
Height (m) of best friend	1·72	1·69	1·82	1·70	1·74	1·64	1·58	1·68	1·60	1·70

a Plot this data on a scatter graph. Have Height of pupil on the horizontal axis.
b Could you use this graph to estimate the height of the best friend of a pupil who is 171 cm tall? Explain your answer.

5 The scatter graph on the next page shows information about trees called poplars.   [SATs Paper 1 Level 6]
a What does the scatter graph show about the **relationship** between the diameter of the tree trunk and the height of the tree?
b The height of a different tree is 3 m. The diameter of its trunk is 5 cm.
Use the graph to explain why this tree is **not** likely to be a poplar.
c Another tree **is** a poplar. The diameter of its trunk is 3·2 cm.
Estimate the height of this tree.

392

Analysing and Displaying Data

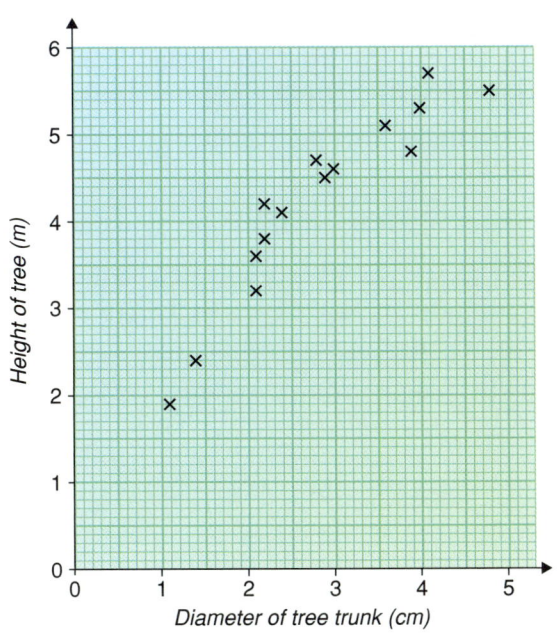

d Below are some statements about drawing lines of best fit on scatter graphs. [Level 7]
For each statement, tick (✓) to show whether the statement is True or False.

Lines of best fit must always ...

    go through the origin. ☐ True ☐ False
    have a positive gradient. ☐ True ☐ False
    join the smallest and the largest values. ☐ True ☐ False
    pass through every point on the graph. ☐ True ☐ False

*6 The goldcrest is Britain's smallest species of bird. [SATs Paper 2 Level 7]
On winter days, a goldcrest must eat enough food to keep it warm at night.
During the day the mass of the bird increases.
The scatter diagram shows the mass of goldcrests at different times during winter days.
It also shows the line of best fit.

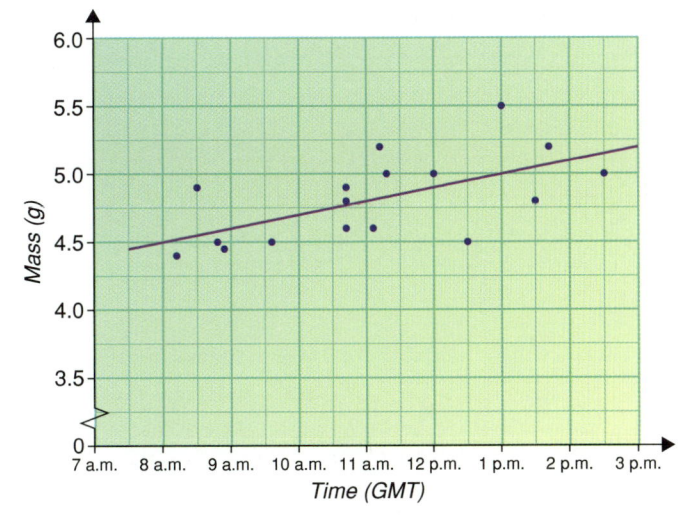

a Estimate the mass of a goldcrest at **11:30 a.m.**
b Estimate how many grams, on average, the mass of the goldcrest **increases** during **one hour**.
c Which goldcrest represented on the scatter diagram is **least likely** to survive the night if it is cold?
Show your answer by giving the coordinates of the correct point on the scatter diagram, then explain why you chose that point.

393

Handling Data

***7** Lauren thinks that as water gets hotter, more sugar will dissolve in it. If this is true, sketch what a graph of temperature of water versus mass of sugar dissolved would look like.

8 Hannah did a survey to see if practice resulted in better shot-put distances thrown. She plotted her results on this scatter graph.

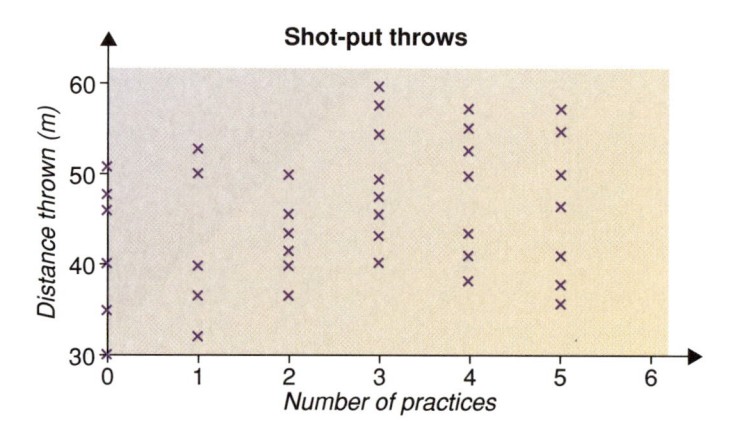

Shot-put throws

Is there enough evidence to show that as the number of practices increase from 1 to 5 the distance the shot is thrown increases? Explain.

[T] **Review 1** The table lists the ages of some children and their heights in centimetres.

Age (years)	2	6	8	10	7	3	5	4	8	7	9	6
Height (cm)	80	110	122	136	114	95	104	100	126	120	130	112

a Use a copy of the grid.
Use the information in the table to draw a scatter graph.

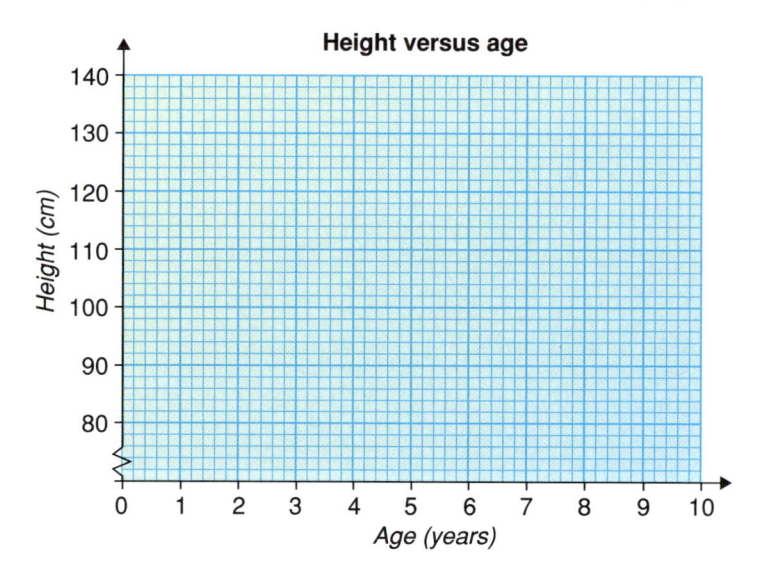

Height versus age

b What sort of correlation between height and age does the graph show?
c Copy and finish this.
 Older children tend to be _____
d Callum is $5\frac{1}{2}$ years old. Estimate how tall he is.
e Charlotte is 85 cm tall. Estimate how old she is.

Analysing and Displaying Data

Review 2 The lengths and wingspans of a selection of aircraft are given below.
a Use the information to draw a scatter graph on a copy of this grid. Put the length on the horizontal axis.

Aircraft type	Length (m)	Wingspan (m)
Boeing 747	70	60
Boeing 767	60	48
Boeing 737–400	36	29
Airbus 330	58	60
Airbus 320	38	34
Boeing 737–800	40	36

b Which aircraft seems out of place?
c What type of correlation does the graph show, positive correlation, negative correlation or no correlation?
*d Draw the line of best fit through **5** points. Another type of aircraft has length 50 m. About what would you expect its wingspan to be?

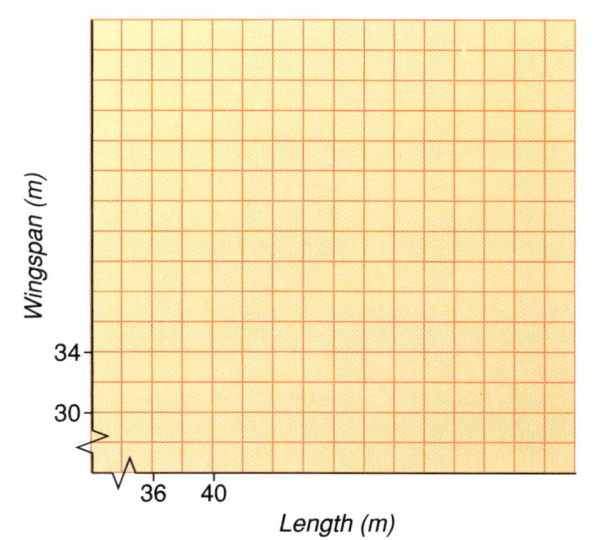

Practical

Collect some data which is suitable for displaying on a scatter graph. Some suggestions follow.
Before you gather the data, make a statement about likely correlation between the variables.
Display your data on a scatter graph.
*Draw in a line of best fit if there seems to be a correlation.
Write a report. Include statements on how you gathered the data, on any correlation between the variables and on whether your data confirmed your statement about likely correlation.

Suggested data – about the students in your class
 armspan and handspan
 circumference of head and circumference of wrist
 time spent travelling to school and time spent on homework
 number of brothers and number of sisters
 number of letters in forename and number of letters in surname
 time spent watching TV and time spent on homework
 long jump distance and high jump height
 time taken to do 50 calculations with and without the calculator

Suggested data – to be gathered from the newspaper or library.
 goals scored by home teams and goals scored by away teams
 runs scored in 2-innings of cricket
 engine size of cars and petrol consumption

Handling Data

Interpreting graphs and diagrams

Discussion

- **Holiday destinations 1971**
  - Spain 34%
  - Other countries 33%
  - France 16%
  - Italy 9%
  - Greece 4%
  - Portugal 3%
  - United States 1%
  - Irish Republic 0%

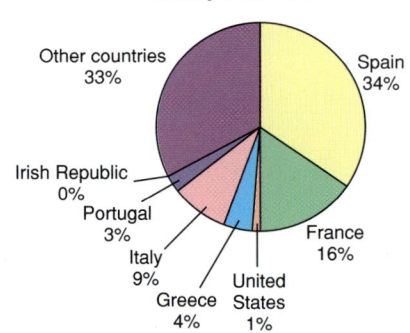

  Holiday destinations 2001
  - Spain 28%
  - Other countries 27%
  - France 18%
  - United States 7%
  - Greece 7%
  - Irish Republic 5%
  - Portugal 4%
  - Italy 4%

  These pie charts show the holiday destinations chosen by British people in 1971 and 2001.

  a **Discuss** a possible reason why a greater proportion of people holidayed in the United States in 2001 than in 1971.

  b The Spanish claim that more British people visited Spain in 2001 than in 1971. Is this possible if the graphs above are correct? **Discuss**.

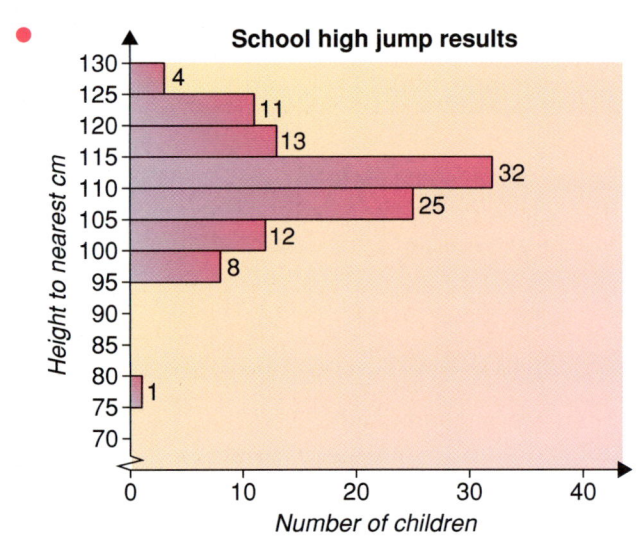

- **School high jump results**

Height to nearest cm	Number of children
130	4
125	11
120	13
115	32
110	25
105	12
100	8
80	1

  This frequency diagram shows the high jump results for Chisnalwood school. The jumps were measured to the nearest cm and put into class intervals $70 \leqslant h < 75$, $75 \leqslant h < 80$, ...

  a Jenni jumped 122 cm.
  She told her mother that she came fifth in the school.
  Could she be right? Explain.

  *__b__ Ruben jumped 107 cm.
  He said 'I was above the median'.
  Explain how you can tell from the graph that he is wrong.

Analysing and Displaying Data

Exercise 4

1 The diagrams show the amount of rain that fell each day in two different months.

Number of mm of rain in month 2

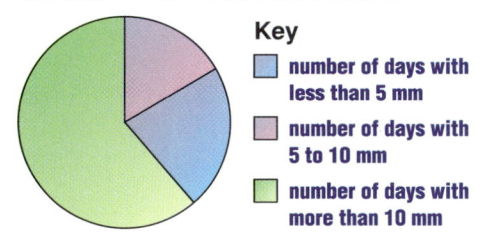

Key
- number of days with less than 5 mm
- number of days with 5 to 10 mm
- number of days with more than 10 mm

Number of mm of rain in month 1

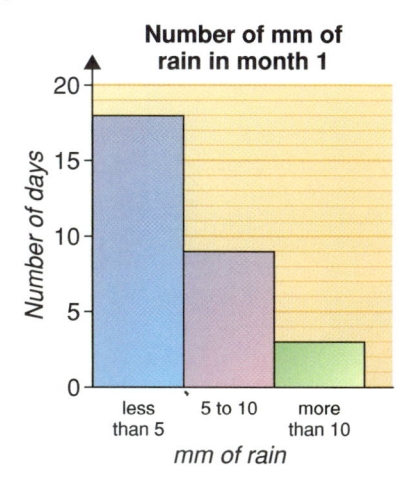

a How many days are there in month 1?
  A 28 **B** 30 **C** 31 **D** Can't tell
b How many days are there in month 2?
  A 28 **B** 29 **C** 30 **D** 31 **E** Can't tell
c Which month had more mm of rain? Explain how you know.

2 This frequency diagram shows the weight of the luggage of people on a coach tour.
  a How many people were on this coach tour?
  b Is the following statement true? 'Most people's luggage weighed between 15 and 20 kg.'
  c Mrs Lunn and Mr Piper both had luggage weighing 20 kg. Can you tell from the graph which class interval they would have been put in?

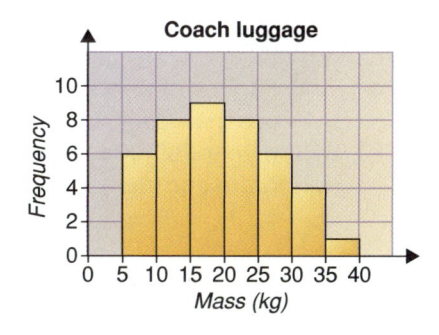

3 This data shows the aircraft movements (in thousands) at five British airports in 1991, 1996 and 2001.

Aircraft movements (000s)

Airport	1991	1996	2001
Heathrow	362	428	464
Gatwick	163	212	252
Stansted	36	77	170
Manchester	124	144	181
Birmingham	66	78	112

Paula drew this graph of the data.
a Which do you think illustrates the trends in aircraft movement better, the table or the graph?
b Which airport had the greatest increase in aircraft movements from 1991 to 2001?
c Give two reasons why aircraft movements might have increased over this time.

397

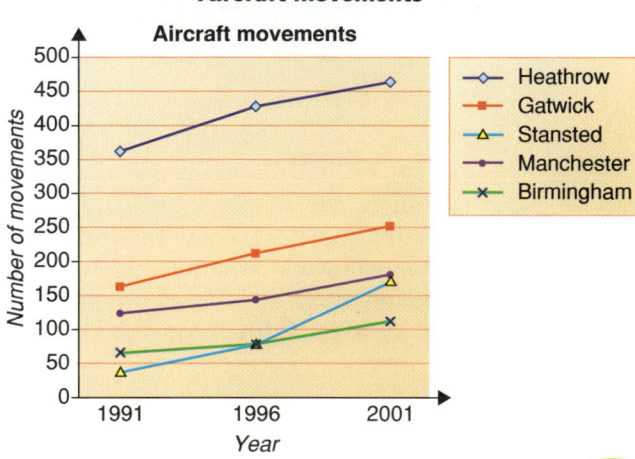

Handling Data

4 The swimming association wrote an article about public swimming pools. This graph was in the article.

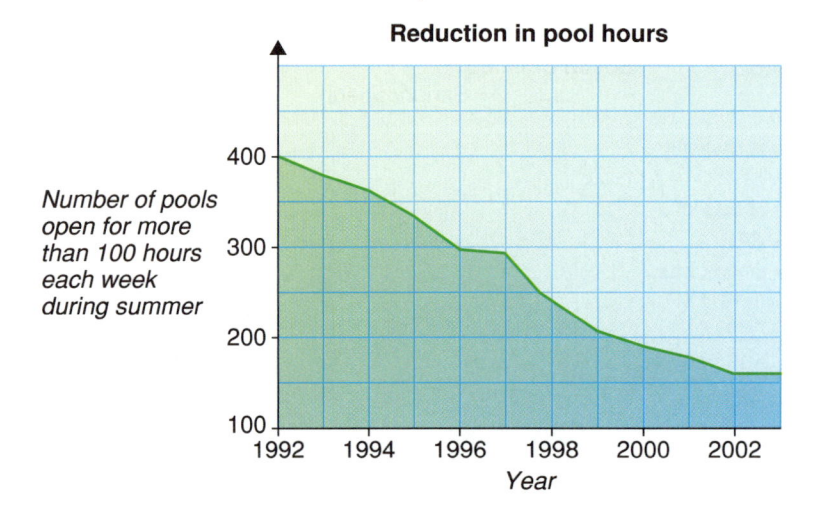

Reduction in pool hours

Number of pools open for more than 100 hours each week during summer (y-axis, 100 to 400)
Year (x-axis, 1992 to 2002)

Use the graph to decide whether these statements from the article are true or false or you cannot tell.

a The number of pools open for more than 100 hours each week during the summer fell by more than half from 1992 to 2002.
b By the year 2006, only about 100 pools will be open for more than 100 hours each week during the summer.

5 These graphs show the maximum and minimum temperatures and the mean temperatures (°C) in Madrid.

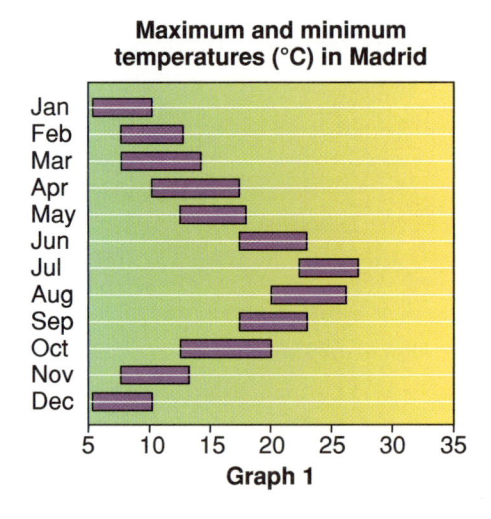

Maximum and minimum temperatures (°C) in Madrid
Graph 1

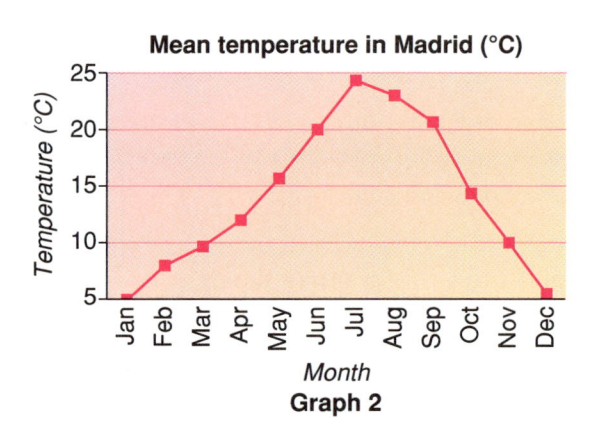

Mean temperature in Madrid (°C)
Graph 2

a Estimate the maximum and minimum and mean temperatures for April?
b 'Madrid Promotions' was making an advertising brochure to give to visitors to Madrid. There is only room for one of the graphs in the brochure.
Which do you think gives visitors better information about the temperatures in Madrid? Explain why.

Analysing and Displaying Data

6 Two beaches are very similar. [SATs Paper 2 Level 6]
A survey compared the number of animals found in one square metre on each beach.
One beach had not been cleaned.
The other beach had been cleaned.

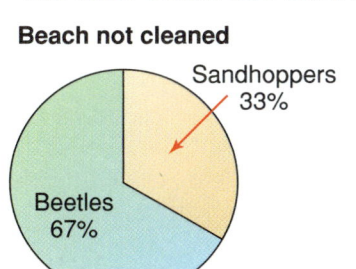

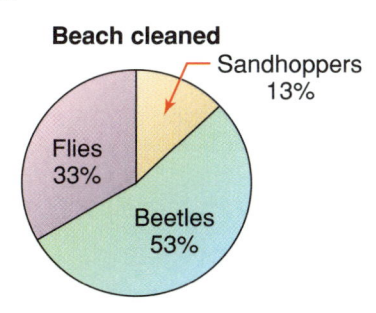

Beach not cleaned
- Sandhoppers 33%
- Beetles 67%

Beach cleaned
- Sandhoppers 13%
- Flies 33%
- Beetles 53%

a The data for the beach that had **not been cleaned** represent **1620** animals.
Copy and complete the table to show how many of each animal were found.

Beach not cleaned

	Number found
Sandhoppers	
Beetles	
Flies	

b The data for the beach that had been **cleaned** represent **15** animals.
Copy and complete the table to show how many of each animal were found on the cleaned beach.

Beach cleaned

	Number found
Sandhoppers	
Beetles	
Flies	

c Cleaning the beach changes the numbers of animals and the proportions of animals.
Write a sentence to describe **both** these changes.

7 This graph shows cinema attendance by age.

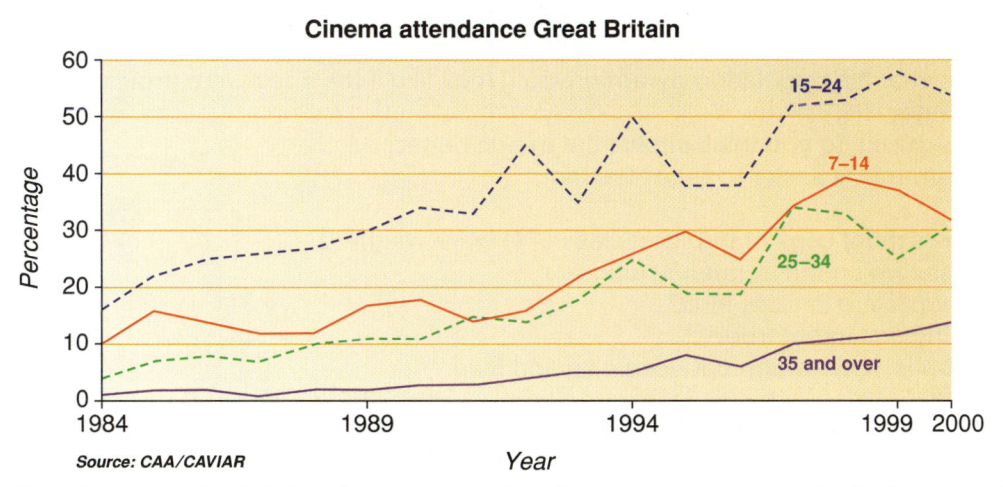

Cinema attendance Great Britain

Source: CAA/CAVIAR

People were asked if they had gone to the cinema once or more in the last month.
a Which age group has had the greatest increase in cinema attendance since 1984?
Give a reason why this might be.
b Give a possible reason why some age groups have 'peaks' in attendance.

399

Handling Data

8 A study was carried out on 100 000 people. This two-way table shows the number who died from coronary heart disease, their age and the number of cigarettes they smoked in a day.
Explain how these figures support the argument that smoking causes coronary heart disease.

Age	No. of cigarettes smoked per day			
	0	1–14	15–24	25+
45–54	118	220	368	393
55–64	531	742	819	1025

*9 The percentage charts show information about the wing length of adult blackbirds, measured to the nearest millimetre.   [SATs Paper 2 Level 7]

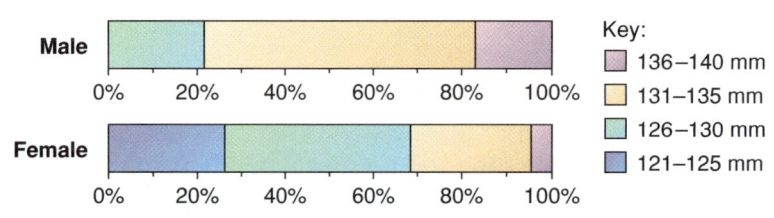

Key:
- 136–140 mm
- 131–135 mm
- 126–130 mm
- 121–125 mm

Use the data to decide whether these statements are true or false, or whether there is not enough information to tell. Explain your answer.
a The smallest male's wing length is larger than the smallest female's wing length.
b The biggest male's wing length is larger than the biggest female's wing length.

*10 This is a population pyramid for Bangladesh in the year 2000.

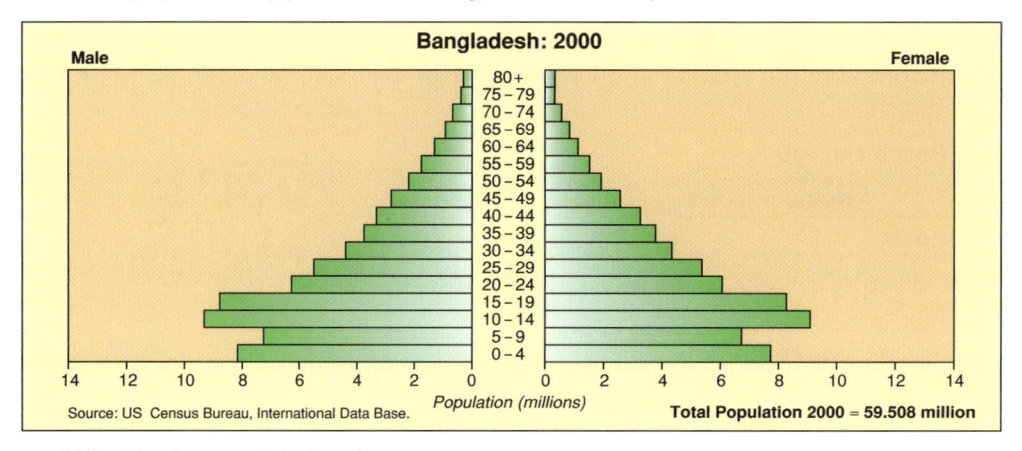

Bangladesh: 2000
Source: US Census Bureau, International Data Base.
Total Population 2000 = 59.508 million

a What is the modal class?
b A newspaper headline said 'Explosion in teenage population in Bangladesh'. Comment on the accuracy of this headline.
c **Sketch** what the population pyramid would look like if the ages were grouped in 15-year intervals.
Which pyramid do you think shows the trends better?
Which pyramid is easier to read? Explain.

Review 1 The school bags of pupils in class 9PQ were weighed and the results shown on the frequency diagram.
a How many pupils are in class 9PQ?
b Is the following statement true?
   'Most pupils' bags weigh between 4 kg and 6 kg.'
   Explain.
c Jane's bag weighs 6 kg. Can you tell from the graph which class interval it would be in? Explain.

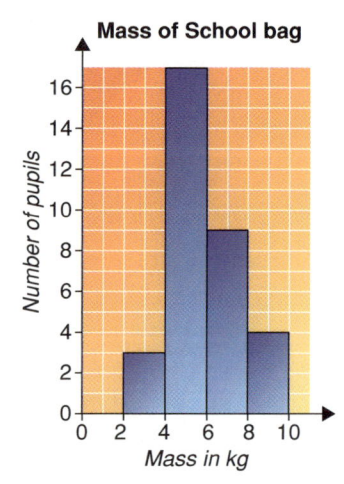

400

Review 2 The number of fatal road accidents occurring in two countries of similar size are shown on the graph.

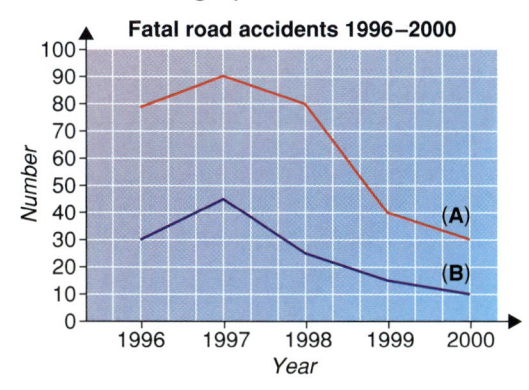

Fatal road accidents 1996–2000

a What is the most obvious difference between the road deaths in the two countries?
b One country ran an aggressive road safety campaign in 1998. Which country was it?
c Comment on the general trend of road deaths in the two countries.

Review 3 This chart shows the percentage of animals, reptiles and birds at a zoo.
a About what percentage of females are birds?
b About what percentage of males are not birds?
c The blue bars show the percentages for animals.
One blue bar is longer than the other.
Does this mean that there **must** be more male animals than female animals at the zoo?
Explain your answer.

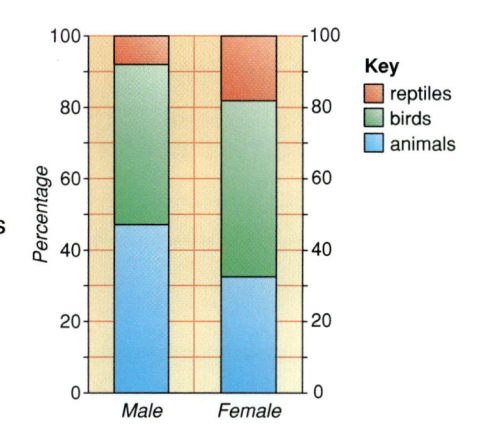

Key: reptiles, birds, animals

Misleading graphs

Discussion

● **Discuss** how each of these graphs is misleading.
Think about these questions.
Is the graph complete?
Is the scale appropriate?
Are conclusions made from very small samples?
Is the data graphed appropriately?

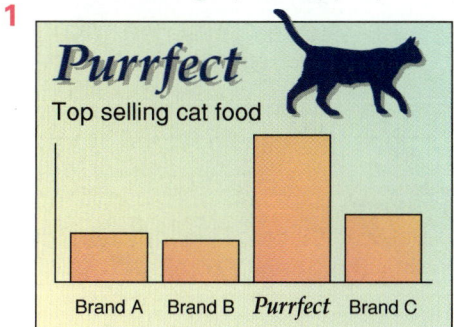

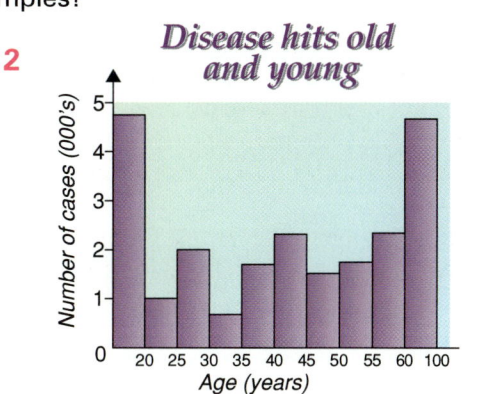

1 *Purrfect* Top selling cat food
Brand A   Brand B   *Purrfect*   Brand C

2 *Disease hits old and young*
Number of cases (000's) vs Age (years)

Analysing and Displaying Data

401

Handling Data

3 *Huge increase in output*

1·5 tonnes — Year 1
1·8 tonnes — Year 2
2·2 tonnes — Year 3

4 *Slow population increase*

(graph showing values from 2000 to 2003, y-axis 1000, 5000, 6000, 7000)

- What is misleading about these statements?
  1 Brite Colour washes your clothes 50% better.
  2 Tests prove Kittydins is best.
  3 Come to the Sunshine Resort. Annual mean rainfall only 200 mm.

Practical

You will need a spreadsheet package.

Ask your teacher for the **Misleading Graphs** ICT Worksheet.

Comparing data

We can **compare data** by looking at the 'shape' of distributions.

Example Robyn drew these graphs of the Year 7 and Year 9 high jump results.

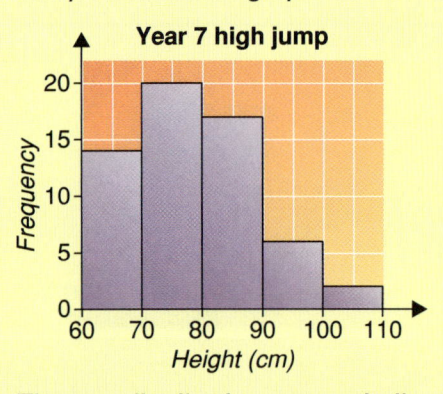

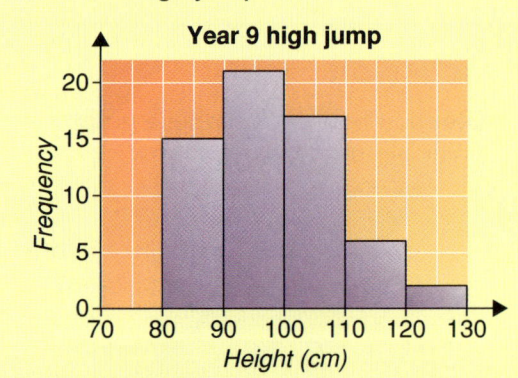

Year 7 high jump
(histogram: Frequency vs Height (cm), bars at 60, 70, 80, 90, 100, 110 with frequencies 14, 20, 17, 6, 2)

Year 9 high jump
(histogram: Frequency vs Height (cm), bars at 70, 80, 90, 100, 110, 120, 130 with frequencies 15, 21, 17, 6, 2)

The two distributions are a similar shape with a similar range.
This indicates that there is a similar pattern of poor, average and good jumpers in each year.
Robyn also calculated the mean of each year's jump.
For Year 7 the mean was 79 cm and for Year 9 it was 98 cm. This indicates that generally, Year 9 pupils jump about 19 cm higher than Year 7 pupils.

Analysing and Displaying Data

Exercise 5

1 Mrs Burrows asked each pupil in her class to estimate when one minute was up.
She then gave them practice at estimating one minute and tested them again.
These graphs show the results before and after practice.
Write true or false for these.
  a The range of estimates was the same before and after practice.
  b More pupils estimated more closely to one minute after practice.

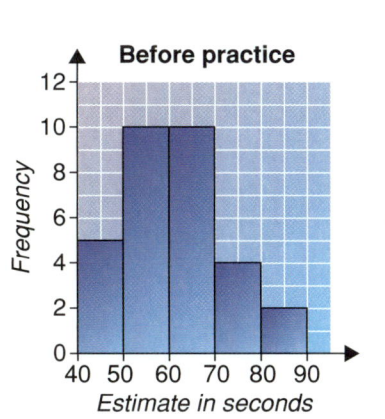

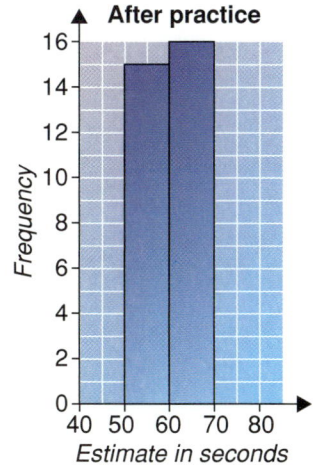

2 Jasmine was investigating the contents of two brands of 50 g bars of chocolate.
She summarised the data she collected in this table.

	Mean mass (g)	Range (g)
Spoil U chocolate	50·2	3·7
Can't resist chocolate	51·1	1·4

Which brand of 50 g chocolate bar would you buy?
You could choose either as long as you justify your answer using the information in the table.

3 Tammy timed the length of advertisements on two different radio stations. The advertisements were timed to the nearest second.

Radio Station One (time in seconds)

28	15	34	23	8	19	43	26	34	54	48
19	21	18	25	16	41	30	51	46	35	29
28	18	27	33	36	26	19	9	40	43	24

Radio Station Two (time in seconds)

26	25	22	23	19	18	21	31	24	17	12
18	27	33	9	13	17	24	35	37	29	30
20	29	33	25	32	40	29	16	19	18	11

  a Find the mean, median and range of each set of data.
  b Draw a frequency table like this one for each radio station.
  c Draw a bar chart for each radio station.
  You could put both sets of data on the same chart.
  d Which radio station would you rather listen to? Explain your answer.
  Refer to your answers to **a** and **c**.

Time (secs)	Tally	Frequency
0–9		
10–19		
20–29		
30–39		
40–49		
50–59		

Handling Data

4 Population Pyramid Summary for United Kingdom

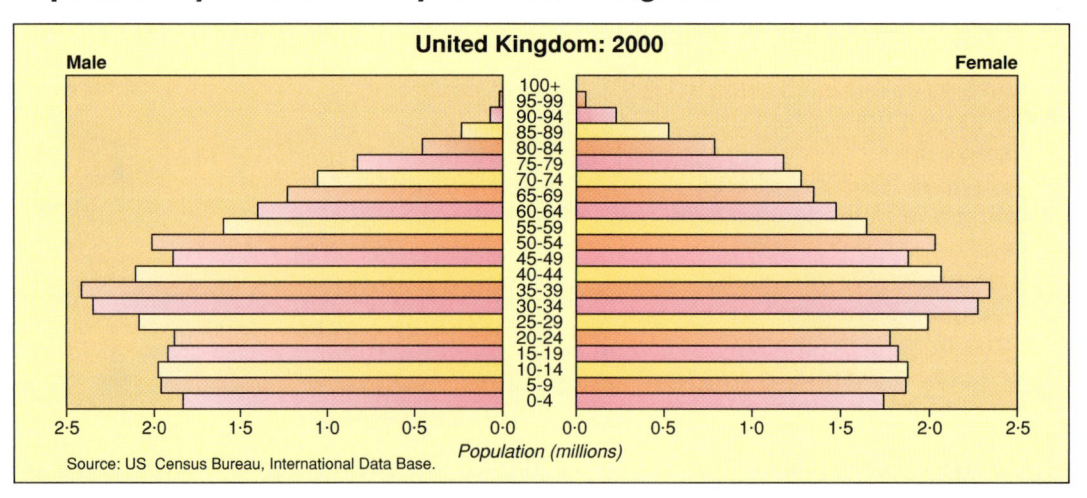

United Kingdom: 2000 population pyramid, Male/Female, age groups 0–4 to 100+, Population (millions) 2.5 to 2.5. Source: US Census Bureau, International Data Base.

Population Pyramid Summary for Thailand

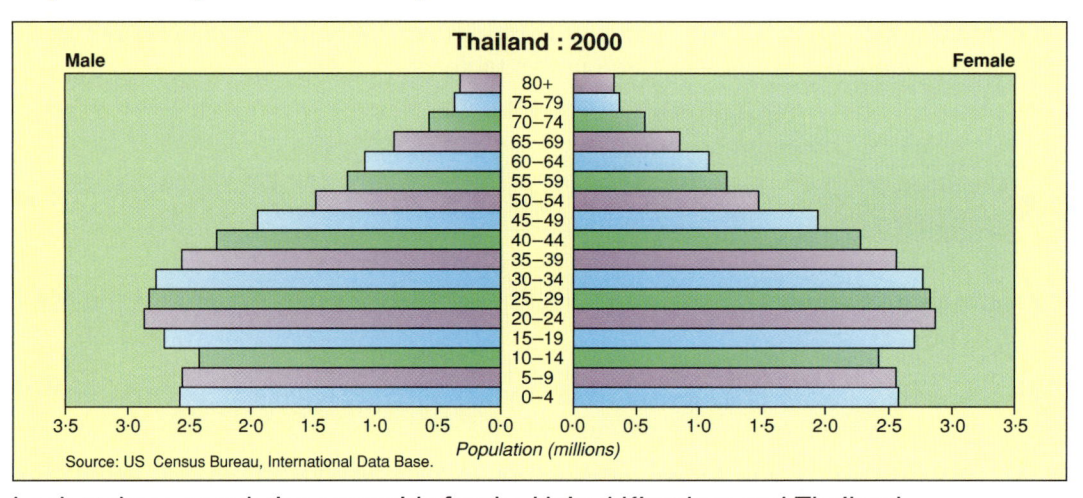

Thailand: 2000 population pyramid, Male/Female, age groups 0–4 to 80+, Population (millions) 3.5 to 3.5. Source: US Census Bureau, International Data Base.

Look at these population pyramids for the United Kingdom and Thailand.
- **a** Write true or false for these.
  - **i** About the same **number** of people in Thailand as the United Kingdom live to be over 80.
  - **ii** People in the United Kingdom generally live to be older than people in Thailand.
- **b** Write another two sentences comparing the populations of the United Kingdom and Thailand.

Review Granny Smith is experimenting with a new fertiliser for her apple orchard. She chooses an area of 40 trees and uses the new fertiliser on half the apple trees (set A). The number of apples on each tree is recorded.

Set A (new fertiliser)

| 24 | 28 | 35 | 30 | 30 | 28 | 36 | 43 | 68 | 51 |
| 52 | 45 | 42 | 47 | 50 | 45 | 30 | 24 | 28 | 21 |

Set B (old fertiliser)

| 23 | 40 | 42 | 35 | 25 | 28 | 35 | 40 | 35 | 32 |
| 46 | 32 | 36 | 38 | 28 | 21 | 31 | 29 | 20 | 33 |

- **a** Calculate the mean, median and range for each set of trees.

b Draw a frequency table like this for each set of trees.

No. of apples	Tally	Frequency
20–29		
30–39		
40–49		
50–59		
60–69		

c Draw a bar chart for each set of trees. You could put both sets of data on the same chart.

d Should Granny Smith use the new fertiliser throughout her orchard?

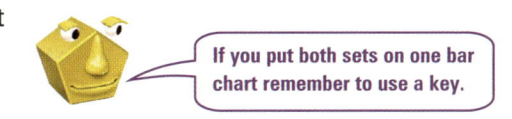

If you put both sets on one bar chart remember to use a key.

Surveys

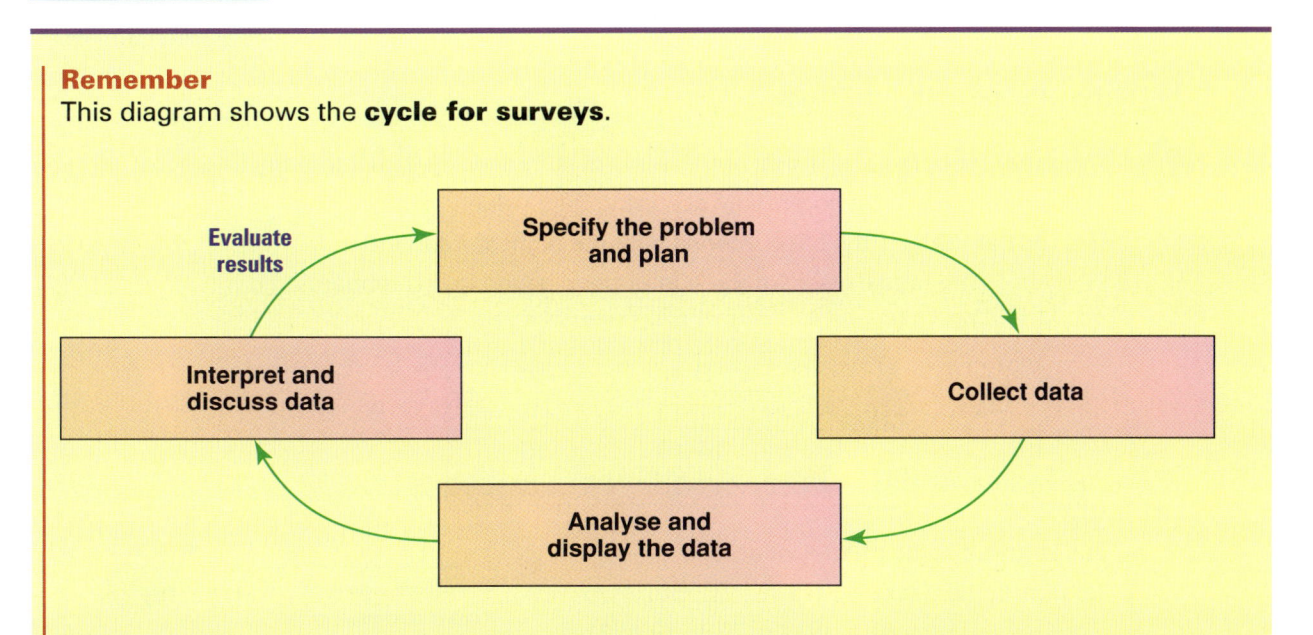

Remember
This diagram shows the **cycle for surveys**.

Specify the problem and plan → Collect data → Analyse and display the data → Interpret and discuss data → Evaluate results → (back to Specify the problem and plan)

Sometimes when we evaluate the results at the end of a statistical investigation, this leads to further questions that need investigating. The cycle begins again.

When **planning a survey, remember to decide on the answers to these questions**:

- What do you want to find out?
- Are there any related questions?
- What might you find out? Make up a conjecture to test.
- What data do you need to collect?
- How accurate does the data need to be?
- How will you collect the data and who from? You may choose a primary source or a secondary source.
- How many pieces of data do you need (sample size)?
- When and where will you collect the data?
- How will you display the data? Is using ICT appropriate or best?
- How will you interpret the data? Is finding the mean, median, mode or range appropriate?

Handling Data

Practical

1 Choose a problem to investigate. You could choose one of the suggestions given in the Discussion on page 369, or a topic of your own.
2 Plan a survey using the steps above.
3 Carry out your survey.
4 Analyse and display the results using ICT if appropriate.
  Use the mean, median, mode and range if appropriate.
5 Write a report on what you found out. Include your conclusions.
  Make sure your conclusions relate to the original problem you set out to investigate.
  In your report, write about any difficulties you had and how you solved these difficulties.

Use ICT to display your results and present your report.

Summary of key points

A The **mean**, **median** and **mode** are all ways of summarising data into a single number.

The **mode** is the most commonly occurring data value.

The **modal class** is the class interval with the highest frequency.

Example The modal class for the age of people who go skateboarding is 14–16 years.

Age (yrs)	Frequency
8–10	11
11–13	19
14–16	27
17–19	17

The **median** is the middle value of a set of ordered data.

Example The median of 14 g, 17 g, 19 g, 21 g, 22 g and 27 g is $\frac{19 + 21}{2} = 20$.

When there is an even number of values we find the mean of the two middle values to find the median.

The **mean** = $\frac{\text{sum of data values}}{\text{number of values}}$

The mean is affected by extreme values.

Often one of the mean, median or mode represents the data best.

B Data collected in tables is often then **displayed** as one of these types of **graphs**.

Categorical data	– pictogram, pie chart, bar chart
Discrete data	– pictogram, pie chart, bar chart, bar-line graph
Grouped discrete	– bar chart
Continuous data	– frequency diagram
Data over time	– line graph

A graph highlights particular features and trends that a table does not.

Analysing and Displaying Data

C   A **scatter graph** displays two sets of data.

Example   This scatter graph shows the marks some students got in maths and in science.

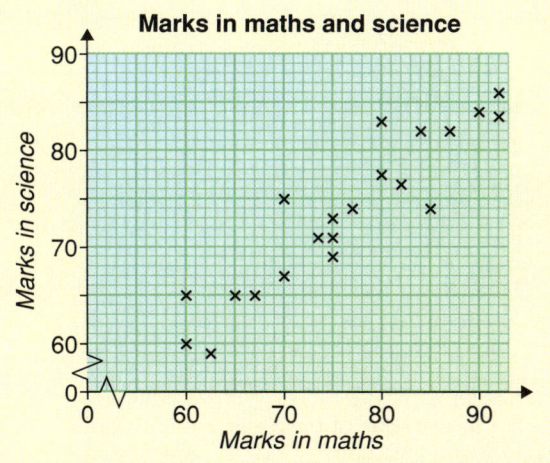

Marks in maths and science

A scatter graph sometimes shows a **correlation** (relationship) between the variables.

Example

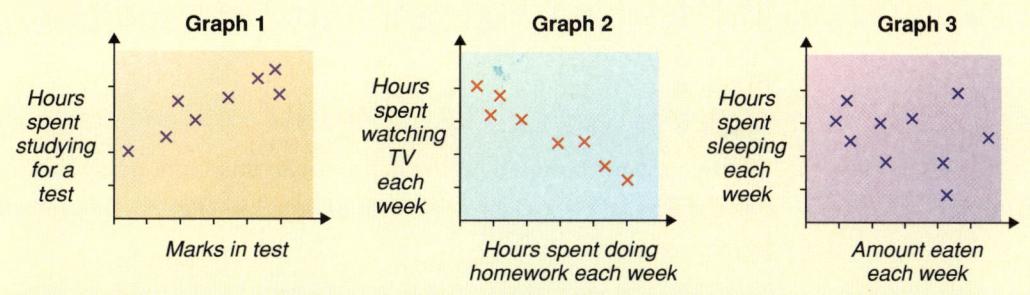

Graph 1 — Hours spent studying for a test vs Marks in test

Graph 2 — Hours spent watching TV each week vs Hours spent doing homework each week

Graph 3 — Hours spent sleeping each week vs Amount eaten each week

Graph 1 shows there is a **positive correlation** between the hours spent studying for a test and the marks gained in the test. As the number of hours increases so do the marks in the test.

Graph 2 shows a **negative correlation** between hours spent watching TV and hours spent doing homework. As the number of hours spent watching TV increases, the hours spent doing homework decreases.

Graph 3 shows there is no correlation between the hours spent sleeping and the amount eaten in a week.

D   We often use graphs and tables to help **interpret** data.

E   Sometimes graphs, diagrams or statements can be **misleading**.

Example   **Packets of biscuits sold**

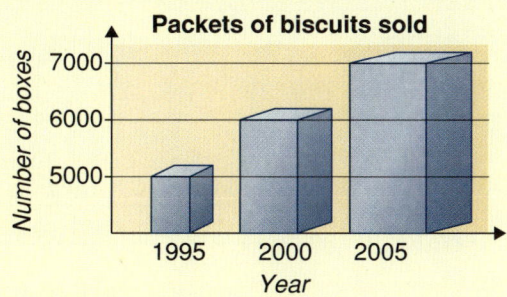

This graph is misleading because the volume of the boxes makes it look like the increase has been massive. Also the vertical scale does not start at zero, again exaggerating the increase in number sold.

407

Handling Data

F We can **compare data** by
- looking at the 'shape' of distributions

Example

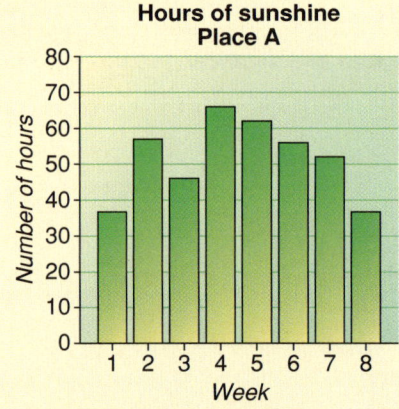

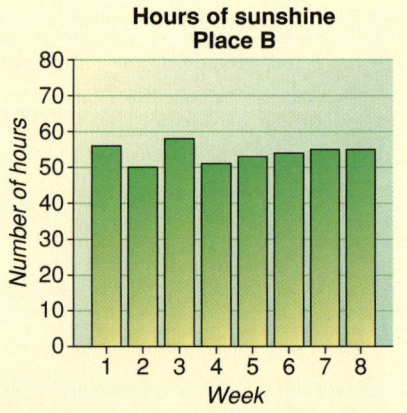

Hours of sunshine Place A

Hours of sunshine Place B

The two distributions have a different shape.

For place A the number of hours of sunshine per week is much more variable than for place B.

- using the range and either the mean, median or mode.

Example Robert found the mean, median, mode and range of the hours of sunshine per week in two places.

Place A   mean 53   range 24

Place B   mean 54   range 8

The two places have about the same mean sunshine hours but place A has a much less consistent number of sunshine hours, shown by the bigger range.

Test yourself

1 Rachel was goalkeeper for her hockey team.
   She wrote down the number of goals she stopped in each game.
        2   4   2   6   3   3   2   10
   a Find the mean, median and mode of this data.
   b Does the mean represent the data well?
      Explain your answer.
   c Which of the mean, median or mode would Rachel be more likely to use in an application for a place in a team to represent her area.
      Would this be a fair 'average' to quote?

2 This table shows the marks that class 9L got in a test.
   a In which class interval will the median lie?
   b What is the modal class?
   c What sort of graph could you use to display this data? Explain your choice.

Mark	Tally	Frequency
31–40	II	2
41–50	IIII	4
51–60	IIII II	7
61–70	IIII IIII III	13
71–80	III	3
81–90	I	1

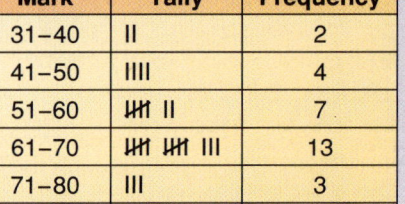

Analysing and Displaying Data

3   Is it possible to find a data set with five values with a mean of 4, a range of 2 and a mode of 6?

T

4   Every day Jamie practised his goal shooting for basketball. At the end of each week he checked to see how many goals out of 50 he could get through the net. This table shows his results.

Week	1	2	3	4	5	6	7
Number of goals out of 50	12	20	26	32	36	40	42

a   Use a copy of the grid.

Goals out of 50

Draw a line graph to show this information.

b   Could you use the graph to estimate how many goals Jamie was able to shoot after three and a half weeks?
Explain your answer.

5   This table gives the results for the Year 8 long jump competition at Ryan's school.

Distance jumped d (in cm)	Frequency
$180 \leq d < 190$	2
$190 \leq d < 200$	6
$200 \leq d < 210$	10
$210 \leq d < 220$	11
$220 \leq d < 230$	14
$230 \leq d < 240$	16
$240 \leq d < 250$	9
$250 \leq d < 260$	4

a   Draw a frequency diagram for the data.
b   How many jumped 230 cm or more?
c   How many jumped less than 220 cm?
d   Ryan jumped 243 cm. He thought he came fifth.
Is this possible? Explain your answer.
*e   The school magazine reported that over half of Year 9 students jumped further than 233 cm.
Explain how you can tell from the graph or table that this is not correct.

409

Handling Data

6 These three graphs show three ways of displaying data about what makes people start playing golf.

   a Which graph do you think shows the data best? Explain.

 * **b** Compare the reasons given by under 16 year olds and those given by adults.

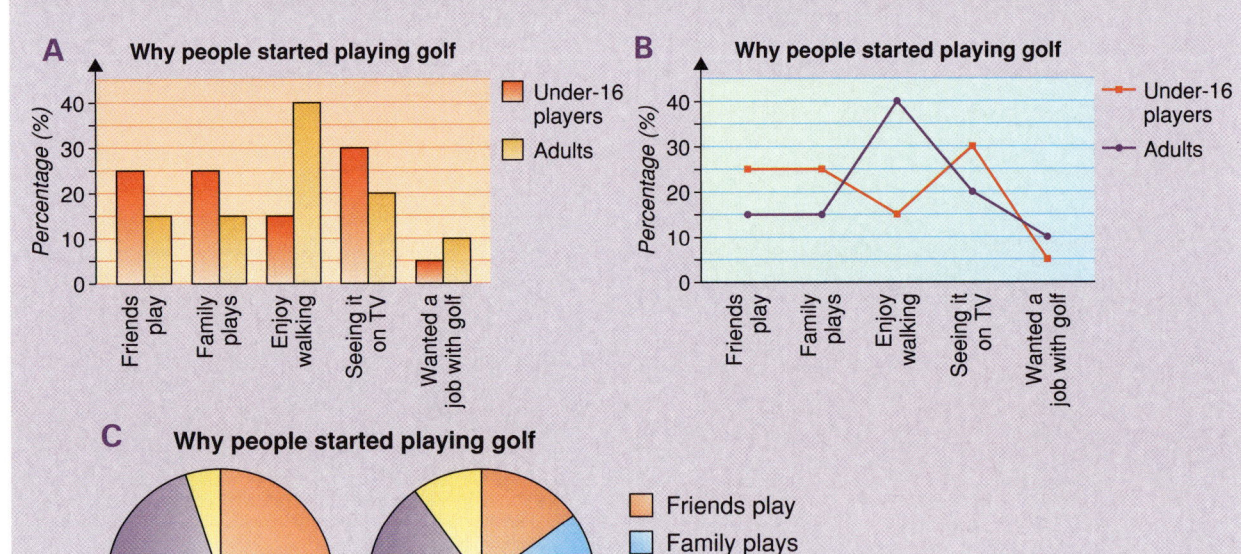

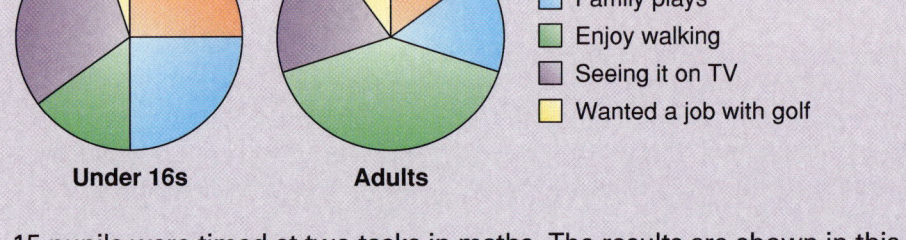

A Why people started playing golf

B Why people started playing golf

C Why people started playing golf

- Friends play
- Family plays
- Enjoy walking
- Seeing it on TV
- Wanted a job with golf

Under 16s   Adults

7 15 pupils were timed at two tasks in maths. The results are shown in this table.
The first task was to complete 25 calculations without a calculator.
The second task was to complete 25 similar calculations using a calculator.

Time (sec) for 1st task	75	64	83	63	72	67	82	74	61	78	66	73	81	68	77
Time (sec) for 2nd task	53	45	55	47	50	44	52	49	43	53	48	49	52	49	50

  a Use a copy of the grid.
Draw a scatter graph for the data. The scales have been started for you.

  b Another pupil took 48 seconds for the 2nd task. Estimate the time this pupil would take for the 1st task.

  c Estimate the time taken for the calculations using a calculator if a pupil took 76 seconds without a calculator.

  d Does the scatter graph show any correlation between the time taken to complete the two tasks?
If so, what sort of correlation is it?

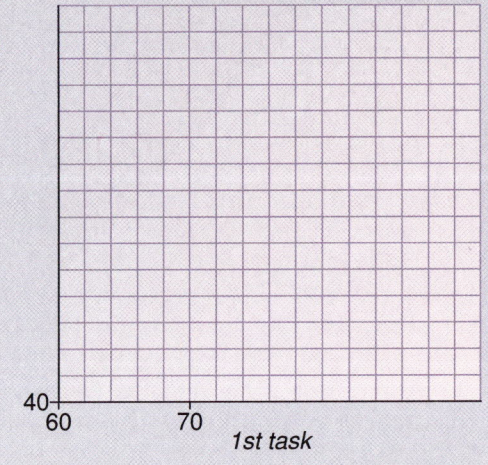

You could draw a line of best fit to help.

410

Analysing and Displaying Data

8 Jordan thinks that people with longer arms also have longer legs. If this were true, what would the scatter graph look like? Draw a sketch.

9 The median score of three people in a test is 35. The mean is 38 and the range is 41. What are the three scores?

10 a Four patients were in a room together at St George's hospital. One of these patients worked out that the mean of the number of visitors they each had one day was 3, the mode was 3 and the range was 4. Is this possible? If it is, what is the number of visitors each patient could have had that day?

b In the same hospital, a ward manager kept a record of the number of visitors one day for every patient in the ward.

Visitors per patient	0	1	2	3	4	5	6
Frequency	3	4	6	5	5	3	4

  i What is the mean number of visitors?
  ii What is the modal number of visitors?

11 This graph appeared in an article claiming that we had beaten tooth decay in children. Explain why it is misleading.

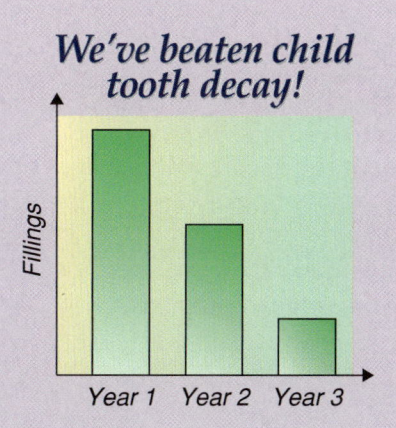

We've beaten child tooth decay!

(Bar chart: Fillings vs Year 1, Year 2, Year 3)

12 Every day Jamie and Simon practised their cricket bowling. They each timed how long they practised.

Jamie (time in minutes)
15 16 20 24 10 12 15 15 25 17

Simon (time in minutes)
9 30 26 17 15 22 10 29 16 22

a Find the mean, median and range of each set of data.
b Draw a frequency table like this for Jamie and Simon.
c Draw a bar chart for Jamie and Simon. Put their data on the same chart.
d Compare the amount of time that Jamie and Simon spent practising.

Time (minutes)	Tally	Frequency
8–11		
12–15		
16–19		
20–23		
24–27		
28–31		

Handling Data

T

13 Lee collected information on the favourite type of movie for boys and girls.

B

	Drama	Romance	Science fiction	Adventure	Horror
Boys	3	2	8	10	7
Girls	8	12	2	6	2

He started working out the angles and drawing two pie charts for the data.

Boys
Drama $\frac{3}{30} \times 360° = 36°$

Girls
Drama $\frac{8}{30} \times 360° = 96°$

Use a copy of the diagrams.
Finish them.
Show your working and draw your angles accurately.

Boys

Girls

14 The school netball team has a final next week.
The coach had to choose whether Lela or Gwen should play as goal shoot.
The following list shows their goals for their last 6 games.

A F

| Gwen: | 12 | 10 | 12 | 14 | 12 | 12 |
| Lela: | 10 | 2 | 4 | 30 | 2 | 24 |

a Find the mean, median and range for each girl.
b Which girl do you think the coach should choose?
Explain why using your results from **a**.

16 Probability

You need to know
✓ probability   page 359

Key vocabulary
event, experimental probability, mutually exclusive, $p(n)$ probability of event n, relative frequency, sample space, theoretical probability

▶▶ Spiralling out of control

We can draw a spiral in two directions.

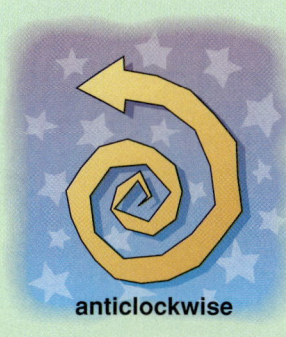

anticlockwise   clockwise

Ask about 50 people to draw a spiral. Collect the results on a table like this one.

Is it equally likely that the next person you ask to draw a spiral will draw a clockwise one or an anticlockwise one?

	Tally	Frequency
Clockwise		
Anticlockwise		

Handling Data

Language of probability

We often describe **probability** using these words.

certain, possible, impossible, 50% chance, even chance, better than even chance, less than even chance, very likely, likely, very unlikely, equally likely

Example This fair spinner is spun.
Each of the outcomes are **equally likely**.
There is the same chance the spinner will stop on each colour because there is the same proportion of each colour.

If an event is **random**, the outcomes are **unpredictable**.
In the above example the outcomes could be red, green, purple or yellow. It is unpredictable.

Worked Example
Jan likes dark chocolates.
Which box should she take a chocolate from to have the greatest probability of getting a dark chocolate?

Answer
In box 1 there are 5 dark chocolates out of 15.
In box 2 there are 7 dark chocolates out of 24.

We need to find which box has the greater **proportion** of dark chocolates.

$\frac{5}{15} = \frac{1}{3} = 0.\dot{3}$ $\frac{7}{24} = 0.29$ (2 d.p.)   and $0.29 < 0.\dot{3}$

There is a greater proportion of dark chocolates in box 1 so Jan has the greater probability of getting a dark chocolate from this box.

We can use a calculator to find 7 ÷ 24.

Exercise 1

1 Gabrielle's class has been divided into two groups, blue and yellow.
A spinner is spun.
If it stops on blue, the blue group gets a point.
If it stops on yellow, the yellow group gets a point.
The teacher has these three different spinners.
One game is played using each spinner.

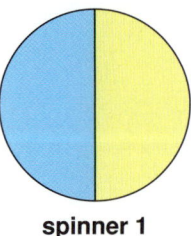

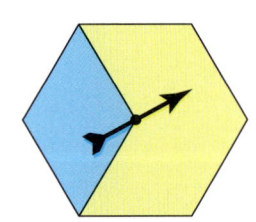

spinner 1   spinner 2   spinner 3
game 1   game 2   game 3

   a Which game is the yellow group most likely to win? Why?
   b Which game is the blue group most likely to win? Why?
   c Which game is one group certain to win? Which group?
   d Which game is it equally likely that yellow and blue will win? Why?

Probability

2 Paulo and Eliza are playing a game of High/Low. Ten cards with the numbers 1 to 10 are placed face down in random order.
Paulo and Eliza take turns to turn a card over.
If the card turned over by a player has a higher value than the previous card turned over, that player gets a point.

The cards look like this after one turn each.

| 8 | 6 | | | | | | | | |

a It is Paulo's turn.
Does he have a less than 50% chance or greater than 50% chance of turning over a card higher than 6? Explain.

b Paulo turns over a 4.
Now it is Eliza's turn.
Does she have a less than 50% chance or greater than 50% chance of turning over a card higher than 4?

| 8 | 6 | 4 | | | | | | | |

3 A game in an arcade has a grid with some squares coloured.
When you press 'enter', one square is randomly chosen.
If a coloured square is 'hit' you get 1000 points. With each game you get three tries.
If you get 3000 points you win ten times your money back.
A different card is displayed for each game.

a On which of these cards are you most likely to score 3000 points? **Explain**.

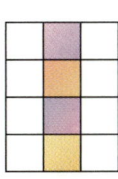

card 1   card 2   card 3

*b On which of these cards are you most likely to score 3000 points? Explain.

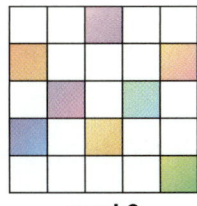

card 1   card 2   card 3

Use a calculator if you need to.

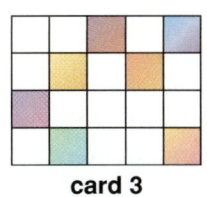

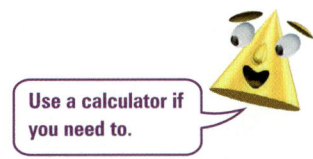

*c On which of these cards would you be most likely to win?
A   10 coloured squares and 54 white squares
B   40 coloured squares and 216 white squares
C   99 coloured squares and 381 white squares.

4 Molly, who is 5, likes red jet planes.
At a party there are two bags of jet planes.
a In bag one there are 8 red jet planes and 10 planes of other colours.
In bag two there are 6 red jet planes and 12 of other colours.
Which bag should she pick from? Why?

*b A third bag has 5 red jet planes and 6 planes of other colours.
Which bag should Molly pick from now? Why?
Show your working.

415

Handling Data

5 I have two bags of counters. [SATs Paper 2 Level 7]

Bag A contains
12 **red** counters and
18 **yellow** counters.

Bag B contains
10 **red** counters and
16 **yellow** counters.

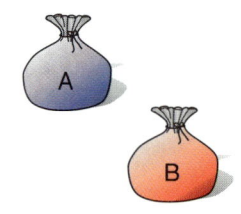

I am going to take one counter at random from either bag A or bag B.

I want to get a **red** counter.
Which bag should I choose?

Show working to explain your answer.

Review 1

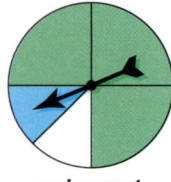

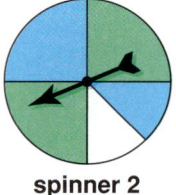

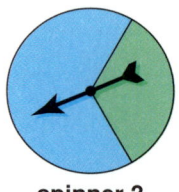

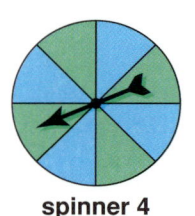

spinner 1   spinner 2   spinner 3   spinner 4

a Which spinner is equally likely to stop on blue or green?
b Which spinner is the most likely to stop on blue?
c Which spinner is least likely to stop on blue?
d What goes in the gap?
Spinners ___ and ___ are more likely to stop on green than any other colours.

Review 2
I have two bags of counters.

Bag A contains 14 red counters and 21 yellow counters.
Bag B contains 10 red counters and 16 yellow counters.

I am going to take one counter at random from either bag A or bag B.
I want to get a red counter.
Which bag should I choose? Explain your answer.

Discussion

Discuss the truth of these statements.

a A serious road accident happens nearly every day in Britain. There are so many cars on the road today, an accident is **certain** to happen.

b For the last three days, each time I tossed a fair coin I got a head. When I toss the coin today I can't **possibly** get a head.

c The next person to walk through the school gate could be a teacher or a pupil. So there is a 50% chance it will be a pupil.

d Taylor buys a ticket each week in the National Lottery. She said 'I'm not lucky, I'll **never** win.'

e The risk of being killed in an accident is about 1 in 400 and of dying of cancer is 1 in 3. You are much more likely to die of cancer next year than in an accident.

Mutually exclusive events

This spinner could stop on 1 or 2 or 3 or 4 or 5 or 6 or 7 or 8.
It can only stop on *one* of the numbers.

If event A is 'stops on an odd number' and event B is 'stops on the 2', event A and event B cannot happen at the same time.

Event A and event B are called **mutually exclusive**.

If event C is 'stops on an odd number' and event D is 'stops on a multiple of 3', event C and event D can happen at the same time.
If the spinner stopped on 3, this is an odd number **and** a multiple of 3.
Events C and D are *not* mutually exclusive.

Events which cannot happen at the same time are called **mutually exclusive**.

Exercise 2

State whether or not the following events A and B are mutually exclusive.

1. A dice is rolled.
   Event A : an even number
   Event B : an odd number

2. Two coins are tossed.
   Event A : two heads
   Event B : one head and one tail

3. A dice is rolled.
   Event A : a number greater than 4
   Event B : an odd number

4. Two coins are tossed.
   Event A : two heads
   Event B : at least one head

5. A card is drawn from a full pack.
   Event A : a spade
   Event B : an ace

6. A day dawns.
   Event A : it is a fine day
   Event B : it is windy

7. A sheep has lambs.
   Event A : the lambs are twins
   Event B : the lambs are triplets

8. Two pupils are chosen at random.
   Event A : one pupil wears glasses
   Event B : one pupil is tall

9. A counter is drawn from a box containing red, blue and white counters.
   Event A : a red counter
   Event B : not a red counter

Review 1 A dice is rolled.
Event A : a number less than 4
Event B : the number 4

Review 2 Salina goes shopping.
Event A : Salina goes shopping with Kate
Event B : Salina goes shopping with Shannon

Handling Data

> **Discussion**
> - Think of pairs of events that are mutually exclusive. **Discuss**.
>   Think of pairs of events that are not mutually exclusive. **Discuss**.
> - A card is drawn from a pack.
>   **Event A** : an ace   **Event B** : the king of spades
>   What might **event C** be if the three events A, B and C are mutually exclusive? **Discuss**.
>   What might **event C** be if the three events A, B and C are not mutually exclusive? **Discuss**.

Calculating probabilities of mutually exclusive events

Remember
If the outcomes of an event are **equally likely**,

> **Probability of an event** = $\dfrac{\text{number of favourable outcomes}}{\text{number of possible outcomes}}$

Example   There are 80 people at a dinner.
24 are men, 26 are women and 30 are children.
One seat is chosen at random and the person on it receives a prize.
The probability it is a child's seat is given by

probability (child) = $\dfrac{30}{80}$ ← number of children
                                      ← total number of people
= $\dfrac{3}{8}$ or 0·375 or 37·5%

Probability can be given as a fraction, decimal or percentage.

Note   Do not give the answer as 3 out of 8 or 3 in 8 or 3 : 8.

An event will either happen or not happen.

Always give fractions in their simplest form.

> **Probability of an event not happening** = 1 − probability of it happening

If the probability of an event happening is p, the probability of it not happening is $1 - p$.

Example   If the probability of drawing a circle from a pack of shape cards is 0·65 then the probability of **not** drawing a circle is 1 − 0·65 = 0·35.

If all the outcomes of an event are **mutually exclusive**, then one of them **must** happen.

Example
There are red, green and yellow counters in a bag. I take one at random.
It is certain that I will get red **or** green **or** yellow.
The sum of the probabilities of getting each colour must add to 1.
p(red) + p(green) + p(yellow) = 1

> **The sum of probabilities of all the mutually exclusive outcomes of an event is 1.**

Worked Example

In a game there are just four types of card.
These are the probabilities of getting each card:

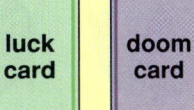

luck card	$\frac{1}{8}$
doom card	$\frac{1}{4}$
wealth card	$\frac{1}{2}$
lose money	?

a What is the probability of getting a lose money card?
b What is the probability of not getting a luck card?

Answer
a The four outcomes, luck card, doom card, wealth card and lose money card are mutually exclusive.
The probabilities of getting a luck card **or** a doom card **or** a wealth card **or** a lose money card must add to 1.
$p(\text{luck}) + p(\text{doom}) + p(\text{wealth}) + p(\text{lose money}) = 1$

$$\frac{1}{8} + \frac{1}{4} + \frac{1}{2} + ? = 1$$
$$? = 1 - \frac{1}{8} - \frac{1}{4} - \frac{1}{2}$$
$$= \frac{1}{8}$$

The probability of getting a lose money card is $\frac{1}{8}$.

b $p(\text{not luck}) = 1 - p(\text{luck})$
$= 1 - \frac{1}{8}$
$= \frac{7}{8}$

The probability of not getting a luck card is $\frac{7}{8}$.

Exercise 3

1 This spinner has eight equal sections.
   a What is the probability of the spinner landing on a circle?
   b What is the probability of the spinner landing on a blue shape?
   c A different spinner has six equal sections.
   It has numbers between 0 and 10 on it.
   The probability of scoring an odd number is $\frac{2}{3}$.
   The probability of scoring 5 is $\frac{1}{3}$.
   What numbers could be on the spinner?

2 A garage has ten cars in the yard waiting for repairs.
   This table shows how many of each make.
   a One car is chosen at random to be repaired.
   What goes in the gap?
   i The probability that the car is a _____ is $\frac{1}{2}$.
   ii The probability that it is a Nissan is _____.
   b The first two cars to be repaired that day were both Toyotas.
   Now a third car is chosen at random from the cars left.
   What is the probability it will be the Nissan?

Make	Number of cars
Toyota	5
Ford	2
Mitsubishi	2
Nissan	1

Handling Data

14 Arshad has a bag that contains only blue, green, red and orange sweets.
Arshad is going to take one sweet at random.
This table shows the probability of each colour being taken.

	blue	green	red	orange
Probability		0·05	0·35	0·2

    a What is the probability of a blue sweet being taken?
***b** Explain why the number of orange sweets cannot be 10.
***c** What is the smallest number of each colour sweet in the bag?

***15** Two classes, K and Y, at a school each have the same number of pupils.
The probability of choosing a boy at random from class K is 0·5.
The probability of choosing a boy at random from class Y is 0·3.
The classes join together to go on a class trip.
What is the probability of choosing a boy at random from all the pupils on the class trip?

Review 1 Janine has two pen holders.
Pen holder A has 2 red, 4 blue and 3 black pens.
Pen holder B has 1 red, 5 blue and 4 black pens.
a Janine takes a pen at random from holder A.
   What is the probability it is   **i** blue   **ii** not red?
b Janine's friend takes a pen at random from holder B.
   What is the probability it is black?
c Janine puts all her pens into a box and chooses one from the box at random.
   What is the probability it is red?

Review 2 A bag of fruit has oranges, apples and bananas.
The probability of James taking an apple at random from the bag is $\frac{5}{8}$.
a What is the probability that James does *not* take an apple?
b If there are 16 pieces of fruit in the bag, what is the greatest number of oranges there could be in the bag?

Review 3 Can you find the name of these towns in England?
a $p(\text{letter E}) = \frac{2}{5}$ $p(\text{letter D}) = \frac{1}{5}$ $p(\text{letter L}) = \frac{1}{5}$ $p(\text{letter S}) = \frac{1}{5}$
b $p(\text{letter L}) = \frac{3}{7}$ $p(\text{letter A}) = \frac{2}{7}$ $p(\text{letter W}) = \frac{1}{7}$ $p(\text{letter S}) = \frac{1}{7}$

Review 4 In an arcade game, one of three options appears in the final window.
The probability of each appearing is
    $p(\text{win}) \quad\quad\quad = \frac{1}{12}$
    $p(\text{consolation}) = \frac{1}{4}$
    $p(\text{lose}) \quad\quad\,\, = ?$

a What is the probability of 'lose' appearing?
b Which is most likely to appear?
c What is the probability of not getting 'win'?
***d** After many games 'win' had appeared 4 times. About how many games do you think had been played?

Calculating probability by listing all the mutually exclusive outcomes

> **Discussion**
>
> This spinner is spun twice.
> How many possible outcomes are there? **Discuss**.
> Are all of the outcomes mutually exclusive? **Discuss**.

Before we can calculate probability we need to identify all the **mutually exclusive outcomes**.

Worked Example
Three pupils, Bryce, Taisia and Aine are running for sports captain and deputy sports captain.
The names are drawn from a hat.
List all the possible outcomes.

Answer

Sports captain	Deputy
Aine (A)	Bryce (B)
Aine (A)	Taisia (T)
Bryce (B)	Taisia (T)
Bryce (B)	Aine (A)
Taisia (T)	Bryce (B)
Taisia (T)	Aine (A)

It is a good idea to list the outcomes in a table or list.

This table is called the sample space.

We could list the outcomes as
AB, AT, BT, BA, TB, TA.

Once all outcomes have been listed we can calculate probabilities.

Example The probability of Aine being sports captain or deputy in the example above is.

$p(\text{Aine}) = \frac{4}{6}$ ← number of outcomes where Aine is captain or deputy
← total number of outcomes

$= \frac{2}{3}$ or $66\frac{2}{3}\%$ or 0·67 (2 d.p.)

Exercise 4

1. A fair counter is red on one side (R) and blue on the other (B).
   This counter and a fair dice are thrown together.
   List all the possible outcomes.

   Remember: When a fair dice is thrown all the outcomes are equally likely.

2. These two spinners are spun at the same time.
   a Write down all the possible outcomes.
   b What is the probability of getting
      i two As   ii at least one A   iii an A and a B?

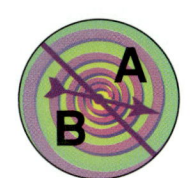

Handling Data

3 These spinners are spun at the same time and the numbers are added.
Use a copy of this table.

+	1	3	5	7	9	11
2						
4						
6						
8						
10						
12						

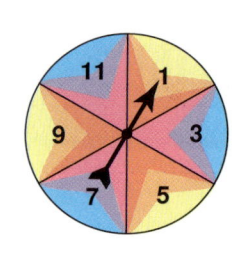

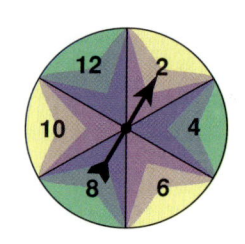

a Fill in the sample space to show all the possible outcomes.
b What is the most likely total? Why?
c Use the sample space to find the probability of getting
 i a total of 3
 ii a total less than 9
 iii both spinners stopping on their highest number
 iv a total of more than 11.

4 a How many possible outcomes are there when three coins are tossed together?
*__b__ What about if four coins are tossed?
*__c__ For each of **a** and **b**, what is the probability of getting two heads?

5 Two children are playing 'paper, scissors, stone'.
They each choose one of paper, scissors or stone and at the count of three, show their choice using a hand.
a Copy and finish this sample space to show all the possible outcomes.

	Paper (P)	Scissors (S)	Stone (O)
Paper (P)	PP		
Scissors (S)			
Stone (O)			

b What is the probability of
 i both children showing the same hands
 ii at least one scissors **iii** no stones?

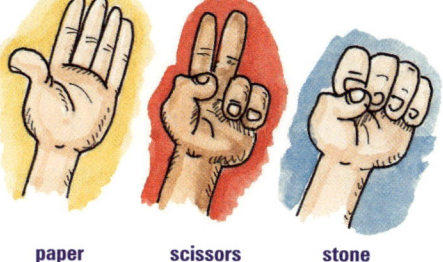

6 These spinners are spun at the same time.
The two numbers spun are added.
a Use a copy of this table to show the sample space for the outcomes.

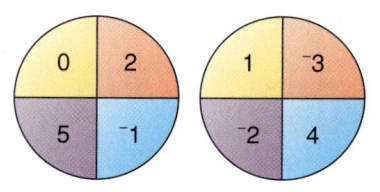

+	0	2	5	⁻1
1		3	6	0
⁻3				
⁻2				
4				

b Find the probability of getting a total of
 i 1 **ii** 3 **iii** less than 5 **iv** more than 6 **v** at least 2.
c What is the most likely total?
d What is the probability of getting 2 on one spinner and ⁻3 on the other?
e What is the probability of getting a negative total?

424

Probability

*7 Stella and Paolo each have three cards numbered 1, 2 and 3.
They each take one of the other person's cards and put it down on the table.
They then add together the numbers on the four cards left in their hands.
What is the probability the total will be an odd number?

*8 Sanjay is choosing subjects for next year.
He must choose one subject from each of these blocks.

Block 1	**Block 2**	**Block 3**
French (F)	Italian (I)	Spanish (S)
Art (A)	Computers (C)	Food Technology (FT)

a List all the possible combinations Sanjay could choose.
b Sanjay decides to choose his subject from each block randomly.
What is the probability his choice will
  i be French, computers and food technology
  ii have at least one language
  iii have neither art nor food technology
  iv have French and food technology but not computers?

*9 At a fair if you toss 6 dice and get 6 sixes you win £300.
What is your chance of winning?

Review 1 A group are going out for a meal. To keep the cost down they have agreed to a random choice of only 4 main courses and 2 desserts.
The main courses are: a chicken dish, a beef dish, a fish dish and a vegetarian dish.
The desserts are: ice cream sundae or plum pudding.
a Using the initials, C, B, F, V and I, P list all possible combinations of a main course and dessert.
b What is the probability that a person randomly chooses chicken and plum pudding?
c What is the probability that a person randomly chooses chicken or fish and ice cream sundae?
d What is the probability that a person randomly chooses ice cream sundae and not beef?
e What is the probability that a person randomly chooses neither beef nor plum pudding?

Review 2 Certain conditions are hereditary, for example, left-handedness. There is a dominant gene, R, and a recessive gene, r. A child gets one gene from each parent. Children are left-handed if they inherit rr, right-handed but a carrier of left-handedness if they inherit Rr and right-handed and not a carrier if they inherit RR.
If both of the parents are carriers, they are both Rr.
a Copy and fill in this table to show the possible outcomes for their children.
What is the probability a child born to these parents will
  i be left-handed
  ii be a carrier of left-handedness
  iii not be left-handed nor be a carrier?
b Repeat **a** for one parent being a carrier and the other left-handed.

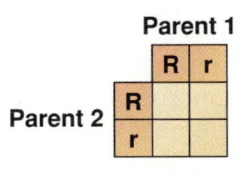

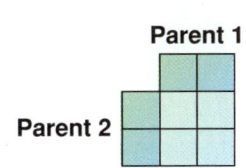

Handling Data

Review 3 A computer game shows two cards.
Each card is equally likely to be a cherry, a strawberry or a plum.

Card 1   Card 2   cherry (c)   strawberry (s)   plum (p)

a List all the possible outcomes.
b What is the probability of getting
   i two identical fruits   **ii** at least one strawberry   **iii** no cherries?

Estimating probabilities from relative frequency

Rani wanted to know the probability that she would shoot a goal successfully in a netball match.
In the next ten netball games, she kept a count of how many attempts at goal she had. She noted how many of these were successful.
She successfully shot 126 out of 154 attempts.

The **relative frequency** of a successful shot $= \frac{126}{154} = \frac{9}{11}$.

The relative frequency is the number of times the event occurs in a number of trials.

$$\text{Relative frequency} = \frac{\text{number of times an event occurs}}{\text{number of trials}}$$

We often use the relative frequency as an **estimate of probability**.
In the above example, the probability that Rani will successfully shoot a goal is about $\frac{9}{11}$.

★ Practical

You will need a spinner like this or a similar one.

1 Spin the pointer twice. Add the two scores.
Do this 50 times. Record the results in a tally chart.
Draw a bar chart to show the results.
Compare your results with another group.
Are they different? Why?

What is the relative frequency of a total of 4?

Use the relative frequency to estimate the probability of getting a total of 4 the next time you spin it twice and add the scores.

Predict what might happen if you repeat the experiment.

Repeat spinning and adding the scores another 50 times.
Combine the results together on another table.
What effect do the extra throws have on the results?

Use the combined results of your experiment to estimate the probability of getting a total of 4 the next time you spin the spinner twice and add the results.
How could you get a more accurate estimate?

If you repeated the experiment 1000 times, how many times would you expect to get a total of 4?

2 Now change the numbers on the spinner to 3, 3, 1 and repeat part **1**.

What if you changed the numbers to 2, 2, 2?

When **estimating probability** from an experimental result it is important to note that

1 when an experiment is repeated, there may be, and usually will be different outcomes
2 increasing the number of times an experiment is repeated usually leads to better estimates of probability.

Worked Example
Nathan tossed two coins together a number of times. He recorded the results on the following table.

Event	Tally	Frequency
HH	|||| |||| ||||	15
HT	|||| |||| |||| |||| ||||	24
TH	|||| |||| |||| |||| |||| ||||	29
TT	|||| |||| |||| |||	18

a Find
  i the number of times Nathan tossed the two coins
  ii the relative frequency of the event 'two heads'.
b Estimate the probability of getting 'one head and one tail' the next time these coins are tossed.
c What would happen if Nathan tossed the two coins together again, the same number of times?
d If these two coins are tossed 48 times, about how many times would you expect to get two heads?

Answer
a i Number of tosses = 15 + 24 + 29 + 18
         = **86**
  ii 'Two heads' occurred 15 times.
     Relative frequency of 'two heads' = $\frac{15}{86}$
b 'One head and one tail' occurred 53 times (24 HT and 29 TH).
  Relative frequency of 'one head and one tail' = $\frac{53}{86}$
  Probability of getting one head and one tail = $\frac{53}{86}$
c **The results would be different but probably similar.**
d An estimate of the probability of getting two heads is $\frac{15}{86}$.
  So you would expect to get 2 heads $\frac{15}{86}$ of 48 times.
  $\frac{15}{86} \times 48 = $ **8 times (nearest whole number)**.

Handling Data

Exercise 5

1 This tally chart gives the number of pictures on each of the pages of a newspaper.

Number of pictures	Tally	Frequency
0												10
1									7
2											9
3								6
4								6
5						4
6								6

a How many pages were there in this newspaper?
b Find the relative frequency of a page having just one picture.
c Estimate the probability of there being 5 pictures on a page chosen at random.
d How could you make a more accurate estimate of probability?

2 A card was drawn at random from a pack and the shape on it noted. The card was put back and the pack shuffled. This was done 250 times. The results are shown in the table.

Shape	Square	Triangle	Circle	Star
Frequency	52	67	61	70

a Find the relative frequency of a
  i square **ii** star **iii** triangle **iv** circle.
  What is the sum of these relative frequencies?
b Estimate the probability of getting a star the next time a card is drawn at random from this pack.
c If a card is drawn at random from this pack 1000 times and put back each time, how many times would you expect to get a circle?

3 Some pupils tossed three coins. This table shows their results.

Name	No. of tosses	Two the same	All the same
Tony	50	42	8
Huw	150	112	38
Jane	100	71	29

a Whose data is most likely to give the best estimate of the probability of getting each result? Explain.
b Use this person's results to estimate the probability of getting all the same the next time you toss three coins.
  How could you improve the accuracy of this estimate?
c If the coins were tossed together 500 times, how many times would you expect to get just two the same?

4 A dice was thrown 200 times and the results were as shown in this table.

Number on dice	1	2	3	4	5	6
Frequency	24	29	32	41	39	35

a Find the relative frequency of getting a
  i 1 **ii** 2 **iii** 3 **iv** 4 **v** 5 **vi** 6.
  What is the sum of these relative frequencies?
b Estimate the probability that the next time this dice is thrown it will land on a 6.
c If the dice is tossed 500 times, about how many times would you expect to get a 6?

Review This table shows what happened to calls made by a telemarketer one day.

Result of call	Frequency
Answered	76
Not answered	34
Answer machine	25
Out of order	3
Engaged	12

A telemarketer is a person who phones people at home trying to sell them something.

a Find the relative frequency of each result.
b Estimate the probability of the phone being answered.
c Estimate the probability of the telemarketer not being able to talk with the person at home.
d If the telemarketer phones 600 people in the next week, how many times would she expect to get an answer machine?

Practical

1 Take one column of your local telephone book.
   - Use a copy of this table. Record the number of times the digits 0, 1, ... 9 occur.

Digit	0	1	2	3	4	5	6	7	8	9
Frequency										
Relative frequency										

   - Find the relative frequency of each of the digits and complete the last line of the table.
   - Use your results to estimate the following probabilities.
       $p(0)$ $p(3)$ $p(7)$ $p(9)$
   - Take another column and repeat.
   - Were the estimates of $p(0)$, $p(3)$, $p(7)$, $p(9)$ about the same in both cases? Did you expect them to be?

2 Select a page of this book which has a lot of numbers on it.
   - What would you expect the relative frequency of the digit 4 to be?
   - Find the relative frequency of the digit 4 on the page you selected. (Only consider the *digits* on this page, not the letters.)
   - Discuss your results with the other students in your group or your class.
   - Using the results of your group or class, estimate the probability of a digit on a page of this book being a 4.

3 Conduct an experiment of your choice to estimate the probability of an event, using relative frequency as an estimate. You could use one of the following suggestions:
   - probability that a buttered piece of toast will fall butter side down when dropped
   - probability that the next person to try to throw a piece of screwed up paper into a rubbish bin from a distance of 3 m will succeed
   - probability that the next person leaving the library will wear glasses.

   If you did the same experiment on another day would you expect to get about the same estimate for the probability?

Handling Data

Comparing experimental and theoretical probability

Practical

1 **You will need** computer software that can simulate rolling a dice and tossing a coin.
Ask your teacher for the Simulation ICT worksheet.

If you don't have computer software for this, you could do it as a class in groups and combine the results to get 1000 tosses.

   a What is the probability of getting a head when a coin is tossed?
   If a coin is tossed 1000 times, how many times do you expect to get a head?
   If a coin is tossed 10 times, how many times do you expect to get a head?

   Toss a coin 1000 times. Find the relative frequency of a head after 100 tosses, after 200 tosses, ... after 1000 tosses. You could use a tally chart to record each time a head comes up, or you could work with a partner and have your partner count the number of heads.
   Summarise your findings in a table such as that shown below.

Number of tosses	100	200	300	400	500	600	700	800	900	1000
Number of heads										
Relative frequency of a head										

   Did the relative frequency of a head get closer to $\frac{1}{2}$, the more trials you did?
   Did you expect it to get quite close to $\frac{1}{2}$?

   What if the coin was tossed 5000 times?
   What if the coin was tossed 10 000 times?

   b What is the probability of getting a 2 when you roll a dice?
   If you rolled a dice 240 times, how many times would you expect to get a 2?

   Roll a dice 240 times and collect the results on a table such as the one below.

Number on dice	1	2	3	4	5	6
Tally						
Frequency						
Relative frequency						

   Did you get the number of 2s you expected? Did you expect each of the relative frequencies to be close to $\frac{1}{6}$? Were the relative frequencies all close to $\frac{1}{6}$?
   If you rolled the dice 24 000 times, would you expect each of the relative frequencies to be very close to $\frac{1}{6}$?

*2 **You will need** a set of dominoes.
   Put the dominoes in a bag or box.
   Draw out a domino, record the total score of the dots and put it back. Do this many times.
   Use a tally chart to record the totals.
   Draw a bar chart for your results.
   Use this to calculate the relative frequency for each possible total.
   Calculate the theoretical probability of getting each total.
   Compare your theoretical probability with the experimental probability.

Probability

When we **compare experimental probability with theoretical probability**, the greater the number of trials in the experiment, the closer the experimental probability is to the theoretical probability.

Exercise 6

1 Jade and Kira were asked to roll a fair dice 90 times each and record the results.
One of them made up the results.
Which one? Explain.

	1	2	3	4	5	6
Jade	15	16	14	17	13	15
Kira	15	15	15	15	15	15

*2 Design an experiment so that you could compare the theoretical probability with the experimental probability of guessing the missing digit in this combination. It could be any digit from 0 to 9.

*3 Jasmine worked out the probability of getting a total of seven when she spun this spinner twice and added the scores.
   a What theoretical probability should she have got?
   b She did an experiment to test the theoretical probability.
     She spun the spinner twice and added the scores.
     She repeated this 90 times.
     She got a total of seven 33 times.
     She said 'The experimental probability is not the same as the theoretical probability so I must have done something wrong.'
     Is she correct? Explain.

Review Toby rolled a dice 200 times. He got a six 34 times.
Do you think the dice is biased? Explain.

Dice Totals – a game for a group or class

You will need   36 counters for each player,
                    a strip of paper about 30 cm long for each player and 2 dice.

To play
- Each player writes the numbers 1 to 12 along the strip of paper.
  Now each player spreads all 36 counters above the 12 numbers.

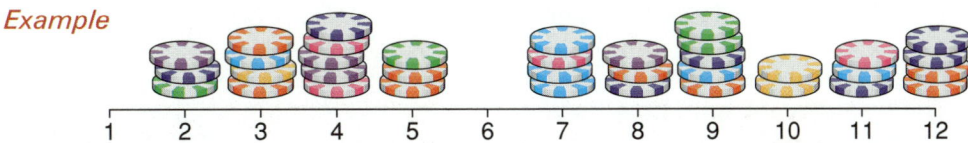

  Example

- One player rolls the two dice and calls the total.

  Example   If the dice land as shown the total called is 9.

  Players who have counters placed on 9, remove one of these counters.
  Take turns to keep rolling the dice and calling the total.
- The winner is the first player to have removed all 36 counters.

Handling Data

Note: You could use dots instead of counters.

Instead of removing a counter, a dot could be crossed out.

Once you have played the game a few times think about these.

1. Is this game mainly luck? Is it sensible to place counters on 1?
2. Should you put more counters on some numbers than others? If so, which ones?
3. Why does each student have 36 counters rather than 20 or 50 or ...?
4. If you had 360 counters rather than 36, could you place them so that they would all be removed after 360 tosses of the dice?
5. **What if** you had 3600 counters? **What if** you had 36 000 counters?

Some games are **fair** and others are **unfair**.
If a game is fair, it means that all players have the same chance of winning.

Example In a game of Even/Odd, two dice are rolled and the total is added.
One player gets a point if the total is even and the other player gets a point if the total is odd.

To decide if this game is fair, we need to look at the sample space of all the possible outcomes. To be a fair game there needs to be the same number of even outcomes as odd outcomes. There are 18 odd outcomes and 18 even outcomes so it **is** a fair game.

+	1	2	3	4	5	6
1	2	3	4	5	6	7
2	3	4	5	6	7	8
3	4	5	6	7	8	9
4	5	6	7	8	9	10
5	6	7	8	9	10	11
6	7	8	9	10	11	12

Exercise 7

You could do this exercise in pairs or groups and actually play the games.

1. In the game given in the example above, would the game be fair if the numbers on the dice were multiplied instead of added? Justify your answer by drawing a sample space of all possible outcomes.

    You need to draw the sample space for multiplication.

2. A game is played with three players and these two spinners.
The spinners are spun together.
The difference between the numbers is found.
If the result is even, player 1 gets a point. If it is odd player 2 gets a point and if it is zero player 3 gets a point.
    a Draw a sample space of all the possible outcomes. 
    b Is this a fair game? Explain.

432

*3 Eight players play a game using these two spinners.

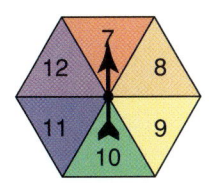

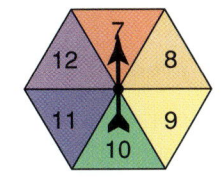

Eight rule cards are put in a bag.
Each player chooses a rule card at random. Then the spinners are spun together. If the rule is satisfied, that player gets a point.
This shows the rule each player got.

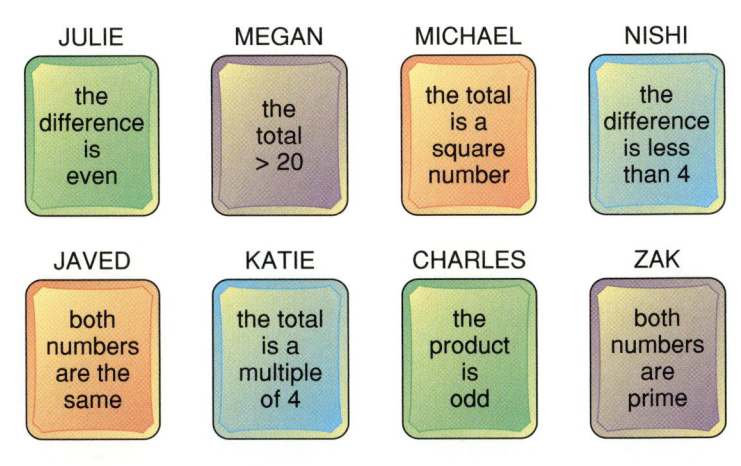

JULIE	MEGAN	MICHAEL	NISHI
the difference is even	the total > 20	the total is a square number	the difference is less than 4

JAVED	KATIE	CHARLES	ZAK
both numbers are the same	the total is a multiple of 4	the product is odd	both numbers are prime

a Draw a sample space for all the possible outcomes of spinning the spinners.
b Who is most likely to win?
c Who is least likely to win?

*4 Ralph and Sasha play a game with five coins. It costs 10p to play.
If you get exactly two heads you get 20p plus your 10p back.
If you get anything else you lose.
Justify, using mathematical reasoning, whether you are more likely to win or lose.

*5 Make up a game such as the one in question **3** and test the rules. Predict then test the results after 36 spins.

Review Two players play a game using two dice. The dice are thrown and the difference between the two numbers is calculated.
Player A wins if the answer is 0, 1 or 2 and Player B wins if the answer is 3, 4 or 5.
a Draw a sample space of all possible outcomes.
b Explain why this game is not fair.
c How could you change the rules so it is fair?

Handling Data

Summary of key points

A When an event is **random**, the outcome is **unpredictable**.

Some events have **equally likely** outcomes.
Example Tim takes a marble out of this bag at random.
It is **equally likely** to be a pink or green marble because there is the same number of green and pink marbles in the bag.

Some outcomes are **more likely** to happen than others.
Example Jody takes a marble out of each of these bags at random. She is **more likely** to take a red marble from Bag A than Bag B because there is a greater proportion of red marbles in Bag A than Bag B. $\frac{3}{6} > \frac{3}{8}$

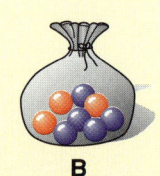

B Events that cannot happen at the same time are called **mutually exclusive**.
Example A is the event 'getting an even number' when a fair dice is rolled.
B is the event 'getting a 3' when a fair dice is rolled.
These events cannot happen at the same time.
They are mutually exclusive events.

C If the probability of an event occurring is p, then the **probability** of it **not** occurring is $1 - p$.
Example If the probability of Sophie successfully shooting a goal in netball is $\frac{5}{7}$, then the probability of her not getting the shot is $\frac{2}{7}$.

D **The sum of the probabilities of all the mutually exclusive outcomes of an event is 1.**
Example There are four different colours of counters in a bag, red, green, blue and yellow.
One is taken at random.
The probabilities of getting three of the colours are
  red 0·2   green 0·25   blue 0·4
The sum of all four probabilities must equal 1.
So p(yellow) = 1 − 0·2 − 0·25 − 0·4
           = 0·15
The probability of getting yellow is **0·15**.

E To **calculate a probability** we often record all the possible **outcomes** using a list, diagram or table. The set of all the possible outcomes is called the **sample space**.  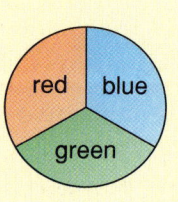
Example These two spinners are spun.
The possible outcomes are
  red 1, red 2, blue 1, blue 2, green 1, green 2.
The probability of getting an outcome with blue = $\frac{2}{6}$ ← ways of getting blue
                              ← total number of possible outcomes
              = $\frac{1}{3}$

F From the results of an experiment we can find the **relative frequency** of an event.

$$\text{Relative frequency} = \frac{\text{number of times an event occurs}}{\text{number of trials}}$$

We often use the relative frequency as an **estimate of probability**.

Example A student dropped a piece of toast with honey on it 50 times.

It landed honey side up 19 times.

The relative frequency of it landing honey side up is $\frac{19}{50}$

We can use this to estimate that the probability of this toast landing honey side up is $\frac{19}{50}$.

1 When an experiment is repeated, there may be, and usually will be different outcomes.
2 Increasing the number of times an experiment is repeated usually leads to better estimates of probability.

G When we compare **experimental probability** with **theoretical probability**, the greater the number of trials in the experiment, the closer the experimental probability is to the theoretical probability.

Test yourself

1 These four spinners are spun.

A (blue, red, red, red, green)
B (green, green, red, blue, blue)
C (blue, blue, yellow, yellow, red)
D (blue, green, green, blue, blue)

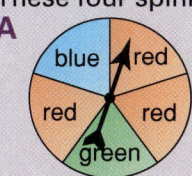

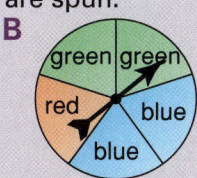

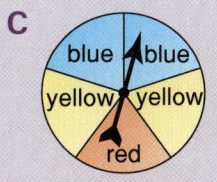

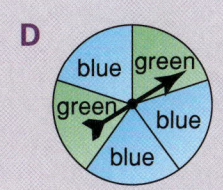

a With which spinner are you most likely to spin blue?
   Explain using proportion.
b With which two spinners are you equally likely to spin green?
   Explain.
c With which spinner are you least likely to spin blue?

2 A sports shop had a promotion and had the following giveaways.
a A giveaway is chosen at random to be given to customers who spend over £100 at the shop.
   What goes in the gap?
   i The probability that the first giveaway is a netball ball is ___.
   ii The probability that the first giveaway is a _____ is $\frac{1}{4}$.
b The first three giveaways were 2 cricket bats and 1 netball ball.
   A fourth giveaway is chosen at random from what is left.
   What is the probability that it will be a cricket bat?

Giveaways	Numbers
tennis rackets	2
cricket bats	5
netball balls	2
footballs	3

435

Handling Data

3 The sports shop also had 8 balls in a bag. Some are squash balls and some are golf balls. They chose some customers to take a ball at random from the bag. If a customer takes a ball at random, the probability it will be a squash ball is $\frac{1}{2}$.
   a What is the probability the ball will be a golf ball?
   b How many squash balls are in the bag?
   c The first customer takes a ball at random out of the bag and keeps it. It is a squash ball. The next customer also takes a ball at random from the bag. What is the probability it is also a squash ball?

4 The probability of a fisherman catching an under-sized lobster is 0·08.
If under-sized lobsters are caught, they must be thrown back to sea.
Find the probability that a lobster is not thrown back to sea.

5 Gareth likes white chocolates.
He can choose a chocolate at random from one of three boxes.
Box A has 4 white and 8 milk chocolates.
Box B has 10 white and 22 milk chocolates.
Box C has 16 white and 42 milk chocolates.
From which box should Gareth take his chocolate? Explain.

6 In which of the following are events **A** and **B** mutually exclusive?
   a **Event A**: John goes to the football match.
       Event B: Jessie goes to the football match.
   b **Event A**: A diamond is drawn from a pack of cards.
       Event B: A picture card is drawn from a pack of cards.
   c **Event A**: You get a prime number when you roll a dice.
       Event B: You get a six when you roll a dice.

7 A cube-shaped biased dice is numbered 1, 2, 3, 4, 5 and 6.
The probabilities of it landing on a particular number are:
   $p(1) = 0·1$
   $p(2) = 0·2$
   $p(3) = 0·15$
   $p(4) = 0·05$
   $p(5) = 0·25$
   a What is the probability of it landing on 6?
   b What is the probability of it not landing on 3 or 4?

8 There are some cubes in a bag. They are either blue or green.
If a cube is taken at random, the probability it is blue is $\frac{1}{6}$.
   a What is the probability it is green?
   b What is the probability it is not green?
   c I take a cube at random. It is blue.
       What is the smallest number of green cubes that could be in the bag?
   d I take another cube. It is also blue.
       Now what is the smallest number of green cubes that could be in the bag?
   *e A different bag has red (R), yellow (Y) and purple (P) cubes in it. There is at least one of each of the three colours. If a cube is taken at random, the probability it will be red is $\frac{5}{8}$.
       There are 24 cubes in the bag.
       What is the greatest number of purple cubes there could be in the bag?
   *f Two bags, A and B, each have the same number of cubes.
       The probability of taking a blue cube from bag A is 0·6.
       The probability of taking a blue cube from bag B is 0·3.
       All the cubes from bags A and B are put in a new bag.
       What is the probability of taking a blue cube from the new bag?

9 Each pupil on a camp could choose two pieces of fruit, one for breakfast and one for lunch.
They could choose from bananas (b), apples (a) and oranges (o).
  a List all the possible choices they could make for their two pieces.
  b What is the probability that a pupil chosen at random will have
    i the same fruit for breakfast and lunch
    ii at least one orange
    iii no apples?

10 These two spinners are spun.
The totals are added together. 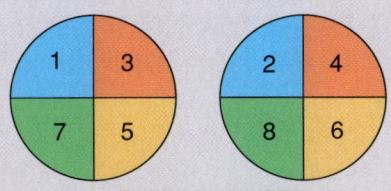
  a Use a copy of the table.
    Fill in the sample space to show all the possible outcomes.
  b What is the most likely total? Why?
  c Use the sample space to find the probability of getting
    i a total of 3
    ii a total of less than 11
    iii an even total
    iv a total of 7 or 13.

+	2	4	6	8
1				
3				
5				
7				

11 The hands on these spinners are spun at the same time.
The two scores are added together.
What is the probability that the total score is negative?

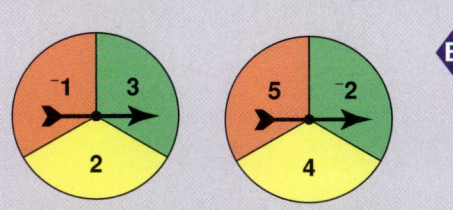

12 Four full packs of cards (52 cards in each) are shuffled together. A card is chosen at random, then put back and the pack shuffled again. This is done 260 times.
How many picture cards (Aces, Kings, Queens and Jacks) do you expect there to have been in the 260 cards chosen? Show your working.

13 54 out of 720 shirts sewn at the Shirt Factory last month were rejected.
  a What is the relative frequency of a shirt being rejected?
  b Estimate the probability that the next shirt sewn will be rejected.

14 Melanie was going to estimate the probability of a page, chosen at random, from a magazine (published 25 May) having an advertisement. She began by counting the pages with advertisements and recording her results on this table.

	Frequency
Advertisements	
No advertisement	

  a Explain how Melanie could continue.
  b If she had chosen the 18 May publication instead of the 25 May would you expect Melanie to get the same estimate?
  c Would you expect the two estimates to be quite close?

Handling Data

15 a Richard has estimated that the probability of winning a computer game is 0·25.
He plays 20 games.
How many of these games should he expect to win?

b Sally played the same game.
She won 15 times and estimated the probability of winning each game to be 0·3.
How many games did Sally play?
Show your working.

c It is claimed that the probability of winning a different computer game is 0·45.
Kit played this game 50 times and won it 42 times.
He says that the claim is wrong.
Do you agree? Explain your answer.

Test yourself answers

Chapter 1 page 35

1. **a** 10 000 **b** 1 **c** 0·001 **d** 0·0001
2. **a** 10^3 **b** 10^1 **c** 10^{-2} **d** 10^{-4}
3. **a** Eight point eight four eight times ten to the power of three
   b Four times ten to the power of negative twenty-three
4. **a, d** and **e**
5. **a** 10^3 **b** 10^6 **c** 10^{-3} **d** 10^{-9}
6. **a** D **b** F **c** B **d** C **e** A **f** E
7. **a** 602 **b** 0·602 **c** 0·0602 **d** 6020
8. $9·5 \times 0·1 = 9·5 \times \frac{1}{10}$
   $= 9·5 \div 10$
9. **a** 0·0435 **b** 43·5 **c** 435 **d** ⁻0·435 **e** ⁻435
10. 480 metres
11. **a** 600 **b** 70 000 **c** 1000 **d** 2 **e** 80 **f** 3
12. **a** 330 **b** 4700 **c** 22 000 **d** 4 700 000
13. **a** 14 500 **b** 15 499 **c** 15 150 and 15 249
14.

Number	Nearest whole number	to 1 d.p.	to 2 d.p.
46·075	46	46·1	46·08
0·625	1	0·6	0·63
16·995	17	17·0	17·00

15. **a** 5·12̇7 or 5·13 (2 d.p.) **b** 0·86 (2 d.p.) **c** 3·5̇1 or 3·51 (2 d.p.) **d** 0·01 (2 d.p.)
16. **a** 0·43 kg (2 d.p.) **b** 4·9 m (1 d.p.)
17. 40% to the nearest percentage

Chapter 2 page 56

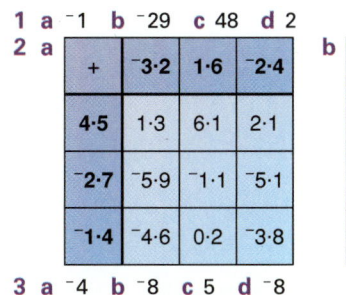

1. **a** ⁻1 **b** ⁻29 **c** 48 **d** 2
2. **a**

+	⁻3·2	1·6	⁻2·4
4·5	1·3	6·1	2·1
⁻2·7	⁻5·9	⁻1·1	⁻5·1
⁻1·4	⁻4·6	0·2	⁻3·8

b

×	⁻7	6	⁻8
⁻3	21	⁻18	24
5	⁻35	30	⁻40
4	⁻28	24	⁻32

3. **a** ⁻4 **b** ⁻8 **c** 5 **d** ⁻8
4. Possible answers are:
   a 2 + ⁻19 = ⁻17 **b** ⁻7 − ⁻2 = ⁻5 **c** ⁻9 × 4 = ⁻36 **d** ⁻12 ÷ ⁻3 = 4
5. **a** 6 and ⁻3 **b** ⁻6 and ⁻2
6. **a** ⁻15 **b** ⁻26 **c** ⁻14 **d** 3
7. $5(3 - {}^-2) = 25$
8. **a** + **b** ⁻8 and 3, ⁻12 and 7 **c** 6 and ⁻5 **d** 7 + 9 − ⁻12 = 28 **e** (see diagram: ⁻5, ⁻8, 3, ⁻2, ⁻6, 9)
9. **a** 6 **b** 12 **c** 14 **d** 16
10. **a** $\frac{4}{7}$ **b** $\frac{5}{8}$ **c** $\frac{4}{7}$ **d** $\frac{5}{9}$
11. **a** 180 **b** 120 **c** 240
12. **a** $\frac{103}{180}$ **b** $\frac{91}{120}$ **c** $\frac{133}{240}$
13. 4 and 24
14. **a** x **b** a **c** $3d$ **d** $4xy$
15. 6
16. **a** 4 or 6 **b** No. Because the square root will always end in 4 or 6
17. **a** 279 936 **b** 8·3521 **c** 0·02 **d** 1296 **e** 1
18. 2
19. **a** +6 and ⁻6 **b** 8 **c** 3·63 **d** 20·86 **e** 7·51
20. ⁻27

439

Test yourself answers

21 a 3·32 **b** 3·56
22 a 4^{11} = 4 194 304 **b** 8^7 = 20 971 52 **c** 7^5 = 16 807 **d** 5^6 = 15 625 **e** 5^5 = 3125
23 a $x^3 \times x^4 = (x \times x \times x) \times (x \times x \times x \times x)$ **b** $x^9 \div x^4 = \dfrac{x \times x \times x \times x \times x \times x \times x \times x \times x}{x \times x \times x \times x}$
$= x^7$ $= x^5$
So $x^3 \times x^4 = x^{(3+4)} = x^7$ So $x^9 \div x^4 = x^{(9-4)} = x^5$
24 $4^4 = 4^2 \times 4^2 = 16 \times 16 = 16^2$. 4^4 is a square number.
25 a $4^3 - 3^3 = 37$ **b** 9 and 11
26 Let the three-digit number be $100h + 10t + u$.
When repeated the number is $100\,000h + 10\,000t + 1000u + 100h + 10t + u$
$= 100\,100h + 10\,010t + 1001u$.
$= 7(14\,300h + 1430t + 143u)$ which is divisible by 7.

Chapter 3 page 89

1

50p	20p	10p	5p
1	1		1
1		2	1
1		1	3
	3	1	1
	3		3
	2	3	1
	2	2	3
	1	5	1
	1	4	3

2 c and d
3 a 20 **b** 42 **c** 7 **d** ⁻4 **e** ⁻3 **f** 9 **g** 6 **h** 3
4 a 939 = 324 + 615. There are other possible answers. **b** 258 = 612 − 354
5 56·928 g
6 £1·20
7 18
8 a 800 **b** 8 **c** 12 000 **d** 1·2 **e** 0·02 **f** 0·009 **g** 0·54 **h** 60 **i** 240 **j** 500 **k** 90
l 0·324. The shading gives the letter O.
9 50·8 cm
10 a 0·75 **b** 40% **c** $\frac{3}{5}$ **d** $\frac{33}{5}$ **e** $5\frac{7}{8}$ **f** 37·5% **g** $\frac{13}{20}$
11 a 10 × 5 **b** 10 ÷ 0·01 **c** 10 × 0·1
12 a £540 **b** 374 **c** £56·25
13 A possible answer is:

```
          25·9
        14·3  11·6
      7·7  6·6  5·0
    4·5  3·2  3·4  1·6
```

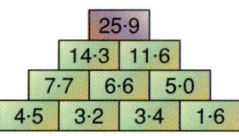

14 a 15 **b** 10·3 **c** 20
15 He did not use brackets around the ③ × ④.
16 £4·65
17 a 66 **b** 140 mℓ **c** 27 **d** 14 **e** 54 **f** 48 **g** $8\frac{3}{4}$ or 8·75
18 a 6 and 7 **b** 5 and 15
19 26, 28 and 30
20 a B **b** A **c** C
21 a Possible estimates are: area = 1200 cm²; perimeter = 140 cm
b Area = 1167·48 cm²; perimeter = 139·2 cm
22 Possible answers are: **a** 4520 ÷ 8 **b** 69·4 ÷ 7
23 a 36·7 **b** 153·2
24 a 4·33 **b** 69·40 **c** ⁻1·16 **d** 12·65 **e** ⁻95·44 **f** $8\frac{9}{35}$ **g** $2\frac{2}{39}$ **h** 29·93 **i** 2·72
25 Boxes of 18 pens by £9·90.

Chapter 4 page 116

1 a $\frac{3}{4}$ **b** $\frac{2}{3}$ **c** $\frac{3}{2}$ or $1\frac{1}{2}$ **d** $\frac{1}{3}$ **e** $\frac{1}{4}$ **f** $\frac{7}{12}$
2 a $\frac{4}{9}$ **b** $\frac{2}{3}$

440

Test yourself answers

3 a 80%, 70%, 75%
   b $\frac{1}{3}$ of the diagram is shaded
      $\frac{1}{3}$ = 0·33333333 ...
      $\frac{1}{3} \times 100\% = 33\frac{1}{3}\%$

4 $\frac{2}{5}$ or 40% or 0·4

5 a $\frac{1}{2}$ b $\frac{11}{24}$

6 Shape B because it has $\frac{3}{4}$ shaded. Shape A has $\frac{2}{3}$ shaded.

7 a $\frac{7}{25}, \frac{3}{10}, \frac{17}{50}, \frac{2}{5}, \frac{1}{2}$ b $\frac{12}{20}$, 0·9, 130%, $\frac{35}{25}$

8 The lunchtime club

9 a Sport b Drama c Only $\frac{3}{20}$ of boys liked music, whereas $\frac{3}{10}$ of the girls liked music. d Sport

10 a 46·6% b In 2004 the proportion was 43·7%. So the rainfall in June as a percentage of the rainfall in January was greater in 2002.

11 a 1 b $\frac{13}{12}$ or $1\frac{1}{12}$ c $1\frac{13}{40}$ d $\frac{1}{24}$ e $\frac{1}{8}$ f $3\frac{3}{4}$ g $4\frac{7}{15}$ h $2\frac{9}{40}$

12 a $\frac{13}{63}$ b $1\frac{11}{40}$

13 $\frac{1}{6}$

14 104

15 20 g

16 a 36 ℓ b 56 km c £270 d £360 e 6 m f 19·5 ℓ g 127·5 km h 6 m

17 a £10·20 b £16·20 c £114·84

18 a $\frac{1}{10}$ b 30 c $7\frac{1}{2}$ d $\frac{1}{10}$ e $\frac{3}{20}$ f $4\frac{8}{15}$ g $2\frac{1}{4}$

19 $11\frac{3}{8}$ m^2

20 a $\frac{2}{3}$ b 20 c $\frac{3}{50}$ d $1\frac{1}{2}$ e $1\frac{1}{4}$ f $3\frac{9}{10}$ g $8\frac{1}{3}$ h $1\frac{1}{4}$

21 22

22 20

23 £1·45

24 78·5% (1 d.p.)

Chapter 5 page 142

1 3·12 g

2 a 3 : 2 b 13·8 cm

3 a 2·7 m^2 b 26·7% (1 d.p.)

4 a 60 b 60 c 177·6 d 111·6

5 No. Because ×0·8 × 1·2 is the same as ×1·2 × 0·8.

6 67·7% (1 d.p.)

7 a 8 : 9 b $\frac{8}{17}$

8 12·5%

9 300 kg

10 300 g flour, 4 tsp baking powder, 1 cup milk, 1 egg, 160 g sugar, $1\frac{1}{2}$ chopped apples, 60 g butter

11 a 35·7% (1 d.p.) b 18·4% (1 d.p.) c Packets of 6 cookies

12 a 3·36 g b Fruit Bars

13 Cash by £18.

14 a 2 : 3 b 1 : 3 c 1 : 5 : 9 d 3 : 8 e 5 : 12 f 1 : 3 g 3 : 4 h 9 : 2 i 5 : 11

15 300 mℓ

16 £968

17 £144

18 Yes

19 Area of red paint = 6 × 2 + 8 × 2
                        = 28 cm^2
    Area of blue paint = 6 × 12 − 28
                         = 44 cm^2
    Area of red : area blue = 28 : 44
                            = 7 : 11

20 a 5 : 6 b 19 : 21
   c No. Olivia will always be older than Alex so her age cannot be the smaller one in the ratio.

21 £190

22 500 mℓ

23 Katie. The ratio for Rebecca is 0·71 : 1 and for Katie is 0·83 : 1.
    0·83 > 0·71 so Katie scores more goals for each goal attempted. Katie is the better goal shooter.

Test yourself answers

Chapter 6 page 178

1 $a + 7 = 15$ and $6(x + 5) = 20$ are equations; $A = \pi r^2$ and $s = \frac{D}{T}$ are formulae; $y = 2x + 3$ and $2y - x = 7$ are functions.

2
$p = 3$	Tim gets £3 pocket money
$p + q = 11$	Tim and Lisa get £11 pocket money altogether
$q = 2r$	Lisa gets twice as much pocket money as Kit
$\frac{p+q+r}{3} = 5$	The average amount of pocket money Tim, Lisa and Kit get is £5

3 a $n = 3$ b $n = 2$ c $n = 12$ d $n = 20$ e $n = 1$ f $n = 5$ g $n = 16$ h $n = {}^-13$ i $n = 4$ The letter I.

4 a i $4(x - 3) = 4(2 - 3) = 4({}^-1) = {}^-4$ ii $4(x - 3) = 4(7 - 3) = 4 \times 4 = 16$
       $4x - 12 = 4 \times 2 - 12 = {}^-4$ $4x - 12 = 4 \times 7 - 12 = 28 - 12 = 16$
    iii $4(x - 3) = 4({}^-1 - 3) = 4 \times {}^-4 = {}^-16$
         $4x - 12 = 4 \times {}^-1 - 12 = {}^-4 - 12 = {}^-16$
   b An identity

5 a D b B
6 $2(2a + 4 + 6) = 48$, $a = 7$
7 $x + 2 + 3x + 1 + 2x - 1 = 32$
   or $2x + 7 + 3x + 1 + x - 6 = 32$;
   $x = 5$.
8 $3x + 8 = 6x - 4$, $x = 4$
9 c and e
10 $a = 9$, $b = 4\frac{1}{2}$ or $4\cdot5$
11 a $t = 3$ b $y = \frac{8}{3} = 2\frac{2}{3}$ c $y = 1$ d $m = {}^-1\frac{1}{2}$ e $x = 2\frac{1}{2}$ f $k = {}^-1$
12 a $x = +5$ or $x = {}^-5$ b $k = +12$ or $k = {}^-12$ c $n = +6$ or $n = {}^-6$
13 a $p = 4\cdot2$ b $m = +2\cdot9$ or $m = {}^-2\cdot9$
14 a $y = 7\cdot3$ b $w = 4\cdot47$
15 a

| Number of chocolates (n) | 1 | 2 | 3 | 4 | 5 | 6 |
| Money earned (p) | 20 | 40 | 60 | 80 | 100 | 120 |

   b Yes, because the ratio of number of chocolates : money earned is constant $\frac{1}{20} = \frac{2}{40} = \frac{3}{60} = \frac{4}{80} = \frac{5}{100} = \frac{6}{120}$
   c Yes, because money earned and number of chocolates are directly proportional.
   d

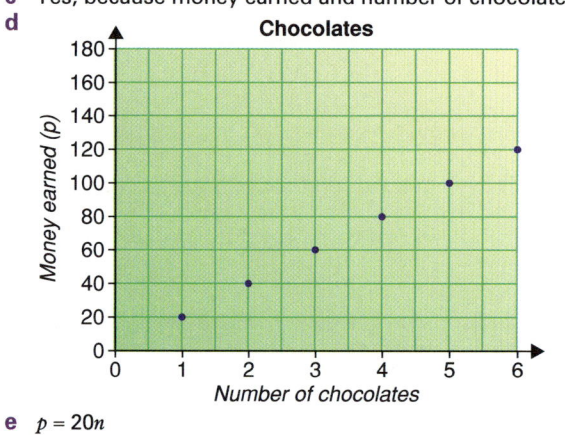

   e $p = 20n$
   f 10

Chapter 7 page 206

1 a $8m + 8$ b $2n + 8$ c $8x + 5$ d $3k + 14$ e $3a + 3$ f $5n$ g $2y^2 + 5$ h $8x^2 + 3x$
2 a $6 + 5y$, $5y + 6$
   b Yes, because if $5y + 6 = 56$, y would equal 10, which is possible, or yes because if we take the single mints away from 56, there are 50 mints left and 50 is divisible by 5.

Test yourself answers

3 a

3x − 3	7x − 5	4x − 2
5x − 2		7x − 2
2x + 1	5x + 1	3x

b

x − 4	5x − 1	4x + 3
6x − 7		7x + 5
5x − 3	8x − 1	3x + 2

4 a $8y − 1$ **b** $14x + 4$

5 a $20x$ **b** $6n$ **c** $10m^2$ **d** ^-12ab **e** n **f** $2p$ **g** $5k$ **h** $3b^6$ **i** n^5 **j** $\frac{4x^3}{3}$

6 a i 58 **ii** 66 **iii** 850   **b i** $^-1.4$ **ii** 6·6 **iii** 50·08

7 a £455 **b** 13 days

8 a pqr and $6r^2$, $2p + q$ and $6 + q$, $3q$ and $6r$, q^2 and $4r^2$, $4p − q$ and $2(6 − r)$

9 a 40 m **b** 18·75 m

10 a $9(y + 3)$ **b** $5(3x + 1)$ **c** $x(8x + 3)$ **d** $k^2(k + 1)$ **e** $8(d − 3)$ **f** $9(3\ell − 2)$ **g** $m^2(2m + 1)$ **h** $y(y^2 + 2y − 4)$

11 $8(2p + 3)$

12 a Total number of people $= 2 \times 1 + 3 \times 5 + 4 \times x + 5 \times 7 + 6 \times 8 + 7 \times 4 + 8 \times 2$
$= 2 + 15 + 4x + 35 + 48 + 28 + 16$
$= 4x + 144$

  b $27 + x$ **c** 9

13 a $r = \frac{C}{2\pi}$ **b** $T = \frac{PV}{nR}$ **c** $h = \frac{2A}{a+b}$

14 a $2c$ **b** A possible answer is: $5c + 2$ and $5c − 2$ **c** $3c − 5$

15 a $z = \frac{y}{3} − x$ **b** $p = n − 3m$ **c** $x = \sqrt{\frac{5y}{3}}$

16 Surface area $= 2 \times \frac{1}{2}ab + bd + cd + ad = ab + bd + cd + ad$

17 a $\frac{1}{m} + \frac{3}{n} = \frac{n}{mn} + \frac{3m}{mn} = \frac{3m + n}{mn}$ **b** $\frac{x}{4} − \frac{y}{3} = \frac{3x}{12} − \frac{4y}{12} = \frac{3x − 4y}{12}$

18 a $\frac{7}{y}$ **b** $\frac{x}{12}$ **c** $\frac{ad + bc}{bd}$ **d** $\frac{x}{15}$

19 a n^2 is even; $n + 3$, $2n − 1$, $(n + 1)^2$ and $(n − 1)(n + 1)$ are odd.

  b Not possible to tell. If you add 4 to an even number you get an even number. When you divide an even number by 2 you can get an even **or** odd number.

Chapter 8 page 229

1 a 10, 9·5, 9, 8·5, 8 **b** 2, 2, 4, 6, 10
2 a 1·4, 1·7, 2 **b** 32, 64, 128 **c** 18, 24, 31 **d** 8, 13, 21
3 a add 0·3 **b** multiply by 2 **c** add 1, 2, 3, 4, ... **d** add the two previous terms
4 a 2, 6, 10, 14, 18, 22 **b** 1·5, 3·5, 5·5, 7·5, 9·5, 11·5 **c** 0·2, 0·4, 0·6, 0·8, 1, 1·2 **d** 32, 28, 24, 20, 16, 12
5 a $T(n) = 4n − 2$ has terms with a common difference of 4. All terms are 2 more or 2 less than a multiple of 4. It starts at 2 and ascends.
  b $T(n) = 36 − 4n$ has terms with a common difference of 4. All terms are a multiple of 4. It starts at 32 and descends.
6 a 3, 6, 11, 18, 27, 38 **b** $^-1$, 5, 15, 29, 47, 69
7 a 61 **b** 15 **c** $m = 7h + 1$
8 a $T(n) = 2n + 3$ **b** $T(n) = 8n + 24$ **c** $T(n) = 7 − 4n$
9 One possible answer is: The sequence starts at 10. The rule is subtract 0·2

10 a

Input	Output
5	12
7	18
10	27

b

Input	Output
12	9
20	13
24	15

12 a $x \rightarrow$ multiply by 2 $\rightarrow$ add 5 $\rightarrow 2x + 5$

  b $x \rightarrow$ divide by 2 $\rightarrow$ subtract 4 $\rightarrow \frac{x}{2} − 4$

  c $x \rightarrow$ subtract 2 $\rightarrow$ multiply by 3 $\rightarrow 3(x − 2)$

443

Test yourself answers

13 a Add 1   **b** Multiply by 4

14 a The number is 9. $3x + 5 = 32$ or $3(x + 5) = 42$ **b** $3(x + 5) - (3x + 5) = 3x + 15 - 3x - 5$
$3x = 27$ $x + 5 = 14$ $= 10$
$x = 9$ $x = 9$ The difference will always be 10.

15 a $x \to \frac{x-3}{2}$ **b** $x \to \frac{x}{2} + 1$ **c** $x \to 2(x + 3)$

16 $d = \frac{n \times (n-3)}{2} = \frac{n(n-3)}{2} = \frac{n^2 - 3n}{2}$

Chapter 9 page 252

1 a C   **b** D   **c** B   **d** A   **e** D and E

2 a (2, 4), (0, −2), (−3, −11)   **b**

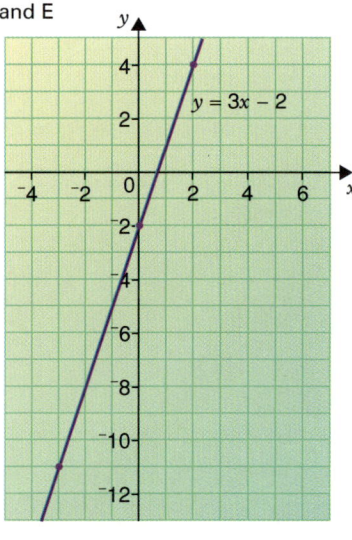

3 a i B   **ii** A   **iii** D   **iv** C
  b Yes. Because (4, 8) satisfies the equation $y = 3x - 4$. $8 = 3 \times 4 - 4$.
  c 4

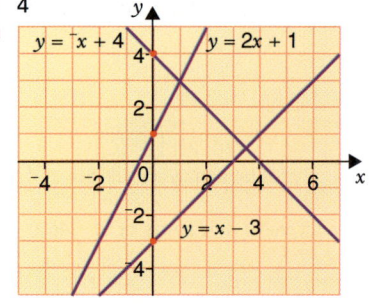

4 a

  b Yes because (2, 5) satisfies the equation $y = 2x + 1$. $2x + 1 = 2 \times 2 + 1$
$= 4 + 1$
$= 5$
$= y$
  c 0
  d $y = ^-x + 4$

5 $\ell_1\ ^-1$, $\ell_2\ ^-3$, $\ell_3\ \frac{3}{2}$, $\ell_4\ \frac{1}{3}$

6 a C   **b** D   **c** E   **d** A   **e** B

7 a $y = ^-2x + 3$ **b** $y = \frac{^-x}{2} + 3$ **c** $y = 3x - 1$

8 a 2 times   **b** He went back home.   **c** Alan   **d** Yes. The gradient stays the same.

9 a About 190 m   **b** About 70 seconds   **c** About 48 seconds   **d** C

10 a The skier skied downhill, stopped for a while then skied on down to the lodge.
  b Some water was put in a kettle. After a while some water was taken out but then more water was put into the kettle straight away. Then nothing happened for a while.
  c The newborn baby lost weight for the first few days then slowly started to put weight on. The weight gain slowed down a bit after a while.

11 a Yes. $2x = 2 \times 35 = 70$. So for (35, 70) y does $= 2x$.
  b (2, 5)
  c $y = ^-2x + 4$ and $y = ^-2x - 3$ have the same gradient. This means the graphs are parallel and will never meet.

12 a $y = 5x$ **b** $y = ^-2$ **c** $y = x^2 + 1$ **d** $y = x - 2$ **e** $y = 5x$ **f** (−6, −8)

Test yourself answers

Chapter 10 page 283

1 **a** Convention **b** Derived property **c** Convention **d** Definition **e** Derived property **f** Definition

2 **a** $x = 135°$ — vertically opposite angles equal
$y = 67°$ — exterior angle equals sum of the two opposite interior angles

b $a = 70°$ — alternate angles on parallel lines
$b = 110°$ — angles on a straight line add to 180°
$d = 70°$ — alternate angles on parallel lines
$c = 110°$ — angles on a straight line add to 180°

c $e = 180° - 95° - 25°$ — angles of a triangle add to 180°
$= 60°$
$f = 95°$ — corresponding angles on parallel lines
$d = 25°$ — alternate angles on parallel lines

d $g = 88° - 47°$ — vertically opposite angles equal
$= 41°$
$i = 180° - 41° - 72°$ — angles of a triangle add to 180°
$= 180° - 113°$
$= 67°$
$h = 67°$ — corresponding angles on parallel lines

e $a = 180° - 15° - 15°$ — angles in a triangle add to 180° and isosceles triangle
$= 150°$
$b = 150°$ — identical isosceles triangles and 1 line of symmetry
$l = 360° - 150° - 150°$ — angles at a point add to 360°
$= 60°$

3 **a** 88° **b** 123° **c** 95° **d** 47°

4 **a** A quadrilateral can be divided into two triangles as shown.
$a + b + c + f + d + e = 180° + 180°$ — angle sum of triangle is 180°
$= 360°$
So interior angles of a quadrilateral add to 360°.
b 540°
c A heptagon can be divided into 5 triangles.
Angle sum $= 5 \times 180°$
$= 900°$

5 **a** 45° **b** 135° **c** No. The sum of the exterior angles of a polygon is 360°. 54° will not divide exactly into 360°.

6 The pattern is made up of squares, equilateral triangles and rhombuses.
The angles in the square are 90°.
The angles in the equilateral triangle are 60°.
In the diagram the angles in the ring add to 360° (angles at a point).
$90° + 60° + 60° + x = 360°$
$x = 360° - 90° - 60° - 60°$
$= 150°$
$2y + 2x = 360°$ — angle sum in rhombus is 360°
$2y + 300° = 360°$
$2y = 360° - 300°$
$= 60°$
$y = 30°$
The 4 angles in the rhombuses are 30°, 30°, 150°, 150°.

7 **a** $3x + 86° + x + 46° = 180°$ — angles on a straight line add to 180°
$4x = 180° - 132°$
$= 48°$
$x = 12°$
b $x - 30° + x - 15° + x + 15° = 180°$ — angles in a triangle add to 180°
$3x - 30° = 180°$
$3x = 210°$
$x = \mathbf{70°}$

Chapter 11 page 307

1 **a** False **b** True **c** True **d** False

2 **a** Red length = 7 cm, a parallelogram has rotation symmetry of order 2
$b = 116°$, a parallelogram has rotation symmetry of order 2

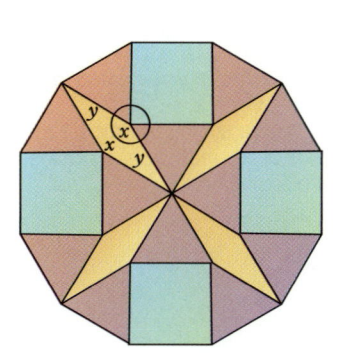

445

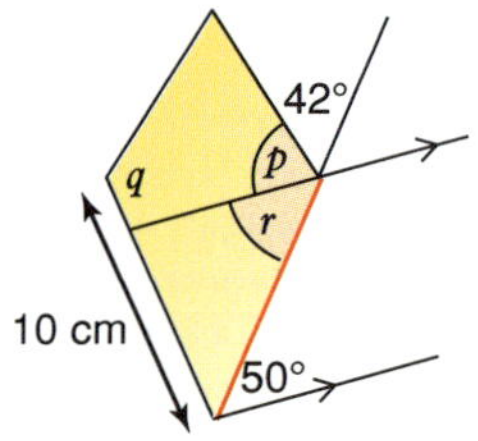

Test yourself answers

b Red length = 10 cm, a kite has a line of symmetry
$r = 50°$ alternate angles parallel lines
$p = 180° - 42° - 50°$ angles on a straight line add to 180°
   $= 88°$
$q = p + r$ a kite has a line of symmetry
   $= 88° + 50°$
   $= 138°$

c $\angle DCB = 25°$ base angles isosceles triangle
$\angle ACD = x$ an arrowhead has a line of symmetry
$82° + x + 25° + x + 25° = 180°$ angle sum of triangle is 180°
           $2x = 48°$
           $x = 24°$

kite

3 a Rectangle, rhombus   **b** Rectangle, rhombus
4 a No   **b** No   **c** No   **d** Yes
5 a △PQS is isosceles
    i $\angle PSQ = 63°$ base angle of isosceles triangle
    ii $\angle RQP = \angle SQR + \angle PQS = 126°$ sides of a rhombus are parallel and alternate angles parallel lines
   b $\angle CBE = 75°$ sides of a parallelogram are parallel and corresponding angles parallel lines are equal
     $\angle CEB = 75°$ angles of a triangle add to 180°
     Since $\angle CBE = \angle CEB = 75°$
     △CBE is isosceles
6 This tessellation is made by rotating the shape.

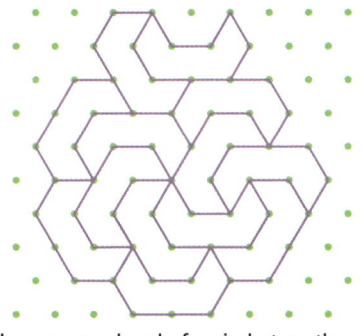

7 A regular pentagon can be constructed in this way because a chord of a circle together with two radii form an isosceles triangle. If further chords of the same length are drawn, the triangles are congruent and angles between successive chords are equal. If the succession of equal chords divides the circle without remainder, a regular pentagon is drawn inside the circle. 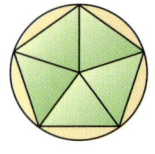
8 Check your answer using the diagram on page 000.
9 a C   **b** A   **c** B   **d** A   **e** B
11 a About 60°   **b** About 8·1 m
12 a Yes   **b** No. The sum of the 2 shorter sides in the triangle must be longer than the longest side.
13 Possible answers are: **a**   **b**

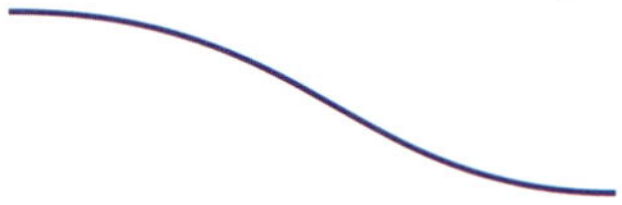

14 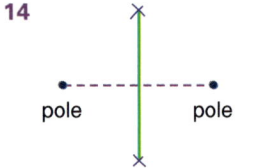
pole   pole   The locus is the perpendicular bisector of the line joining the poles.

15 A ii   B iii   C iv   D i
16 a i View D   **ii** View C   **iii** View A   **iv** View B   **b**   **c** 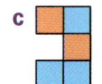   or 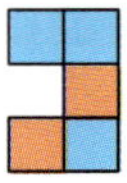
17

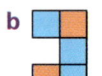

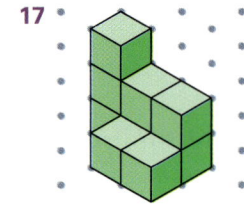

446

18 a A triangle b A triangle
19 A possible shape is:

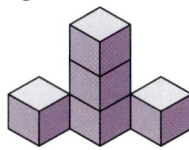

Chapter 12 page 329

1 a Lengths and angles b Lengths and angles c Lengths and angles d Yes e Yes
2 a 30° b 6 cm c C
3 a b c   d Rectangle

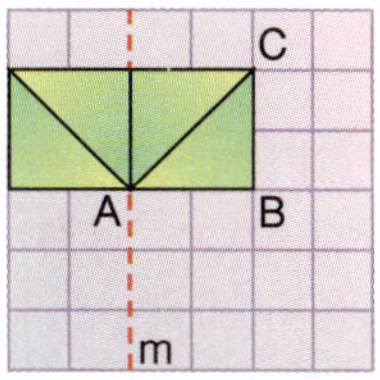

4 b (−2, 2), (0, 4), (1, 4), (1, 2) c (−2, 2), (−2, −1), (0, −1), (0, 0) d Yes
5 a 4 cm b 98° c 90°
6 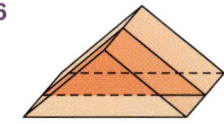 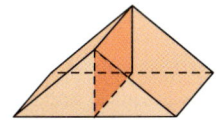
7 3
8 a   b i 40° ii 3 cm iii 3 cm

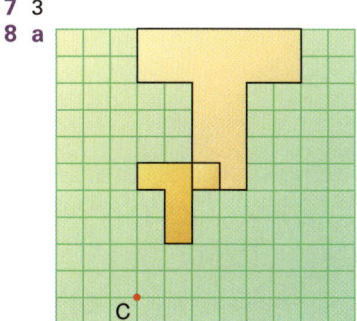

9 a i 12 ii 54° b 36 cm
10 About 10·8 m
11 a 40 m b 155 m
12 a 10 cm b 70 cm c 66 cm by 10 cm d 58 cm e 66 cm

Chapter 13 page 352

1 a 40 000 m² b 0·08 ha c 5000 ℓ d 52 mℓ e 5·8 ℓ f 4·9 m³ g 50 000 cm²
   h 4000 mm³ i 850 cm³ j 800 mm² k 650 000 cm³ l 528 cm²
2 a 9000 cm³ b 9 000 000 mm³ c 9000 mℓ d 9 ℓ
3 a 2700 cm² b 270 000 mm²
4 2 kg
5 150 m
6 a 10 miles, 8·8 lb, 0·75 pints
   b 8 km, 1200 mℓ, 120 g
7 Possible answers are:
   a 8 m ⩽ width of house ⩽ 20 m
   b 1 kg ⩽ mass of 10 apples ⩽ 3 kg
   c 20 ℓ ⩽ capacity of washing machine ⩽ 50 ℓ
8 a i 6 cm ii 60 m b i 065° ii 245°
9 B, A, C   Area of square = 25 cm²
               Area of triangle = $\frac{1}{2} \times 6 \times 8$ = 24 cm²
               Area of rectangle = 8 × 4 = 32 cm²
10 a Area = 113·1 cm² (1 d.p.), circumference = 37·7 cm (1 d.p.)
   b Area = 201·1 cm² (1 d.p.), circumference = 50·3 cm (1 d.p.)
   c Area = 211·2 cm² (1 d.p.), circumference = 51·5 cm (1 d.p.)

Test yourself answers

11 a 314 cm²   **b** 62·8 cm or 63 cm
12 a 159·27 m²   **b** 65·7 m
13 a 234 cm³   **b** 0·336 cm³   **c** 216 cm³
14 301·2 cm²
15 a 1·5 ℓ   **b** 14·5 cm   **c** 3, because if the jugs are a little more than 15 cm wide, 4 will not fit in.
16 a 4 hours   **b** 83 m.p.h   **c** 73·5 miles

Chapter 14 page 378

1 Possible answers are:
  a People sprint faster when the temperature is lower than 15 °C.
    Sprinters don't get such fast times at very high temperatures.
  b Warm conditions help the seeds germinate and grow faster.
    Moist conditions help the seeds germinate and grow faster.

2 A i Data on the power rating of hairdryers needs to be collected. Time taken to dry the same hair needs to be measured to the nearest 15 seconds.
   ii Data on the power rating would be collected from the instructions that go with the hairdryer. This is a secondary source. Data on time taken to dry hair would be obtained by experiment. This is a primary source.
   iii Information about 10 different hairdryers could be collected. This should give a good selection of hairdryers.
   iv A possible collection sheet would be:

   Power rating _____
   Time taken to dry hair _____

  B i Data on number of hours teenagers usually watch TV each week in winter and also in summer.
    The accuracy should be within 2 hours a week.
   ii The data source is primary. You would use a questionnaire.
   iii To get a representative sample you would ask 30 to 50 teenagers.
   iv A possible questionnaire would be:

Number of hours you watch TV each week in winter.	0 up to 4 ☐ 4 up to 8 ☐ 8 up to 12 ☐ 12 up to 16 ☐ 16 up to 20 ☐ 20 up to 24 ☐ > 24 ☐
Number of hours you watch TV each week in summer.	0 up to 4 ☐ 4 up to 8 ☐ 8 up to 12 ☐ 12 up to 16 ☐ 16 up to 20 ☐ 20 up to 24 ☐ > 24 ☐

3 A possible answer is:

Price (nearest £)	Pascoes rings sold	Morten's rings sold
< 100		
100–199		
200–299		
300–399		
400–499		
500–599		
≥ 600		

  The class intervals chosen would give a good spread of values so that it would be easy to see the differences between the two jewellers.

4 a The question does not give a great enough range of possible responses. It is possible that someone might like all except one person in their family. The answer is then 'No' but this does not give good data about attitudes to family.
  b A possible answer is: I consider I generally have a good relationship with
    my mother ☐   my father ☐   sibling 1 ☐   sibling 2 ☐   sibling 3 ☐   sibling 4 ☐   sibling 5 ☐
    Tick to agree, cross to disagree, dash for not applicable.
  c Mia's family is unlikely to be representative of the whole population.
    Giving the questionnaire to one family is not a big enough sample to be representative.

5 Possible answers are: At what age do you think teenagers should be allowed to smoke if they choose to?
    13 ☐   14 ☐   15 ☐   16 ☐   17 ☐   18 ☐   19 ☐   not at all ☐
  Tick agree or disagree
    Teenagers should be fined for smoking.   Agree ☐   Disagree ☐
    Teenagers should smoke if they want to.   Agree ☐   Disagree ☐
    Teenagers should be educated about the dangers of smoking.   Agree ☐   Disagree ☐
    Teenagers who smoke should be made to visit people dying of lung cancer. Agree ☐   Disagree ☐

7 a 17 b 30 c 22 d There are the same number of boys and girls in the drama club. There are more boys than girls in the computer club and there are more girls than boys in the dance club.

8

Age	Men	Women
60–		
70–		
80–		
90+		

9 a

	Rained	Cloudless	Total
June	9	6	15
July	11	7	18
Total	20	13	33

b 13 c 9

Chapter 15 page 408

1 a Mean = 4, median = 3, mode = 2
  b No, because there are two extreme values, 6 and 10, which make it higher.
  c Mean. No, because only two of the data values are greater than the mean.
2 a 61–70 b 61–70 c A bar chart for grouped data would be best to display the data as it would show the spread of data very clearly.
3 No
4 a *(graph: Goals out of 50)*
  b Yes, we can use the graph to estimate that Jamie would be able to shoot about 29 out of 50 goals after $3\frac{1}{2}$ weeks.
5 a *(bar chart: Long jump results)*
  b 29 c 29
  d Yes, because it is possible that all the other 8 people in the class interval $240 \leqslant d < 250$ jumped less than the 243 cm that Ryan jumped.
  e There are 72 results. Over half would be more than 36.
    The 36th jump is in the class interval $220 \leqslant d < 230$ which is less than the 233 cm quoted.

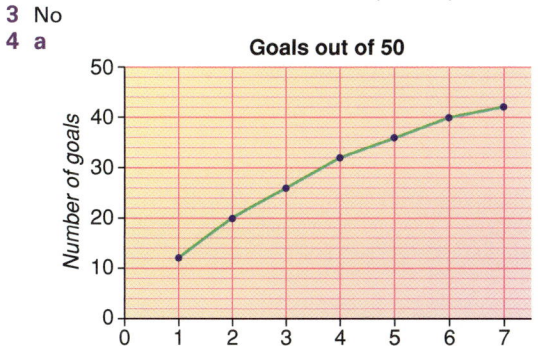

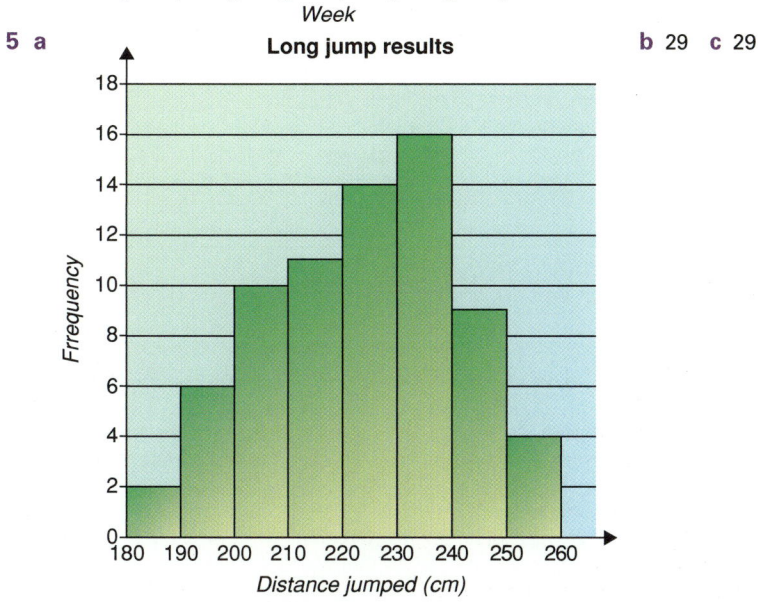

Test yourself answers

6 a The line graph is not a suitable graph to show the data because line graphs are used for showing changes over time. It doesn't matter whether you choose the bar chart or pie chart as long as you explain why you chose it.

b For adults, the main reason was that they enjoyed walking. Next was seeing it on TV. For the under 16s, friends, family and seeing it on TV were the main reasons they started playing golf.

7 a

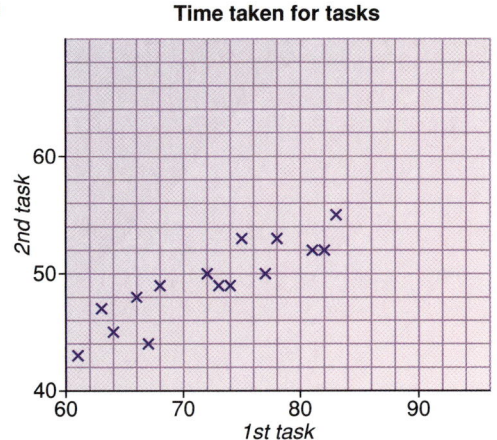

Time taken for tasks (scatter graph: 1st task vs 2nd task)

b 68–74 seconds

c 48–54 seconds

d Yes it is a positive correlation. The longer the pupils took to complete the 1st task, the longer they took to complete the second task.

8 A possible answer is:

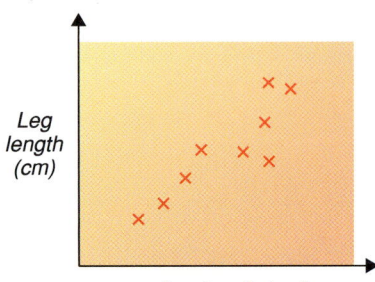

Leg length (cm) vs Arm length (cm) — scatter graph showing positive correlation

9 19, 35, 60

10 a Yes. The number of visitors could have been 1, 3, 3 and 5.

b i 3 **ii** 2

11 There is no scale on the vertical axis. It is impossible to tell by how much tooth decay has decreased.

12 a Jamie – mean is 16·9 minutes, median is 15·5 minutes, range is 15 minutes

Simon – mean is 19·6 minutes, median is 19·5 minutes, range is 21 minutes

b

Jamie

Time (minutes)	Tally	Frequency
8–11	I	1
12–15	IIII	4
16–19	II	2
20–23	I	1
24–27	II	2
28–31		0

Simon

Time (minutes)	Tally	Frequency
8–11	II	2
12–15	I	1
16–19	II	2
20–23	II	2
24–27	I	1
28–31	II	2

c A possible answer is:

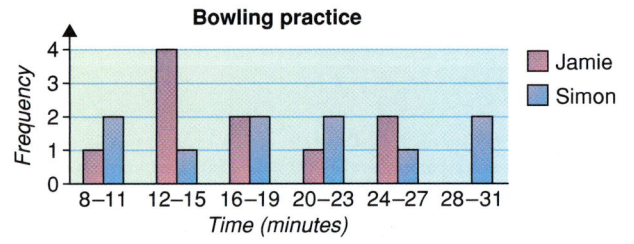

Bowling practice — bar chart comparing Jamie and Simon frequencies across time intervals

d Although the mean and median of the times Jamie practises are less than Simon's, his range of times is smaller, which means the length of his practices is less variable. Simon sometimes practises for a long time and sometimes for a short time.

13

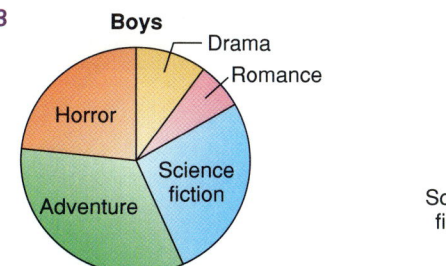

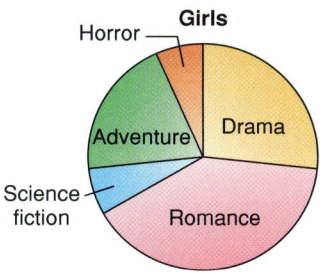

Boys pie chart: Drama, Romance, Science fiction, Adventure, Horror

Girls pie chart: Horror, Drama, Romance, Science fiction, Adventure

14 a **Gwen** mean = 12, median = 12, range = 4
   Lela mean = 12, median = 7, range = 28
   b The coach could choose Gwen because she has the same mean as Lela, a high median and she has more consistent scores shown by her smaller range.
   The coach could choose Lela because there is a possibility she will score a lot of goals, because of her big range.

Chapter 16 page 435

1 **a** D, $\frac{3}{5}$ of spinner D is blue **b** B and D. The same proportion of each spinner is green. **c** A

2 **a i** $\frac{2}{12}$ or $\frac{1}{6}$ **ii** Football **b** $\frac{3}{9}$ or $\frac{1}{3}$

3 **a** $\frac{1}{2}$ **b** 4 **c** $\frac{3}{7}$

4 0·92

5 Box A, because this has the greatest proportion of white chocolates. $\frac{4}{12} > \frac{10}{32}$ and $\frac{4}{12} > \frac{16}{58}$

6 c

7 **a** 0·25 **b** 0·8

8 **a** $\frac{5}{6}$ **b** $\frac{1}{6}$ **c** 5 **d** 10 **e** 8 **f** 0·45

9 **a** ba, bo, bb, ab, ao, aa, ob, oa, oo **b i** $\frac{3}{9}$ or $\frac{1}{3}$ **ii** $\frac{5}{9}$ **iii** $\frac{4}{9}$

10 **a**

+	2	4	6	8
1	3	5	7	9
3	5	7	9	11
5	7	9	11	13
7	9	11	13	15

   b 9, because there are more 9s than any other total.
   c i $\frac{1}{16}$ **ii** $\frac{10}{16}$ or $\frac{5}{8}$ **iii** 0 **iv** $\frac{5}{16}$

11 $\frac{1}{9}$

12 About 80

13 **a** $\frac{54}{720}$ or $\frac{3}{40}$ **b** $\frac{54}{720}$ or $\frac{3}{40}$

14 **a** She could calculate the relative frequency of a page having advertisements then use this as an estimate of the probability.
   b No
   c Yes

15 **a** 5 **b** 50 **c** It is probably wrong because $\frac{42}{50}$ = 0·84 which is a lot higher than 0·45. To be sure, a lot more trials would need to be done.

Index

accidental deaths 388
accuracy, degree of 72–3, 260, 370, 378
adding 2, 38, 55
    0·01, 0·001 etc 1
    algebraic fractions 193, 205
    decimals 6, 76
    fractions 8, 44, 55, 102, 115
    mentally 4–5, 63, 87
    mixed numbers 105, 115
algebra 172–3, 177, 184
    common factors 45, 55
    divisibility 46, 47, 55
    fractions 193, 205
    operations 146
angles 255
    adjacent 255
    alternate 255, 274
    bisector 257, 297, 300
    complementary 255
    corresponding 255, 274
    exterior 255, 274
    finding 273, 274
    naming 255
    made with parallel lines 255, 274
    at a point 255, 273
    of a polygon 255, 278, 279, 282
    reflex 256
    on a straight line 255, 273, 282
    supplementary 255
    of a triangle 255, 273, 274, 282
    vertically opposite 255, 273, 279
annulus 204
answers 439–51
answers, checking 7, 78, 88
arc of a circle 291, 306
area 259, 260–1, 332, 338, 350, 351
    of a circle 75, 331, 342, 343, 344, 351
    of an ellipse 199
    of a parallelogram 261, 338
    of a rectangle 69, 338, 339, 344
    of a trapezium 75, 198, 261
    of a triangle 260, 261, 338, 339
arrowheads (deltas) 256

balancing act 157
bar charts 357, 358, 406
    compound 357, 364, 385
bar-line graphs 357, 366, 406, 410
base numbers 50, 56
bearings 260, 335, 351
bedroom change 311
BIDMAS 7, 61, 86
bisector of an angle 257, 297, 300
blood cells 337
boxes 267
brackets 7, 47, 61, 147, 181, 191

calculators, graphical 42, 215
calculators, using 85, 89, 169–70
capacity 259, 260, 332, 350
car hire 150

centicubes 319
centre of enlargement 320
certainty 359, 414
changing the subject of a formula 200, 206, 234, 251
characters v
checking answers 7, 78, 88
chord of a circle 292, 306
cigarettes 386, 388, 400
circles 258, 291, 292, 341–2
    area 75, 331, 342, 343, 344, 351
    parts of 306
circumference 200, 331, 341, 342, 344, 351
class intervals 93, 355–6, 358, 371, 381
coins, tossing 427, 428, 430
collecting like terms 147, 181, 205
collection sheets 355, 371, 372
common denominator 193, 205
common factors 45, 55, 191
compasses 257
compensating 5
complements in numbers 4
cones 317, 347
congruence 259, 286, 348
congruent pieces of 3-D shapes 328
congruent shapes 259, 312, 317, 327
conjecture 368, 378
consecutive terms 211, 213, 214, 221, 228
constant multiplier 131, 142
constant of proportionality 239, 251
constructions 257, 294–5
conventions 273, 282
conversions, metric/imperial 155, 269, 336
coordinate pairs 149, 258
correlation 389, 390–1, 407
counting on and back 4, 148
cross-section 305, 307, 347, 348, 352
cube numbers 4, 47, 85
cube roots 4, 52, 54, 56, 85
cubes (shapes) 352
cuboids 261, 305, 317, 332, 333, 348
currency conversion 232, 335, 336
cylinders 159, 317, 341

data
    categorical (non numerical) 357, 385, 406
    collecting 369, 371, 378, 406
    collection sheet 378
    comparing 358, 402, 408
    continuous (measurement) 355, 356, 358, 361, 371, 385
    discrete 355, 357, 361, 385, 406
        grouped 358, 385, 406
    displaying 357, 384, 385, 406
    grouped 355, 358, 385, 406
    interpreting 357, 396, 407
    raw 384
    more than one set 385, 389, 407
    skewed 381
    sources 355, 369, 378
    over time 385, 406
    value 356

452

Index

decade 259, 332
decimals
    adding and subtracting 6, 76
    dividing 7, 60, 77, 78, 86, 88
    to fractions 9–10, 66, 87
    multiplying 6, 25, 60, 77
    putting in order 2
    to percentages 9, 10, 66, 87
    places, rounding to 31, 34
    recurring 9, 31, 93, 114
    terminating 9, 93, 114
definitions 273, 282
degree of accuracy 72–3, 260, 370, 378
deltas (arrowheads) 256
denominator 7–8, 44, 55, 93, 115
derived properties 273, 282
diagonals in polygons 197, 231, 256, 278, 318
diagrams, interpreting 396
diameter 292, 306, 342, 343, 351
dice 423, 428, 430, 431, 432
difference in a sequence 211, 213, 214, 221, 227, 228
diseases 388
distributions, shape 402, 408
dividing 2, 38
    by 10, 100, 1000 etc 1, 25, 34
    algebra 184
    decimals 7, 60, 77, 78, 86, 88
    fractions 112–13, 116
    numbers with indices 50, 184
    mentally 5, 63, 87
    by zero 81
divisibility 3, 46, 47, 53, 55
divisor 78, 81
dodecahedrons 258
dominoes 430
dot paper 189, 204, 302
doubling and halving 6

electrical circuits 77, 173, 198
elevation 302, 307
ellipse, area 199
enlargement 259, 320, 324, 328
    centre of 320
equally likely 359, 414, 418, 434
equations 146, 158
    linear 176
    non-linear 168–70, 177
    solving 146, 162, 168–70, 177, 197
    of a straight line 149, 172, 240, 251
    with unknowns on both sides 166
    writing 163, 276
equivalent calculations 7, 78, 88
Escher, Maurits 285
estimating 6, 7, 28, 72–4, 334, 391
    probability 426, 427, 435
evaluating 166
even chance 359, 414, 418, 434
even numbers 3
events 359, 414, 426, 427
    mutually exclusive 417, 418, 419, 423, 434
expanding the product 181
experiments 359, 369, 426, 427, 431, 435
exponents (indices, powers) 4, 7, 21, 47, 49–50, 184
expressions 146, 147, 186, 195, 205
    for the nth term 227

    simplifying 181, 184, 205
exterior angles of polygons 278, 279, 282
extreme values 381

factorising 191, 205
factors and factor trees 3, 5, 45
fair games 414, 417, 423, 430, 432
Fibonacci sequence 210
first term 211, 216
flow charts 152, 212
formulae 147, 156, 158, 159, 176, 202
    diagonals in polygons 197
    speed 176, 206, 207, 334
    changing the subject of 200, 206, 234, 251
    substituting into 197, 206
fractions 7–10, 85
    adding 8, 44, 55, 102
    algebraic 193, 205
    comparing 10, 97–8
    to decimals 9, 10, 66, 87
    dividing 112–13, 116
    equivalent 8, 102, 115, 193, 205
    improper 8, 105, 115
    multiplying 8, 110, 115
    to percentages 9, 10, 66, 87, 92, 93
    of a quantity 7, 8, 10, 107, 115
    simplest form (cancelling) 7, 8, 44, 55, 110
    subtracting 8, 44, 55, 102
    unit 103
frequency diagrams 93, 95, 116, 208, 358, 396
frequency tables 355–6, 371
function machines 148, 158, 176, 222, 228, 229
    inverse 225, 229, 234, 335
functions 148–9, 158, 176, 222, 233, 228
    inverse of 225
    linear 233, 239

games 431–2
gear ratio (bicycle) 140
geometrical reasoning 274, 282
goat, tethered 301
golden ratio 119
gradient/slope (m) of a line 149, 234, 239–40, 251
graphs 149–50
    bar-line 357, 366, 406, 410
    distance-time 243, 252
    drawing 233, 247
    of a function 233
    interpreting 247, 252, 396
    line (statistics) 357, 385, 386, 406
    misleading 401–2, 407
    plotting on 172–3
    of real-life situations 150, 232
    scatter 358, 389, 390, 407
    sketching 247, 252
    straight line 149, 172, 233, 251
greener than green 331

hectare 259, 332
hemispheres 258
heptagons 256, 279
hexagonal numbers 37
hexagons 256, 264, 282, 291
highest common factor (HCF) 3, 8, 42, 43, 44, 191
hypotenuse 288, 294

Index

identities 159, 176
identity functions 222, 228
images 312
imperial and metric equivalents 260
impossibility 359, 414
'impossible' drawings 285
index laws 49–50, 56, 184, 205
index notation 43
indices (powers, exponents) 4, 7, 21, 47, 49–50, 184
inequalities 160, 176
infinite sequences 147
input 149, 222, 228
integers 2, 8, 38, 55
interest rates 159
interpreting data 357, 396, 407
inverse of a function 225, 229
inverse operations 7, 38, 51, 146, 169, 200
    in algebra 177, 191
    in function machines 222, 225, 229
inverse rule 113, 116
inverses 112, 113
isometric drawings 302, 307

kites 256, 306

lawn mowing business 331
leap year 259, 332
length 259, 260, 332
like terms 147
    collecting 147, 181, 205
likeliness 359, 414, 418, 434
line graphs 357, 385, 386, 406, 410
line of best fit 391, 393
line symmetry 317
linear functions 233, 239
lines and line segments 255, 257, 292
lines of symmetry 256, 258, 318
loci 258, 297, 300, 301, 306
lowest common multiple (LCM) 3, 42–3, 44, 55

magic squares 12, 106, 181, 183
mapping diagrams 149, 222, 225
maps 325, 326, 327
mass 259, 260, 332
mean 198, 356, 358, 381, 406, 408
measures 259, 334–5
median 356, 381, 406
memory on calculators 85
mental calculation 4–6, 63, 67, 69, 87
metric conversions 25, 27, 259, 332
metric measures 23, 33
metric/imperial equivalents 260
mirror line 259
mission impossible 285
mixed numbers 8, 105, 115
modal class 356, 381, 406
mode 356, 381, 406
multiple of mysteries! 59
multiplying 2, 8, 38
    by 10, 100, 1000 etc 1, 25, 34
    algebra 184
    decimals 6, 25, 60, 77, 86
    fractions 8, 110, 115
    numbers with indices 49–50, 184
    mentally 5–6, 63, 87

mutually exclusive events 417, 418, 419, 423, 434

nautical miles 75
nearly numbers 5
negative numbers 2, 38, 51, 55, 85, 160
negative slope 239, 240
nets 258, 266, 349
nomograms 92
nth term 148, 211, 227, 228, 235
    rule for 210–11, 213, 216, 221, 227, 228
number chains 214
number lines 2, 112
number systems 20, 21
numerator 7–8, 44, 55

octagons 256, 291
octahedrons 258
order of operations 7, 61, 86–7, 205
order of rotation symmetry 258, 317
origin (graphs) 258
outcome 359, 414, 418, 427
    possible 359, 423, 432, 434
    unpredictable 434
output 149, 222, 228

paper sizes 323
parallel lines 255, 273, 274
parallelograms 256, 261, 318, 338
Parthenon 119
partitioning 4, 5
patterns, tile 155, 190, 216, 284
pentagonal numbers 37
pentagons 256, 278, 279
percentage
    change 120, 122, 125, 141
    to decimals 8, 10, 66, 87
    to fractions 8, 10, 66, 87
    of a quantity 10, 107, 115
perimeter 186, 260, 338, 351
perpendicular bisector 257, 297
perpendiculars 257
photos 272
pi 32, 75, 342, 351
pictograms 357, 406
pie charts 357, 360, 384, 385, 387, 396
place value 1, 5, 25
    charts 1, 21
plan view 302, 307, 326
planes of symmetry 317, 328
Planet X 20
plotting on a graph 172–3, 233, 251
plumber charges 147
polygons 256, 282
    angles of 278, 279, 282
    diagonals in 197, 231, 256, 278, 318
    regular 256, 281, 291
    tessellating 291
population 28, 30, 34, 36, 400, 404
    pyramids 400, 404
position-to-term rule 211, 213, 216, 221, 227, 228
possibility 414
posters 130
powers (indices, exponents) 4, 7, 21, 47, 49–50, 184
    of ten 1, 21, 25, 28, 34
    of zero 47, 56

454

Index

primary data sources 355, 369, 378
prime factors and tables 3, 43
prime numbers 3
prisms 209, 258, 317, 347, 348, 352
probability 359, 414, 418–19, 434
    calculating 418, 423, 434
    comparing experimental and theoretical 430, 431, 435
    estimating from relative frequency 426, 427, 435
    experiments 359, 369, 426, 427, 431, 435
proportion 10, 11, 66, 130, 414
    comparing 97–9, 114
proportional reasoning 142, 335
proving 46
pyramids 258, 317
Pythagoras' theorem 288

quadratic sequences 214, 228
quadrilaterals 256, 257, 273
questionnaires 355, 369, 371, 378
quotient 64

radius 291, 306, 331, 343, 351
random 359, 414, 434
range 356, 358, 381, 408
ratio 10, 11, 131, 134, 137, 142
    gear (bicycle) 140
ratio, golden 119
recipes 19, 132, 133, 138, 143, 337
rectangle, golden 119
rectangles 69, 186, 256, 338, 339, 344
reflection 259, 312, 317
reflection symmetry 258, 317
relative frequency 426, 427, 435
remainder 7, 9, 78
rhombuses 256, 273, 318
rotation 259, 312
rotation symmetry 258, 317, 318
rounding 1, 6, 28, 31, 34, 77
rule for the nth term 210–11, 213, 216, 221, 227, 228
rule, term-to-term 148, 210, 211, 213, 227
running track 347

sale price 69
sample size 370, 378, 423, 432, 434
samples 355, 378
scale 324
scale drawings 295, 324, 325, 328, 331
scale factor 259, 320, 321, 328
scales, reading 260
'scaling' 131
scatter graphs 358, 389, 390, 407
secondary data sources 355, 369, 378
sector of a circle 291, 306
segments of a circle 292, 306
self-inverse 259
semicircles 292, 306, 344, 347
sequences 147–8, 202, 211
    Fibonacci 210
    infinite 147
    linear (arithmetic) 148, 211, 213, 221, 227
    in practical situations 148, 216, 228
    quadratic 214, 228
    rules for 210–11, 213, 216, 221, 227, 228
set squares 257

shapes
    2-D 256, 260–1, 306
    3-D 258, 261, 302, 307, 328
    construction of 257
    similar 320, 328
shirt pieces 330
simplifying expressions 181, 184, 205
skeleton 180
slope of a line on a graph (m) 149, 234, 239–40, 251
speed formula 176, 206, 207, 334
spheres 317
spinner, fair 414, 417
spirals 413
spreadsheets 170
square numbers 4, 21, 47, 85
square roots 4, 51, 52, 53, 54, 85
squares (figures) 256, 338
standard form 23, 33
steepness of a line (m) 149, 234, 239–40, 251
stem-and-leaf diagrams 362
subject of a formula 200, 206, 234, 251
substituting into formulae 197, 206
subtracting 2, 38, 55
    0·01, 0·001 etc 1
    algebraic fractions 193, 205
    decimals 6, 76
    fractions 8, 44, 55, 102, 115
    mentally 4–5, 63, 87
    mixed numbers 105, 115
sun cream 360
sunshine hours 93, 101, 408
surface area 261, 348, 352
surveys 361, 367, 405
    planning 355, 368, 369, 378, 405
symbols, mathematical 13, 73, 130, 159, 160, 162, 273
    on Planet X 20
symmetry 258, 317, 328
    lines of 256, 258, 318
    planes of 317, 328
    reflection 258, 317
    rotation 258, 317, 318
        order of 258, 317

tangent to a circle 292, 306
telemarketer 429
telescopes 345
temperature conversion 156, 198
terms 147, 148
    consecutive 211, 213, 214, 221, 228
    first 148, 210, 227
    like, collecting 147, 181, 205
    nth, rule for 227
term-to-term rule 148, 210, 211, 213, 227
tesselations 290, 291, 306
tetrahedrons 258, 347
tile patterns 155, 190, 216, 284
time 259, 332
transformations 259, 312, 314, 328 *see also* enlargement, reflection, rotation, translation
transforming both sides 146, 166, 177, 235
translation 259, 312
trapeziums 75, 198, 256, 261, 287, 338
tree diagrams 43
trial and improvement 169–70, 177
trials *see* experiments

455

Index

triangles
    angles of 255, 273, 274, 282
    area 260, 261, 338, 339
    constructing 257
    equilateral 256, 274
    isosceles 256, 274, 282
    naming 256, 282
    properties of 256
    right-angled 256, 288, 294–5
    scalene 256
triangular numbers 4
trundle wheel 345
two-way tables 375, 376, 378, 385

unitary method 125, 131, 141, 142
unlikeliness 359
unpredictability 414, 434

variables 158, 176, 247, 389, 390, 407
    in direct proportion 172–3, 177
Venn diagrams 3, 43
vertices 255, 256

volume 261, 332, 333, 350
    of a prism 347, 348, 352

websites 210
weekly earnings 101
wind speeds 14, 387
word search 380
written calculations 6–7, 76

x-axis 258
    lines parallel to 149
x-coordinate 149

y-axis 234, 251, 258
    lines parallel to 149
y-intercept (c) 234, 240, 251
$y = mx + c$ 234, 239, 240, 251

zero
    dividing by 81
    power of 47, 56